DELPHI

A Developer's Guide

Bill Todd and Vince Kellen

with

Ray Novak and Brad Saenz

M&T Books
A Division of MIS:Press, Inc.
A Subsidiary of Henry Holt and Company, Inc.
115 West 18th Street
New York, New York 10011

Library of Congress Cataloging-in-Publication Data

```
Kellen, Vince.
    Delphi, a developer's guide / Bill Todd and Vince Kellen with Ray
  Novak and Brad saenz.
      p.   cm.
    ISBN 1-55851-455-4
    1. Client/server computing.  2. Computer software--Development.
  3. Delphi (Computer file)  I. Todd, Bill.  II. Title
QA76.9.C55K45    1995
005.265--dc20                                            95-30440
                                                            CIP
```

10 9 8 7 6 5 4 3 2 1

Associate Publisher & Vice President: *Paul Farrell*

Managing Editor: *Cary Sullivan*
Development Editor: *Michael Sprague*
Copy Edit Manager: *Shari Chappell*

Production Editor: *Maya Riddick*
Technical Editor: *Oktay Amiry*
Copy Editor: *Judith Katz*

CONTENTS

CHAPTER 6 • Data Types   101

CHAPTER 10 • Objects 205

CHAPTER 11 • Flat File Input and Output 229

CHAPTER 12 • Units 259

CHAPTER 13 • Dynamic Link Libraries   273

CHAPTER 14 • Anatomy of a Component   291

CHAPTER 15 • Delphi Controls   313

x

CHAPTER 18 • Understanding SQL   445

CHAPTER 19 • Delphi Query Component   473

CHAPTER 20 • Error Handling   501

xii

CHAPTER 21 • Building a Simple Database Application   527

CHAPTER 22 • Direct Calls to the Borland Database Engine   547

CHAPTER 26 • Data Integrity Overview   619

CHAPTER 27• Using Interbase   631

CHAPTER 28 • Using Microsoft SQL-Server   673

CHAPTER 29 • Improving Performance   695

CHAPTER 33 • Database Desktop Background and Overview 751

CHAPTER 1

Overview of Delphi's Features

Borland's newest programming product, Delphi, has so much to offer. It is completely object-oriented. It is fast (an optimizing compiler and a smart class library makes this possible). It has oodles of visual controls and plenty of database-aware controls. It can use existing Visual Basic controls (VBX). Its integrated development environment sports an excellent editor with color syntax highlighting, fast syntax checking, and an excellent debugger. It can connect to a variety of database servers via Microsoft's Open Database Connectivity (ODBC), or through the Borland SQL-Link drivers.

Many people have asked us what it is that we like so much about Delphi and how we rank its features. Our top 10 list follows:

1. Speed
2. Speed
3. Speed
4. Great extensibility
5. True object orientation
6. Scalable database choices
7. Speed
8. Multi-programmer and version-control support
9. A good integrated development and debugging environment
10. Speed

Even in today's environment of fast computers with lots of memory and large hard drives, performance matters. Delphi delivers some of the fastest performance ever in an incredibly easy-to-use programming environment. Users are demanding smarter software. In response, software continues to increase in complexity. As software gets more complex, developers will need fast object-oriented tools. For the foreseeable future, performance will continue to matter.

In many ways Delphi is deceiving. Novice programmers can use it to turn out more than just trivial applications. Programmers who do not know a lick of object-oriented programming can use it immediately. Many are doing so right now. Windows programming gurus who need to dig deeper into the Windows event model and write some complex object-oriented applications will also find it exciting. After all, the Borland software engineers who wrote Delphi needed advanced Windows event control; and they got that control using Delphi. Object-oriented programmers will find Delphi valuable too. Delphi delivers the performance and ease of use without sacrificing control and power; programmers of all skill levels can use it.

Regardless of how Borland or others target Delphi, we are finding it useful for the following types of programmers and development environments:

- Rapid application development and prototyping. Delphi lets you build user interfaces quickly and easily with minimum coding. One word of warning is in order: If you prototype in Delphi and deliver your application in another language, your users may be disappointed. Delphi applications run fast.

- Corporate developers and consultants who write applications that need to access existing file server, client/server, or mainframe databases.

- Commercial software developers. Delphi is a viable alternative to C or C++ developer tools. Delphi's programming language, ObjectPascal, gives access to assembler and low-level Windows event handling to satisfy any commercial software application needs. After all, Delphi is written in Delphi.

- Vertical market developers. With Delphi, you do not have to be locked into a particular single-vendor solution. You can mix and match database environments, report writers, VBX controls and other tools to build the best possible application for your clients. Since Delphi supports a wide variety of database formats, you can choose the database format that works best for your clients.

Delphi is a Compiler

Unlike other environments, such as Visual Basic and Paradox for Windows, Delphi is the product of years of compiler research and experience that Borland has gained in their Turbo Pascal language. The language inside Delphi, ObjectPascal, makes some additional improvements over the last version of Pascal that Borland shipped. All these years of compiler experience has made Delphi an excellent environment.

In fact, nearly all of Delphi is written in Delphi. We say nearly because a handful of routines are written in assembler for speed. However, the user-interface and all the dialogs and windows in Delphi are written in Delphi. The result of this is that Delphi is a programming environment, written by programmers for programmers. Borland programmers wrote Delphi so that they could create Delphi quickly without sacrificing performance. Subsequently you will be using the very same facilities that Borland programmers used when writing Delphi.

Fast Optimizing Compiler, Fast Applications

The Delphi compiler is an optimizing compiler. Borland has had years to enhance it so that it produces the tightest and fastest code possible. This results in an application that performs better. However, a smart compiler alone does not make for a fast product.

Delphi's visual component library (VCL) is also written with speed in mind. The VCL is a collection of routines which provide you with all the tools to create user-interfaces and access data. The VCL contains the code for buttons, fields, labels, graphics, dialog boxes, and table access. The algorithms Borland implements in the VCL are designed for speed. In fact, you get the source code in the client/server edition. You can read the source code and examine the exact algorithms Borland employed in the VCL.

Easy Application Distribution

Delphi produces a standalone EXE file. Unless your application needs to access data in tables, this executable does not require any other runtime libraries or Dynamic Link Libraries (DLLs). If you application needs to access data, Borland includes the Borland Database Engine distribution kit which includes all the necessary files and DLLs. If you need to ship reports with your applications, Delphi comes with *ReportSmith* and *ReportSmith Runtime*. You can use ReportSmith to create the report and ReportSmith Runtime to distribute the report without giving all your users a copy of ReportSmith.

You can distribute your executable, the Borland Engine and ReportSmith Runtime all without paying any royalties or licensing fees.

Rapid Application Development

Delphi is suitable for rapid application development techniques. You can quickly create tables using the Borland Database Desktop; you can prototype

4

data entry forms with little or no code; and you can display these prototypes to the user during the design process. As with many other development tools such as Borland's Paradox for Windows, Microsoft Visual Basic
and Access, the prototype does not need to be discarded once implementation begins. Instead, more code and functionality can be added to the prototype as it slowly grows into a production system.

Delphi allows rapid application development through various tools.
These include visual tools to create the user interface, control data access,
and to produce reports. Delphi comes with several experts which make creating complex application objects easy. Delphi enables easy integration with
version control facilities, such as Intersolv's PVCS package.

Visual User-Interface Development

Delphi sports a visual design development environment in which the various controls the user interacts with are displayed as objects on a toolbar (see
Figure 1.1).

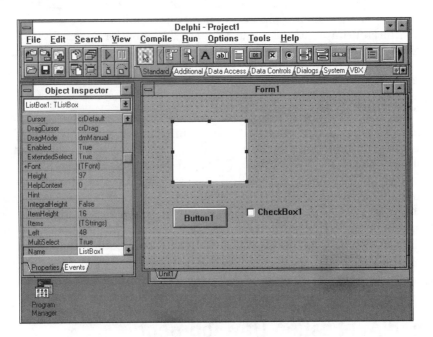

FIGURE 1.1 THE DELPHI IDE AND COMPONENT PALETTE.

To create the user interface, you place a component, from the component
palette, onto the form. You resize and position each component until the

user interface meets the user's requirements. What makes Delphi unique is that the visual development environment is constantly scanning the source code you write to ensure that the two match. Any changes you make visually are automatically made in your source code. Any changes in your source code are reflected visually. In this regard, Delphi is a two-way tool. You can work with it visually and look at the code, or you can work only with code and inspect the visual result.

Visual Data Objects

Like Visual Basic and Paradox for Windows, Delphi includes visual objects you place on your form that you can see during design-time, but the user cannot see when the form is running. The objects which manage data access fall into this category. Figure 1.2 is just like Figure 1.1 except that 1.2 contains two objects on the top of the form: a table object and a data-source object.

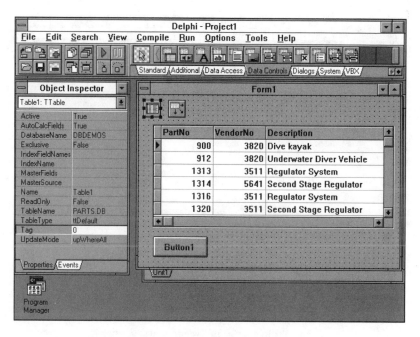

FIGURE 1.2 VISUAL DATA OBJECTS.

The table object is connected to a data table on disk. The data-source object is connected to the table object and the list box is connected to the data-source object, which sets up the following dependencies:

6

```
Table on disk -> Table object -> Data source -> Data control
```

The data-control object needs a data-source object, which needs a table object, which needs a table on disk to access. Other chapters (see Chapter 17 on connecting controls to databases, Chapter 19 on using TQuery objects, and Chapter 21 on a sample database application) in this book explain the virtues of this model.

More importantly, you can see your data while you are designing it. You do not need to run your form just to see if you have the connections set right.

Visual Report Development With ReportSmith

Delphi comes with a report writing tool called ReportSmith (shown in figure 1.3). Like Delphi, ReportSmith let's you design your reports while you are viewing the data. You do not need to run the report just to see if the data in correct. Chapter 23 discusses reporting and using ReportSmith and Delphi in more detail.

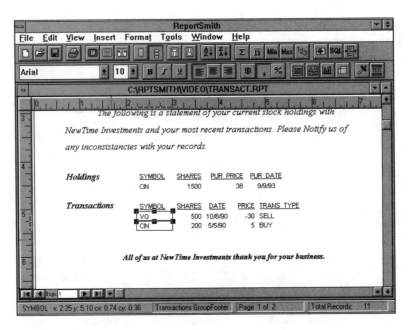

FIGURE 1.3 REPORTSMITH REPORT IN DESIGN MODE.

Again, just like in Figure 1.2, Delphi has a component which you can see at design time but not at runtime. This control lets you interactively specify the report directory and name, whether the report should go to the printer or screen, and other properties.

Experts

Delphi comes equipped with several experts that automate parts of the application development environment. Figure 1.4 shows the form expert, which will automatically create some basic forms or dialog boxes for you. Figure 1.5 shows a sample customer/orders form the expert built.

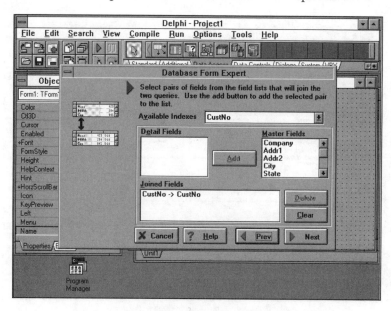

FIGURE 1.4 THE DELPHI FORM EXPERT.

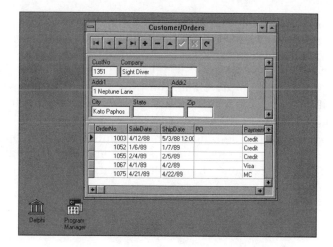

FIGURE 1.5 FORM CREATED BY THE DELPHI FORM EXPERT.

Delphi includes a dialog box expert to make the job of created dialog boxes easy. In addition, it also comes with eight different form templates (which you can easily add to) which make creating forms with default properties a snap (see Figure 1.6).

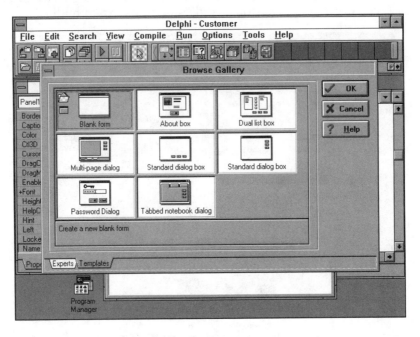

FIGURE 1.6 THE DELPHI FORM TEMPLATES.

Delphi also includes a project expert which asks you a series of questions so that it can help build basic parts of your application (see Figure 1.7). Also included are four project templates: a blank project, an MDI project, an SDI project, and a DOS-like CRT project. Like the form templates, they do not ask you questions but simply create the project according to some prede-fined defaults. In addition you can add your own templates to the list of project templates.

These tools make prototyping and rapid application development easy. In addition, for larger applications, these experts and templates let you ensure that all the developers will be creating consistent user interfaces.

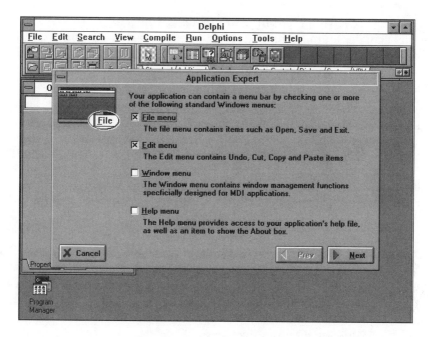

FIGURE 1.7 THE DELPHI PROJECT EXPERT.

Version Control Integration

Delphi integrates with the Intersolv PVCS version control software to provide automatic check in and check out of source code files to support team programming support. If Intersolv's PVCS is installed on your PC, you can make a simple one-line entry in your Delphi INI file and Delphi will automatically add a Workgroup menu to the Delphi menu bar. This menu lets you check in and check out source code units via custom dialog boxes that know exactly how to interface with PVCS. Intersolv's PVCS package is sold separately and, if you wanted, you could use any one of a number of version control packages available.

Unlike Paradox for Windows and other environments which maintain binary representations of your application objects, all of Delphi is converted to text-based source code. In Delphi you store all your source code in a file with a .PAS extension. Delphi also creates a file with a .DFM extension· which is actually a binary file, but can be opened up in Delphi in text form and saved in a text form, if needed. This DFM file contains all the properties for each object on the form. Delphi includes routines which would allow any third party tools developer to read and write the DFM file.

Since all your code is stored in a text file, version control is fast and compact. Since the differences are text based, the differences between versions of your source code have semantic meaning. You can view the lines of code that have been added or changed. With other development environments where forms are purely binary objects (and rather large ones at that), version control loses meaning because the differences cannot be converted to source code differences.

True Object Orientation

Delphi is a truly *object-oriented programming* (OOP) environment with full support for object identity, inheritance, polymorphism and encapsulation. Chapter 10 on objects and Chapter 30 on object-oriented issues cover Delphi's OOP implementation.

Develop Reusable Components and Code

Because Delphi is truly object-oriented, you can reuse more of your code more easily than you can in non-object-oriented environments. With Delphi it is a snap to create your own components which inherit properties and behavior from an existing component class (see Chapter 31 on creating components).

When you build complex applications which have large numbers of forms, it becomes necessary to centralize complex code so that multiple forms and modules can make use of it. When you need to modify this complex code, you need to modify it in one place only. Delphi lets developers attain this goal easily.

Delphi Components Written in ObjectPascal

To prove the point about code reuse, Borland wrote Delphi in Delphi itself. When you create your own components, forms and dialogs, you will be doing what nearly every Borland developer who wrote Delphi did. Since Borland developers had to use Delphi to create Delphi, the quality of the components is high, and the effort required to create your own components is quite low.

If you are new to OOP, OOP requires thinking about programming in a new way. You have to start thinking in terms of objects that inherit certain properties and behavior from other objects (see Chapter 3, "Object Oriented Programming: What is it?"). This naturally decomposes the application into smaller, more manageable units, making your application more robust and easier to maintain. Perhaps the best testament to virtue is Delphi's VCL, which is written in ObjectPascal.

Supports O/S Standards

Delphi lets you tap into various Windows operating system resources, including *Object Linking and Embedding* (OLE), *Dynamic Data Exchange* (DDE), and *Open Database Connectivity* (ODBC).

Delphi includes an OLE client object (which has many properties and methods) which lets you activate and control other OLE server applications. Delphi supports OLE2 in place activation in which the embedded application shares the menus and toolbars with the client application. Delphi also includes objects to control DDE client and server applications. DDE lets you send text between running applications. With DDE you can send another application commands (macros) which let you control the other application.

Extensibility

Because Delphi is written in Delphi, Delphi is entirely customizable. If you do not like one of the components, you can roll your own. Or you can purchase third-party components that provide enhanced versions of the standard controls. Delphi is so extensible that it can even create components which represent large portions of your application. Traditional programming environments have a sharper distinction between the programming environment and the application. Through new components, form templates, and application templates, the development environment can contain a rather large number of application objects. This lets you jump start application development by taking advantage of a body of existing code.

Delphi also lets you add existing VBX controls to the component palette. When you add a VBX control (see Figure 1.8) (which must conform to the VBX 1.0 specification), Delphi creates an ObjectPascal wrapper around the control so that it is a normal Delphi object which fits into the VCL class hierarchy. This means that you can include a VBX control and derive new classes based on the VBX control.

12

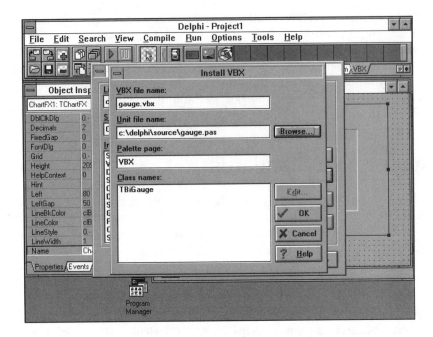

FIGURE 1.8 ADDING A VBX CONTROL IN DELPHI.

Scalable Database Environment

With Delphi you have lots of choices for database formats. Delphi provides native support for Paradox and DBase file formats. If you purchase the client/server edition of Delphi, you receive a copy of the Local Interbase Server and you can get the SQL Link drivers for Oracle, Sybase, Microsoft SQL Server, Informix, or Interbase.

If you want to do client/server development that's SQL-92 compatible, you can use the Local Interbase Server (Local Interbase is SQL-92 compatible) to create your tables, declare referential integrity, establish rules and triggers, and then port your database to any other SQL-92 compatible back end. Or, you can start development using local Paradox or DBase file formats and later port the database to any of the back-end databases.

In addition, for a nominal fee, you can purchase from Microsoft ODBC 2.0 drivers for Access, Btrieve, Excel, FoxPro, and SQL Server. Or, you can purchase ODBC drivers from other vendors for access to a wide variety of mainframe and minicomputer databases. Delphi can use any ODBC 2.0 driver for data access. Delphi offers so many database choices that should let you build applications of just about any size or complexity.

Summary

Because Delphi is a truly object-oriented, visual development tool with plenty of database extendibility and scalability, there is not much that it cannot do. All programmers, beginners, journeymen, and experts can use it effectively.

This book focuses on those areas of the product that either the on-line help or manuals do not emphasize enough, or that we consider critical for proper application development. It discusses relational database design and object-oriented programming concepts. After all, these are two areas where Delphi excels. The early chapters give a quick overview of the language syntax and the development environment. The middle part of the book reviews various user-interface controls and database controls. Towards the end, the book goes into more detail concerning client/server application development, additional OOP concepts, and writing your own components.

CHAPTER 2

Database and Object Design

In order to build successful Delphi applications, you are going to need to do two things well: properly design the tables in your application, and design the data entry and report objects with which the user will work. Of these two, perhaps properly designing the tables that store your data is the more important. Properly designed tables are easily queried and modified. This keeps system maintenance costs down. Properly designed form and report objects require less code, thus making programming the user interface that much easier.

This chapter discusses database design and object design. Relational database design has a rather distinguished history with hundreds of books and thousands of articles explaining every aspect of the relational model. This chapter does not attempt to give a detailed analysis. Instead, it provides you with a straightforward overview on the key relational concepts that will help you develop Delphi applications. In addition, the chapter also discusses object design. While designing tables is important, properly designing your main user-interface objects is vital.

This chapter does not discuss object-oriented design. That is reserved for the next chapter. Instead, this chapter focuses on object design, which is a method of identifying the major forms and reports a Delphi application may need. Once the main objects have been identified and listed, you will need to devise ways of properly presenting and sequencing these objects to the user. In Delphi, as in many other visual programming environments, a good database design and a good user interface object design are both crucial attributes of successful projects.

Relational Database Design

If you want to learn more about building Delphi database applications, then read other books too. The more you understand relational database design, the better a developer you will become. Our experience has shown that developers with significant relational database knowledge build better database applications. Whether you are new to relational databases or experienced, you should learn more about the relational model.

T I P

There is no substitute for a thorough understanding of relational database design. Developers with significant relational database knowledge build better applications.

Developers often shy away from relational database design discussions assuming that the endeavor is too theoretical and not applicable in the real world. Nothing could be further from the truth. Relational database theory helps us solve practical, real-world problems in efficient and elegant ways.

Some Terms

The first thing you must do in order to understand relational database design is to understand some basic terms. Relational theory and practice have introduced dozens of terms, some understood, some not.

Databases, Tables, Rows, Columns, Domains

These basic terms refer to fundamental components of a database. Before diving into these terms, it is important to understand the term *database*. In the context of this book, a database is a collection of files that store information needed by an application or a user. The term does not denote the level or quality of organization of those files. For example, a series of disorganized text files could be called a database, although not a very nice one. The term database does not try to assign a judgmental value to the files. It simply refers to a collection of files.

Tables, records, rows, columns and fields are terms thrown about so often that many times one assumes that everyone knows what they mean. For clarity's sake, these terms are explained in Table 2.1.

TABLE 2.1 SOME RELATIONAL TERMS

Table	A file (or files) which holds related data. A table has rows of data, like a spreadsheet row, and each row is divided up into columns. Each row has exactly the same number of columns.
Row	A *row* contains information about a particular item. For example, one row in an Employee table will hold information about one employee. If an Employee table has 20,000 rows, then it has 20,000 employees. *Record* is another word for row. Another term for a row is *tuple*, although this terms is more frequently used in relational theory than in database practice.

Field A *field* holds a piece of information of a record. For example, a row in the Employee table can have the following fields: Name, Pay Rate, Address, City, State and Zip. Another name for a field is column or attribute.

Domain A *domain* is a more of a concept than a tangible thing. A domain represents the range of possible values for a field. For example, a US_State field in a customer table has 50 states as the possible range of values for it. Each field in a table has a domain. Many fields can share domains. In fact, this is the great advantage for using domains: the database system can easily identify fields that share domains, and can prevent users from making invalid entries when querying or entering data.

While the term table is easy to understand and appreciate, the term *relation* is not. The term table and relation are very often used to refer to the same thing. However, a table is *one possible* representation of a relation. In relational database theory, using the two terms interchangeably is perfectly acceptable. Understanding exactly what a relation is can help you understand a bit more about relational databases. In fact the phase *relational model* came from the word *relation*.

A relation has the following properties:

- It is composed of a header which includes a listing of each attribute(field), and its corresponding domain.
- It is composed of a body which includes a series of sets, with each set listing each attribute (field) and its corresponding value.

The header of a relation is represented as a set of field/domain pairs:

```
{(FieldA:DomainA), (FieldB:DomainB), (FieldZ:DomainZ)}
```

Clearly the header of a relation can be compared with a field list from a relational table, with one major difference. Many database systems don't provide full support for domains, so the header of a table often does not contain field/domain pairs. The header usually contains a listing of the valid fields in the table.

Domains are eminently useful. If every field was assigned a name domain with validation properties, then not only could the database system perform field-level validation, it could also inform the user when he or she tries to link two tables using fields from different domains. For example, if the user tried to link a customer table with an orders table by linking the customer name field in the customer table to the customer number field in the orders table, than the database system could inform them of their error.

The body of a relation is represented as a set of tuples (rows) of field/value pairs:

```
{(((FieldA:"J. Smith"),(FieldB:"122 W. Michigan")),
((FieldA:"I. Chang"), (FieldB:"30 S. Oak")))}
```

Clearly the body of a relation can be compared with the records in a table. Just as a tuple in a relation has a set of fields and field values, each record in a table has a set of fields and field values.

Since the header of a relation is a set, there is no order in the set elements implied. The field/domain pairs can be listed in any order. Since the body of a relation is also a set, there is no order implied in the set of records.

In other database systems, this unordered list aspect of relations is sometimes ignored. For example, in a spreadsheet (and in many database packages), columns (fields) have a specific order which means something to the spreadsheet and its calculations. Fields in a table should be considered an unordered list. They can appear in any order in the physical structure of the table without changing the application which uses the table. As developers, you always have the ability to display the fields to the user in a particular order, but underneath, the actual ordering of the fields in the actual table is unimportant. Instead of referring to fields by number, in a relational database you can refer to fields by name.

 According to the relational model, the fields in a table structure and the records in the table are considered an unordered list. In practice, some relational database systems assume that fields are in a specific order and that records are in a certain order. When designing database applications, it is always wise to assume that both fields and records are *unordered* lists.

T I P

Programmers and users often think in terms of spreadsheets, where the rows imply a certain order because of their physical placement. You need to avoid this approach when designing relational databases. While the order that records display is important when programming the user interface, the actual physical ordering of the records on disk should not matter. The developer should be able to refer to a specific record in a table by a unique identifier, just like field names are unique identifiers for field values. This name is called the primary key.

Primary Key

Of all the terms in relational database theory, this one has the most significance. A *primary key* uniquely identifies a record in a table. Each of us have primary keys. Social Security numbers uniquely identify us. (If they did not we would have problems collecting social security checks!) Drivers' license numbers do, too. When you design and build relational databases, each table must have a primary key, otherwise you will have no way of referring to an individual record.

T I P

When designing tables, think long and hard when choosing a primary key. A properly selected primary key will keep the cost of maintenance down and will let you easily change and enhance your database application. Bad primary key selection turns potentially good applications into bad ones.

A field, or any number of fields, can serve as a primary key. Primary keys are best when they are short. For example, using a simple number field for the primary for an Employee table is better than trying to make a primary key out of the employee's first and last name. Since primary keys determine uniqueness, you will not be able store two employees named Robin Smiths in the Employee table if the first and last name fields are used as primary key fields.

Primary keys are also best when they are stable. Primary key fields tend to show up as fields in other tables (foreign keys). If the primary key values need to change frequently, then the database system, or your application, will need to cascade these changes to other tables. This can be a performance bottle neck.

While all data tables must have one primary key, it is possible for tables to sometimes have multiple primary keys. Additional primary keys are called alternate keys (or candidate keys). Tables need alternate keys when businesses use two or more numbers to uniquely identify a transaction or record. If you have a table that has many primary key candidates, try to choose the shorter and more stable of the primary key candidates. In the long run, a primary key with these attributes will be less expensive to maintain.

Foreign Keys

When a table's primary key appears as a non-primary key field in another table, it is called a *foreign key*. For example, consider a table with the following structure:

Field	Type	Width	Primary Key?
State_code	Alphanumeric	2	Y
State_name	Alphanumeric	40	N

This table serves as a master table containing the valid list of states. Consider the following table, Company, which contains a State code field:

Field	Type	Width	Primary Key?
Company_code	Alphanumeric	10	Y
Name	Alphanumeric	40	N
City	Alphanumeric	20	N
State_code	Alphanumeric	2	N
Zip	Alphanumeric	10	N

In this case, the [State_code] field in the Company table is the foreign key. Why? Because it is not a primary key field in the Company table, but it is the primary key field in the State table. In database application development, it is common to have many tables like the State table. Developers use these tables to validate data entry in foreign key fields through the use of drop-down lists in the user-interface or through triggers in the database server.

Maintaining Database Integrity

Over time, database developers and researchers have identified basic rules which maintain a database system's integrity. Without these rules, the database can easily contain bad information leading to inaccurate results or results that are costly to make accurate. These integrity features include:

- Entity integrity
- Referential integrity
- Domain integrity
- Column integrity
- User-Defined integrity

If the underlying database system provides good support for all of these integrity features, then you will invariably end up writing less code to manage these issues in the user interface. If these rules are specified as part of the underlying database system, then *it will be impossible for any programmer to violate these rules.* After all, programmers and developers, as well as users, can damage data.

Entity Integrity

The entity integrity rule states that primary key values can not be missing. Simply put, this means that each record must have a primary key and that primary key must be completely entered. If the primary key is a compound primary key (composed of multiple fields), then each field in the primary key must be supplied. Many database systems provide some measure of support for entity integrity.

For example, in the Paradox file format, you can specify a table's primary key and you can *optionally* specify that each field in the primary key is required—blanks are not allowed. The entity integrity rule ensures that we can always access a record by its primary key and that the primary key is never ambiguous.

Referential Integrity

In the prior example (foreign keys), the Company table and the State table have a relationship. Each state can have many companies in it. Therefore, each State record in the State table can have multiple Customer records; a one-to-many relationship exists between the State and Company tables.

Suppose a user was editing the State table and the user accidentally deleted the state Illinois, which had 230 companies in it. The company records have been orphaned. Conversely, their parent records (the State records) have been killed. The next time anyone tries to add a customer in the state of Illinois, he or she will be prevented because Illinois no longer exists in the State validation table.

Referential integrity ensures that your application can not have parent killers. It ensures that foreign key relationships can't be usurped. When designing your application's database, make sure you understand how your database system handles referential integrity. Both the Paradox for Windows and Microsoft Access file formats provide support (although slightly different flavors) for referential integrity, whereas the dBASE file format does not. In addition, most SQL servers, such as Interbase, Sybase, and Oracle provide mechanisms for referential integrity support.

The nice thing about having referential integrity supported in the database is that the user would be prevented from deleting the state Illinois from the State table if that state had dependent records in the Company table, *regardless of what application the user was in.*

A database environment should let the developer establish exactly how and when parent records can be changed. Database environments should let the developer prohibit the user from changing a primary key, if the record has depended records in another table. The database environment also should have an option for automatically cascading the change in the parent record's primary key to all dependent records. This feature is often called a *cascading update*. If the user tries to delete a parent record with dependent children, the database environment should let the developer prohibit the delete or cascade the delete, and remove all dependent records. This feature is often called a *cascading delete*.

As you design your application's database, determine what referential integrity relationships exist. If you have a choice, select a database platform which provides full support for referential integrity, including the option to choose prohibited or cascading deletes and updates. If the referential integrity rules are established as part of the database layer, not the user interface layer, then you will only need to create these rules once when you create the database. As you begin to proliferate various user-interfaces (which you will be able to do quite easily with Delphi), you won't have to write any code to enforce referential integrity. The database server will inform Delphi that the user can or can't change or delete the parent record.

Domain Integrity

Since multiple fields can be assigned a single domain, it would be nice if the database environment let us establish integrity rules for the domain. Then all fields for that domain would inherit this constraint. This would save work, since you could simply establish constraints on the domain, rather than on each dependent field. For example, a domain called Bonus_amount could be constrained to allow only values between 0 and $1,000,000. Every field assigned to the Bonus_amount domain would inherit this constraint.

Column Integrity

Although domain integrity is useful, it does not go far enough. Very often developers need to add additional constraints on a field independent of the domain. For example, in a table called Executive_staff, the Yearly_Bonus field (assigned to the Bonus_Amount domain) could be constrained to allow a range of values from $25,000 and $1,000,000. In no way should column integrity rules conflict with domain integrity rules.

User-Defined Integrity

Column integrity rules go further, but often business rules can not be adequately expressed in terms of domain or column integrity features in a given database system. Many database systems let developers write code or SQL (structured query language commands, discussed in Chapter 18) which can further constrain the data in records. Again, many database systems have anywhere from straightforward to intricately involved ways of implementing user-defined integrity.

T I P

If database integrity is high on your list of features when evaluating a database system for your application, be sure to check how easily the environment supports each of the integrity rules.

Normalizing Data

Understanding relational database theory is important to building solid database applications. You get to apply the theory when you sit down and design your tables. When you begin designing an application, many questions come to mind. How many tables should there be? What fields should they contain? What relationships between them need to exist? The process of answering these questions is often called *database normalization*.

The rules of database normalization help you create databases that are robust, efficient, and easily modified. If you follow the rules carefully, accessing the data through your application's user-interface will be much easier. Your application will be more flexible to allow for changes, and more reliable since redundant data will be removed from your tables. Good relational database design can save thousands of lines of code. Since your relational data model will ripple through every facet of the application, building it right is a number one priority.

First Normal Form

The first step in normalizing your data is to make sure all your tables are in first normal form. A table is in *first normal form* if each field in it contains a single value (each field must be *atomic*, representing one thing). For example, a field such as Company_Address which holds both the city, zip code, and state in one field would violate first normal form. Why? Because the field contains three distinct values: city, state, and zip code, which should be split into three fields.

Some developers like to have some sort of structure within a particular field. For example, consider a table holding a list of courses, with each course identified uniquely with a Course_Id field:

```
Course_Id      Description
27-1183        Calculus
```

In this example, the Course_Id field's fist two characters refer to a building code, and the last four digits refer to the room number. The Course_Id field contains two pieces of information. Do you think the Course_Id field should be split into two? If splitting the field into two will add value to the system for the user or the application developer, then the field should be split into two. If splitting the field does not add value, then leave it alone. By adding value, we mean that the alteration will make it easier for the users to manipulate, query, or search that field, or that it will facilitate construction of the system for the developer. This is a judgment call that you will have to make each time you decide on what data goes into what field.

Another violation of the first normal form is the *repeating groups* problem. The table in Figure 2.1 violates first normal form. This table, which holds personal addresses and phone numbers contains the following offending fields: Address1, Phone1, Address2, Phone2, Address3, Phone3. These fields comprise a repeating group and is actually a variation of the atomicity problem stated earlier. If you view the repeating group fields as one single field containing a list of values, then you can see that a repeating group violates the condition that fields must be atomic.

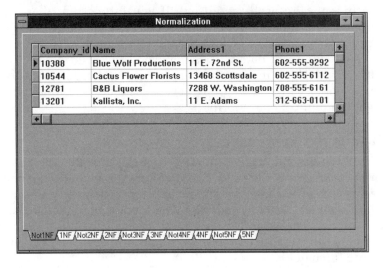

FIGURE 2.1 NOT1NF.DB - REPEATING GROUPS.

This problem can be quickly solved by splitting the repeating groups off to a separate table, so that the data is now in two separate tables (see Figure 2.2).

Repeating groups is an especially bad problem because it introduces many querying problems. For example, to find an address at 11 W. Adams, you will need to query three fields: Address1, Address2, and Address3. If you decide to create ten fields to hold up to ten different addresses for someone, you will need to search each of these fields to find an address.

Beginners in relational database application development frequently make the mistake of not eliminating repeating groups. Why? Probably because repeating groups are often representative of a spreadsheet framework where data can be entered in a free-form way, and relationships (expressed as calculations), are entered referencing cells from anywhere on the spreadsheet. While this is convenient for the spreadsheet developer, it is a real problem for the database developer.

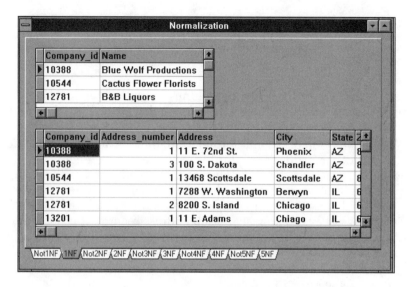

FIGURE 2.2 SOLVING REPEATING GROUPS: 1NFCUST.DB, 1NFADDR.DB.

Second Normal Form

Getting tables into first normal form is easy. Getting them into second normal form is just a bit more work because violations of second normal form are just a bit harder to spot. In order to understand second normal form, we need to talk more about primary keys.

As stated earlier, primary keys uniquely identify records. Primary keys also determine all the other fields in the record. In other words, all the non-primary key fields depend entirely on the primary key for proper interpretation of their value. Consider the following table, NOT2NF2.DB. This table, designed to hold a list of company addresses, has the following structure:

Field	Primary key?
Company_id	Y
Address_number	Y
Address	
City	
State	
Zip	
Phone	
Company_CEO_	

We can depict this relationship between the primary key fields (Person_id and Address_number) and the city field like this:

```
(Company_id, Address_number) -> City
```

This states that the primary key determines a single value for the field City, or this is the city for this primary key. Notice that the full primary key completely determines what city means.

When tables violate second normal form, they have fields which depend on only part of the primary key. In this example, the Company_CEO field is supposed to represent the last name of the person who is the company's chief executive officer, where each company has one *CEO*. The problem with this field is that if one company has multiple addresses, that company's CEO will have to appear in each address record. The Company_CEO field is not completely determined by the primary key. It depends on only a portion of the primary key. We can depict the relationship like this:

```
Company_id -> Company_CEO
```

Clearly the Company_CEO field belongs in a separate table: the company table depicted in Figure 2.2 (1NFCUST.DB). Tables that have a single primary key field can never violate second normal form. Why? Because a table which violates second normal form has non-key fields dependent on a portion of a multi-field primary key.

Figure 2.3 shows the unnormalized version of the tables while Figure 2.4 shows the normalized versions of NOT2NF1.DB and NOT2NF1.DB.

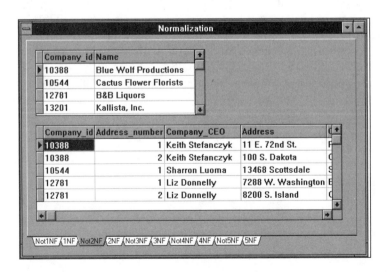

FIGURE 2.3 TABLES NOT IN SECOND NORMAL FORM

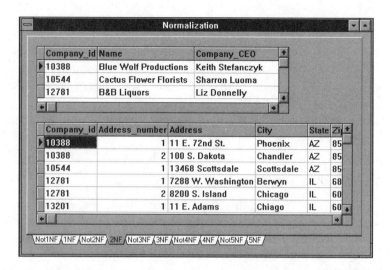

FIGURE 2.4 TABLES IN SECOND NORMAL FORM (2NFCUST.DB AND 2NFADDR.DB).

Third Normal Form

In order for a table to be in third normal form, all the fields in the table must be entirely dependent on the primary key. Sometimes developers get into trouble by creating *transitive dependencies*. These are dependencies where one field is dependent on another field in the table which in turn is dependent on the primary key.

Consider the following table structure for a table NOT3NF.DB, which is supposed to hold a list of company addresses:

Field	Primary key?
Company_id	Y
Address_number	Y
Address	
City	
State	
State_name	
Zip	
Phone	

In this table structure, the field State_name appears to be redundant. Why? Because if we have ten addresses in one state, the state name is repeated ten times. If the state name was entered incorrectly and needs to be changed, then it must be changed ten times. Although it is not likely that you would need to delete a state from the Address table, if you did, you would have to find all occurrences of a state name and delete the state name as well as the two character abbreviation. Tables not in third normal form suffer from update and delete problems like this.

If you look closely at the State_name field, you will notice the following two relationships between this field and the State field and the primary key:

```
(Person_id, Address_number) -> State
State -> State_name
```

In this example, the State_name field is transitively dependent on the primary key. Why? because it is fully dependent on the State field, which in turn, is fully dependent on the primary key. To correct this problem, you will need to move the State_name field to it's own table. This table serves as a lookup table holding the full state name so that all other tables that need the full state name can use the two character state abbreviation instead. Figure 2.5 shows the incorrect versions and Figure 2.6 shows the corrected versions of NOT3NF1.DB and NOT3NF2.DB.

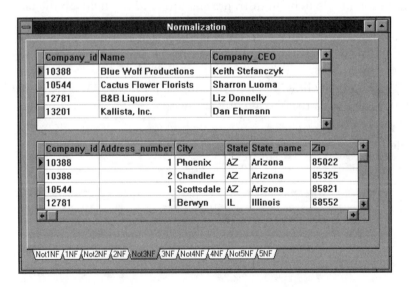

FIGURE 2.5 TABLES NOT IN THIRD NORMAL FORM

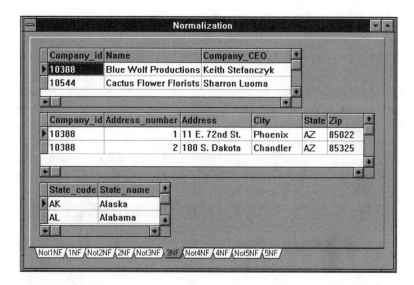

FIGURE 2.6 TABLES IN THIRD NORMAL FORM

Boyce-Codd Normal Form

While 3NF (third normal form) goes further to reduce redundancies, update, and delete anomalies in database systems, it does have a weakness. Specifically, if the table in question has multiple candidate keys (keys which could be primary), and each of the candidate keys are composite (comprised of two or more fields), and the candidate keys overlapped (have at least one field in common), the original description of 3NF is not strict enough.

The revised definition for 3NF, call BCNF (for Boyce-Codd Normal Form) is actually simpler than the definition for 3NF. In the example in the section on 3NF, table NOT3NF.Db contained a transitive dependency: the State_name field depends on the State_code field. In other words, the State_code field determines the State_name field, or the State_code field is a *determinant*.

In order for a relation to be in BCNF, all determinants must be candidate keys. If a table has multiple primary keys, then all fields in the table must depend entirely on the candidate keys. As you can see, the definition for BCNF is simpler than that for 3NF and it is easier to determine if a table is in BCNF or not.

However, since the limitations for BCNF occur very rarely in real-world applications, you may never have tables not in BCNF. Most experienced database developers intuitively detect unwanted dependencies and design tables properly without ever having to think about normalization. Normalization simply makes explicit what good database developers implicitly do.

Fourth Normal Form

Tables not in 4NF (fourth normal form) have at least three key fields. Consider the table in Figure 2.7 representing examiners, exam types and exam course for a mythical ski school.

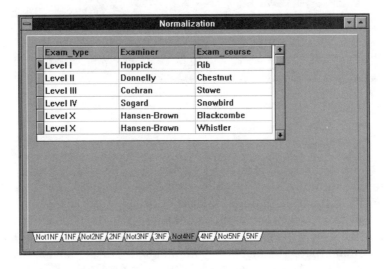

FIGURE 2.7 TABLE NOT IN FOURTH NORMAL FORM (NOT4NF.DB).

The structure for this table includes three fields, which together comprise the primary key:

Field	Primary key?
Exam_type	Y
Examiner	Y
Exam_course	Y

In this example, each exam type has multiple examiners associated with it, as well as multiple test courses the examiner may need to use. Each exam can have many different examiners independent of the courses the exam uses. In addition, each examiner must give the exam at all exam courses.

Placing this information in one table introduces update inserts and deletes anomalies. For example, if you delete the record with examiner "Cochran" in it from this table, by definition we lose the information that Level 1 exam uses the course at Stowe. If you need to assign examiner Harness-Brown's to a different exam, then we need to make the change in several rows. Or, if you need to add information to the table to indicate that a new examiner can teach a new course, you need to insert as many rows as there courses for that exam type.

It is useful to depict the relationship between the fields in NOT4NF.DB the following way:

```
Exam_type ->> Examiner
Exam_type ->> Exam_course
```

The ->> symbol means that the field Exam_type determines a set of Examiner values (called a *multi-valued dependency*), not just a single examiner value. Whenever this relationship exists between fields in a table, redundant data can exist. Clearly, this table needs to be broken down into smaller tables in order to store the data non-redundantly (see Figure 2.8).

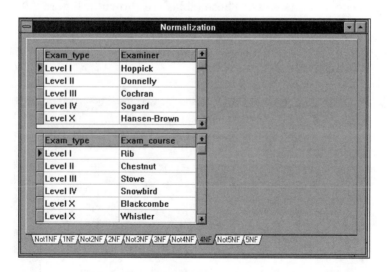

FIGURE 2.8 TABLES IN FOURTH NORMAL FORM.

While it is useful to store the data as shown in Figure 2.8, it is still useful to sometimes view the data as it is shown in Figure 2.7. Such a view is always possible, with the use of queries to manipulate the stored data. Data normalization does not proscribe how the data should be viewed, only how the data should be stored.

Fifth Normal Form

To understand 5NF (fifth normal form), it will be useful to start with the table in Figure 2.8, but change the constraints on the table. Instead of assuming that each examiner must give the exam at each course, a new constraint will be supplied: each course has a list of available examiners. In other words, there exists a cyclic constraint:

```
If
Examiner "Sogard" is assigned Exam_course "Snowbird"
        and
Exam_course "Snowbird" is used for Exam_type "Level IV"
        and
Exam_type "Level IV" is given by Examiner "Sogard",
        then
Examiner "Sogard" gives Exam_type "Level IV" at Exam_course "Snowbird."
```

Rather than trying to represent these data relationships in a single table, it is better to decompose the table into three tables, with each table representing the constraints given. These tables are shown in Figure 2.9. The first table on top in Figure 2.9 represents the list of examiners assigned to exam courses. The second table (in the middle of Figure 2.9) is the list of exam courses assigned to exam types. The third table on the right is the list of exam types each examiner can give.

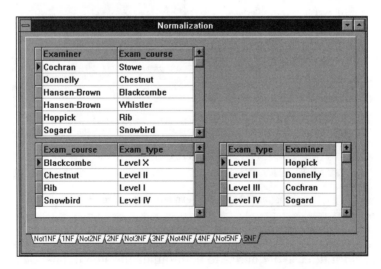

FIGURE 2.9 TABLES IN FIFTH NORMAL FORM

When tables with compound primary keys contain these sorts of cyclical constraints, they can always be decomposed into at least three tables, thereby eliminating awkward and redundant data storage.

Normalizing Conclusions

Normalizing databases is simply an exercise in finding and removing all redundant data. During this process, you will find that the number of fields in your tables will decrease, and the number of tables in your application will increase. This is a good sign. Do not let the growing number of tables bother you. Good relational database design often produces lots of simple tables. In fact, this is one of the most important goals of relational database design: to simply the practice of representing data.

You might have heard some people say that you should keep the number of fields in your tables small. While the process of normalization of your data often does this, not all tables are simple. Some tables can have a rather large number of fields, often as many as 75 or 100. This is not necessarily a bad thing.

The most important consideration in the design of a table is this: Do all fields in this table depend entirely on the primary key? If any fields are partially or transitively dependent on the primary key, then they should be moved to another table. If not, then the fields can stay where they are.

Now if a table or two still has a large number of fields, you might consider breaking the table down into a series of smaller tables joined in one-to-one relationships. Why? For performance, security, or other considerations. In some database systems, such as Paradox, tables with smaller record sizes perform better than tables with larger record sizes. The reason for this is that tables with large record sizes can have much larger primary key indexes. The larger the primary key index is, the longer the database system takes reading the index. If your table contains a large number of fields, or several fields with widths of 80-255 characters, consider shortening your field sizes, or moving some of the other fields to another table.

When a table has a large number of fields, it often means that the table is complex. If you can break the table down into a series of simpler tables, joined with one-to-one relationships, then data is segregated into smaller simpler tables. When creating applications, simpler is almost always better.

When creating Delphi database applications, if you understand the first three normal forms well, you are doing better than most developers. If you understand and apply the fourth and fifth normal forms, then you are developing databases with the least amount of redundancy.

Relational Database Rules

In 1985, E.F. Codd, one of the pioneers in establishing the relational database model, proposed a set of 12 rules for determining how relational a so-called relational database product might be. These rules are useful when considering which database system to use for Delphi applications. These rules, however, represent a very high hurdle over which any database system has to jump. Few relational database systems, if any at all, provide complete support for all 12 rules.

Information Rule

This rule states that the information in a database is represented as relations—as tables with rows and columns. The system should not use internal links or pointers to access links between data elements. Instead, the database system should link data based on common field values.

Guaranteed Access Rule

Users must be able to access every data value in the database by using the table name, the primary key value for the record in question, and the column name. This clarifies access which is hinted at in the information rule.

Systematic Treatment of Nulls

The system must have some way to consistently handle missing information so that it can be distinguished from supplied information. Fields with a blank value in them can be considered to have a known blank value (as in no middle name for a middle name field), or unknown value, (*as in the middle name for the person has not been determined yet*). The term null value is frequently used to refer to this latter description of missing information. Null values are particularly important when summarizing numeric data. For example, if you were averaging employee salaries to determine a mean company salary, what should you do with a record in which the employee salary is blank? Should the field value be considered 0 with the amount included in the total and the average salary adjusted? Or should the record be discarded as if it were never seen?

In a perfect world, a database would never have missing information. Since we do not live in a perfect world, the database must somehow allow us to keep missing information distinct from information with a blank value, or a 0 value. In other words, a missing value should not be considered a value at all.

Systematic treatment of nulls gets sticky because there might be multiple classifications for a null value. Fields with either-or constraints between them introduce an additional meaning to the term *null value*. Regardless of how the null value debate turns out, many database packages at least let you tell the difference between a null value and a blank, or 0 value.

Active On-Line Relational Catalog

The database system must employ relations (tables) to describe the database and its tables, domains, fields and integrity rules. This catalog must be maintained on-line so that as the database structure is changed, the catalog which describes that structure is also maintained. Users (in most cases database developers) should be able to query various parts of the database catalog as easily as they query regular data tables.

High-Level Insert, Delete , and Update

The system must allow the user to insert, delete, and update sets of records at a time, rather than just one record at a time.

Comprehensive Data Sublanguage

The system must support at least one relational language which can be used to retrieve, update, delete, and insert data, define data (such as creating tables and views), establish security and integrity constraints, and manage transactions.

Physical Data Independence

The database system hides the physical implementation of the data. The physical mechanisms used to implement the database must be irrelevant to the user and the use of the database system. Changes in the physical mechanisms underlying the database must not affect querying, or manipulating the data in the database or the catalog.

Logical Data Independence

If the underlying tables in the database are changed, such as adding fields to a table, or breaking up data in one table into two or more tables, the application that uses the data must not be affected. Stated conversely, the application should not directly manipulate the base tables in the system. Instead, the application (or user) should manipulate *views* of the base tables. So long as a change does not remove information from the database, the application and user must be unaffected by the change.

From the users' perspective, views must be indistinguishable from tables. In practice, views are implemented as SQL statements which return information from one or more tables presented to the user as a single table.

View Updating Rule

While the idea of views is quite powerful in that they can insulate an application from logical changes in the base tables, they come at a price. Certain views are not updatable. Views which do not return primary key values are not updatable because the view removes the very thing (the primary key) that would be used to update the base table. Also, summary operators, such as average, make it impossible to update the records with the numeric field upon which the average is based.

The database system should automatically know which views are updatable and which are not, and notify as well as prevent the user from trying to update a non-updatable view.

Integrity Independence

The various integrity constraints, entity, domain, referential, domain, column, and user-defined, must be defined as part of the database catalog and certainly independent of application logic.

Distribution Independence

While most database systems are stored centrally in one computer or device, some relational database systems are distributed and stored on multiple devices in multiple locations. Distributing the database across multiple platforms must not affect applications that depend on the database. If a particular table is stored on a computer in Chicago, it should not affect the application if the table is moved to another computer in Phoenix.

Nonsubversive Rule

A programmer (or user) cannot be able to bypass any of the integrity constraints or security using low-level access facilities or any other mechanism, that the database system might provide.

Formal Object Role Modeling

Various tools to help construct relational databases are available. One such tool, call *InfoModeler* is produced by the Asymetrix company. InfoModeler lets developers model the relationships in their data in a way that is more easily communicated to end users, yet still preserving all the technical benefits of the relational database model. InfoModeler uses an approach, called object-role modeling (ORM) and a language, called Formal Object Role Modeling Language (*FORML*, pronounced FORM-EL). While the acronyms ORM and FORML may sound difficult, they really are not. One of the important benefits to the ORM methodology is that it can produce database design documents that can be easily validated and reviewed by end users as well as application developers.

Object role modeling views the world as object playing roles. Objects, being nouns, play roles in relation to each other. An object might be a person, company, an address. An object might correspond to a table or a field in a table. A role how the object interacts with another object.

Consider an object Instructor and an object Math 101. The statement *Instructor 44 teaches Math 101* includes two objects and a role that each object plays. The role is defined by the verb *teaches*. In FORML, the term predicate is used to denote the phrase that describes the role an object plays. If you turn the phrase around like this: *Math 101 is taught by Instructor 4,* the predicate *is taught by* describes the role Math 101 plays. In FORML it is common to use the sentences like the following to depict the two roles that exist between two objects: *Instructor 44 teaches/is taught by Math 101.* The / character in the predicate is used to separate the role when reading the sentence forward and the role when reading the sentence in reverse.

You can see from this small example, that simple, English-like sentences are used to describe the roles that objects play. Since objects can be fields and tables, if you aggregate enough of these small facts, you eventually have enough information to create an accurate data mode.

Identifying Objects

Figure 2.10 shows an example of the Object Browser window in InforModeler. The diagram shows a simple relation: an object called Name2 which has a relationship with six other objects representing first name, middle initial, last name, date of birth (DOB), social security number, and work phone. Each object in this diagram represents a field, with the object Name, referring to a primary key identifier for the other fields.

The Name object has several facts associated with it: *Name2 (ID) has First_Name, Name2(ID) has Middle_Init* among others. In this case, First_Name and Middle_Init are fields in the Name2 table. In FORML parlance, First_Name and Middle_Init are objects that play a role in regards to Name2 and vice versa.

With FORML, you do not have to design your databases first. Instead, you identify the objects you need to include in your database and then you identify the roles these objects play. When you are finished identifying objects and roles, you are then ready to produce a relational database model which accurately reflects the list of objects and roles.

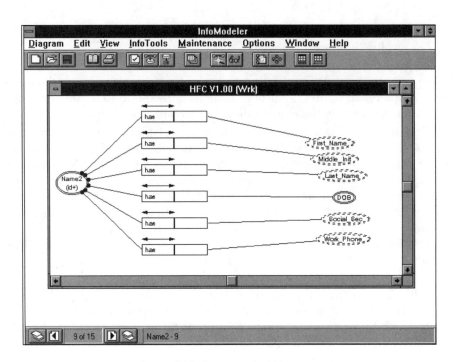

FIGURE 2.10 OBJECTS IN INFOMODELER.

Identifying Roles

Once you get a list of objects defined, its a simple matter to start linking objects together via roles.

Figure 2.11 is an example of the Verbalizer Dialog which InfoModeler can display for the objects in your model. This dialog is very useful to review the facts contained within the application. These facts include the predicates which describe the roles your objects play.

Predicates are depicted as rectangles with a vertical dividing line separating the rectangle into two halves (see Figure 2.10). Each half of the predicate box depicts one side of a role. Reading from left to right, the left half of the predicate box describes the role for the left object and the right half of the predicate box describes the role for the right object.

After you identify the roles objects play, you begin to accumulate a series of facts about objects. These facts can be printed out and verified rather easily.

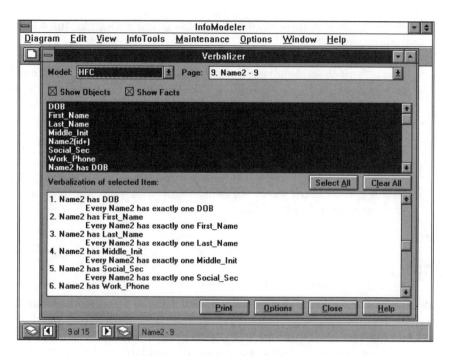

FIGURE 2.11 VERBALIZER DIALOG.

Notice the facts listed for the Name2 object:

```
Each Name2(ID) has exactly one First_Name.
Every Name2(ID) has exactly one First_Name.
```

These facts contain the predicate **has** which describes the role Name2 plays with First Name. The phrase **exactly** is a constraint which clarifies the role one object has with another object. With InfoModeler, you can identify several constraints which clarify and restrict the types of relationships objects can have. These constraints appear as simple qualifiers in a predicate. Any user or developer can read the two facts listed above and understand quickly and easily what is being said. If these facts can be verified, then they accurately reflect the business requirements for the application and can be automatically incorporated into the database design.

Once the objects and roles have been identified, InfoModeler has enough information to automatically build a logical relational database model. Defining constraints, which are a key component to FORML, are not discussed here but are important in building complex and robust data models in InfoModeler. It is important to note that using a tool like InfoModeler has several advantages:

- Communicating database design with the end user is easier since the reports that InfoModeler prints to document the facts in your data model use simple, easy to read sentences.
- Verifying the database design is much simpler than other methods.
- Using a tool like InfoModeler helps ensure that you have a complete design that is not missing essential features.
- The InfoModeler design tool can be used to actually construct the tables (even client/server tables) to be used by your application, saving a small modicum of time.

Object Design

Once the you have completed a data model for your application, the next step is to enumerate all the other objects your application will need. How many reports are needed? How many data entry forms? How many special purpose dialog boxes? Do you need any additional tables, such as configuration tables? You will need to develop a list of these objects, which can also serve as a checklist to ensure that you do not forget any important piece. After all, a short pencil is more powerful than a long memory.

As you work through the list of potential objects the user requires, think about the user interface. Since Delphi gives you many tools to implement a user-interface, you will need to carefully consider which tools you want to use. Does your application require a tabbed notebook type of interface? Does the main data entry screen need to be split up into three or four smaller dialog boxes? Should an outliner control be used to represent hierarchical relationships?

While designing database involves matching the needs of the application with the goal of relational database design—reducing redundancy, object design is not so concrete. Often, objects must be hand crafted to meet the skills and expectations of the user and the demands of the application. The goals in object design are many. Their measures are not always so easily measured. Nonetheless, an application must be built and objects must be designed. Perhaps the best place to look for user-interface design ideas is from any good Windows software package.

Identify Each Object's Behavior and Purpose

Once you have listed each object, you will then need to start thinking about how you want that object to behave and to what end it will be put. This is often the most difficult part of creating Delphi applications. Since Delphi has an enormous wealth of tools for forms and reports creation, you will need to weigh many alternative object designs that will determine how well your application meets the requirements at hand.

Fortunately, many of these data entry and report objects fall into well defined categories. Data entry forms typically fall into three main categories: key data entry forms which the user will interact with most of the time; secondary data entry forms the user will interact with infrequently; and dialog boxes which are used to prompt the user for simple information or display messages.

Key data entry forms are the ones that will require the most time since ease of use and performance will be important. And to provide ease of use, ObjectPascal code will be required. Secondary data entry forms are usually very simple to create and program. Simple dialog boxes occupy a middle ground in terms of complexity, because in order to use dialog boxes to prompt the user for information, you need to communicate information between forms.

Reports, on the other hand, have a very different requirement than forms. And since ReportSmith is such a powerful report-writing tool, often no programming is required. In order to produce reports, you will frequently need to create a series of queries to select the relevant records that you wish to include, and to transform the data with calculations of some kind. As you list out each report, it is important to keep in mind exactly how the report should be sorted, exactly what records need to be included in the report, and precisely what calculations or summarizing needs to be performed.

Since designing and programming forms is often the most critical part of creating Delphi applications, we recommend the following ideas to help with this process:

- Keep your forms simple. Do not try to have one form do too much. You will run into conceptual difficulties in trying to understand exactly what the form needs to do, and you will run into implementation difficulties because the form will be too large and complex. Although Delphi applications can range from trivial to enormously complex, your forms do not have to. The hallmark of a good application is that it comprises many relatively simple components.

- Let your forms serve as windows to the data. As with any powerful application development tool, Delphi's object-oriented environment gives you lots of ways to do the same thing. If you think of your forms as windows to the data, your forms will be easier to construct and require less code. Conversely, if you need to perform intricate transformations of your data in order to present it, the coding effort will be higher.

- Think in an object-oriented way. If you need a form or object with slightly different behavior than another object, then use Delphi's object-oriented facilities to reuse code in that other object. Object-oriented design is critical in minimizing code effort.

- Seek out stellar user-interface design examples and imitate them. Or, consult one of the many texts available about good user interface design for ideas.

With Delphi, programmers have enormous power to create absolutely intricate and complex database applications with maximum performance and minimum coding. If you carefully enumerate and design your user-interface objects and take advantage of the Delphi's object-oriented tools, form construction will proceed smoothly.

Summary

When building database applications, the first priority is to design the database properly. Relational database theory can help you design easy to use, efficient, and robust databases that will require less maintenance. Anything you can do to learn more about relational database theory will help you construct better applications.

Since Delphi has a wealth of user-interface tools, it is important to carefully design the forms and reports the user will interact with. After all, the forms and reports are the windows to the application's database.

Bibliography

An Introduction to Database Systems, C.J. Date, Addison-Wesley Publishing Company, 1990.

SQL and Relational Basics, Fabian Pascal, M&T Publishing, 1990.

The Relational Model for Database Management: Version 2, E.F. Codd, Addison-Wesley Publishing Company, 1990.

CHAPTER 3

Object-Oriented Programming: What is It?

When the concept of object-oriented programming (OOP) caught fire over the past decade, learned software developers quickly realized that it was not just a fad. OOP was here to stay and would find its way into mainstream products. While this has been a boon for OOP enthusiasts, market-savvy software houses have taken the term OOP and used it loosely, so that many developers are not sure exactly what it means anymore. It seems that every software development package claims to be object-oriented, whether or not it is.

For those new to object-oriented programming, read on. For the experienced, feel free to skim this chapter; it briefly explains the key concepts of OOP. This chapter will clearly explain exactly what OOP means and how Delphi is object-oriented.

Object-oriented programming is a way of programming that differs substantially from traditional programming, such as COBOL, C, Pascal, and Basic. While you can now purchase object-oriented flavors of each of these languages, the original versions were not object-oriented. In fact, ObjectPascal, the language used in Delphi, is based on the non-object-oriented language Pascal.

What makes OOP different is that rather than writing a program by writing a main loop and then all the subroutines that constitute the application, you start by deciding which objects your application requires and then you endow each object with properties and behavior. Objects fall into a class hierarchy, like a hierarchy of the animal kingdom. Just as wealth can be passed on from generation to generation in many cultures in the world, in OOP an object's wealth (its properties and behavior) can be passed on to descendant objects.

In order for a language to be considered object-oriented, it must support the following key concepts:

- Classes
- Encapsulation
- Polymorphism
- Inheritance

Unlike other products (for example, Visual Basic and PowerBuilder), Delphi supports all four of these features extremely well. In fact, if you have C++ experience, you should feel right at home in the Delphi OOP environment, because it implements OOP in a very similar manner.

While Delphi is fully object-oriented, you do not need to know anything about object-oriented programming to use it. Delphi is a powerful tool in the hands of both experienced and inexperienced OOP programmers.

NOTE

What is an Object?

In order to understand how all this OOP stuff works, you need to clearly understand an *object*. In OOP, an object is like a variable, except the object comes packaged with properties that define it and code that causes the object to do something or react to something. Just as dogs have properties (color, weight, size of tail) and behavior (barking, digging, sleeping, eating), programming objects also have properties (color, position, a value, a name) and behavior (deactivate, open, close, make invisible, execute). Lastly, objects have unique names that make it possible to refer to them unambiguously. After all, we name our dogs for the same reason.

In summary, objects have:

- Properties
- Behavior
- Identity

Properties require space in the computer and represent data that can be potentially accessed by other objects. *Behavior* requires the writing of code in modules (called *methods*) that act on the objects and sometimes on its properties. While these two concepts (data and programs) are often treated separately in traditional programming languages, in OOP they are clasped together into one entity: an object. That object has at least one property that separates it from the other objects: a name. An object must have some property that uniquely identifies it.

Consider the following programming object, called Invoice. In this example, an invoice is a tangible object in the real world; it is the piece of paper telling the cost of a service or product that is sent to a customer. Table 3.1 lists the properties and behavior for this Invoice object.

TABLE 3.1 INVOICE PROPERTIES AND BEHAVIOR

45

Properties

NetAmount
Tax
TotalAmount
Customer#
Date

Behavior

Print
CalculateTax
MarkAsPaid
Post

Using this short list of properties, in ObjectPascal, you would refer to the properties and behavior in the following manner (each line is commented, with the curly braces surrounding the comment):

```
Invoice.NetAmount := 100.00; {Assign $100 to the net amount}
Invoice.CalculateTax(.075); {Calculate the tax}
Invoice.Print; {Print the invoice to a printer}
Invoice.Post; {Post the invoice, updating balances}
Invoice.MarkAsPaid; {Upon receipt of payment, mark paid}
```

In these code examples, the first line assigns a value to a property. The next four lines invoke methods (CalculateTax, Print, Post, and MarkAsPaid) to cause the object to do something. As you can see, the object's properties and behavior are bound together to make the object.

Inheritance

As far as OOP is concerned, inheritance is the critical feature. Without inheritance, encapsulation, and polymorphism do not have much meaning. *Inheritance* simply means that an object can pass on some or all of its properties and behavior to a descendant object. Just like inheritances in the world of humans, the descendant object does not have to do any work on its own to deserve the inheritance. It receives the inheritance simply because it is a descendant object.

Inheritance is the key to code reuse, which is another important OOP goal. If you can design a clever inheritance hierarchy, you can maximize your code reuse by ensuring that each generation in the inheritance tree passes on exactly what the next generation needs. Each generation adds its own little bit, thereby enhancing and enriching the family line.

If you look at the animal kingdom classification scheme, you will find that OOP is really based on this sort of hierarchical ordering. Humans tend to naturally classify objects into hierarchical relationships. OOP takes advantage of this and makes programming easier to understand. For example, the classification of mammals encompasses a rather large number of other subordinate classifications. Mammals have many subtypes, one of them is a dog. And there are large numbers of types of dogs: spaniels, setters, and retrievers, to name a few.

Dogs inherit several properties from the mammal class, including their warm bloodedness and the fact that they do not lay eggs like birds. In addition, each type of dog inherits attributes from the dog class, such as the barking behavior and the animals' morphology (skeletal structure and shape). However, each type of dog has distinguishing characteristics. A Brittany Spaniel is a certain color, height, and weight, for example, which is quite different from a Boston Terrier. Boston Terriers are much shorter and are black and white in color; Brittany Spaniels are larger and white with tan spots in color.

In OOP, you must establish a hierarchy of object types (called *classes*) and decide what properties and behavior each generation in the hierarchy adds and passes on to the next generation. In fact, the people at Borland who built Delphi did exactly that: they designed an intricate object hierarchy that we can browse and use as we wish. Moreover, *Borland staff used Delphi to write Delphi*. Delphi is such a powerful OOP tool that most of what constitutes it is written using Delphi. It's object-oriented nature makes this possible.

Polymorphism

Polymorphism means that different objects can respond to the same message appropriately. Just as different dogs can respond to the same message "Bark," objects can do the same. Polymorphism makes inheritance easy. Since you do not need to write a differently named routine to respond to the same message, the code you write is easier to understand. For example, without polymorphism, in order to get different dogs to bark, you would have to write the following code:

```
Doberman.DobermanBark;
IrishSetter.IrishSetterBark;
Spaniel.SpanielBark;
```

With polymorphism, you do not need to have a different method for each type of object. You can simply write the following:

```
Doberman.Bark;
IrishSetter.Bark;
Spaniel.Bark;
```

In this example, the three different dog types have three different barks, yet the same method name is used to invoke the different barks. In the code for these mythical objects, you would need to write three different Bark methods: one for each type of dog. Although you would have to write three different routines for three different barks, *the routines would share the same name.*

Polymorphism obviously does not help us reuse code. Instead, it helps us comprehend our programs. Since a great many objects share the same classification of behavior with slightly different implementations, finding a way to decrease the number of terms used to invoke the behavior helps immensely. Programmer's don't need to know that a Doberman's bark is different from a Spaniel's bark. All programmers need to know is that if they want the dog to bark, they just invoke the Bark method.

Consider a real-world example. Most businesses write different kinds of checks: paychecks to employees and checks to vendors. Checks share similar behavior. They need to print and they need to be calculated. The employee check differs from the vendor check in that the employee check stub includes withholding information. The vendor check stub usually includes the list of invoices paid. The way the checks are calculated is quite different. Employee checks need to have the federal, state, and local taxes computed.

However, because vendor and employee checks both need to be calculated and printed, they can share the same method names: Print and Calculate. The programmer who needs to cause the check to be printed does not need to know the difference between the two printing methods, just the method name.

Since similar behaviors will share the same method name (or property name), from the programmer's perspective the application will look simpler since the number of methods to memorize is substantially smaller. In effect, the application appears somewhat smaller.

Encapsulation

Contrary to the common misconception, encapsulation does not mean that an object has properties and behavior. Rather, *encapsulation* literally means information hiding. Parts of the object are placed in a capsule that *seals* those parts from view. You may be asking why you would want to prevent others from seeing an object's properties or behavior. The reason is that some complex objects, like humans, have private parts, which you would rather not expose to view.

One of the goals of OOP is to build objects that are blank boxes. Like a car, you may have no knowledge about what is inside it and how it works. All you know is that it works and that you have enough skill to drive it. If we had to know all about the internal workings of the combustion engine in order to drive a car, our freeways would be a lot less jammed.

So it is in programming. With one programmer creating objects and another programmer implementing the object in part of the application, the second programmer is free to ignore messy details involved with that object. The second programmer does not get bogged down in unimportant (at least from his or her perspective) details.

In Delphi, encapsulation is fully supported. You can create objects with the following levels of protection assigned to the objects' internals:

- Private
- Protected
- Public
- Published

If an object has a *private* method or property, that item is completely hidden from view from all other objects. Only that object can access that item. This provides the greatest level of security. If an object's method or property is *protected*, then only that object and any descendant objects can access that item. Objects outside the family line are forbidden access. *Public* items are visible to any other object regardless of family relationships. *Published* items are the same as public ones, except that the published items are available to the Object Inspector. The Object Inspector lets the developer set an object's properties and attach code to events for that object. Without the published classification, you would not be able to enhance the Delphi environment with your own controls.

Objects and Classes

So far the distinction between an object and a class has been not quite clear. The terms are different, and the difference is important. A class is a blueprint used to create an object. It is a description of an object's behavior and properties. A class hierarchy describes the inheritance relationship between each generation of classes.

An object is a class created or instantiated. It is the real-world entity you will manipulate. In Delphi, one creates an object with the following syntax:

```
var
     Mylist: TList;
```

The variable (or object) is MyList and the object's type (or class) is TList.

If you are new to object oriented terminology, it is important to keep the distinction between class and object clear. The facilities in ObjectPascal to deal with classes and objects are quite different.

The Object Browser

One of the best ways to learn about OOP is to observe the work of others, and what better way to learn than looking at what the bright people at Borland created in Delphi. The tool to do this is called the Object Browser (see Figure 3.1).

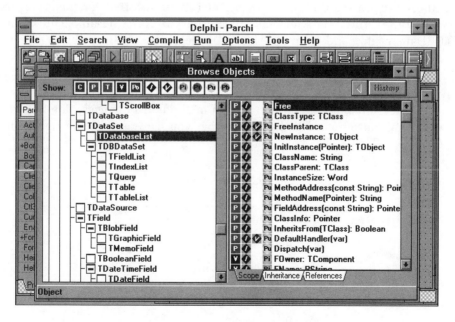

FIGURE 3.1 THE OBJECT BROWSER.

To bring up the Object Browser, simple compile any project, even a blank new project, and use the **View | Browser** menu.

N O T E   In order to view the Object Browser, you need to successfully compile a project. In Delphi, the Object Browser shows not only the Delphi VCL (Visual Component Library) class hierarchy, but the relationships between your code and the library. This is why a project must be compiled before viewing the Object Browser.

In Figure 3.1, you can see the following object types:

- TDataSet
- TDatabaseList
- TDBDataSet
- TDBFieldList
- TDBIndexList
- TQuery
- TTable
- TTableList

In the left-hand window the Browser clearly shows that for this group of object types, the TDataSet class is the parent class. TDatabaseList and TDBDataSet descend from it. Also, TDBFieldList, TDBIndexList, TQuery, TTable, and TTableList all descend from TDBDataSet.

The right side of the Browser lists the various methods and properties available to the selected object type. As you scroll through the list of classes on the left-hand side, the properties and methods list changes. The Browser has several buttons on top that limit what you can view on the right-hand side. These buttons are explained in Table 3.2.

TABLE 3.2 BROWSER BUTTONS

Button Heading	Button Meaning
C	show/hide constants
P	show/hide procedure/functions (methods)
T	show/hide types
V	show/hide variables

show/hide properties

show/hide inherited items

show/hide virtual methods

show/hide private items

show/hide protected items

show/hide public items

show/hide published items

Do not worry about what each of these items mean right now. The important two to examine now are the Inherited Items button and the Private Items button. Figure 3.2 shows the Browser with the inherited and private items turned off for the TDataSet class. This means that the Browser will not show items that have been inherited or items are meant to be encapsulated or hidden from view (private items). In this context, the term *items* refers to constants, procedures, types, variables, or properties. With private and inherited items off, you can observe what each class contributes to the family line and makes available to descendent classes.

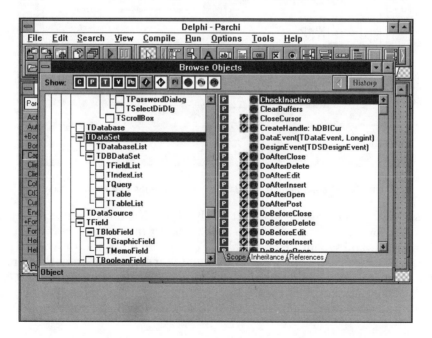

FIGURE 3.2 BROWSER VIEWING TDATASET WITH INHERITED AND PRIVATE ITEMS OFF.

The TDataSet class has quite a few items associated with it. Some of the methods include DoAfterClose and DoAfterDelete. These are methods that Borland engineers wrote and decided to give to the TDataSet class. Since these methods are protected, any class that is a descendant of TDataSet has access to these methods. While you will never need to access any of these methods for the TDataSet class, they are there to service a family of related objects. Borland designed the hierarchy so that its development staff's efforts are maximized as code is reused. You will be working with descendants of the TDataSet object, especially the TTable object and the TQuery object.

Moving further down the family line, Figure 3.3 shows the Browser with the inherited and private items turned off for the TDBDataSet class.

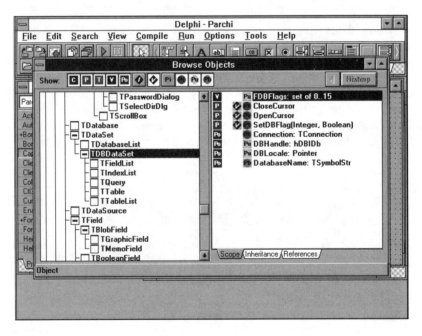

FIGURE 3.3 BROWSER VIEWING **TDBD**ATA**S**ET WITH INHERITED AND PRIVATE ITEMS OFF.

This class, which is a descendant of the TDataSet object, inherits all the methods for TDataSet and adds a few items to the family line, including CloseCursor and OpenCursor. Finally, Figure 3.4 shows the Browser listing for the TTable object, which is a component you can access from the component palette. TTable inherits all the non-private items from TDataSet and TDBDataSet and adds its own. Some of the methods it adds that you can directly use in your code include CreateTable, DeleteTable, and EmptyTable.

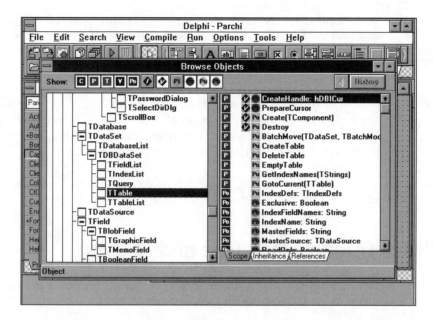

FIGURE 3.4 BROWSER VIEWING TTABLE WITH INHERITED AND PRIVATE ITEMS OFF.

The Browser clearly shows the hierarchical relationships between classes and enumerates exactly what each generation passes off to the next generation. Spend some time with the Browser, as it shows you object-oriented programming at work within Delphi.

Delegation

You might hear and read about the term *delegation* as you work with Delphi. Delegation is a technique in OOP whereby one object delegates its behavior to another object. In Delphi, it means that a visual component can choose to delegate to another object the responsibility for responding to an event. For example, if you have a form with five field objects, you can choose to write one procedure to respond to the OnClick event for each of the five fields. In this case, the field objects have delegated responsibility for the OnClick event to another object.

Event delegation helps eliminate code redundancy. If many different objects need to respond identically to different events, there is no need to write a separate function for each object.

NOTE

The objects that share an event delegation relationship do not need to be within the same family line in the class hierarchy. Event delegation is not tied to the class hierarchy. All that is required is that all objects need to respond to the event in the same manner.

54

Event delegation, if improperly used, can work against an object-oriented approach. Remember that in OOP, if a group of objects needs to respond in a similar manner to the same message, then those objects should be in an inheritance relationship of some kind. Delegation can circumvent this requirement. Spontaneous delegation code can degenerate into non-object-oriented code, which might not be what you want. Delphi gives you tools to construct applications; it is up to you to decide what is appropriate for your application.

Object-Oriented Analysis and Design

Just as object-oriented programming is different from structured programming, so object-oriented analysis and design are different from structured analysis and design.

In structured analysis and design, code and data are considered two very separate things. A structure chart of a program shows how routines are called from one another. A data-flow diagram, another structured analysis tool, shows how routines transform data and pass the data on to other routines. A data dictionary describes the structure of the data independent of the routines that process and transform it.

In object-oriented analysis and design (OOA and OOD), you dispense with the usual structured formalities and proceed to identify your objects and the relationships that exist between them. Just like structured analysis and design, OOA and OOD have notations you can use to illustrate the relationships between classes of objects graphically. Peter Coad and Edward Yourdon describe a notation in their book *Object-Oriented Analysis.* Grady Booch also describes an object-oriented notation in his book *Object Oriented Design with Applications.* Sally Shlaer and Stephen J. Mellor describe yet another notation scheme in their books *Object-Oriented Systems Analysis: Modeling the World in Data* and *Object-Oriented Systems Analysis: Modeling the World in States.*

Each of the OOA and OOD methods discussed in the aforementioned books helps in defining in detail, a class hierarchy for an application. As with structured analysis and design, OOA and OOD are sometimes difficult processes, often requiring an iterative approach with step-wise refinement of the model. Several problems present themselves. How do you interview application users in order to determine what the objects for this application are? Once you have determined the important objects, how do you go about deciding what the class hierarchy should look like? How similar do two classes need to be in order for them to belong to the same parent class? What properties should each class have? What methods? Which methods should be passed on to the next generation? Which ones should be enhanced or modified by the next generation? The list of questions goes on.

If anything can be learned from OOA and OOD, it is that it requires the developer to make a fundamental shift in thinking. The developer must stop thinking in terms of processes transforming data and start thinking of objects joined together in an inheritance hierarchy. For developers new to OOP, this is sometimes difficult and awkward, but it is a significant first step.

Advantages of OOP

OOP has done well because it has some marked advantages. These include:

- Code reuse
- Application scalability
- Maintainability
- Appropriateness

One of the biggest driving forces behind OOP is code reuse. The inheritance hierarchy forms a structure that promotes code reuse more readily than other programming environments. OOP naturally forces developers to think in terms of inheritance hierarchies, and they subsequently tend to create class hierarchies that share code.

Larger applications can be developed with OOP techniques more easily than without. Code reuse is of obvious benefit, but so are polymorphism and encapsulation. Without polymorphism, the developer would be faced with an unending list of methods with different names but similar behavior. Or the developer would be left with large blocks of code with switch-case statements simulating polymorphism. Either solution is fraught with error. Without encapsulation, developers would have no way of knowing what an object's essential and inessential details are. With the object totally exposed, developers would *need to understand too much* about an object in order to use it. Or they would take advantage of the exposure for short-term expediency, risking long-term maintainability.

Applications developed with OOP techniques are more easily maintained than without. If the application needs additional functionality, you do not need to change existing code; you simply create a new generation of a class, inherit the old behavior, and add new behavior or redefine old behavior. In fact, this feature is so important to developers that you will find you can completely redefine the Delphi application environment by creating new generations of classes and placing them on the component palette. Delphi is an application you are free to enhance using OOP techniques.

Another advantage of OOP techniques is also a disadvantage: appropriateness (see the next section). Problems in the real world are often easily solved by transforming the problem using OOA and OOD techniques. Our minds are natural classifiers of things. Typically we classify things in hierarchies of inheritance. OOP takes advantage of this fact and gives us a framework that works more like the way our minds work. In this manner, OOP is more appropriate to solving systems problems than other approaches are.

Disadvantages of OOP

Despite all the hype, OOP does have some disadvantages. These include:

- Appropriateness
- Brittleness
- Development linearity

Appropriateness is listed as both an advantage and a disadvantage because OOP does not always solve problems neatly. While the human mind appears to classify objects into categories (classes) and to group these categories into inheritance relationships, what it really does is not so simple. Instead, objects with *roughly* similar features, not precisely defined ones, get lumped together into a classification. OOP requires precise definitions of classes, not softly defined ones. In the human mind, these classifications can change over time. New objects can be placed in old categories. The criteria as to what gets placed into a category can change significantly. Whether OOP exactly mimics the way our brain works is a highly debatable point.

In addition, real-world problems sometimes do not decompose neatly into a hierarchy of classes. Businesses and people often have rules for operations on objects that defy clean hierarchical and object-oriented decomposition. The object-oriented paradigm does not deal well with problem domains that require fuzzy boundaries and dynamic ad hoc rules for object classification. Ironically, in this world of organizations that are embracing nonrigid, easily changing rules, even the best of OOP techniques might not be able to keep pace with the changes.

This leads to the next problem with OOP: brittleness. Since an object-oriented hierarchy requires precise definitions, if the fundamental relationships between the key classes change, the original object-oriented design is largely lost. You must reanalyze the relationships between your key objects and redesign a new class hierarchy. If there is a fundamental flaw in the class hierarchy, the problem is not easily fixed. It requires hard work to get it right. The human mind was designed by nature to be anything but brittle. It adapts continuously, and usually appropriately, to new situations. It finds ways of classifying objects in the environment automatically. While our minds work this way, OOP environments are not so well-equipped.

Because of this brittleness, OOP requires up-front analysis and design to ensure that the solution is proper. This tends to lead to a linear development approach, rather than a cyclical one. Unfortunately, some problems are *wicked*, which means that you don't know how to solve the problem until you have actually solved it. Such problems defy even the best analysts and designers. Using a rapid application development approach with iterations between prototype design, construction, and user feedback is sometimes a good way to solve wicked problems. OOP, however, still requires a careful design of the class hierarchy, which can raise the cost of using OOP in a rapid application development environment. The class hierarchy may undergo substantial revision and change. Fundamental assumptions in the class hierarchy may change.

Despite these limitations, which may sound severe, OOP, especially as Delphi delivers it to us, is a sound problem-solving approach and an important advancement in developing computer systems. Delphi is not just a good OOP tool, it is a good prototyping tool. Programmers do not need to understand OOP techniques to build solid simple and advanced applications with Delphi. Delphi can help with rapid application development in which fundamental design objectives might change drastically. But, because Delphi is object oriented, it can serve when precise and up-front object–oriented analysis and design is needed.

Summary

Delphi provides full support for the most important parts of OOP: inheritance, polymorphism, and encapsulation. Although you do not need to understand OOP in order to use Delphi, programmers that do understand it will not only be able to build superior complex applications, they will also be able to enhance the Delphi development environment by adding their own new classes to the Delphi VCL class hierarchy. Because of this, developers with OOP knowledge and experience will have a significant advantage in creating sophisticated database applications.

Bibliography

Object-oriented Software Construction, Betrand Meyer, Prentice Hall International, Englewood Cliffs, N.J., 1988.

Object Oriented Design with Applications, Grady Booch, The Benjamin/ Cummings Publishing Company, Inc., Redwood City, CA, 1991.

Object Oriented Analysis, P. Coad and E. Yourdon, Prentice Hall International, Englewood Cliffs, NJ, 1991.

Object Oriented System Analysis: Modeling the World in Data, S. Shlaer and S.J. Mellor, Prentice Hall International, Englewood Cliffs, NJ, 1988.

CHAPTER 4

The Delphi Development Environment

Like all programming books this one faces the challenge of where to start. With Delphi, the starting point is clearly the interactive development environment (IDE). This chapter introduces you to all of the features of the IDE including the Main Menu, Speedbar, Component Palette, Code Editor, Debugger, Project Manager, Bitmap Editor, Menu Designer more.

Along the way you will also get your first taste of creating applications in Delphi. Although you will be amazed at what Delphi does for you, will also discover quickly that you need to know Delphi's programming language, Object Pascal, to build sophisticated programs. The next section of this book will introduce you to Object Pascal.

Changing the Default Directory

The default Delphi installation makes the DELPHI\BIN directory the working directory. If you create a new project in Delphi, save it, and forget to specify a different directory, your project files will be mixed in with over 80 other files in the DELPHI\BIN directory. Sorting them out and moving them is a nuisance, and the problem gets worse if you accidentally move or delete a file that is not part of your project. If that happens Delphi may not run until you restore the file, or reinstall.

To avoid these problems create a directory for your Delphi projects. Then open the Delphi group in Program Manager, select the Delphi icon, choose **File | Properties** from the menu, and change the working directory to the new project directory you created. Now when you start Delphi any projects you save will be placed in your project directory by default, and will not become mixed in with Delphi's program files.

Exploring the Main Window

When you start Delphi you will see the Delphi IDE as shown in Figure 4.1.

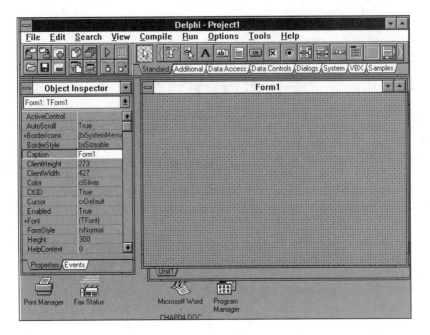

FIGURE 4.1 THE DELPHI IDE.

The Speedbar

At the top of the screen is the main menu. Below the main menu on the left is the double row of buttons that comprise the Speedbar. To find out what each of the buttons on the Speedbar does just point to it with the mouse and a help box will appear to identify the button. The buttons on the Speedbar are shortcuts to choices on the menus.

You can customize the Speedbar to contain any combination of menu choices you prefer. To change the size of the Speedbar move the mouse over the dividing line at the right hand end and drag the divider.

To change its contents right-click anywhere on the Speedbar to display the speed menu and select **Configure**. The Speedbar Editor dialog shown in Figure 4.2 will appear. Using the Speedbar Editor you can add any menu choice to the Speedbar by dragging its button from the Commands list and dropping it on the Speedbar. To remove a button drag it off of the Speedbar.

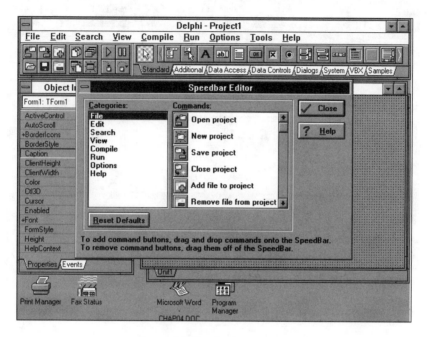

FIGURE 4.2 THE SPEEDBAR EDITOR

The Component Palette

To the right of the Speedbar is the Component Palette. The Component Palette is organized as a notebook with tabs along the bottom to allow you to select the various pages of components. The Component Palette is filled with components that you can drop onto your forms to add the features and functions that you want. Components run the gamut from simple buttons to data grids that let you easily display a database table in tabular format. To place a component on the form just click the component on the palette then click on the form where you want to place the component.

You can customize the Component Palette in the same way you customized the Speedbar. Just right-click to display the speed menu and select **configure**. Figure 4.3 shows the **Environment Options dialog** with the P**alette page** selected. You can also display this dialog from the **O**ptions menu.

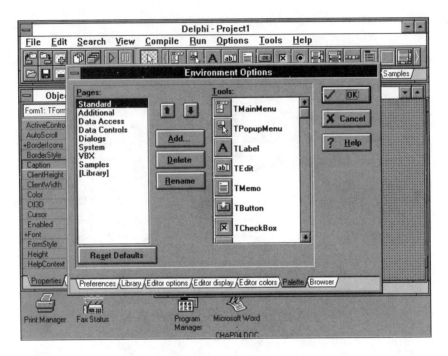

FIGURE 4.3 CUSTOMIZING THE COMPONENT PALETTE.

Exploring the Default Form

When you start Delphi or open a new project Delphi automatically creates a new form. Forms are the vehicle for all user interaction in Delpi applications. Associated with each form is a Pascal unit, a file that contains Pascal code related to the form. The form is named Form1 by default, and the associated unit is named UNIT1.PAS.

To see the unit associated with the form click the **Unit1** notebook tab below the form, or click the **Toggle Form/Unit** button on the Speedbar. It is the middle button in the bottom row. You will now be looking at the unit file in the Delphi Code Editor as shown in Figure 4.4.

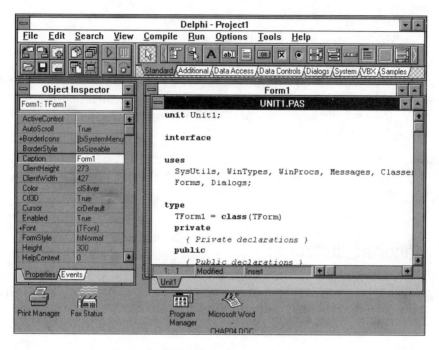

FIGURE 4.4 THE DELPHI CODE EDITOR.

Exploring the Code Editor

The Delphi Code Editor is a full featured configurable editor with the following features,

- Multiple keyboard maps
- Syntax highlighting
- Multi-file editing
- Block indent and undent
- Unlimited undo and redo
- Bookmarks

- Symbol browsing
- Regular expression searches
- Context sensitive help

Many of the Code Editor's features are only available through *hot keys*. To make it easy to look up the hot keys, until you learn them, search for the name of the keyboard map you use in the on-line help and set a bookmark for the list of hot keys.

The keystrokes in this section are for the default keyboard. If you use the Classic, Brief, or Epsilon keyboard search for the keyboard name in the on-line help to find correct keys.

N O T E

Configuring the Editor

You can change the Code Editor's configuration by selecting **Options|Environment** from the main menu and selecting the **Editor options**, **Editor display** or **Editor colors** page in the Environment options dialog shown in Figure 4.5.

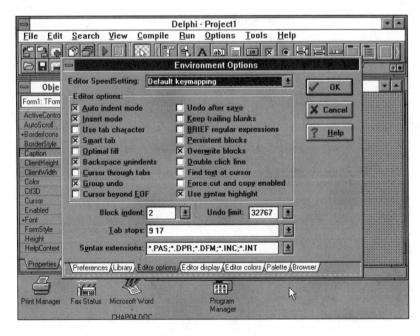

FIGURE 4.5 CONFIGURING THE CODE EDITOR.

For a detailed explanation of the options on each page just click the **help** button.

Using the Editor

You can open any text file in the Code Editor from the File menu by selecting **Open File**. You can also open any unit in the current project, including
the project file, by clicking the Select Unit From List button in the top row
of the Speedbar. You can also open a new unit by selecting **New Unit** from
the File menu. Each file is shown on a different page in the Code Editor
window and you can quickly switch from file to file by clicking the tabs at
the bottom of the window.

Right click anywhere in the Code Editor window to display the Code
Editor speed menu shown in Figure 4.6.

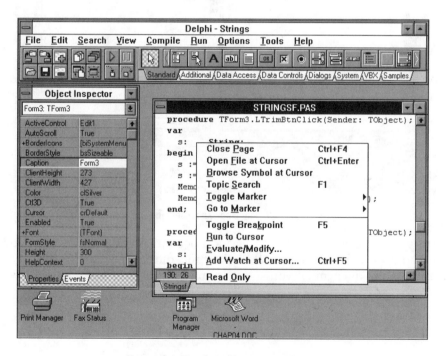

FIGURE 4.6 THE CODE EDITOR SPEED MENU.

The first choice, Close Page, closes the file being edited in the current page.
Whenever you close a page, the Code Editor window, or the entire project,
Delphi always prompts you to save any unsaved changes.

Open File at Cursor lets you point to a file name in the text of the file
you are editing, and open that file.

Browse Symbol at Cursor is one of the most useful features of the Code Editor. It allows you to place the insertion point on the name of any symbol in your code, such as a variable, procedure, function, or object name, and display the **Browse Symbol** dialog shown in Figure 4.7.

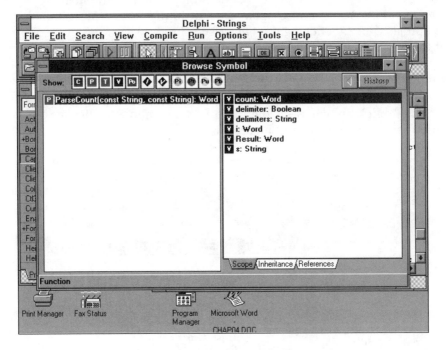

FIGURE 4.7 THE BROWSE SYMBOL DIALOG.

In this case the symbol selected was a procedure so the Scope page shows all of the variables defined within the procedure. The Inheritance page is empty unless the symbol you select is an object. If you select an object the

Inheritance page will show the objects from which the selected object is descended. For example, Figure 4.8 shows the Inheritance page when a button object named **LTrimBtn** is selected.

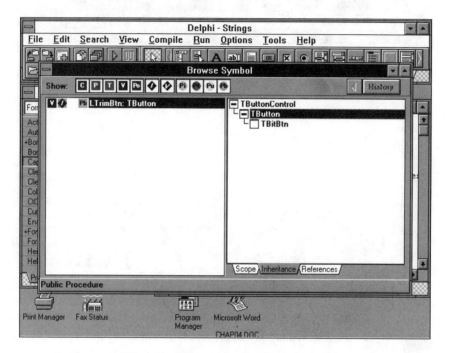

FIGURE 4.8 THE INHERITANCE PAGE FOR A BUTTON OBJECT.

If you are new to object-oriented programming you will understand the meaning of objects and inheritance after you read chapter 10, "Objects." The third page, "References," shows each line where the selected symbol is referenced as shown in Figure 4.9.

68

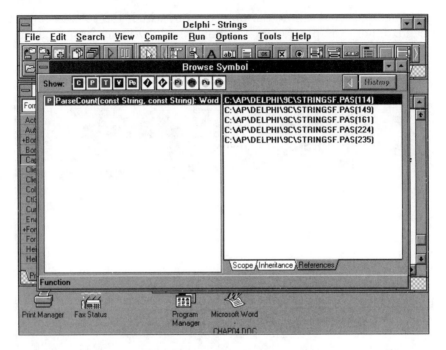

FIGURE 4.9 THE REFERENCES PAGE.

If the **Browse Symbol at Cursor** choice is dimmed press **Ctrl+F9** to compile your project. There must be a current symbol table for the unit you
are editing to use **Browse Symbol at Cursor**.

T I P

The next option on the Code Editor speed menu, Topic Search, has the same
effect as pressing the F1 key. It searches for on-line help for the word that
contains the insertion point and displays the **Search All** dialog with all relevant topics shown.

Toggle Marker and Go to Marker let you set up to ten bookmarks in the
file and instantly jump to any one of them. When you select **Toggle Marker**
the menu in Figure 4.10 appears so that you can pick the marker you want
to place on the line that contains the insertion point. Once you have set the
marker its number appears in the left margin of the Code Editor as shown
in Figure 4.11.

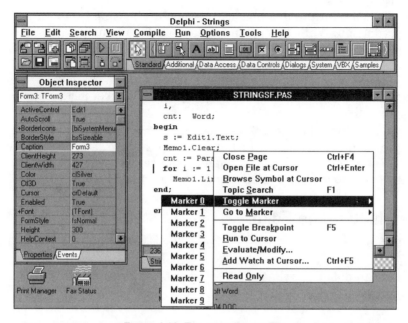

FIGURE 4.10 THE SET MARKER MENU.

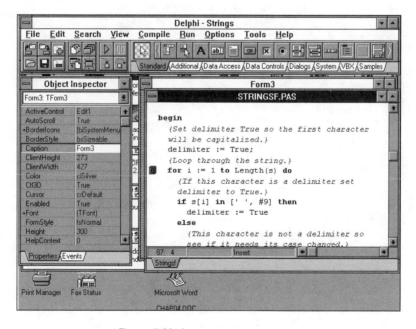

FIGURE 4.11 A LINE WITH A MARKER SET.

Now you can return to this line at any time by choosing **Go to Marker** from the speed menu. While this feature is nice what really makes it useful is that you can set, clear, and go to markers with a single keystroke. To set a marker, place the insertion point on the line you want to mark, and press **Shift+Ctrl+** the number of the marker you want to set. Press **Shift+Ctrl+** the number again to clear the marker. To jump to any marker just press **Ctrl+** the marker number.

The next four choices on the speed menu are used with the interactive debugger and are discussed in the debugger section later in this chapter. The last choice is Read **O**nly. Toggle this choice on when you want to make sure that you do not accidentally make changes to this file.

Searching in the Editor

The Delphi Code Editor offers two ways to search through a file and both of them are available from the Search menu as well as the keyboard. If you use the default keyboard **Ctrl+F** displays the find text dialog shown in Figure 4.12.

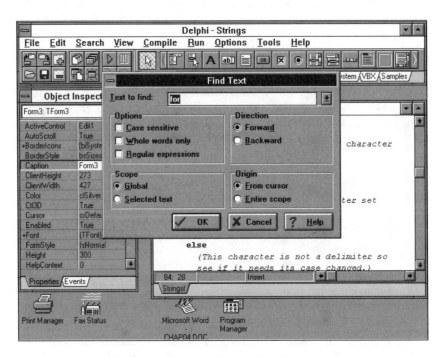

FIGURE 4.12 THE CODE EDITOR'S FIND TEXT DIALOG

Enter the text to find, select the options you want, and click the **OK** button to begin the search. To find the next occurrence of the text you are searching for, press **F3**. Regular expressions provide a powerful set of wildcard characters you can use in your search strings. If you are not familiar with regular expressions, search for **Regular Expressions** in the on-line help.

The Delphi Editor also supports incremental searches, invoked by pressing **Ctrl+E**. Once you have invoked incremental searching, Delphi adds each character you type to the search string, and searches for a match. The characters being sought are shown on the status line at the bottom of the Code Editor window. The search process continues until you press **Enter**, **Tab,** or a function key that invokes some other function. Once again, you can find the next occurrence of the search string by pressing **F3**.

You can also search and replace from the menu, or by pressing **Ctrl+R**. The Replace Text dialog offers a set of options almost identical to those shown in the Find Text dialog in Figure 4.12.

N O T E

The Code Editor does not support multi-file searches or search and replace.

Using the Object Inspector

All of the objects that you can place on a form, as well as the form itself, have properties that you can change in the IDE, or with your code. Objects also respond to events and you can customize the way that they respond to an event by writing code that executes when the event occurs. The Object Inspector lets you do both of these things.

Figure 4.13 shows a form with a button and the Object Inspector to the left of the form. To create this form just click the button component on the palette, then click on the form to place the button. This form is also on your code disk as the project PROP.DPR.

The Object Inspector displays the properties and events for whichever component is selected in the form. The selected component appears with selection handles as the button does in Figure 4.13. In addition, the name of the selected component appears in the drop-down list at the top of the Object Inspector. The component's name is just one more property. You can change the name of any component in the Object Inspector's properties page to make it more meaningful when you refer to the component in your code. You can select a component by clicking on it in the form, or using the drop-down list in the Object Inspector.

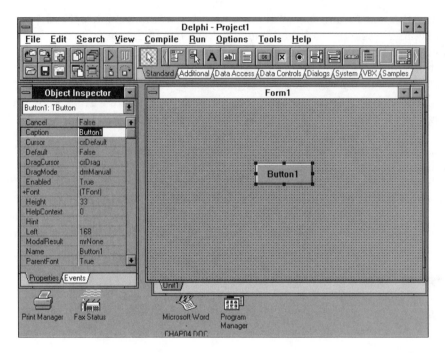

FIGURE 4.13 THE OBJECT INSPECTOR PROPERTIES PAGE

The connection between the Object Inspector and the form is alive. To see this select the button and change its Caption property by typing **Test** in place of **Button1**. Notice that as you type the text in, the button in the form changes. You change different properties in different ways. Notice that the button's Font property has a plus sign to the left of the word **Font**. Double click the **Font** property and it expands to show the indented list of sub-properties shown in Figure 4.14. Select the form, then click the **Color** property in the Object Inspector and a button appears indicating a drop-down list of choices. Select **clTeal** to change the form's color.

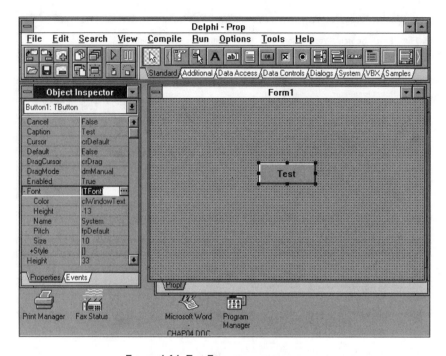

FIGURE 4.14 THE FONT PROPERTY EXPANDED.

Now click the **Events** tab to display the Events page of the Object Inspector and select the button. Double click in the edit area of the OnClick event and the code editor will appear showing a new procedure that Delphi has added to the form's code unit for you. This procedure is called an *event handler* because it will be executed whenever the button receives a click event. Add the following line of code to the procedure so it looks like Figure 4.15.

```
Color := clNavy;
```

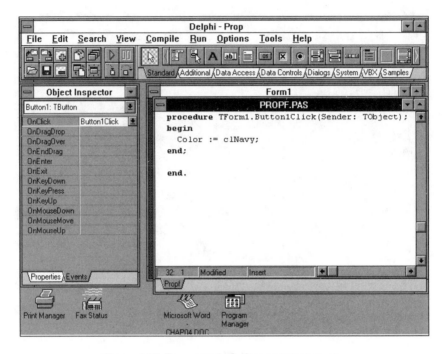

FIGURE 4.15 THE BUTTON'S ONCLICK EVENT HANDLER.

Next, select the form itself, double-click the edit area of its OnClick event and add this line of code.

```
Color := clTeal;
```

Now press **F9** to compile and run the program. Click the button, then the form, to see the form change color. When you are done close the form by double clicking its control-menu icon in the upper-left corner to return to the IDE.

With this simple program you have explored the basic steps in creating all Delphi applications.

1. Create a form.
2. Add components to the form.
3. Set the properties of the components.
4. Add code to respond to events.

Building Menus with the Menu Designer

Using the Component Palette and the Menu Designer you can quickly add custom menus to your forms. The easiest way to learn the Menu Designer is to build a couple of menus. Start by creating a new project, then add a MainMenu component, and a Memo component to the form so that it looks like Figure 4.16. To open the Menu Designer double click on the **MainMenu** component.

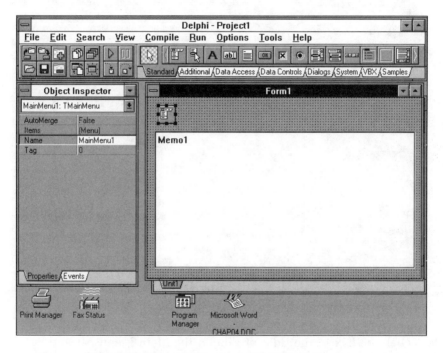

FIGURE 4.16 FORM WITH MEMO AND MAINMENU COMPONENTS.

The Menu Designer opens with a highlight where the first menu choice goes. Type **&File** and press **Enter**. The ampersand (**&**) designates the following letter as the accelerator key for the menu item. Notice that when you typed **&File** you were actually changing the Caption property of the menu item in the Object Inspector. When you press the **Enter** key the highlight moves down so you can enter the first choice on the File submenu.

Type **&Open** then click on the **ShortCut** property in the Object Inspector. Type **Ctrl+O** and press **Enter**. Notice that you have added a shortcut key to the menu. Enter the rest of the menu choices so that your menu looks like Figure 4.17. To add the separator bar between **&Save** and **&Exit** just type a hyphen for the caption of the menu item.

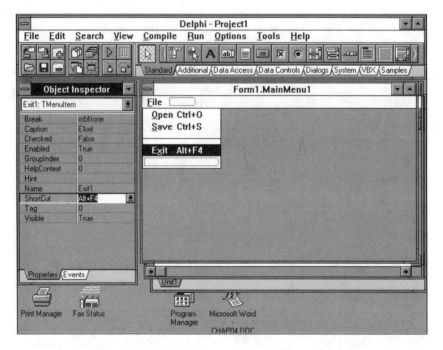

FIGURE 4.17 THE COMPLETE FILE MENU.

Next click the box to the right of File on the Main Menu bar and enter the Edit menu as shown in Figure 4.18. To add the submenu for the Align choice press **Ctrl+Right Arrow** when **Align** is highlighted. You can also create a submenu by right clicking to display the Menu Designer's speed menu, and selecting **Create Submenu**. To make the choices in your menu do something click the Events tab in the Object Inspector. Each menu choice has an OnClick event to which you can attach code. The OnClick event is generated no matter how users make a menu selection, even if they use the shortcut key instead of the menu.

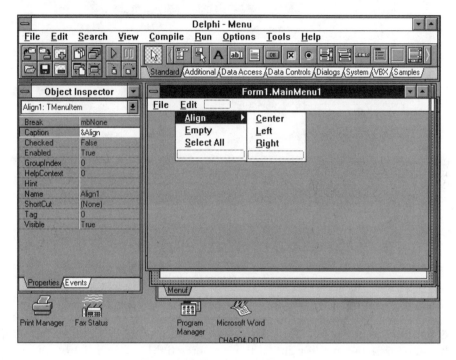

FIGURE 4.18 THE COMPLETE EDIT MENU.

You can also use the Menu Designer to add a Speed menu to any component. Close the Menu Designer window and add a PopUpMenu component from the Standard page of the Component Palette. Double click the **PopUpMenu** component to open the Menu Designer, build the Popup menu in Figure 4.19 and close the Menu Designer.

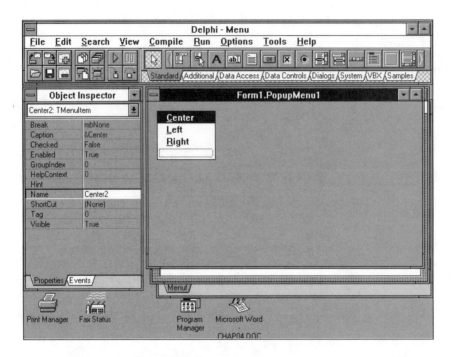

FIGURE 4.19 THE COMPLETE POPUP MENU.

You can attach a Popup menu to any component to create a Speed menu for that component by setting its PopupMenu property in the Object Inspector. Select the **Menu** component then select its **PopupMenu** property. Click the drop-down arrow at the right of the property field to see a list of all of the PopUpMenu components in the form, and select the one you want. Save your project, and press **F9** to compile and run it. If you did not actually build this project use **MENU.DPR** on your code disk. Right click the **Memo** to see the Speed menu appear.

Changing menus is as easy as building them. To remove an item from the menu just click on it, and press the **Del** key. To add a new item press the **Ins** key. If the highlighted menu item is in the Main Menu bar the new item will be added to its left. If the highlighted item is in a submenu the new item will be added above it. To move an item to a new location, just drag and drop it where you want. You can also insert or delete menu choices using the Menu Designer speed menu.

To save time creating menus with standard choices Delphi ships with several menu templates. You can add a menu template to your menu object from the speed menu. You can also create a menu and save it as a template for future use.

Using the Integrated Debugger

When your run your program in the IDE it is running under the control of the Integrated Debugger. When your program is executing it behaves as if it were running outside of the IDE. However, if an error occurs the debugger takes control and shows you, in the editor window, the line of code that caused the error. To use the debugger the compiler must generate symbolic debugging information, which it does by default. If you ever need to turn debugging information on select **Options | Project** from the main menu and check the Debug Information and Local Symbols check boxes on the Compiler page. Using the debugger you can:

- Single step through each line of your code.
- Watch the values of variables.
- Set breakpoints to stop execution at any location.

If your program uses command line arguments you can supply them in the IDE by selecting **Run | Parameters** from the menu, and entering the parameters in the Run Parameters dialog box.

Giving the Debugger Control

When something in your program does not work right you can usually guess about where in your code the problem must be, based on what you are doing when the problem occurs. There are several ways you can give control to the debugger when your program begins executing code that you want to troubleshoot.

Running to a Breakpoint

One way to do this is to set a breakpoint in the editor. To set a breakpoint double-click the left margin of the Code Editor window next to the line where you want execution to stop. The line will be highlighted and the breakpoint symbol will appear in the margin as shown in Figure 4.20. You can set as many breakpoints as you wish.

NOTE

If you set a breakpoint on a line of code that is not an executable statement, for example, a comment or a variable declaration, the breakpoint will be ignored.

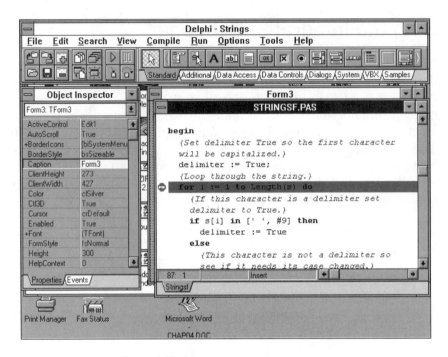

FIGURE 4.20 A BREAKPOINT SET IN THE EDITOR.

Once you have set a breakpoint you can run your program and it will stop when it reaches the breakpoint.

When your program reaches a breakpoint, execution halts before the line of code that contains the breakpoint is executed, and the Editor window gets focus with the line that contains the breakpoint highlighted. You can step through your code one line at a time using the **Step Over** or **Trace Into** commands on the **Run** menu, the corresponding **F8** and **F7** keys, or the **Step Over** and **Trace Into** buttons on the speedbar.

Step Over and Trace Into do the same thing except when the line of code to be executed is a procedure or function call. For a procedure or function call, Step Over executes the call as a single statement. Trace Into takes you into the code for the procedure, or function, so you can step through it.

When you are stepping through code the execution point marks the next line of code that will be executed. Figure 4.21 shows some code that contains a breakpoint, after the line that contains the breakpoint was executed, by clicking the Step Over button on the speedbar. The execution point, the solid triangle in the left margin, is now positioned at the next line of code that will be executed.

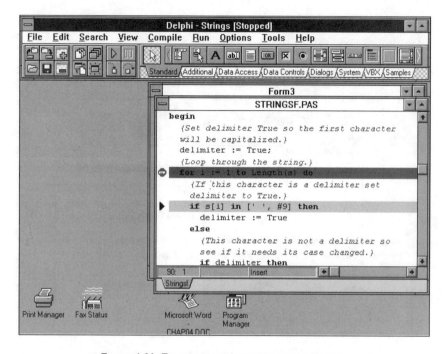

FIGURE 4.21 THE EXECUTION POINT IN A DEBUG SESSION.

Running to the Cursor

Another way to stop program execution at the spot you want to begin debugging is to place the insertion point in the Code Editor on the line where you want to stop. Then, select **Run | Run To Cursor** from the menu, or **press F4**. Your program will run at full speed until it reaches the line that contains the cursor.

At that point it is just as though you had a breakpoint set on that line. The Editor window gets focus, and the execution point points to the line that contains the cursor.

Using Breakpoints

The BreakPoint List and its Speed menu lets you see and manage all of the breakpoints you have set in all of the source files for your project. Select **View | Breakpoints** from the menu to display the Breakpoint List. Right-click the list to display the Speed menu as shown in Figure 4.22.

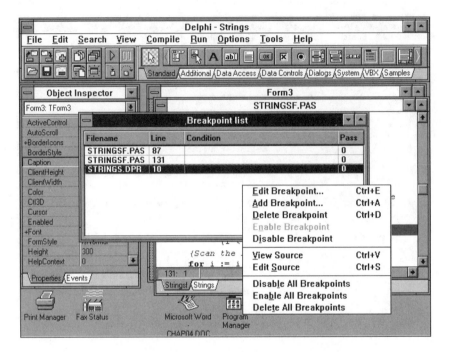

FIGURE 4.22 THE BREAKPOINT LIST AND SPEED MENU.

Many of the choices on the Breakpoint List should be self-explanatory and will not be discussed here. If you need additional information, see the *Delphi Users Guide*. Disabling a breakpoint causes it to be ignored when you run your program without deleting it. A disabled breakpoint appears grayed in both the Breakpoint List and the Code Editor. The View Source and Edit Source choices both display the line that contains the breakpoint in the Code Editor. The difference is that when you choose **View Source** the Breakpoint List retains focus. If you choose **Edit Source** focus shifts to the **Code Editor**.

Choosing **Edit Breakpoint** from the speed menu opens the **Edit Breakpoint** dialog shown in Figure 4.23.

You can edit all of the fields in the Edit Breakpoint dialog including the file name and line number. If you change these values you will move the breakpoint to a new location.

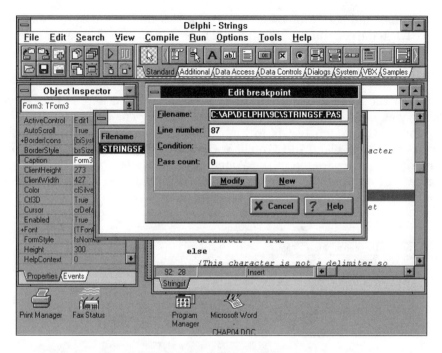

FIGURE 4.23 THE BREAKPOINT LIST AND SPEED MENU.

The Condition and Pass Count values are very valuable. You can enter a conditional expression in the Condition field and the breakpoint will only become active when that condition is true. An example would be the line:

```
i > 20
```

Once this condition is entered the breakpoint will only become active when the value of the variable *i* is greater than **20**. For the breakpoint to become active the expression you enter must evaluate to either Boolean True, or a nonzero value. The only limitations on the expression you enter is that it cannot contain a procedure or function call, and all variables in the expression must be in scope at the point in your code where the breakpoint is set.

A pass count causes the breakpoint to become active after the line in which it is contained has been executed the specified number of times. You can use pass counts and conditions together. When you do the breakpoint becomes active when the condition has been found to be true pass count number of times.

Watching Values

You can watch the value of any number of variables or expressions as you debug your code by adding them to the Watch List. The easiest way to add a variable to the Watch List is to highlight it in the Code Editor and either press **Ctrl+F5** or select **Add Watch At Cursor** from the editor's Speed menu. When you add a variable to the Watch List the Watch Properties dialog in Figure 4.24 appears. This dialog also appears when you select **Edit Watch** from the Watch List Speed menu.

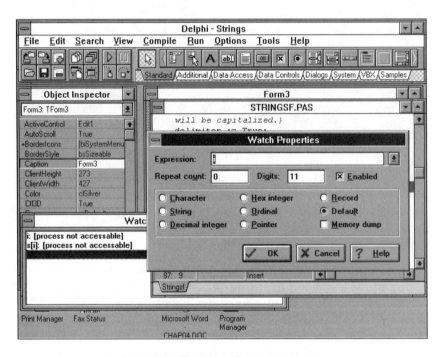

FIGURE 4.24 THE WATCH PROPERTIES DIALOG.

You can change the expression by typing a new expression or variable name in the Expression field. Count is handy when you are watching an element in an array. For example, if you enter **5** in Count you will see the value of the current element of the array, and the next four elements in order. The radio buttons let you change how the value is interpreted. Checking the Memory Dump check box shows the value of each byte of the value in hex.

When you click the **OK** button, the Watch List Window shown in Figure 4.25 appears. Figure 4.25 also shows the Watch List speed menu.

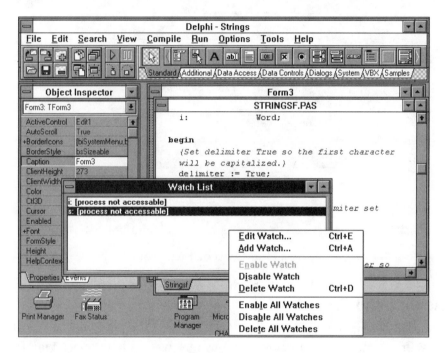

FIGURE 4.25 THE WATCH LIST AND ITS SPEED MENU.

You can also evaluate expressions and change the value of variables during a debugging session by selecting **Evaluate/Modify** from the **Run** menu, or the **Code Editor** speed menu, or pressing **Ctrl+F7**. Type the name of the variable, or type the expression you want to evaluate in the Evaluate/Modify dialog shown in Figure 4.26.

To evaluate an expression or view the value of a variable enter it in the **Expression** field, and click the **Evaluate** button. To change the value of the variable in the Expression field, type the new value in the **New Value** field, and click the **Modify** button. You can now continue your debugging session with the variable set to its new value.

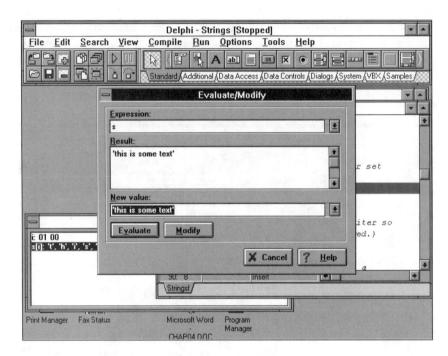

FIGURE 4.26 THE EVALUATE/MODIFY DIALOG.

Viewing the Call Stack

When you are debugging code in a function or procedure you may want to know from where the function or procedure was called. Select **View | Call Stack** from the menu to see the **Call Stack** window, shown in Figure 4.27 with its Speed menu.

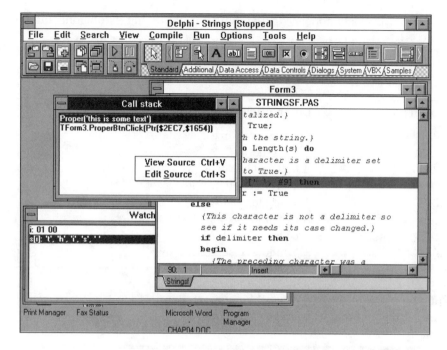

FIGURE 4.27 THE CALL STACK WINDOW.

Managing Projects

Since a Delphi project can consist of many files, the the best way to manage projects is by putting each project in a separate directory. With that in mind, remember the suggestion at the beginning of this chapter to change Delphi's default working directory so you will not accidentally save a project in the DELPHI\BIN directory.

Delphi projects consist of files with the following extensions shown in Table 4.1.

TABLE 4.1 DELPHI FILE EXTENSIONS

Extension	Description
.PRJ	The project source code file
.FRM	A form file
.PAS	A unit's source code file
.OPT	The project options file
.DSK	The desktop status file
.DLL	A dynamic link library
.DCU	A compiled unit
.RES	A Windows resource file

You can use the Delphi Project Manager, shown in Figure 4.28, by selecting **View | Project Manager** from the main menu.

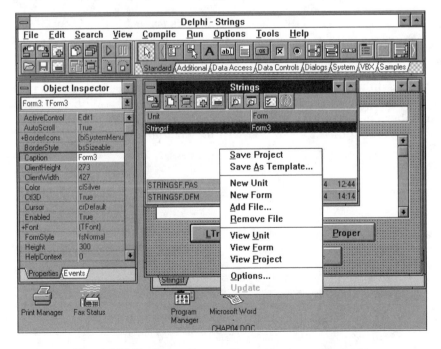

FIGURE 4.28 THE DELPHI PROJECT MANAGER AND ITS SPEED MENU.

The Project Manager lists the files the make up the project on which you are working. Using the Project Manager speedbar and Speedmenu you can add files, or remove files from your project, switch between units and forms, and create new source code units and forms.

That concludes the tour of the Delphi IDE, with one exception. The IDE also includes a Bitmap Editor which you can access from the **Tools** menu if you want to draw your own bitmaps, icons, and cursors. The IDE makes creating and debugging programs in Delphi fast and easy. Now on to the second section of this book and the Object Pascal language.

Summary

The time you spend mastering all of the features of the Delphi IDE including the editor, debugger, menu builder, project manager and object inspector, will pay big dividends in productivity as you begin to develop applications. The IDE is highly configurable so you can customize it to fit your work style and increase your productivity even more.

You have had an overview of Delphi's features and a tour of the IDE. The next section of this book introduces you to the ObjectPascal language. As you work through the examples in this section you will not only learn ObjectPascal but also put what you have learned about Delphi so far to use.

CHAPTER 5

Program Components

The programming language in Delphi is Object Pascal. Chapters five through thirteen introduce you to the Object Pascal language. If you are familiar with standard Pascal you may want to skip or skim Chapters five through nine. If you program in Borland Pascal 7.0 With Objects you may want to skip, or skim all of the chapters in this section, except Chapter 10, "Objects." Delphi introduces some changes to Pascal objects that you will not want to miss.

This chapter introduces the basic structure and elements of an Object Pascal program. You will see the structure of the program file including the location of constant and variable declarations, procedures and functions, and the main block of program code. You will also learn the rules for using blanks and whitespace, comments and labels.

The demonstration programs in this chapter and many of the subsequent chapters are very simple. Each of the demonstration programs is set up as a Delphi project. They all have one form and one unit for the form. Many of the forms contain a single memo control, and single button. In some of the later chapters an edit control is added so you can enter values to test the code. The code samples are in the click procedure of the button. These programs do not focus on forms or the visual aspects of Delphi. That will come later in the book. The goal now is to master the basics of the Pascal language without which you will not be able to understand how Delphi works.

Structure of a Pascal Program

Figure 5.1 shows the minimum program file that will compile without errors in the Delphi editor window. The first line is the program heading. It consists of the key word Program, followed by the name you assign to your program, followed by a semicolon.

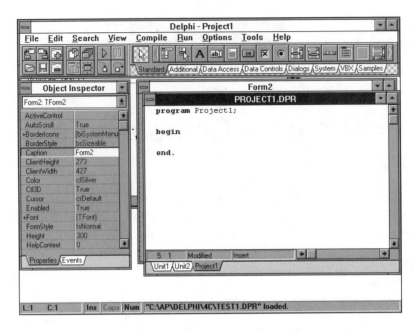

FIGURE 5.1 THE BASIC STRUCTURE OF A PASCAL PROGRAM.

The second part of this program is the section that contains your program code. This section starts with the key word *begin* and ends with the key word *end* followed by a period. Of course this program does not do anything since it contains no code.

Units

One of the most useful features of Object Pascal is units. In any large application, development is much faster if you can create and test the code for one part of the application, and then move on to the next part. You can also save vast amounts of time if you can easily develop routines that can be used over and over in future projects without the need to copy them into each program.

Units allow you to do both of these things. Although units are covered in detail in Chapter 12, it is important that you understand the basic concept now since you cannot write a Windows program that does anything without using units.

A unit is a separate file from your main program file that contains code and may also contain variable declarations, constant declarations, objects, and anything else that a Pascal program can contain. The source code file for a unit has a .PAS file extension. Each unit is compiled to create a file with the same name as the unit source file and a .DCU extension. Once you have compiled a unit any program you create can use the code in the unit. Note that in order to use the code in a unit you do not need to have the source code file for the unit. All you need is the compiled .DCU file. This makes units an ideal way to create standard routines and share them with other programmers. If you wish to retain control of the source code you can distribute just the compiled .DCU file. To share the source code, distribute the .PAS file.

Most Delphi programs will interact with the user. The medium for user interaction is a form. Each form has two associated files. The first has a .DFM extension and contains the description of the physical layout of the form and any components you place on the form. The second file has a .PAS extension, and contains the unit associated with that form. Therefore, a simple one form Delpi program consists of the form, its associated unit file, the main program, or project file, which has a .DPR extension, and the resource and options files. The resource file (.RES) contains the program icon and other resources. The options file (.OPT) contains the compiler project options settings.

You start a new program in Delphi by Selecting **New Project** from the File menu. When you do Delpi automatically creates a blank form, a unit file for the form, and a project file. Figure 5.2 shows the project file, and Figure 5.3 shows the form's unit file.

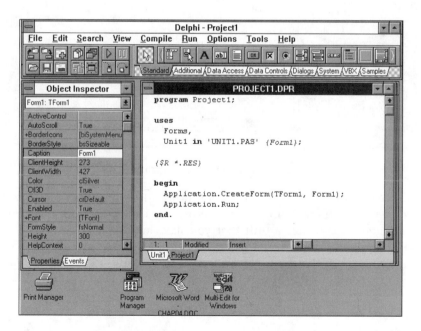

FIGURE 5.2 A NEW PROJECT FILE CREATED BY DELPHI

In Figure 5.2 notice that Delpi has automatically placed a uses clause in the project file and added the unit for the form to the uses list. The uses clause is the way you identify units that program, or units you are writing will use. The form's unit in Figure 5.3 has many units in its uses clause. All of these units come with Delphi and contain procedures and functions used by forms.

Note that nobody has written any code yet. Delphi wrote all of the code in the project file and the form's unit file for you. As you learn more about Delphi you will be amazed at how little code you have to write.

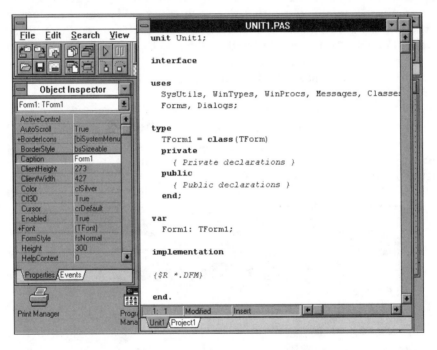

FIGURE 5.3 A FORM'S UNIT FILE CREATED BY DELPHI

You can write your own units to contain procedures and functions you plan to use in many different projects, or to organize your code for easy design and maintenance. To use a unit that you have written you need to add its name to the uses clause in the project, or unit that calls one or more of its procedures or functions. As you can see from Figure 5.3 the **uses clauses** can wrap onto multiple lines if the number of units is large. Note that the maximum line length allowed in Object Pascal is 126 characters. When the length of a line nears this limit you must begin a new line.

Runtime Library

Pascal is actually a very simple programming language. There are not many commands and control structures to learn. What makes the language powerful is that it includes a runtime library that contains many procedures and functions to perform special operations that extend the language. The runtime library includes routines for program flow control, string manipulation, mathematics, memory allocation, file access, and many others.

The sample program in Figure 5.2 includes two lines of code between the keywords **begin** and **end**. These two lines are calls to the runtime library procedure Writeln which is used to write two lines of text to the screen. Note that Object Pascal statements end with a semicolon.

Whitespace

The general category of whitespace includes spaces, tabs, and blank lines in your program code. You can use whitespace to improve the readability of your code.

Blank lines can be inserted between Pascal statements to provide visual separation of groups of statements, or for any other purpose. You can use spaces to separate elements (called tokens) within a statement. You can also insert spaces at the beginning of lines to indent statements as you read the rest of this book, and the Delphi manuals. Notice how indenting and whitespace are used to make the code easy to understand. One of the great features of Pascal is that well written Pascal code tends to be self documenting. That reduces the amount of time you must spend commenting your code now and makes maintenance easier later on.

Comments

You can include comments in your code by enclosing the comment in either braces, {}, or parentheses asterisk pairs, (**). You cannot start a comment with a { and close it with *) or vice versa. Everything contained in a comment is ignored by the compiler. Figure 5.4 shows the button click procedure for the Demo1 program, a sample program with a comment added.

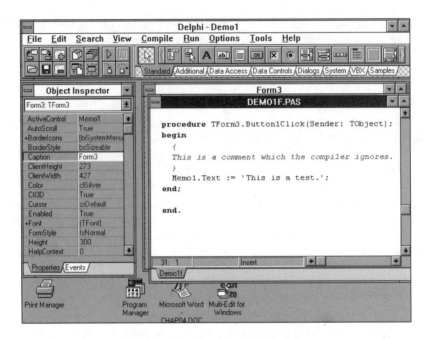

FIGURE 5.4 A PROGRAM WITH COMMENTS.

Although this example shows the opening and closing braces on separate lines, this is not required. For example, the following line is also a valid comment.

```
{This is a valid comment with the braces on the same line.}
```

You do not have to place comments on a line by themselves. The following line includes a comment after the Pascal statement.

```
Writeln('This is a test.');    {Display a message on the screen.}
```

N O T E

You cannot include a } or *) within a comment. The compiler will always see this as the end of the comment. If the first character after the { or (* is a dollar sign the compiler will interpret this as a compiler directive, not a comment.

Compiler directives, although enclosed in a comment, are not ignored by the compiler. Instead they are interpreted by the compiler, and affect the compilation process. For example,

```
{$R+}
```

turns on range checking so that any attempt to address an array with an invalid subscript will cause an error. For more information about compiler directives search for *compiler directives* in the Delphi on-line help.

Labels

Labels should be used rarely in Pascal because their only purpose is to allow you to use a goto statement. A goto allows you to unconditionally transfer control from one location in your code to another. Using goto statements is generally considered bad programming practice but the code in Figure 5.5 shows how to use a label, and goto if you need to.

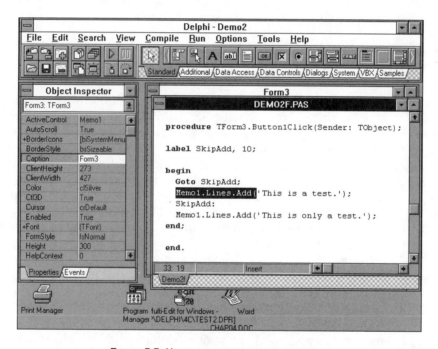

FIGURE 5.5 USING A LABEL AND GOTO STATEMENT.

Notice that the label must be declared following the label keyword before it can be used. The program in Figure 5.5 declares two labels, SkipWrite and 10, but only uses SkipWrite. If you run this program you will see that the first Memo1.Lines.Add() call is bypassed, and only the second line of text appears on the screen when you click the **Run** button on the form.

Tokens

A token is the smallest element of a program that means something to the compiler. In Object Pascal tokens can be reserved words, labels, numbers, strings, special symbols, compiler directives, or identifiers such as variable names.

For example, in Figure 5.5 you see the line

```
label SkipAdd, 10;
```

as two words and a number. However, to the compiler this line consists of four tokens. The first, **label**, is a reserved word. The second and third, **SkipAdd** and **10**, are identifiers. The third token, the **semicolon**, is a special symbol. Tokens must be separated from each other by whitespace. To the compiler your program is a series of tokens and separators.

Procedures and Functions

Procedures and functions are covered in detail in Chapter nine. The purpose of discussing them here is to describe their purpose and where they fit into the basic structure of a Pascal program. Procedures and functions in Pascal are analogous to subroutines in some other programming languages.

Procedures and functions are named blocks of code that can be executed by calling their name. They are used for two purposes. First is to break your program into small discreet sections that perform a single function. Developing your code as a series of discreet operations makes writing a large complex program easier, because you write and test small modules that are easy to understand and test.

The second reason for using procedures and functions is to encapsulate a series of statements that must be executed in several different places in your program. Instead of replicating the same code each time it is needed, you write the code once in a procedure or function, and call it wherever you need it. Figure 5.6 shows the button click procedure from a simple demonstration program.

This program has a single form which contains a memo object named Memo1, and a button labeled Run. The button click procedure, TForm3.Button1Click, is called automatically by Delphi when the user clicks the button. Once again Delphi will create the entire procedure for you with the exception of the code between begin and end. In this case the two lines of code add two lines of text to the memo object on the form.

The procedure almost looks like a small program. It begins with the key word procedure followed by the procedure's name. Next, comes a begin-end block that contains the statements that execute each time the procedure is called. The only difference from the begin-end block in the main program (project file) is that in the procedure the keyword end is followed by a semi-colon, while in the main program end is followed by a period. A function is similar to a procedure except that it returns a value that can be assigned to a variable. You should now have a good understanding of the basic structure of a Pascal program and its major components.

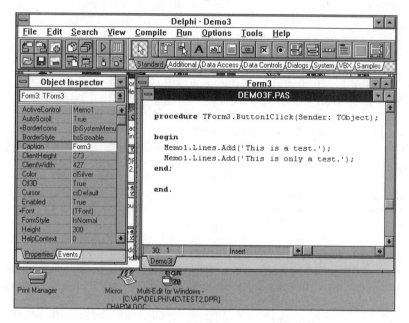

FIGURE 5.6 A BUTTON CLICK PROCEDURE.

Memory Management

Windows memory management is a complex subject that is beyond the scope of this book. However, to use Delphi there are a few things you need to know about how Pascal programs use memory.

Code

The compiled code for your program is stored in the code segment. The code segment is limited to 64k in size for the main program. You can over-come this limitation easily by dividing your program into units, which are discussed in Chapter 12, because each unit has its own 64k code segment. By using multiple units in addition to the main program you can write a program that includes as much code as you need.

Data

Data is stored in three different memory areas, the data segment, the stack, and the heap. Each program has a 64k data segment that is divided into three areas. The first area contains all global variables and typed constants and is called the static data area. The size of the static data area is 64k, minus the size of the local heap, minus the size of the stack.

The second area, the local heap, is used by Windows when it needs temporary storage for various controls. The default size of the local heap is 8k and it should never be set to zero. If you do need to change the size of the local heap you can use the $M compiler directive, or by selecting **Options | Project** from the Delphi Main menu, and then choosing the **Linker** page.

The third area is the stack. The stack contains all local variables declared in procedures and functions, all parameters passed to procedures and functions, and the return address that tells the program where to resume execution after a procedure or function has been called.

By default, the stack is set to 16k but you can change it by using the $M compiler directive, or by selecting **Options | Project** from the Delphi main menu, and then choosing the Linker page. You may need to increase the size of the stack if you have procedures calling each other to a great depth, or if a procedure calls itself recursively many times.

At first the 64k limit for data may sound very restrictive, but it is not. As you will learn in Chapter 6, you can dynamically allocate data using the New and GetMem runtime library procedures. The memory that dynamic variables use comes from the Windows global heap which is limited only by the amount of real and virtual memory available to Windows. By allocating large data structures, such as *arrays*, dynamically you can easily bypass the 64k data segment limitation.

Now that you understand the basic structure of a Pascal program, it is time to start looking at the details. The next chapter describes the data types available in Object Pascal.

Summary

This chapter introduced the basic structure of an ObjectPascal program. Using units you can write portable reusable modules that you can use in each program you write. As you begin developing Delphi applications look for opportunities to write solutions to problems as reusable tools in units.

One approach that works well is to have a subdirectory that contains your generic units and create units by the type of procedures they contain. You might have a string unit that contains string manipulation routines that you have written and a math unit with various computational routines. With Delphi's smart linker you do not have to worry about units that contain many routines bloating the size of your application. Since the linker links only those procedures and functions that your program actually calls into the compiled program your program's size will always be minimized.

CHAPTER 6

Data Types

ObjectPascal supports many different data types. If you have experience in prior versions of Pascal, most of this will be redundant. If you have experience in other languages like C or C++, then this chapter is worth a look. This chapter discusses the basic data types available within Delphi. It also illustrates, with plenty of examples, how to declare and use each data type.

For database programmers used to manipulating data in tables, it is easy to skip over data types. Do not. The wealth of data types available in ObjectPascal means that you can use data structures other than tables: linked lists, stacks, queues, trees, multi-dimensional arrays and more. In order to create variables of different types, you will need to understand how to declare variables, types, and constants in ObjectPascal.

All of the techniques demonstrated in this chapter are included on the accompanying code disk. The project name is DTYPES.DPR and the form (shown in Figure 6.1) is called DataTypes. To illustrate how to use variables, this chapter makes use of the fundamental ObjectPascal statements, including the **if** and the **for** statements. Statements are covered fully in Chapter 8. However, if you have experience in another computer language, you should have no problem following the examples.

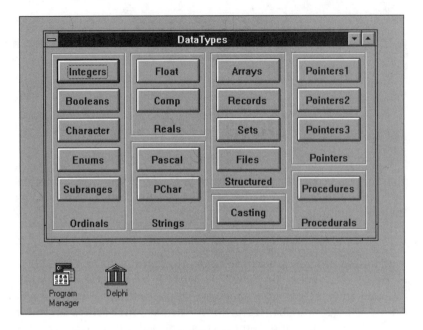

FIGURE 6.1 DATA TYPES FORM.

Variables

Declaring a variable is easy. You simply place the variable in a function or procedure's var statement:

```
procedure MyProc;
var
    x,y,z : Integer;
begin

end;
```

The word **var** is not a required part of the procedure or function declaration. If it is not there you can always add it. When you place variables in the var block in a procedure or function, then only that procedure or function can access that variable. You can also declare variables global to many (or all) functions or procedures. This is discussed in Chapter 11. "Units."

Type Declarations

Variables are of a certain type. In the last example, three variables were created: x,y,z. These variables are of the type *Integer*. Most of this chapter is dedicated to explaining the various data types within Delphi. You can create your own types as well. In fact, some of the examples in this chapter define their own types. To do this, simply declare the data type in a **type** block, which appears above the **var** block:

```
procedure MyProc;
type
   MyInteger = Integer;
var
   x,y,z : MyInteger;
begin

end;
```

Declaring your own type can be an important way of hiding the actual data structure used to implement the variable. For example, Delphi has several different types of integers: integer, shortint, longint, byte, and word. If you have a family of related variables in your application that share the same data type (integer) and you need to change the data type to longint, with a user-defined type it is easy. You can simply change the type declaration from integer to longint, rather than changing each variable's declaration.

Ordinal Types

Ordinal types include integers, booleans, char, enumerated, and subrange types. You can consider ordinals a finite set of ordered elements. In the case of short integers, the ordered set begins at -128 and increases by one, up to 127. ObjectPascal supports a wide variety of ordinals. Some of the ordinal types serve simply as compatibility types so that ObjectPascal can deal with types in a different format in other languages.

Integers

The integer family of ordinals is shown in Table 6.1.

TABLE 6.1 INTEGER TYPES

Type	Range	Format
Shortint	-128 to 127	Signed 8 bit
Integer	-32,768 to 32,767	Signed 16 bit
Longint	-2,147,483,648 to 2,147,483,647	Signed 32 bit
Byte	0 to 255	Unsigned 8 bit
Word	0 to 65,535	Unsigned 16 bit

A signed integer can store negative numbers. An unsigned integer can not. In a signed integer, an extra bit is used to denote the sign of the number. Unsigned integers do not reserve an extra bit for a sign. Listing 6.1 shows how to declare and manipulate the various integer types. In this listing the Low() and High() functions return the lowest and highest value for the integer type. The High() and Low() functions can be used on any ordinal type to return the lowest and highest value in the set of ordinals for that type. The Inc() function increments the integer by one, or by an optionally specified amount. The Inc() function can also be used on any ordinal type.

As you read through the listings, you will see the procedure MessageDlg() is used liberally. This procedure displays a dialog box displaying text.

LISTING 6.1 USING INTEGER TYPES

```
procedure TDataTypes.IntegersButtonClick(Sender: TObject);
var
    c : Longint;
    d : Byte;
    e : Word;
begin
    { display the high and low values on a,b,c}
    MessageDlg('Low(shortint) = '+ IntToStr(low(Shortint)),
            mtInformation,[mbOK],0);
    MessageDlg('High(shortint) = '+ IntToStr(high(Shortint)),
            mtInformation,[mbOK],0);
    MessageDlg('Low(Integer) = '+ IntToStr(low(Integer)),
            mtInformation,[mbOK],0);
    MessageDlg('High(Integer) = '+ IntToStr(high(Integer)),
            mtInformation,[mbOK],0);
    MessageDlg('Low(Longint) = '+ IntToStr(low(Longint)),
            mtInformation,[mbOK],0);
```

```
MessageDlg('High(Longint) = '+ IntToStr(high(Longint)),
          mtInformation,[mbOK],0);

{ make c equal to high(integer) * 2 }
c:= Longint(high(Integer)*2);
MessageDlg('C = '+ IntToStr(c),
          mtInformation,[mbOK],0);

d := 3 * 2; {perform math on two literals, store in d}
MessageDlg('D = '+ IntToStr(d),
          mtInformation,[mbOK],0);

e:=0;       {initialize e}
Inc(e);     {increment e by 1, e=1}
Inc(e,10);  {increment e by 10, e=11}
MessageDlg('E = '+ IntToStr(e),
          mtInformation,[mbOK],0);

end;
```

As you work with integers of different types within the same operation, keep in mind that the Delphi compiler will warn you when you can not assign one type to another. However, for clarity, you can perform explicit typecasting to convert from one type to another. The following line of code, taken from Listing 6.1 illustrates this:

```
c:= Longint(high(b)*2);
```

Boolean

Variables of boolean type equate to two values: True or False. Table 6.2 lists ObjectPascal's boolean types.

TABLE 6.2 BOOLEAN TYPES

Type	Size
Boolean	1 byte
ByteBool	1 byte
WordBool	2 bytes
LongBool	4 bytes

The ByteBool, WordBool, and LongBool boolean types accept more than two values (True or False). Any nonzero value for these types is interpreted as true, and zero (0) is considered false. The reason for this is that in other languages, especially C and C++, boolean variables are implemented this way. Listing 6.2 shows how to declare and manipulate the various boolean types. In this listing the WordBool() and ByteBool() functions convert a variable from a Word and a Byte to a Boolean value. These are two of several typecasting functions available in ObjectPascal.

LISTING 6.2 USING BOOLEAN TYPES

```
procedure TDataTypes.BooleansClick(Sender: TObject);
var
   a : Boolean;
   b : ByteBool;
   c : WordBool;
   d : LongBool;
   e : Longint;
   ByteVar : Byte;
   WordVar : Word;
begin

   { assign True to a, evaluate a }
   a := True;
   if a = True then
      MessageDlg('A = True',mtInformation,[mbOK],0)
   else
      MessageDlg('A = False',mtInformation,[mbOK],0);

   { assigned value to b, evaluate b }
   ByteVar := 100;
   b := ByteBool(ByteVar);
   if b = True then
      MessageDlg('B = True',mtInformation,[mbOK],0)
   else
      MessageDlg('B = False',mtInformation,[mbOK],0);

   { assigned value to c, evaluate c }
   WordVar := 32000;
   c := WordBool(Wordvar);
   if c = True then
      MessageDlg('C = True',mtInformation,[mbOK],0)
   else
      MessageDlg('C = False',mtInformation,[mbOK],0);
```

```
{assign value to d, evaluate d}
d := High(d);
if d = True then
   MessageDlg('High(D) = True',mtInformation,[mbOK],0)
else
   MessageDlg('High(D) = False',mtInformation,[mbOK],0);

{ get the next value for the ordinal }
d := Succ(d);
if d = True then
   MessageDlg('Succ(D) = True',mtInformation,[mbOK],0)
else
   MessageDlg('Succ(D) = False',mtInformation,[mbOK],0);

{ show the integer representation of d }
e := Longint(d);
MessageDlg('E = '+InttoStr(e),mtInformation,[mbOK],0);

{ decrement ByteVar from 10 to 0,
  stop when b is false }
ByteVar := 10;
repeat
     dec(ByteVar);
     b := ByteBool(ByteVar);
     MessageDlg('ByteVar = '+IntToStr(ByteVar),
                mtInformation,[mbOK],0);
until not b;

end;
```

Listing 6.2 uses the **Succ()** function to determine the next item in the set of ordinals, which in the listing is a boolean ordinal. When you are at the last item in a set of ordinals, **Succ()** does not return the first item in the set of ordinals. In Listing 6.2, the variable **d** is set to High(**d**), which sets **D** to **True**. The successor of **D** is also True (Succ(**d**)=True). When traversing a set of ordinals with the Succ() and Pred() functions, be careful to detect the upper and lower bounds for that ordinal.

Char

The Char type is used to represent a single character. For example, the following line of code stores the letter **Z** in the variable CurrentChar:

```
CurrentChar := 'Z';
```

Listing 6.3 shows how to declare and use a variable of Char type. In this listing, the **Chr()** function returns a character corresponding to an ASCII integer.

LISTING 6.3 USING CHAR TYPES

```
procedure TDataTypes.CharacterClick(Sender: TObject);
var
    c, newc : Char;
    s : Shortint;
begin
    c := 'A';              {assign 'A' to c}
    s := Ord(c);           {get the ASCII integer of 'A'}
    newc := chr(66);       {get the Char of 66 - 'B'}
    MessageDlg('C = '+c+'; Ord(c) = '+IntToStr(s)+
               '; Chr(66) = '+newc, mtInformation,[mbOK],0);

end;
```

Enumerated

An enumerated type is an ordered collection of constants. Listing 6.4 shows how to declare and use an enumerated type. The type **CustomerClass** is an enumerated type with the following list of identifiers: **Active, Inactive, Terminated,** and **Purged**. The compiler assigns the Active identifier a value of **0**, the Inactive identifier a value of **1** and so on, until the last enumerated identifier is assigned a value.

Enumerated types make your code more readable and reliable. The compiler can determine if you are using a valid identifier or not. And if you use descriptive identifiers, then your code will be much easier to read than if you used integer literals. In addition, you can use the Inc() function to increment an enumerated variable (as you can with any ordinal variable), the **Dec()** function to decrement an enumerated variable, the **Succ()** function to determine what is the next value for the ordinal and the **Pred()** function to find out the previous value.

LISTING 6.4 USING ENUMERATED TYPES

```
procedure TDataTypes.EnumsClick(Sender: TObject);
type
    { declare an enumerated type }
    CustomerClass = (Active,Inactive,Terminated,Purged);
var
    CustomerStatus,x : CustomerClass;
```

```
begin
  { get and display the highest value in the enumerated type }
  x := High(CustomerStatus);
  MessageDlg('High(CustomerStatus) = '+IntToStr(Ord(x)),
             mtInformation,[mbOK],0);

  { loop through all the customer status types
    and display a message listing the status }
  for CustomerStatus := Active to Purged do
  begin;
    case CustomerStatus of
      Active :
        MessageDlg('Customer is Active',mtInformation,[mbOK],0);
      Inactive :
        MessageDlg('Customer is Inactive',mtInformation,[mbOK],0);
      Terminated :
        MessageDlg('Customer is Terminated',mtInformation,[mbOK],0);
      Purged :
        MessageDlg('Customer is Purged',mtInformation,[mbOK],0);
    end;
    { display the integer representation for each identifier }
    MessageDlg('Ord(CustomerStatus) = '+IntToStr(Ord(CustomerStatus)),
               mtInformation,[mbOK],0);
  end;
  { display the successor of the last enumerated identifier (purged) }
  MessageDlg('Ord(Succ(Purged)) = '+IntToStr(Ord(Succ(Purged))),
             mtInformation,[mbOK],0);

end;
```

Subrange

Subrange types let you restrict the range for an ordinal type. The code in Listing 6.5 has a subrange variable called **ValidYears**, which is restricted to the range 1990 to 1994. The subrange type has the advantage that the compiler will make sure that only values within the specified range get assigned. For example, the following line of code will fail to compile:

```
ValidYears := 1988;
```

The range can be specified as a literal or as a formula involving literals. For example, the *MaxHeight* variable is limited to the range 180 to 1600, except the range is expressed as the following formula:

```
2*(100-10)..800*2;
```

If the formula was expressed like this:

```
(100-10)*2..800*2;
```

the subrange declaration would not compile. The reason for this is because the compiler thinks the first parenthesis is declaring an enumerated type. As long as the subrange calculation does not begin with a parenthesis (the '(' character), then the subrange will compile.

Listing 6.5 Using Subrange Types

```
procedure TDataTypes.SubrangesClick(Sender: TObject);
type
     TValidYears = 1990..1994;
var
    ValidYears : TValidYears;
    Letters : 'A'..'Z';
    LowYear, HighYear : Integer;
    MaxHeight : 2*(100-10)..800*2;
begin
    { can only assign Letters something between 'A' and 'Z' }
    Letters := 'C';

    { get the lowest year possible in ValidYears }
    LowYear := Low(ValidYears);

    { get the highest year possible in ValidYears }
    HighYear := High(Validyears);

    { display the range of possible years }
    MessageDlg('Low Year = '+IntToStr(LowYear)+
               ' High Year = '+IntToStr(HighYear),
               mtInformation,[mbOK],0);

end;
```

Notice that in Listing 6.5, you can either specify a type as a subrange and then create a variable using the new type, or you can simply declare the variable without creating a new type. The type declaration below shows how to create a subrange type. It is a good idea to preserve the ObjectPascal notation in which type names begin with a capital T.

```
type
     TValidYears = 1990..1994;
```

You always have the option of creating the type first. in fact, it makes sense to do this, especially if you expect to reuse the type elsewhere in your application.

Real Numbers

Of all the types, perhaps real numbers are most important for database applications. After all, financial and scientific applications use real numbers. Delphi supports four types of floating point numbers and one special type called Comp.

Float

Real numbers, often called floating point numbers (or float for short) require either a math coprocessor, or software emulation to perform floating point calculations. ObjectPascal comes with software emulation of floating point numbers, so you do not have to worry if your computer or the client's does not have an FPU (floating point unit). ObjectPascal supports several different flavors of real numbers. Table 6.3 lists the various real numbers available.

TABLE 6.3 REAL TYPES

Type	Range	Size	Precision
Real	2.9×10^{-39} to 1.7×10^{38}	6 bytes	11-12
Single	1.5×10^{-45} to 3.4×10^{38}	4 bytes	7-8
Double	5.0×10^{-324} to 1.7×10^{308}	8 bytes	15-16
Extended	3.4×10^{-4932} to 1.1×10^{4932}	10 bytes	19-20

Normally, you would only need to use the real type. However, if you are dealing with very large or very small numbers with a specific number of digits of precision required, the other types are available. Also, please note that the result of some integer mathematical operations return real numbers, such as diV1sion. Code Listing 6.6 shows how to declare and use real numbers. In this listing integer division is demonstrated using the keyword **div** and the Trunc() and **Round()** functions. The **div** keyword ensures that the result of diV1sion between two integers results in an integer. However, the result is not rounded, it is truncated. In this respect, doing diV1sion with **div** is the same as using the Trunc() function as shown in Listing 6.6. This listing uses the str() function to convert real numbers to strings with a given width and number of decimal digits. For example, the following line of code

```
str(3.33:4:2,Result)
```

converts the real number 3.33 into a string Result with a width of four and two decimal places.

LISTING 6.6 USING REAL NUMBERS

```
procedure TDataTypes.FloatButtonClick(Sender: TObject);
var
    r1 : Real;
    r2 : Single;
    r3 : Double;
    r4 : Extended;
    i1 : Longint;
    Result : String;
begin

    { perform diV1sion on various types of reals }

    i1 := Round(27/7);  { diV1sion of 2 ints gives a real }
    str(i1,Result);
    MessageDlg('Result Round(27/7) = '+Result,
                mtInformation,[mbOK],0);

    i1 := Trunc(27/7);
    str(i1,Result);
    MessageDlg('Result Trunc(27/7) = '+Result,
                mtInformation,[mbOK],0);

    i1 := 27 div 7;
    str(i1,Result);
    MessageDlg('Result 27 div 7 = '+Result,
                mtInformation,[mbOK],0);

    r1 := 27/7;
    str(r1:20:18,Result);
    MessageDlg('Result 27/7 (real) = '+Result,
                mtInformation,[mbOK],0);
    r2 := 27/7;
    str(r2:20:18,Result);
    MessageDlg('Result 27/7 (single) = '+Result,
                mtInformation,[mbOK],0);
```

```
r3 := 27/7;
str(r3:20:18,Result);
MessageDlg('Result 27/7 (double) = '+Result,
          mtInformation,[mbOK],0);

r4 := 27/7;
str(r4:20:18,Result);
MessageDlg('Result 27/7 (extended) = '+Result,
          mtInformation,[mbOK],0);

end;
```

When you run this code, the first three dialog boxes display the results of three forms of diV1sion. Table 6.4 shows the results of the integer diV1sion and Table 6.5 shows the results of real diV1sion using the different real data types.

TABLE 6.4 RESULTS OF INTEGER DIVISION

Operation	Result
Round(27/7)	4
Trunc(27/7)	3
27 div 7	3

TABLE 6.5 RESULTS OF REAL DIVISION

Type	Operation	Result
Single	27/7	3.857142925262451170
Real	27/7	3.857142857141298010
Double	27/7	3.857142857142857210
Extended	27/7	3.857142857142857140

In Table 6.5 you can see the difference in precision between single (which has the least precision) and real, double and extended.

Comp

The comp data type is an integer data type with a range between $-2^{63}+1$ and $2^{63}-1$. This is roughly between $-9.2*10^{18}$ and $9.2*10^{18}$. The comp data type is useful for handling very large integers. The comp data type does not handle the fractional component of a real number. While you can assign real numbers with fractional components to a comp data type, the number is rounded when it is assigned to the comp variable. Code Listing 6.7 shows how to declare and use comp variables.

LISTING 6.7 USING COMPNUMBERS

```
procedure TDataTypes.CompButtonClick(Sender: TObject);
var
    a,b,r1 : Comp;
    Result : String;
begin

    { perform various math routines on Comp numbers }

    r1 := 20/3;
    str(r1:10:7,Result); {result = 7}
    MessageDlg('Result (comp) 20/3 (real diV1sion) = '+Result,
                mtInformation,[mbOK],0);


    a:=3.14;b:=14.24; {a=3, b=14}
    r1 := a+b;
    str(r1:10:3,Result); {result = 17}
    MessageDlg('Result (comp) 3.15+14.24 (comp addition) = '+Result,
                mtInformation,[mbOK],0);

    a:=3.5;b:=14.6; {a=4, b=15}
    r1 := a+b;
    str(r1:10:3,Result); {result = 19}
    MessageDlg('Result (comp) 3.5+14.6 (comp addition) = '+Result,
                mtInformation,[mbOK],0);

    r1 := 3.5+14.6; {lets see the result after real addition}
    str(r1:10:3,Result); {result = 18}
    MessageDlg('Result (comp) 3.5+14.6 (real addition) = '+Result,
                mtInformation,[mbOK],0);
    a:=24;
    r1 := Sqrt(a);
    str(r1:10:7,Result); {result = 5}
    MessageDlg('Result (comp) Sqrt(24) = '+Result,
                mtInformation,[mbOK],0);

    a:=256;b:=16;
```

```
    r1 := a/b;
    str(r1:10:7,Result); {result = 16}
    MessageDlg('Result (comp) 256/16 = '+Result,
               mtInformation,[mbOK],0);
end;
```

When working with comps, keep in mind that real numbers get rounded when they are stored in a comp variable. This is why 3.5 + 14.6 = 19 in Listing 6.7.

Strings

For database developers, the string data type is also important. Strings come in two flavors in ObjectPascal: Pascal strings and Pchar strings (also known as null-terminated strings, the kind of strings used in C and C++). Pascal strings are easier to use but are incompatible with C and C++ strings and are limited in size (only 255 characters versus 64k for PChar strings). If you have C or C++ programming experience, the PChar data type will be very familiar. It is almost a direct implementation of the C string functionality.

Pascal Strings

A Pascal string is stored, internally, as an array of characters. Declaring a string is easy:

```
var
   CustomerName : String[25];
```

In the CustomerName variable, ObjectPascal reserves the first byte (position 0 in the array) to hold the actual length of the string. So if you assign 'ACME' to CustomerName, four (4) will be stored in the first byte. This scheme automatically limits the size of string arrays to 255 characters. (An unsigned short integer, which is what the 0th byte is treated as, can have a range of values from 0 to 255).

You can declare Pascal strings with no size specified:

```
var
   CustomerName : String;
```

In this case, ObjectPascal automatically assigns it a size of 255 characters. Code Listing 6.8 shows how to declare and traverse through a Pascal string variable.

LISTING 6.8 USING PASCAL STRINGS

```
procedure TDataTypes.PascalButtonClick(Sender: TObject);
var
   s : String[10];
   x,y : Byte;
begin
   {assign the string s a value}
   s:='Hello';
   {get the length of s}
   {y:=Length(s) is the preferred approach}
   y:=Byte(s[0]);
   {display the length of the string in s}
   MessageDlg('Position 0 = '+IntToStr(y),
              mtInformation,[mbOK],0);
   {display each character in s}
   for x:=1 to y do
      MessageDlg('Position '+IntToStr(x)+' = '+s[x],
                 mtInformation,[mbOK],0);

end;
```

In Listing 6.8, the actual size of the string is retrieved with the following line of code:

```
y:=Byte(s[0]);
```

This is a long-winded way getting the length of a string. A better approach would be to use the System function Length() which returns a string's length. The Pascal-style strings have a host of functions and procedures you can use to manipulate them. Table 6.6 lists these.

TABLE 6.6 PASCAL-STYLE STRING MANIPULATION METHODS

Method	Description
AssignStr	Assigns a string to a specified variable.
CompareStr	Compares two strings.
CompareText	Compares two strings.
Concat	Concatenates a sequence of strings.
Copy	Returns a substring of a string.
Delete	Deletes a substring from a string.
DisposeStr	Disposes of a string created with NewStr.
Format	Formats a string.

Insert	Inserts a substring into a string.
IntToHex	Converts an integer value to a hexidecimal value.
IntToStr	Converts a integer value to a string.
Length	Returns the dynamic length of a string.
LowerCase	Converts the entire string to lowercase.
NewStr	Returns a pointer to the string allocated on the heap.
Pos	Searches for a substring in a string.
Str	Converts a numeric value to a string.
StrToInt	Converts a string to an integer value.
StrToIntDef	Converts a string to an integer value.
UpperCase	Converts the entire string to uppercase.
Val	Converts a string value to its numeric representation.

PChar (Null-Terminated) Strings

You can create null-terminated strings if you need the size and structure they provide. For example, some third-party DLLs require that you pass null-terminated strings, not Pascal-style strings. In addition, if you need to pass a string to any of the Windows API calls, you will need to use a PChar variable.

Null-terminated strings do not store the size of the string anywhere in the array of characters. Instead, a null character (ASCII 0) is placed at the end of the string. Normally, you do not need to use null-terminated strings. But if you do, Listing 6.9 shows how to declare and use a null-terminated string.

LISTING 6.9 USING NULL-TERMINATED STRINGS

```
procedure TDataTypes.PCharButtonClick(Sender: TObject);
var
   s,p : PChar;
   u : String;
begin
   {assign a null-terminated string}
   s:='Hello';

   {assign p the address to s
    p and s now point to the same string}
   p:=s;

   {check to see if the address to which s and p
    point to is identical }
```

```
if ( Seg(p^)=Seg(s^) ) and ( Ofs(p^)=Ofs(s^) ) then
    MessageDlg('P=S', mtInformation,[mbOK],0);

{copy string pointed to by p to
 a Pascal-style string u}
u:=StrPas(p);
{display the Pascal style string}
MessageDlg(u, mtInformation,[mbOK],0);

{start at the beginning of the string
 and process it one character at a time.
 p^ returns the character the pointer p
 is looking at. Ord(p^) converts that to
 the ordinal number. If it is 0, then
 we have reached the end of the string}

while p^<>#0 do
    begin
        {display the character p is pointing to}
        MessageDlg(p^, mtInformation,[mbOK],0);
        {move the pointer 1 byte over}
        Inc(p);
    end

end;
```

Listing 6.9 introduces a concept, pointer, which is discussed in the "Pointers" section of this chapter. In this case, the variable **p** is actually a pointer to an array of characters (type **pchar**). In fact, the compiler interprets PChar as a pointer to char, like this:

```
type
    PChar = ^Char;
```

Like all pointers, it must be initialized to point to a valid memory address. In Listing 6.9, the following line of code

```
s:='Hello';
```

initializes the pointer variable s to the literal string 'Hello.' The compiler converts the literal string 'Hello' into a null-terminated string, allocates six bytes for it, and then assigns the address of those six bytes to the pointer variable **s**. In order to properly initialize **PChar** variables, you need to do one of the following:

- Assign a literal to the **PChar** variable.
- Assign the **PChar** variable the address of another data structure, such as an array of **Char** or an address in another **PChar** variable.
- Using **strNew()** to allocate memory on the heap for a string.
- Using **GetMem.**

Later the code listing points the variable **p** to the first character of the string literal 'Hello' (p:=s;). The code then steps through each character in the string to which p points. The following line of code

```
while p^<>#0 do
```

does two things as it attempts to control stepping through a null-terminated string one letter at a time. First, it *dereferences* what p points to, in this case the first letter 'H' (dereferencing is also discussed later in this chapter in the "Pointer" section). The ^ character is the dereferencing symbol. Second, it gets the ordinal position of H in the set of characters to determine if it is 0. If so, then the end of the string has been reached. The line of code

```
Inc(p);
```

moves the pointer one byte over, so that it points to the next letter in the string. The PChar data type is actually considered a pointer to an array of char.

Delphi has several methods to manipulate null-terminated strings besides StrCopy(), including one to convert a null-terminated string into a Pascal-style string: the function **StrPas()**. Table 6.7 lists some of these methods.

TABLE 6.7 NULL-TERMINATED STRING MANIPULATION METHODS

Method	Description
StrCat	Appends a copy of one string to the end of another and returns the concatenated string.
StrComp	Compares two strings.
StrCopy	Copies one string to another.
StrDispose	Disposes a string on a heap.
StrECopy	Copies one string to another and returns a pointer to the end of the resulting string.
StrEnd	Returns a pointer to the end of a string.
StrLCat	Appends characters from one string to the end of another and returns the concatenated string.
StrlComp	Compares two strings without case sensitivity.

StrLComp	Compares two strings, up to a maximum length.
StrLCopy	Copies characters from one string to another.
StrLen	Returns the number of characters in Str.
StrLIComp	Compares two strings, up to a maximum length, without case sensitivity.
StrLower	Converts a string to lower-case.
StrMove	Copies characters from one string to another.
StrNew	Allocates a string on a heap.
StrPas	Converts a null-terminated string to a Pascal-style string.
StrPCopy	Copies a Pascal-style string to a null-terminated string.
StrPos	Returns a pointer to the first occurrence of a string in another string.
StrScan	Returns a pointer to the first occurrence of a character in a string.
StrRScan	Returns a pointer to the last occurrence of a character in a string.
StrUpper	Converts a string to upper-case.

Structured Types

ObjectPascal lets you define more than just simple types that allow a single value. You can declare variables that refer to arrays, records, sets and files. These types of variables contain data with a more complex structure than the data types previously discussed.

Arrays

Arrays are one of the standard structured types most programming languages support. An array is a block of memory designed to hold multiple values in numbered slots. Just like post office boxes which have a number that uniquely identifies a particular box in an array of boxes, array elements are also accessed by a number. Code Listing 6.10 shows how to declare and access an array.

LISTING 6.10 USING ARRAYS

```
procedure TDataTypes.ArrayButtonClick(Sender: TObject);
var
   LettersArr : array[1..5] of char;
   MultiDimArr : array[1..10,1..10,1..10] of Shortint;
   x,y,z : ShortInt;
begin
```

```
{assign letters to the array}
LettersArr[1]:='a';
LettersArr[2]:='b';
LettersArr[3]:='c';
LettersArr[4]:='d';
LettersArr[5]:='e';

{assign the number 1 to all entries in
 this 3-dimensional array}
for x:=1 to 10 do
   for y:=1 to 10 do
      for z:=1 to 10 do
         MultiDimArr[x,y,z] := 1;

{display the contents of index 3,4,7}
   MessageDlg('Index 3,4,7 = '+IntToStr(MultiDimArr[3,4,7]),
mtInformation,[mbOK],0);

end;
```

Listing 6.10 declares a simple array of characters (LettersArr) and a 3-dimensional array of short integers (MultiDimArr). To access elements in either array, you need to reference the element number.

Records

ObjectPascal supports a record structure which lets you place many different data types in a named container. The named container is the record structure. Listing 6.11 shows how to declare and use a record structure. In this example, two record structure types are declared: TTaxRec and TEmpRec. The TTaxRec type is designed to hold a tax code, a tax rate, and a maximum taxable amount. This is a simple record structure.

The TEmpRec type is designed to hold an employee id, their first name, their last name, an employee type classification (one of Hourly, Exempt, or Executive) and some pay information which varies depending on the type of employee. This is called a *variant* record structure. While an executive employee has Compensation, DeferredComp, and SharesOwned as additional fields, an Hourly employee has HourlyRate, and OTRate as additional fields.

As soon as you assign the EmpType field a value of Hourly Exempt or Executive, the other fields become available. This conserves space. Rather than creating a record structure which always allocates space for all of the variant field, the record structure is remapped depending on the variant field.

LISTING 6.11 USING RECORDS

```
procedure TDataTypes.RecordButtonClick(Sender: TObject);
type
   {declare an enumerated type for the variant record}
   TEmpType = (Hourly,Exempt,Executive);
   {state tax record type}
   TTaxRec = record
      State : String[2];
      TaxRate : Real;
      MaxTaxAmount : Real;
   end;
   {employee record type}
   TEmpRec = record
      Id : Longint;
      Fname : String[20];
      LName : String[20];
      case EmpType : TEmpType of
         Hourly :
           (HourlyRate : Real;
            OTRate : Real);
         Exempt :
           (Salary : Real);
         Executive :
           (Compensation : Real;
            DeferredComp : Real;
            SharesOwned : Longint);
   end;
var
   ILTaxRec : TTaxRec;
   EmployeeArr : array [1..3] of TEmpRec;
   DisplayStr : String;
begin
   {setup the IL tax record}
   with ILTaxRec do begin
      State := 'IL';
      TaxRate := 0.03;
      MaxTaxAmount := 30000;
   end;

   {assign the first record without 'do'}
   EmployeeArr[1].Id := 2134;
   EmployeeArr[1].Fname := 'Tom';
   EmployeeArr[1].Lname := 'Lucas';
   EmployeeArr[1].EmpType := Executive;
```

```
EmployeeArr[1].Compensation := 250000;
EmployeeArr[1].DeferredComp := 75000;
EmployeeArr[1].SharesOwned := 630000;

{assign the next two using 'do'}
with EmployeeArr[2] do begin
    Id := 3981;
    Fname := 'Mary Ann';
    Lname := 'Maslanka';
    EmpType := Exempt;
    Salary := 59500;
end;

with EmployeeArr[3] do begin
    Id := 2774;
    Fname := 'Ira';
    Lname := 'Blumen';
    EmpType := Hourly;
    HourlyRate := 7.40;
    OTRate := 7.40*1.5;
end;

{display the contents of the tax record}
str(ILTaxRec.TaxRate*100:5:2,DisplayStr);
MessageDlg(ILTaxRec.State+' = '+DisplayStr+'%',
        mtInformation,[mbOK],0);

{display the contents of an employee record}
with EmployeeArr[3] do begin
    str(EmployeeArr[3].HourlyRate:5:2,DisplayStr);
    MessageDlg(Fname+' '+Lname+' rate = '+DisplayStr,
            mtInformation,[mbOK],0);
end;

end;
```

Sets

ObjectPascal also lets you create sets, which are collections of values. You declare a set in the **var** section just like the other data types:

```
var
    ValidResponse : set of char;
begin
    ValidResponse := ['Y','N'];
```

In this example, the variable ValidResponse is a set variable which contains Y and N as its members. Unlike enumerated types, there is no order implied with a set. The entries in a set can be in any order. This is why sets are not considered ordinals. In addition, like enumerated types, sets are limited to 256 items in the set.

The usefulness of sets is in the operations you can perform on them. For example, if you do see a particular character is in a given set, all you need to do is the following:

```
if 'Y' in ValidResponse then
        MessageDlg('Y is in the Valid Response set',
mtInformation,[mbOK],0);
```

Other operations are allowed. For example, you combine two sets (of the same set type) into a third set (union). You can find out what two sets have in common (intersection) and you can find out what two sets do not have in common (difference). In addition, you can determine if two sets are equal (they contain the same elements), or if one set is a subset of another. These are illustrated in Listing 6.12.

LISTING 6.12 USING RECORDS

```
procedure TDataTypes.SetsButtonClick(Sender: TObject);
type
   TCustomerTypes = (Education,NonProfit,Retail,Wholesale);
var
   CustomerTypeArr : array[1..3] of Set of TCustomerTypes;
   DiffSet, CommonSet, CombinedSet : Set of TCustomerTypes;
begin
   {assign three customer type sets three different sets}
   CustomerTypeArr[1] := [Education,NonProfit,Retail];
   CustomerTypeArr[2] := [Wholesale,NonProfit];
   CustomerTypeArr[3] := [Education,Retail];

   {perform the set union operation on customer sets 2 and 3
    CombinedSet = [Education,NonProfit,Retail,Wholesale]}
   CombinedSet := CustomerTypeArr[2] + CustomerTypeArr[3];

   {perform the set intersection operation on customer sets 1 and 2
    CommonSet = [NonProfit]}
   CommonSet := CustomerTypeArr[1] * CustomerTypeArr[2];

   {perform the set difference operation on customer sets 1 and 2
    DiffSet = [Education,Retail]}
   DiffSet := CustomerTypeArr[1] - CustomerTypeArr[2];
```

```
{test each of the set operations:
  = equality
  <> inequality
  <= subset
  >= superset
  in contains}

if DiffSet = CustomerTypeArr[3] then
   MessageDlg('DiffSet = Set 1', mtInformation,[mbOK],0);

if CommonSet <> CustomerTypeArr[2] then
   MessageDlg('CommonSet <> Set 2', mtInformation,[mbOK],0);

If DiffSet <= CombinedSet then
   MessageDlg('DiffSet is a subset of CombinedSet',
mtInformation,[mbOK],0);

If CombinedSet >= CommonSet then
   MessageDlg('CombinedSet is a superset of CommonSet',
mtInformation,[mbOK],0);

If Retail in CombinedSet then
   MessageDlg('Retail is in the CombinedSet', mtInformation,[mbOK],0);

end;
```

Files

ObjectPascal has a file type which lets you read and write files on disk at a low level. You can manipulate two types of files: typed and untyped. Typed files expect the file to have a structure which can be mapped to one of the previously discussed data types. Untyped files let you read and write blocks of data to and from files without regard for how the data in the file is stored. Chapter 11, "Flat-File I/O" goes into much more depth concerning the file types. The file type is introduced here with a simple example. Listing 6.13 shows how to create both a typed and untyped file variable.

LISTING 6.13 USING FILE TYPES

```
procedure TDataTypes.FilesButtonClick(Sender: TObject);
type
   TFtype = char;                 {typed file type}
var
   MyFile : File of TFType;       {typed file}
```

```
  GenFile : File;                {untyped file}
  Buffer : TFType;               {buffer for typed file}
  Block : array [1..50] of char; {buffer for untyped file}
  RecsRead : Word;               {count of records read}
begin

  {assign MyFile to MYFILE.TXT}
  AssignFile(MyFile,'MYFILE.TXT');
  {create a new file, overwriting an old one}
  ReWrite(MyFile);
  {Write 'H' then 'i' then '!' to MYFILE.TXT}
  Buffer := 'H';
  Write(MyFile,Buffer);
  Buffer := 'i';
  Write(MyFile,Buffer);
  Buffer := '!';
  Write(MyFile,Buffer);

  {assign GENFILE to CONFIG.SYS}
  AssignFile(GenFile,'CONFIG.SYS');
  {Open CONFIG.SYS with a record size of Block}
  Reset(GenFile,SizeOf(Block));
  {Read in 1 records of size Block into Block}
  BlockRead(GenFile, Block, SizeOf(Block), RecsRead);
  {Display the first 50 characters in Block}
  MessageDlg(Block, mtInformation,[mbOK],0);

end;
```

In Listing 6.13, the typed file is called 'MYFILE.TXT' and is assigned a handle with the Assign() procedure. *This does not open the file.* The Reset() procedure opens a new file, overwriting what was previously there. To write to a typed file, use the Write() procedure.

Untyped files can be assigned and opened just like typed files. However, in order to read and write untyped files, you will need to use the BlockRead() and BlockWrite() procedures. These procedures expect a file handle, a buffer to read into or write from, the number of records to read, and a variable to hold the result of how many records were read.

While file variables are useful, if you need to read and write text files, look into the TStrings, TStringList, and TFileStream classes. These classes are designed to read and write data to and from files.

Pointers

Variables declared in a var statement are static. Only the compiler can allocate space for these variables. There are times, however, when you may want to dynamically allocate memory, at run time, that the compiler can not possibly know about. In order to access this dynamically created memory, you will need pointers.

For experienced C and C++ programmers, pointers are nothing new. To database programmers used to Paradox, Access, or V1sual Basic, pointers can be confusing. The reason they can be difficult is that environments like Access and Paradox insulate the programmer from the difficulties of handling pointers, and allocating and deallocating memory. After all, improperly handled pointers are the cause of a large number of bugs in existing C and C++ code (including Windows itself).

Allocating with New

Declaring a pointer to a variable is easy. You need to do two things: declare a pointer to a variable and then create the variable. The top of code Listing 6.14 shows how to declare a pointer to a variable.

LISTING 6.14 USING POINTERS

```
procedure TDataTypes.PointerButtonClick(Sender: TObject);
type
    TBigArray = array [1..100,1..100] of Shortint;
var
    Intp : ^Shortint;
    BigArrayp : ^TBigArray;
    MemLeft, TotalAmt : Longint;
    x,y : Shortint;
begin

    {find out how much memory is left}
    MemLeft := MemAvail;
    MessageDlg('MemAvail = '+IntToStr(MemLeft), mtInformation,[mbOK],0);

    {allocate a pointer to a shortint}
    new(intp);

    {assign a value to the variable}
```

```
Intp^ := 3;
MessageDlg('Intp = '+IntToStr(Intp^), mtInformation,[mbOK],0);

{create the memory for the 100x100 array}
new(BigArrayp);

{find out how much memory is left}
MemLeft := MemAvail;
MessageDlg('MemAvail = '+IntToStr(MemLeft), mtInformation,[mbOK],0);

{assign values to the array}
for x:=1 to 100 do
   for y:=1 to 100 do
      BigArrayp^[x,y]:=x+y;

{get the total for the items in the array}
TotalAmt:=0;
for x:=1 to 100 do
   for y:=1 to 100 do
      TotalAmt := TotalAmt + BigArrayp^[x,y];

{display the total for the items}
MessageDlg('TotalAmt = '+IntToStr(TotalAmt), mtInformation,[mbOK],0);

{free up the memory the pointers access}
Dispose(intp);
Dispose(BigArrayp);
```

```
end;
```

When you create variables with New(), you need remove them as well. The Dispose() procedure handles this.

Dereferencing

In order to access the actual data a pointer points at, you need to *dereference* the pointer. With normal variables, this is not required. To access the value in a variable, you simply refer to the variable by name:

```
a:=100;
c:=a;
```

Listing 6.13 shows how to set and get a value with a pointer:

```
Intp^ := 3;
MessageDlg('Intp = '+IntToStr(Intp^), mtInformation,[mbOK],0);
```

In the first line, the value 3 is stored at the address *to which Inpt points*. This is indicated by the carat (^) character after the pointer name Intp. The second line (MessageDlg()) retrieves what Intp points to. Again, you simply place the ^ character at the end of the pointer name to dereference the pointer.

When developing database applications, you do not usually need to create pointer variables. Database applications typically access data in tables, not in dynamically allocated memory variables. On the other hand, pointers open up a whole new world of data structures for database developers.

Using nil

Delphi has an important keyword, called *Nil*. You can assign pointer variables of any type the value Nil. This is useful in determining if a pointer variable actually points at anything. It is good practice to assign all your pointer variables the value of Nil before assigning them a memory address. If you do not, the pointer will have a random number stored in it and if you access the pointer without initializing it with New(), your code will compile and run, but your pointer will most likely be pointing off into deep space somewhere. This can cause system crashes.

Accessing Typed and Untyped Pointers

A common data structure that programmers manipulate with pointers is a linked list. Listing 6.15 shows an example of creating a linked list dynamically, one node at a time, and then traversing the linked list in order. This example uses a typed pointer to manage the allocation and accessing of memory.

LISTING 6.15 USING TYPED POINTERS

```
procedure TDataTypes.Pointers3Click(Sender: TObject);
type
   TDataPtr = ^TData;
   TData = Record
      Value : Integer;
      Next : TDataPtr;
   end;
var
   Head, Prior, Temp : TDataPtr;
   x : Integer;
begin

   {create 10 nodes in a linked list}
   for x:=1 to 10 do begin
```

```
    {create a spot of memory, assign to Temp}
    New(Temp);
    {set the value in the node to x}
    Temp^.Value := x;
    {set the next pointer to nil}
    Temp^.Next := nil;
    if x=1 then
        {store the address of the 1st node in Head}
        Head:=Temp
    else
        {save the address of temp in the prior node's next slot}
        Prior^.Next := Temp;

    {save the address to the node just setup as Prior}
    Prior := Temp;
end;

{get temp pointing to the first node}
Temp:=Head;
{navigate the linked list until Temp is nil,
 at the same time, clean up memory}
while Temp <> nil do begin
    MessageDlg('Node '+IntToStr(Temp^.value), mtInformation,[mbOK],0);
    {save the address of the node visited}
    Prior:=Temp;
    {get temp pointing at the next item}
    Temp := Temp^.Next;
    {dispose of the old node}
    Dispose(Prior);
end;

end;
```

Listing 6.15 creates a type TDataPtr, which is a pointer type to the record structure TData. A field, **Value**, holds an integer which is used to number the nodes created. Notice that one of the fields in the record structure is of type **TDataPtr**. The code creates 10 nodes in memory and uses the **Next** field in the record structure to link the nodes together.

The **for** loop in Listing 6.14 creates each node with slightly different processing for the first node. When the first node is created, its address must be saved so that the list can be referenced later. If you do not save the address to the first node in the list in some variable, you will not be able to traverse the list. As each of the other nodes are created, the **Next** slot on each prior node needs be set to point to the node just created (**Temp** points to this node). With this setup, **Node1's Next** slot points to **Node2**. **Node2's Next** slot points to **Node3** and so on. The last node's **Next** slot points to **nil**.

Traversing the linked list is easy. Listing 6.14 uses the Temp variable to point from node to node. At first, it starts out by pointing to the start of the linked list (**Temp:=Head**). The lines of code while in loop continue to execute until Temp is equal to nil, which means the end of the list has been reached. As each node is visited, the code in Listing 6.14 cleans up memory, deleting each node after its value is displayed.

Listings 6.13 and 6.14 shows how to dynamically create memory for an array of fixed size or a record structure of fixed size. But what if you do not know how big a structure needs to be? In database programming, sometimes you might want to read values from a table into an array but you do not know exactly how many values there will be until run time.

ObjectPascal is not as flexible as C when it comes to pointers. For example, the pointer arithmetic discussed earlier with the PChar data type only works with PChar pointers. In addition, ObjectPascal is a strongly typed language which restricts pointer assignment. Fortunately, ObjectPascal has enough tools to let us dynamically allocate memory of varying quantity at runtime. Listing 6.15 shows how to declare a variable of type *Pointer*. This is different than creating a variable which is a pointer to some other type. In the latter case (as demonstrated in prior listings), you declare the variable as follows:

```
var
    Intp : ^Integer;
```

You declare a general purpose, untyped pointer as follows:

```
var
    ptr : Pointer
```

Unlike the typed pointers, you can not allocate memory for it with New(). Instead, you need to use GetMem(), as shown in Listing 6.16.

LISTING 6.16 USING UNTYPED POINTERS

```
procedure TDataTypes.Pointer2ButtonClick(Sender: TObject);
type
    TData = LongInt;            {'array' base data type}
var
    BiggerArrayP : Pointer;     {general memory pointer}
    TempP : ^TData;             {pointer to base data type}
    y, ArrSize : Integer;       {counter vars}
    OfsAddr, SegAddr : Word;    {address locations}
begin
    {Establish the array size, allocate memory for it}
    ArrSize := 1000;
```

```
GetMem(BiggerArrayP,SizeOf(TData)*ArrSize);

{Store the address to the array in memory -
 these addresses are used to move through the array}
SegAddr:=Seg(BiggerArrayP^);
OfsAddr:=Ofs(BiggerArrayP^);

{Assign each spot in the array the value of y}
for y:=0 to ArrSize-1 do begin
    {using the saved addresses, increment the pointer TempP by y.
     You can't do PChar pointer math here!}
    TempP := Ptr(SegAddr,OfsAddr+y*SizeOf(TData));
    {store y+1 at the address TempP points to}
    TempP^ := y+1; {start the numbering at 1 to 1000}
end;

{Retrieve what was stored in the 503rd position in the array}
TempP := Ptr(SegAddr,OfsAddr+(503-1)*SizeOf(TData));
MessageDlg('503 = '+IntToStr(TempP^), mtInformation,[mbOK],0);

{free up the memory for the array access}
Freemem(BiggerArrayP,SizeOf(TData)*ArrSize);
```

```
end;
```

In Listing 6.15, two pointers variables are being used: BiggerArrayP which is an untyped pointer and TempP which is a typed pointer to the TData type. Once the block of memory is allocated with GetMem, the address to which BiggerArrayP points to is stored into two variables: OfsAddr and SegAddr. These two variables store the memory segment and offset where the array of memory starts.

The functions Seg() and Ofs() are used to retrieve the address. Please note that Seg() and Ofs() get the address for *BiggerArrayP^* not BiggerArrayP. BiggerArrayP must be dereferenced with the ^ symbol otherwise Seg() and Ofs() would return the address of the memory pointer BiggerArrayP, not the address for the start of the newly allocated memory structure. This is a very subtle difference in notation which makes a big difference in this example. Getting the address to BiggerArrayP is a very different thing from getting the address to what BiggerArrayP points at.

Be very careful when working with untyped pointers, Ofs(), Seg() and Ptr(). If you do not get your memory pointer arithmetic all correct, you can cause GPFs in your code which can blow you right out of Windows. Make sure nothing important is running in Windows, and save your work early, and save often when using the techniques described here. Very rarely does one get the pointer arithmetic just right the first time.

The array is filled by positioning the pointer TempP to the address saved in OfsAddr and SegAddr plus the value of counter **y** (less 1) times the size of Tdata using the Ptr() function. If you give Ptr a segment and offset address, it will return a pointer to that address. This ensures that on the first pass through the loop, TempP points to the 0th byte in the array of memory. On the second pass, TempP is moved down x number of bytes, where x is the size of the Tdata type. In this case, the size of TData is 4 bytes.

Notice that the pointer TempP is a pointer to the Tdata type. When Ptr() returns a pointer to an area of memory to TempP, the program V1ews the area of memory through the eyes of TempP. This means that TempP thinks the area of memory is a long integer. This lets us use any of the functions and procedures that work on long integers on any element within this V1rtual array. With TempP happily thinking that the memory it is looking at is a long integer, we can freely assign and retrieve values using it, just like this line from Listing 6.14:

```
TempP^ := y+1; {start the numbering at 1 to 1000}
```

The last thing you need to do when working with untyped pointers is to free up the memory GetMem() allocated for them. Use the FreeMem() function to do this. Make sure that the amount of memory freed up using FreeMem() is identical to the amount allocated with GetMem().

Procedural Types

Procedural variables let you store the address to a function or procedure and pass the function or procedure as a variable. Typically you only need to pass data between functions and procedures, however, you can pass a function and execute that function *under a different name*. Listing 6.17 shows how to declare and use a procedural type.

LISTING 6.17 USING PROCEDURAL TYPES

```
procedure Msg; far;
begin
    MessageDlg('In msg procedure', mtInformation,[mbOK],0);
end;

function Add2(x : Integer) : Integer; far;
begin
  Add2 := x+2;
end;

procedure TDataTypes.ProcedureButtonClick(Sender: TObject);
var
    p : procedure;
    f : function(x : Integer) : Integer;
    z : Integer;
begin

    z:=0;
    {assign p the address of procedure Msg}
    p:=Msg;
{The following also assigns p the address of procedure Msg, but with the
@ operator. This approach tells the compiler to not execute Msg, but to
assign its address tp the address of p. The @ operator has the highest
order of precedence, so the compiler will always properly compile this
code if it is mixed with other operators.}
@p:=@Msg;
    {assign f the address of function Add2}
    f:=Add2;
    {Call Msg}
    p;
    {call Add2, display result}
    z:=f(3);
    MessageDlg('Z was 2 is now '+IntToStr(z), mtInformation,[mbOK],0);

end;
```

To use procedural variables, you need to declare the assigned functions or
procedures with the **far** keyword so that they are always locatable. If you do
not use the **far** keyword, your code will not compile.

Type Compatibility

ObjectPascal is a strongly typed language. In order for two variable types to be compared with each other, they must be *type compatible*. Two types are considered compatible if any one of the following conditions is true:

- Both types are the same.
- Both types are real.
- Both types are integers.
- One type is a subrange of the other.
- Both types are subranges of the same host type.
- Both types are set types with compatible base types.
- One type is a string type and the other is either a string type or Char type.
- One type is Pointer and the other is any pointer type.
- One type is PChar and the other is a zero-based character array of the form array[0..X] of Char. (This applies only when extended syntax is enabled with the {$X+} directive.)
- Both types are pointers to identical types. (This applies only when type-checked pointers are enabled with the {$T+} directive.)
- Both types are procedural types with identical result types, an identical number of parameters, and a one-to-one identity between parameter types.

Assignment Compatibility

It is one thing to be type-compatible and quite another to be assignment-compatible. Variable V2 can be assigned to variable V1 (V1:=V2;) if both are type compatible and any one of the following rules is true:

- V1 and V2 are identical types and neither is a file type or a structured type that contains a file-type component at any level of structuring.
- V1 and V2 are compatible ordinal types, and the values of type V2 falls within the range of possible values of V1.

- V1 and V2 are real types, and the value of type V2 falls within the range of possible values of V1.
- V1 is a real type, and V2 is an integer type.
- V1 and V2 are string types.
- V1 is a string type, and V2 is a Char type.
- V1 is a string type, and V2 is a packed string type.
- V1 and V2 are compatible set types, and all the members of the value of type V2 fall within the range of possible values of V1.
- V1 and V2 are compatible pointer types.
- V1 is a PChar and V2 is a string constant. (This applies only when extended syntax is enabled {$X+}.)
- V1 is a PChar and V2 is a zero-based character array of the form array[0..X] of Char. (This applies only when extended syntax is enabled {$X+}.)
- V1 and V2 are compatible procedural types.
- V1 is a procedural type, and V2 is a procedure or function with an identical result type, an identical number of parameters, and a one-to-one identity between parameter types.
- V2 is assignment-compatible with an object type V1 if V2 is an object type in the domain of V1.
- A pointer type P2, pointing to an object type V2, is assignment-compatible with a pointer type P1, pointing to an object type V1, if V2 is in the domain of V1.

Type Casting

Variables can be assigned to other variables of a different type using type casting functions. For example, you can convert between many of the ordinal types using the type name as a function name. Code Listing 6.18 shows an example of some variable type casting.

LISTING 6.18 VARIABLE TYPE CASTING

```
procedure TDataTypes.CastingButtonClick(Sender: TObject);
const
    c
var
    x,y : Integer;
```

```
   b : Boolean;
   c : Char;
   r : Real;

begin
```

```
   {store 65 in x}
   x:=65;
   MessageDlg('X='+IntToStr(x), mtInformation,[mbOK],0);
   {cast x to a character variable c}
   c:=Char(x);
   MessageDlg('Char(x) = '+c, mtInformation,[mbOK],0);
   {cast it back to another integer variable}
   y:=Integer(c);
   MessageDlg('Y [Integer(Char(x))] = '+IntToStr(y),
mtInformation,[mbOK],0);

   {cast y to a boolean, using C-style boolean integer evaluation}
   b:=WordBool(y);
   if b then
       MessageDlg('WordBool('+IntToStr(y)+' = True',
mtInformation,[mbOK],0);

end;
```

Constants

Like most other programming languages, ObjectPascal lets you define constants. Constants have their values fixed at compile time and can not be changed during program execution. In addition, constants enhance the readability of your code. To declare a constant, simply include a **const** section after the procedure or function name:

```
procedure ConstExample;
const
   c = 1;
   Name = 'George';
   YearCreated = 1995;
begin
   MessageDlg('Name = '+Name, mtInformation,[mbOK],0);
end;
```

Typed Constants

The term typed constant is misleading, because it is not a constants at all. A typed constant is a variable, declared in constant section, which contains initialization code along with the type declaration. Typed constants are initialized only once, at the beginning of the call to the routine. The following example shows how to declare and use a typed constant.

```
procedure TypeConstExample;
const
    Name : String[10] = 'George';
    YearCreated = 1995;
begin
    Name :='Hello';
    MessageDlg('Name = '+Name, mtInformation,[mbOK],0);
end;
```

Summary

Delphi gives programmers a wealth of data types. While database programmers usually deal with data in tables and other visible objects on a form, having a variety of data types available is quite useful. These fundamental data types let you implement various abstract data types, such as stacks, queues, linked lists, binary trees, hash tables, and multi-dimensional arrays. These kinds of tools help solve non-relational data problems. And from time to time, database developers need to grapple with these problems. Having a detailed knowledge of ObjectPascal's data types helps.

CHAPTER 7

Expressions

An *expression* is composed of operands and operators. A very simple expression is A + B. In this expression the variables A and B are the *operands* (the values that are operated upon), and + is the *operator* which determines what is done to the operands.

To program in Pascal you must be familiar with each of the operators, and the types of operands with which they are used. You must also understand the order in which operations take place. For example, in the expression 2 + 3 * 2 you must know which operation takes place first. If the addition occurs first, the result is 10. However, if the multiplication is performed first, the answer is 8. You must also understand the concept of short circuit evaluation in logical expressions to understand how your code will run. This chapter will cover all of these topics and more.

Operators

Pascal includes a large array of operators to manipulate various data types. The following sections describe the various types of operators and how you use them.

Arithmetic Operators

Pascal has six arithmetic operators. The first four are the standard + for addition, - for subtraction, * for multiplication, and / for division. All of these operators can be used with both real and integer numbers, or any combination of the two.

In Pascal the division operator, /, always yields a real number as the result. To perform integer division use the **div** operator. To understand the difference take a look at the program in Figure 7.1.

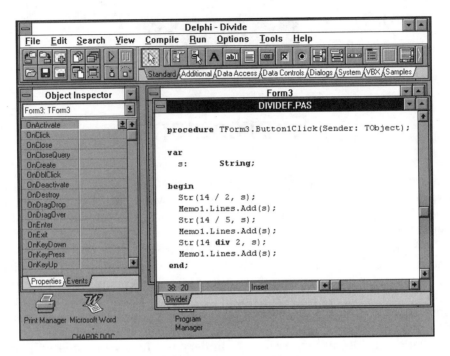

FIGURE 7.1 REAL VERSUS INTEGER DIVISION.

This code uses the runtime library Str procedure to convert the numeric result of the division to a String so that it can be displayed in the Memo object on the form. Str takes two parameters. The first is the value to be converted and the second is the String variable to put the result into. Memo1.Lines.Add(s) calls the Add method of the Memo object's Lines to add the Strings to the end of the text in the memo. The first two statements display the result of dividing one integer by another. Since 14 is evenly divisible by 2, the result should be the integer 7. The second Str call divides 14 by 5 using the real or floating point division operator (/). The third Str call divides 15 by 4 using the integer division operator (div). Figure 7.2 shows the results that this program produces.

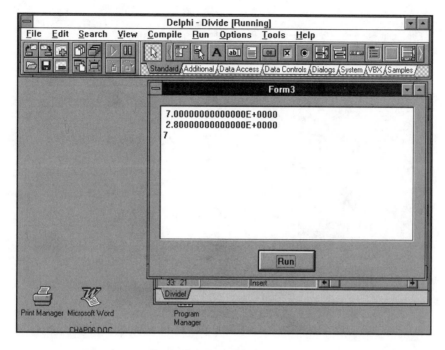

FIGURE 7.2 RESULTS OF DIVISION.

Note that the result of dividing the integer 14 by the integer 2 using the / operator is 7.0000000000E+00, a floating point value even though 14 is evenly divisible by 2. The second line shows the result of dividing the integer 14 by the integer 5. This is the floating point value 2.8 as you would expect, since 14 is not evenly divisible by 5. The third line shows that the result of dividing 14 by 5 using the integer division operator, div, is 2. Notice that integer division does not produce a rounded result since the actual answer is 2.8, which would round to the integer 3. When you perform integer division using the div operator, any fractional part of the result is discarded.

The sixth arithmetic operator is mod. Mod computes the remainder when one integer is divided by another. The program in Figure 7.3 shows how it works.

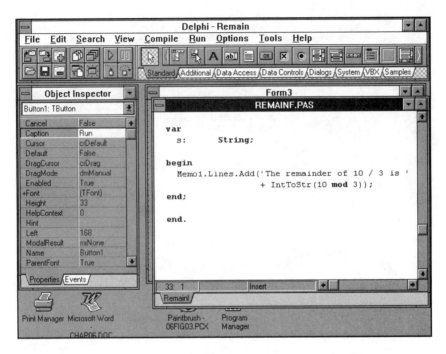

FIGURE 7.3 THE MOD OPERATOR.

This program, Remain, computes the remainder of dividing 10 by 3. In this case the runtime library function IntToStr converts the integer result to a string, so it can be displayed in the Memo object on the form. Figure 7.4 shows the result. Notice that when converting numbers, to strings use Str to convert real numbers and IntToStr to convert integers. If you use Str to convert an integer value the compiler will first convert it to a real number, and then to a string.

Most operators are binary, that is, they require two operands. However, there are some exceptions such as the + and - operators. Plus and minus can also be used as unary operators to indicate the sign of a value. In the expression

```
x := -3
```

the - operator has only one operand, 3, and denotes that the value of 3 is negative. You can also use the + operator in the same way, although there is no reason to do so since all numeric values are assumed to be positive, unless preceded by the unary - operator.

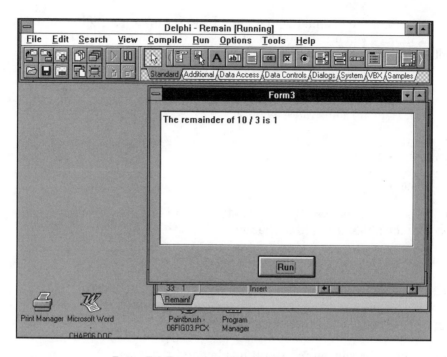

FIGURE 7.4 THE OUTPUT OF THE REMAIN PROGRAM.

Binary Numbers

Pascal includes a set of operators that allow you to manipulate the individual bits in an integer value. To understand what they do you have to understand how numbers are stored in binary form. If you are familiar with binary numbers, skip to the next section, "Bitwise Operators."

Binary integers consist of some number of bits. Each bit can have only two values, zero or one. The Byte type in Pascal is an eight bit value. Both the Integer and Word types are 16 bit values. For simplicity all of the examples in this section will use the Byte type. When you work with binary numbers each digit represents one bit, so a byte whose value is zero, is represented as eight zeros or 00000000. Each bit represents a power of two starting from the right. The first bit has the value 2 raised to the zero power or 1, the second bit the value 2 raised to the 1st power or 2, the third bit the value 2 raised to the 2nd power or 4, the fourth the value 2 raised to the 3rd power or 8, and so on.

To assign the decimal value 1 to a byte, set the first (rightmost) bit to 1 so the binary value is 00000001. To assign the decimal value 4 to the byte set the third bit to 1 so the binary value is 00000100. Decimal 3 in binary is 00000011 because the first bit represents 1 and the second bit represents 2, and 2 + 1 = 3. So, to determine the decimal number that a binary value represents all you have to do is sum the values of each of the bits that they are set to 1. Here are some more examples.

```
00000101 = 5
00000110 = 6
00000111 = 7
00001000 = 8
```

What is the decimal value of 11111111? To find the answer sum the value of each of the bits starting from the right.

```
1 + 2 + 4 + 8 + 16 + 32 + 64 + 128 = 255
```

This means that the largest value you can store in an 8 bit byte is 255.

Bitwise Logical Operators

Pascal provides operators to shift bits left and right, set the value of any bit, or combination of bits, and detect the value of any bit or combination of bits.

The shl and slr Operators

The first two bit-wise operators are shl and shr. These operators shift the bits in an integer to the left or right, respectively. If you have a byte with the decimal value 1 its binary value is 00000001. If you shift the bits to the left one position, the result is 2. Or, in binary:

```
00000001 shl 1 = 00000010 = 2
00000001 shl 2 = 00000100 = 4
```

Shifting bits to the left has the effect of multiplying the value by 2, raised to the power of the number of bits. In other words, shifting the bits in an integer two bits to the left is the same as multiplying the value by 2, raised to the 2nd power or 4. Shifting bits to the right divides the value by the power of 2 equal to the number of bits you shift. Figure 7.5 shows a simple program to demonstrate this.

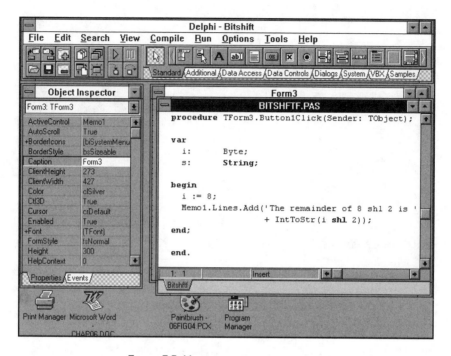

FIGURE 7.5 MULTIPLICATION BY BIT SHIFTING.

This program, BITSHIFT, Displays the result of shifting the bits in the Byte variable i with the value of 8 two places to the left. If you change the program and enter **128** for the integer and **2** for the number of bits to shift left, you may be surprised by the result. As you have seen, shifting 2 bits to the left multiplies the value by 4. However, 128 times 4 is 512, and the largest value a single byte can hold is 255, so what happens? In this case the program displays the right answer because Pascal promotes the result from an 8-bit byte to a 32-bit long integer which can hold the value 512.

However, if you assigned the result to another Byte variable and displayed its value, the value is zero. Why? Because 128 in binary is 10000000. If you shift this value to the left then the bit falls off the end of the byte, and leaves only zeros. Figure 7.6 shows a modified version of the BITSHIFT program in Figure 7.5 that does store the result in a Byte variable.

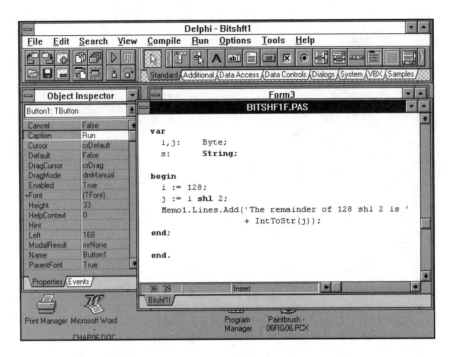

FIGURE 7.6 A BIT SHIFTING EXAMPLE THAT DEMONSTRATES OVERFLOW.

Unlike most programming languages, Pascal does not use the equal sign to assign a value to a variable. Instead, Pascal uses := as its assignment operator. This is read as "gets the value of" or just "gets" for short. So A := B is read, "A gets B".

NOTE

The and Operator

The and operator lets you determine if a particular bit in an integer value is set to 1. When changing the bits in a value you use a second value called the *mask*. Each bit that you want to operate on in the value must be set to 1 in the mask. In other words, the mask identifies the bits on which to operate. If you and two integer values together the only bits that will be set to 1 in the result are those that were set in both values.

Figure 7.7 shows a program that demonstrates the and operator by and-ing the value 7 with a mask of 2.

Run this program and you will see that the result is 2. This means that you can find out if any bit is set to 1 in an integer by anding the integer with a mask that has that bit set to 1. If the result is zero, the bit is set to zero. If not, the bit is set to 1.

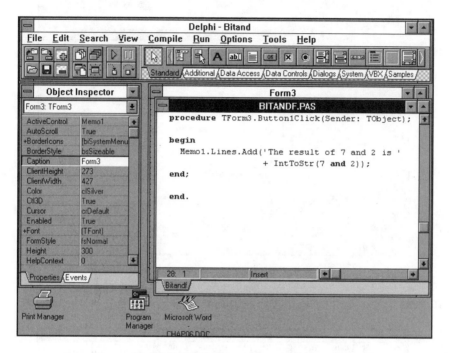

FIGURE 7.7 THE BITWISE AND OPERATOR.

The or Operator

The or operator is most often used to turn a bit on (set it to 1). This is because the result of an or operation is 1 if the value of the bit in either operand is 1. Therefore, if you or the value 5 with a mask that has the bit whose value is 2, set 2 to 1, the result is 7. You can see this more clearly if you look at the binary values.

```
00000101 or 00000010 = 00000111
```

Notice that in the result, 00000111, every bit that was set to 1 in either of the two values on the left of the equal sign, is set to 1. Therefore, if you want to turn a particular bit on (set it to 1), or the value with the value of that bit. Figure 7.8 shows a program that demonstrates setting a bit using the or operator.

148

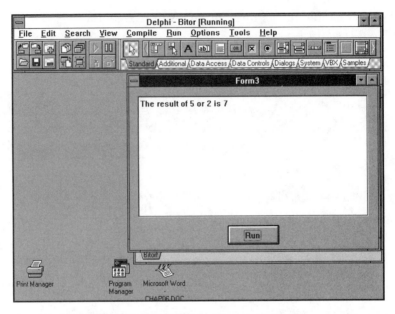

FIGURE 7.8 SETTING A BIT WITH THE OR OPERATOR.

Running this program yields the results shown in Figure 7.9.

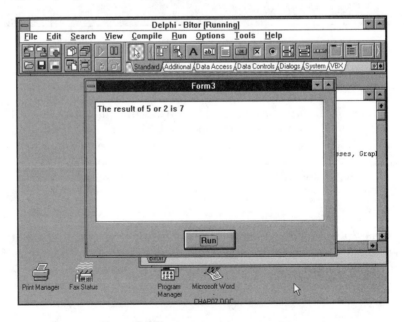

FIGURE 7.9 THE RESULT OF AN OR OPERATION.

Turning a bit on adds the value of that bit to the value of the number, if the bit was not already on. In this example 5 or 2 is the same as 5 + 2, which equals 7.

The xor Operator

The exclusive or operator, xor, toggles the value of bits. That is, it changes the bits that are 1 to 0 and the bits that are 0 to 1. For example if a variable has the value 5 in binary it would be 00000101. If you want to toggle the state of the first four bits xor it with a mask that has the first four bits set to 1. The decimal value of the mask 00001111 is 15. The result will be binary 00001010, or decimal 10. The bits that were 1 have been changed to zero and the bits that were zero have been changed to 1. The program in Figure 7.10

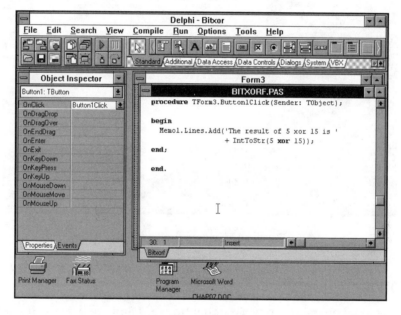

FIGURE 7.10 THE XOR OPERATOR.

String Concatenation

There is only one String operator, the + sign, used to combine two strings. For example, 'abc' + 'def' = 'abcdef'. Figure 7.11 shows a Pascal program that lets you combine strings.

Since string literals are delimited by single quotes (apostrophes) you cannot include an apostrophe in a string literal directly. To include the word dog's in the string assigned to s2, the apostrophe is inserted by using the pound sign, followed by its ANSI code. You can include any character in a string using this technique. For apostrophes, there is also a shortcut. Just use two consecutive apostrophes as in 'dog' 's'.

The string type in Pascal is limited to 255 characters. If the total length of the strings you concatenate is greater than 255 the result will be truncated to 255 characters.

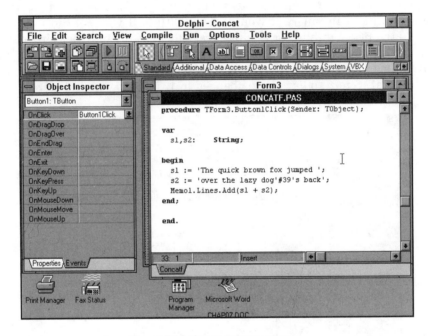

FIGURE 7.11 CONCATENATING STRINGS.

Relational Operators

The relational operators are very straightforward and are listed in Table 6.1.

TABLE 7.1 RELATIONAL OPERATORS

Operator	Description
=	Equal to
<>	Not equal to

>	Greater than
<	Less than
>=	Greater than or equal to. When used with sets tests if one set is a superset of another.
<=	Less than or equal to. When used with sets tests if one set is a subset of another.
in	Tests if a value is a member of a set.

Using the relational operators you can construct expressions that evaluate to the logical values True or False. Figure 7.12 shows a simple program that compares two integers to see if the first is greater than the second, and displays the result.

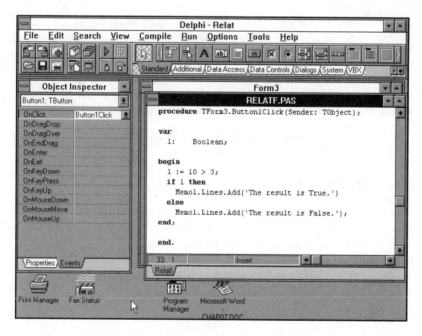

FIGURE 7.12 USING THE RELATIONAL GREATER THAN OPERATOR.

This program uses the if keyword to examine the value of the Boolean variable l, and displays the correct answer in the Memo object. Figure 7.13 shows the output produced when you run this program.

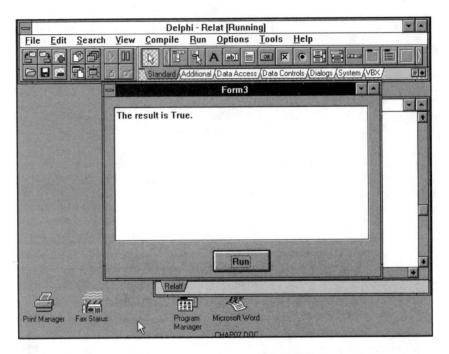

FIGURE 7.13 OUTPUT FROM RELAT.EXE.

Boolean Operators

The Boolean operators, and, or , not, and xor, combine Boolean values in various ways. When two values are combined with the and operator, the result is True only if both of the values are True. Figure 7.14 shows a simple example of using the and operator. This program compares two integers to see if they are both greater than zero. Since the second value, -1, is not greater than zero, the result is False.

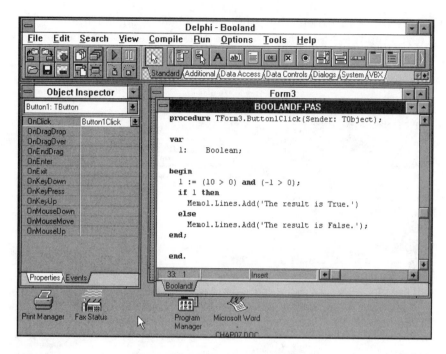

FIGURE 7.14 USING THE AND OPERATOR.

The parentheses in the expression

```
1 := (10 > 0) and (-1 > 0);
```

are required. To understand the reason why, read the next section, "Operator Precedence."

Combining two Boolean values using the or operator results in True if either one, or both of the values are True. Figure 7.15 shows the sample program which demonstrates logic. This is the same program used in the example in Figure 7.14 except the operator has been changed from and to or. When you run this program the result is True, because one of the numbers is greater than zero.

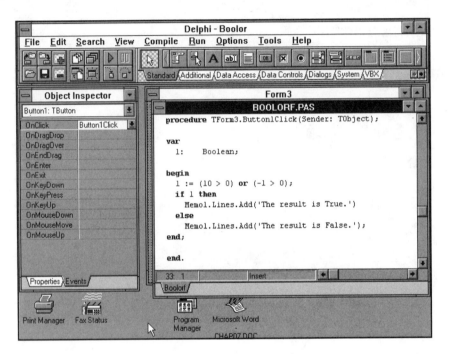

FIGURE 7.15 USING THE OR OPERATOR.

The exclusive or operator, xor, combines two values such that if both values are True, the result is False, and if both values are False, the result is False, however, if one value is True and the other is False the result is True. Put another way, when you combine two Boolean values with xor the result is True if the two values are not the same, and False if the two values are the same. Figure 7.16 shows the test program modified to use the xor operator.

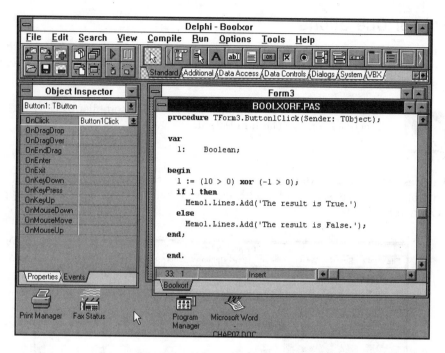

FIGURE 7.16 USING THE XOR OPERATOR.

The last of the Boolean operators is not. Not is a unary operator and it simply reverses the value of the operand. If the value of a Boolean variable, i, is True the statement:

```
l := not i;
```

assigns False to the boolean variable l. If the value of i is False then the statement:

```
l := not i;
```

assigns True to l.

Pointer Operations

There are two types of operations you can perform on pointers. You can get the address of an object in memory and assign it to a pointer, and you can perform addition and subtraction on pointers of type PChar.

To use the PChar type you must use the {$X+} compiler directive. This directive is on by default in Delphi.

N O T E

The easiest way to understand pointer operators is with an example. The program in Figure 7.17 declares three variables, a string, a pointer of type PChar, and a byte.

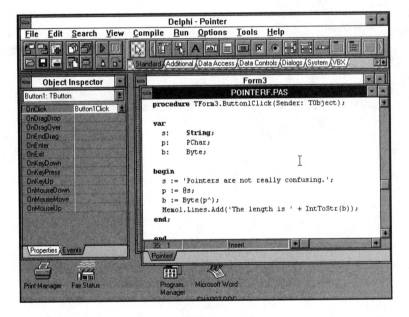

FIGURE 7.17 USING POINTERS.

The first statement in the program assigns a value to the string variable s. Next, the statement:

```
p := @s;
```

uses the address of operator, @, to assign the address of the string variable, s, to the pointer p. The pointer now points to the beginning of the string in memory. Remember that Pascal strings store the length of the string in the first byte and the text starts in the second byte so the pointer, p, now points to the length of the string. To display the length of the string as a number it must be assigned to one of the integer variable types. The statement:

```
b := Byte(p^);
```

gets the value pointed to by the pointer p, casts it to the byte type, and stores it in the byte variable b. Finally, the Add call displays the string's length on the screen. Note that this is not the easy way to find the length of a string. Instead, it is easier to use the runtime library Length function.

The next thing to examine is the use of the + and - arithmetic operators as they apply to pointers. Figure 7.18 shows a program that declares two pointers of type PChar. The statements

```
p := @s;
p := p + 1;
q := p + 4;
```

assign the address of the string, s, to p. Adding one to p makes it point to the first character of the string instead of the length byte. Adding four to p and assigning the result to q provides a second pointer that points to the fifth character in the string.

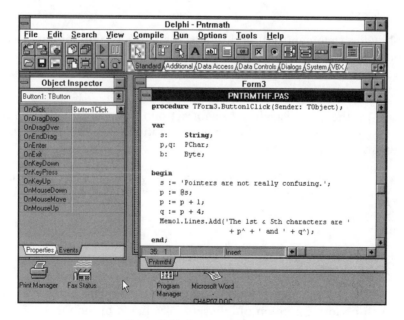

FIGURE 7.18 POINTER ARITHMETIC.

In addition to adding integer values to character pointers to change the character to which they point, you can also subtract one pointer from another to determine the number of bytes between two locations in the same string, as shown in the following statement.

```
i := q - p;
```

Make sure that you subtract the lower memory address from the higher memory address. In this example q - p is 4 but p - q is 65532 because the pointers are unsigned numbers.

When you subtract one pointer from another make sure that they both point to the same string. If they do not, the result is undefined.

T I P

You can also subtract an integer from a pointer to make it point to a lower memory address.

It is possible to increment and decrement the value of pointers whose type is other than PChar using the Inc and Dec runtime library procedures. So, given the pointer declaration:

```
ptr:    ^Char;
```

the following statement will add one to the value of the pointer, so that it will point to the next byte in memory.

```
Inc(ptr)
```

You can use the Dec procedure to subtract one from a pointer value in the same way. These are the only arithmetic operations that you can perform on pointers whose type is other than PChar.

Using Inc and Dec on pointers whose type is not PChar is an undocumented feature. It may not work in future versions of Delphi.

WARNING

Set Operators

Pascal includes three operators for working with sets. The first is the + operator which performs a union of two sets. A value is in the result of a union if it is in one of the two sets.

The second is the difference operator, -. A value is in the result of a difference operation only if it is in the set on the left side of the operator, and not in the set on the right. The final set operator, *, performs an intersection of two sets. A value is in the result of an intersection only if it is in both sets.

Operator Precedence

Now that you are familiar with all of the operators, it is vital to understand how the compiler decides how to process expressions that contain two or more operators.

The introduction to this chapter asked what the result of 2 + 3 * 2 should be. If the addition is done first, the result is 10, however, if the multiplication is done first, the result is 8. The compiler resolves this question with a simple set of rules. First, all of the operators are assigned a precedence ranking as shown in Table 6.2.

TABLE 7.2 OPERATOR PRECEDENCE

Operators	Precedence
@,not	First
*,/,div,mod,and,shl,shr	Second
+,-,or,xor	Third
=,<>,>,<,>=,<=,in	Fourth

When the compiler evaluates an expression, the operation with the highest precedence is performed first. Therefore, in the example 2 + 3 * 2, since * has precedence over +, the compiler multiplies first, and the correct answer is 8. If the operators have equal precedence as in 2 + 3 - 2, they are evaluated from left to right.

You can change the order of evaluation in an expression by adding parentheses to group operators and their operands. When an expression contains parentheses, the compiler evaluates the sub-expressions within the parentheses first to get a single value, and then evaluates the rest of the expression. The following statement is used in the sample program for the and operator in the preceding section.

```
l := (i > 0) and (j > 0);
```

You can see from Table 6.2 that the and operator has higher precedence than > and <. Without the parentheses, this expression will not work because the compiler tries to evaluate 0 and j first to get a Boolean value, and then tries to evaluate i >, the Boolean value. Since it is not valid to test if an Integer is greater than a Boolean, the compiler will produce an error if you remove the parentheses.

Adding the parentheses solves this problem. Since the compiler evaluates the expressions in the parentheses first, it now evaluates (i > 0) to get a Boolean result, next it evaluates (j > 0) to get a Boolean result, and finally it ands the two Boolean values and assigns the result to l.

You can nest parentheses within parentheses to any depth. The compiler evaluates them from the inside out. For example, in the expression:

```
l := (a > b) and ((c < d) or (e = f))
```

the order of evaluation is (c < d), (e = f), (a > b), then the or operation and finally the and operation.

Short Circuit Evaluation

Make sure that you do not construct complex relational expressions that require every sub-expression to be evaluated. To optimize performance the compiler generates code that uses short circuit expression evaluation. Consider the expression:

```
(a > b) and (c < d)
```

If a is less than or equal to b then the first sub-expression evaluates to False. When the compiler sees the and operator it is smart enough to realize that if the first term is False then the whole expression is False. It makes no difference whether (c < d) is True or False.

In this case, to save time, the compiler does not bother to evaluate the parts of the expression following the and operator. Normally this is not a problem. However, if the expression includes a call to a user written function that not only returns a value but also does other things, you need to be aware that you cannot be sure the function will be called. Functions are discussed in more detail in Chapter 9.

You cannot depend on an expression being processed in the order that you write it. Delphi uses an optimizing compiler and the compiler may rearrange the order of evaluation to improve performance.

You can disable short circuit evaluation with the {$B+} compiler directive. The default setting is {$B-} which tells the compiler to generate short circuit evaluation code and which provides the best performance.

Typecasting a Value

As part of an expression you can cast the type of a value to make it compatible with other elements of the expression. For example, suppose you need to add the character whose code is 238 to a string. The program in Figure 7.19 shows how to cast the number 238 to a character, and concatenate it with a string.

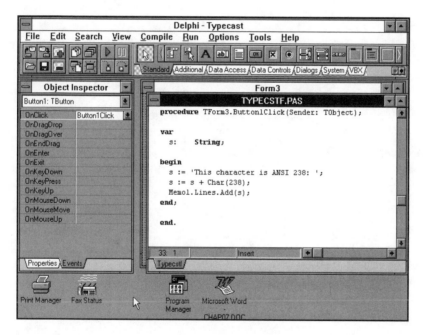

FIGURE 7.19 A VALUE TYPECAST.

The next step in mastering Pascal is to combine expressions into statements, and control the order of execution of those statements. *Statements* are the fundamental building blocks of Pascal programs. Once you master them, the following chapter will introduce you to procedures and functions, and you will start writing truly useful code.

CHAPTER 8

Statements

In addition to being an object-oriented language, ObjectPascal is a stuctured programming language. Therefore, it has all the structured constructs you would expect: two basic switching consructs to manage the flow of control in your application, and three basic looping constructs to manage iterative processes. It also includes a programming structure, the **goto** statement, which structured programming enthusiasts frown upon.

All of the techniques demonstrated in this chapter are on the accompanying code disk. The project name is STMT.DPR, and the form (shown in Figure 8.1) is called Statements.

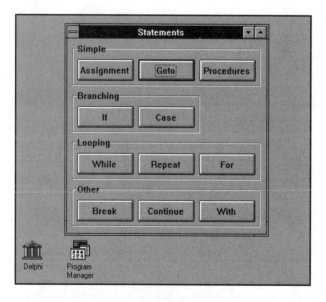

FIGURE 8.1 STATEMENTS FORM.

Simple Statements

Simple statements do one of the following: assign variables values, transfer control of the program to another location, or invoke a procedure, or function. These tasks correspond to the assignment statement, the goto statement, and procedure statements.

Assignment

The assignment statement is perhaps the most fundamental in all of programming. It associates some value, a number, character, or string, with a variable. In ObjectPascal, the assignment operator is :=. Listing 8.1 shows some sample assignment statements.

LISTING 8.1 ASSIGNMENT STATEMENTS

```
procedure TStatements.AssignmentClick(Sender: TObject);
type
   TCharges = (Phone,Service,Relay,Tax,Delivery);
var
   i: Integer;
   s: String[20];
   r: Real;
   l: Boolean;
   q: set of TCharges;
begin

i := (1+3)*6;
s := 'Hello '+'World!';
r := Pi;
l := (i=25) and (s='Hello world');
q := [Phone,Relay,Delivery];

end;
```

Goto

The goto statement is to be avoided. You do not need it to write code. The problem with the goto statement is that if you use it indiscriminately, your code will be unreadable and unmaintainable. In addition, the ObjectPascal language has language constructs that eliminate the need for the goto statement. Nonetheless, it is shown here in Listing 8.2.

LISTING 8.2 GOTO STATEMENT

```
procedure TStatements.GotoButtonClick(Sender: TObject);
label Starter,Ender;
begin
MessageDlg('Before the Starter label',
           mtInformation,[mbOk],0);
Starter:
MessageDlg('After the Starter label, before the goto',
           mtInformation,[mbOk],0);
goto Ender;
MessageDlg('After the goto statement',
           mtInformation,[mbOk],0);
Ender:
MessageDlg('After the Ender label',
           mtInformation,[mbOk],0);

end;
```

In order to use the goto statement, you need to use the **label** keyword. This key-word is used to inform the compiler of the names of placemarks that the goto statement can use. In Listing 8.2, message which is listed after the statement

```
goto Ender;
```

is never executed. The goto statement causes the program to jump to the command after the Ender label.

Procedure Statements

You use procedure statements to invoke a procedure or function. *Procedures* are different from functions. A procedure does not return a value, whereas a function does. In Listing 8.1, **Pi** is a function that returns the value of Pi. Listing 8.3 shows some sample procedure and function invocations.

LISTING 8.3 GOTO STATEMENT

```
{ The following functions/procedures are called
  from TStatements.ProceduresButtonClick:

        function Bigger(x,y : Longint) : Longint;
        procedure IncreaseLots(var x : Longint);
        function AnyNumber : Integer; }

procedure TStatements.ProceduresButtonClick(Sender: TObject);
```

```
var
    z: Longint;
begin

z:=Bigger(10,100);
MessageDlg('Which is bigger, 10 or 100? '+
            IntToStr(z),mtInformation,[mbOk],0);

IncreaseLots(z);
MessageDlg('Z was 100, increased a lot to: '+
            IntToStr(z),
            mtInformation,[mbOk],0);

z:=AnyNumber;
MessageDlg('Any number '+IntToStr(z),
            mtInformation,[mbOk],0);

end;
```

Notice that you can not include the () for procedures and functions without arguments. Unlike C and C++, ObjectPascal forbids this. When you look at parameterless functions for the first time, you will notice that they are indistinguishable from constants or variables. In addition, paramerterless procedures are indistinguishable from standard ObjectPascal statements. If you are a C programmer, this may take some getting used to.

Structured Statements

ObjectPascal has the following structured statements: **if**, **case**, **while**, **repeat** and **for**. Three other statements, **break**, **continue** and **with** are used in conjunction with the set of looping structured statements.

Compound Statements

The compound statements, or branching statements, direct your program's flow of control. For programmers, the if and case statements are what mortar is to the bricklayer: the stuff that keeps the bricks in place.

If

ObjectPascal has a standard **if-then-else** statement. You can nest several if statements to implement an if-then-elseif construct. Listing 8.4 demonstrates both versions of the if statement.

LISTING 8.4 IF STATEMENT

```
procedure TStatements.IfButtonClick(Sender: TObject);
var
   x,y : Integer;
   d : TDateTime;
   Year, Month, Day : Word;
begin

{simple if statement}
if 1<>1 then
   MessageDlg('Something fundamental in the universe has changed',
            mtError,[mbOk],0)
else
   MessageDlg('All''s well with the universe',
            mtInformation,[mbOk],0);

x:=1;
y:=22;
d:=Date;
DecodeDate(d,Year,Month,Day);
{nested if-then-else if statement which
 evaluates several variables}
if x=10 then
   MessageDlg('X='+IntToStr(x),mtInformation,[mbOk],0)
else if y=25 then
   MessageDlg('y='+IntToStr(y),mtInformation,[mbOk],0)
else if Year<1995 then
   MessageDlg('Year is < 1995',mtInformation,[mbOk],0)
else if (x=1) and (y=22) and (Year>=1995) then
   MessageDlg('X=1, Y=22 and Year is >= 1995',mtInformation,[mbOk],0);

end;
```

Case

The case statement is a cleaner form of nested if-then-else statements. But unlike nested if-then-else statements, the case statement evaluates a single variable. And case statements can only evaluate byte and word-sized ordinal expressions, so strings, reals and long integers are not useable here. Code Listing 8.5 demonstrates the case statement.

LISTING 8.5 CASE STATEMENT

```
procedure TStatements.CaseButtonClick(Sender: TObject);
type
    TDaysOfWeek = (Sunday,Monday,Tuesday,
                    Wednesday,Thursday,Friday,Saturday);
    TMeals = (PorkRoast,Hamburger,PattyMelt,Linguini,
            BroiledChicken,Veal,BLT);
var
    MealDesc : array [0..6] of String;
    MealOfTheDay : TMeals;
    Today : TDaysOfWeek;
    d : TDateTime;
begin

{setup the meal descriptions array}
MealDesc[0]:='Pork Roast';
MealDesc[1]:='Hamburger';
MealDesc[2]:='Patty Melt';
MealDesc[3]:='Linguini';
MealDesc[4]:='Broiled Chicken';
MealDesc[5]:='Veal';
MealDesc[6]:='BLT';

{get today's date}
d:=Date;
{store the number of the day of the week in Today}
Today := TDaysOfWeek(DayOfWeek(d)-1);

{Find out the meal of the day}
case Today of
    Sunday      : MealOfTheDay :=BroiledChicken;
    Monday      : MealOfTheDay :=Hamburger;
    Tuesday     : MealOfTheDay :=PorkRoast;
    Wednesday   : MealOfTheDay :=Linguini;
    Thursday    : MealOfTheDay :=PattyMelt;
    Friday      : MealOfTheDay :=Veal;
```

```
    else           MealOfTheDay :=BLT;
end;

{display the meal of the day}
MessageDlg('Today''s meal is
'+MealDesc[Integer(MealOfTheDay)],mtInformation,[mbOk],0);

end;
```

Loops

Loop statements let you iterate through sections of code for a certain duration. ObjectPascal has three looping constructs: **while**, **repeat** and **for**.

While

The while loop repeats a single statement, or a series of statements enclosed in a begin..end block, as long as the controlling Boolean expression remains true. Unlike the repeat statement (discussed in the next section), whose code executes at least one time, the while statement's code can execute zero or more times. This is because the while statement checks the Boolean expression before executing it's code. Listing 8.6 shows an example of a while statement.

LISTING 8.6 WHILE STATEMENT

```
procedure TStatements.WhileButtonClick(Sender: TObject);
var
   c,b: Byte;
begin
b:=0;
c:=0;
while b<=200 do
  begin
    {increase b a random number between 1 and 25}
    Randomize;
    Inc(b,Random(25));
    {increment c by 1}
    Inc(c);
  end;

MessageDlg('It took '+IntToStr(c)+' interations to make B = '+
          IntToStr(b),mtInformation,[mbOk],0);

end;
```

Repeat

The repeat statement is very much like the while statement, except the Boolean expression which controls the iteration is evaluated *after* each iteration, not before. But unlike the while statement, you do not need a begin..end block to contain multiple statements. Listing 8.7 demonstrates an example of the repeat statement.

LISTING 8.7 REPEAT STATEMENT

```
procedure TStatements.RepeatButtonClick(Sender: TObject);
var
    c,b: Byte;
begin
b:=0;
c:=0;
repeat
    {increase b a random number between 1 and 25}
    Randomize;
    Inc(b,Random(25));
    {increment c by 1}
    Inc(c);
until b>200;

MessageDlg('It took '+IntToStr(c)+' interations to make B = '+
         IntToStr(b),mtInformation,[mbOk],0);

end;
```

For

The for loop is a more constrained looping construct. It is designed to iterate a precisely controlled number of steps by incrementing a variable from a starting value up to an ending value. A for loop manipulates an ordinal variable only, and the start and end values must be assignment compatible with that ordinal variable. Listing 8.8 shows the for statement in action.

LISTING 8.8 FOR STATEMENT

```
procedure TStatements.ForButtonClick(Sender: TObject);
var
    x: Integer;
    Total: Longint;
```

```
begin
Total:=0;
for x:=1 to 100 do
   Inc(Total,x);

MessageDlg('The Fibonacci sequence from 1 to 100 is '+
          IntToStr(Total),mtInformation,[mbOk],0);

{decrease x back down to 0}
for x:=100 downto 1 do
   Dec(Total,x);

MessageDlg('Total is back down to '+
          IntToStr(Total),mtInformation,[mbOk],0);

end;
```

Break and Continue

The two procedures, Break and Continue control execution of while, repeat, and for blocks. Break causes the program flow to exit a looping construct. Continue causes the program to ignore subsequent commands in a looping construct and perform the loop's next iteration. Listing 8.9 shows how to use Beak and Continue.

LISTING 8.9 BREAK AND CONTINUE STATEMENTS

```
procedure TStatements.BreakButtonClick(Sender: TObject);
var
   x: Longint;
begin
x:=1;
{'while True' is an infinite loop,
 however, with break, there's a way out}
while True do
  begin
    Inc(x);
    if x>100 then begin
       MessageDlg('Break encountered. Leaving while loop',
                 mtInformation,[mbOk],0);
       break;
    end;
  end;

end;
```

```
procedure TStatements.ContinueButtonClick(Sender: TObject);
var
   x: Integer;
   Total: Longint;
begin
Total:=0;

for x:=1 to 100 do begin
   {if the number is divisible by 3, leave it out}
   if (x mod 3)=0 then Continue;
   Inc(Total,x);
end;

MessageDlg('The Fibonacci sequence from 1 to 100 is '+
           ' (excluding numbers divisible by 3) '+
           IntToStr(Total),mtInformation,[mbOk],0);

end;
```

With

The with statement introduces a short-hand way of referencing record structures and objects. Rather than repeating the report variable name when
assigning or accessing record fields, you can use the with statement. Listing
8.10 shows an example of the with statement.

LISTING 8.10 WITH STATEMENT

```
procedure TStatements.WithButtonClick(Sender: TObject);
type
   TPayCheck = Record
      Name : String;
      CheckDate : TDateTime;
      Amount : Real;
   end;
var
   MyPayCheck : TPayCheck;
begin

{assign the fields in the record structure a value}
with MyPayCheck do begin
   Name := 'Keith Stefanczyk';
   CheckDate := Date;
   Amount :=23750.00;
```

```
MessageDlg('Check for '+Name+' is assigned.',
          mtInformation,[mbOk],0);
end;

end;
```

Summary

The various statements in ObjectPascal support all the fundamental structured programming constructs you would expect: branching, looping, assigning values to variables, invoking functions and procedures, and even the goto statement. Compared with other languages, especially C and C++, ObjectPascal has a particular philosophy and style when it comes to statements. ObjectPascal relies less on symbols and more on statements with linguisitic references. This makes ObjectPascal code more readable and understandable.

CHAPTER 9

Procedures and Functions

Procedures and functions are the building blocks of modular maintainable reusable code. A *procedure* is a named block of code within your main program. You can execute this code from any place at any time using its name. Like the main program block a procedure can contain variable, type, and constant declarations as well as code. A *function* is identical to a procedure except that it is called as part of an expression, and returns a value that is used in the expression.

This chapter explores how to declare and call procedures and functions, pass data to them, and get values back. It also explores what you can do in procedures and functions, and develops examples you will find useful in your applications.

Declaring Procedures and Functions—The Basics

A *procedure declaration* starts with the reserved word procedure, followed by the procedure name, and the procedure's parameter list, if any. The following example shows a procedure that reverses the order of a string, and displays it in a memo object on a form. This procedure is from the sample program REVERSE.DPR.

```
procedure ReverseStr(s: String);

var
   r:        String;
   i:        Byte;

begin
  {
  Set the string variable r to null.
  }
  r := '';
  {
  Loop through the string from the last
  character to the first.
  }
  for i := Length(s) downto 1 do
    {
    Concatenate the character in s to the
    end of r
    }
    r := r + s[i];
  {
  Empty the Memo object and display the
  result.
  }
  Form3.Memo1.Lines.Clear;
  Form3.Memo1.Lines.Add(r);
end;
```

A *function declaration* is identical to a procedure declaration except that a
function declaration must include the type of the value the function returns.
The following function, Reverse, is the same as the preceding example,
except it returns the reversed string instead of displaying it. This function is
also in REVERSE.DPR.

```
function Reverse(s: String): String;
{Reverses the order of the characters in a
string}
var
   r:        String;
   i:        Byte;
```

```
begin
  {
  Set the string variable r to null.
  }
  r := '';
  {
  Loop through the string from the last
  character to the first.
  }
  for i := Length(s) downto 1 do
    {
    Concatenate the character in s to the
    end of r
    }
    r := r + s[i];
  {
  Return the reversed string;
  }
  Reverse := r;
end;
```

There are two ways that a function can return the value it computes. The one shown above is to assign the value to the function name. However, all functions also have a system declared local variable named Result. You can assign the value to return to Result instead of to the Function name.

In this example the return value is assigned to the function name in the last line of code, but this is not required. You can assign a value to the function name, or to Result as often as you wish anywhere in the functions code. The last value you assigned before the function ends, is the value that the function returns.

Figure 9.1 shows the statements that call the ReverseStr procedure and the Reverse function. A *procedure call* is a statement that consists of nothing but the procedures name, followed by any parameters the procedure requires in parentheses. When you call a function you can call it in exactly the same way as a procedure, and ignore the value that it returns, or you can call it within an expression that uses the value. In Figure 9.1 the call to Reverse is used as a parameter to the call to the Add procedure for the memo's lines object, so the value returned by Reverse is what gets added to the memo object.

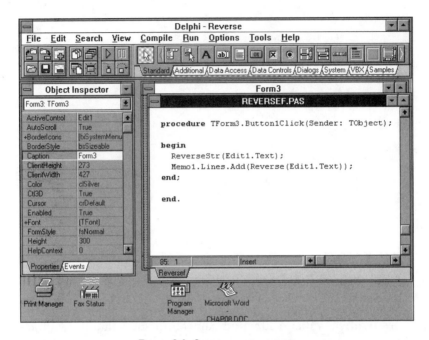

FIGURE 9.1 CALLING A PROCEDURE.

You can declare variables within a procedure or function using exactly the same syntax the you use in a main program. The function Reverse begins with

```
function Reverse(s: String): String;
{Reverses the order of the characters in a
string}
var
  r:       String;
  i:       Byte;
```

which declares two variables. However, variables declared within a procedure or function are local to that procedure or function. The variables are created on the program stack when the procedure or function is called, and they are destroyed when the procedure or function ends. Local variables do not retain their value between calls.

Passing Parameters

When you call a procedure or function you can pass any information it needs as a *parameter*. There are two types of parameters. The parameters in the procedure or function declaration are the formal parameters. The parameters you supply when you call the procedure or function are the actual parameters. In the declaration for ReverseStr

```
procedure ReverseStr(s: String);
```

s is the formal parameter. In the call to ReversStr in Figure 9.1

```
ReverseStr(Edit1.Text);
```

Edit1.Text is the actual parameter. Within the procedure or function you refer to the formal parameters to access the data provided by the actual parameter. This allows you to call a procedure or function as many times as you wish within your program, and provide different values in each call. You can pass as many parameters as necessary. For example, the procedure declaration

```
procedure MyProc(i, j: Word; TestName: String);
```

includes three formal parameters. The first two, i and j, are both of type Word. The third parameter, TestName, is a string. When you call a procedure or function, Pascal matches the actual parameters to the formal parameters by position, so you must use the required number of actual parameters and you must have them in the correct order. If you do not, you will get an error if the types do not match, or unexpected results.

There are three ways to pass a parameter depending on the effect you want. A parameter can be a value parameter, a constant parameter, or a variable parameter. There are also two special cases. The first is untyped parameters. The second is open parameters for strings and arrays.

Value Parameters

Value parameters, like local variables, are created on the program's stack when the procedure or function is called. Each formal value parameter is assigned the value of the corresponding actual parameter. Therefore, when you use a value parameter you are working with a local copy of the actual parameter. This means that you can change the formal parameter in any way you wish within the function or procedure and the actual parameter will not be changed.

Value parameters cannot be of type File, or of any structured type that includes a variable of the File type. If a value parameter is a String the compiler automatically allocates 255 bytes when it creates the formal parameter.

When you call a procedure or function that takes a value parameter the actual parameter can be an expression that evaluates to an assignment compatible type. For example,

```
ReverseStr('abc' + 'def');
```

is a valid call to the ReverseStr procedure. Your formal parameters are value parameters by default. To specify constant or variable parameters, you must precede the parameter with a keyword as described in the following sections.

Value parameters have two possible disadvantages. First, for large values such as large arrays or PChars performance will suffer slightly because of the time it takes to copy the value of the actual parameter. Second, value parameters consume additional memory to hold the copy of the value. Where the memory is consumed depends on the size of the parameter. If the size is less than four bytes the copy is made on the stack. If the size is greater than four bytes the calling routine creates the copy and a pointer to the copy is pushed onto the stack. The default stack size for a Delphi program is 16k. If you need to pass many parameters or call procedures or functions recursively you can increase the size of the stack up to 64k by selecting **O**ptions | **P**roject from the main Delphi menu and choosing the Linker page.

Variable Parameters

From a practical standpoint, the difference between a value parameter and a variable parameter is that if your procedure or function changes the value of a formal variable parameter then the value of the actual parameter is changed. Consider the following procedure from PARAMTST.DPR.

```
procedure ParamTest(a: String; var b: String);

begin
  a := 'xxxxx';
  b := 'xxxxx';
end;
```

The procedure declaration includes two formal parameters. The first, a, is a value parameter. The second, b, is a variable parameter because it is preceded by the key word var. Figure 9.2 shows the code from the button's click procedure which assigns the contents of the edit component to two variables, calls ParamTest, and displays the result in the memo.

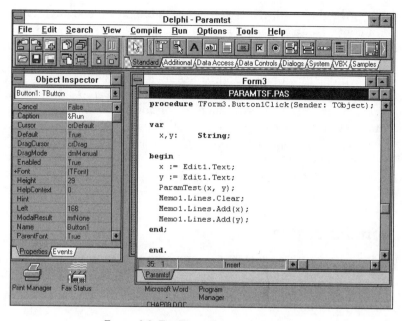

FIGURE 9.2 THE PARAMTST DEMO PROGRAM.

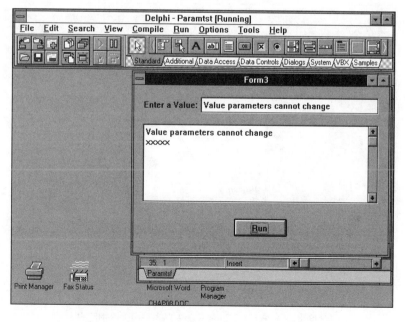

FIGURE 9.3 THE VARIABLE PARAMETER HAS CHANGED.

Figure 9.3 shows the result when you enter, **Value parameters cannot change**, in the edit control, and press the **run** button. The reason that you can change the value of the actual parameter when the formal parameter includes the var key word, is that Pascal does not create a copy of the actual parameter on the stack for the procedure or function to use as it does with value parameters. Instead, a pointer to the actual parameter is placed on the stack. Within the procedure or function, every reference to the formal parameter dereferences the pointer and accesses the value of the actual parameter.

This has another benefit besides allowing you to write procedures and functions that change their actual parameters. If you need to pass a large structure such as a string, array, or record as a parameter, and you pass it by value, Pascal has to make a copy of the entire structure.

Constant Parameters

If you need to pass a parameter to a procedure or function and the procedure or function will not change the value of the formal parameter, you should use a constant parameter. A constant parameter is read only. You cannot assign a value to it.

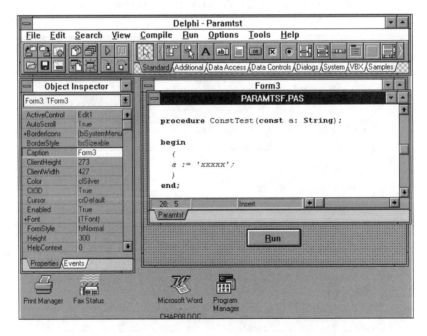

FIGURE 9.4 A PROCEDURE WITH A CONSTANT PARAMETER.

Figure 9.4 shows a procedure, ConstTest, that has a single formal constant parameter, a. Constant parameters are preceded by the key word const. If you uncomment the line:

```
a := 'xxxxx';
```

by removing the curly braces and compile the ParamTst project you will get the error shown in Figure 9.5, **Invalid variable reference**.

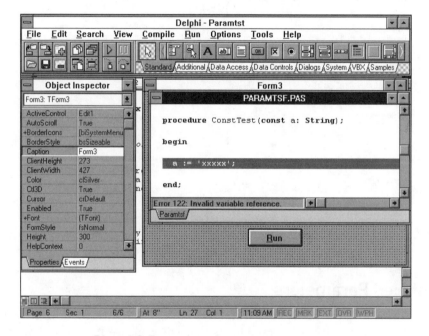

FIGURE 9.5 TRYING TO CHANGE A CONSTANT PARAMETER.

Using a constant parameter in a procedure or function where the value of the parameter should never be changed protects you from accidently changing the formal parameters value, because the compiler will not compile any program that contains an assignment to a constant parameter.

There is another advantage to using a constant parameter. Constant parameters, just like variable parameters, are implemented by passing a pointer on the stack, so they generate more efficient code for arrays, strings, and other structured variables.

There is one limitation to using formal constant parameters. A procedure or function cannot pass a constant parameter to another procedure or function as a variable parameter since the procedure that gets the variable parameter, may try to change it. However, you can use a constant parameter as the actual parameter to a procedure or function whose formal parameter is a value parameter. Therefore, the code

```
procedure Foo(var a: String);
begin
end;

procedure Caller(const a:String);
begin
  Foo(a);
end
```

will not compile because the actual parameter a that is passed in the call to Foo is a constant parameter in Caller and a variable parameter in Foo. However, the code

```
procedure Foo(a: String);
begin
end;

procedure Caller(const a:String);
begin
  Foo(a);
end
```

will work because the formal parameter in Foo has been changed from a variable parameter to a value parameter.

Untyped Parameters

You can also pass untyped parameters to a procedure or function. The advantage of an untyped parameter is that you can use it to pass a value of any type to a procedure or function. Within the procedure or function the value of an untyped parameter is incompatible with any type. To use the untyped parameter you must cast it to the type you need. The following code from the UnType project shows a procedure that you can use to copy anything to anything else.

```
procedure TypelessCopy(const src; var target;
                       nBytes: Word);
type
  TByte = array[0..65534] of Byte;

var
```

```
   i:        Word;

begin
  for i := 0 to nBytes do
    TByte(target)[i] := TByte(src)[i];
end;
```

Untyped parameters must be declared as either variable or constant parameters. You cannot use an untyped value parameter. In the declaration for the TypelessCopy procedure above, src is a constant parameter because you do not want to change the source, just copy it. Target is a variable parameter since it will be changed when the contents of src are copied to it. The third parameter, nBytes, tells the procedure how many bytes to copy from src to target.

Notice the type declaration for TByte in TypelessCopy. Although no variables of type TByte are declared, this type is required so you can cast src and target to type TByte. This allows you to treat the two untyped parameters as arrays of bytes, regardless of the type of the actual parameters. The for loop performs the actual copy from src to target.

The following code from the Run button's click procedure calls TypelessCopy to copy the contents of a string to an array of bytes.

```
procedure TForm3.Button1Click(Sender: TObject);
var
  codes:    array[0..255] of Byte;
  s:        String;
  i:        Word;

begin
  s := Edit1.Text;
  TypelessCopy(s, codes, Length(s));
  Memo1.Lines.Clear;
  Memo1.Lines.Add('The bytes are:');
  For i := 0 to Length(s) do
    Memo1.Lines.Add(IntToStr(codes[i]));
end;
```

The for loop displays the decimal value of each byte in the form's memo control. Since the first byte of a Pascal string is not a letter but the length of the string, the first value displayed in the memo is the length of the string, and the second is the code for the first letter of the string. Figure 9.6 shows the result when you type "abc" and press the **run** button.

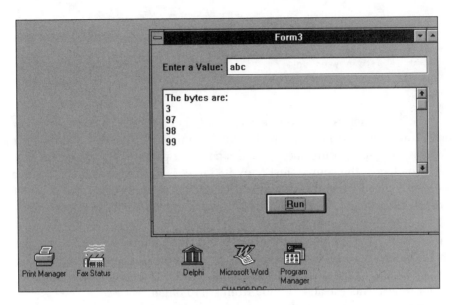

FIGURE 9.6 A STRING CONVERTED TO AN ARRAY OF BYTES.

Be very careful when you use untyped parameters because the compiler has no way to check for invalid operations. In this example, if target is not large enough to hold the required number of bytes you will overwrite some part of your programs memory, and will either corrupt other data, or cause a crash.

Open Parameters

Open parameters are very handy because they allow strings and arrays of varying size to be passed to a procedure or function. This makes it easy to write reusable procedures and functions that will work with any string or array.

Open Strings

One of the compiler directives on the Compiler page of the Project Options dialog shown in Figure 9.7 is the Open Parameters checkbox. It is the last checkbox under Syntax Options. To display the Project Options dialog choose **Options | Project** from the Delphi menu.

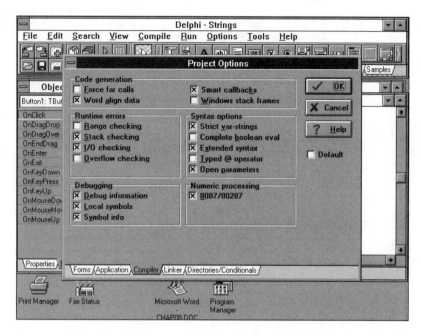

FIGURE 9.7 COMPILER OPTIONS.

This option is on by default, which is the same as using the $P+ compiler directive. The easiest way to understand the benefits of open string parameters is to look at an example. The following code implements a procedure named LTrim that removes any leading whitespace from a Pascal string. You will find the complete program in the LTrim project on disk.

```
procedure LTrim(var s: String);
{
Remove leading whitespace from a string.
Whitespace is defined as blanks or tabs.
}
var
  i:      Word;

begin
```

```
  i := 1;
while (s[i] in [' ', Chr(9)]) and
        (i <= Length(s)) do Inc(i);
  s := copy(s, i, 255);
end;
```

This procedure takes a string as a variable formal parameter. The while loop takes advantage of the ability to access strings as arrays by scanning the string starting with the first character, and continuing until the end of the string is reached, or a character is found that is not in the set [' ', Chr(9)], which has two members, the space and tab characters. As long as the character being checked, s[i], is in the set, the while loop increments i and continues to the next character.

The button-click procedure that calls LTrim is shown below.

```
procedure TForm3.Button1Click(Sender: TObject);
var
  n:    Word;
  s:    String[64];
begin
  s := Edit1.Text;
  LTrim(s);
  Memo1.Clear;
  Memo1.Lines.Add('*'+s+'*');
end;
```

Notice that the string variable, s, that is used as the actual parameter to LTrim is declared with a maximum length of 64 characters. If the open parameter option were not on, the fact that the actual parameter and the formal parameter are of different size causes a "Type mismatch" error when you compile the program. Open string parameter option allows you to pass strings of any length to a procedure with a variable formal parameter.

If, for any reason, you turn the Open Parameters option off you can still use open string parameters when you need them. To use an open string parameter make the type of the formal parameter OpenString as shown below.

```
procedure LTrim(var s: OpenString);
```

OpenString is a special type that can only be used to declare a formal parameter in a procedure or function.

The Open Parameter setting only affects variable parameters. You can always use actual string parameters of any size if the formal parameter is a value or constant parameter.

N O T E

Open Arrays

An open array parameter lets you pass an array of any size as a parameter to a procedure, or function. Suppose you need to work with arrays of integers and you need a function to compute the sum of all of the integers in an array. This function will sum an integer array of any size.

```
function SumInt(const i: array of Integer): Integer;
{
Returns the sum the integers in the array i.
}
var
   s:        Integer;
   j:        Word;

begin
  s := 0;
  for j := 0 to High(i) do s := s + i[j];
  Result := s;
end;
```

Notice the formal parameter declaration. By declaring i as **array of Integer** without specifying a size **i** becomes an open array parameter and the actual parameter can be an array of any size. The High runtime library function in the for loop

```
for j := 0 to High(i) do s := s + i[j];
```

returns the highest value of the index of the array i. Once computed, the sum is returned by assigning it to the special variable Result. This code is from the SumInt project on disk. The following code is from the Run button's click procedure.

```
procedure TForm3.Button1Click(Sender: TObject);
var
   n:     array [1..64] of Integer;
   s:     String[64];
   i:     Word;
begin
  s := Edit1.Text;
  {Assign zero to each element of the array.}
  for i := 1 to 64 do n[i] := 0;
  {Convert each character of the string to
  an integer and store it in the array n.}
  for i := 1 to Length(s) do
    n[i] := Ord(s[i]) - Ord('0');
```

```
{Call SumInt to compute the sum of the array.}
i := SumInt(n);
{Display the sum.}
Memo1.Clear;
Memo1.Lines.Add('The sum of the digits is ' + IntToStr(i));
end;
```

This program allows you to type a series of digits into the edit control, and computes the sum of those digits when you press the **Run** button. Since the digits you type are text, the first step is to convert them to integer numbers and put them in an array. This is done by the second for loop.

```
for i := 1 to Length(s) do
    n[i] := Ord(s[i]) - Ord('0');
```

This statement loops through the characters in the string s and converts them to integers by subtracting the ordinal value of zero, from the ordinal value of the digit. You must do this because the value of the ANSI character zero is 48, one is 49, and so on.

Notice that the array n, which is the actual parameter in the call to SumInt, is declared with a subscript range from 1 to 64. However, in the procedure SumInt the first element of the formal parameter array, i, is zero. No matter how the actual parameter array is declared, the index of a formal open array parameter is always zero based.

Declaring Procedures and Functions Forward

You may have noticed that in all of the programs so far each function or procedure always appears physically before the procedure that calls it. This is a requirement in Pascal so that the compiler can examine the procedure or function declaration and make sure that the call is correct.

Obviously this would be a very limiting requirement in complex programs so you can eliminate it when you need to with a forward declaration. The following code from the Forward project is identical to the LTrim example earlier in this chapter, except that the LTrim procedure is now after the button-click procedure that calls it.

```
procedure LTrim(var s: String); forward;

procedure TForm3.Button1Click(Sender: TObject);
```

```
var
  n:     Word;
  s:     String[64];
begin
  s := Edit1.Text;
  LTrim(s);
  Memo1.Clear;
  Memo1.Lines.Add(s);
end;

procedure LTrim(var s: String);
{
Remove leading whitespace from a string.
Whitespace is defined as blanks or tabs.
}
var
  i:       Word;

begin
  i := 1;
  while (s[i] in [' ', Chr(9)]) and
        (i <= Length(s)) do Inc(i);
  s := copy(s, i, 255);
end;
```

The reason that this version works is the first line which is called a forward declaration.

```
procedure LTrim(var s: String); forward;
```

It is identical to the procedure declaration except that it is followed by the key word forward. The forward declaration tells the compiler everything it needs to know about the procedure or function to validate any calls. It also tells the compiler that the procedure or function will be declared later in the code.

NOTE When you declare a procedure or function forward you do not have to include the parameters and return value in the defining declaration later in your code. Only the name is required in the defining declaration.

By using forward declarations you can arrange your procedures and functions in any order with respect to the code that calls them. You can even have two procedures call each other.

Passing Procedures and Functions As Parameters

Object Pascal allows you to assign a procedure or function to a variable, and pass that variable as a parameter to another procedure or function. The procedure or function which receives the procedure or function as a parameter can then call it.

The variable is called a *procedural variable* and to declare it you must first declare a procedural type. All of the sample code in this section is in the PVal project on disk. The following are samples of *procedural type declarations.*

```
type
  TStrProc = procedure(var s: String);
  TStrFunc = function(var s: String): String;
```

The first, TStrProc, is from the sample project PVal. The second, TStrFunc, is just an example of a procedural type declaration for a function. In both cases the declaration looks exactly like a procedure or function declaration except that there is no name. The names used for the parameters have no meaning. They are just place holders so the compiler can ensure that the type declaration matches the procedure or function declaration, when you try to assign a procedure or function to a variable of this type. If the procedure or function declaration does not match the type declaration the compiler will generate a **Type mismatch** error. The following code includes the procedural type declaration and two procedures.

```
type
  TStrProc = procedure(var s: String);

procedure LTrim(var s: String); far;
{
Remove leading whitespace from a string.
Whitespace is defined as blanks or tabs.
}
var
  i:        Word;

begin
  i := 1;
  while (s[i] in [' ', Chr(9)]) and
        (i <= Length(s)) do Inc(i);
  s := copy(s, i, 255);
```

```
end;

procedure Capitalize(var s: String); far;
begin
  s := UpperCase(s);
end;
```

The click procedure for the Run button on the form contains the following code.

```
procedure TForm3.Button1Click(Sender: TObject);
var
  sProc:  TStrProc;
  s:      String[64];
begin
  s := Edit1.Text;
  sProc := Capitalize;
  RunProc(s, sProc);
  Memo1.Clear;
  Memo1.Lines.Add(s);
  sProc := LTrim;
  RunProc(s, sProc);
  Memo1.Lines.Add(s);
end;
```

The var block of this procedure declares sProc of type TStrProc making sProc a procedural variable. You can assign any procedure to sProc whose declaration matches the declaration of TStrProc. The statement:

```
sProc := Capitalize;
```

assigns the procedure Capitalize to the variable sProc. The next line,

```
RunProc(s, sProc);
```

passes the string variable s and the procedural variable sProc to the procedure RunProc as parameters. This is the code for RunProc.

```
procedure RunProc(var s: String; proc: TStrProc);
begin
  proc(s);
end;
```

Notice that the second parameter, proc, is declared to be of type TStrProc. The formal parameter proc is now a surrogate name for whatever procedure was passed to RunProc. The result is that the statement:

```
proc(s);
```

calls the Capitalize procedure the first time it is called in the Run button's click procedure, and the LTrim procedure the second time it is called. Figure 9.8 shows the output produced by PVal.exe when you enter several spaces followed by the letters abcd.

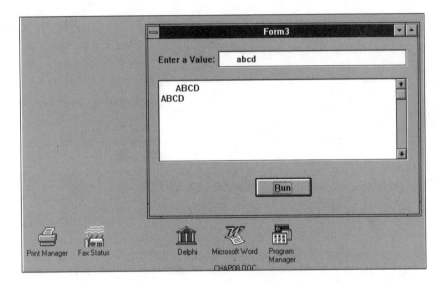

FIGURE 9.8 THE OUPUT OF PVAL.EXE.

You can see that Capitalize is indeed called first, because the first line of text in the memo control was converted to upper-case while the second line shows that LTrim was called to remove the leading whitespace.

If you examine the Capitalize and LTrim procedures closely you will notice something new. At the end of both procedure declarations is the key word far as shown below.

```
procedure Capitalize(var s: String); far;
begin
  s := UpperCase(s);
end;
```

You can declare procedures and functions as either near, the default, or far. Calling near procedures and functions is a bit faster, but they can only be called from within the program or unit that they are declared in. Units will be covered in detail in Chapter 12. Procedures and functions that use the far call model can be called from other program units. Normally you do not have to worry about this because the compiler automatically determines the correct call model for each procedure and function, and generates either near or far calls as required. However, you cannot assign a procedure or function to a procedural variable unless the procedure or function uses the far calling model.

You must declare procedures and functions as far if you will assign them to a procedural variable.

TIP

For additional examples of using procedural variables search for the topic **Procedural Types** in the Delphi on-line help.

Putting It All Together

Had enough of the useless demonstration programs? You should know enough now to write some useful procedures and functions. This section will look at five routines that provide string manipulations that are not built into Pascal. They are:

LTrim	Removes leading whitespace characters
RTrim	Removes trailing whitespace characters
Proper	Capitalizes the first letter of each word and makes the other characters lower case.
ParseCount	Counts the number of substrings delimited by one or more characters in a string.
ParseString	Returns a substring delimited by one or more characters

These routines are in the Strings project on your disk. Figure 9.9 shows the form you can use to test them.

The form contains a label and an edit control that you can type a string of text in. There is a button for each of the five string manipulation routines. Each button's click procedure contains the code to call the routine and display the result in the memo control on the form.

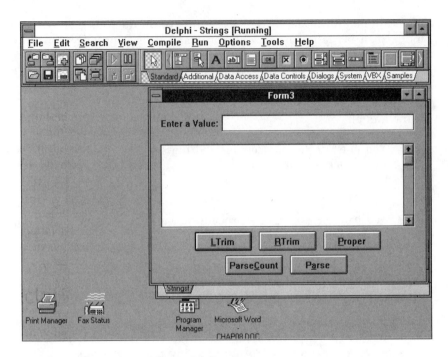

FIGURE 9.9 THE STRINGS FORM.

LTrim

This is very similar to the LTrim procedure developed earlier in this chapter, except that it has been converted to a function. Here is the code.

```
function LTrim(const s: String): String;
{
Remove leading whitespace from a string.
Whitespace is defined as blanks or tabs.
}
var
  i:      Word;

begin
  i := 1;
  {Skip all leading whitespace characters.}
  while (s[i] in [' ', #9]) and
        (i <= Length(s)) do Inc(i);
  {Return the rest of the string.}
```

```
    LTrim := copy(s, i, 255);
end;
```

This function takes advantage of the ability to access strings as arrays of characters in Pascal. The while loop examines each character of the string in turn. If the current character, s[i], is a member of the set of whitespace characters, [' ', #9], the subscript, i, is incremented by calling the runtime library Inc procedure, and the loop continues to check the next character. In the set [' ', #9] the #9 is the ANSI code of the tab character. The while loop ends when it finds a character that is not a member of the set, or when it reaches the end of the string.

When the while loop ends the subscript, i, points to the first non-white-space character in the string. The copy runtime library procedure copies the characters starting at s[i] through the end of the string, and returns them. You do not have to worry about how many characters have to be copied because of the number of characters, the third parameter in the call to copy, exceeds the length of the string copy copies all characters up to the end of the string. Since the maximum length of a Pascal string is 255 characters, using 255 for the number of characters ensures that the balance of the string is copied.

RTrim

The RTrim function is similar to LTrim but it removes whitespace characters from the end of a string.

```
function RTrim(const s: String): String;
{
Remove trailing whitespace from a string.
Whitespace is defined as blank, tab,
carriage return, line feed or form feed.
}
var
   i:        Word;

begin
   i := Length(s);
   {Skip all trailing whitespace characters.}
   while (s[i] in [' ', #9, #10, #12, #13]) and
         (i > 0) do Dec(i);
   {Return the rest of the string.}
   RTrim := copy(s, 1, i);
end;
```

In this function the Length function is used to set the variable used to index the array to the length of the string. Since the first character of the string is s[1], then s[Length(s)] is the last character of the string.

The while loop scans backward starting with the last character of the string and checking each character in turn to see if it is in the set [' ', #9, #10, #12, #13]. In addition to space and tab, the carriage return, line feed, and form feed characters have been added to the set since they may occur at the end of a string.

The while loop ends when it finds a character that is not in the set, or when it reaches the beginning of the string. When the while loop ends the array index, i, points to the last non-whitespace character, and copy extracts the characters up to and including the last non-whitespace character.

Proper

The Proper procedure converts a string so that the first letter of each word is uppercase and all of the others are lowercase. This is the code.

```
procedure Proper(var s: String);
{
Converts a string to proper case, that is,
the first letter of each word is capitalized.
The word delimiters are space and tab.
}
var
   delimiter:    Boolean;
   i:            Word;

begin
   {Set delimiter True so the first character
   will be capitalized.}
   delimiter := True;
   {Loop through the string.}
   for i := 1 to Length(s) do
     {If this character is a delimiter set
     delimiter to True.}
     if s[i] in [' ', #9] then
       delimiter := True
     else
       {This character is not a delimiter so
       see if it needs its case changed.}
       if delimiter then
       begin
         {The preceding character was a
```

```
        delimiter so if this letter is
        lower case make it upper case.}
        if s[i] in ['a'..'z'] then
          s[i] := Chr(Ord(s[i]) - 32);
        {Set the flag to False so the next
        character will be made lower case.}
        delimiter := False;
      end
    else
      {This character is not the first in a
      word so make it lower case if it is
      a letter.}
      if s[i] in ['A'..'Z'] then
        s[i] := Chr(Ord(s[i]) + 32);
end;
```

This procedure uses two variables. The first, delimiter, is a Boolean and is set to True whenever a delimiter character is found. The delimiter characters are space and tab. When a non-delimiter character is found delimiter is set to False. The second variable, i, is used as the array index to access individual characters in the string.

The key to this procedure is the statement:

```
if s[i] in ['a'..'z'] then
  s[i] := Chr(Ord(s[i]) - 32);
```

which converts a letter to uppercase if it is a lowercase letter. This works because the ordinal value of a lowercase letter in the ANSI character set is the ordinal value for the uppercase letter plus 32. For example, the ANSI code for "A" is 65 and the ANSI code for "a" is 97. Ord(s[i]) converts the character to its ordinal number so you can subtract 32 from it to get the ordinal value of the uppercase letter. The Chr function converts the result back to a character which is assigned to the current character in the string.

The same technique is used in the statement:

```
if s[i] in ['A'..'Z'] then
  s[i] := Chr(Ord(s[i]) + 32);
```

to convert the other letters in the word to lowercase.

Note that while adding or subtracting 32 to the ordinal value of a character is a fast way to change the case of ASCII characters it is not the best way in Windows applications. A better choice is the AnsiLowerCase and AnsiUpperCase runtime library functions because they use the Windows language driver installed on your system to perform the conversion.

ParseCount

One common task in dealing with data is the need to parse a string into its component parts based on one or more delimiter characters. For example, you might encounter a name stored as Last, First and need to break it into separate first and last name strings. Before you can extract the substrings you need to know how many there are and that is what the ParseCount function will tell you. ParseCount takes two parameters. The first, s, is the string to scan. The second, delimiters, is a string that contains all of the delimiter characters you want to use. Any occurrence of one or more of the delimiter characters marks the end of one substring, and the beginning of the next. This is the code for ParseCount.

```
function ParseCount(const s, delimiters: String): Word;
{
Count the number of substrings in the string s
delimited by one or more of the characters in
the string delimiters.
}
var
  delimiter:      Boolean;
  count, i:       Word;
begin
  count := 0;
  delimiter := True;
  if Length(s) > 0 then
  begin
    {Skip delimiters at the beginning of the
    string.}
    i := 1;
    while (Pos(s[i], delimiters) <> 0) and
          (i <= Length(s)) do Inc(i);
    {Scan the rest of the string.}
    for i := i to Length(s) do
      {If this character is a delimiter set
      the delimiter flag.}
      if Pos(s[i], delimiters) <> 0 then
        delimiter := True
      else
      begin
        {If this character is not a delimiter
        and the previous character was then
        this is the first character of a new
        substring so increment the count.}
        if delimiter = True then Inc(count);
```

```
        delimiter := False;
      end;
  end;
  ParseCount := count
end;
```

This function begins by setting the count variable to zero. This variable counts the number of substrings found in the string parameter s. The Boolean delimiter variable is set to True because the string will either start with delimiters or you want to pretend that it does so that the first substring will be counted. The while loop

```
i := 1;
while (Pos(s[i], delimiters) <> 0) and
      (i <= Length(s)) do Inc(i);
```

skips any delimiter characters at the beginning of the string and leaves the variable i pointing to the first non-delimiter character in the string. The Pos runtime library function checks to see if the current character, s[i], is contained in the string parameter delimiters. If it is, Pos returns the position of s[i] in delimiters. If s[i] is not in delimiters Pos returns zero.

The for loop

```
for i := i to Length(s) do
```

scans from the first non-delimiter character through the end of the string. If the current character is a delimiter, the delimiter flag is set to True. If the current character is not a delimiter but the delimiter variable is True, then the preceding character was a delimiter and this character is the first character of a substring so the value of count is incremented by one. When the for loop has scanned the entire string the function returns the value of count.

ParseString

ParseString lets you retrieve any substring delimited by one or more characters from within a string. This function has three parameters. The first, s, is the string to search, the second, delimiters, is the delimiter characters to use to separate the substrings in s. The third parameter, num, identifies which substring you want. Here is the code for ParseString.

```
function ParseString(const s, delimiters: String; num: Word): String;
var
  delimiter:      Boolean;
  count,
```

```
    j,
    sLength,
    sStart,
    sEnd:            Word;
begin
    if ParseCount(s, delimiters) >= num then
    begin
        {Skip delimiters at the beginning of the
        string.}
        sStart := 1;
        while (Pos(s[sStart], delimiters) <> 0) and
              (sStart <= Length(s)) do Inc(sStart);
        {Find the first character of the requested
        substring.}
        for j := 1 to num - 1 do
        begin
            while Pos(s[sStart], delimiters) = 0 do Inc(sStart);
            while Pos(s[sStart], delimiters) <> 0 do Inc(sStart);
        end;
        {Find the end of the substring.}
        sEnd := sStart;
        while Pos(s[sEnd], delimiters) = 0 do Inc(sEnd);
        {Compute the length of the substring.}
        sLength := sEnd - sStart;
        {Extract and return the substring.}
        ParseString := copy(s, sStart, sLength);
    end
    else
        ParseString := '';
end;
```

The first line of ParseString calls ParseCount to verify that the string, s, really contains the substring identified by num. If you try to return the fifth substring in a string that has less than five substrings, ParseString returns an empty string. Next, the same while loop that was used in ParseCount is used again to skip any delimiter characters at the beginning of the string. When this loop finishes sStart is the index of the first non-delimiter character in the string s.

Having found the beginning of the first substring the next step is to find the beginning of the requested substring. The for loop

```
for j := 1 to num - 1 do
begin
    while Pos(s[sStart], delimiters) = 0 do Inc(sStart);
    while Pos(s[sStart], delimiters) <> 0 do Inc(sStart);
end;
```

finds the requested string using two while loops. The first skips all characters that are not delimiters. This moves sStart to the end of the current substring. The second while loop skips all delimiter characters. This moves sStart to the beginning of the next substring. In other words, each pass through the for loop moves the index, sStart, to the first character of the next substring in the string s.

Now that the first character of the requested substring is found you must find the end of the substring. The two statements:

```
sEnd := sStart;
while Pos(s[sEnd], delimiters) = 0 do Inc(sEnd);
```

set sEnd to point to the first character past the end of the substring by setting sEnd equal to sStart, and then skipping all non-delimiter characters. Now that the function has found the beginning and end of the requested substring it is a simple matter to compute the length of the substring and extract it with a call to Copy. Figure 9.10 shows the result of parsing a name using space and comma as the delimiters.

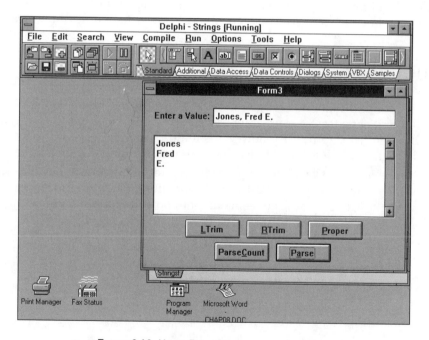

FIGURE 9.10 USING PARSESTRING TO PARSE A NAME.

The code in the Parse button's click procedure, shown below, shows how you can use ParseCount and ParseString to extract substrings from a delimited string.

```
procedure TForm3.ParseBtnClick(Sender: TObject);
var
   s:     String;
   i,
   cnt:   Word;
begin
   s := Edit1.Text;
   Memo1.Clear;
   cnt := ParseCount(s, ' ,');
   for i := 1 to cnt do
     Memo1.Lines.Add(ParseString(s,' ,',i));
end;
```

In this code the text in the edit control, Edit1, is saved in the string variable s. Then ParseCountis called to determine how many substrings s contains. Finally, the for loop calls ParseString to retrieve each substring in turn, and add it to the memo control.

Now that you have explored procedures and functions you have learned all of the basic concepts of Pascal. The remaining chapters in this section show you how to use these concepts in more powerful and flexible ways.

Summary

Procedures and functions are the heart of ObjectPascal programming. They let you write and test your program as a series of small modules that are easy to write and easy to test. By now you should clearly see Pascal's roots as a language that was developed to teach structured programming techniques.

Now that you have explored procedures and functions you have learned all of the basic concepts of Pascal. The remaining chapters in this section show you how to use these concepts in more powerful and flexible ways.

CHAPTER 10

Objects

In Delphi, objects rule. Nearly everything that you will deal with while programming in Delphi is an object. Every time that you design a form that accesses tables and queries, you will be programming with objects. Of course, variables and traditional data types are still important. But relative to objects, their importance fades. Subsequently, understanding objects is yet another critical requirement for building database applications.

ObjectPascal directly implements the following OOP concepts:

- Encapsulation
- Inheritance
- Polymorphism

However, ObjectPascal does not support multiple inheritance and *parametric polymorphism*, otherwise known as overloading. *Multiple inheritance* lets a single object inherit traits from two non-related ancestor classes. Multiple inheritance is sometimes considered too complex and fraught with ambiguity (how should the new object handle duplicate methods from two unrelated parent classes?). On the other hand, some consider multiple inheritance quite useful. Regardless of how this debate rolls on, ObjectPascal does not support multiple inheritance.

Overloading, however, is such a useful feature in C++ that experienced C++ programmers will undoubtably feel disappointed in not finding it in ObjectPascal. If Delphi did support overloading, you would be able to declare two methods with the same name but with a varying number of arguments with different argument types, like this:

```
procedure TMyObject.Init(const X : Integer);
procedure TMyObject.Init(const X : Real);
procedure TMyObject.Init(const X : Integer; Y : Integer);
```

Delphi will not compile these procedure declarations. You will get a "Duplicate identifier" compiler error message. Overloading has been deliberately *not* implemented in ObjectPascal. Unlike C and C++, ObjectPascal is highly typed. Variable assignments must meet strict assignment compatibility rules. Perhaps because of this strict type assignment philosophy, overloading was left out of ObjectPascal. In addition, Unlike C++, Delphi does not allow for operator overloading either.

Unlike Chapter 3, "Object Oriented Programming: What Is It?" which reviewed the theoretical basics of OOP, this chapter will demonstrate exactly how Delphi implements OOP. All of the techniques demonstrated in this chapter are on the accompanying code disk. The project name is OBJECTS.DPR.

Object Declaration

Declaring an object type is easy. In the **type** section of a unit, simply declare an object type using the **class** keyword (Listing 10.1).

LISTING 10.1 DECLARING AN OBJECT TYPE

```
type
  TCheck = class
  private
  protected
     Amount : Real;
     PayTo : String[30];
     Date : TDateTime;
  public
     constructor Create;
     destructor Destroy;
     procedure Calc;
     function Print: real;
  published
  end;
```

This example declares an object type, TCheck with several fields and methods in four parts:

- private
- protected
- public
- published

These four parts are discussed in the section entitled "Encapsulation" so you do not have to worry about them right now. The important thing is that to declare an object type, you need to use the **class** keyword. Within the four parts are some data fields and methods. The data fields for TCheck include Amount, PayTo, and Date. The methods include Calc and Print. Methods typically set, get, or otherwise transform the data fields. The data fields contain values pertinent to that object. You can declare as many data fields and methods (procedures or functions) as you want.

All objects declared as shown in Listing 10.1 are considered to be descendents of type TObject. The declaration in Listing 10.2 is identical to the listing in 10.1.

LISTING 10.2 DECLARING AN OBJECT TYPE

```
type
  TCheck = class(TObject)
  private
  protected
     Amount : Real;
     PayTo : String[30];
     Date : TDateTime;
  public
     constructor Create;
     destructor Destroy;
     procedure Calc;
     function Print: real;
  published
  end;
```

Delphi ObjectPascal still supports the Borland Pascal **object** keyword, so it is possible to declare an object type as shown in Listing 10.3.

LISTING 10.3 DECLARING AN OBJECT TYPE USING THE OBJECT KEYWORD

```
type
  TCheck = object
  private
  protected
     Amount : Real;
     PayTo : String[30];
     Date : TDateTime;
  public
     procedure Calc;
     function Print: real;
  published
  end;
```

This creates an object type which is *not* a descendant of TObject. If you declare a type using the object keyword, you will not be able to take advantage of any enhancements Delphi has made to the Pascal language, such as properties (discussed later in this chapter in the section entitled "Properties"). The object keyword is included in Delphi so that it could compile Borland Pascal code.

Use the **class** keyword when creating object types in Delphi. This will ensure that your new class will inherit all the properties and behavior included in the Delphi TObject type. The **object** keyword is supported only so that older Borland Pascal code could be compiled.

WARNING

Using an object is also easy. After the object type has been declared, create a variable which refers to the object in a var block:

```
var
   MyCheck : TCheck;
```

Keep in mind that when you declare an object variable *you are not initializing or creating that object.* You are only creating a pointer to the object type. In fact, Delphi considers the MyCheck variable as a pointer to type TCheck, as in:

```
var
   MyCheck : ^TCheck;
```

Fortunately, Delphi's object reference model removes the need for any pointer symbols. It always assumes that an object variable needs to be dereferenced before accessing individual fields or methods. Keep in mind, however, that each time you declare an object variable, you are actually declaring a pointer to an object type, *which will need to be initialized sooner or later.* If you want to pass an object variable as an argument to another procedure or function, pass it by reference using the **var** keyword. This is discussed in Chapter 9 "Procedures and Functions."

Initializing an object variable is also easy. The following line of code initializes the object pointer MyCheck:

```
MyCheck := TCheck.Create;
```

Notice that this line of code initializes the object variable with TCheck.Create, not MyCheck.Create. Since prior to this line of code, the object MyCheck does not yet exist, you need to use the Create method by referencing the object's type. The TObject Create method (which TCheck inherits since it is a descendant of TObject) is considered a class method. Class methods do not require a specific instance of an object to operate. Class methods operate on the type of an object variable, not instances of an object.

This is one of the benefits of creating objects which descend from TObject: they inherit the **Create** method, among many others. The Create method establishes space in memory for the object and calls it *constructor*, which initializes any additional memory (constructors are discussed in detail later in the section entitled "Constructors").

If you want to create objects independent of components on the component palette, you will need to do the following: a) declare an object type using the **class** keyword, b) declare an object pointer variable in a **var** block, and c) initialize the object pointer variable using the **Create** method. The create method is referenced using the name of the object variable's type, not the object variable's name.

Inheritance

When you declare an object type using the class keyword, you are actually utilizing Delphi's inheritance capabilities. Inheritance lets ancestor classes pass on to future generations accumulated wisdom (methods and data).

The code in Listing 10.4 demonstrates four object types: TCheck, TAPCheck, TPayrollCheck and TPettyCashCheck. TCheck is the ancestor class and the other three all descend from TCheck.

LISTING 10.4 TCHECK INHERITANCE RELATIONSHIP

```
type
  TCheck = class
  private
  protected
    Amount : Real;
    PayTo : String[30];
    Date : TDateTime;
  public
    constructor Create;
    destructor Destroy;
    procedure Calc;
    function Print: real;
  end;

  TAPCheck = class(TCheck)
  private
  protected
  public
  end;
```

```
TPayrollCheck = class(TCheck)
private
protected
   TaxRate : Real;
   GrossAmount : Real;
public
   constructor Create;
   destructor Destroy;
   procedure Calc;
   function Print: Real;
end;

TPettyCashCheck = class(TCheck)
private
protected
public
end;
```

In this example, TAPCheck, TPayrollCheck, and TPettyCashCheck are declared as types based on TCheck, using the class keyword. You can view the relationship between these classes by compiling the project and using the Browse Objects window (use the View | Browser menu item). Figure 10.1 shows Browser Window.

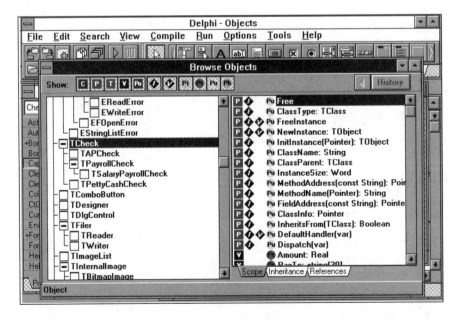

FIGURE 10.1 BROWSER WINDOW SHOWING TCHECK AND DESCENDANT TYPES.

Listing 10.4 shows how to create two generations of objects. In practice, you can create as many generations as you need. In fact, Delphi's VCL (Visual Component Library) inheritance tree is several generations deep in certain parts.

Polymorphism

While inheritance is nice, polymorphism makes it even nicer. In Listing 10.4, notice that a method, Print, is defined in the TCheck type and the TPayrollCheck type. The reason for this is so that TPayrollCheck objects can use a Print method which is different from the ancestor class. In this regard, objects of TPayrollCheck type respond slightly differently to the Print message.

Without polymorphism, the TPayrollCheck type Print method would have to be named something different. Polymorphism eliminates the need to do this.

Encapsulation

Hiding parts of your objects from other sections of code, otherwise known as encapsulation, is an important part of OOP. Delphi implements encapsulation through the four P's: the private, protected, public, and published keywords.

These four keywords control how other units can access parts of an object. In Delphi, a unit is a collection of data types, variables, and methods or procedures which is compiled separately into linkable code. All but the smallest applications will have multiple units, so you will need to understand units as well (see Chapter 12 for a full discussion of units). Obviously, if you have spent hours creating a form in a unit which will be reused elsewhere in your application, you might want to hide certain parts of implementation details in your form. This will ensure that whoever else uses your form will manipulate it via the appropriate methods and fields.

Private Section

The best way of ensuring incorrect tampering with an object is through the private keyword. Only code in the current unit can access private data fields and methods. Consider the TCheck type declaration below:

```
type                        {type part in Checks unit}
  TCheck = class
  private
    Number : Integer;
  protected
```

```
      Amount : Real;
      PayTo : String[30];
      Date : TDateTime;
   public
      constructor Create;
      destructor Destroy;
      procedure Calc;
      function Print: real;
   published
   end;
```

In this example, the Number field is defined as private. Only the code in this unit (which includes the Calc and Print procedures) can access the Number data field. Suppose this type were declared in a unit called Checks and from another unit (let's say Unit1) you created an object variable and tried to access the Number field as shown below:

```
unit Unit1;              {unit name}
interface                {list what this unit needs and exports}
uses Checks;             {this unit needs the Checks unit}

var
   MyCheck : TCheck;     {this unit makes available the MyCheck var}

implementation

begin
   MyCheck:=TCheck.Create;
   MyCheck.Number := 3;      {code will not compile}
end.
```

This code would not compile, because unit Unit1 would be attempting to access a private data field in the TCheck type defined in unit Checks. The only way private data fields can be accessed from other units is to write public methods which access the private data fields. In this way, the public methods serve as an "official" conduit between the object's private data fields and other parts of your application.

Please remember that you can always refer to an object type's private data fields and methods from code within the unit that defines the type. In C++, it is possible to declare functions as *friends* of a class with the friend keyword. Friend functions can access private parts. In Delphi, all code in a unit is considered "friends" of any classes defined.

Code listing 10.5 lists the final version of the Checks (CHECKS.PAS) unit in the Objects project. This chapter will refer frequently to this listing, as some parts of the listing are discussed in later sections. The part that is important here is the CheckForm.OnCreate event at the very end of the listing. This event occurs when the form is created.

Listing 10.5 Checks Unit (CHECKS.PAS)

```
unit Checks;

interface

uses
   SysUtils, WinTypes, WinProcs, Messages, Classes, Graphics, Controls,
   Forms, Dialogs, StdCtrls, Mask;

type
   TCheck = class                {base class for checks}
   private
   protected
      Amount : Real;
      PayTo : String[30];
      Date : TDateTime;
   public
      constructor Create;
      destructor Destroy;
      procedure Calc; virtual;
      function Print: real; virtual;
   end;

   TAPCheck = class(TCheck)       {account payable check class}
   private
   protected
   public
   end;

   TPayrollCheck = class(TCheck) {payroll check class}
   private
   protected
      TaxRate : Real;
      GrossAmount : Real;
   public
      constructor Create;
      destructor Destroy;
      procedure Calc;
      function Print: Real; override;
   end;
```

```
  TPettyCashCheck = class(TCheck) {petty cash check class}
  private
  protected
  public
  end;

  TCheckForm = class(TForm)    {form to test check classes}
    PaytoEdit: TEdit;
    PaytoLabel: TLabel;
    AmountLabel: TLabel;
    CheckType: TGroupBox;
    Payroll: TRadioButton;
    AccountsPayable: TRadioButton;
    PettyCash: TRadioButton;
    AmountEdit: TMaskEdit;
    DateEdit: TMaskEdit;
    DateLabel: TLabel;
    NetEdit: TEdit;
    OkButton: TButton;
    NetLabel: TLabel;
    CalcButton: TButton;
    TaxRateEdit: TMaskEdit;
    TaxRateLabel: TLabel;
    procedure CalcButtonClick(Sender: TObject);
    procedure SetTaxRateVisibility(Sender:TObject);
    procedure FormCreate(Sender: TObject);
    procedure FormDestroy(Sender: TObject);
  private
    { Private declarations }
  public
    { Public declarations }
  end;

var
  CheckForm: TCheckForm;
  APCheck: TAPCheck;
  PCCheck: TPettyCashCheck;
  PRCheck: TPayrollCheck;

implementation

{$R *.DFM}

procedure TCheck.Calc;
begin
{awaiting future functionality}
```

```
end;

function TCheck.Print: Real;
begin
Print:=Amount;
end;

constructor TCheck.Create;
begin
inherited Create;
end;

destructor TCheck.Destroy;
begin
inherited Destroy;
end;

constructor TPayrollCheck.Create;
begin
inherited Create;
TaxRate:=0.11;
end;

destructor TPayrollCheck.Destroy;
begin
inherited Destroy;
end;

procedure TPayrollCheck.Calc;
begin
{save the amount in GrossAmount}
GrossAmount:=Amount;
{calculate the net amount}
Amount:=Amount - Amount*TaxRate;
end;

function TPayrollCheck.Print: Real;
begin
Calc;
Print:=Amount;
end;

procedure TCheckForm.CalcButtonClick(Sender: TObject);
var
   ValCode: Integer;
   NetAmt: Real;
```

```
      Result: String;
      Check : TCheck;
  begin

  if Payroll.Checked then
      begin
        {convert the tax rate from a string to a real,
         store it in PRCheck.TaxRate}
        val(TaxRateEdit.Text, PRCheck.TaxRate, ValCode);
        {Point Check at the PRCheck object}
        Check:=PRCheck;
      end
      else if AccountsPayable.Checked then
          {Point Check at the APCheck object}
          Check:=APCheck
          else if PettyCash.Checked then
              {Point Check at the PCCheck object}
              Check:=PCCheck;

  {using the Check pointer, print the results to screen}
  Check.Date:=StrToDate(DateEdit.Text);
  Val(AmountEdit.Text, Check.Amount, ValCode);
  Str(Check.Print:3:2,Result);
  NetEdit.Text := Result;

  end;

  procedure TCheckForm.SetTaxRateVisibility(Sender: TObject);
  begin
  if Payroll.Checked then
    begin
     TaxRateEdit.Visible:=True;
     TaxRateLabel.Visible:=True;
    end
  else
    begin
     TaxRateEdit.Visible:=False;
     TaxRateLabel.Visible:=False;
    end

  end;

  procedure TCheckForm.FormCreate(Sender: TObject);
  var
      Result : String;
  begin
```

```
{create the three check objects}
PRCheck:=TPayrollCheck.Create;
APCheck:=TAPCheck.Create;
PCCheck:=TPettyCashCheck.Create;
```

```
{assign the TaxRate edit field the value
contained in the PRCheck.TaxRate field}
Str(PRCheck.TaxRate:3:2,Result);
TaxRateEdit.Text:=Result;

end;

procedure TCheckForm.FormDestroy(Sender: TObject);
begin
PRCheck.Destroy;
APCheck.Destroy;
PCCheck.Destroy;
end;

end.
```

In the CheckForm.OnCreate event, you can freely access any private fields or methods (if any were defined) for any of the three object variables: PRCheck, APCheck, and PCCheck. However, code in another unit *cannot* access a private field or method in either of these three variables (which are available to other units). In addition, suppose you had code in another unit which creates a local object variable of any of the four check types. That code would not be able to access any private fields or functions for that check object.

Protected Section

Protected methods and fields behave just like private ones, with one important distinction. The protected keyword ensures that new descendant objects can reference data fields or methods. The protected keyword defines the developer's interface. For example, consider the following class definition discussed earlier:

```
type                          {type part in Checks unit}
  TCheck = class
  private
    Number : Integer;
  protected
    Amount : Real;
    PayTo : String[30];
```

```
    Date : TDateTime;
  public
    constructor Create;
    procedure Calc;
    function Print: real;
  published
  end;
```

The TCheck type has three protected fields: Amount, PayTo, and Date. Consider the following implementation section in another unit, Unit1, which uses the Checks unit:

```
unit Unit1;              {unit name}
interface                {list what this unit needs and exports}
uses Checks;             {this unit needs the Checks unit}

var
  MyCheck : TCheck;      {this unit makes available the MyCheck var}

implementation

begin
  MyCheck:=TCheck.Create;
  MyCheck.Amount := 100;   {code will compile}
end.
```

By instantiating a new variable, MyCheck, the protected fields are available for access. However, consider the following code example in which the variable MyCheck is instantiated in the Checks unit, and not in Unit1, yet referred to in Unit1:

```
unit Unit1;              {unit name}
interface                {list what this unit needs and exports}
uses Checks;             {this unit needs the Checks unit}

implementation

begin
  MyCheck.Amount := 100;   {code will not compile}
end.
```

In this example, because MyCheck.Amount is a protected field, the line of code which assigns it a value of 100 will not compile. The compiler has no idea what the MyCheck.Amount is.

Public Section

The public section is the easiest to understand. All items in the public section can be referenced from any other unit. In this regard, the public section identifies the runtime interface to an object. In the TCheck object type discussed above, the Calc procedure and the Print function are public. Any other units which use the Checks unit can freely use these methods on local object variables. Other units can also access these methods on global variables declared in other units.

The public section is perhaps the most important section to consider. It defines the public interface to the object. When you design objects, you will need to carefully consider exactly what methods and data ought to be public. If the public interface is designed properly, you can make extensive revisions in the object's internal data structures and methods without having to change the public interface. If the public interface is stable, changes in the object's source code will not involve source code changes in parts of the application that use the object type.

Published Section

The published section is identical to the public section with one major difference. Any properties listed in the published section can be made available at form design time through the component palette. Properties are discussed in detail later in this chapter. They are used primarily to create reusable design components. It is through the published section that you can extend and enhance Delphi's design interface.

Properties are the only thing that need to be listed in the published section. Putting functions or procedures there does nothing more than making those methods public. The Delphi design interface makes only properties available in the visual component.

Managing Object Details

When you work with objects, important details pop up. For example, you might want to initialize variables or allocate additional memory when an object is created. You might also want to delay, until runtime, the exact determination of an object's type. Delphi has facilities to handle these and other issues.

Constructors and destructors are two blocks of code which are invoked when the object is created and when it is destroyed, respectively. Virtual methods let you design objects in which the object's type is determined at runtime rather than compile time. Properties and event methods are two mechanisms to help you create objects which can be placed on the component palette and reused.

Constructors

Declaring a constructor is simple. Listing 10.5 contains a constructor declaration for the TPayrollCheck type:

```
TPayrollCheck = class(TCheck)
  private
  protected
    TaxRate : Real;
    GrossAmount : Real;
  public
    constructor Create;              {constructor}
    procedure Calc;
    function Print: Real; override;
  end;
```

When declaring a constructor, you need to use the **constructor** keyword. Constructors typically take the form of procedures, with or without parameters. Creating a constructor is also simple. The following code fragment from Listing 10.5 shows a constructor for the TPayrollCheck class:

```
constructor TPayrollCheck.Create;
begin
inherited Create;
TaxRate:=0.11;
end;
```

Constructors execute when the object is created. In Delphi, objects which descend from TObject inherit a Create function, which returns a pointer to the object just created. The TObject Create method allocates space in memory for the object. You can create your own version of Create for your own objects and still get the benefits of the TObject.Create method.

The constructor shown above, calls the inherited Create method. The TCheck type also has a constructor Create defined. This constructor does nothing except call the inherited Create method for the TObject type. When you run the Objects project included in the book's disk, the TCheck constructor gets called three times and the TPayrollCheck constructor once. The following lines of code, at the end of Listing 10.5 invoke the constructors:

```
PRCheck:=TPayrollCheck.Create;
APCheck:=TAPCheck.Create;
PCCheck:=TPettyCashCheck.Create;
```

The first line of code invokes the TPayrollCheck constructor, which invokes
(via the **inherited** keyword) the TCheck constructor. The other two lines of
code call the TCheck Create constructor as well.

To help understand constructors, use the debugging tools in Delphi to
step through code execution one line at a time as objects get created.

T I P

In this example, the TPayrollCheck constructor, Create, simply assigns 11%
to the TaxRate field. Constructors are not always that simple. In fact, you
can allocate memory and create other objects from within a constructor. As
constructors get more complex, you may have to trap for errors. For example, if the TCheck constructor dynamically allocated memory (see Chapter
6, Data Types, for examples of dynamically allocating memory) that was
unavailable due to a low memory situation, you would need to cancel the
construction process. Delphi comes equipped with system procedure, *Fail*,
which cancels a constructor. Fail takes no arguments and simply cancels the
current construction process. It does not undo anything your code has done
during the construction process. You must handle that yourself.

Before you get too deep in creating complex constructors, make sure that
you understand Delphi's exception handling mechanisms, which are
explained in Chapter 20, "Error Handling."

WARNING

Constructors can take arguments. For example, the TComponent Create
method accepts an argument: an object variable that points to some other
TComponent object. If you create an object which descends from
TComponent, you can pass the Create method an object variable which points
to an object considered the owner of the newly created one. The owner of an
object takes responsibility for disposing of that object when the owner object
is destructed. Arguments passed to constructors can serve other purposes as
well. You might want to pass a constructor the initial value of a field.

Destructors

If you give birth to an object, you will need to get rid of it sooner or later.
Destructors help in that role. Destructor methods are invoked when an

object disappears. Objects which descend from TObject inherit two methods which help in the destruction process: *Free* and *Destroy*. The Free method looks like this:

```
AnObject.Free;
```

What Free does is check to make sure the object pointer variable is not nil. If it is, nothing happens. If the object variable is assigned, the Free method then invokes the Destroy method.

Virtual Methods

Normally, Delphi resolves address to variables and methods at compile time, including what methods to call for a given object. The form in code listing 10.5 does not yet know which type of check object that it will need to perform calculations. The code fragment below is the CalcButtonClick method for the form. This code is called every time the user presses the Calculate net button shown in Figure 10.2. Notice that this code assigns one of the three check objects (PRCheck, APCheck or PCCheck) to the Check variable, which is of type TCheck.

LISTING 10.6 USING VIRTUAL METHODS, CALCBUTTONCLICK()

```
procedure TCheckForm.CalcButtonClick(Sender: TObject);
var
    ValCode: Integer;
    NetAmt: Real;
    Result: String;
    Check : TCheck;
begin

if Payroll.Checked then
    begin
      {convert the tax rate from a string to a real,
       store it in PRCheck.TaxRate}
      val(TaxRateEdit.Text, PRCheck.TaxRate, ValCode);
      {Point Check at the PRCheck object}
      Check:=PRCheck;
    end
    else if AccountsPayable.Checked then
        {Point Check at the APCheck object}
        Check:=APCheck
        else if PettyCash.Checked then
            {Point Check at the PCCheck object}
            Check:=PCCheck;
```

```
{using the Check pointer, print the results to screen}
Check.Date:=StrToDate(DateEdit.Text);
Val(AmountEdit.Text, Check.Amount, ValCode);
Str(Check.Print:3:2,Result);
NetEdit.Text := Result;
```

```
end;
```

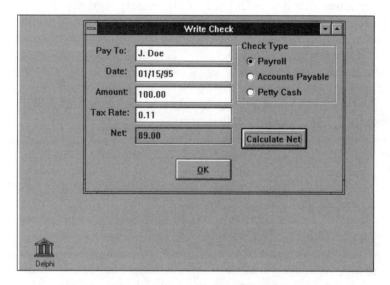

FIGURE 10.2 THE WRITE CHECK FORM

Using one variable to handle multiple types of check objects makes the code in Listing 10.6 much simpler. We do not need to handle each type of check object separately, even for common processing, such as printing the check amount. The function Print is declared as a **virtual** method in the TCheck type and as **override** in the TPayrollCheck type, as shown below.

```
type
  TCheck = class            {base class for checks}
    ...
    function Print: real; virtual;
  end;

  TPayrollCheck = class(TCheck) {payroll check class}
    ...
    function Print: Real; override;
  end;
```

If Print was not declared as virtual, Delphi would call the Print method for the TCheck type, not the TPayrollCheckType in the following line of code in the TCheckForm.CalcButtonClick method:

```
Str(Check.Print:3:2,Result);
```

The reason for this is because the compiler thinks Check is of TCheck type. It does not know that it is pointing to a different type of object, in this case a TPayrollCheck object. By declaring Print virtual in the parent class and as override in the child class, you are instructing Delphi to resolve the address for Print at run time, not compile time.

Each object in Delphi has a VMT (virtual method table). This table is created and maintained at runtime and includes the address for all virtual methods of the object and any inherited virtual methods. This table is used to determine what method to call at runtime.

Since the Print method is declared as virtual, and the Check variable points to a TPayrollCheck object (and it is associated VMT), at runtime Delphi looks up the Print method in the VMT that Check points to and calls that Print method. If listing 10.5 was changed so that print is not declared as virtual in the TCheck type and as override in the TPayrollCheck type, then when a payroll check is printed, it would not take the tax rate into consideration when performing the calculation.

Obviously virtual methods are of great importance in an object-oriented environment. However, to make use of them, you need to keep in mind the following rules. To use override, the method must exist in the ancestor object, be declared as virtual, and have an identical declaration as the ancestor method with the same number and types of arguments.

You can create polymorphic objects without using virtual methods. Methods which are duplicated in a descendant class without the override directive are *static*. Delphi does not place these methods in the object's VMT. Instead, the addresses to those methods are resolved at compile time. This is often called *replacing* an ancestor method rather than overriding it. Methods declared statically do not need to have the same number of arguments in both the ancestor and descendant classes.

Properties

Delphi introduces the keyword *properties* into the ObjectPascal language. A property is a special kind of data field. All of the objects you place on a form in the Delphi designer have properties. Since most of Delphi is written in ObjectPascal, you have the same ability as the software engineers at

Borland do to create your own components. Properties figure prominently in that capability.

Properties not only are a design-time interface to the object, they are also a runtime interface to the object. Having a design-time interface is important if you want to create your own components. However, properties also provide a superior means of hiding implementation details at runtime.

Listing 10.7 demonstrates how to implement properties.

LISTING 10.7 USING PROPERTIES, PROPS UNIT (PROPS.PAS)

```
unit Props;

interface
uses Classes;

type
  TMyObject = class(TObject)
  private
    FAccountKey : String;   {Account primary key}
    function GetAccountKey : String;
    procedure SetAccountKey(const AKey : String);
  protected
  public
    property AccountKey : String
      read GetAccountKey write SetAccountKey;
  published
  end;
implementation

function TMyObject.GetAccountKey;
begin
GetAccountKey:=FAccountKey;
end;

procedure TMyObject.SetAccountKey(const AKey : String);
begin
FAccountKey:=AKey;
end;

end.
```

In this listing, one property is declared: AccountKey. The property is defined as a String and two methods are used to read and write the property: GetAccountKey and SetAccountKey. These two methods store and retrieve a string into the FAccountKey field.

By using properties, you can change how properties are internally stored without changing the public interface. This gives you plenty of flexibility which lets you change the implementation with no disruption to other code which uses the object. Because the methods which set and get the property are private, code in other units can not access them. The only way to get at the field the property represents is to use the property as if it were a data field:

```
var
   MyObject : TMyObject
begin
MyObject:=TMyObject.Create;
MyObject.AccountKey:='100';
end;
```

In this example, you simply assign the property the string '100.' This calls the SetAccountKey procedure, which stores the string '100' in the FAccountKey Field.

Naming Conventions

Keeping track of all the bits and pieces on an object gets a bit heady. We strongly recommend that you decide on a naming convention so that other programmers (or yourself six months later) can better understand what the code is doing. Borland software engineers came up with a naming convention which is used throughout Delphi and which we have adopted in this book where appropriate. Here are some of the naming guidelines:

- Types begin with a capital T, as in TMyObject.
- All objects are in proper case.
- All Methods and fields are in proper case.
- Fields accessible via properties are given the same name as the property, except they begin with F to denote field, as in FMyName.
- The methods to get and set the property are also given the property name prefixed with Set or Get, as in GetMyName.
- Wherever possible, use names and conventions similar to that found in Delphi's VCL source code. This will help other programmers understand the Delphi VCL code as well as you code.

Summary

Delphi objects are truly object-oriented, providing full support for inheritance, polymorphism, and encapsulation. This chapter introduced you to the basics of how to declare and use nonvisual Delphi objects. The visual objects, such as tables, grids, radio buttons, and so on, are objects as well and they have the same code structure as the nonvisual objects discussed here. Learning how to implement your own objects not only helps ensure that your code will be well-written, it prepares you for understanding and using Delphi objects.

CHAPTER 11

Flat File Input and Output

Although this book is about databases it is common in database applications to need to import data from or export data to sequential files. You may also want to include a .INI file in your application to provide a way to save and retrieve settings between sessions.

No matter what your needs, Pascal offers routines to meet them. You can read and write text and fixed length files. You can even define your own file types. Delphi even includes routines specifically for managing .INI files. This chapter will look at Delphi's support for text files, typed files, untyped files, and .INI files.

Working with Text Files

Figure 11.1 shows the form for the sample project TextFile. The code in this project demonstrates text file input and output by allowing you to select a file and view it in the memo component on the form. You can also write a copy of the text in the memo control to the file COPY.TXT. To run the sample program double-click a directory entry, then click a text file in the file list box, and click the Open button. Clicking the Copy button copies whatever is displayed in the memo control to the file COPY.TXT. Clicking Numbers loads the integers in NUMBERS.TXT into the memo.

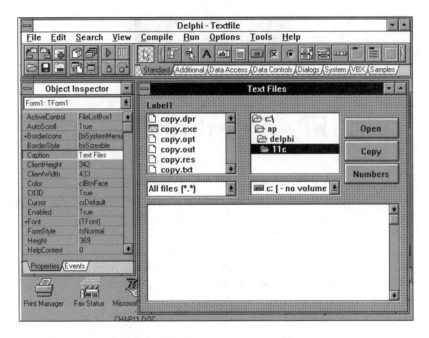

FIGURE 11.1 TEXTFILE SAMPLE PROGRAM.

The list and combo boxes used to select the drive, directory and file are covered in Chapter 15. This chapter is focused on how the files are accessed. Before you can read or write a text file you must declare a file variable of type Text.

```
var
  txtFile:    System.Text;
  txtLine:    String;
  filePath:   String[80];
```

If you have programmed in Pascal before you are used to declaring your text file variables as just Text. However, you cannot do that in Delphi because Text is also a property of many of the Delphi visual components. To resolve this ambiguity you must specify the unit that the file type is defined in and declare the variable to be of type System.Text. Here is the code from the Open button's click method.

```
procedure TForm1.OpenBtnClick(Sender: TObject);
var
  txtFile:    System.Text;
  txtLine:    String;
  filePath:   String[80];
```

```
begin
  {Get the directory path from the file list.}
  filePath := FileListBox1.Directory;
  {If the path does not end with \ add one.}
  if filePath[Length(filePath)] <> '\' then
    filePath := filePath + '\';
  {Add the file name to the path.}
  filePath := filePath + FileListBox1.FileName;
  {Open the file.}
  Assign(txtFile, filePath);
  Reset(txtFile);
  {Empty the memo and read the file.}
  Memo1.Lines.Clear;
  while not EOF(txtFile) do
  begin
    Readln(txtFile, txtLine);
    Memo1.Lines.Add(txtLine);
  end;
end;
```

Before you can open a file you have to have its name. In this case, you can browse your directory structure and pick any file you need to have the full path to the file. The following lines of code build the path from properties of the file list control on the form.

```
{Get the directory path from the file list.}
  filePath := FileListBox1.Directory;
  {If the path does not end with \ add one.}
  if filePath[Length(filePath)] <> '\' then
    filePath := filePath + '\';
  {Add the file name to the path.}
  filePath := filePath + FileListBox1.FileName;
```

The first line retrieves the directory. You need the if statement due to an inconsistency in the way the directory path is returned. If the directory is the root, then it will already contain a trailing backslash, for example, C:\. However, if the directory is a subdirectory the path will not have a backslash at the end, for example, C:\DELPHI. The if statement checks the last character of the filePath variable and if it is not a backslash one is appended. Finally, the FileName property of the file list box is added to provide the full path to the file.

Opening a text file in Pascal is a two step process. The first step is to call the runtime library AssignFile procedure to assign the file name to the file variable. This does not open the file. The second step is to call either Reset or Rewrite to open the file. Reset opens the file for reading while Rewrite opens the file for writing. The following code performs these steps.

```
{Open the file.}
  AssignFile(txtFile, filePath);
  Reset(txtFile);
```

WARNING

If you call Rewrite and the file already exists Rewrite will overwrite it without warning.

The rest of the code in this procedure reads each line of the text file and adds it to the memo control on the form.

```
{Empty the memo and read the file.}
  Memo1.Lines.Clear;
  while not EOF(txtFile) do
  begin
    Readln(txtFile, txtLine);
    Memo1.Lines.Add(txtLine);
  end;
```

The EOF runtime library function in the while statement returns True when you reach the end of the file.

When you read a text file you will probably want to use the Readln procedure. Readln reads one line of text at a time. In this example the text is read into the String variable txtLine. If the line contains more than 255 characters, the variable is truncated at 255 and the remaining characters are skipped.

T I P

If you need to read text lines longer than 255 characters use a PChar or character array instead of a String.

You do not have to use a String variable with Readln. You can use any valid type. Suppose you have a text file that contains an integer at the beginning of each line followed by other text you are not interested in. The following code will read the integer from each line into the integer variable num and ignore the remaining text on each line. Readln is even smart enough to skip any leading whitespace in front of the integer.

```
var
  num:        Integer;
  txtFile:    System.Text;
begin
  {Open the file.}
```

```
AssignFile(txtFile, 'numbers.txt');
Reset(txtFile);
{Empty the memo and read the file.}
Memo1.Lines.Clear;
while not EOF(txtFile) do
begin
  Readln(txtFile, num);
  Memo1.Lines.Add(IntToStr(num));
end;
```

If each line in the file contains three integers separated by whitespace just change the Readln call to

```
Readln(txtFile, num1, num2, num3);
```

to get them all.

You can also read text files with the Read runtime library procedure. Read does not read the file one line at a time but instead reads one or more values at a time. What kind of values? I depends on the type of variable you read the value into. Suppose you have a file that has an unknown number of integers on each line. The following code will read all of the integers and display them in the memo control. This code is from the Numbers button's click procedure.

```
procedure TForm1.NumBtnClick(Sender: TObject);
var
  num:       Integer;
  txtFile:   System.Text;
begin
  {Open the file.}
  AssignFile(txtFile, 'numbers.txt');
  Reset(txtFile);
  {Empty the memo and read the file.}
  Memo1.Lines.Clear;
  while not EOF(txtFile) do
  begin
    Read(txtFile, num);
    Memo1.Lines.Add(IntToStr(num));
  end;
end;
```

To write data to a text file use the Writeln or Write runtime library procedures. Here is the code from the Copy button that writes the contents of the memo control to the file COPY.TXT.

```
procedure TForm1.CopyBtnClick(Sender: TObject);
var
  txtFile:    System.Text;
  i:          Word;
begin
  {Open the output file. Overwrite if it
   exists}
  AssignFile(txtFile, 'copy.txt');
  Rewrite(txtFile);
  {Write all of the lines in the memo.}
  for i := 0 to Memo1.Lines.Count - 1 do
    Writeln(txtFile, Memo1.Lines[i]);
  {Close the output file to save what was
   written.}
  System.Close(txtFile);
end;
```

This procedure is almost identical to code from the Open button with two exceptions. First, Rewrite is used to open the file for output. Second, Writeln is used to write the text from the specified line of the memo to the file. Note that you can also use the Write procedure to write individual values to a text file just as you can read individual values with read.

The last statement of the procedure closes the output file. Since Close is also the name of a method in several of Delphi's visual components you must specify the unit name, System, in the call. To avoid this name conflict use the new CloseFile(FileVar) procedure.

WARNING

You must call Close to close any text file you write to. If you do not the file's memory buffer will not be flushed to disk and you will lose some text at the end of the file. In addition, DOS will not properly update the file's size.

In addition to the information in this section you should read the descriptions and examples for Read, Readln, Write, and Writeln in the Delphi on-line help. These procedures are very flexible and will meet all of your text file processing needs.

Working with Typed Files

Typed files are files that consist entirely of components of a single type. To declare a typed file you must specify the type. For example, the following statement declares two files, one whose type is Integer and one whose type is String with a length of 80 bytes.

```
var
  intFile:    file of Integer;
  strFile:    file of String[80];
```

At first it might seem that a file that can only hold a single type is of very limited use. However, remember that in Pascal you can define your own types and they can be very complex. The simple phone list manager shown in Figure 11.2 uses a typed file to store a list of names and phone numbers. The name of this project is TYPED.DPR.

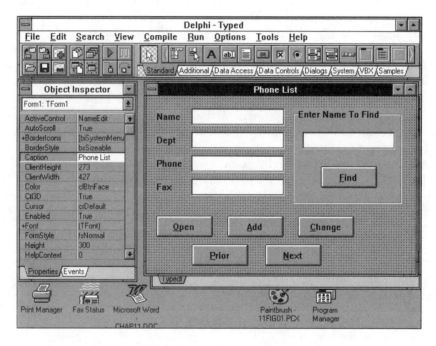

FIGURE 11.2 A PHONE LIST USING A TYPED FILE.

To use the phone list you must click the open button to open the file before you use any of the other controls. Before looking at the code that manipulates the typed file you need to see how it is declared.

```
type
  Person = record
    name:     String[30];
    dept:     String[30];
    phone:    String[12];
    fax:      String[12];
  end;
```

```
var
  rec:         Person;
  phoneFile:   file of Person;
```

You can declare a typed file to be of any type except File so it is possible to declare a file of Integer or a file of String or any other Pascal type. However, you can store more than a single type in a typed file by declaring a record that consists of multiple fields of different types. The type declaration above declares a record that includes four string fields of varying sizes to hold the persons name, department, phone number, and fax number. Next, the var block declares two variables. The program will use the first, rec of type person, to hold values read from or written to the file. The second is the file variable, phoneFile, of type Person. When you look at the complete program notice that these declarations are not inside a procedure. This makes them visible (global in scope) to all of the procedures and functions for this form.

A *typed file* consists of records of the type specified in the file variable declaration. The records have a fixed size and no record delimiter between adjacent records. While records in a *text file* end with the carriage return and line feed characters, records in a typed file are identified only by their length. In this case the length of each record is 88 bytes. Remember that each Pascal string includes an extra byte at the beginning that stores the string's length so the record length is 30 + 30 + 12 + 12 + one extra byte for each of the four strings. In this file the first 88 bytes are the first record, the second 88 bytes are the second record, and so on.

If you need to read a file that contains character fields that were not written using Pascal strings you cannot use Pascal strings because the length byte will not be present. To read character fields written by other languages use arrays of Character as shown below.

```
type
  Person = record
    name:    array[1..30] of Char;
    dept:    array[1..30] of Char;
    phone:   array[1..12] of Char;
    fax:     array[1..12] of Char;
  end;
```

Using fixed length records gives typed files two advantages that text files do not have. First, you can open a typed file for read and write access, which means you can change the contents of an existing record in the file. Second, you can read any record, if you know its number, without having to read all of the preceding records sequentially to find it. Random reads are possible because Pascal can compute where any record starts in the file by multiplying the record number, times the number of bytes per record. Giving the number of bytes from the beginning of the file the operating system knows how to calculate the physical location on disk of that part of the file. The phone list program demonstrates all of these features. The following code is from the click procedure for the Open button.

```
procedure TForm1.OpenBtnClick(Sender: TObject);
begin
  AssignFile(phoneFile, 'phone.dat');
  {Set FileMode for Read/Write};
  FileMode := 2;
  try
    Reset(phoneFile);
  except
    on EInOutError do
      Rewrite(phoneFile);
  end;
  {If there is anything in the file copy the
   first record to the form.}
  if not EOF(phoneFile) then
  begin
    Read(phoneFile, rec);
    CopyRecToEdit;
  end;
end;
```

The AssignFile call associates the file name with the file variable just as it did for a text file. The second statement

```
FileMode := 2
```

needs some explanation. FileMode is a global variable that is built into Pascal. You do not need to declare it. The value of FileMode determines whether typed and untyped files opened by calling Reset will be opened in read only, write, or read write mode. Assigning zero to FileMode sets read only mode, 1 sets write and 2 sets read write. Files created by calling Rewrite are always opened in read write mode.

The next group of statements,

```
try
    Reset(phoneFile);
except
  on EInOutError do
    Rewrite(phoneFile);
end;
```

calls Reset to open the file. However, if PHONE.DAT does not exist Reset will fail and generate a runtime error, called an exception in Delphi. Enclosing Reset in the try/except tells the compiler that if an exception occurs while executing the statements in the try block execution should continue with the statements in the except block. In this case, if the Reset fails due to an input/output error execution moves to the Rewrite statement which will create the file. This is part of Delphi's error handling mechanism which is covered in detail in Chapter 25.

The final step in opening the file is to see if it contains any records and, if it does, display the first record on the form.

```
if not EOF(phoneFile) then
begin
  Read(phoneFile, rec);
  CopyRecToEdit;
end;
```

This code checks to see if the file variable is positioned to the end of the file. If so, then the file is empty. If not the call to Read reads the first record into the variable rec and the call to the custom procedure CopyRecToEdit copies the values from rec to the edit controls on the form as shown below.

```
procedure CopyRecToEdit;
{
Copy values from the record variable rec to the
form's edit controls.
}
begin
  with rec do
  begin
    Form1.NameEdit.Text := name;
    Form1.DeptEdit.Text := dept;
    Form1.PhoneEdit.Text := phone;
    Form1.FaxEdit.Text := fax;
  end;
end;
```

This code was isolated in a separate procedure because it is called from several different places in the program.

N O T E

Text files are accessed using Read and Write only. You cannot use Readln and Writeln as you can with text files because typed files are not composed of lines that end with carriage return/line feed.

The Next and Prior buttons on the form let you scroll forward or backward through the records. Here is the code from the Next button's click procedure.

```
procedure TForm1.NextBtnClick(Sender: TObject);
begin
  {If you are not at the end of the file read
   the next record and display it.}
  if not EOF(phoneFile) then
  begin
    Read(phoneFile, rec);
    CopyRecToEdit;
  end;
end;
```

Moving to the next record is deceptively simple. Pascal maintains a pointer to your current location in a typed file. When you read a record the pointer is positioned at the end of that record so that you are ready to read the next record. Therefore, all the Next button has to do is read the next record. Moving to the prior record is a bit more complex as shown in the following code from the Prior button's click procedure.

```
procedure TForm1.PriorBtnClick(Sender: TObject);
begin
  if FilePos(phoneFile) > 1 then
  begin
    {Since the file position is at the end of
     the record being displayed, move back 2
     to read the prior record.}
    Seek(phoneFile, FilePos(phoneFile) - 2);
    {Read the record and display it.}
    Read(phoneFile, rec);
    CopyRecToEdit;
  end
end;
```

Since the file position is at the end of the last record that was read you need to back up two records to be at the beginning of the record before the one that is currently displayed on the form. Before you can move back you need to know if there is a record in front of the one that is currently being displayed, or if this record is the first one in the form. For a typed file the FilePos runtime library function returns the number of the last record that was read. If the file pointer is at the beginning of the file FilePos returns zero. Therefore, if FilePos is greater than 1 the file position is at the end of the second or later record and you can move back to the prior record.

To move to any record in a typed file call the Seek procedure. Seek positions the file pointer to the end of the specified record so that the next call to Read will read the next record. Therefore,

```
Seek(phoneFile, FilePos(phoneFile) - 2);
```

moves the file pointer to the beginning of the record before the last one that was read. The last two lines in the procedure read the record and display it on the form just as in the code for the Next button.

Once you understand FilePos and Seek, the code for the Add and Change buttons is straightforward. Here is the code for the Add button.

```
procedure TForm1.AddBtnClick(Sender: TObject);
begin
  {Copy the edit controls to the record.}
  CopyEditToRec;
  {Seek to the end of the file.}
  Seek(phoneFile, FileSize(phoneFile));
  {Write the new record.}
  Write(phoneFile, rec);
end;
```

This code calls the custom procedure CopyEditToRec which copies the values from the edit controls on the form to the record variable rec and then moves the file pointer to the end of the file. The move to the end of the file uses the FileSize function which returns the number of records in a typed file. Therefore,

```
Seek(phoneFile, FileSize(phoneFile));
```

positions the pointer at the end of the last record in the file. Once the pointer is at the end of the file a call to Write adds the new record. The CopyEditToRec procedure is exactly the reverse of the CopyRectToEdit procedure shown earlier. Here is the code.

```
procedure CopyEditToRec;
{
Copy values from the form's edit controls to
the record variable rec.
}
begin
  with rec do
  begin
    name := Form1.NameEdit.Text;
    dept := Form1.DeptEdit.Text;
    phone := Form1.PhoneEdit.Text;
```

```
    fax := Form1.FaxEdit.Text;
  end;
end;
```

The code for the Change button is almost identical as shown below.

```
procedure TForm1.ChangeBtnClick(Sender: TObject);
begin
  {Copy the values in the edit controls to the
   rec variable.}
  CopyEditToRec;
  {Move to the end of the prior record.}
  Seek(phoneFile, FilePos(phoneFile) - 1);
  {Write the changed record over the old one.}
  Write(phoneFile, rec);
end;
```

The only difference is that you want to write this record over the last record that you read by calling

```
Seek(phoneFile, FilePos(phoneFile) - 1);
```

to move the file pointer back one record before calling Write.

The last feature of the phone list is the Find button which lets you search for any record by name. The code below is from the Find buttons click procedure.

```
procedure TForm1.FindBtnClick(Sender: TObject);
begin
  {Move to the beginning of the file.}
  Seek(phoneFile, 0);
  {Read each record looking for the name.}
  while not EOF(phoneFile) do
  begin
    Read(phoneFile, rec);
    {If you find the name display the record
     and clear the Find edit control.}
    if rec.name = FindEdit.Text then
    begin
      CopyRecToEdit;
      FindEdit.Clear;
      {Break out of the while loop.}
      break;
    end;
  end;
end;
```

This procedure calls Seek to move to the beginning of the file then uses a while loop to read each record in the file. If the name in the rec variable matches the name in the FindEdit edit control on the form CopyRecToEdit displays the data in the record, FindEdit.Clear empties the edit control and the break command ends the loop.

Working with Untyped Files

Untyped files are similar to typed files in that they have a fixed record length, can be opened in read, write, or read write mode, and can be randomly positioned to any record in the file. What makes untyped files unique is that you can read or write more than one record at a time and reading and writing is done with special low level high performance procedures. The sample project COPY.DPR uses untyped files to allow you to copy any file regardless of its type. Figure 11.3 shows the form for the copy program.

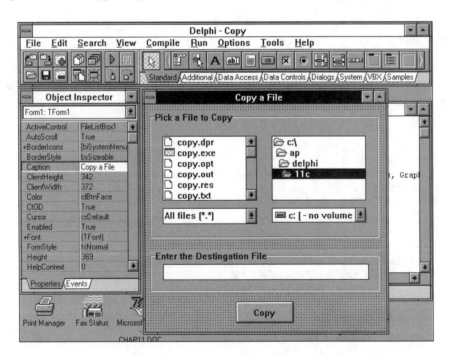

FIGURE 11.3 THE SAMPLE FILE COPY PROGRAM.

The work of the copy program is done in the CopyFile procedure shown below.

```
procedure CopyFile(srcName, DestName: String);
{
Copies the source file to the destination
file.
}
var
  buff:        array[1..8192] of Char;
  srcFile,
  destFile:    File;
  readCount,
  writeCount:  Word;
begin
  {Open the source file.}
  AssignFile(srcFile, srcName);
  Reset(srcFile, 1);
  {Open the destination file.}
  AssignFile(destFile, destName);
  Rewrite(destFile, 1);
  {Copy a buffer full at a time until the
   end of the file is reached or a write
   error occurs.}
  repeat
    BlockRead(srcFile, buff, SizeOf(buff), readCount);
    BlockWrite(destFile, buff, readCount, writeCount);
  until (readCount = 0) or (writeCount < readCount);
  {Close the files.}
  System.Close(srcFile);
  System.Close(destFile);
end;
```

The first thing you will notice that is different about untyped files is that the Reset procedure takes an optional second parameter. This parameter is the record size in bytes. If you omit the record size it defaults to 128. The purpose of this program is to copy any file of any type and size. The record size must be set to one byte so that the size of the copy will match the size of the original file exactly.

The actual copying is performed by the following repeat loop.

```
repeat
  BlockRead(srcFile, buff, SizeOf(buff), readCount);
  BlockWrite(destFile, buff, readCount, writeCount);
until (readCount = 0) or (writeCount < readCount);
```

You must use BlockRead to read untyped files and BlockWrite to write to them. BlockRead takes four parameters. The first is the file variable. The second is the name of the variable or structure to use as a buffer for the data. The buffer contains that data to be written and can be of any size up to 65,535 bytes. In this example buff is an 8k array of Char. The third parameter is the number of records to read. The number of records times the record size must be less than or equal to the size of the buffer. The final parameter, readCount, is set to the number of records actually read. This will always equal the number of records to read, the third parameter, except when you reach the end of the file when it may be less.

In the call to BlockRead above the number of records to write is given as SizeOf(buff). The SizeOf functions will return the size in bytes of any simple or structured variable. Since the record size is one byte in this example the size of the buffer array is equal to the number of records to read.

Always use SizeOf anywhere that your Pascal code requires the size of a variable or structure so the code will still be correct if you change the size of the variable.

TIP

BlockWrite uses the same parameters as BlockRead except that the last parameter is set to the number of records actually written. This will always equal the number of characters to write, the third parameter, unless an error occurs. In this example the number of records to write, the third parameter, is set to readCount which is the number of records read.

The repeat loop continues until the number of records read, readCount, equals zero, indicating the end of file, or until all of the records cannot be written which means an error, such as a full disk, has occurred. The last two statements close the source and destination files.

The following code is from the Copy button's click procedure and is identical to the example given earlier in this chapter in the "Working with Text Files."

```
procedure TForm1.CopyBtnClick(Sender: TObject);
var
  filePath:    String[80];
begin
  {Get the directory path from the file list.}
  filePath := FileListBox1.Directory;
  {If the path does not end with \ add one.}
  if filePath[Length(filePath)] <> '\' then
    filePath := filePath + '\';
  {Add the file name to the path.}
  filePath := filePath + FileListBox1.FileName;
  CopyFile(filePath, DestEdit.Text);
end;
```

This procedure gets the directory path and file name from the file list control and concatenates them to create the full path to the source file. The last statement calls the FileCopy procedure and passes the source file path and the destination file path.

Untyped files appear virtually identical to typed files except that they are more complicated to use because you must worry about sizing the record buffer and extracting individual records from the buffer, if you need to do anything with them other than copy them to another file. When should you use untyped files? The answer is, when you need speed. BlockRead and BlockWrite are low level routines that transfer data directly from the disk with no intermediate buffering or processing of any kind so they are faster than Read and Write on typed files. In addition, using BlockRead and BlockWrite allows you to transfer many records at one time which also improves performance. To see how fast untyped files are try the sample project FAST.DPR. The form is shown in Figure 11.4.

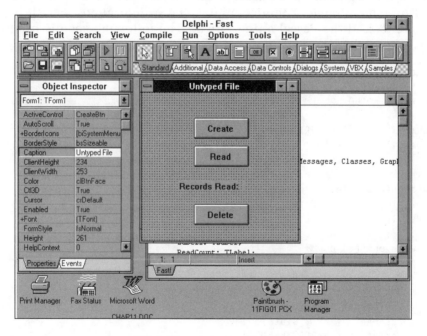

FIGURE 11.4 WRITE AND READ 10,000 RECORDS.

This program lets you create and read a 10,000 record 1 megabyte file. You will be astounded at the speed. After you write the file get out of Windows and reboot your computer to make sure the file is not in your disk cache before you click the read button, so you will get an accurate demonstration of how long it takes to read the file from disk. This program also demonstrates how to process a file of multifield fixed length records using the following record structure as an example.

```
type
  TAddress = record
    name:      array[1..35] of Char;
    addr:      array[1..35] of Char;
    city:      array[1..18] of Char;
    state:     array[1..2] of Char;
    zip:       array[1..10] of Char;
  end;
```

This defines the TAddress type with a total size of 100 bytes. This record uses character arrays instead of Pascal strings to eliminate the length byte at the beginning of a Pascal string. If you were writing a file to be read by a mainframe or minicomputer they would almost certainly not be able to read the Pascal string format. The following code is from the Create button's click method.

```
procedure TForm1.CreateBtnClick(Sender: TObject);
const
  MaxRecs = 100;
var
  buff:       array[1..MaxRecs] of TAddress;
  addrFile:   File;
  i, count:   Word;
begin
  Assign(addrFile, 'addr.dat');
  Rewrite(addrFile, SizeOf(TAddress));
  {Put 100 records into the buffer.}
  for i := 1 to MaxRecs do
    with buff[i] do
    begin
      PasToArray('John Doe', name);
      PasToArray('123 East Main Street', addr);
      PasToArray('New York', city);
      PasToArray('NY', state);
      PasToArray('55555-5555', zip);
    end;
  {Write 100 buffers (10,000 records.}
  for i := 1 to 100 do
    BlockWrite(addrFile, buff, MaxRecs, count);
  System.Close(addrFile);
end;
```

This procedure begins by declaring an array of 100 TAddress records to use as the buffer. The AssignFile and Rewrite statements assign the file name to the file variable and open the file with a record size of SizeOf(TAddress). Using SizeOf ensures that if you change the structure of TAddress the record size in the Rewrite call will adjust automatically. Notice the use of the constant MaxRecs throughout this code to define the number of records in the buffer. This also makes changes easier. If you want to change the number of records in the buffer all you have to change is the constant declaration and the rest of the code takes care of itself. The for loop

```
for i := 1 to MaxRecs do
  with buff[i] do
  begin
    PasToArray('John Doe', name);
    PasToArray('123 East Main Street', addr);
    PasToArray('New York', city);
    PasToArray('NY', state);
    PasToArray('55555-5555', zip);
  end;
```

loads the buffer with 100 identical records. PasToArray is a custom procedure that assigns the value of a Pascal string to a type Char array using the following code.

```
procedure PasToArray(const str: String;
                     var arr: array of Char);
{
Copies a Pascal String to a Char array. The
array is padded with blanks.
}
var
  i:     Word;
begin
{Fill the array with spaces in case the
   string is shorter than the array.}
for i := 0 to High(arr) do arr[i] := ' ';
{Copy the string to the array.}
for i := 1 to Length(str) do arr[i - 1] := str[i];
end;
```

Notice the use of an open array parameter for the array as described in Chapter 9. This lets you pass an array of any size. The first for loop copies the contents of the string to the array. The subscript of the array is computed as [i - 1] because the subscript of an open array formal parameter is always zero based regardless of how the actual parameter is defined. The second for loop fills the remainder of the array elements with spaces.

The following for loop,

```
for i := 1 to 100 do
  BlockWrite(addrFile, buff, MaxRecs, count);
```

Writes the buffer to disk 100 times to create the 10,000 record test file. The Read button's click method, shown below, is similar except that it dynamically allocates a 500 record buffer on the heap.

```
procedure TForm1.ReadBtnClick(Sender: TObject);
const
  MaxRecs = 500;
type
  Tbuff =        array[1..MaxRecs] of TAddress;
var
  buff:          ^Tbuff;
  addrFile:      File;
  total,
  count:         Word;
begin
  try
    New(buff);
  except
    on EOutOfMemory do Exit;
  end;
  try
    Assign(addrFile, 'addr.dat');
    Reset(addrFile, SizeOf(TAddress));
    {Read the file MacRecs records at a time.}
    total := 0;
    repeat
      count := 0;
      BlockRead(addrFile, buff^, MaxRecs, count);
      total := total + count;
    until count = 0;
    System.Close(addrFile);
    ReadCount.Caption := IntToStr(total);
  finally
    Dispose(buff);
  end;
end;
```

Start by looking at the declarations in this procedure, particularly the following statements.

```
const
  MaxRecs = 500;
type
  Tbuff =        array[1..MaxRecs] of TAddress;
var
  buff:          ^Tbuff;
```

Here the constant MaxRecs is set to 500 and a type, Tbuff, is declared as an array of 500 TAddress records. The pointer variable, buff, is declared as a pointer to type TBuff. Since each TAddress record is 100 bytes this array will consume 50k bytes of memory. Because the data segment is limited to a total of 64k you need to allocate this large array on the heap by calling the New procedure.

The remaining code is enclosed in a try/finally block to ensure that the Dispose procedure will be called to release the memory allocated by New if an exception (runtime error) occurs.

The next two lines open the file and the repeat loop reads 500 records at a time until it reaches the end of file. The repeat loop also counts the number of records read in the variable total. After the file has been read the statement

```
ReadCount.Caption := IntToStr(total);
```

displays the number of records in the label component, ReadCount.

Working with Fixed-Length Text Files

While fixed-length files on mainframes and minicomputers do not have record delimiters, that is usually not the case in the PC world. Many PC programs that produce fixed-length files append a carriage return/line feed pair to the end of each record so that the files are actually text files even though each record has a fixed length.

However, you can still read or write the file as either a typed or untyped file, and you will probably want to because both typed and untyped file processing is faster than text file processing. The FIXTEXT.DPR project is identical to FAST.DPR except that it creates a text file. Here is the revised type declaration for the record.

```
type
  TAddress = record
    name:        array[1..35] of Char;
    addr:        array[1..35] of Char;
    city:        array[1..18] of Char;
```

```
  state:       array[1..2] of Char;
  zip:         array[1..10] of Char;
  delimiter:   array[1..2] of Char;
end;
```

The only change is to add the two-character array named <u>delimiter</u> to the end of the record to hold the carriage return and line feed. The only other change is in Create button's click method shown below.

```
procedure TForm1.CreateBtnClick(Sender: TObject);
const
  MaxRecs = 100;
var
  buff:       array[1..MaxRecs] of TAddress;
  addrFile:   File;
  i, count:   Word;
begin
  Assign(addrFile, 'addr.dat');
  Rewrite(addrFile, SizeOf(TAddress));
  {Put 100 records into the buffer.}
  for i := 1 to MaxRecs do
    with buff[i] do
    begin
      PasToArray('John Doe', name);
      PasToArray('123 East Main Street', addr);
      PasToArray('New York', city);
      PasToArray('NY', state);
      PasToArray('55555-5555', zip);
      delimiter[1] := #13;
      delimiter[2] := #10;
    end;
    {Write 100 buffers (10,000 records.}
    for i := 1 to 100 do
      BlockWrite(addrFile, buff, MaxRecs, count);
    System.Close(addrFile);
end;
```

Here the two lines

```
delimiter[1] := #13;
delimiter[2] := #10;
```

have been added to assign the carriage return character, ASCII 13, and the line feed character, ASCII 10, to the two elements of the delimiter array at the end of each record. If you have an editor that can read large files take a look at ADDRESS.DAT after you run this program and you will see that each record appears as a separate line.

251

Working with .INI Files

Most Windows programs, like Windows itself, use .INI files to save various settings between sessions and initialize them again the next time you run the program. You can easily use .INI files in your programs in the same way because Delphi includes a special object, TIniFile, with all of the features you need. Figure 11.5 shows the form for the INI.DPR project which creates and reads TEST.INI in your Windows directory. Figure 11.6 shows the contents of TEST.INI.

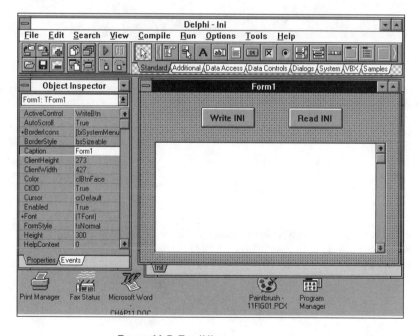

FIGURE 11.5 THE INI FILE TEST PROGRAM.

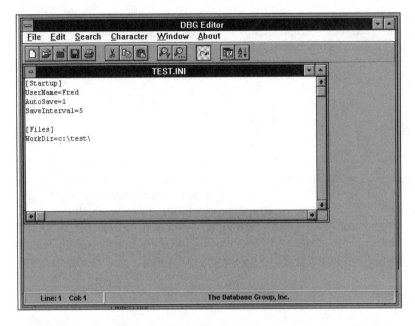

FIGURE 11.6 THE **TEST.INI** FILE.

The code that creates TEST.INI is in the Create button's click procedure and is shown below.

```
procedure TForm1.WriteBtnClick(Sender: TObject);
var
  TestIni:    TIniFile;
begin
  TestIni := TIniFile.Create('test.ini');
  with TestIni do
  begin
    WriteString('Startup','UserName','Fred');
    WriteBool('Startup','AutoSave',True);
    WriteInteger('Startup','SaveInterval',5);
    WriteString('Files','WorkDir','c:\test\');
    Free;
  end;
end;
```

This code declares TestIni as an instance of TIniFile and opens the file by calling its constructor in the statement:

```
TestIni := TIniFile.Create('test.ini');
```

The following lines write values to the INI file by calling the WriteString, WriteBool and WriteInteger methods of TIniFile. Each of these methods takes three parameters. The first is the section name that will contain the value, the second is the identifier that appears on the left side of the equal sign, and the third parameter is the value that appears on the right of the equal sign. WriteString and WriteInteger store the values you would expect in the INI file. WriteBool puts a zero in the file if the Boolean value is False and a one if the Boolean value is True. The last line of code calls TIniFile's Free method to destroy the object and release its memory.

The Read button reads the values from the INI file and displays them in the memo control. Here is the code from the Read button's click procedure.

```
procedure TForm1.ReadBtnClick(Sender: TObject);
var
  TestIni:    TIniFile;
  workDir,
  uName:      String[80];
  autoSave:   Boolean;
  saveInt:    Integer;
  mainTitle:  String[48];
begin
  TestIni := TIniFile.Create('test.ini');
  with TestIni do
  begin
    uName := ReadString('Startup','UserName','');
    autoSave := ReadBool('Startup','AutoSave',False);
    saveInt := ReadInteger('Startup','SaveInterval',0);
    workDir := ReadString('Files','WorkDir','c:\');
    mainTitle := ReadString('Files','Title','INI Test');
    Free;
  end;
  with Memo1 do
  begin
    Clear;
    Lines.Add(uName);
    if autoSave then
      Lines.Add('True')
    else
      Lines.Add('False');
    Lines.Add(IntToStr(saveInt));
    Lines.Add(workDir);
    Lines.Add(mainTitle);
  end;
end;
```

The first line creates the TIniFile instance just as before. The code in the first with block reads the values from TEST.INI and the code in the second with displays the values in the memo control.

The values are read by calling the ReadString, ReadBool, and ReadInteger methods. Like their write counterparts these methods take three parameters and like the write methods the first two are the section and identifier to read. However the third parameter is the default value to return if there is no corresponding entry in the INI file. The statement

```
mainTitle := ReadString('Files','Title','INI Test');
```

has no entry in the file so the value 'INI Test' is returned. Figure 11.7 shows the values displayed by clicking the read button.

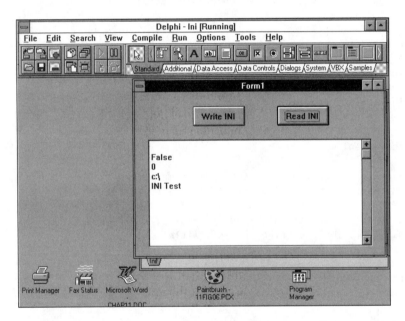

FIGURE 11.7 THE .INI FILE VALUES.

Working with Objects that Use Files

Now that you have seen the rich set of features that Pascal provides to work with files, it is time to point out that you frequently do not need to write file access code in Delphi. Why? The answer is that all of the following objects in Delphi have their own built-in methods for reading data from and writing data to files. These methods are LoadFromFile and SaveToFile.

- TBitmap
- TGraphic
- TIcon
- TMemoryStream
- TMetaFile
- TPicture
- TStringList
- TString

In addition, the following components also have their own methods for file I/O.

- TOLEContainer
- TOutline

However, this list tells only part of the story because all of the components that include any of the objects above also include their file I/O routines. For example, the lines in a Memo component are actually a TStringList object so you can load the memo by calling LoadFromFile and save the memo's contents by calling SaveToFile. Figure 11.8 shows the form from the TSTRING.DPR project.

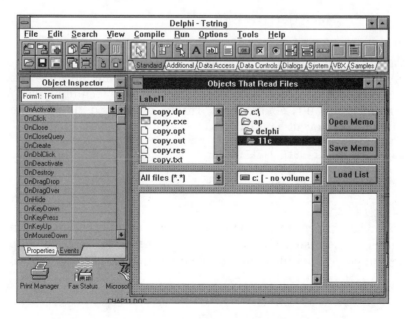

FIGURE 11.8 THE FORM FROM **TSTRING.DPR**

The following code is from the Load Memo button's click procedure and shows how the text from the file is loaded into the Memo component on the form.

256

```
procedure TForm1.OpenBtnClick(Sender: TObject);
begin
  {Get the directory path from the file list.}
  filePath := FileListBox1.Directory;
  {If the path does not end with \ add one.}
  if filePath[Length(filePath)] <> '\' then
    filePath := filePath + '\';
  {Add the file name to the path.}
  filePath := filePath + FileListBox1.FileName;
  {Empty the memo and read the file.}
  Memo1.Lines.Clear;
  Memo1.Lines.LoadFromFile(filePath);
end;
```

This is the same code you saw earlier in the discussion of text file processing, except for the last line which calls the LoadFromFile method of the memo's Lines property to read the contents of the text file into the memo. The following code is from the Save Memo button's click procedure.

```
procedure TForm1.SaveBtnClick(Sender: TObject);
begin
  Memo1.Lines.SaveToFile(filePath);
end;
```

Here a call to the SaveToFile method saves the contents of the memo. You can see these methods in action by running the program, opening a text file, making some changes, and saving the file. The same technique works with TList and TComboBox components. The following code is from the Load List button's click event handler.

```
procedure TForm1.LoadBtnClick(Sender: TObject);
begin
  ListBox1.Items.LoadFromFile('months.txt');
end;
```

You can also perform this same type of string manipulation in your code behind the scenes using TStringList objects. The following code is from the click event handler for the button in the project UPPER.DPR.

```
procedure TForm1.UpperBtnClick(Sender: TObject);
var
```

```
  UpList:      TStringList;
  i:           Word;
begin
  UpList := TStringList.Create;
  UpList.LoadFromFile('upper.txt');
  for i := 0 to UpList.Count - 1 do
    UpList[i] := UpperCase(UpList[i]);
  UpList.Sorted := True;
  UpList.SaveToFile('upper.txt');
  UpList.Free;
end;
```

This code declares an instance of TStringList called UpList and begins by calling its constructor in the statement:

```
UpList := TStringList.Create;
```

Next the code loads the contents of the text file UPPER.TXT into the string list then uses a for loop to iterate through the list and convert each string in the list to upper case. The line

```
UpList.Sorted := True;
```

sets the string list's Sorted property to True which causes the string list to sort itself. The call to SaveToFile saves the uppercase text back to UPPER.TXT. The last statement in this code

```
UpList.Free;
```

is perhaps the most important. Remember that when you are done with the object you must always call an object's destructor to release the memory it uses.

Notice that the for loop uses the string list's Count property to determine the number of strings in the list and access each string like an element in an array. Since the first string in a string list always has an index of zero the last string's index is always Count-1.

Summary

With the features described in this chapter you should be able to handle any sequential file access problem you encounter whether it is importing a file from a mainframe or managing an INI file for your application. You can even create your own file objects.

CHAPTER 12

Units

If you are new to ObjectPascal, you might scratch your head and be slightly confused when you create your first Delphi application and save your project. As part of saving a project, Delphi asks you what name you want to give to UNIT1.PAS. And you might have asked yourself: 'Exactly what is a unit?'

A *unit* is a file which contains ObjectPascal code. All the code you write in Delphi is stored in units. All the code for Delphi itself, written in ObjectPascal, is also stored in units. Whenever you create a new form, Delphi automatically creates a unit just for that form. As you design the new form and add controls, Delphi makes sure that all the appropriate Delphi units are automatically linked in.

Since Delphi creates a unit for each form, units serve to group like procedures together in one package. If you need to create units without forms (nearly all of the units internal to Delphi are units without forms!), it is a good idea to package like procedures and functions together. This makes your application and your code more understandable.

Clearly Delphi is handling a lot of unit management for you. Many developers will create all sorts of applications without getting too deep into units. However, if your applications get complex you will need to understand how to work with units.

All of the techniques demonstrated in this chapter are on the accompanying code disk. The project name is UNITS.DPR.

Structure of a Unit

In order to understand units, you need to understand their structure. A unit has the following sections:

- Heading
- Interface
- Implementation
- Initialization

The heading identifies the unit's name. The interface identifies what items in the unit are public. The implementation section holds the code for the unit and the initialization section is designed to initialize any data structures the first time the unit is opened.

Unit Heading

The unit heading is short and sweet. It includes the keyword **unit** followed by the unit name. The unit name must be unique and should not collide with any other identifiers, including object names, variable names, types, functions, procedures, or other keywords. The unit name can be of any length but Delphi considers only the first 63 characters as significant. In addition, the unit name does not have to match the .PAS file name which contains it. It is a good programming practice to keep the .PAS file name and the unit name the same or nearly the same.

Interface Part

The interface part serves two purposes. It lists all the items in the unit that other units can see and it lists all the other units that it needs to see. The interface part states what resources the unit has to offer the outside world, and what resources it needs from the outside world.

The very first keyword, which is optional, that can appear after the interface keyword, is the **uses** clause. The uses clause identifies what other resources the current unit needs. Each unit is listed with a comma separating them:

```
Unit Unit1;

interface

uses Unit2, Unit3;
```

In this example, Unit1 needs items from Unit2 and Unit3. What follows the uses clause, if one is needed, is a listing of items visible to other units. Any variables, types, constants, procedures, or functions declared in the interface part are available to other units for use.

If any declarations in your interface section require resources in other units, then those units must be referenced in the interface section's uses clause. For example, if you create a class which is a subclass of TComponent, you will need to use the Classes unit so that the compiler can understand how to construct a subclass in your unit. An interface part can contain var, const, and type clauses, but it cannot contain the body of a function or procedure.

Code Listing 12.1 shows an example interface part.

LISTING 12.1 AN INTERFACE PART

```
unit Sample;

interface

Var
   UserLoggedIn : String;

function GetAppName: String;
function GetAppDate: String;
```

In Listing 12.1, because no uses clause exists, the interface section requires nothing from other units. It makes available to other units, however, the variable UserLoggedIn, and the functions GetAppName, and GetAppDate. The code which implements these functions will be contained in the "Implementation Part," which follows.

Implementation Part

The guts of what a unit does is contained within the implementation part. All the code needed to implement what the interface part says will be implemented needs to be contained here.

The implementation part can also contain a uses clause, too. In many ways, it is always preferable to place the other units referenced in the implementation part's uses clause. If the uses clause is in the implementation part, then only the code in the implementation part can access the unit. The implementation part serves to hide important pieces of information from other units. This protects the implementation of the unit. Other units can access the resources in unit only through the 'published interface' spelled out in the interface section.

> When designing units and objects *hide everything you possibly can* by placing as many features as you can in the implementation section or by making as much as possible of your object, private or protected. Encapsulation (information hiding) is one of the most powerful tools to help you write and maintain robust code.

T I P

The implementation part can contain variables, types, constants, and of course, the body of functions and procedures. Listing 12.2 shows an example implementation section for Listing 12.1.

LISTING 12.2 AN IMPLEMENTATION PART

```
implementation
Const
    ApplicationName = 'Sample unit';
    ApplicationDate = '1/10/95';

function GetAppName;
begin
    GetAppName:=ApplicationName;
end;

function GetAppDate;
begin
    GetAppDate:=ApplicationDate;
end;
```

Initialization Part

The initialization part serves to initialize any variables or data structures within the unit. The initialization part is executed once and only once: the first time the unit is accessed as part of another unit's uses clase.

Listing 12.3 shows a sample initialization part for Listing 12.1.

LISTING 12.3 AN INITIALIZATION PART

```
initialization
    UserLoggedIn :='Test User';
end.
```

The code in listing 12.3 simply initializes a global variable, UserLoggedIn. Listing 12.4 shows the entire unit from listings 12.1, 12.2, and 12.3.

LISTING 12.4 A COMPLETE UNIT

```
unit Sample;

interface

Var
   UserLoggedIn : String;

function GetAppName: String;
function GetAppDate: String;

implementation
Const
   ApplicationName = 'Sample unit';
   ApplicationDate = '1/10/95';

function GetAppName;
begin
   GetAppName:=ApplicationName;
end;

function GetAppDate;
begin
   GetAppDate:=ApplicationDate;
end;

initialization
   UserLoggedIn :='Test User';
end.
```

Circular Unit References

It is possible to get yourself in a catch-22 situation with units. If unit A requires resources from Unit B and Unit B requires resources in Unit A, *and each unit refers to the other in the interface part uses clause*, you will not be able to compile your code. You will get a circular unit reference error. You can solve this problem by moving one or both of the unit references from the interface part to the implementation part.

Two units that refer to each other, either through the implementation or the interface part, are mutually dependent. Delphi can successfully compile two units mutually dependent via their implementation part's uses clause, but *not* through their interface part. While mutually dependent units are necessary in certain circumstances, this should be the exception rather than the rule. It is harder to understand and debug mutually dependent units.

Implementing Global Variables

One of the common things that many applications need is an area of global memory which different parts of the application can share. Typically, global memory is used to hold information which is not appropriate to store in, or repeatedly read from a table or file either for performance reasons, or because the information does not need to persist between sessions of the application. Global data can include:

- The name of the person logged into the application.
- Application version information.
- Security rights to different parts of the application, which may be stored in a table or an INI file.
- Configuration settings, stored in a table or an INI file, which affect how the application should start up.

While many Windows applications use INI files to hold this information, database developers are often more comfortable using system tables in the database environment to hold this data. Making the frequently used pieces of information into global variables makes accessing the information much quicker.

Creating a unit specifically for holding global information makes sharing data easy. Each unit that needs to access the global data simply needs to reference the unit in a uses clause. Constructing the global unit is relatively straightforward and you have some design options to consider.

You can store the global information in a series of variables or a record structure. Or you can combine the global variables and the routines which setup and retrieve those values into an object. For the object-oriented programming novice, creating a non-object-oriented global unit would be easier. But since Delphi is an object-oriented tool, creating an object-oriented version of a global variable object will enhance the object's robustness by letting you clearly specify the private parts to your object and its published interface.

Code listing 12.5 shows a sample global unit (called Globals in GLOB-ALS.PAS) and global object (called AppGlobals). The Globals unit is designed to hold information about an application version number, the name of the user who owns the application, an internal build number (which can be maintained independent of the external version number), and copyright information. Some of this information is stored in a table (called SYSCFG.DB) so that it can be maintained dynamically and some of the information is stored in constants so that it can be maintained by changing the source code. The information contained within the AppGlobals object is designed to be read when the application is initialized and shared by any other unit in the application.

LISTING 12.5 GLOBALS UNIT

```
unit Globals;
interface
uses DBTables,Classes;

type
   {create a subclass to hold global info}
   {TGlobalComponent is the ancestor of TApplication}
   TAppGlobals = Class(TGlobalComponent)
     private
        {fields, methods not visible to others}
        FOwner : String;
        FVersion : String;
        FName : String;
        FConfigTable : String;
        FConfigDb : String;
        ProfileTable : TTable;
        function GetConfigTable: String;
        procedure SetConfigTable(const TableName: String);
        function GetConfigDb: String;
        procedure SetConfigDb(const Db: String);
        function GetVersion: String;
        function GetName: String;
        function GetOwner: String;
        function GetBuild: String;
        function GetCopyright: String;
     protected
     public
        Constructor Create;
          Procedure ReadCfg;
     published
        property Version: String read GetVersion;
        property Name: String read GetName;
        property Owner: String read GetOwner;
        property Build: String read GetBuild;
```

```
        property Copyright: String read GetCopyright;
        property ConfigTable : String read GetConfigTable
                                   write SetConfigTable;
        property ConfigDb : String read GetConfigDb
                                   write SetConfigDb;
    end;

Var
  {global variable}
  AppGlobals : TAppGlobals;

implementation
const
    {constants used by some of the properties}
    CCopyright = 'Copyright @ 1995, The Developer';
    CBuild = '1.50b';

constructor TAppGlobals.Create;
begin
    {execute the ancestor constructor}
    inherited Create(nil);
    {assign the config table name and database}
    FConfigTable:='SYSCFG.DB';
    FConfigDb:='';
    {create the TTable object using self as the owner
     with self as the owner, when the owner is destroyed
     ProfileTable will be destroyed}
    ProfileTable := TTable.Create(self);
    {set the tablename property}
    ProfileTable.TableName := FConfigTable;
    {if a database name is given, use it}
    if FConfigDb <> '' then
        ProfileTable.DatabaseName := FConfigDb;

    {read the config table settings}
    ReadCfg;

end;

procedure TAppGlobals.ReadCfg;
begin
    {Open the profile table}
    ProfileTable.Open;
    {store the field values into the object fields}
    FOwner := ProfileTable.FieldByName('Owner_name').AsString;
    FVersion := ProfileTable.FieldByName('Version_number').AsString;
```

```
    FName := ProfileTable.FieldByName('Application_name').AsString;
    {close the profile table}
    ProfileTable.close;
end;

function TAppGlobals.GetVersion;
begin
    GetVersion:=FVersion;
end;

function TAppGlobals.GetBuild;
begin
    GetBuild:=CBuild;
end;

function TAppGlobals.GetName;
begin
    GetName:=FName;
end;

function TAppGlobals.GetOwner;
begin
  GetOwner:=FOwner;
end;

function TAppGlobals.GetCopyright;
begin
    GetCopyright:=CCopyright;
end;

function TAppGlobals.GetConfigTable;
begin
    GetConfigTable:=FConfigTable;
end;

procedure TAppGlobals.SetConfigTable(const TableName: String);
begin
    FConfigTable := TableName;
end;

function TAppGlobals.GetConfigDb;
begin
    GetConfigDb:=FConfigDb;
end;

procedure TAppGlobals.SetConfigDb(const Db: String);
```

```
begin
   FConfigDb := Db;
end;
```

```
initialization
   AppGlobals:= TAppGlobals.Create;
end.
```

The Globals unit requires the services of the DBTables and the Classes units. The DBTables unit lets Globals create a TTable object. The TTable object is a database object which lets you access tables. This object is discussed fully in Chapters 16, "Delphi Database Controls" and Chapter 17, "Connecting Controls to Databases," so you do not have to worry about it here. Globals needs a TTable object to access the SYSCFG.DB table. The Classes unit lets Globals declare TAppGlobals as a subclass of another object, TGlobalComponent.

GLOBALS.PAS not only demonstrates how to create a unit with global information, it also shows you how to create an object within the framework of existing objects in Delphi. The TAppGlobals type is declared as a subtype of TGlobalComponent. The reason for this is that a global unit that is initialized when the application starts has a lot in common with the TApplication component. However, it is different enough that we need to make it a descendant from TApplication's parent class: TGlobalComponent. Since TAppGlobals is also a descendant from TComponent, it can contain a published interface with properties that might be useful in future, if the class becomes a design component. Published properties are available in design mode.

The TAppGlobals type has several properties:

- Version
- Name
- Owner
- Build
- Copyright
- ConfigTable
- ConfigDb

These properties are set and retrieved using the functions and procedures listed immediately after the write and read keywords in the property description. These properties are also available to all client units at runtime. *The client units can be totally unaware of exactly how the properties are stored.* This is a big benefit of object-oriented programming. If you need to change the internal representation of a property, you do not have to change the published interface to that property. Therefore you do not have to modify the code in all the client units.

The Globals unit declares a variable, AppGlobals, which is initialized by the following line of code in the unit's initialization part:

```
AppGlobals:= TAppGlobals.Create;
```

This line of code calls the Create constructor method and passes back a pointer to the object for the AppGlobals variable. Remember, that object variables are actually pointers to objects. The Delphi compiler automatically dereferences object variables for you.

The AppGlobals constructor method goes about the hard word of creating a TTable object (ProfileTable), assigning it a database name (if one is provided) and a table name. It then opens the profile table and retrieves the information about the application stored in the table.

In addition to properties to change the default configuration table and database names, the TAppGlobals type contains a procedure to re-read the configuration table and load new values. This is useful if your application lets the user change the contents of the table and you want the global variable values refreshed immediately after a change.

Accessing the Globals unit is easy. The client unit needs to list Globals in its uses clause, preferably in the implementation section. Once there, it can freely reference the AppGlobals object and its properties. Figure 12.1 shows a two client forms. The main form accesses some of the information contained in the AppGlobals object, the subform accesses some more information.

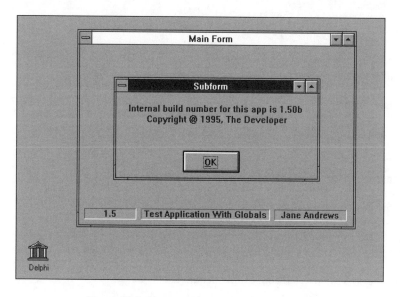

FIGURE 12.1 FORMS WHICH USE THE GLOBALS UNIT.

The code on the main form's unit is shown in Listing 12.6.

LISTING 12.6 MAINF UNIT

```
unit Mainf;

interface

uses
  SysUtils, WinTypes, WinProcs, Messages, Classes, Graphics, Controls,
  Forms, Dialogs, StdCtrls, DB, DBTables;

type
  TMainForm = class(TForm)
    AppName: TPanel;
    Who: TPanel;
    Version: TPanel;
    Button1: TButton;
    RefreshButton: TButton;
    procedure FormCreate(Sender: TObject);
    procedure Button1Click(Sender: TObject);
    procedure RefreshButtonClick(Sender: TObject);
  private
    { Private declarations }
  public
    { Public declarations }
  end;

var
  MainForm: TMainForm;

implementation
uses Globals,Subf;
{$R *.DFM}


procedure TMainForm.FormCreate(Sender: TObject);
begin
  Version.Caption:=AppGlobals.Version;
  AppName.Caption:=AppGlobals.Name;
  Who.Caption:=AppGlobals.Owner;
end;

procedure TMainForm.Button1Click(Sender: TObject);
begin
```

```
SubForm.showModal;
SubForm.hide;
end;

procedure TMainForm.RefreshButtonClick(Sender: TObject);
begin
   AppGlobals.ReadCfg;
end;

end.
```

Notice that the implementation part's uses clause lists the Globals unit and the Subform unit. The Globals unit is there so that it can reference the AppGlobals variable in TMainForm.Create() and in the Refresh Button's click event. The Refresh button is there to demonstrate calling one of the AppGlobal variable's procedures. The Subform unit is listed in the uses clause so that the main form can display the subform when the user presses the Subform button.

Listing 12.7 shows the Subform unit's code.

LISTING 12.7 SUBF UNIT

```
unit Subf;

interface

uses
  SysUtils, WinTypes, WinProcs, Messages, Classes, Graphics, Controls,
  Forms, Dialogs, StdCtrls;

type
  TSubForm = class(TForm)
    MessageArea: TLabel;
    Button1: TButton;
    procedure FormActivate(Sender: TObject);
  private
    { Private declarations }
  public
    { Public declarations }
  end;

var
  SubForm: TSubForm;
```

```
implementation
uses Globals;
{$R *.DFM}


procedure TSubForm.FormActivate(Sender: TObject);
begin
MessageArea.Caption:='Internal build number for this app is '+
                 AppGlobals.Build+' '+
                 AppGlobals.Copyright;

end;

end.
```

The subform also lists the Globals unit in its implementation part's uses clause. As you can see, accessing global information in another unit is very easy to do, once you set up the globals unit properly.

Summary

To those unfamiliar with ObjectPascal, units can seem confusing and difficult. They are not. They are actually quite easy to work with and fairly easy to understand. Units provide another layer of encapsulation which lets you write more reliable and more maintainable applications. Understanding units is essential if you want to take full advantage of the Delphi environment, especially if you want to design your own reusable components that can appear on the component palette in design mode. In fact, one of the best ways to learn about units is to carefully read through the Delphi source code for all the built-in units.

CHAPTER 13

Dynamic Link Libraries

Dynamic link libraries, DLLs for short, let several Windows programs share the same code when they are running simultaneously. Delphi enables you to write DLLs that you can use in your own applications, or with any Windows application that can call procedures and functions in a DLL.

This chapter explores the structure of a DLLs and how to create them in Delphi. It also examines the advantages and disadvantages of using DLLs and discusses exactly when you should use them.

Understanding DLLs

A DLL is similar to a Pascal unit in many ways. It contains functions, procedures, types, constants, variables, and objects. However, the way DLLs are used is very different.

Units are said to be statically linked. That means that when you compile your program the unit is linked into, and becomes part of the executable program file. If you run two copies of your program at the same time under Windows then two separate copies of the code in the unit will be in memory at the same time. When your program calls a procedure or function in the unit it knows the memory address where the procedure is located because the linker determined the address when it linked the unit into your program.

DLLs use a different process called *dynamic linking*. When you create a DLL it is compiled and linked into a file with a .DLL extension. When you write a program that uses the procedures and functions in a DLL the DLL does not have to be present, or even exist, when you compile and link your program. However, the DLL must be present when you run your program. When your program calls a procedure or function in a DLL, Windows looks to see if the DLL is already in memory. If not, Windows loads it. Then Windows determines the address of the procedure or function you are calling and execution begins.

If a second program calls a procedure or function in the same DLL it is not loaded again. Instead its use count is incremented. When a program that is using a DLL terminates, the DLLs use count is decremented. When the use count reaches zero Windows unloads the DLL. The advantage is that many programs can share a single copy of the code in the DLL which conserves memory.

Deciding When to Use DLLs

There are three cases when you should use a DLL instead of a unit. The first is when you get a DLL from an outside source and you want to use the code it contains. There are numerous commercial DLLs that you can use to add features to your programs much more easily and economically than if you had to write the code yourself. For example you can purchase communications DLLs that will let your program send and receive files by modem or acquire data from laboratory instruments that have an RS-232 interface. There are also DLLs that you can use to compress files to Zip format to save disk space or data transmission time. The list is almost endless.

You are more likely to find the functionality you want in a DLL than in a Pascal unit because DLLs are a Windows standard, while units are unique to Borland Pascal. You can write a DLL in many different languages and any other language or program that can call functions in a DLL can use it.

The second situation when you should use a DLL is when you are writing an application that consists of several programs that need to share procedures and functions, and users may run more than one of these programs at the same time. In this case a DLL is a better choice than a unit because only one copy of the code will need to be in memory, which saves memory, and can reduce swapping, and improve performance.

The third situation where a DLL is the right choice is when you are writing code in Delphi that will be used by someone programming in another language. Since DLLs are a Windows standard they can be used by most Windows development environments.

This discussion of when to use DLLs has also pointed out their advantages. What are the disadvantages? The first is that while units can share procedures, functions, types, constants, variables, and objects DLLs can only share procedures and functions. If you need to get the value of a variable in a DLL you can do it by calling a function in the DLL that returns the variables value. You can also set the value of a variable in a DLL by calling a procedure in the DLL that takes the value as a parameter and assigns it to the variable.

Another potential problem with DLLs is that any files they open belong to the application that called the DLL. That means that any global file variable in a DLL can become invalid at any time if the application that called the DLL procedure that opened the file terminates. Therefore, you should either open and close files within a single procedure or function or pass the file variable as a parameter to the DLL procedure or function, you are calling, and make the caller responsible for opening and closing the file.

In some languages when you allocate global memory blocks the memory blocks belong to the calling application just as file variables do and they can become invalid if the calling application terminates. However, in Delphi global memory allocated by calling the New or GetMem procedures is allocated in such a way that the memory belongs to the DLL and will only be deallocated if you explicitly deallocate them in your code or when Windows unloads the DLL.

Creating DLLs

The basic structure of a DLL is very similar to a Pascal program except that it begins with the key word library as shown below.

```
library MyLib;

uses
  Testu;

exports

begin
end.
```

You can build a DLL using one or more units just as you can with a program. Just include the units your DLL uses in the uses clause.

Your global constant, type and variable declarations follow the uses clause. These constant type and variable declarations are global to the DLL but they cannot be seen by any program that uses the DLL. The exports section contains a list of all of the procedures and functions that you want programs that use the DLL to have access to. You can include procedures and functions in the DLL that are not listed in the exports block but they can only be called from within the DLL. The begin end block is where you put the initialization code for the DLL.

The best way to understand writing and using DLLs is to look at examples. In Chapter 9 the Strings project developed five procedures and functions for manipulating Pascal strings. This chapter will put those strings into a DLL and modify the project, STRINGD.DPR, to use the DLL. The first few examples will use two of the functions, LTrim and RTrim, to keep the length of the code listings short. The final example will use all five routines.

A DLL in a Single File

Creating a DLL in Delphi is a bit complicated in the beginning because Delphi assumes that each time you start a new project it will involve forms. The result is that a blank Delphi project consists of a project file, a form, and a unit for the form. For a simple DLL all you need is the project file and an empty unit file.

To create a DLL first create a new project. Next, close the windows that contain the form and the forms unit. When you are asked if you want to save the changes choose **No**. Now select **File | New Unit** from the menu and save the empty unit by selecting **File | Save As**. While you are at it you may as well save the project too. The unit should now look like Figure 13.1.

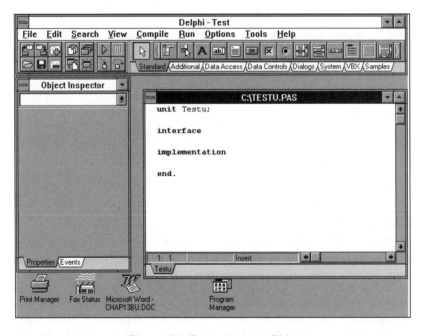

FIGURE 13.1 EMPTY UNIT FOR A DLL.

Now that you have created and saved this empty unit you can close its window. You will not need to change it again. The only reason for this empty unit is that the Delphi IDE requires a uses clause in all project files. Using an empty unit keeps the DLL as small as possible.

The next step is to switch to the project file which should look like Figure 13.2.

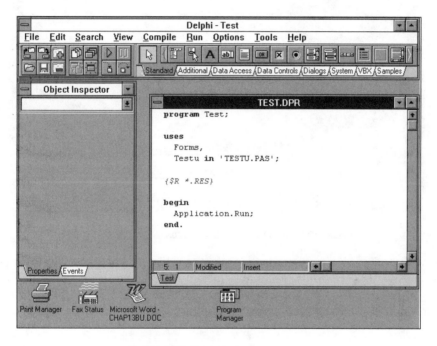

FIGURE 13.2 THE DEFAULT PROJECT FILE.

To turn the project file into a DLL make the following changes. When you are done the project file should look like Figure 13.3.

1. Change the key word program in the first line to library.
2. Remove the Forms unit from the uses clause.
3. Delete the {$R *.RES} compiler directive if your DLL does not use any resources.
4. Delete the Application.Run call in the begin end block.
5. Add the exports keyword above the begin end block.

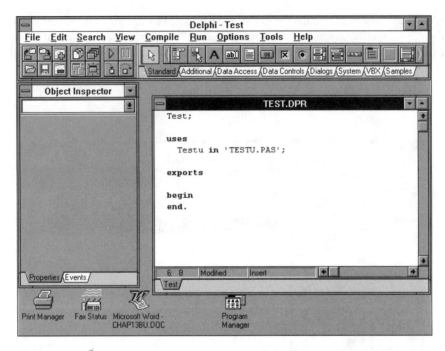

FIGURE 13.3 THE PROJECT FILE AFTER CONVERSION TO A DLL.

Now that you have converted the project to a library you can compile it just as you would any other program. The only difference is that the result of compiling is a .DLL file instead of a .EXE. The next step is to add the procedures and functions to the project file to produce the code shown below.

```
library Strp;

uses
  Strpu in 'STRPU.PAS';

function LTrim(const s: String): String; export;
{
Remove leading whitespace from a string.
Whitespace is defined as blanks or tabs.
}
var
  i:      Word;

begin
  i := 1;
  {Skip all leading whitespace characters.}
```

```
  while (s[i] in [' ', #9]) and
        (i <= Length(s)) do Inc(i);
  {Return the rest of the string.}
  LTrim := copy(s, i, 255);
end;

function RTrim(const s: String): String; export;
{
Remove trailing whitespace from a string.
Whitespace is defined as blank, tab,
carriage return, line feed or form feed.
}
var
  i:        Word;

begin
  i := Length(s);
  {Skip all trailing whitespace characters.}
  while (s[i] in [' ', #9, #10, #12, #13]) and
        (i > 0) do Dec(i);
  {Return the rest of the string.}
  RTrim := copy(s, 1, i);
end;

exports
  LTrim index 1,
  RTrim index 2;

begin
end.
```

279

The Export Procedure Directive

The RTrim and LTrim functions in the code above are identical to the functions described in Chapter 9 with one exception. The declaration of every procedure or function in a DLL that will be called from outside the DLL must include the Export directive. The function declaration for LTrim is

```
function LTrim(const s: String): String; export;
```

The addition of the export key word at the end of the function declaration makes it possible to export the function. When the compiler sees the export key word it knows that it must use the far call model for this function so that it can be called from any other code segment no matter where in memory the calling code is located. It also tells the compiler to generate the special entry and exit code required by routines in a DLL.

Using the export procedure directive in the procedure or function declaration does not make the procedure or function accessible from outside the DLL. It only makes it possible to make the routine available. To make a procedure or function available to programs that use the DLL you must list it in the exports clause.

The Exports Clause

You can have one or more exports clauses in your DLL. Each exports clause can list one or more procedures or functions that you want to make available to programs that use the DLL. There are just two rules that govern the location and content of the exports clause.

1. The procedure or function declaration must be before the exports clause.
2. The declaration for the procedures or functions in the exports clause must contain the export directive discussed in the last section.

The following exports clause exports the LTrim and RTrim functions and assigns an index number to each. Note that the list of procedures and functions in the exports clause is comma separated. The only semicolon appears at the end of the list.

```
exports
  LTrim index 1,
  RTrim index 2;
```

The index number must be an integer in the range of 1 through 32,767. When you use a function or procedure from a DLL in your program identifying it by its index number allows Windows to call it faster.

Assign index numbers to all of your DLL procedures and functions so you can take advantage of the faster calls generated by identifying your DLL routines by number in your programs.

In addition to specifying an index number you can also specify a name in the exports clause. The following code shows the same exports clause with new names specified for LTrim and RTrim.

```
exports
  LTrim index 1 name 'LeftTrim',
  RTrim index 2 name 'RightTrim';
```

This feature lets you assign a different name for calling programs to use for any of the routines in your DLL.

The last option in an exports entry is the resident keyword. If a program that uses a DLL calls the procedures and functions in the DLL by name then Windows must look up the name in the DLLs names list to find the routines index before it can complete the call. That is why calling by index is faster. If you are going to call DLL routines by name the exports entry for those routines should include the resident keyword. This tells Windows to keep the names list in memory which makes calls by name much faster than they would otherwise be. The following shows the exports clause with the resident keyword.

```
exports
  LTrim index 1 name 'LeftTrim' resident,
  RTrim index 2 name 'RightTrim' resident;
```

TIP

Always use the resident keyword for procedures and functions that will be imported and called by name to make the calls faster.

Initialization and Exit Code

Any code you place in the begin end block of your DLL is executed once when the library is first loaded. The main use for initialization code is to assign initial values to global variables in the library. The first time a program calls a procedure or function in the DLL, Windows will load the DLL into memory and the initialization code will run. When other programs make calls to routines in the DLL the DLLs use count is incremented but the initialization code does not run again.

You can use the variable ExitCode, which is defined for you in the System unit, to handle errors that occur in your DLL startup code. By default ExitCode is set to 1 which indicates that the DLL was successfully loaded. If an error occurs in your initialization code set ExitCode to zero. This tells Windows to unload the DLL from memory and notify the calling program that the DLL could not be loaded.

By using another system defined variable, ExitProc, you can also identify a procedure that Windows should run when your DLL is being removed from memory. The following code fragment shows an example of how to use ExitProc.

```
library exitTest;

uses
  exitu;

var
  OldExitProc:    Pointer;
```

```
{$S-}
procedure Cleanup; far;
begin
  {
  Your cleanup code goes here.
  }
  ExitProc := OldExitProc;
end;

begin
  {
  Your initialization code goes here.
  }
  OldExitProc := ExitProc;
  ExitProc := @Cleanup;
end.
```

This library has some initialization code in its begin end block. At the end of the initialization code it saves the current ExitProc pointer and assigns the address of the Cleanup procedure to ExitProc. When Windows removes the library from memory it will call Cleanup. The last thing Cleanup does is restore ExitProc to its original value.

WARNING

If you use an exit procedure in your library the exit procedure must be compiled with the {$S-} compiler directive to turn stack checking off because Windows switches to it own stack when unloading a DLL.

TIP

Make sure you include thorough error checking in your exit procedure. A runtime error in a DLL exit procedure will crash Windows.

DLLs and the Stack

Although DLLs have their own code segment and data segment they do not have their own stack. Instead routines in a DLL use the stack of the program that calls them.

This means that you must not only have room on your program's stack for all of the automatic variables and parameters for its functions and procedures but also for any library procedures and functions the program calls.

A DLL Using Units

The main difference between creating a DLL in a single file and creating a DLL that uses units is where the procedures and functions go. If you are writing a complex DLL with many routines, units offer the same advantages that they offer in a complex program.

If you use units to develop your DLL the library itself will look like the following code from the project STRINGL.DPR.

```
library Stringl;

uses
  Stringlu in 'STRINGLU.PAS';

exports
  LTrim index 1,
  RTrim index 2,
  Proper index 3,
  ParseCount index 4,
  ParseString index 5;

begin
end.
```

The library contains nothing but the uses clause and the exports clause. All of the procedures and functions are in the unit files. The following code is from the unit file STRINGLU.PAS in this project.

```
unit Stringlu;

interface

function LTrim(const s: String): String; export;
function RTrim(const s: String): String; export;
procedure Proper(var s: String); export;
function ParseCount(const s, delimiters: String): Word; export;
function ParseString(const s, delimiters: String; num: Word): String;
export;

implementation

function LTrim(const s: String): String;
{
Remove leading whitespace from a string.
```

```
Whitespace is defined as blanks or tabs.
}
var
   i:        Word;

begin
  i := 1;
  {Skip all leading whitespace characters.}
  while (s[i] in [' ', #9]) and
        (i <= Length(s)) do Inc(i);
  {Return the rest of the string.}
  LTrim := copy(s, i, 255);
end;

function RTrim(const s: String): String;
{
Remove trailing whitespace from a string.
Whitespace is defined as blank, tab,
carriage return, line feed or form feed.
}
var
   i:        Word;

begin
  i := Length(s);
  {Skip all trailing whitespace characters.}
  while (s[i] in [' ', #9, #10, #12, #13]) and
        (i > 0) do Dec(i);
  {Return the rest of the string.}
  RTrim := copy(s, 1, i);
end;

procedure Proper(var s: String);
{
Converts a string to proper case, that is,
the first letter of each word is capitalized.
The word delimiters are space and tab.
}
var
   delimiter:    Boolean;
   i:            Word;

begin
  {Set delimiter True so the first character
  will be capitalized.}
  delimiter := True;
```

```
{Loop through the string.}
for i := 1 to Length(s) do
  {If this character is a delimiter set
  delimiter to True.}
  if s[i] in [' ', #9] then
    delimiter := True
  else
    {This character is not a delimiter so
    see if it needs its case changed.}
    if delimiter then
    begin
      {The preceding character was a
      delimiter so if this letter is
      lower case make it upper case.}
      if s[i] in ['a'..'z'] then
        s[i] := Chr(Ord(s[i]) - 32);
      {Set the flag to False so the next
      character will be made lower case.}
      delimiter := False;
    end
    else
      {This character is not the first in a
      word so make it lower case if it is
      a letter.}
      if s[i] in ['A'..'Z'] then
        s[i] := Chr(Ord(s[i]) + 32);
end;

function ParseCount(const s, delimiters: String): Word;
{
Count the number of substrings in the string s
delimited by one or more of the characters in
the string delimiters.
}
var
  delimiter:     Boolean;
  count, i:      Word;
begin
  count := 0;
  delimiter := True;
  if Length(s) > 0 then
  begin
    {Skip delimiters at the beginning of the
    string.}
    i := 1;
    while (Pos(s[i], delimiters) <> 0) and
```

```
            (i <= Length(s)) do Inc(i);
      {Scan the rest of the string.}
      for i := i to Length(s) do
        {If this character is a delimiter set
        the delimiter flag.}
        if Pos(s[i], delimiters) <> 0 then
          delimiter := True
        else
        begin
          {If this character is not a delimiter
          and the previous character was then
          this is the first character of a new
          substring so increment the count.}
          if delimiter = True then Inc(count);
          delimiter := False;
        end;
    end;
    ParseCount := count
end;

function ParseString(const s, delimiters: String; num: Word): String;
var
    delimiter:        Boolean;
    count,
    j,
    sLength,
    sStart,
    sEnd:             Word;
begin
    if ParseCount(s, delimiters) >= num then
    begin
      {Skip delimiters at the beginning of the
      string.}
      sStart := 1;
      while (Pos(s[sStart], delimiters) <> 0) and
            (sStart <= Length(s)) do Inc(sStart);
      {Find the first character of the requested
      substring.}
      for j := 1 to num - 1 do
      begin
        while Pos(s[sStart], delimiters) = 0 do Inc(sStart);
        while Pos(s[sStart], delimiters) <> 0 do Inc(sStart);
      end;
      {Find the end of the substring.}
      sEnd := sStart;
```

```
    while Pos(s[sEnd], delimiters) = 0 do Inc(sEnd);
    {Compute the length of the substring.}
    sLength := sEnd - sStart;
    {Extract and return the substring.}
    ParseString := copy(s, sStart, sLength);
  end
  else
    ParseString := '';
end;

end.
```

Notice that since the routines in this unit will be exported by the DLL the function and procedure declarations in the interface section must include the export directive. However, you do not include the export directive in the actual procedure and function declarations in the implementation section of the unit.

The code for the procedures and functions in the implementation section is exactly the same code that was described in detail in Chapter 9 where these routines were developed. This means that you can easily build DLLs from exiting procedures and functions since the procedures and functions themselves do not have to be changed in any way.

Using DLLs

This section demonstrates how to use DLLs. It will modify the Strings program from Chapter 9 to use the DLL described in the preceding section. To use the procedures and functions in a DLL you must import them into your program using the external keyword as shown below.

```
function LTrim; external 'stringl' index 1;
function RTrim; external 'stringl' index 2;
procedure Proper; external 'stringl' index 3;
function ParseCount; external 'stringl' index 4;
function ParseString; external 'stringl' index 5;
```

These declarations import the five routines from STRINGL.DLL into the program they appear in by index number. If you want to import a routine by name instead of index number you can do it in one of two ways. The following statement imports LTrim by name.

```
function LTrim; external 'stringl';
```

You can also specify a new name that the routine will be known by within this program using the following syntax.

```
function LTrim; external 'string1' name 'LeftTrim';
```

However, remember that calling a routine that has been imported by index number is faster so that is the recommended method.

There is one problem with this approach. Suppose you are working on a program that includes several units or a system that includes several programs. Now suppose that more than one of these units or programs needs to use the routines in your DLL. It is a nuisance to have to recreate the import declarations in each program or unit. Worse yet is what happens if you need to change the declaration for one of your library routines. If that happens you must then find every program and unit that includes the routine's import declaration and change it.

A much better technique is to use an import unit for your DLL such as the one shown below.

```
unit StringId;

interface

function LTrim(const s: String): String;
function RTrim(const s: String): String;
procedure Proper(var s: String);
function ParseCount(const s, delimiters: String): Word;
function ParseString(const s, delimiters: String; num: Word): String;

implementation

function LTrim; external 'string1' index 1;
function RTrim; external 'string1' index 2;
procedure Proper; external 'string1' index 3;
function ParseCount; external 'string1' index 4;
function ParseString; external 'string1' index 5;

end.
```

This unit contains the import declaration for each procedure and function in its implementation function and the function or procedure declaration in the interface section. Now all you have to do is add the name of this import unit to the uses clause in any program or unit that needs to use the library's routines. If you need to make changes the only file you have to change is this import unit.

To convert the Strings program from Chapter 9 to use STRINGL.DLL, all you have to do is remove the code for the five routines from the Stringsf unit and add the import unit to the uses clause as shown below.

```
unit Stringsf;

interface

uses
  SysUtils, WinTypes, WinProcs, Messages, Classes, Graphics, Controls,
  Forms, Dialogs, StdCtrls, StringId;
```

Run the program and try it. You will find that it works exactly like the original version in Chapter 9. Figure 13.4 shows the program after running the LTrim function on a string that contains leading blanks.

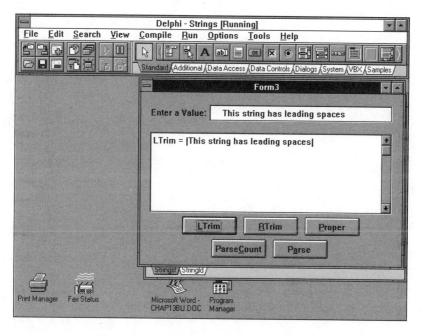

FIGURE 13.4 THE STRINGS PROGRAM USING A DLL.

Summary

Dynamic Link Libraries extend the power of Delphi in two ways. First, in large projects where the user may be running several programs at once DLLs let you maintain a single copy of shared code in memory. This reduces memory consumption and can improve the performance of your application by reducing disk swapping.

The ability to write DLLs also allows you to write libraries that can be used by others working in other development environments such as Paradox, dBase, and C/C++. Since DLLs are a Windows standard they are very portable and flexible.

CHAPTER 14

Anatomy of a Component

When you work in Delphi, you work with components. This chapter reviews all the important component parts: properties, events, aligning them on a form, attaching code to them, changing their properties, and other topics.

What are Components?

Components are visual and nonvisual objects which you can manipulate at design time. Almost all of the components available to you are on the component palette (Figure 14.1).

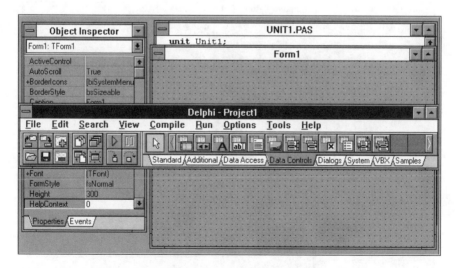

FIGURE 14.1 THE COMPONENT PALETTE.

Components make programming in Delphi easy. Rather than manipulating an object purely in code, Delphi gives us a highly visual representation of the object. This gives us something real to touch, move, adjust, change, and delete. Our code, therefore, is organized visually. You can quickly determine what a form is doing simply by looking at the components it includes while in design mode.

Components have two parts: properties and events. Properties are component characteristics which you can change at design time or run time, depending on the property. Properties such as color, name, and caption are common properties. Components also participate in the Windows event stream. You can attach code to these events so that your code is invoked in response to an event.

What are Properties?

We all have properties: age, weight, name, among others. Components have properties too. Let us look at a typical component: the TEdit object (Figure 14.2).

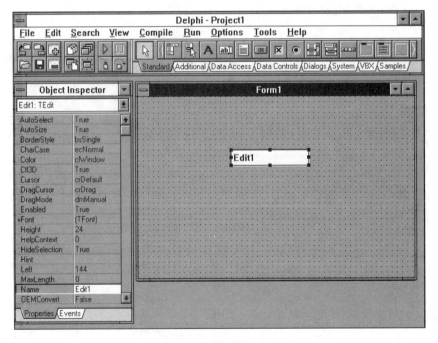

FIGURE 14.2 THE TEDIT COMPONENT.

By default, the Object Inspector appears as a separate window to the left of the current form, as Figure 14.2 shows. The Object Inspector has two pages: a properties page and an event page. The properties on a TEdit object's property page are listed in Table 14.1.

TABLE 14.1 TEDIT PROPERTIES

Property	Description
AutoSelect	Determines if the text in the object is selected, by default, when the user tabs into the object.
AutoSize	Will the object resize itself to fit the contents? For edit boxes, if the property is true, increasing the font size will cause the component to increase in height.
BorderStyle	What type of border does the object have?
CharCase	Lower, normal, or upper-case characters?
Color	The object's color, which can be a pre-set color or based on another Window object's color.
Ctl3D	Does the object display with a 3-D effect?
Cursor	What should the mouse cursor look like as it passes over the object?
DragCursor	What should the mouse cursor look like as it passes over the objects that will accept the dragging component.
DragMode	Used to control object drag and drop.
Enabled	Will the object respond to mouse, keyboard, and timer events?
Font	Font name for the text in the object.
Height	The object's visual height, in pixels.
HelpContext	A number used to display the proper help context screen in the help system.
HideSelection	If True, then the object does not appear as selected if it does not have focus.
Hint	The hint text for the object. Hints are text which appears just below or near the object when the mouse temporarily pauses on the object. In order to get hints to appear, the object's ShowHint property must be true and you must set the application's ShowHint property to true at runtime with ObjectPascal code.
Left	The object's position relative to the form window's left edge, in pixels.
MaxLength	Maximum number of characters the user can type in. If 0, the number is unlimited.
Name	The name of the object.
ParentColor	If true, the object uses the parent object's color.

ParentCtl3D	If true, the object uses the parent object's 3-D property.
ParentFont	If true, the object uses the parent object's font.
ParentShowHint	If true, the object uses the parent object's ShowHint property.
PasswordChar	Normally set to null (#0). If set to another character, that character is used as a password display character.
PopupMenu	The name of the PopupMenu component to invoke when the user right-clicks on the object with the object selected.
ReadOnly	Is the object read-only?
ShowHint	Should the object show hint text?
TabOrder	What is the object's position in the tab order?
TabStop	Can the user tab into the object?
Tag	An integer property which Delphi does not use, but leaves available for the programmer.
Text	The text in the object.
Top	The object's position relative to the top of the form's window, in pixels.
Visible	Is the object visible at runtime?
Width	The object's width, in pixels.

Obviously this is a rather lengthy list! Before you can master programming components, you need to understand the various component properties. Each component has a different list of properties. In Chapter 15, "Delphi Controls" and Chapter 16, "Delphi Database Controls," we discuss properties for various different components with specific examples.

T I P

Spend some time building some sample forms with various components. Experiment with various properties. It is easy to forget or not even be aware that a specific property, such as ParentHint, exists. Review the property list for each component from time to time so that you remember what properties are available. In Windows development, the list of options and properties available to you is quite large. What you do not know *can* hurt you.

Remember that properties in the Object Inspector are published properties. Nearly all of these properties are read/write; that is, you can change them. Keep in mind, however, that all components might have public and protected properties. These properties are not available at design time, but are available at runtime. For example, the Align property is not available at design time for the TEdit control, but it is available at runtime. *When in doubt about the availability of a property at runtime, use the Object Browser or read the Visual Component Library source code.* These two tools illuminate a great number of unpublished properties.

What are Events?

Events are actions that either the user or some piece of software takes. For example, whenever the user presses a key on the keyboard, he or she is generating an event. Whenever a Delphi application attempts to lock a record, it generates an event. Like most Windows development environments, Delphi lets us attach code at various points so that our application can respond to these events.

When developing Delphi client-server applications, you will find yourself intimately involved with all sorts of events. You will have to handle database events, such as updating records and committing transactions. You will have to handle Windows events, such as mouse clicks or mouse moves so that you can perform user-interface programming tricks.

You can see a list of events for a component by clicking on the Events tab in the Object Inspector. Figure 14.3 shows the events page for a TEdit control.

All the controls in Delphi share many events, such as OnClick, OnDoubleClick, OnEnter, OnExit, OnKeyDown, OnKeyPress, OnKeyUp, OnMouseDown, OnMouseMove, OnMouseUp. In Delphi, you can write code which executes when the event occurs. It is through these event entry points that you can enhance, override, or cancel the default Windows behavior for the event.

Database controls such as TTable, which manage inserting, deleting, posting records, and navigating through data sets, have database oriented events. These events are discussed in Chapter 17, "Connecting Controls to Databases."

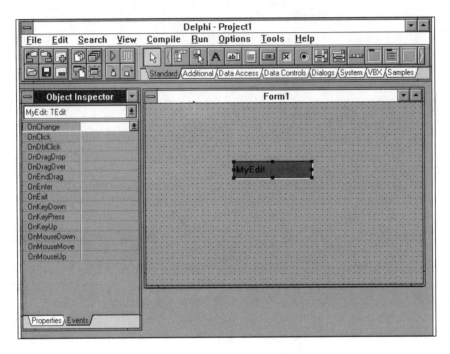

FIGURE 14.3 TEDIT COMPONENT EVENTS.

Working with Components

Some of the components on the components palette are visible at runtime. The TEdit control previously discussed is a visual component. Visual components are those components that the user interacts with. Nonvisual components, such as the TOpenDialog component (see Figure 14.4) are visible only at design time. At run time, they are invisible. These components provide a visual way of setting up properties that we would otherwise have to set up by writing code. They exist as a programming convenience so that we don't have to go through the bother of writing code to set all the properties for the non-visual component.

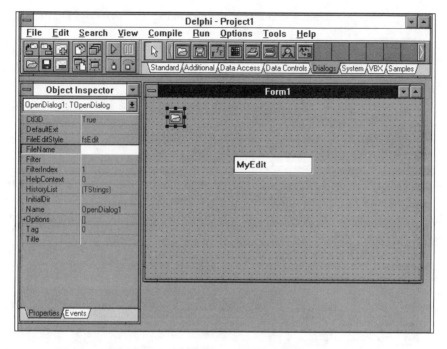

FIGURE 14.4 TOPENDIALOG NONVISUAL COMPONENT.

Adding Components to a Form

Adding components to a form is easy. First you select the component page that you need. Delphi comes with 8 component palette pages and 78 components. Table 14.2 lists each page and their components.

TABLE 14.2 COMPONENT PALETTE PAGES AND CONTENTS

Standard	MainMenu, PopupMenu, Label, Edit, Memo, Button, CheckBox, RadioButton, ListBox, ComboBox, Scrollbar, GroupBox, RadioGroup, Panel
Additional	BitButton, SpeedButton, TabSet, Notebook, TabbedNotebook, MaskEdit, Outline, String Grid, DrawGrid, Image, Shape, Bevel, Header, ScrollBox
Data Access	DataSource, Table, Query, StoredProc, Database, BatchMove, Report
Data Controls	DBGrid, DBNavigator, DBText, DBEdit, DBMemo, DBImage, DBListBox, DBComboBox, DBCheckBox, DBRadioGroup, DBLookupList, DBLookupCombo

Dialogs	OpenDialog, SaveDialog, FontDialog, ColorDialog, PrintDialog, PrinterSetupDialog, FindDialog, ReplaceDialog
System	Timer, PaintBox, FileListBox, DirectoryListBox, DriveComboBox, FilterComboBox, MediaPlayer, OleContainer, DdeClientConv, DdeClientItem, DdeServerConv, DdeServerItem
VBX	BiSwitch, BiGauge, BiPict, Chart
Samples	Gauge, ColorGrid, SpinButton, SpinEdit, DirectoryOutline, Calendar

Delphi lets you configure the component palette by adding and reordering palette pages as well as components on a page. Figure 14.5 shows the palette page of the Environment Options dialog. You can access this page directly by right-clicking on the component palette and choosing **Configure** from the popup menu.

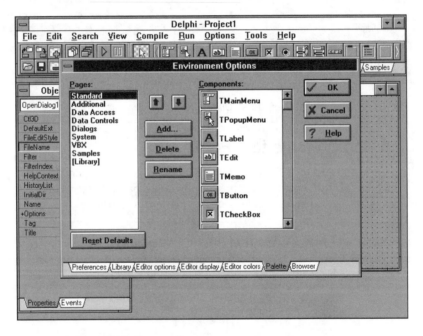

FIGURE 14.5 PALETTE PAGE OF ENVIRONMENT OPTIONS DIALOG.

To add a component to a form, simply click on the component on the palette page and then click on the form at the spot where you want the component. Each time you place a component on the form, you must reselect a component from the component palette. If you need to place several components at a time to your form, such as three buttons, hold down the shift key while you click the component on the component palette. Each time you click on the form, another component appears on the form and the component on the component palette stays depressed. This indicates that the next time you click on the form, the depressed component will be placed on the form.

Selecting One or More Components

You can select a single component and manipulate it simply by clicking on the component on the form. Just like most Windows applications, Delphi lets you select multiple components as well. To do this, hold down the shift key while you click on the components. With multiple components selected, you can move or manipulate the components at the same time.

In addition, you can use the mouse to select multiple components. To do this, hold the mouse down and drag a rectangle surrounding (or at least touching) all the components you wish to select. Figure 14.6 shows an example of this.

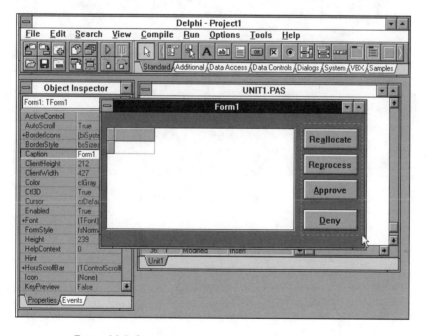

FIGURE 14.6 SELECTING MULTIPLE COMPONENTS WITH A MOUSE.

Sizing and Aligning Components

Delphi has several tools to help size and align components. As with most Windows applications, there is more than one way to accomplish a task. Of course you can use the mouse to select, resize, and align any number of components. However, when your form accumulates lots of components, this can get tedious.

You can use the menu choice Edit | Align to align components. This brings up Alignment dialog (Figure 14.7). Using the Edit | Size menu choice brings up the Size dialog (Figure 14.8).

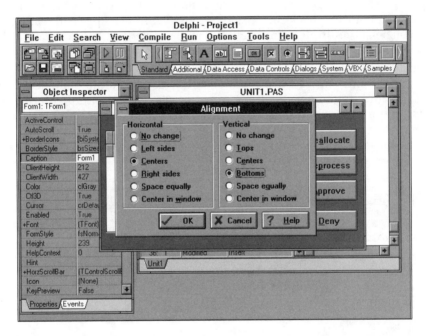

FIGURE 14.7 ALIGNMENT DIALOG

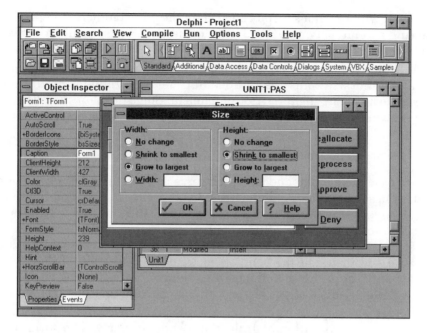

FIGURE 14.8 SIZE DIALOG

These two dialogs can save you time because they let you quickly align and size multiple items. You can also use the Alignment Palette. To display the Alignment Palette, choose the View | Alignment Palette menu choice. This brings up a toolbar which remains on the workspace during the design session. It has buttons for all the alignment options in the Alignment dialog.

You can also use the design grid as a mechanism for sizing and aligning components. You can set the grid options by choosing Options | Environment from the menu and selecting the Preferences page. You can display the grid if you want or turn grid snap on. If grid snap is on, all objects will align to the defined grid coordinates when you move or resize the object with the mouse. You can also set the grid granularity, in pixels, by entering a value between 2 and 128 in the Grid Size X and Grid Size Y fields in the Preferences page.

Whether you use the grid to align and size objects or whether you use the align and size tools really does not matter, although the debate as spurred many a late-night religious argument. Some developers prefer using the grid while others prefer not to. What matters is what works best for you.

Grouping Components

Delphi has several components which serve as containers for other components. These container components let you group a collection of components together. These include the GroupBox, Panel, Notebook, TabbedNotebook, and ScrollBox containers. In order to get controls into these container objects, you will need to first place the container object, on the form and then add the component from the component palette to the container object or use the clipboard to cut and paste into the component. You will not be able to drag existing components into the container object.

Container components are the parent for the objects they contain. The parent property is different from the owner property. The form object remains the owner of all components on it. The parent property is most frequently used in ObjectPascal to identify which object should be responsible for creating and destroying other objects. The parent property is useful for basing an object's color, font, and hint property on its parent, as discussed previously.

Figure 14.9 shows an example of three fields placed in a GroupBox component. The three radio buttons on the right are not in a container component. That control is called the RadioGroup control. It lets you establish radio buttons inside a box without having to place individual radio buttons inside. Hence, that control does not really contain any other components, although it looks like it does.

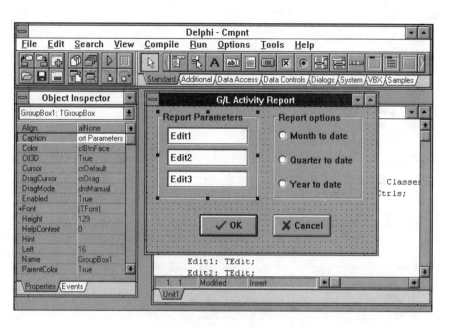

FIGURE 14.9 GROUPED EDIT FIELDS

You can move grouped components around at design and run time as a single unit. If you delete a container component at design or runtime, you delete the contained components as well.

Using the Clipboard

Of course you can use the clipboard to cut and paste components to and from a form. What is not immediately obvious is that when you cut a component to the clipboard, you can paste it into Windows Notepad and it appears as source code (Figure 14.10). The reason for this is that all objects and their properties are converted to source code.

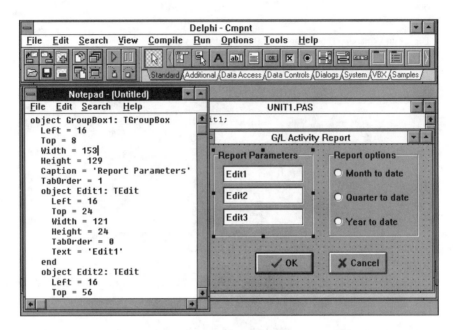

FIGURE 14.10 COMPONENT COPIED AND PASTED INTO NOTEPAD.

In Delphi, you do not see each component's design-time properties because Delphi writes this out to a special binary file with a .DFM extension. You can edit this file in Delphi by using the File | Open File menu option (Figure 14.11). If you change the contents of this file and save it, *its as if you changed the form using the form designer tools.* As you make changes to the form interactively using the design tools or by changing the source code, Delphi keeps both the source code and the form up to date and in sync.

In Delphi, you can alter your form using the interactive design tools, or you can edit the PAS file contents and the DFM file contents. Delphi will always make sure the visual properties of the form and the source code files are synchronized. In fact, Delphi was designed this way up front so that you can alter your forms by changing source code, or by using interactive design tools.

TIP

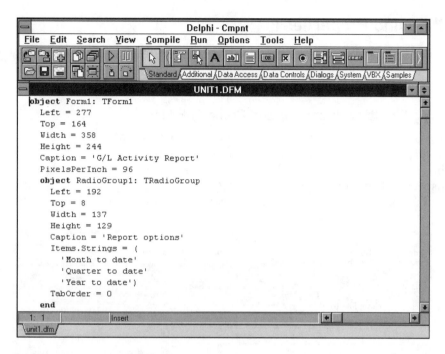

FIGURE 14.11 DFM FILE OPENED IN DELPHI.

Because of this dynamic convertibility between source code and visual objects, Borland is calling Delphi a *two-way tool*. Another benefit to this two-way tool design is that version control is easy to implement. Since all forms can be reduced 100% to source code (in the PAS file and the DFM file), these text files can be run through a version control facility. Version control utilities let you compare different versions of the same object to see exactly what changed between versions. In other development environments, form objects are strictly binary objects. They do not contain meaningful textual or semantic information. While these binary objects can be placed in a version control package, you can not get meaningful semantic difference information out of the version control tool.

Changing Properties

Since Delphi is a two-way tool, you can change properties for an object using the property edit or by altering code. You can alter the code contained in the DFM file, or at run time you can write ObjectPascal code to set object properties.

Using the Object Inspector and Property Editor

The object inspector is the most productive way to set properties. If you have programmed in other Windows development environment, you have learned this. If you are new to Windows development, learn how to use the Object Inspector. Some properties have property editor dialogs which you can access. For example, the font property has its own property editor (see Figure 14.12)

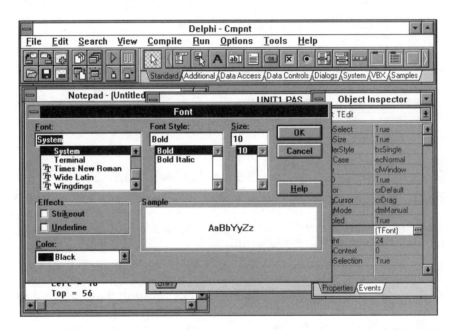

FIGURE 14.12 FONT PROPERTY EDITOR.

Other properties, including the Font property, have several levels inside of them. These properties have the + character right next to them. If you double-click on the property name, the list will expand to show the embedded properties (see Figure 14.13).

You can access property values on properties with drop-down lists, such as fsBold in Figure 14.13, by clicking on the combo-box drop-down arrow, or by double-clicking on the property value. When you double-click on the property value, Delphi will change the property value to the next item on the list. Hence, you can change between False and True property values simply by double-clicking on the property value.

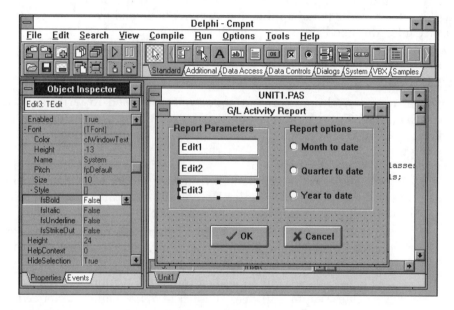

FIGURE 14.13 FONT PROPERTIES EXPANDED

Using Code

If you feel comfortable changing an object's property in code, you can open the form's DFM file and change any property using the Delphi editor. You will not be able to use another editor to edit a DFM file however. Delphi writes the DFM file in a binary format and converts it to text when you use the Delphi editor to open it.

Additionally, you can write code to change an object's properties at run-time. Properties with single values, such as the Caption property, are easy to change. The following code example sets the Report Parameters group box caption to "Report Settings" in the form's OnCreate event.

```
procedure TForm1.FormCreate(Sender: TObject);
begin
GroupBox1.Caption := 'Report Settings';
end;
```

Events

To gain a high level of proficiency in Delphi, you are going to need to understand events. Although Delphi is so easy to use and program that many developers will not need to understand events in detail, those that do will be able to write better applications. Do not be fooled by Delphi's ease of use. Under the hood are some very interesting, somewhat complex, and extremely useful low-level features, particularly in the area of events.

Event Handlers

In order to do anything useful in code, you will need to write code in event handlers. *Event handlers* are procedures which Delphi creates for you or that you create yourself. You can access an event handler in the following ways

- Double-click on the component in design mode. Most components have a default event handler Delphi automatically displays in an editor window in response to a double-click.
- Double-click on or press **Ctrl-Enter** while in the value for the event property in the Object Inspector window. Delphi will display the event handler procedure in an editor window.
- Select a procedure name from the drop-down list for the event property's value. Delphi will display a list of valid methods. Notice that you will not see the same list of methods for different events. Delphi has a slightly different argument list for different events. The drop-down list will contain procedures that match the current event's argument list.
- Type in a procedure name in the event's property value field in the object inspector, and then move to the next property by pressing the tab key, or clicking on another property. Return to the event value and double-click or press **Ctrl-Enter**. Delphi will automatically create an event handler with the name of the procedure you typed in earlier.

In addition, you can simply read the source code behind the form and add your own event handlers without using the Object Inspector.

If you accidentally create event handlers and do not add any code to them, Delphi will remove them for you the next time you compile your application.

NOTE

Figure 14.14 shows an event handler for the form's OnCreate event. Notice that the code for the event handler is between the begin..end block.

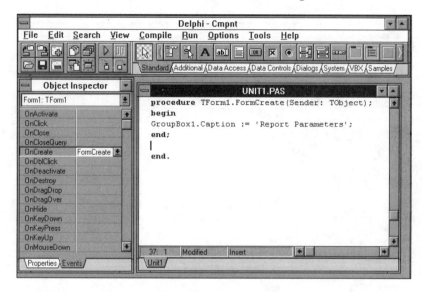

FIGURE 14.14 FORM OBJECT ONCREATE EVENT HANDLER.

Delegation of Event Handling

Components can share event handlers. For example, you can write one routine to handle a single event for multiple objects. The following procedure is attached to the OnExit event for the three edit components:

```
procedure TForm1.EditAllExit(Sender: TObject);
begin
   If Sender = Edit1 then
      MessageDlg('Edit 1 called me',mtInformation,[mbOk],0)
   else if Sender = Edit2 then
      MessageDlg('Edit 2 called me',mtInformation,[mbOk],0)
   else if Sender = Edit3 then
      MessageDlg('Edit 3 called me',mtInformation,[mbOk],0);

end;
```

Each of the edit objects has this procedure name as the OnExit event value (Figure 14.15). You can determine which object is calling the procedure by using the Sender argument. Sender is a TObject variable which points to the object which received the event. In other words, it is the object calling the shared event handler.

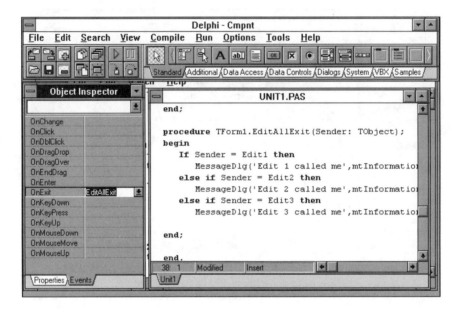

FIGURE 14.15 A SHARED EVENT HANDLER.

Components can share event handlers provided that all the events that use the event handler have the same number and type of arguments. For example, a TEdit object's OnExit event can't call an event handler designed for the key down event. Event handlers for the key down event must have the following three arguments:

```
Sender: TObject; var Key: Word;Shift: TShiftState;
```

If you try and use an invalid event handler for a given event, Delphi will prevent this and display an error message.

Right-Clicking a Component

If you right-click on a component, Delphi displays a popup menu which contains some items from the Edit menu (Figure 14.16).

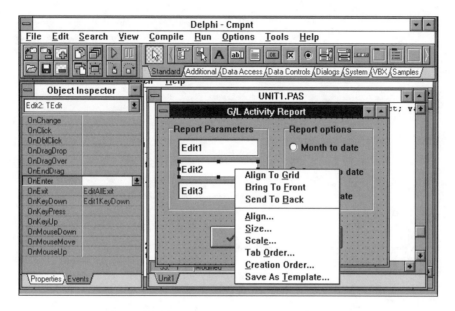

FIGURE 14.16 COMPONENT RIGHT-CLICK POPUP MENU.

Summary

Understanding component properties and events is essential to programming effectively in Delphi. While most components are visual, that is visible at design and runtime, some components are nonvisual. These components are only visible at design time. Nonvisual components provide a convenient way of accessing services without programming. Visual components are the objects with which the user will interact. In Delphi, the number of properties, both published and available in design mode, and unpublished yet available at runtime, is quite large. Be prepared to spend some time learning these properties and how to access them.

Components also have events and Delphi lets us establish shared and non-shared event handlers for events. Learning how to write shared and non-shared event handlers is critical in developing client-server applications. In client-server development, you will invariably find the need to write both shared and nonshared event handlers for all sorts of database events.

CHAPTER 15

Delphi Controls

Anyone who has used or programmed Windows has seen controls such as edit boxes, pushbuttons, drop-down lists, and so on. These can be quite tedious to program, with messages to be sent and received, 'wParams' and 'lParams' to be deciphered, resource files to link, and on and on.

Delphi control objects, or components, encapsulate the standard Windows controls, and provide many new ones. Messages are translated into events and properties allowing simple response functions without the elaborate switch-case statements of standard Windows programming. Control properties can be set at design time, and easily modified at runtime. The programmer never has to get involved in the Windows message stream at all.

This chapter builds on the discussion in Chapter 14 by demonstrating most of the standard Delphi components, showing how to use properties, methods, and event handlers in real programs. These controls are demonstrated in five example projects: SORTER.DPR, COLORS.DPR, MEDIA.DPR, NOTEBOOK.DPR, and TASKMAN.DPR.

The Sorter Example

The Sorter project demonstrates edit controls, memo controls, pushbuttons, string lists, the common font dialog, and 'fly-by' hints. Load and run the SORTER.DPR project. You will see the form shown in Figure 15.1.

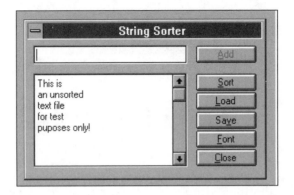

FIGURE 15.1 THE SORTER EXAMPLE.

Pushbuttons

Pushbuttons perform their actions in response to an OnClick event. This event occurs whenever the button is pressed, either by clicking with the mouse, pressing its hot key, or pressing the Enter key when the button has focus.

The CloseButtonClick method is entered as the OnClick event handler for the CloseButton control in the Object Inspector. This means that the Close button calls the CloseButtonClick method when it is pressed. In this example, the code simply call the form's Close method.

LISTING 15.1 CLOSE BUTTON ONCLICK EVENT HANDLER

```
procedure TSortForm.CloseButtonClick(Sender: TObject);
begin
   Close;
end;
```

Sometimes a button should not be available to the user. Enable or disable a button by setting its Enabled property to True or False, as shown in Listing 15.2. Display or hide a button by setting its Visible property to True or False.

Edit Controls

Edit controls allow you to enter a single line of text of up to 255 characters in length. The Text property of the control retrieves and sets the value displayed in the control. Whenever the text in the control changes, whether by user action or program code, an OnChange event occurs. Listing 15.2 is the

OnChange event handler for the edit control. The code disables the Add button when the edit control is empty, and enables it when there is some text entered.

LISTING 15.2 EDIT CONTROL ONCHANGE EVENT HANDLER

```
procedure TSortForm.SorterEntryChange(Sender: TObject);
begin
   if SorterEntry.Text = EmptyStr then
      AddButton.Enabled := False
   else
      AddButton.Enabled := True;
end;
```

Memo Controls

Memo controls are similar to edit controls, but they allow you to enter multiple lines of text. The text in a memo control can be accessed in two ways. The Text property provides access to the entire contents of the control, up to 255 characters. The Lines property provides access one line at a time. Each line is limited to 255 characters, but there is no limit to the number of lines. Listing 15.3 is the OnClick event handler for the Add button. It adds the contents of the edit control to the memo control.

LISTING 15.3 ADD BUTTON ONCLICK EVENT HANDLER

```
procedure TSortForm.AddButtonClick(Sender: TObject);
begin
   { add the text - added at the end of the memo }
   SorterMemo.Lines.Add(SorterEntry.text);

   { clear out the edit control and move focus back to it }
   SorterEntry.Clear;
   SorterEntry.SetFocus;
end;
```

The memo control's Lines property and its Add method are used to add the contents of the edit control. The string is added to the end of the memo control. Use the Insert method to insert a string at a particular location. Since the strings will be sorted later, the Add method is used for this example.

The edit control's Clear method is called next, to empty the control in preparation for the next string. Since pressing a button moves input focus to the button, as a convenience to the user, the SetFocus method is called to move focus back to the edit control.

TStrings and TStringList Objects

The memo control's Lines property is an object of type TStrings. Many controls (memos, combo boxes, radio groups, and so on) use TStrings objects to maintain their lists of items. TStrings objects provide string manipulation methods enabling you to easily alter the contents of the controls at runtime. For example, you can insert and delete items into a list box, reorganize an outline, or add a button to a radio group.

The Add method used in Listing 15.3 belongs to the Lines property of the memo control, and not to the memo control itself. Writing 'SorterMemo.Add(SorterEntry.Text)' would produce a syntax error because the memo control does not have an Add method.

The TStrings object also provides quick and easy methods for saving and retrieving text in a disk file. The developer does not have to worry about file structures. The TStrings object knows how to save and retrieve its own text. Listing 15.4 shows the OnClick event handlers for the Load and Save buttons (a similar example is shown in Chapter 11 covering file I/O). In this example, a hard coded file name is used for brevity. In a real application, you would probably use the common file open and save dialogs (covered in the Colors example project.) A test file is provided on the sample code disk.

LISTING 15.4 LOAD AND SAVE BUTTON ONCLICK EVENT HANDLERS

```
procedure TSortForm.LoadButtonClick(Sender: TObject);
begin
    SorterMemo.lines.loadFromFile('chap15.txt');
end;

procedure TSortForm.SaveButtonClick(Sender: TObject);
begin
    SorterMemo.lines.saveToFile('chap15.txt');
end;
```

Sorting the lines in the memo control is almost as easy as loading and saving, as shown in Listing 15.5.

LISTING 15.5 SORT BUTTON ONCLICK EVENT HANDLER

```
procedure TSortForm.SortButtonClick(Sender: TObject);
var
    MemoStringList: TStringList;
begin
```

```
try
    { create a TStringList object and add the contents of the
      memo to it }
    MemoStringList := TStringList.Create;
    MemoStringList.AddStrings(SorterMemo.Lines);

    { sort the strings, clear the memo, and replace with the sorted
strings }
    MemoStringList.Sort;
    SorterMemo.Lines.Clear;
    SorterMemo.lines.AddStrings(MemoStringList);
finally
    { release the memory allocated for the string list }
    MemoStringList.Free;
end;
end;
```

TStringList objects are very similar to the TStrings objects already discussed. The difference is that TStrings objects are used only in association with controls, whereas TStringList objects are used to manage lists of strings not associated with a control. For this example, the benefit of the TStringList object is that it has a Sort method.

The code first creates a TStringList object. This is done inside a try-finally block to ensure that the memory used by the new object is released no matter what else happens. Since Windows resources and memory are precious, it is good practice to ensure that all objects created in code are released when no longer needed.

The AddStrings method is used to copy the strings from the memo control Lines property (which is a TStrings object) to the new TStringList object. The Sort method is called to do the real work. The memo is cleared, and the AddStrings method is used again to transfer the sorted text back to the memo. Finally, the TStringList object's memory is released by calling Free.

In addition to managing text strings, TStrings and TStringList objects can manage lists of other objects through the Objects property. Since the Objects property is of type TObjects, an object of any type can be attached to each item in a string list. The Colors example links the items in a combo box to several other controls on the form.

Font Dialog Box

Windows provides a number of common dialog boxes for opening and saving files, search and replace, printing, and so on. The FontDialog is used in the Sorter example to change the font of the memo control. The FontDialog is a nonvisual component, visible on the form only at design time. The Font button displays and responds to this dialog. Listing 15.6 is the OnClick event handler for the Font button.

LISTING 15.6 FONT BUTTON ONCLICK EVENT HANDLER

```
procedure TSortForm.FontButtonClick(Sender: TObject);
begin
    if FontDialog.execute then
        SorterMemo.Font := FontDialog.Font;
end;
```

The FontDialog Execute method displays the standard Windows font selection dialog box and waits for the you to press the OK or Cancel buttons. If you press **OK**, the selected font is assigned to the font property of the FontDialog object, and the method returns True. The selected font is then assigned to the memo control.

The Font property of the FontDialog and the memo field is an object of type TFont. TFont objects encapsulate the windows font structures. All the usual font parameters (typeface, style, point size, and so on) are properties of this object.

Hints

Delphi enables you to display helpful hints to the users of your applications. The Sorter example shows the easiest way to accomplish this. Each control on the form has a Hint property,which takes a string of up to 255 characters, and a ShowHint property which takes a value of True or False. When you move and pause the mouse pointer over a control which has ShowHint set to True, the text in the Hint property will be displayed in a small box near the control. No code is necessary. The Media example shows a more elaborate use of hints.

The Colors Example

The Colors example demonstrates panels, bevels, labels, combo boxes (drop-down lists), scroll bars, shapes, the common open, save and color dialog boxes, bitmap and graphics, drag and drop, and attaching objects to string lists. It will even draw a picture of one of the authors, load and run the COLORS.DPR project. You will see the form shown in Figure 15.2.

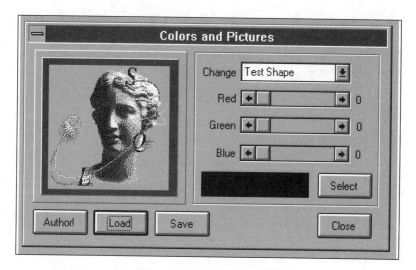

FIGURE 15.2 THE COLORS EXAMPLE.

Panels and Bevels

A panel is a container object for other control objects you place on a form (container objects were discussed in Chapter 14); with a border (set with the BorderStyle, BorderWidth, BevelInner, and BevelOuter properties), the panel serves to visually group controls. In the Colors example the two frames around the image control are panels. Each of the examples in this chapter use a panel as the background of its form. The Align property of the background panels is set to alClient, which causes the panel to fill the entire form area. The Media example shows how to use panels as status bars.

Bevels are similar to panels, except that they do not serve as containers for other controls. A bevel is used when the you need a visual grouping, but you do not want to group the controls in a container like a panel. The border around the combo box, scroll bars, and shape control on the Colors example is a bevel object.

Labels

Label controls display static text, contained in its Caption property. There is no user interaction with a label control, and it cannot get input focus. The

Caption property can be assigned at design time or runtime. In this example, the numbers displayed to the right of the scroll bars are labels. Listing 15.7 shows how the labels' Caption property is changed to display the position of the scroll bars.

Scroll Bars

The scroll bar is a standard Windows control which returns a range of values based on the position of the scroll box. It is generally used to scroll a region on a form, but this example uses the three scroll bars to set the red, green, and blue color values for the object selected in the combo box. The Position property of a scroll bar sets or returns the current value, or position, of the scroll box. The Min and Max properties set the values for the extreme ends of the scroll box travel. The SmallChange property sets the amount of position change when you click on one of the arrows at the ends of the scroll bar. The LargeChange property sets the amount of position change when you click on either side of the scroll box within the scroll bar.

The OnChange event is triggered whenever the scroll box position changes, either through user action or code. Listing 15.7 is the OnChange event handler for the 'Red' scroll bar. It sets the Caption property of its label to the new position value, then calls the SetColors procedure to paint the appropriate area of the form. Each of the scroll bars has a similar OnChange event handler.

LISTING 15.7 RED SCROLL BAR ONCHANGE EVENT HANDLER

```
procedure TColorForm.RedScrollBarChange(Sender: TObject);
begin
    RedValue.Caption := IntToStr(RedScrollBar.Position);
    SetColors;
end;
```

Combo Boxes

A combo-box control is an edit control with an associated list of available items. You can type into the edit control, or select an item by clicking the arrow to drop down a list (depending on the value selected for the style property). Like an edit control, the contents of the combo box is accessed with the Text property. The Items property is a TStrings object containing the entries in the drop-down list. The ItemIndex property is the ordinal number of the selected item, with the first item being 0.

In order to change the color of the selected object when the scroll bars are moved, those objects are attached to the corresponding entry in the combo box. This is done as the form opens, in the OnCreate event handler (Listing 15.8).

LISTING 15.8 COLORS FORM ONCREATE EVENT HANDLER

```
procedure TColorForm.FormCreate(Sender: TObject);
begin
    { by default, always update the current object colors }
    UpdateColors := True;

    { assign control objects to frame selector Tstrings -
      these objects are used by SetColors to know what to color }
    FrameSelector.Items.Objects[0] := TestShape;
    FrameSelector.Items.Objects[1] := InnerFrame;
    FrameSelector.Items.Objects[2] := OuterFrame;

    { first item in list should be current when form opens -
      set the colors so the test shape color is initialized to black }
    FrameSelector.ItemIndex := 0;
    SetColors;
end;
```

The code first sets a flag to be used later in the example. Then, three of the forms controls are attached to the three elements in the combo-box list. The text string of the first item in the list is 'Test Shape'. The Objects property of the TStrings object is used to connect an object to this text string. The code:

```
FrameSelector.Items.Objects[0] := TestShape;
```

connects the shape control object (named TestShape) to the first item (ItemIndex 0) in the combo-box TStrings object (the Items property). When an item is selected in the combo box, both the text string and the connected object are selected. This enables the code in Listing 15.10 to select the control whose color should be changed with the scroll bars.

The OnCreate code then sets the ItemIndex property of the combo box to 0 (zero) to be sure that the first item in the list is selected as the form opens. If you do not want any item selected by default, set this property to -1.

Listing 15.10 is the OnChange event handler for the combo box. It is called whenever the combo box value changes, whether by typing in some text, selecting from the drop-down list, or through code.

Colors, Brushes, and Pens

In Windows, colors are represented by a 32-bit value calculated from three single byte values for the red, green, and blue components. If all three values are 0, the color is black. If all three are at the maximum of 255, the color is white.

The Colors example uses three scroll bars with a range of 0 to 255 to set colors. The Windows API function RGB takes the red, green, and blue values as parameters, and returns a Windows color value. Many Delphi components have a Color property which can be set using one of the many color constants provided (declared in the Graphics unit, see the TColor topic in the help system for a complete list), or by directly setting the component color to an RGB value. The colors of the panel objects used as picture frames in this example are set directly by the SetColors procedure (shown in Listing 15.9).

Brushes and pens are used when drawing graphics in Windows. A brush is a small bit pattern used to fill an area. A solid brush fills an area with a solid color, whereas a hatched or pattern brush fills an area with a small regular pattern. A pen is used, as you might expect, for drawing lines. Pens can draw solid lines, or various combinations of dotted and dashed lines. Both brushes and pens can be set to any Windows RGB color. If your system can not display the selected color, Windows will pick the nearest matching color in its current palette.

Brushes and pens are GDI objects. In traditional Windows programming, it is necessary to create brushes and pens as needed, then destroy them to avoid using up precious GDI resources. Delphi encapsulates them into TBrush and TPen objects. These objects are properties of canvas objects (discussed in the next section) and are created and destroyed automatically along with the canvas and its parent object.

Canvases, Graphics, and Shapes

The simplest graphics controls are shapes. Shape controls are geometric figures (rectangles, circles, and so on) which can be placed on your form. The shape can be painted using various standard Windows brushes and colors. Listing 15.9 shows how the colors of the shape and panel controls are set by the movements of the three scroll bars.

A canvas is an object used as a drawing surface. It encapsulates the Windows device context. A number of different objects have a Canvas property, including forms, combo boxes and, notably for this example, bitmaps. By selecting appropriate pen and brush properties, almost any sort of drawing can be done on a canvas (see Listing 15.11).

LISTING 15.9 SETCOLORS PROCEDURES

```
procedure TColorForm.SetColors;
var
   ColorObject: TObject;
   NewColor: TColor;

begin
   { only if UpdateColors flag is set }
   if UpdateColors then
      begin
         { get generic TObject handle to current selection }
         ColorObject :=
FrameSelector.Items.Objects[FrameSelector.ItemIndex];

         { get the color specified by the scroll bars -
         'RGB' is a windows API function }
         NewColor := RGB(RedScrollBar.position, GreenScrollBar.position,
BlueScrollBar.position);

         { check the type of the selected object -
           if it is TShape (the test shape) then cast the object type
           and use the brush to set the color }
         if ColorObject is TShape then
            TShape(ColorObject).Brush.Color := NewColor

         { if it is not TShape, then it must be one of the Frames (pan-
els) -
           cast the object type and use the color property }
         else
            TPanel(ColorObject).Color := NewColor;

      end;
end;
```

A local object of type TObject is used to attach to the object selected in the combo box (recall that the objects stored in a TString are of type TObject). The Position property of each scroll bar is used to create a new RGB color.

Actually setting the color of the selected object is a little tricky. To color a shape control, you must set the color of its Brush property. The color of a panel control can be set directly. The object type of the selected object is tested to see which coloring technique to use:

```
if ColorObject is TShape then
```

The same trick is used in the combo box's OnChange event handler (Listing 15.10). When a new object is selected, the existing color of the object is read and loaded into the scroll bars.

NOTE

A TObject does not have a Color property, so in order to read the Color property, the TObject must be cast to the appropriate type. You can also use the 'as' operator to perform the cast.

LISTING 15.10 COMBO BOX ONCHANGE EVENT HANDLER AND LOADCOLOR PROCEDURES

```
procedure TColorForm.FrameSelectorChange(Sender: TObject);
var
    ColorObject: TObject;

begin
    ColorObject := FrameSelector.Items.Objects[FrameSelector.ItemIndex];

    { check the type of the selected object -
      if it is TShape (the test shape) then cast the object type
      and use the brush to get the color }
    if ColorObject is TShape then
        LoadColor(TShape(ColorObject).Brush.Color)

    { if it is not TShape, then it must be one of the Frames (panels) -
      use the color property to get the color }
    else
        LoadColor(TPanel(ColorObject).Color);
end;

procedure TColorForm.LoadColor(NewColor: TColor);
begin
    { do not update until all three scroll bars are set }
    UpdateColors := False;

    { separate a TColor into its red, green, and blue values using
      the windows API calls GetRValue, etc. -
      pop these numbers into the scroll bars }
    RedScrollBar.Position := GetRValue(NewColor);
    GreenScrollBar.Position := GetGValue(NewColor);
    BlueScrollBar.Position := GetBValue(NewColor);

UpdateColors := True;
    SetColors;
end;
```

The red, green, and blue components of an RGB color are extracted with the GetRValue, GetGValue, and GetBValue functions (sort of the inverse of the RGB function discussed earlier). These values are used to set the positions of the scroll bars to reflect the current color of the selected object.

A drawing can be displayed on a form by using an image control. The Picture property of the image control determines the bit map. icon, or metafile which will be displayed. Listing 15.11 demonstrates how a realistic portrait of one of the authors can be drawn and displayed with a few simple method calls.

LISTING 15.11 DRAWAUTHOR METHOD

```
procedure TColorForm.DrawAuthor;
var
   AuthorBitmap: Tbitmap;

begin

   { Create a new bitmap handle }
   AuthorBitmap := TBitmap.Create;

   with AuthorBitmap do
      begin
      { set the bitmap size to match the area on the form }
      Width := 134;
      Height := 123;

      with Canvas do
         begin
         { First, draw a rectangle the color of the underlying panel.
            The brush and pen color are the same so there is no border -
            This rectangle fills the area defined above }
         Brush.Color := Panel1.Color;
         Pen.Color := Panel1.Color;
         Pen.Width := 1;
         Rectangle (0,0, 134,134);

         {    set the pen to black and the brush to yellow-
                 this draws a black figure filled with yellow -
                 also set pen width to get a nice thick line }
         Brush.Color := clYellow;
         Pen.Color := clBlack;
         Pen.Width := 5;

         {    draw an ellipse (circle in this case) which almost fills the area -
                 leave a little space for a border }
```

```
Ellipse (4,4, 130,130);

{   Next, draw an arc, or section of an ellipse -
        the dimensions used here were determined by trial and error   }
    Arc(30,60, 104,110, 30,87, 104,87);

{ set the brush color to black to draw two small black-filled ellipses
}
    Brush.Color := clBlack;
    Ellipse (35,36, 44,45);
    Ellipse (91,36,100,45);
    end;
  end;
{   put the new bitmap into the form's image control -
    this will replace anything already there   }
  ImageDisplay.Picture.Graphic := AuthorBitmap;
end;
```

The code in Listing 15.11 creates a TBitmap object of a size to match the image control on the form. In this example, the size is hard coded. In a real application, you would probably dynamically size the bitmap, or at least use declared constants.

The Canvas property of the bitmap is used to do the actual drawing. First, the Brush and Pen properties are set to the proper colors and line widths. Then, the Rectangle, Ellipse, and Arc methods are used to do the drawing.

Open, Save, and Color Common Dialog Boxes

The Colors example uses three of the common Windows dialog boxes (all the code is shown in Listing 15.12). Pressing the Load button invokes the common file open dialog box. At design time, the file filter is set to display only bitmap (*.bmp), icon (*.ico), and metafile (*.wmf) file types. If you press the **OK** button, the Execute method returns True, and the code attempts to load the selected file into the image control. This is done inside a try-except block in case an invalid file is selected. If the image load fails, an error message is displayed.

The Save button demonstrates the common file save dialog box. Again, the filters are set at design time. The code first checks to see that there actually is a picture in the image control to be saved, by comparing the Picture.Graphic property of the image control to the predefined constant 'nil' (the null pointer). The save dialog is then displayed by calling its

Execute method. If you press the **OK** button, the Execute method returns True, and the code saves the current picture in the selected file.

The common colors dialog boxes allows you to select a predefined color, or create a custom color. The Select button's OnClick event handler calls the LoadColor procedure (shown in Listing 15.10) if you press **OK** in the colors dialog. The selected color is returned in the color dialog's Color property.

327

LISTING 15.12 LOAD, SAVE, AND SELECT BUTTONS ONCLICK EVENT HANDLERS

```
procedure TColorForm.LoadButtonClick(Sender: TObject);
begin
   { display the standard open file dialog - the file filters
     are set at design time - if a selection is made, try to load it }
   if OpenDialog.execute then
      { use try block in case invalid file selected, or some other prob-
lem occurs }
      try
          ImageDisplay.Picture.LoadFromFile(OpenDialog.FileName);

      except
          { nothing fancy, just display a message -
            this will prevent default exception handling from occurring }
          Application.MessageBox('Error displaying selected picture',
'Error', mb_OK);
      end;
end;

procedure TColorForm.SaveButtonClick(Sender: TObject);
begin
   { display the standard save file dialog - the file filters
     are set at design time - if a selection is made, save it }
   if ImageDisplay.Picture.Graphic = nil then
      Application.MessageBox('No picture to save', 'Error', mb_OK)
   else
      if SaveDialog.execute then
          ImageDisplay.Picture.SaveToFile(SaveDialog.FileName);
end;

; procedure TColorForm.SelectButtonClick(Sender: TObject);
begin
   if ColorDialog.execute then
      LoadColor(ColorDialog.Color);
end;
```

Drag and Drop

Drag and drop allows you to use the mouse to drag an object from one place to another in a Windows application. In the Colors example, the color displayed in the shape control can be dragged to either of the two picture frame panels. Pressing and moving the mouse when positioned over the shape control initiates a drag. The mouse cursor changes to let you know that a drag is in process. When the cursor passes over a control which can accept a drop (the picture and its frames, in this example), it changes to the shape specified in that control's DragCursor property. When the cursor is in any other position on the form, it changes to the crNoDrop cursor to let you know that the dragged object can not be successfully dropped in that location. Drag and drop is quite easy to implement in Delphi with just a few lines of code and a couple of properties.

Each control on the form has a DragMode property. Set this property to dmAutomatic to initiate dragging without code. Set this property to dmManual to maintain control of dragging through code, allowing you to allow or prohibit the drag based on conditions in your application. In the example, the manual drag mode is used.

To initiate the drag operation, call the BeginDrag method in the control's OnMouseDown event handler (all drag and drop code is shown in Listing 15.13). BeginDrag takes a single Boolean parameter. When set to True, the drag starts (and the cursor changes) immediately when the OnMouseDown event occurs. In effect, this is the same as setting DragMode to dmAutomatic. This can be distracting, especially if the control can be clicked for some purpose other than dragging. Set the BeginDrag parameter to False to delay the start of dragging until the mouse has been moved a small distance.

As the dragging cursor moves over a control, the control receives an OnDragOver event. This event is asking the control if it can accept a drop. The control can check to see what object is being dragged, and decide whether it can accept a drop of that particular object or not. In the example, the panel control's OnDragOver event handler checks to see if the dragged object (the Source parameter) is of type TShape. If so, the Accept parameter is set to True. The cursor changes to show that the dragged object can now be successfully dropped.

Releasing the mouse button over a control which can accept the drag triggers an OnDragDrop event. Your application must determine what to do with the dropped object. The example responds by setting the color of the panel receiving the drop (the Sender parameter) to the color of the shape control which was dragged (the Source parameter). If the drop occurs on the image control, it responds by changing the color of the inner frame panel. Other applications might respond to a drop by opening or printing a file, setting a paragraph's format, moving a spreadsheet cell to a new location, and so on.

A drag can be ended in code also. The EndDrag method can be called to end a drag operation, whether or not the mouse button has been released. It takes a single Boolean parameter. If set to True, the dragged object is dropped. If set to False, the drag is ended, but the object is not dropped. The OnEndDrag event is triggered when a drag is ended, either with or without a successful drop. This gives you an opportunity to clean up after a drag.

LISTING 15.13 DRAG AND DROP CODE

```
{ Shape control OnMouseDown event handler }
procedure TColorForm.TestShapeMouseDown(Sender: TObject;
  Button: TMouseButton; Shift: TShiftState; X, Y: Integer);
begin
   TestShape.BeginDrag(False);
end;

{ panel control OnDragOver event handler }
procedure TColorForm.OuterFrameDragOver(Sender, Source: TObject; X,
  Y: Integer; State: TDragState; var Accept: Boolean);
begin
   Accept := Source is TShape;
end;

{ panel control OnDragDrop event handler }
{ this code is identical for the inner and outer frame controls }
procedure TColorForm.OuterFrameDragDrop(Sender, Source: TObject; X,
  Y: Integer);
begin
   TPanel(Sender).Color := TShape(Source).Brush.Color;
end;

{ image control OnDragDrop event handler - sets color of inner frame
panel }
procedure TColorForm.ImageDisplayDragDrop(Sender, Source: TObject; X,
  Y: Integer);
begin
   InnerFrame.Color := TShape(Source).Brush.Color;
end;
```

The Media Example

FIGURE 15.3 THE MEDIA EXAMPLE.

The Media example demonstrates the media player, radio buttons, and group boxes, check boxes, status bars (panels), application level events, and scroll boxes. It will play CD audio, wave files, and MIDI files if you have the appropriate hardware and/or software installed. Load and run the MEDIA.DPR project. You will see the form shown in Figure 15.3.

Radio Buttons and Group Boxes

Radio buttons allow you to make a single choice out of a group of mutually exclusive choices. The simplest way to use radio buttons in a Delphi application is the Radio Group control, like the 'Control Button Type' box on the example form. The radio group has an Items property which is a TStrings object. Each entry in the Items list corresponds to a radio button. You can have as many or as few radio buttons as you need in a group. You set the overall size of the control, and Delphi handles the spacing of the buttons. Buttons can be added or deleted at runtime by adding or deleting entries in the Items property.

When one of the radio buttons is selected, the radio group control receives an OnClick event. The selected button can be accessed by the ItemIndex property, as shown in Listing 15.14

LISTING 15.14 RADIO GROUP ONCLICK EVENT HANDLER

```
procedure TMediaPlayerForm.ControlButtonTypeRBClick(Sender: TObject);
begin
   {control type RB = 0 means show the media player buttons otherwise,
    show the scroll box buttons}
   MediaPlayer.Visible := (ControlButtonTypeRB.ItemIndex = 0);
   ScrollBox.visible := not ScrollBox.Visible;
end;
```

The first radio button in the group has an ItemIndex property value of 0 (zero). For this example, if the first radio button is selected, the media player control is displayed and the scroll box is hidden. If the second button is selected (ItemIndex = 1), the opposite is done.

There is also a separate radio-button control available in Delphi. To the user, it doesn't matter which type of radio button is used. The developer, however, has to handle them a little differently. You must manually group individual radio buttons by placing them in a container object. Panels, group boxes, notebook pages, and even the form itself can serve as radio-button grouping containers. All radio buttons in a single container are grouped, so only one of them can be selected by the user. In this example, the 'Media Type' group is three individual radio buttons in a group box. Each of the radio buttons has its own OnClick event handler (instead of a single handler for the entire group as in the radio group control). One of the individual radio button OnClick event handlers is shown in Listing 15.15. Use the Checked property to find the current value of the radio button.

Check Boxes

Check boxes are used to select Yes/No, On/Off choices. In the example, checking the Play Twice check box will cause the selected media to be repeated. Leave it unchecked, and the media will be played only once. The current state of the checkbox can be accessed with the Checked property (True or False), or the State property (cbChecked, cbUnchecked, or cbGrayed). The cbGrayed value of the State property is available only if the AllowGrayed property is set to True. This uncommon usage allows the check box component to represent three states instead of the usual two. Listing 15.15 shows how the checkbox is used to decide whether or not to repeat the selection.

Media Player

The media player component can control devices which provide a *Media Control Interface* (MCI). It provides a set of VCR-like buttons for playing, pausing, recording and so on. The player can be visible on the form so that you can interact directly with the buttons, or it can be invisible so that all media control is done by your code. This example shows both styles of control. Listing 15.15 shows the code concerned with controlling the media player component.

Set the DeviceType property to determine what type of media is to be played. Media which use disk files have a FileName property.

LISTING 15.15 MEDIA PLAYER CONTROL CODE

```
{ wave audio radio button OnClick event handler }
procedure TMediaPlayerForm.WaveAudioRBClick(Sender: TObject);
begin
    { set up file selector for .WAV files -
      if a file is selected (user pressed OK) then
      set up the media player }
    FileSelector.FileName := EmptyStr;
    FileSelector.Filter := 'Wave Audio Files|*.wav';
    if FileSelector.Execute then
        begin
            { close current media player file and assign new one }
            MediaPlayer.Close;
            MediaPlayer.DeviceType := dtWaveAudio;
            MediaPlayer.FileName := FileSelector.FileName;
            MediaPlayer.Open;

            { set up status bar display and enable select button }
            FileNamePanel.Caption := LowerCase(FileSelector.FileName);
            SelectButton.Enabled := True;
            if MediaPlayer.Error <> 0 then
                messageDlg(MediaPlayer.ErrorMessage, mtError, [mbOK], 0);
        end;
end;

{ CD audio radio button OnClick event handler }
procedure TMediaPlayerForm.CDAudioRBClick(Sender: TObject);
begin
    { close current media player file - CD audio does not use file name }
    MediaPlayer.Close;
    MediaPlayer.DeviceType := dtCDAudio;
    MediaPlayer.FileName := EmptyStr;
    MediaPlayer.Open;

    { set up status bar display and disable select button }
    FileNamePanel.Caption := 'CD Audio';
```

```
    SelectButton.Enabled := False;
    if MediaPlayer.Error <> 0 then
        messageDlg(MediaPlayer.ErrorMessage, mtError, [mbOK], 0);
end;

{ play button (in scroll box) OnClick event handler }
procedure TMediaPlayerForm.PlayButtonClick(Sender: TObject);
begin
    { use try block to report error if PC can't play the selected item }
    try
        if PlayTwiceCB.State = cbChecked then
            begin
                MediaPlayer.Wait := True;
                MediaPlayer.Play;
                MediaPlayer.Wait := False;
                MediaPlayer.Play;
            end
        else
            MediaPlayer.Play;
    except
        messageDlg(MediaPlayer.ErrorMessage, mtError, [mbOK], 0);
    end;
end;
```

In the wave audio radio button OnClick event handler, the common file open dialog box (see the Colors example) is used to get a file selection from the user. If a file was selected, the media player is closed, the new file is assigned to the FileName property, the value dtWaveAudio is assigned to the DeviceType property, and the player is opened again. The MIDI radio button OnClick event handler (not shown) is identical except for the open dialog Filter property and the media player DeviceType property.

The CD audio radio button OnClick event handler is similar, except that CD audio does not require a file. Both buttons test the Error property of the MediaPlayer to see if an error occurred (for example, you tried to open a bitmap file as if it were a wave audio file). If the Error property is not zero, the error is displayed in a message box.

When you click on the media player Play button, the selected media is played. To play the media from code, call the media player's Play method (the media player has methods corresponding to each of its buttons). In the example, this is done form the Play button in the alternate button bar.

The Wait property tells the media player whether or not it should finish what it is doing before returning control to your program. A value of False means that control returns to your program immediately. True means that the media player will finish its present task before returning control. This could be dangerous: if you play a CD, you will have to wait 45 minutes or so before the application continues, (or manually eject the CD). Even the media player buttons will not be available. To avoid this problem, the Wait property is set to False as the form is created (see Listing 15.16).

If the Play Twice checkbox is checked, the Wait property is set to True. The application execution will pause after the first call to Play and wait until the media player has finished playing the selection. After the selection is complete, execution moves to the next statement. Wait is reset to False and Play is called again. If Wait had been False for the first call to Play, the second Play would have been called immediately. The media player would have ignored it since the selection was already being played.

Panels and Status Bars

The Media example uses two panel controls at the bottom of the form. One displays the name of the currently selected file. The other displays a hint for the control under the mouse pointer (see the section below on hints for more information). Displaying a message in a panel as a status bar is a simple matter of setting the panel control's Caption property to the desired message. In this example, the Alignment properties of the panels are set to left justify the caption text on the panel.

The panels themselves can be aligned to the bottom of the form by using the Align property. Setting this property to alBottom will cause the panel to move to the bottom of its container (often the form itself) and fill its entire width. The height of the panel is not affected. Align property values of alTop, alLeft, and alRight will cause the panel to move to the top, left, or right of the container and fill the width or height completely. A panel with a value of alClient will fill the entire container. when the form (or container) is resized, the 'Aligned' components will resize also, to maintain their alignment.

By setting the Align properties of controls in the proper order, a form can be 'tiled' with status bars and container panels. In the example, the lowest panel (the hint display panel) was set to alBottom first. Then the current file name panel was also set to alBottom. Since the bottom of the form was already occupied by the first panel, the file name panel filled the area just above it. Finally, the large panel containing the rest of the components was set to alClient, causing it to fill the remaining area of the form.

Application Events and Hints

There is one important component which does not appear on the palette or in the Object Inspector: The TApplication component. The TApplication component encapsulates your entire application. Delphi creates a variable called Application, of type TApplication, when your program runs. Typically, you will see the TApplication component only in your project file:

```
Application.CreateForm(TMediaPlayerForm, MediaPlayerForm);
Application.Run
```

There are a number of useful TApplication methods, properties, and events. Several of the examples in this book have used the MessageBox method to display a simple message dialog box. In this example the TApplication component is used to display hints in the hint panel at the bottom of the form.

Since the TApplication component does not appear in the Object Inspector, its properties and events cannot be directly accessed at design time. The event handlers and properties must be set manually in code. Listing 15.16 shows how the hinting properties are set, and a TApplication OnHint event handler is assigned as the main form is created.

LISTING 15.16 FORM ONCREATE AND APPLICATION ONHINT EVENT HANDLERS

```
procedure TMediaPlayerForm.FormCreate(Sender: TObject);
var
   WinDir: array[0..144] of Char;
begin
   { tell the media player not to finish the selection before
     processing the next code step }
   MediaPlayer.Wait := False;

   { assign application OnHint event handler, hint color, and pause }
   Application.OnHint := DisplayHint;
   Application.HintColor := clAqua;
   Application.HintPause := 200;

   { get windows directory as initial dir in file selector }
   GetWindowsDirectory(WinDir, 144);
   FileSelector.InitialDir := StrPas(WinDir);
end;

{ displays application hints in hint panel -
  application OnHint event handler }
procedure TMediaPlayerForm.DisplayHint(Sender: TObject);
begin
   HintPanel.Caption := Application.Hint;
end;
```

An OnHint event is triggered when the mouse moves over a control with a non-blank Hint property. Since the DisplayHint procedure is assigned as the application OnHint event handler, the hint text will be displayed as the caption of the hint panel.

Several of the controls in the example display fly-by hints as well as panel hints. The Hint property of a control can contain two separate hints by separating them with a ' | ' (pipe or vertical bar character). The first is the fly-by hint, and the second is the application hint.

The HintColor property is set to clAqua. The HintPause property is the length of time the mouse pointer must remain on a control before an OnHint event is generated.

Bitmap Buttons

Delphi bitmap buttons are pushbuttons which can have a bitmap on its face. There are a number of predefined bit-map buttons, available through the Kind property. The example uses the predefined close button. This closes the application without having to write any code.

Scroll Box

Use a scroll box control to provide a scrollable area on a form. The example uses a scroll box to contain the alternate set of media player control buttons. Without the scroll box. the button bar would be much larger than the form. Many applications (Delphi, for example) use this technique for a scrolling toolbar. An image editor or word processor might use a scroll box to display a picture or document larger than the available form or screen space. No programming is necessary to maintain a scroll box, though a number of properties and methods are available if you need to manage it in code.

The Notebook Example

The Notebook example demonstrates notebooks and tabsets, file selection controls, list boxes, masked edit boxes, timers, date manipulation, text file printing, and VBX's and sample controls. Load and run the NOTEBOOK.DPR project. You will see the form shown in Figure 15.4.

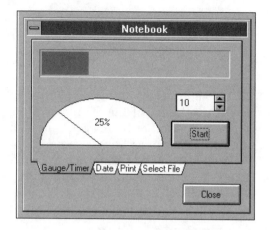

FIGURE 15.4 THE NOTEBOOK EXAMPLE.

Notebooks and Tabsets

Delphi provides two ways to get multiple pages of controls on a single form. The tabbed notebook control provides each page with its own tab. When the tab is clicked, the page is displayed. It is a simple control, with no code required to use it. Many modern applications are using tabbed notebook style controls for setup and configuration dialog boxes.

The notebook example uses the second method of creating multiple pages. The notebook control is a multipage control without tabs. The tabset control is a set of tabs without a notebook. Listing 15.17 shows how the two controls are connected.

LISTING 15.17 TAB SET ONCLICK EVENT HANDLER

```
procedure TNotebookForm.TabSetClick(Sender: TObject);
begin
   Notebook.PageIndex := TabSet.TabIndex;
end;
```

When you select a tab, the tabset control receives an OnClick event. The TabIndex property of the tabset is the ordinal number of the tab selected (starting with 0). The PageIndex property of the notebook is the currently displayed page.

Timers

The first page of the notebook example demonstrates a timer control. A TTimer object is an encapsulation of the Windows timer. Use a timer to delay some processing for a period of time, or to repeat some processing at intervals of time. Listing 15.18 shows how to respond to OnTimer events, and how to set the timing interval of a timer control, and how to turn the timer on and off. Timers are a limited resource, in Windows, and should be used sparingly.

VBX and Sample Controls – Gauges

Delphi can use industry standard VBX (version 1.0) controls on a form without the need for the VB runtime DLL's (the VBX file itself is still required, and must be in the application directory, or in your search path). Several sample VBX's are supplied with Delphi. In this example, the gauge VBX is used to show timer events.

Several sample custom components are also provided with Delphi (developing your own custom components is discussed in Chapter 31). The Delphi sample gauge component is used to show timer events just like the VBX described above. A spin control sample component is used to adjust the value of the timer interval. The VBX and the custom Delphi components are placed on the form and dealt with just like any native components. You do not really need to know that they are custom components or VBX's at all.

LISTING 15.18 TIMER, GAUGE, AND SPIN CONTROL CODE

```
{ OnTimer event handler }
procedure TNotebookForm.GaugeTimerTimer(Sender: TObject);
begin
   { if the gauges are at max (100), reset to 0 }
   if VBXGauge.Value >= VBXGauge.Max then
      begin
         VBXGauge.Value := VBXGauge.Min;
         SampleGauge.Progress := SampleGauge.MinValue;
      end
   else
      { the gauges are not at max, so add 5 }
      begin
         VBXGauge.Value := VBXGauge.Value + 5;
```

```
            SampleGauge.Progress := SampleGauge.Progress + 5;
      end;
end;

{ gauge button OnClick event handler }
procedure TNotebookForm.GaugeButtonClick(Sender: TObject);
begin
   GaugeTimer.Enabled := not GaugeTimer.Enabled;

   if GaugeTimer.Enabled then
      GaugeButton.Caption := 'Stop'
   else
      GaugeButton.Caption := 'Start';
end;

{ spin control OnChange event handler }
procedure TNotebookForm.SpinEditChange(Sender: TObject);
begin
   GaugeTimer.Interval := SpinEdit.Value;
end;
```

The timer runs the gauge values from zero to 100 by fives, then resets them to zero again. You can leave them running while you go to another page on the form, or another program entirely. The start and stop button toggles the Enabled property of the timer, to turn the timer on and shut it off. The spin control assigns its new value to the timer's Interval property to speed up or slow down the gauges.

List Boxes

The Date page of the notebook has a list box control. This is a list of values presented for you to choose from (it is an encapsulation of the standard Windows list box control). The Items property stores the values in the list. It is an object of type TStrings, so the list can be managed using the methods discussed in the Sorter example. The ItemIndex property is the ordinal number of the selected item. The OnClick event is triggered when you select an item from the list. Listing 15.19 shows how the selected item is accessed in response to an OnClick event.

Mask Edit Boxes

A mask edit box is very similar to a normal edit box, except that an input mask can be provided to force the user to enter data in a particular format. The mask used in this example forces entry in date format (99/99/99). The mask enforces only the pattern of characters entered. It cannot insist that you enter a valid date. This is done in the program code shown in Listing 15.19. An OnChange event is triggered whenever the data in the control changes. The details of defining an edit mask are discussed in Chapter 17.

Date Manipulation

Delphi provides a TDateTime data type with a number of methods for date and time manipulation. This example displays the day of the week for any day you enter or select from the list box.

LISTING 15.19 DATE MANIPULATION CODE

```
{ list box OnClick event handler }
procedure TNotebookForm.DateListBoxClick(Sender: TObject);
begin
    DisplayDayOfWeek(DateListBox.Items[DateListBox.ItemIndex]);
end;

{ mask edit OnChange event handler }
procedure TNotebookForm.DateEntryChange(Sender: TObject);
begin
    DisplayDayOfWeek(DateEntry.EditText);
end;

{ translates the input date to a DOW }
procedure TNotebookForm.DisplayDayOfWeek(DOWText: String);
var
    DayValue: Integer;
    DTValue: TDateTime;
    DayName: String;
begin
    try
        { cast the string to a datetime - if this doesn't work,
          an exception will be raised and caught below }
        DTValue := StrToDate(DOWText);

        { get the integer dow and translate to a string }
        DayValue := DayOfWeek(DTValue);
        case DayValue of
            1: DayName := 'Sunday';
            2: DayName := 'Monday';
            3: DayName := 'Tuesday';
            4: DayName := 'Wednesday';
```

```
     5: DayName := 'Thursday';
     6: DayName := 'Friday';
     7: DayName := 'Saturday';
   else
     DayName := 'Error'
   end;
   { set the label caption with the date and dow }
   DayOfWeekLabel.Caption := DOWText + ' is a ' + DayName;
 except
   { on date conversion error, display message }
   on EConvertError do
     DayOfWeekLabel.Caption := 'Invalid date';
 end;
end;
```

The DisplayDayOfWeek procedure receives the entered or selected date as a string. It first tries to cast this value to a DateTime type with the StrToDate function. If this fails, an EConvertError exception will be raised, and will be dealt in the except block.

If the conversion is successful, the DayOfWeek function is called to get the ordinal number of the day of the week for the selected date (1 = Sunday, 7 = Saturday). A case statement converts this to the string name of the day, and the date and day of week are displayed in a label control.

Selecting Files and Directories

The common file open and save dialog boxes have been used in a couple of examples. Delphi also provides controls you can use to create your own file management forms. A directory list box control displays an outline view of the directories on the drive specified in its Drive property (the outline is similar to Windows File manager). The Directory property is the name of the currently selected directory in the outline. The Drive property is the name of the disk drive the directory structure is on.

A file list box control displays a list of files in the directory specified in its Directory property, and conforming to the file filter in its Mask property. Set the FileList property of a directory list box to the name of a file list box, and the file list box display will change as you select directories, without having to write any code.

The drive combo box control is a combo box containing a list of available drives on the system. Set its DirList property to the name of a directory list box to make an automatic connection between them. When a new drive is selected in the combo box, the directory list box will change its display.

Finally, the filter combo box contains a list of file filters (set up by the developer at design time or run time). By setting its FileList property to the name of a file list box, the file list box contents will change when a new filter is selected.

Since these controls are connected automatically by Delphi, the only custom code needed is to display the name of the selected file (Listing 15.20).

LISTING 15.20 FILE LIST BOX ONCHANGE EVENT HANDLER

```
procedure TNotebookForm.FileListBoxChange(Sender: TObject);
begin
    if FileListBox.FileName = EmptyStr then
        SelectedFileLabel.Caption := 'No file selected'
    else
        SelectedFileLabel.Caption := FileListBox.FileName;
end;
```

Printing Text Files

Delphi provides a simple way to print a standard text file. Listing 15.21 shows how to invoke the standard printer setup dialog, read a text file, and send it to the printer.

LISTING 15.21 PRINTING TEXT FILES

```
{ setup button OnClick event handler }
procedure TNotebookForm.SetupButtonClick(Sender: TObject);
begin
    PrinterSetupDialog.Execute;
end;

{ print button OnClick event handler }
procedure TNotebookForm.PrintButtonClick(Sender: TObject);
var
    LineCounter: Integer;
    PrintText: System.Text;
    FileStrings: TStringList;
begin
    { display print dialog - if the user cancels, get out }
    { not using any dialog settings - its just for show }
    if not PrintDialog.Execute then
        exit;
```

```
try
    { create a TStringList and load in the selected file }
    FileStrings := TStringList.Create;
    FileStrings.LoadFromFile(FileListBox.FileName);

    { assign the standard text file to the printer }
    AssignPrn(PrintText);

    { open the std file for printing }
    Rewrite(PrintText);

    { loop thru lines and write each one }
    for LineCounter := 0 to FileStrings.Count - 1 do
        Writeln(PrintText, FileStrings.Strings[LineCounter]);

finally
    { close std text file and free TStringList memory }
    System.Close(PrintText);
    FileStrings.Free;
end;
end;
```

The standard printer setup dialog is called by the Setup button. There is no need to test for a return value, as any user interaction in this dialog is with Windows, and not our application.

This example is similar to the text file example in Chapter 11, except that output is sent to the printer. The AssignPrn method is used (instead of Assign) to assign a standard text file to the printer. Writing to this file causes a line to be sent to the printer. This example uses a TStringList object instead of a memo control. The Rewrite and Writeln methods, and the rest of the example work exactly as discussed in Chapter 11.

Note that this example does not attempt to control the printer in any way. Any changes made in the printer setup dialog box are accepted. Whatever fonts, orientation, and so on, are established are used without modification. The common print dialog is used to initiate the print job, but any changes made (page range, number of copies, and so on) are ignored.

More sophisticated printing can be done by using a TPrinter object in your code. The TPrinter object has a Canvas property, just like the ones discussed in the Colors example. By using Canvas methods like TextOut, LineTo, Ellipse, and so on, you can create any kind of document.

The Task Manager Example

The Task Manager example demonstrates the TOutline component. It also previews some of the data aware controls to be covered in the next few chapters, and custom exceptions, which will be covered in Chapter 25. Copy the two data tables (files task.* and status.*) to the directory in which Delphi will create the TASKMAN.EXE file for the project, then load and run the TASKMAN.DPR project. You will see the form shown in Figure 15.5.

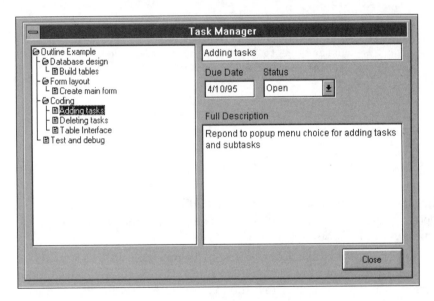

FIGURE 15.5 THE TASK MANAGER EXAMPLE.

Data-Aware Controls

This example uses a Paradox table to store the outline data and another as a data lookup. The group of controls on the right side of the form are connected directly to the data and lookup tables, and display the values from the current data table record. These controls, and the objects and methods used to extract the data from the tables are only briefly covered in this chapter. Chapters 16 and 17 cover databases and data controls thoroughly.

Outlines

The outline control displays a hierarchical tree, similar in appearance to the Windows File Manager. In fact, one of the sample components provided with Delphi is a directory outline, derived from the basic outline component. For this example, the outline control displays a task database. Each task may have many sub-tasks. The detail for each task is displayed in the data controls on the right side of the form.

The TOutline control is a complex component with a number of important properties:

Items	An array of TOutlineNode objects, containing one element for each node in the outline. The outline elements are numbered from top to bottom, starting with one, in the fully expanded outline.
SelectedItem	The Items array index for the currently selected node.
OutlineStyle	An enumerated type providing several constants describing how the node glyphs are displayed.
PictureLeaf	The bitmap to be displayed for nodes which contain no subnodes. Similar properties are PictureOpen, PictureClosed, PictureMinus, and PicturePlus.

Each node is an object of TOutlineNode type. A TOutlineNode also has some important properties:

Text	The text displayed in the outline, up to 255 characters.
Data	A Pointer object which can be used to attach any type of data to the node.
Index	The index into the outline's Items property array.
HasItems	Does the node have sub-nodes?
Level	The hierarchical level (or indentation)of the node, with zero being the top level.
Parent	The TOutlineNode object which is the node's parent node.
Expanded	Is the node expanded to show sub-nodes?

Several TOutline methods are used in this example:

AddObject	Adds a TOutlineNode object to the outline as a sibling (at the same level) as an existing item.
AddChildObject	Adds a TOutlineNode object to the outline as a child of an existing item.
Delete	Deletes an outline node.

The example first declares several types it will need to manage the outline. A new TNodeData record type is defined for use as the Data property to be stored by each outline node. The record contains the key value from the data table and two Boolean variables, flagging whether or not the node has sub-nodes, and if those sub-nodes have been loaded from the table yet.

Two enumerated types are defined. The first is for the three possible node types (child, sibling, and master). The second is a list of data table fields used by the table access routines. A custom exception is declared to allow the application to shut down if it can not find the data tables. Two variables are defined (in addition to the MainForm variable generated by Delphi). UpdateNodeText is used as a flag to prevent some screen flashing when reading outline nodes from the table. CurrentNode is used to keep a handle to the currently selected outline node.

The form's OnCreate event handler (Listing 15.22) calls the GetDatabaseName function (Listing 15.24) to retrieve the name of the directory where the tables should be located. It then tests to be sure that the required tables exist. If they do not, the custom exception is raised to report the error. This will also cause the application to be terminated (see the project file in Listing 15.23).

If all is well, the procedure sets up the data tables, calls LoadTaskGroup (Listing 15.25) to load the first level of outline nodes, and calls SelectNode (Listing 15.28) to set the outline to the first item.

LISTING 15.22 OUTLINE INITIALIZATION

```
type
   { data item record for outline nodes }
   TNodeData = record
      TaskID:          LongInt;  { key value from task table }
      HasSubTasks:     Boolean;  { does this item have sub tasks? }
      SubTasksLoaded:  Boolean;  { have the sub tasks been loaded yet? }
   end;
```

```
{ enum type for task table fields }
   TTaskFields = (fnTaskID, fnParentTaskID, fnHasSubTasks, fnStatus,
fnDueDate, fnShortDesc, fnLongDesc);

   { enum type for new nodes }
   TNewTaskTypes = (ChildTask, SiblingTask, MasterTask);

   { custom exception to report missing table }
   ETableMissing = class(Exception);

var
   MainForm: TMainForm;
   UpdateNodeText: Boolean;
   CurrentNode: TOutlineNode;

{ main form OnCreate event handler }
procedure TMainForm.FormCreate(Sender: TObject);
begin
   try
      { Set flag to prevent updates on short desc OnChange event -
        no need to do it on form open }
      UpdateNodeText := False;

      { get data base name }
      MainForm.TaskDB.DatabaseName := MainForm.GetDatabaseName;

      { make sure the task table exists before running the app - raise
exception if not }
      if not FileExists(TaskDB.DatabaseName + '\' + TaskTable.TableName)
then
         raise ETableMissing.Create('Task table missing');

{ set up and activate tables }
      TaskDB.Connected := True;
      TaskTable.DatabaseName := TaskDB.DatabaseName;
      TaskTable.Active := True;
      TaskTableIndex.DatabaseName := TaskDB.DatabaseName;
      TaskTableIndex.Active := True;
      StatusTable.DatabaseName := TaskDB.DatabaseName;
      StatusTable.Active := True;

      { if the table is not empty, then load up the outline }
      if not TaskTable.EOF then
         begin
         { load up top level tasks - since outline is empty, parent node
and ID is 0 }
```

```
        LoadTaskGroup(0, 0);

        { start at top of outline }
        SelectNode(1);
        end;

    { Set flag to permit updates on short desc OnChange event }
    UpdateNodeText := True;
  except
    on E: ETableMissing do
        MessageDlg(E.Message, mtError, [mbok], 0)
  end;
end;
```

If the data tables are not found, the OnCreate event handler raises the EMissingTable exception. The except block handles this in a very simple manner: it just displays an error message.

N O T E However, if this exception is raised, the code which activates the database and the tables is never executed. This fact is exploited in the project file, as shown in Listing 15.23. If the database component's (TaskDB) Connected property is False, Application.Run is never called, and the application is therefore terminated. See Chapter 25 for more information on exception handling.

LISTING 15.23 OUTLINE EXAMPLE PROJECT FILE

```
program Taskman;

uses
  Forms,
  Main in 'MAIN.PAS' {MainForm};

{$R *.RES}

begin

  Application.CreateForm(TMainForm, MainForm);
  if MainForm.TaskDB.Connected then
    Application.Run;

end;
```

For this example, we assume the data tables are in the same directory as the TASKMAN.EXE file. This directory can be found as shown in Listing 15.24.

The Application.ExeName property contains the full path name of the executable file from which the program is run (in this example TASKMAN.EXE). The directory name ends and the file name starts with the last backslash character in the string.

The code uses the strRScan function to get a pointer to this character. The length of the path portion of the string is calculated by subtracting the pointer to the original string from the pointer to the file name. This length is used in the StrLCopy function to get the path portion of the original string, and return it to the calling procedure. See Chapter 6 for more information on string handling routines and pointer arithmetic.

LISTING 15.24 GETDATABASENAME FUNCTION

```
function TMainForm.GetDatabaseName: String;
var
   ExeDirName,
   ExeFileName: array[0..100] of Char;
   FileNamePtr: PChar;
   NumChars: Word;
begin
   { get .exe file name }
   StrPCopy(ExeFileName, Application.ExeName);

   { find the last '\' in the full path file name to get
     starting point of the file name }
   FileNamePtr := StrRScan(ExeFileName, '\');

   { subtract the pointers to get the number of chars in the path }
   NumChars := FileNamePtr - ExeFileName;
   StrLCopy(ExeDirName, ExeFileName, NumChars);

   { return the path string }
   Result := StrPas(ExeDirName)
end;
```

The example loads groups of sub-tasks only when the parent task is expanded (by double-clicking). The LoadTaskGroup procedure takes the parent node's Index property as well as its ID value in the table. The code reads all tasks from the table having this parent task. The AddTaskToOutline function (Listing 15.30) is called to add each task.

The final step is to set the SubTasksLoaded flag in the parent node so the next time it is expanded, the program does not try to call this procedure again.

LISTING 15.25 LOADTASKGROUP PROCEDURE

```
procedure TTaskForm.LoadTaskGroup(ParentIndex, ParentID: LongInt);
var
    NewDataItem,
    ParentDataItem: ^TNodeData;
    NewNodeIndex: LongInt;
begin
    { set range in indexed task table -
      using the passed in TaskID to filter the parent ID field }
    TaskTableIndex.SetRange([ParentID], [ParentID]);

    { loop through all adding to outline }
    while not TaskTableIndex.eof do
        begin
            { add new item to outline }
            NewNodeIndex := AddTaskToOutline(ParentIndex, ChildTask,
TaskTableIndex);

            { move to next record }
            TaskTableIndex.Next;
    end;

    { get pointer to parent data item - update subs loaded flag -
      skip on form open when index is 0 }
    if ParentIndex <> 0 then
        begin
            ParentDataItem := TaskOutline.Items[ParentIndex].Data;
            ParentDataItem^.SubTasksLoaded := True;
        end;
end;
```

The steps required to add a node to the outline are contained in the AddTaskToOutline procedure (Listing 15.26). It adds the node from the current record in the table object parameter, and returns the new node's Index property. The AtIndex parameter tells the code which existing node the new node should be attached to. The TaskType parameter can assume a value of *ChildTask* for inserting sub-tasks, *SiblingTask* for inserting tasks at the same level as the current task, or *MasterTask* for new top level tasks (see Listing 15.22 for the declaration of this enumerated type). The NewItemTable parameter is the TTable object used to retrieve the task to be added. The LoadTaskGroup procedure (Listing 15.25) and the AddTask procedure (Listing 15.30) call this function.

A new TNodeData item is created and filled with the data from the table record. The SubTasksLoaded field is set to False (since this is a newly loaded item). If a new master or sibling task is being added, the TOutline's AddObject function is used. This function adds a new node at the same level as the node index passed as the first parameter. The text description and the TNodeData information of the new node are also passed to this function, and used in the new node. Notice that a parent value of zero is passed to AddTask if a master task is being added.

If a new child task is being added, the TOutline's AddChildObject function is used. This is identical to the AddObject function, except that the new item is a child of the current node, instead of at the same level. In this case, the parent node's HasSubTasks item is set to True.

The outline control displays different glyphs for nodes which have subnodes and nodes which do not. Since we are loading sub-tasks on demand only, the code has to fool the outline a little bit. A newly loaded parent node has sub-nodes in the table, but not yet in the outline. A temporary sub-node is added to each of these parent nodes so that the proper glyph is displayed. The temporary node is deleted when the parent node is expanded (see Listing 15.26).

LISTING 15.26 ADDTASKTOOUTLINE FUNCTION

```
function TTaskForm.AddTaskToOutline(AtIndex: LongInt;
                                   TaskType: TNewTaskTypes;
                                   NewItemTable: TTable): LongInt;
var
    NewDataItem,
    ParentDataItem: ^TNodeData;
begin
    { create data item for new outline node }
    new(NewDataItem);
    NewDataItem^.TaskID := NewItemTable.Fields[Ord(fnTaskID)].AsInteger;
    NewDataItem^.HasSubTasks :=
NewItemTable.Fields[Ord(fnHasSubTasks)].AsBoolean;
    NewDataItem^.SubTasksLoaded := False;

    if (TaskType = SiblingTask) or (TaskType = MasterTask) then
        { add new sibling or master item to outline - return new index }
        Result := TaskOutline.AddObject(AtIndex,
NewItemTable.Fields[Ord(fnShortDesc)].AsString,
        NewDataItem)
    else
        begin
            { add new child item to outline - return new index }
            Result := TaskOutline.AddChildObject(AtIndex,
NewItemTable.Fields[Ord(fnShortDesc)].AsString,
NewDataItem);
```

```
{ if the new item should have subs, add a phony one
  to fool the outline into using the right glyph -
  only necessary for child objects added by LoadTaskGroup }
if NewDataItem^.HasSubTasks = True then
  TaskOutline.AddChildObject(Result, 'phony', newDataItem);
  end;
end;
```

When a parent node is expanded for the first time, its temporary sub-task must be deleted and its real sub-tasks must be loaded. The HasSubTasks flag is true if the node is a parent, and the SubTasksLoaded flag is true if the sub-tasks have already been loaded. Note that these flags are fields in the TNodeData record set up for this program only. They are not related to the TOutlineNode property HasItems, which is maintained automatically by the outline..

The temporary node is the first and only child node of the current node. The TOutlineNode method GetFirstChild returns the Index property of this node. This Index is used in the TOutline method Delete to delete the temporary node. Then, LoadTaskGroup (Listing 15.25) is called to load the sub-tasks.

LISTING 15.27 EXPANDING A NODE

```
p procedure TMainForm.TaskOutlineExpand(Sender: TObject; Index: Longint);
var
    DataItem: ^TNodeData;
begin
    DataItem := CurrentNode.Data;

    { only load subs if item has subs, and they are not already loaded -
      delete the phony sub first }
    if DataItem^.HasSubTasks and not DataItem^.SubTasksLoaded then
      begin
        TaskOutline.Delete(CurrentNode.GetFirstChild);
        LoadTaskGroup(TaskOutline.SelectedItem, DataItem^.TaskID);
      end;
end;
```

Two things must happen when a task is selected by user interaction or by code. The CurrentNode variable must be updated to the new current node, and the table data display must be synchronized. The SelectNode procedure (Listing 15.28) is used any time that a node is selected.

The test for 'NewIndex > 0' is used in case the outline is empty. If it is, CurrentNode is set to 'nil'. Otherwise, the code sets the SelectedItem property to the new index passed in to the procedure. If a node is selected by code, this is necessary. If a node is selected by user interaction (either mouse or keyboard), the OnClick event handler is triggered, and calls SelectNode. Since the outline's SelectedItem property is already set by the user interaction, this is partially redundant, but it does not cause any problems.

The CurrentNode variable is set to the Items property of the selected node. The Data property of the node is then retrieved, and the LocateTask function is called to synchronize the data display to the new node (since LocateTask is strictly a database function, it is not covered here).

LISTING 15.28 SELECTNODE PROCEDURE AND ONCLICK EVENT HANDLER

```
procedure TMainForm.SelectNode(NewIndex: LongInt);
var
    DataItem: ^TNodeData;
begin
    if NewIndex > 0 then
        begin
            TaskOutline.SelectedItem := NewIndex;
            CurrentNode := TaskOutline.Items[NewIndex];

            { get the data for the current node }
            DataItem := CurrentNode.Data;

            { sync up the table - locate the task ID}
            if not LocateTask(DataItem^.TaskID) then
                MessageDlg('Task not found', mtError, [mbok], 0);
        end
    else
        CurrentNode := nil;
end;

{ outline control OnClick event handler }
procedure TMainForm.TaskOutlineClick(Sender: TObject);
begin
    SelectNode(TaskOutline.SelectedItem);
end;
```

When the description of an outline item is changed by typing in the ShortDesc control, the change should be reflected in the outline itself. This is done in the OnChange event handler for the ShortDesc control (Listing 15.29).

LISTING 15.29 SHORTDESC ONCHANGE EVENT HANDLER

```
procedure TMainForm.ShortDescChange(Sender: TObject);
begin
    { only update if flag is set -
      prevented during form open and adding tasks }
    if UpdateNodeText then
      CurrentNode.Text := ShortDesc.Text;
end;
```

Tasks can be added to the outline by right-clicking and selecting **Insert Task** or **Insert Subtask** from the pop-up menu (pop-up menus are covered in Chapter 4). Both menu choices call the AddTask procedure as shown in Listing 15.30.

After disabling screen updates, the code checks to see if there are any nodes in the outline (if CurrentNode = nil). If not, a master task must be added, no matter what type of task was requested. Next, if a sub-task is being added, the parent's HasSubTasks field in the table is updated. Then, if a sibling task is being added at level 1, the type is changed to MasterTask.

A new task ID number is generated, a new task record is inserted in the task table, and the record is filled with default values. A case statement then adds the parent information to the table. If a sub-task is being added, its parent is the current node. If a sibling task is being added, its parent is the parent of the current node. A master task does not have a parent, so a value of zero is stored in the table.

The AddTaskToOutline procedure (Listing 15.26) is called to insert the new task into the outline control. If a child task is being added, the parent is expanded first so that the SelectNode procedure can make the new task the current node (if a parent node is not expanded, its children cannot be made current). Screen updates are enabled, and focus is moved to the ShortDesc field so that data can be entered for the new task.

LISTING 15.30 ADDTASK PROCEDURE

```
procedure TTaskForm.AddTask(TaskType: TNewTaskTypes);
var
    NewTaskID,
    NewNodeIndex: LongInt;
    ParentDataItem: ^TNodeData;

begin
    { disable text updates and all data source updates }
    UpdateNodeText := False;
```

```
TaskDS.Enabled := False;

{ if the outline is empty (CurrentNode is nil), add a master task instead }
if CurrentNode = nil then
    TaskType := MasterTask;

{ if we are adding a sub-task, be sure the parent record in the table knows it }
if TaskType = ChildTask then
    begin
        TaskTable.Edit;
        TaskTable.Fields[Ord(fnHasSubTasks)].AsBoolean := True;
    end;

{ if we are adding a sibling task, if the current item is a master(level = 1)
  then add a master task instead }
if (TaskType = SiblingTask) and (CurrentNode.Level = 1) then
    TaskType := MasterTask;

{ move to end of table, calc new ID number }
TaskTable.Last;
NewTaskID := TaskTable.Fields[Ord(fnTaskID)].AsInteger + 1;

{ Get new record and fill in ID and default values }
TaskTable.Edit;
TaskTable.Insert;
TaskTable.Fields[Ord(fnTaskID)].AsInteger := NewTaskID;
TaskTable.Fields[Ord(fnHasSubTasks)].AsBoolean := False; { new item does not
have sub-tasks }
TaskTable.Fields[Ord(fnStatus)].AsString := '0'; { assume new item is 'open' }
TaskTable.Fields[Ord(fnShortDesc)].AsString := 'New Task'; { initial short desc
}

{ set up the parent id of the new item }
case TaskType of
    { if this is a new child, its parent is the current item }
    ChildTask:
        begin
        ParentDataItem := CurrentNode.Data;
        TaskTable.Fields[Ord(fnParentTaskID)].AsInteger := ParentDataItem^.TaskID;
        { make sure the parent's HasSubTasks flag is correct }
        ParentDataItem^.HasSubTasks := True;
        end;
    { if this is a new sibling, its parent is the parent of the current item }
    SiblingTask:
```

```
        begin
        ParentDataItem := CurrentNode.Parent.Data;
        TaskTable.Fields[Ord(fnParentTaskID)].AsInteger := ParentDataItem^.TaskID;
        end;
      { if this is a new master, its parent is 0}
      MasterTask:
        TaskTable.Fields[Ord(fnParentTaskID)].AsInteger := 0;
  end;

  { post the data hanges }
  TaskTable.Post;

  { put the new record into the outline }
  NewNodeIndex := AddTaskToOutline(TaskOutline.SelectedItem, TaskType, TaskTable);

  { if the new item is a child, make sure the parent is expanded
    so we can make the new item the current one }
  if (TaskType = Childtask) and (CurrentNode <> nil) then
    if not CurrentNode.Expanded then
      CurrentNode.Expand;

  { make the new node the current one }
  SelectNode(NewNodeIndex);
  { reset data source and text update flag }
  TaskDS.Enabled := True;
  UpdateNodeText := True;

  { move to short desc field for data entry }
  ShortDesc.SetFocus;
end;
```

Tasks can be deleted from the outline by right-clicking and selecting **Delete** from the pop-up menu. This menu choice calls the DeleteTask procedure as shown in Listing 15.31. This procedure first checks to see if the current task has any sub-tasks. If so, an error message is displayed and the delete is cancelled.

If there are no sub-tasks, screen updates are disabled, and the Index and Level properties of the current node are saved. If the current node is not a master node (its Level property is not zero), its parent's Index and table ID are saved as well. The item is then deleted from the table and the outline using the Delete methods.

If there is a parent (SaveLevel <> 1) and the parent no longer has any sub-tasks after deleting the current task (its HasItems property is False), the HasSubTasks flags in the table and in the outline must be reset. In the table, the proper record is located and changed. In the outline, the parent's TNodeData is changed. Finally, screen updates are enabled, and the SelectNode procedure is called to set focus to the node immediately above the deleted node (SaveNode - 1).

LISTING 15.31 DELETING A NODE

```
procedure TMainForm.DeleteTask;
var
   SaveNode,
   SaveParentID,
   SaveParentNode: LongInt;
   SaveLevel: Word;
   DataItem: ^TNodeData;

begin
   { if there are sub tasks, display an error message }
   if CurrentNode.HasItems then
      MessageDlg('Delete sub-tasks first', mtError, [mbok], 0)
   else   { no sub tasks }
      begin
      { turn off the data source and node update to eliminate flashing data }
      TaskDS.Enabled := False;
      UpdateNodeText := False;

      { delete record and node - sync data display to new current node }
      SaveNode := TaskOutline.SelectedItem;
      SaveLevel := CurrentNode.Level;
      if SaveLevel <> 0 then
         begin
         SaveParentID := TaskTable.Fields[Ord(fnParentTaskID)].AsInteger;
         SaveParentNode := CurrentNode.Parent.Index;
         end;
      TaskTable.Edit;
      TaskTable.Delete;
      TaskOutline.Delete(SaveNode);

      { if the parent no longer has sub-tasks, then change the flags }
      if (SaveLevel <> 1) and (not TaskOutline.Items[SaveParentNode].HasItems) then
         begin
            LocateTask(SaveParentID);
            TaskTable.Edit;
            TaskTable.Fields[Ord(fnHasSubTasks)].AsBoolean := False;
            TaskTable.Post;
            DataItem := TaskOutline.Items[SaveParentNode].Data;
```

```
        DataItem^.HasSubTasks := False;
    end;

{ turn on data source and update node flag }
TaskDS.Enabled := True;
UpdateNodeText := True;

{ move to the item above the deleted item }
SelectNode(SaveNode - 1);
    end;
end;
```

Summary

Delphi provides dozens of controls, each with dozens of properties, methods, and events. This chapter has barely scratched the surface. It is important to study the Object Inspector and Object Browser for each control. Find out what is available: try different combinations of properties, trap different events, call different methods. While we have tried to provide meaningful examples for each control, there is no way that everything can be covered. These examples will get you started, but there is no substitute for experimentation on your own.

The next few chapters discuss Delphi's powerful data aware controls which enable you to easily connect your application to desktop and server databases. Chapter 31 will show you how to create your own Delphi controls.

CHAPTER 16

Delphi Database Controls

The database controls in Delphi are the heart of creating database applications quickly and easily. Delphi's database controls connect your program to its data source. It makes no difference whether the data source is a local Paradox, or dBase, table or a remote database server. Your program uses the same components in the same way to connect to the data source and display and edit data.

The database controls fall into two categories, *data access controls* and *data display controls*. The data access controls have no user interface. They simply provide the connection to your data. Data display controls include a rich set of Windows style controls that can display and edit data. The data display controls are the building blocks of your user interface. This chapter introduces you to the Delphi database controls and their properties. The next chapter will focus on using them to build applications and will explore their methods and events.

What is the Borland Database Engine?

To understand Delphi's database controls you need to understand the common architecture of all Borland database products. All Borland database products, except Paradox for DOS and dBASE for DOS, use a middleware layer called the *Borland Database Engine*, or BDE, to access data. It makes no difference where the data is. The BDE has built-in drivers for Paradox and dBase tables and for text files. It has add-on drivers for Oracle, Sybase, Interbase, and Informix. It also has an ODBC socket that allows you to use ODBC drivers to access data. The following list gives some of the major advantages you get from the BDE.

- You can share data with other BDE applications, such as Paradox and dBase, with no fear of locking or other conflicts because all data access is handled by the BDE.
- You can access data using bidirectional scrollable cursors even on database servers that do not support bidirectional cursors.
- You can perform heterogeneous joins of data on different platforms. For example, in a single query you can join an Oracle table, a Paradox table, and an Interbase table.
- You do not have to translate data between the standard Pascal data types and the data types supported by your data source. The BDE handles all translation automatically.
- You can move data quickly and easily from one platform to another.

In Delphi, the data access controls provide the interface to the BDE, and through the BDE to your data.

There is one interesting thing you need to understand about the BDE to understand the behavior of one of the controls. When the BDE positions a cursor within a table the cursor can point to either a record or a crack. A *crack* is the position between two records, before the first record or after the last record. This actually makes sense and leads to some very useful features. For example, if you tell the engine to move the cursor to the beginning of the table it is actually moved to the crack before the first record. This is useful because you can now read ever record in the table by reading the next record. If the cursor were on the first record doing a "read next" it would skip the first record and read the second record. If the cursor is on a record and you delete the record, the cursor is now on the crack where the record used to be. You will see one place where this is important in the discussion of the DBNavigator control later in this chapter.

Data Access Controls

Table 16.1 lists the Delphi Data access controls and provides a brief description of each.

TABLE 16.1 DELPHI DATA ACCESS CONTROLS

Control	Description
TDatabase	Creates a persistent connection to a database. This is particularly useful with remote database servers.
TTable	Reads and writes data in a table and creates tables and indexes.
TQuery	Uses SQL statements to read and write data.
TStoredProc	Lets you pass execute a stored procedure on your database server and pass parameters to it.
TDataSource	Provides the connection between a TTable or TQuery and one or more data display components such as a TDBGrid.
TBatchMove	Copies a table including its structure and its data.
TReport	Prints reports using ReportSmith.

TDatabase

There is no need to use a TDatabase component unless you are working with data on a remote database server. The TDatabase component controls transaction isolation, whether the user is prompted for a user name and password, and it will hold the database connection open while you open and close tables.

When you work with tables on a server and close all of them the connection to the server will also be closed. Opening the connection to the server is a time consuming process so, ideally, you only want to do it once.If you place a TDatabase component in your form the connection to the server will be held open allowing you to open and close tables quickly at will. Table 16.2 describes the most important properties for TDatabase.

WARNING

The only connection between a TDatabase Component and a TTable or TQuery component is the DatabaseName property. If you want a TDatabase to hold a connection open while you open and close the table make sure that the TTable or TQuery component uses exactly the same DatabaseName as the TDatabase component.

TABLE 16.2 IMPORTANT TDATABASE PROPERTIES

Property	Description
Connected	Set to True to open the connection to the database. Set to False to close the connection.
DatabaseName	The alias of the database you want to connect to.
DatabaseType	The database driver type, for example, STANDARD or INTRBASE.
LoginPrompt	Set to True if you want the user to be prompted for their server user name and password. If the driver information for the alias includes a user name the user name will be filled in automatically. Set to False if you will supply the user name and password in the Params property.
Params	This is a string list that contains the parameters from the alias. For example, Figure 16.1 shows the parameters for a local Interbase connection. Note that you can include the password, as shown in Figure 16.1, using the PASSWORD=MYPASSWORD parameter. However, the password will be visible to anyone that examines the .DCU or .EXE files with an editor.
TransIsolation	Set to one of three values as follows. When set to tiDirtyRead uncommitted changes can be read by others. When set to tiReadCommitted other transactions committed changes can be read. When set to tiReapeatableRead other transactions changes to data that has been read are not seen. How, or if, these features are implemented varies from one database server to another, so check your server documentation.

Remember that passwords you enter in the Params property are not secure. Anyone who is determined and has access to the .EXE or .DCU files and a hex editor or disk editor can find them. For security, either set the LoginPrompt property to True and let Delphi automatically prompt the user for their user name and password or prompt the user yourself and add the password to the TDatabase Params property before you open the database. The project DBASE.DPR on your code disk shows how to add a password to the TDatabase component's Params property. This project has a form with a TDatabase component named Database1 and a Get Password button. The following code is from the button's click-event handler.

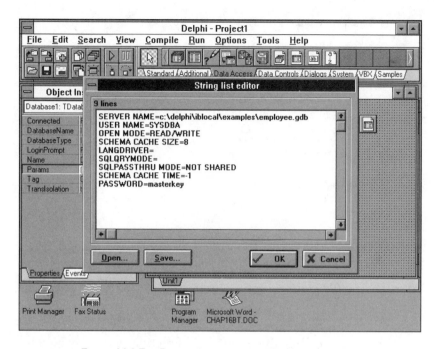

FIGURE 16.1 THE PARAMS PROPERTY OF A TDATABASE CONTROL.

```
procedure TForm1.Button1Click(Sender: TObject);
var
  password: String[32];
  indx:     Word;
begin
  {Initialize the password to null.}
  password := '';
  if InputQuery('Password Please',
               'Enter a test password upto 32 characters.',
               password) then
  begin
    {Add the password to the database component's
     Params property.}
    Database1.Params.Add('password=' + password);
```

```
    {See if the password is really in the Params
     list now.}
    indx := Database1.Params.IndexOf('password=' + password);
    if indx >= 0 then
      MessageDlg('Password stored in Params.',
                 mtInformation,
                 [mbOk],
                 0)
    else
      MessageDlg('Password not stored.',
                 mtWarning,
                 [mbOk],
                 0);
  end
  else
    MessageDlg('You did not enter anything.',
               mtError,
               [mbOk],
               0);

end;
```

This code begins by calling the InPutQuery function to display a dialog and prompt you to enter a test password. InPutQuery returns True if you click the **OK** button and False if you close the dialog any other way. The Params property of a TDatabase component, like the lines in a memo or the items in a list box, is a string list so all of the methods for the TStringList object are available. The statement

```
Database1.Params.Add('password=' + password);
```

calls the string list Add method to add the password to the Database component's Params list. To confirm that the password= line was really added to the Params list

```
indx := Database1.Params.IndexOf('password=' + password);
```

calls the string list IndexOf method. IndexOf searches the string list for the parameter you pass it. If the parameter string is in the string list IndexOf returns its index number. If the parameter is not in the string list IndexOf returns −1. The remainder of the code just uses the MessageDlg procedure to display the appropriate message.

Remember that if you are going to prompt the user for a password and add it to the Params list you must set the TDatabase's Connected property to False when you design the form. Otherwise it will try to open the connection when the form opens and it will fail because there is no password. After you have added the password to the Params list you can use

```
Database1.Connected := True;
```

to open the connection. Also remember to set the TDatabase's LoginPrompt property to False or Delphi will try to prompt the user for a user name and password.

The TDatabase component has a single event, OnLogin. This event occurs when the Connected property is set to True and Delphi attempts to login to the server. This event does not occurr when you connect to a local Paradox or dBase database. It only occurs when Delphi establishes a connection with a database server.

TTable

The TTable component provides a connection between your form and the BDE. Although you can see the TTable in design mode when you place it on your form it is invisible when the form runs. Figure 16.2 shows a new form with a TTable component set to access the Customer table in the DBDEMOS alias.

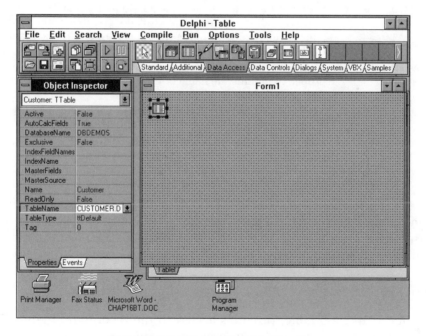

FIGURE 16.2 A TTABLE COMPONENT ON A FORM.

Table 16.3 describes the important properties of TTables.

TABLE 16.3 IMPORTANT PROPERTIES OF TTABLE

Property	Description
Active	Set to True to open the table and False to close it.
BOF	A read only property that is True if the table cursor is positioned before the first record (at the beginning of the file).
CanModify	True if you can make changes to the table.
DatabaseName	The alias of the database that contains the table.
EOF	A read only property that is True if the table cursor is positioned after the last record (at the end of file).
Exclusive	Set to True to open the table with an exclusive lock (sometimes called a Full lock). An exclusive lock prevents any other user from accessing the table in any way.
IndexFieldNames	When you are using a remote database server enter the names of the fields you want the records ordered by separated by a vertical bar (I) character.
IndexName	Enter the name of the index you want to use to access the table. This determines the order in which you will see the records.
MasterFields	If this is the detail table in a one-to-many relationship this property contains the name(s) of the field(s) in the master table to link to. These fields should correspond to the index in the IndexName property.
MasterSource	If this is the detail table in a one-to-many relationship this property contains the name of the TDataSource component for the master table.
ReadOnly	Set this property to True to prevent users from making changes to this table.
TableName	The name of the table you want to access with this TTable component.

The TTable component also includes a rich set of methods that you can use to move through records in a table, search for records in a table, and restrict a users view to a subset of the records in a table using an index. All of these methods will be demonstrated in the next chapter.

TQuery

A TQuery, like a TTable, provides access to the records in a table. The difference is that a TQuery lets you specify a Structured Query Language (SQL) query to the table to restrict which records you will see. Table 16.4 describes the important properties of TQuery components.

TABLE 16.4 IMPORTANT PROPERTIES OF TQUERY

Property	Description
Active	Set to True to open the table and False to close it.
DatabaseName	The alias of the database that contains the table.
EOF	A read only property that is True if the table cursor is positioned after the last record (at the end of file).
DataSource	The TDataSource component which supplies values to parameters that are not supplied in code with the Params property or ParamsByName method.
RequestLive	Set this property to True to request a live answer set. A live answer set is actually a view of the underlying table so changes you make to the data provided by the TQuery will be reflected in the table.
SQL	The SQL property contains the SQL statement that Delphi will execute.
Unidirectional	Some database servers do not support bidirectional cursors. The BDE simulates a bidirectional cursor by buffering records and running new queries as necessary. If your server does not support bidirectional cursors and you do not need a bidirectional cursor set this property to True to improve performance and reduce network traffic.

Because the records you access with a TQuery are the records returned by a SQL query TQuery can provide very flexible views of the data in one or more tables. TQuery is so important and so powerful that an entire chapter, Chapter 20, is devoted to TQuery. In Chapter 20 you will even learn how to create a one-to-many relationship using a SQL query to define the detail record set.

TDataSource

TDataSource is a link between a dataset, that is, a TTable or TQuery, and a data display component. In the section on Data Display Components you will see how to connect one or more data display components to a TDataSource and connect the TDataSource to a dataset to provide interactive access to your data. Table 16.5 introduces the most important properties of TDataSource.

TABLE 16.5 IMPORTANT PROPERTIES OF TDATASOURCE

Property	Description
AutoEdit	If AutoEdit is set to True any component connected to this data source automatically switches to edit mode as soon as the user attempts to change the data displayed by the control.
DataSet	This property contains the name of the TTable or TQuery this TDataSet is connected to.
Enabled	Determines if the data display controls connected to this TDataSoruce will be updated as the table changes or not. Set this property to False if you want to process records in code without the overhead of updating the display.

TBatchMove

The TBatchMove component lets you perform operations with entire datasets at one time; with a TBadtchMove component you can perform any of the following operations:

- Copy a dataset to a table. When you copy a dataset to a table Delphi creates the destination table automatically. If the destination table already exists Delphi overwrites it. If the dataset and destination table are on different platforms, for example, a server dataset and a local Paradox table, Delphi creates the destination table with a structure as close to that of the dataset as possible, and automatically performs any data conversion that is required.

- Delete a dataset from a table. When you delete a dataset from a table you remove each record from the destination table whose primary key matches the corresponding fields of a record in the dataset.

- Append the records from a dataset to a table. Delphi will convert the data as necessary to adjust for differences in field type and size between the tables. If a field type conversion is not possible Delphi generates an exception and no data is appended.

- Update existing records with records from a dataset. If the primary key of a record in the destination table matches the corresponding fields in the dataset the record from the dataset replaces the existing record in the destination table. Records in the dataset that do not match existing records in the destination table are ignored. Once again, as with copy, Delphi will, if possible, convert the data in the dataset to match the field types and sizes in the destination table.

- Append new records and update existing records in the destination table.

For all of these operations Delphi places a Read Lock on the dataset and a Write Lock on the destination table. If the locks cannot be obtained the operation waits until either the locks are obtained, or a timeout occurs. For all TBatchMove operations the source dataset and the destination table can be on different platforms. Table 16.6 describes the important properties of TBatchMove.

TABLE 16.6 IMPORTANT PROPERTIES OF TBATCHMOVE

Property	Description
AbortOnKeyViol	If a TBatchMove operation would violate a referential integrity constraint and this property is True, the operation will abort when the violation is detected.
AbortOnProblem	If a record is found whose data would have to be trimmed in size to fit the field in the destination table and this property is True the operation will abort.
ChangedTableName	If you want to save a copy of records that are changed by an update operation or deleted by a delete operation enter the name of a TTable component. A copy of the original record will be saved in this table.
Destination	The destination TTable component's name.
Mappings	Normally the source dataset's fields are mapped to the destination table's fields from left to right. You can use this property to create your own map in any order.
Mode	The value of Mode determines which operation will be performed. Valid values are batAppend, batAppendUpdate, batCopy, batDelete, and batUpdate.
ProblemTableName	If you enter a TTable name here then records whose data would have to be trimmed to fit the destination tables fields will be placed in this table.
RecordCount	Process all of the records in the source dataset, leave the RecordCount property blank, or set it to zero. If you set this property to any other number then only that many records from the source dataset will be processed. After the TBatchMove operation has finished, RecordCount will be set to the number of records processed.
Source	The source dataset. This can be the name of a TTable or a TQuery.
Transliterate	If True character data will be transliterated from the dataset's character set to the destination's character set if they are different.
TBatchMove	provides a high performance tool for manipulating sets of records. TBatchMove is fast because Delphi simply passes the Mode and other parameters to the BDE and the entire operation is handled by the engine.

TReport

The TReport component provides a link to Borland's ReportSmith report generator. You can design and save reports in ReportSmith and run them from your Delphi application using a TReport Component. Table 16.7 describes the important properties of TReport.

TABLE 16.7 IMPORTANT PROPERTIES OF TReport

Property	Description
AutoUnload	If AutoUnload is True ReportSmith runtime will automatically remove itself from memory when your report finishes running. If this property is False you must explicitly call TReport's CloseApplication method to unload ReportSmith. You will want to keep ReportSmith in memory if your users will run several reports in succession to save the time it takes to load ReportSmith.
EndPage	The last page of the report to print.
InitialValues	This property is a string list that contains the values of any report variables that the report needs when it runs. The strings are of the form VariableName=Value.
MaxRecords	Assign a number to this property to limit the number of records used to create the report. This is useful for testing reports that would be long if the entire database were used.
Preview	If set to True the report will be sent to the screen. Set this property to False to print the report.
PrintCopies	Sets the number of copies to print.
ReportDir	The directory that contains the report you want to run.
ReportName	The name of the saved report that you want to run.
StartPage	The first page to print.

Data Display Controls

Table 16.8 lists the Delphi data display controls, also called data aware controls, and includes a brief description of each.

TABLE 16.8 DELPHI'S DATA DISPLAY CONTROLS

Control	Description
DBGrid	Displays a dataset's data in a tabular format.
DBNavigator	A set of buttons that lets you navigate through a dataset's records with your mouse.
DBText	Lets you display text from a table on your form. You can change the text in code, however, users cannot change the text. DBLabels never get focus.
DBEdit	Displays the data from a single field and lets users change the data unless you restrict their ability to do so.
DBMemo	Displays large amounts of text and lets users edit it. This control is particularly useful for displaying text from memo or large character fields or letting users edit text files.
DBImage	Displays the data from a graphics field.
DBListBox	Displays a list of possible values for a field in a Windows list box.
DBComboBox	Displays a list of possible values for a field in a Windows combo box.
DBCheckBox	Displays the value of a field in a dataset, which can have only two values. You can specify the values for the checked and unchecked state.
DBRadioGroup	Displays a finite set of values in a field as a set of radio buttons.
DBLookupList	Displays the contents of a field in one table, the lookup table, in a list box and lets you select a value to be entered into a field in another table.
DBLookupCombo	Displays the contents of a field in one table, the lookup table, in a combo box, and lets you select a value to be entered into a field in another table.

These controls have many properties in common. The next section describes the common properties for all of these controls. The following sections describe features unique to each control.

Common Properties

Table 16.9 describes the principal properties that are common to all of the data display controls with one exception. The DBNavigator does not actually display data so some of the properties in Table 16.12 do not apply to it.

TABLE 16.9 COMMON PROPERTIES OF DATA DISPLAY CONTROLS

Control	Description
Cursor	Allows you to select the appearance of the mouse cursor when it is in this control.
DataSource	The name of the TDataSource that this control gets its data from.
DragCursor	Allows you to select the shape of the mouse cursor when it is over this control to indicate that the user can drop the object being dragged on this control.
Enabled	If False this control will not respond to keyboard, mouse, or timer events and will not change its display when the data-source it is connected to changes.
Font	Sets the font used to display the data.
Height	Sets the height of the control in pixels.
Hint	Contains a text string that can be displayed when the the mouse cursor passes over the control triggering an onHint event. You can display the hint text in a status bar or as fly-by hints for components in a TPanel.
Left	The position of the left edge of the control relative to the left edge of the form in pixels.
ParentColor	If set to True the control uses its parent's color property. If set to False the control uses its own color property. A control's parent is the object that contains it, usually the form.
ParentFont	If this property is true the control gets its font information from its parent. If not, it uses its own Font property.
PopupMenu	The name of the pop-up menu to display when users right-click on this control.
Top	The position of the top of this control relative to the top of the form in pixels.
Visible	Set to True to make this control visible and False to hide it.
Width	The width of this control in pixels.

The following sections describe properties unique to individual controls. However, many of these properties are also shared by more than one control.

Properties that have already been described for one control will not be repeated for another. To see a complete list of all of the properties for a given control search for the control's type, for example TDBGrid, in the Delphi on-line help.

373

DBGrid

The DBGrid component lets you view the data in a table in a tabular layout similar to a spreadsheet or the tabular view found in most desktop database products. Figure 16.3 shows a form with a DBGrid displaying the sample Parts table that ships with Delphi. Table 16.10 lists the important properties of a DBGrid.

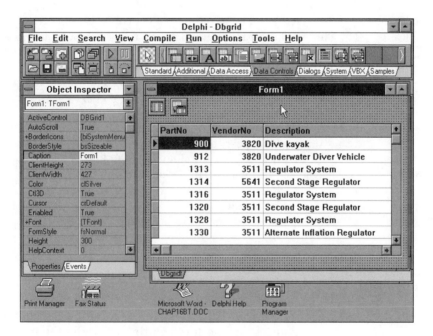

FIGURE 16.3 A DBGRID CONTROL.

TABLE 16.10 MAJOR PROPERTIES OF DBGRID

Control	Description
Align	The value assigned to this property determines how the DBGrid positions and sizes itself within the form. For example, if you select alTop as the Align value the grid moves to the top of the form and sizes itself to fill the form's width.
BorderStyle	Sets the style of the border around the grid.
Color	Sets the color of the DBGrid.
Ctl3D	If True this property gives the control a three-dimensional sculptured look. If False the control has a two dimensional look.
DragMode	Determines if the control can or cannot be dragged or not at runtime.
FixedColor	Sets the color of nonscrolling rows or columns in the grid.
FixedCols	The number of columns that will remain fixed when users scroll the grid horizontally.
FixedRows	The number of rows that will remain fixed at the top of the grid when users scroll the grid vertically.
HelpContext	The context number to be used to call context-sensitive help for this control.
Options	This property has several subproperties that let you control the way the grid appears and behaves. For example, you can turn off the current record indicator or the grid lines if you wish.
ParentCtl3D	If True, the grid will use its parent's Ctl3D property.
ReadOnly	Set this property to True to prevent users from editing the table displayed in the grid.
TabStop	If False, prevents users from tabbing to the control.

DBNavigator

The DBNavigator does not display data. Instead, it is a button bar that lets you move around in a dataset and perform editing operations with your mouse. Figure 16.4 shows a form that contains a DBNavigator and a DBGrid, both connected to the same DataSource. This lets you manipulate the data in the grid using the DBNavigator buttons.

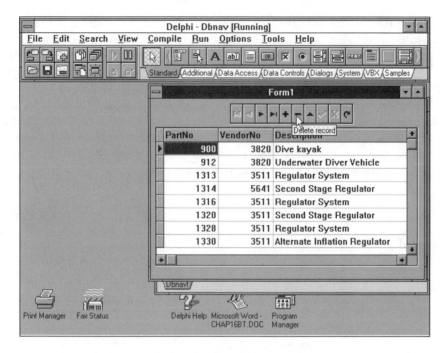

FIGURE 16.4 THE DBNAVIGATOR.

The DBNavigator buttons let you perform the following functions in order, from left to right.

- Move to the beginning of the table.
- Move to the prior record in the table.
- Move to the end of the table.
- Insert a new record in the table.
- Delete a record from the table.
- Edit the current record in the table.
- Post the current record in the table.
- Cancel unposted changes to the current record.
- Refresh your view of the table to show any changes made by other users.

Although the relationship between the symbols on the navigator buttons and the button's function may not be immediately obvious the navigator is very easy to use because it has built-in fly-by help. Just make sure the ShowHint property is true, point to a button with your mouse and its function pops up. You can see the fly-by help window for the Delete button in Figure 16.4.

The DBNavigator is also intelligent in how it displays its buttons. For example, if you click the First Record button to move to the beginning of the table the symbols on the First Record and Prior Record buttons become grayed to indicate that they will not do anything now. Table 16.11 shows the most important properties of the DBNavigator.

TABLE 16.11 MAJOR PROPERTIES OF DBNAVIGATOR

Control	Description
HintColor	This property lets you set the color of the fly-by help.
HintPause	This is the number of milliseconds between the time the mouse cursor arrives over one of the navigator buttons and the time the fly-by help pops up.
ShowHints	If True then fly-by help will appear when the mouse cursor is over a button. Setting this property to False turns the fly-by help off.
VisibleButtons	This property has a subproperty for each button in the navigator so you can control which buttons are included. For example, if you have the AutoEdit property for the DataSource set to True, there is no reason to include the Edit button in the Navigator, since the DataSource will automatically switch to edit mode when the user begins typing in any control.

When you use the DBNavigator you may notice some slightly strange behavior. To see this load and run the DBNAV.DPR project on your code disk. Notice that when you first run the program the Beginning Of Table and Prior Record buttons are grayed. The table cursor is now on the crack before the first record. Now click the **Refresh** button, the last button at the right, and watch what happens. You are still positioned on the first record but the Beginning Of Table and Prior record buttons are no longer grayed. A Refresh positions the cursor on a record so that the cursor is now on the first record, not the crack in front of the record. Click the **Prior Record** button and watch the Beginning Of Table and Prior Record buttons gray again as the cursor moves back to the crack.

Click the **Last Record** button. Notice that you have moved to the last record in the table and the Last Record and Next Record buttons are grayed.

Now click **Refresh** again and watch the buttons un-gray. Clicking the **Last Record** button causes the cursor to move to the crack after the last record, and clicking **Refresh** moves the cursor back to the last record as part of the refresh process.

DBText

A DBText component is similar to the standard label component except that instead of displaying static text it displays the value of a field in a table. A DBText is a good choice to display data that you do not want users to change. It is visually different from a DBEdit control so that it is obvious to users which values they can change, and which they cannot. Figure 16.5 shows the form from the DBTEXT.DPR project with a DBNavigator, a DBText displaying the Part #, and two DBEdit controls displaying the Vendor # and Description fields.

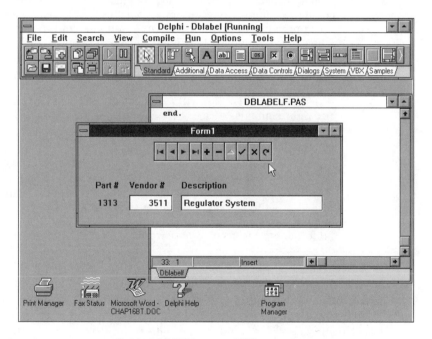

FIGURE 16.5 DBTEXT AND DBEDIT CONTROLS.

DBText has only one property that has not already been described and that is Alignment. The value of the Alignment property determines how the data being displayed will be aligned within the control. The valid values are taLeftJustify, taRightJustify, and taCenter.

DBEdit

DBEdit is a very powerful control for viewing and editing the value from a single field in a table. DBEdit is designed to handle relatively small values that will fit on a single line. For larger amounts of text use a DBMemo. DBEdit includes many powerful properties that let you control what users can and cannot do with the data in a DBEdit. Table 16.12 lists the most useful properties.

TABLE 16.11 MOST USEFUL PROPERTIES OF DBEDIT

Control	Description
AutoSelect	If AutoSelect is True the value in the control is automatically selected when users move to it using the Tab key. If False the contents of the control are not automatically selected. Notice that the value in a DBEdit is never automatically selected when the user moves to the control by clicking it with the mouse. If AutoSelect is True and the user tabs to the field and presses any typable character then the entire contents of the field will be deleted before the new character is entered.
AutoSize	If set to True the DBEdit will automatically resize to match the size of its contents.
MaxLength	This value sets the maximum number of characters that can be entered into the field.
Modified	This read-only property is set to True if the value displayed by the control has been changed.
PasswordChar	If set to #0 (null) then any character the user types will be displayed. If set to any other character then that character will be displayed for each character the user types. This feature is useful for prompting users for passwords.

DBEdit controls include two properties that let you control what a user can enter into this field in the table, EditMask and MaxLength. However, remember that using these tools does not guarantee the integrity of your data if any user can access and modify the data in any way other than by using your application. The best way to ensure domain integrity is to impose restrictions at the database server level using triggers or whatever domain integrity tools your server offers. By enforcing domain integrity at the server you ensure the integrity of your data no matter what tool users use to change it. The EditMask and MaxLength properties are still very powerful and useful tools to use in conjunction with your server's domain integrity enforcement tools, or if your application will be the only means of accessing the data.

DBMemo

The DBMemo control gives you an easy way to handle large volumes of text stored in a memo or BLOb field in your table. Figure 16.6 shows the form from the DBMEMO.DPR project. This form uses a DBMemo to show the notes field in the sample Biolife table that comes with Delphi. It also includes a DBText to display the Common Name field.

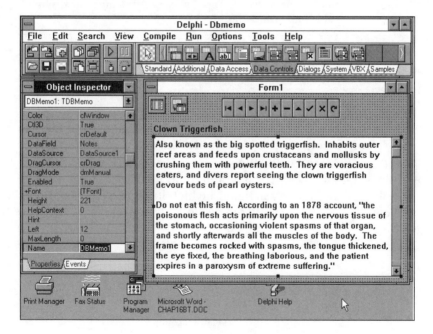

FIGURE 16.6 A DBMEMO CONTROL.

DBmemo has several unique and important properties, which are described in Table 16.13.

TABLE 16.12 MOST USEFUL PROPERTIES OF DBEDIT

Control	Description
AutoDisplay	Set this property to True to automatically display the contents of the memo field as you move from record to record. If you set this value to False the text from the memo field will not be displayed in the DBMemo until the user double-clicks it. This can make scrolling from record to record faster if your data is coming across a network.
ScrollBars	Allows you to specify whether the DBMemo will have scrollbars. Valid values are ssNone, ssBoth, SSHorizontal, and ssVertical.
WordWrap	Set this property to True if you want the memo text wrap to fit within the DBMemo.

DBImage

The DBImage control lets you display graphical data stored in a graphic or BLOb field. Figure 16.7 shows a form with a DBImage control used to display the Graphic field in the sample Biolife table. This form is in the DBGraph project on your code disk.

A DBImage control can display a graphic in .BMP, .WMF, or .ICO format. Its only unique property is Picture which has one of three valid values, Bitmap, Icon, or Metafile. The value of the Picture property determines the image's format.

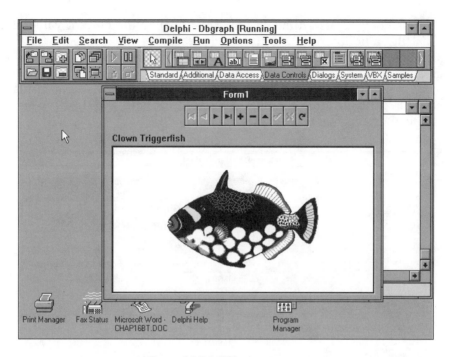

FIGURE 16.7 A DBIMAGE CONTROL.

DBListBox and DBComboBox

Both DBListBox and DBComboBox let users select the value to enter into a field from a list of values contained in the control's Items property. The difference is that DBListBox uses a Windows list box and limits the values the user can enter to those in the list. DBComboBox allows users to select a value from a drop-down list or type in a value that is not in the list.

These controls also differ in how they display the current value of a field. DBComboBox displays the field's value in its edit region, while DBListBox highlights the field's value in its list. If the field contains a value that is not in the DBListBox's list then none of the items in the list are highlighted. Figure 16.8 shows the form from DBLIST.DPR. This form displays records from the sample Country table and has both a DBListBox and a DBComboBox attached to the Continent field.

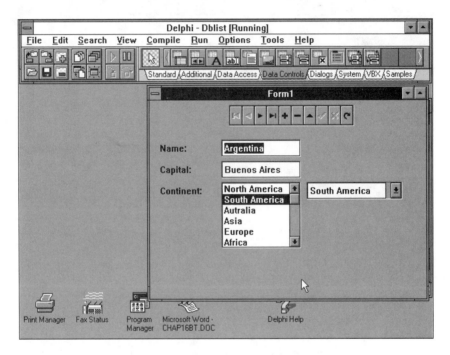

FIGURE 16.8 DBLISTBOX AND DBCOMBOBOX CONTROLS.

The only unique property of these controls is Items. Items is a string list that you can populate either at design time or at runtime. By editing the Items property in your code you can vary the contents of the list as your program runs. To enter values in the list at design time, select the **Items** property in the Object Inspector and click the button in its field to open the string list editor.

DBCheckBox

A DBCheckBox is a good way to let users enter a value into a field that can have only two values. It works well where the values can be True or False, Yes or No, Male or Female, and so on. The form in Figure 16.9 uses the Country table again and shows both a DBCheckBox and a DBRadioGroup connected to the Continent field. Fortunately the DBCheckBox works just fine because all of the countries in this table are either in North or South America.

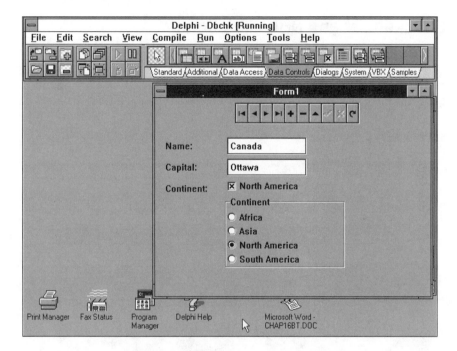

FIGURE 16.9 DBCHECKBOX AND DBRADIOGROUP.

The Caption property of DBCheckBox determines what text appears to the right of the check box itself. Two additional properties, ValueChecked and ValueUnchecked let you set the value that will be entered into the field for the checked or unchecked state of the control. Notice that as you scroll through the records the check appears and disappears depending on the value in the current record. In this example ValueChecked is set to North Americal and ValueUnchecked is set to South America.

DBRadioGroup

DBRadioGroup works exactly like DBListBox. It just provides a different visual effect. It also has an Items property that is a string list of values. The DBRadioGroup will contain one button for each item that you enter into the list.

When you edit data the value of the selected button determines the value from the Items list that will be stored in the table. As you scroll from one record to another the selected button will change to show the value in the Continent field for the current record.

DBLookupList and DBLookupCombo

These components perform the same function as DBListBox and DBComboBox but instead of getting their values from a static list, they get their list of possible values from a table using three special properties. Figure 16.10 shows the form from DBLOOK.DPR on your code disk. This form shows fields from the sample Items table and uses the Parts table as the lookup table.

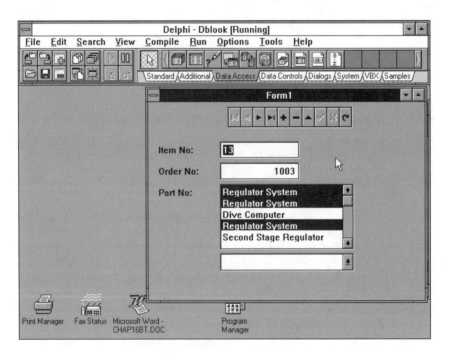

FIGURE 16.10 DBLookupList and DBLookupCombo.

The three properties unique to these controls are LookupSource, LookupDisplay, and LookupField. LookupSource contains the name of the DataSource component that is connected to the Lookup table. LookupField contains the name of the field in the Lookup table whose value will be put into the Data table record. In the example in Figure 16.10 the LookupField property is set to the Part No field in the Parts table. LookupDisplay is set to the field in the Lookup table that you want to display in the list. In the example in Figure 16.10 this property is set to the Description field. This lets users see a list of descriptions, but when they pick a description the corresponding Part No is put into the Part No field in the Items table.

Actually, this is not a very practical example because the Parts table contains the same description for several part numbers but it does work as an illustration.

Summary

Delphi includes a rich set of controls specifically designed to work with data in tables. Although the examples so far have used local Paradox tables there is no difference in the way these controls work in a client server environment. In fact, that is one of the great features of Delphi and the BDE. You can move your data from one platform to another and very little need be changed in your application.

CHAPTER 17

Connecting Controls to Databases

So far in this book, you have been introduced to the concepts and architecture of Delphi, its IDE, its programming language, and the controls in the Visual Control Library. Now it is time to create some database applications. This chapter will show you how to connect all of the components described in the last chapter to both local and server databases. While the last chapter focused on the important properties of each component, this chapter will focus on events and writing code to handle those events.

One of the things you have probably noticed by now is that most of the examples in this book use local Paradox tables. Why is that when this is supposed to be a book about developing client/server systems? The answer is because it is easy and it does not make any difference. It is easy because you do not have to have a server to run the examples. It does not make any difference because there is very little difference between writing an application that uses local tables and writing an application that uses a database server. That is one of the real benefits of using Delphi and other applications that use the BDE.

Throughout this book when a topic is covered where there are differences between the client/server environment and the local table or file server environment, both will be covered. You have already seen one such case in the last chapter in the discussion of TDatabase.

There is one component, TQuery, that was mentioned in the last chapter that is not covered in this chapter. TQuery is so important that it is covered in its own chapter, Chapter 19.

Connecting Datasets to Controls

The first step in creating a database application in Delphi is to place a dataset component on your form. Remember that a dataset can be either a TTable or a TQuery. To create an application to view a table first start by creating a new project, then place a TTable on the form. If you do not want to create this project it is on your code disk as CUST.DPR.

1. Select **File | New Project** from the menu.
2. In the Object Inspector change the form's Caption property to Customer Form. Notice that the form's title bar changes as you type.
3. Click the **Data Access** tab on the Component Palette.
4. Click the **Table** control then click in the upper-left corner of the form to place the TTable.

Your form should now look like Figure 17.1. Next, you need to set the Table control's properties to connect it to the table you want to work with.

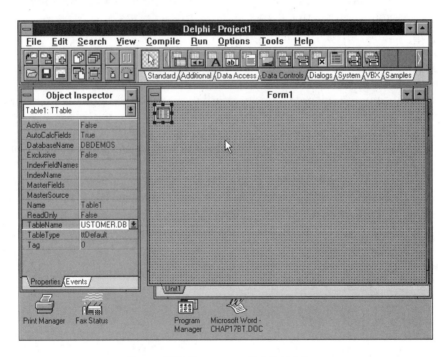

FIGURE 17.1 FORM WITH A TABLE CONTROL.

1. Click on the **Database** property in the Object Inspector, click the drop-down button, and select the **DBDEMOS** alias. This alias should have been created for you when you installed Delphi. DBDEMOS points to the \DELPHI\DEMOS\DATA directory, which contains the sample tables.

2. Next click the **TableName** property, click the drop-down button, and select **CUSTOMER.DB**.

3. Now, click the **Name** property and type in **CustTbl**. You do not have to give controls a name since Delphi automatically creates a unique name for every component you place on a form. However, you will find CustTbl much more meaningful in your code than Table1.

4. Finally, double-click on the Active property's edit area to change the value from False to **True**. This makes the Table active in both design and run mode.

To view the data in the table you need one of the data aware controls on the Data Controls page of the Component Palette. For this example use a DBGrid. To connect any data display control to a dataset you also need a DataSource. Place both of these components as follows.

1. Select the Data Access page of the Component Palette, click on the **DataSource** component, and place it on the form next to the table.

2. In the Object Inspector, click the **DataSet** property, click the drop-down button, and select **CustTbl**. This connects the DataSource to the table.

3. Select the **Name** property and type in **CustSrc**.

4. On the Data Controls page, click the **DBGrid** control. On the form click below the table and drag to the lower right so that the grid files most of the form.

5. In the Object Inspector click the **DataSource** property and select **CustSrc** from the drop-down list. This connects the DBGrid to the DataSource. Because the Table's Active property is True you see actual data from the table as soon as you connect the DBGrid to the DataSource.

6. Change the **Name** property of the **DBGrid** to **CustGrid**.

Before you compile this program and run it it is a good idea to save it. Also, to make it easy to move through your data and edit it, add a DBNavigator as follows.

1. To save your project, select **File I Save Project As** from the menu. You will be asked for names for two files. The first is the unit file for the form. Name it **CUSTF.PAS**. The second file is the project file, that is, the file with an extension of .DPR. This is the name the project will be known by in Delphi. Name the project **CUST.DPR**.

2. To add a DBNavigator, click on it on the Data Controls page of the palette and place it on the form at the top to the right of the DataSource.

3. Center the DBNavigator by selecting **Edit I Align** from the menu and clicking the **Center In Window** radio button at the bottom of the Horizontal column. Click **OK** to close the Alignment dialog box.

4. Change the DBNavigator's DataSource property to **CustSrc** to connect it to the Customer table.

5. Set the Navigator's ShowHint property to True.

6. Press **Ctrl-S** to save the project.

Your project should now look like Figure 17.2.

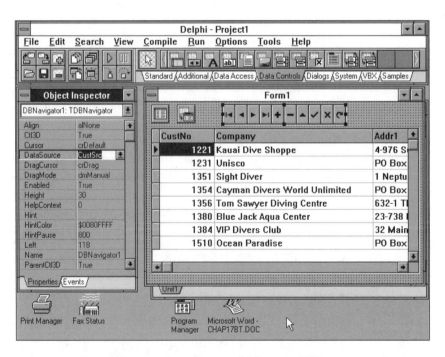

FIGURE 17.2 CUSTOMER FORM WITH DBGRID AND DBNAVIGATOR.

Press **F9** to compile and run your project. Use the navigator buttons to move around through your data. Click on the **Name** column for any record and start typing. Notice that all you have to do to edit the data in the customer table is type a new value in any column. Click the **Cancel Edit** button on the navigator to undo your changes. If you are not sure what the buttons on the navigator do then just hold the mouse cursor over a button and help will appear. The DBNavigator component has built-in fly-by help for all of its buttons.

Now that you have compiled your program you do not need Delphi to run it. If you look in the directory where you saved your project you will find an executable file (.EXE) with the same name as your project. Close Delphi then select **File|Run** from the Program Manager menu and enter the path and name to the .EXE file. You now have a compiled Windows database access program. All you need to run it is the .EXE file and the Customer table, and the Borland Database engine.

Connecting Datasets in a Client/Server Environment

The CS.DPR project on your code disk is identical to CUST.DPR described in the preceding section except that it uses the Customer table from the sample Interbase database EMPLOYEE.GDB. The remainder of this section assumes that you have the Windows version of Interbase installed, and that the alias IbLocal points to the EMPLOYEE.GDB database. To convert the CUST.DPR project to client/server do the following.

1. Open the CUST.DPR project. Select **File|Save As** and save the form unit as CSF.PAS. Select **File|Save Project** As and save the project as CS.DPR.
2. Select the **Table** component and change its Active property to False in the Object Inspector. You must do this because you cannot change its DatabaseName or TableName properties while it is active.
3. Change the **DatabaseName** to **IbLocal**.
4. Change the **TableName** to **Customer**.
5. Change the **Active** property back to **True** and you will see the records from the Customer table in EMPLOYEE.GDB appear in the grid.

That is all there is to connecting to a table on a database server. CS.DPR also contains a Database component on the form with its Alias and Database properties set to IbLocal. The Database component is used to hold the connection to the database server open if you close the tables in the form for any reason. This provides faster performance since establishing the server connection is a relatively slow process.

This project has the Database component's Connected property set to False and the TTable's Active property set to False so you can open the project in the IDE and look at the form without having local Interbase installed. If you have local Interbase installed and want to run the program you do not need to set these properties to true because the following code in the Form's OnCreate event handler takes care of it for you.

```
procedure TForm1.FormCreate(Sender: TObject);
begin
  {Connect the Database and open the Table.}
  Database1.Connected := True;
  CustTbl.Active := True;
end;
```

The OnCreate event occurs before the form is displayed so this code establishes database connection by setting the Database components Connected property to True. This will cause the Database component to prompt you for the password. Next, setting the TTable components Active property to True opens the table so that data appears in the DBGrid as soon as the form is displayed.

Remember that in a client/server program where you will be opening and closing tables by changing their Active property you should include a Database component on your form to hold the server connection open even if no tables are open.

T I P

Working with Linked Cursors

Although it sounds like a cliche, one of the most common needs in relational database applications is to relate tables. If you examine the sample tables that come with Delphi you will see that there is a one-to-many relationship between Customer and Orders, a one-to-many relationship between Orders and Items, and a many-to-one relationship between Items and Parts. Delphi makes it easy to create a form that implements a view of the data based on these relationships by using linked cursors.

Using Notebooks and TabSets

Before you worry about linked cursors there is another problem to concern us. In the example above you used up all of your form real estate with the DBGrid that displays the Customer table. To add more tables to the form you need more room. One of the easiest and most elegant ways to handle this problem is to add a Notebook and a TabSet to the form and link them. A Notebook provides a work space composed of multiple pages and a TabSet is a convenient way to switch from page to page.

This project is on your code disk as CUSTORD.DPR if you do not want to create it. Otherwise, create a new form and follow the steps below. Figure 17.3 shows the result of these steps.

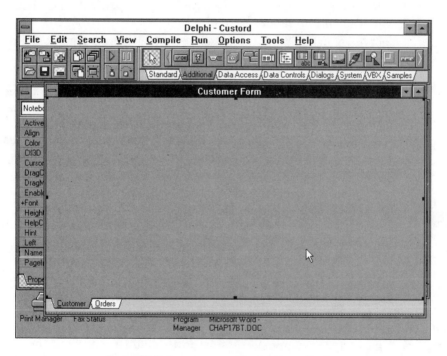

FIGURE 17.3 A FORM WITH A NOTEBOOK AND TABSET.

1. Select the form and drag its sides to make it larger. Enlarge it until it covers about three-fourths of the screen in both directions.

2. In the Object Inspector change the form's Name to **CustForm** and its Caption to **Customer Form**. Since this project only has one form you do not really need to change its name, but it is a good habit to name every object that will appear in your code to make the code easier to understand.

3. Place a Notebook from the Additional page of the palette on the form and drag it to fill the entire form except for about 3/8" at the bottom. Change the Notebook's Name property to **CustBook**.

4. Place a TabSet from the Additional page in the area below the Notebook at the bottom of the form and name it **CustTab**.

5. Set the Align property for both the Notebook and the TabSet to **alTop**. This will make the Notebook move to the top of the form and fill the width and make the TabSet move up against the Notebook's lower edge and fill the form's width.

6. Select the **Notebook** and double-click its **Pages** property to open the String List Editor. Enter **Customer** on the first line and **Orders** on the second to name the pages in the Notebook.

7. Select the **TabSet** and double-click its **Tabs** property in the Object Inspector. The names of the tabs are also stored in a string list. Enter **&Customer** and **&Orders** for the tab names, as shown in Figure 17.4. Preceding a letter in a tab name with an ampersand (&) makes that letter appear underlined in the tab and lets users select that tab from the keyboard by pressing **Alt** and the letter.

When you are working on a form that is so wide that it covers the Object Inspector you can jump to the Object Inspector by pressing **F11** and to the form by pressing **F12**.

T I P

The next step is to connect the TabSet and the Notebook so that clicking a tab, or pressing its accelerator key, moves to the correct page in the notebook. This is easy because the tabs in a TabSet are identified by a zero-based index property, TabIndex, and the pages in a Notebook are identified by a zero-based property, PageIndex. To move to the right page when the user selects a different tab all you have to do is set the Notebooks PageIndex to the value of the TabSets TabIndex. This requires adding two lines of code, one in each of two event handlers.

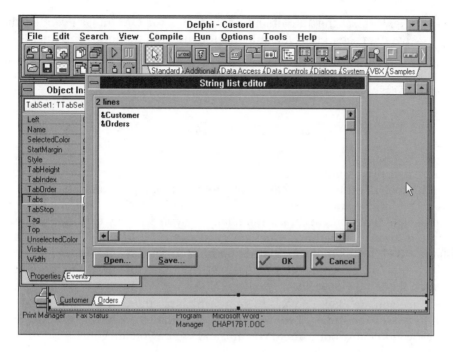

FIGURE 17.4 SETTING THE TABS PROPERTY OF A TABSET.

1. Select the form then click the tab for the Events page in the Object Inspector. Next double-click the **OnCreate** event to open the Code Editor and create the OnCreate event handler. The OnCreate event occurs each time the form is initially opened and you will use it to make sure that the TabSet and Notebook are synchronized.

2. Add the line

```
CustBook.PageIndex := CustTab.TabIndex;
```

to the procedure as shown in Figure 17.5. The active page of the NoteBook is stored in its PageIndex property. The active tab in a TabSet is stored in its TabIndex property. This line sets the NoteBook's PageIndex to the same value as the TabSet's TabIndex to ensure that the active page in the Notebook corresponds to the active tab.

3. Next, select the **TabSet** and double-click the **OnChange** event on the Events page of the Object Inspector, and add the following line.

```
        procedure TCustForm.CustTabChange(Sender: TObject;
NewTab: Integer;
        var AllowChange: Boolean);
        begin
          CustBook.PageIndex := NewTab;
        end;
```

Notice that this is not the same code that you used in the form's OnCreate handler to synchronize the Notebook and the TabSet. The reason is that the TabSet's OnChange event occurs before the active tab is actually changed. This means that you can block the change if you wish by calling the Abort runtime library procedure. Blocking events will be discussed in detail in Chapter 20. This also means that if you refer to the TabSet's TabIndex property in the OnChange event you will get the index of the currently active tab, not the tab the user just clicked.

Since you are likely to want to know which tab the user is trying to select, Delphi passes the index of the new tab as a parameter named NewTab. This allows you to know both where you are, and where you are going.

You could also put the statement:

```
CustBook.PageIndex := CustTab.TabIndex;
```

in the TabSet's OnClick event handler to detect the user's selection of a tab and synchronize the Notebook. However, as you can tell from this code, the OnClick event occurs after the new tab has been made active so CustTab.TabIndex provides the index of the newly selected tab. There is another subtle difference between these two events.

The OnChange event only occurs when the active tab in a TabSet changes. OnClick occurs any time that the user clicks a tab in the TabSet. If the user clicks the active tab then an OnClick event will occur, but OnChange will not.

TIP

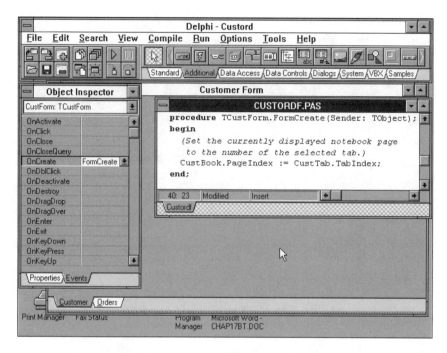

FIGURE 17.5 THE CODE IN THE FORM'S ONCREATE EVENT HANDLER.

Now you can add a Table and a DataSource component to the form and connect them to the Customer table just as you did in the section entitled "Connecting Controls to Databases" earlier in this chapter.

If this was a real application there would be no reason to use a DBGrid to display multiple Customer records. In fact, it makes a lot more sense to use DBEdit controls for the Customer record so that only one record will be displayed at a time and all of the columns will be visible on the screen at once. When you use DBEdit controls for each column, you need a way to identify the columns for the user and the standard Label component is the tool for this. Figure 17.6 shows what the finished Customer page in the form should look like and the following steps detail how to add the DBEdit and Label controls.

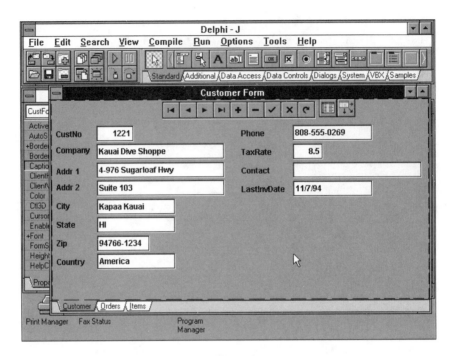

FIGURE 17.6 THE FINISHED CUSTOMER PAGE.

1. To add the 13 Label controls you will use to label the columns, first Shift-click the label control on the Standard page of the palette, then click on the form in each place that you want a label. Place eight labels in the left column and five in the right column as shown in Figure 17.6. After you have placed the labels, next click the arrow icon at the left to the palette to restore the mouse cursor to its normal shape and function.

2. Select the labels one at a time and change their Caption properties to the names of the columns in the Customer table. There is no need to change the Name property of the labels since you will never refer to them in your code.

3. Select all of the labels in the left column by clicking on each one while holding the **Shift** key down.

4. Right-click the form to display its Speed Menu and select **Align**. In the Align dialog box, select **Left Sides** in the Horizontal column and click **OK** to align the left edge of all of the labels.

5. Drag the labels to the location you want relative to the left edge of the form. With all of the labels in the left column selected dragging one of them makes them all move.

6. Repeat steps 2 through 5 for the labels in the right column.

7. Now go to the Data Controls page of the palette, Shift-click the DBEdit control and place 13 of them on the form in columns next to the labels.

8. Select all of the DBEdits then press **F11** to display the Object Inspector. When you select multiple controls, the Object Inspector shows the properties that all of the selected controls have in common. Select **CustSrc** for the DataSource property. This sets the DataSource property for all 13 DBEdit controls at once.

9. Select each DBEdit one at a time, set its DataField property to the column that you want it to display, and set its Name property to the name of the column it displays. You can set the Name property to anything, however, since you may refer to the DBEdit controls in your code the name should be descriptive.

10. Select all of the DBEdit controls in the left column, select **Align** from the form's speed menu, and align the left sides horizontally.

11. Display the alignment dialog box again and select **Space Equally** in the Vertical column to adjust the spacing between the DBEdits.

12. Drag the DBEdits in the left column to position them next to the Labels, then drag each label as necessary to align it with its corresponding DBEdit.

13. Repeat steps 8 through 12 for the DBEdit controls in the right column.

14. Place a DBNavigator control at the top center of the page and set its DataSource property to **CustSrc**. Since the AutoEdit property of CustSrc is True there is no need for an Edit button in the navigator. To remove it, double-click the **VisibleButtons** property to open the list of subproperties for each button, and change nbEdit to **False**.

When you are working on a form that is so wide that it covers the Object Inspector you can jump to the Object Inspector by pressing **F11** and to the form by pressing **F12**.

T I P

You do not have to move back and forth between the form and the Object Inspector to select successive components and change their properties. You can select components using the drop-down list at the top of the Object Inspector.

The next step is to add the data access and data display controls to the Orders page of the Notebook. To do that select the **Notebook** and use the Object Inspector to change the Notebook's ActivePage property to **Orders**.

You can also change the active page of the Notebook by changing its PageIndex property. The page numbers start with zero.

N O T E

To make the Orders Page look like Figure 17.7, do the following:

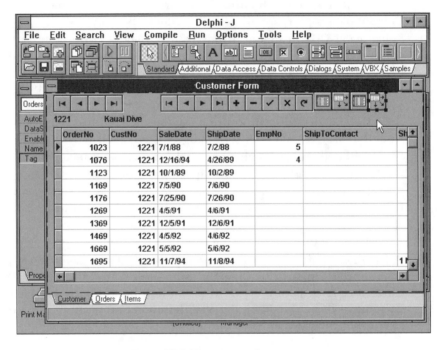

FIGURE 17.7 THE FINISHED ORDERS PAGE.

1. Add a TTable and TDataSource. Connect the TTable to the Orders table in the DBDEMOS Database and name it **OrdersTbl**.

2. Name the TDataSource **OrdersSrc** and change its DataSet property to **OrdersTbl**. You may want to move the TTables and TDataSources to the upper-right corner of the form, where they will be out of the way.

3. Add a DBNavigator to the top center of the page and set its DataSource property to **OrdersSrc**. Remove the Edit button from this navigator the same way you did for the one on the Customer page.

4. It might be handy for users to be able to scroll from one customer to another without returning to the Customer page, so add another DBNavigator in the upper-left corner, set its DataSource to **CustSrc**, and remove all of the buttons except First, Last, Next, and Previous.

5. Users should also be able to tell which customer's orders they are viewing. Add two DBText controls to the form and position them below the navigator for the customer table. Set both of their DataSource properties to CustSrc.

6. Set the DataField property for the first DBText to CustNo and for the second one to Company. This will show users the customer number and company name but they will not be able to change them.

7. Add a DBGrid and set its DataSource to **OrdersSrc**.

Creating One-To-Many Links

To make this form work the way you want it to you need to link the cursors for the Customer and Orders table so that the Orders page shows only the orders for the current customer. Link the cursors as follows.

1. Select the **OrdersTbl TTable** component and press **F11** to show the Object Inspector.

2. Set the MasterSource property to **CustSrc**.

3. Set the MasterFields property to link the CustNo columns in both tables by pressing the **ellipsis** button in the MasterFields property to display the **Field Link Designer Dialog**.

4. From the drop-down Available Indexes list choose the **ByCustNo** index. Notice that you can only link on columns in the detail table, Orders in this case, that are indexed.

5. Click the **CustNo** column in both the Detail Fields and Master Fields lists. The dialog should look like Figure 17.8.

6. Click the **Add** button to create the link then the **OK** button to close the dialog.

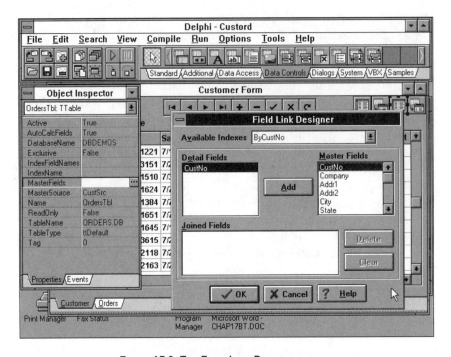

FIGURE 17.8 THE FIELD LINK DESIGNER DIALOG.

Compile and run the project by pressing **F9**. As you scroll from customer to customer the Orders grid should change to show only the orders for the current customer.

Figure 17.9 shows the completed Items page. To create this page follow the same steps that you used to create the Orders page. If you have a problem take a look at the completed project, CUSTORD.DPR on your code disk.

Once you have completed the Items page compile and test your program. You should now have a complete form that shows a one-to-many-to-many relationship and you have only written two lines of code.

You can change the display order of the records in a linked detail table by adding columns to the index used in the link.

T I P

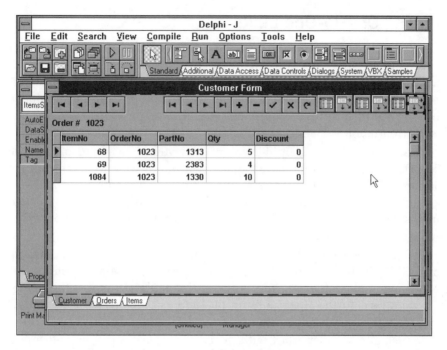

FIGURE 17.9 THE COMPLETED ITEMS PAGE.

To control the order in which the linked detail tables display their records add columns to the index used for the link. For example, suppose you want the Items records to display in alphabetical order by the Description. The Items table has a secondary index on the OrderNo column named ByOrderNo. This must be the active index for Items so that Delphi can quickly find the Order records for the current customer. Since ByOrderNo is the active index it is also the index used to determine the order in which the records will display.

To change the display order of the Items records use the Database Desktop to restructure the Items table and change the ByOrderNo index to include two columns, OrderNo and Description. Now run the form and look at the Items records. Since they all have the same OrderNo, the number of the current Order, they appear in order by Description.

Creating One-to-One Links

One of the most common needs in database applications is to identify codes. One example is a table that contains part numbers. When you display the table's data in a form you would like to display a description that identifies the part number to the user. Another example might be a job code in an employee table that requires a description from a job description table.

This is easy to do in Delphi if you display your data one record at a time using DBEdit components. Unfortunately, it is not easy to do if you use a DBGrid to display multiple records at one time. The example in this section uses the Customer page of the form where data is displayed in DBEdit components. Later in this chapter in the section on calculated fields you will see how to display a lookup value in a DBGrid.

On your code disk the subdirectory for this chapter contains a table named STATE.DB that contains the two character state abbreviations and the full name of each state. You will use this table to display the name of each state next to the State column on the customer page of a form. The sample project is CUSTATE.DPR.

To create this project start with the CUSTORD.DPR project and proceed as follows.

1. Save the project under a new name by selecting **File | Save As** from the menu and save the form and its unit as CUSTATEF.PAS. Next, select **File | Save Project As** and save the project as CUSTATE.DPR.

2. Add a TTable to the form and set its properties as follows.

    DatabaseName = the path to the directory that contains STATE.DB.
    TableName   = STATE.DB
    Name   = StateTbl
    MasterSource = CustSrc
    MasterFields = State (using the primary index of STATE.DB)
    Active   = True

3. Add a TDataSource to the form. Set its DataSet property to **StateTbl** and its name to **StateSrc**.

4. Add a TDBText component from the Data Controls page of the palette and place it after the State DBEdit component. Using a TDBText component assumes that you do not want users to change the value of the State Name column in the State table. If you did want users to be able to edit the value you could use a TDBEdit instead.

5. Set the TDBText component's DataSource property to StateSrc and its DataField property to State Name.

When you run the program you will see the name of the state appear if there is a matching entry in the State table.

Using the Fields Editor

One of the things that can be improved about this form is to remove some redundant columns. For example, on the Items page the OrderNo column is redundant because all of the records have the same order number and it is shown at the top of the page. The same is true of the CustNo column on the Orders page.

When you activate a TTable at design time or when you run a form the code that is built into the data display components dynamically creates a TField object for each column in the dataset you are displaying. To control which columns are displayed and how they are displayed use the Fields Editor to create a static list of TField objects that will be used every time your form runs.

Using the Fields Editor you can:

- Select which columns in the table will be displayed.
- Select a field and use the object Inspector to change its properties.
- Define calculated fields whose value is determined by code you write.

Controlling Which Columns Are Displayed

Start the Fields Editor by right-clicking on a TTable or TQuery and selecting Fields Editor from the Speed Menu. The Fields Editor window should look like Figure 17.10 the first time you open it for a table.

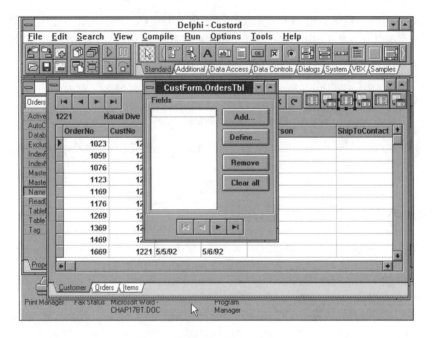

FIGURE 17.10 THE FIELDS EDITOR.

The fields list is empty because all of the field objects are being dynamically created. The buttons in the Fields Editor window are described in Table 17.1

TABLE 17.1 THE FIELDS EDITOR BUTTONS

Button	Description
Add	Lets you add fields to the static field list.
Define	Lets you create calculated fields or new fields based on columns in the dataset.
Remove	Lets you remove a field from the static field list.
Clear All	Lets you remove all fields from the list.

Start by opening the Fields Editor for the Orders table by selecting and then right-clicking the OrdersTbl TTable on the form.

You can also open the Fields Editor for a TTable by double-clicking the TTable component on your form.

T I P

To remove the CustNo column proceed as follows.

1. Click the **Add** button to display the highlighted list of all of the columns in the Orders table.
2. Click the **OK** button to add all of the fields to the static field list in the Fields Editor.
3. Click the **CustNo** field in the list to select it. The Object Inspector now shows the properties for the CustNo Field.
4. In the Object Inspector set the field's Visible property to **False**.

You cannot remove the CustNo field from the form by removing it from the static field list in the Fields Editor because this is the column used to link the Orders table to the Customer table. To remove other columns that are not part of the link just remove them from the list.

N O T E

You can remove the Order Number from the Items DBGrid the same way that you removed CustNo. Since the ItemNo is an artificial key value with no meaning for the user there is no reason to display it either. To remove the ItemNo from the Items DBGrid just select it in the static fields list of the Fields Editor and click the Remove button.

You can change the order of the columns in a DBGrid by dragging the field names in the Fields Editor to new positions in the field list.

T I P

Setting Field Properties

Table 17.2 shows the properties for TField objects. Note that not all of these properties apply to all TField objects. For example, only alphanumeric objects have the EditMask property, only integer number fields have the MinValue and MaxValue properties and only floating point numbers have the Currency property.

TABLE 17.2 TFIELD PROPERTIES

Property	Description
Alignment	Determines if the value is displayed left-justified, right-justified, or centered.
Calculated	True if the value for this field is calculated by code in the CalcFields event handler, otherwise False.
Currency	True if the field should be displayed as a monetary amount. If True the value is displayed with a leading dollar sign and two digits to the right of the decimal.
DisplayFormat	This property lets you control the way a value is displayed when it is not being edited.
DisplayLabel	The column label of the field is displayed in a DBGrid.
EditFormat	This property lets you control the way a value is displayed when it is being edited.
EditMask	Restricts the values users can enter in the field. See the Using EditMasks section later in this chapter.
FieldName	The name of the field in the table.
Index	The order that the field will appear in a DBGrid. The first column in the grid has zero for its Index, the second column 1, and so on. To rearrange the order of the columns just drag the field names to the location you want in the Fields Editor static field list.
MaxValue	Sets the largest value you can enter.
MinValue	Sets the smallest value you can enter.
Name	The TField component's name.
ReadOnly	If True, users cannot edit the value being displayed.
Required	If True, users must enter a value in this field.
Size	The maximum number of characters that can be entered or displayed.
Visible	True if the field should be displayed by a DBGrid.

Using EditMasks

The EditMask property lets you construct a mask using the special characters in Table 17.3 to limit what users can enter in an alphanumeric field.

TABLE 17.3 EDIT MASK CHARACTERS

Character	Description
!	If a ! character appears in the mask, leading blanks don't appear in the data. If a ! character is not present, trailing blanks don't appear in the data.
>	If a > character appears in the mask, all characters that follow are converted to upper case until the end of the mask or until a < character is encountered.
<	If a < character appears in the mask, all characters that follow are converted to lower case until the end of the mask or until a > character is encountered.
<>	If these two characters appear together in a mask, no case checking is done and the data is formatted with the case the user uses to enter the data.
\	The character that follows a \ character is a literal character. Use this character when you want to permit any of the mask special characters as a literal in the data.
L	The L character requires an alpha character only in this position. For the US, this is A-Z, a-z.
l	The l character permits an alpha character in this position, but doesn't require it.
A	The A character requires an alphanumeric character only in this position. For the US, this is A-Z, a-z, 0-9.
a	The a character permits an alphanumeric character in this position, but doesn't require it.
C	The C character requres a character in this position.
c	The c character permits a character in this position, but doesn't require it.
0	The 0 character requires a numeric character only in this position.
9	The 9 character permits a numeric character in this position, but doesn't require it.
#	The # character permits a numeric character in this position or a plus or minus sign, but doesn't require it.
:	The : character is used to separate hours, minutes, and seconds in times. If the character that separates hours, minutes, and seconds is different in the International settings of the Control Panel utility on your computer system, that character is used instead of :.

/	The / character is used to separate months, days, and years in dates. If the character that separates months, days, and years is different in the International settings of the Control Panel utility on your computer system, that character is used instead of /.
;	The ; character is used to separate masks.
Underscore	The __ character automatically inserts a blank the edit box. When the user enters characters in the field, the user's cursor skips over the blank character. When using the EditMask property editor, you can change the character used to represent blanks. You can also change this value programmatically.

Setting an edit mask is an easy way to validate data entry for any value that has a fixed format. For example, suppose you had a part number that always consists of three letters, four numbers, a hyphen, and three more numbers. The EditMask !>LLL0000-000 will let the user enter only values that have that format, remove any leading blanks, and force the letters to uppercase.

To create an edit mask select the **field name** in the Fields Editor or from the drop down list in the object inspector then click the **EditMask** property in the Object Inspector, and click the **ellipsis** button in the field to display the Input Mask Editor dialog shown in Figure 17.11. Do this for the Customer table and select the **Zip** field.

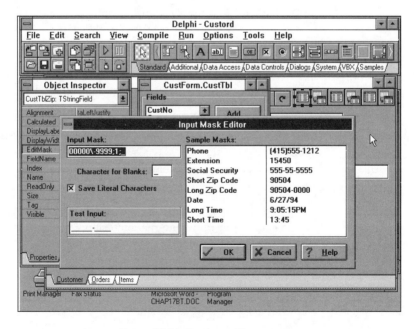

FIGURE 17.11 THE INPUT MASK EDITOR.

In the Input Mask editor you can enter your own mask or select one from the Sample Masks list at the right. Select Long Zip Code to insert the mask

```
00000\-9999;1;_
```

in the Input Mask field. Each mask consists of three parts, or fields, separated by semicolons. The first part is the mask itself. The second part is either 0 or 1. If the second part of the mask is 1 then any literal characters in the mask, such as the hyphen in this example, will be saved in your table as part of the data. If the second field of the mask is 0 the literal characters will not be stored. You can see this digit change as you check and uncheck the Save Literal Characters checkbox. The third field of the mask contains the character that represents a space in the mask itself. Normally this is the underscore character.

You can type values into the Test Input field and see if they are acceptable based on the mask in the Input Mask field.

Another good example of using an EditMask is the State field in the Customer table. The EditMask >LL;1;_ converts the characters that are entered to uppercase and only allows users to enter letters.

As useful as input masks are in Delphi they have some serious limitations because there is no way to specify optional parts or alternate masks. This means that you cannot construct a mask that will allow any of the following.

1. Either a valid five digit or a valid nine digit U.S. zip code.
2. Either a valid U.S. zip code or a valid Canadian postal code.
3. A phone number with or without an area code.

Creating a Calculated Field

Calculated fields let you display values that do not exist in any table in your database. Instead these values are computed at runtime.

Delphi lets you write Object Pascal code to compute values that you can then display in fields on your form. Computing the values automatically is easy because Delphi provides an event for TTable and TQuery components, OnCalcFields, that is triggered any time that your calculated fields need to be updated.

This section looks at two examples of calculated fields. The first one is straightforward and illustrates the basic techniques. The second is more complex. It demonstrates a weak area in Delphi's handling of calculated fields and shows how to get around it.

An Amount Due Field

A good example of a calculated field is to add an AmountDue field to the Orders DBGrid. This will show the ItemsTotal minus the AmountPaid.

1. Select the OrdersTbl TTable component and display the the Fields Editor.
2. Click the Define button to display the Define field dialog.
3. Enter Amount in the Field name edit box. Notice that Delphi automatically generates the Component name for you.
4. Select CurrencyField for the Field type.
5. Click the **OK** button.
6. Drag the AmountPaid field up until it is just after ItemsTotal in the list. Drag AmountDue up until it is after AmountPaid.
7. Close the Fields Editor window.

T I P

The Size field in the Define field dialog can only be used with alphanumeric field types. To limit the size of the value that can be entered in a numeric field use MinValue and MaxValue.

Now that you have created the new field you must add the code to perform the calculation to the TTable's OnCalcFields event handler as follows.

1. Select the ItemsTbl TTable component in the form.
2. In the Object Inspector select the Events page and double-click the OnCalcFields event to open the code editor.
3. Add the following code to this event handler.

```
procedure TCustForm.OrdersTblCalcFields(DataSet: TDataset);
begin
  {Calculate the balance due.}
  OrdersTblAmountDue.Value :=
    OrdersTblItemsTotal.Value -
    OrdersTblAmountPaid.Value;
end;
```

Notice that this code uses the component names, not the field names. Also, notice how the Value property of the TField components is used to perform the calculation and store the result in the newly calculated field. You can find the component names you need in the drop-down list at the top of the Object Inspector.

Adding a Lookup Field to a DBGrid

In the section entitled "Working with Linked Cursors" earlier in this chapter you saw an example of a one-to-one link used to look up the name of a state using the two character abbreviation in the Customer record.

You can do the same thing in a DBGrid but not as easily. The problem is that there is no way to add a field to a DBGrid that is bound to a DataSource other than the DataSource the Grid is bound to. The solution is to use a calculated field. In this example you will add two calculated fields to the ItemsTbl, ListPrice and ExtendedPrice, get the ListPrice from the Parts table, and calculate the ExtendedPrice. Follow these steps.

1. Add a TTable component to the form in the CUSTORD.DPR project. Change its name to PartsTbl and set its Database Property to DBDEMOS, and its TableName property to PARTS.DB.

2. Open the Fields Editor for the Parts table and add the PartNo and ListPrice fields to the list of field objects.

3. Select the **ItemsTbl TTable** component, right-click and open the Fields Editor.

4. Click the **Define** button, enter **ListPrice** for the field name, and select **CurrencyField** for the type. Leave the Calculated checkbox checked, and click **OK**.

5. Click the **Define** button, enter **ExtendedPrice** for the field name, and select **CurrencyField** for the type. Leave the Calculated checkbox checked, and click **OK**.

6. Close the Fields Editor.

Next, add the following code to ItemsTbl's OnCalcFields event handler.

```
procedure TCustForm.ItemsTblCalcFields(DataSet: TDataset);
var
  DiscountFactor:     Real;
begin
  {Find the record for this part in the Parts table.}
  if PartsTbl.FindKey([ItemsTblPartNo]) then
  begin
    {Get the value for the ListPrice field from the
     Parts table.}
    ItemsTblListPrice.Value := PartsTblListPrice.Value;
    {Convert the discount percentage to a discount
     factor.}
    DiscountFactor := 1.0 - (ItemsTblDiscount.Value / 100.0);
```

```
    {Compute the extended price.}
    ItemsTblExtendedPrice.Value :=
      (ItemsTblListPrice.Value *
      ItemsTblQty.Value) * DiscountFactor;
  end;
end;
```

This code searchs the Parts table for a record whose PartNo matches the PartNo in the current Items record, and copies its ListPrice to the ListPrice calculated field in the Items DBGrid. The statement

```
if PartsTbl.FindKey([ItemsTblPartNo]) then
```

calls the PartsTbl TTable's FindKey method. FindKey searches the current index for the value or values you specify. Notice that the parameter for FindKey is an array. If you were searching a composite index composed of three fields and you wanted to find records that matched the first two fields you would use:

```
FindKey([value1, value2]);
```

If you want to search an index other than the current index you must make the index you want to search current by assigning its name to the TTable's IndexName property before you call FindKey. FindKey returns True if a matching record is found and False if a matching record is not found.

If a record was found the statement

```
ItemsTblListPrice.Value := PartsTblListPrice.Value;
```

puts the value from the Parts record's ListPrice field into the calculated field named ListPrice in the Items table.

While this works fine it has two disadvantages. First, it is more work than it should be. Putting a value from the detail table in a one-to-one link into a DBGrid should be as easy as it is using DBEdit components. Second, you cannot give users the ability to edit the field.

The remainder of the code computes the extended price by multiplying the Qty times the ListPrice times the DiscountFactor. In a real application you would probably also want to add a calculated field to display the Description for the item which, like the ListPrice, is in the Parts table.

WARNING

Do not do anything in a table's OnCalcFields event handler that will change the current record in the TTable.

Summing Values from a Detail Table

The Orders sample table has a column named ItemsTotal that contains the total extended price for all of the items for each order. Since you usually do not want to store data in a table that you can calculate from other values in your database, you can remove the ItemsTotal field and calculate the total extended price for the items using a calculated field called OrderTotal.

This looks like a simple task. Since the Items table is already on the form and is linked to the orders table you should be able to add the OrderTotal field to the OrdersTble TTable component and put the following code in its OnCalcFields handler.

```
var
  orderTotal:     Real;
begin
  orderTotal := 0.0;
  with ItemsTbl do
  begin
    First;
    while EOF = False do
    begin
      orderTotal := orderTotal +
        ItemsTblExtendedPrice;
      Next;
    end;
    OrdersTblOrderTotal.Value := orderTotal;
  end;
end;
```

Unfortunately, this code produces the wrong answer because Delphi generates OrdersTbl's OnCalcFields event before it updates the link to the Items table. This means your calculation will be based on Items records for the wrong order.

To solve this problem you need to perform the following steps.

1. Add another TTable to the form and set its properties as follows.

Active	= True
DatabaseName	= DBDEMOS
IndexName	= ByOrderNo
Name	= ItemsTbl2
TableName	= ITEMS.DB

    Note that you do not link this TTable to the Orders table.

2. Use the Fields Editor to add a calculated field named OrderTotal to the orders table. Select CurrencyField as the type.

Now add the following code to OrdersTbl's OnCalcFields event handler.

```
procedure TCustForm.OrdersTblCalcFields(DataSet: TDataset);
var
  OrderTotal:     Real;
begin
  {Computer the total extended price for all items
   in this order.}
  orderTotal := 0.0;
  with ItemsTbl2 do
  begin
    {Filter the Items table so that only those
     records for the current order are visible.}
    SetRange([OrdersTblOrderNo.Value],
      [OrdersTblOrderNo.Value]);
    {Loop through all of the records and compute
     the total amount.}
    while EOF = False do
    begin
      {Find the Parts record for this Item so you
       can get the ListPrice.}
      if PartsTbl.FindKey([ItemsTbl2PartNo.Value]) then
      begin
        {Compute the extended price for this item and
         add it to the total.}
        orderTotal := orderTotal +
          (ItemsTbl2Qty.Value * PartsTblListPrice.Value) *
            (100 - ItemsTbl2Discount.Value) / 100.0;
      end;
      Next;
    end;
    {Assign the total amount to the calculated
     field.}
    OrdersTblOrderTotal.Value := orderTotal;
  end;
  {Calculate the balance due.}
  OrdersTblAmountDue.Value :=
    OrdersTblOrderTotal.Value -
    OrdersTblAmountPaid.Value;
end;
```

This code begins by setting a range on the ItemsTbl2 table so that only the item records for the current order will be accessible. When you set a range you specify a range of values in the current index. Only records that fall within the range of values that you specify will be accessible. Once a range is applied to the table it appears to your code and to the users as though the records in the range are the only records in the table. To set a range you must perform the following steps.

1. Set the TTable's IndexName property to the index you want to use if you want to use, a different one.
2. Call the TTable's SetRange method and pass two arrays to it as parameters. The first array contains the values that define the lower boundary of the range. The second array contains the values that define the upper boundary of the range. You can provide values for the first N fields in the active index. For example, if the current index contains three fields you can supply values for the first, first and second, or first, second, and third fields.

In this example the range is set with the statement

```
SetRange([OrdersTblOrderNo.Value], [OrdersTblOrderNo.Value]);
```

which sets the starting and ending value of the range to the order number of the current order record.

By default the range includes any records that match the starting and ending values. To exclude records that match the starting and ending values set the TTable's KeyExclusive property to True before you call SetRange.

T I P

Finally, the while loop computes and sums the extended price for each item, and the the last statement assigns the total to the calculated field OrdersTblTotalAmt.

There are just two problems left. If you run the form now you will get an immediate runtime error that says, "Cannot perform operation on closed dataset." The problem is that the Orders table is opened and its OnCalcFields event is generated before the ItemsTbl2 table is opened. This happens because you placed the ItemsTbl2 component on the form after you placed the OrdersTbl component on the form.

Fortunately Delphi provides an easy way to change the creation order of the non-visible components on the form. Just select **Edit I Creation Order** from the menu to display the Creation Order dialog and move the ItemsTbl2 component above the OrdersTbl component in the list. Now ItemsTbl2 will be opened before OrdersTbl, and your code will work perfectly.

The second problem is that OrdersTbl's OnCalcFields event handler is not called when you change the value of a column in a table that contributes to the value of one of the calculated fields. To see this, run the CustOrd project and change the quantity for one of the items in an order. Now look at the Orders page and you will see that the OrderTotal calculated field has not been updated. You can force the calculated fields to recalculate by calling the OnCalcFields event handler from your own code. To demonstrate this add a Button to the Orders page of the form. Set its name to RecalcBtn and its Caption to Recalc. Then add the following code to the buttons OnClick event handler.

```
procedure TCustForm.RecalcBtnClick(Sender: TObject);
begin
  OrdersTbl.Edit;
  OrdersTblCalcFields(OrdersTbl);
  OrdersTbl.Post;
end;
```

This code puts the OrdersTbl component into edit mode, calls its OnCalcFields event handler and then calls the Post method to return the table to Browse mode. You could do the same thing from the OnChange event handler, of a field involved in the calculation of the value for one of the calculated fields.

There is another way to update the values in a Table's calculated fields and that is to call its Refresh method. Calling Refresh not only updates any values stored in the table to reflect changes made by other users. It also generates an OnCalcFields event so that all calculated fields will be up to date. Since calling Refresh also requires a reread from the table it may be slower depending on the performance of your network and server.

NOTE

You can only assign values to calculated fields in an OnCalcFields event handler.

Changing Properties On-The-Fly

One of the most useful features of an object-oriented environment like Delphi is that you can change the properties of Objects at any time in your code. The sample Customer table has two indices, its primary index and a secondary index on the Company field. You can easily add two buttons to the Customer page of the form so that user can change the viewing order of the customer table at any time. This will make the Customer page look like Figure 17.12.

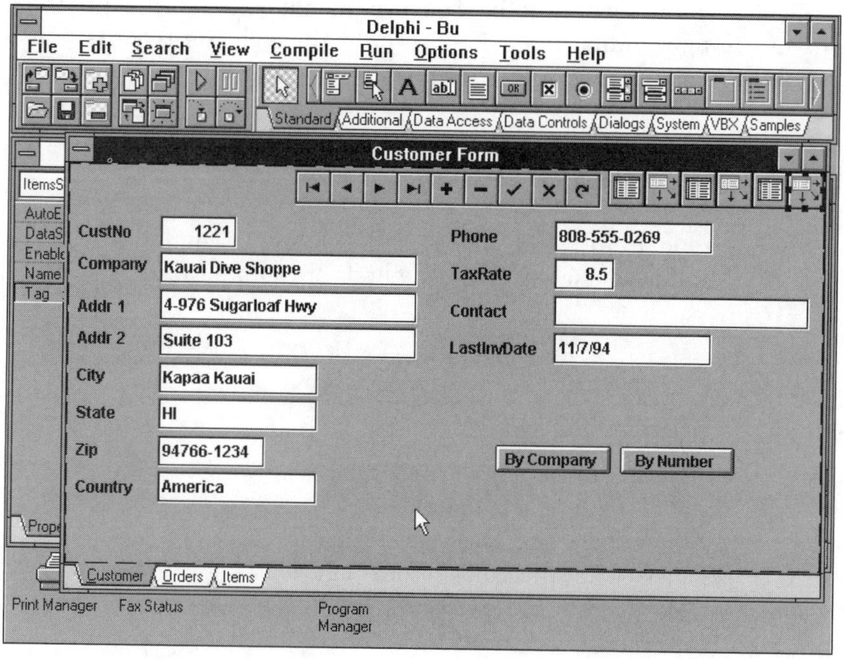

FIGURE 17.12 THE CUSTOMER PAGE WITH BUTTONS TO CHANGE INDICES.

Select the **Notebook** then change its ActivePage to Customer. Add two buttons and change their captions to By Company and By Number, and their Names to ByCompanyBtn and ByNameBtn. Next, add the following line of code to the By Company button's OnClick event handler.

```
CustTbl.IndexName := 'ByCompany';
```

This statement changes the CustTbl TTable's IndexName property to ByCompany, the name of the secondary index on the Company field. The code for the By Number button's OnClick handler is as follows.

```
CustTbl.IndexName := '';
```

Since the Customer table is a Paradox table and the primary index of a Paradox table has no name you switch to the primary index by setting the

IndexName property to null. Run the program and click the **By Company** button. You will not see any of the data on the Customer page change because Delphi preserves your position on the current record when you change the current index, however, you will see the First and Prior buttons on the DBNavigator become active because the current record is not the first record in the new index order. If you scroll through the records you will also find that they are now in alphabetical order by Company.

Moving through a Table

The TDataSet type, from which TTable and TQuery descend, has methods to let you move around in a table. These methods are summarized in Table 17.4.

TABLE 17.4 NAVIGATION METHODS

Method	Description
First	Move to the beginning of the table.
Last	Move to the end of the table.
Next	Move to the next record in the table.
Prior	Move to the preceding record in the table.
MoveBy	Move forward or backward a specified number of records.

In addition, two properties, BOF and EOF, tell you if you are at the beginning or end of the table, respectively.

To see these methods in action add two buttons to the Customer page so it looks like Figure 17.13. Change their Captions to Find State and Next State, and their Name property to FindStateBtn and NextStateBtn.

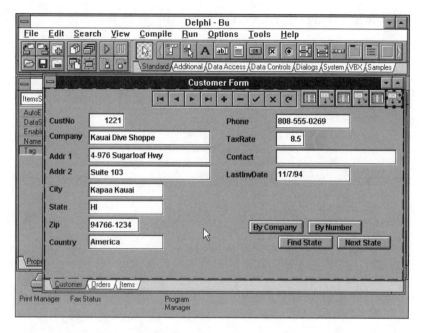

FIGURE 17.13 THE CUSTOMER PAGE WITH THE FIND STATE AND NEXT STATE BUTTONS.

Next, add the following variable declaration at the beginning of the implementation section of the form unit. The variable stateToFind will be used to
hold the state code of the state you are looking for.

```
implementation

{$R *.DFM}

var
   stateToFind:       String[2];
```

Now add the following code to the OnClick handler for the Find State button.

```
procedure TCustForm.FindStateBtnClick(Sender: TObject);
var
  ok:         Boolean;
begin
  stateToFind := '';
  {Prompt the user for the State to find.}
  ok := InputQuery('Which State?',
                   'Enter the State to find',
                   stateToFind);
  if ok then
  begin
    {Disable the DataSource component so the
     screen will not update as you search the
     table.}
    CustSrc.Enabled := False;
    FindState(stateToFind, True);
    {Update the screen.}
    CustSrc.Enabled := True;
  end;
end;
```

This code calls the run-time library function InputQuery to display a dialog box and prompt the user for the state to find. If the user presses the **OK** button the code then sets the CustSrc DataSource components enabled property to False. This prevents the data display components from being updated while your code scans the records in the table. This not only avoids an annoying display but also increases the speed of the search dramatically.

Next the code calls the custom procedure FindState and then re-enables CustSrc to update the screen. The code for FindState is shown below.

```
procedure FindState
          (var stateToFind: String;
          findFirst: Boolean);
{Searches the Customer table for the specified
 State code.}
var
  thisState:      String[2];
begin
  with CustForm do
  begin
    stateToFind := UpperCase(stateToFind);
    {If you are looking for the first occurrence
     move to the beginning of the table.}
```

```
      if findFirst then
        CustTbl.First;
      {Search the table until the end or until
       a matching State is found.}
      while (CustTbl.EOF = False) do
      begin
        {Get the value from the State field.}
        thisState := CustTbl.FieldByName('State').AsString;
        if thisState = stateToFind then break;
        {Move to the next record in the table.}
        CustTbl.Next;
      end;
  end;
end;
```

This procedure takes two parameters. The first, stateToFind, is the code for the state to search for. The second, findFirst, is a Boolean value. If it is True then the search should start at the beginning of the table. If it is False the search will start from the current record. Therefore, if findFirst is True CustTbl.First is called to move to the beginning of the table.

N O T E Note the use of the with CustForm statement at the beginning of this procedure. Without the with you would have to prefix the name of every component in the form with the form name, for example, CustForm.CustTbl.First.

The while loop actually performs the search. The loop continues until the end of the table is reached. The first statement in the while loop

```
thisState := CustTbl.FieldByName('State').AsString;
```

retrieves the value from the State field of the current record. The if statement

```
if thisState = stateToFind then break;
```

checks to see if the value in the current record matches the value you are looking for and, if so, the break command ends the while loop. Otherwise

```
CustTbl.Next;
```

moves to the next record and the search continues. The following code is from the OnClick event handler for the Next State button.

```
procedure TCustForm.NextStateBtnClick(Sender: TObject);
begin
  if stateToFind <> '' then
  begin
    {Disable the DataSource component so the
     screen will not update as you search the
     table.}
    CustSrc.Enabled := False;
    {Move to the next record so you will not
     find this one again.}
    CustTbl.Next;
    FindState(stateToFind, False);
    {Update the screen.}
    CustSrc.Enabled := True;
  end;
end;
```

Like the code for the Find State button this code also sets the Enabled property for the datasource to False to improve performance. The call to CustTbl.Next moves to the next record. Without this statement the FindState procedure would start its search with the current record and find it a second time.

Returning to a Record Using a Bookmark

The search routine in the preceding section has one problem. If the search fails you will be left on the last record of the table. You can correct this by setting a Bookmark on the current record before you start the search. Then if the search fails you can return to the original record. Here is the revised code for the FindState procedure.

```
procedure FindState
        (var stateToFind: String;
         findFirst: Boolean);
{Searches the Customer table for the specified
 State code.}
var
  thisState:    String[2];
  startingRec:  TBookmark;
begin
  with CustForm do
  begin
```

```
      stateToFind := UpperCase(stateToFind);
      {Mark the current record so you can return
       to it.}
      startingRec := CustTbl.GetBookmark;
      {If you are looking for the first occurrence
       move to the beginning of the table.}
      if findFirst then
        CustTbl.First;
      {Search the table until the end or until
       a matching State is found.}
      while (CustTbl.EOF = False) do
      begin
        {Get the value from the State field.}
        thisState := CustTbl.FieldByName('State').AsString;
        if thisState = stateToFind then break;
        {Move to the next record in the table.}
        CustTbl.Next;
      end;
      {If the search failed return the record
       where you started.}
      if thisState <> stateToFind then
      begin
        CustTbl.GoToBookmark(startingRec);
        MessageDlg('No matching record found.',
          mtInformation, [mbOK], 0)
      end;
      {Release the memory used by the bookmark.}
      CustTbl.FreeBookmark(startingRec);
   end;
end;
```

The first step in implementing a bookmark is to declare a variable of type TBookmark. Next, the statement

```
startingRec := CustTbl.GetBookmark;
```

creates the bookmark for the current record in the TTable CustTbl. After the while loop the code

```
if thisState <> stateToFind then
    begin
      CustTbl.GoToBookmark(startingRec);
      MessageDlg('No matching record found.',
        mtInformation, [mbOK], 0)
    end;
```

checks to see if the search failed and if so calls GoToBookmark to return to the starting location and displays a message by calling MessageDlg.

Finding Records Using an Index

While you can find records using the sequential search described in the last two sections it is much faster on large tables or when using servers to search using an index if one exists for the field or fields that you want to search. The Customer table has a secondary index on the Company field. To find a record by Company name start by adding a button to the Customer page as shown in Figure 17.14.

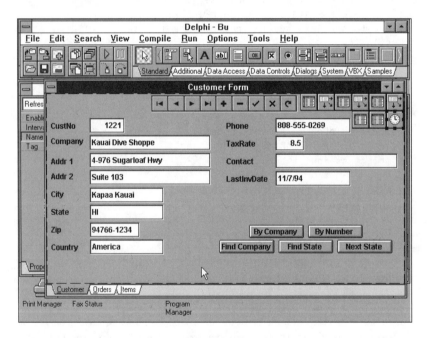

FIGURE 17.14 THE CUSTOMER PAGE WITH THE FIND AND NEXT COMPANY BUTTONS.

Change the button's Caption to Find Company and its name to FindCompanyBtn then add the following code to its OnClick event handler.

```
procedure TCustForm.FindCompanyBtnClick(Sender: TObject);
var
  ok:              Boolean;
  companyToFind:   String[30];
```

```
begin
  companyToFind := '';
  {Prompt the user for the Company to find.}
  ok := InputQuery('Which Company?',
                   'Enter the Company to find',
                   companyToFind);
  if ok then
    with CustForm do
      with CustTbl do
      begin
        {Switch to the ByCompany index.}
        IndexName := 'ByCompany';
        {Open a special record buffer for
         searching.}
        SetKey;
        {Put the value to find into the search
         buffer.}
        FieldByName('Company').AsString := companyToFind;
        {Find the closest match.}
        GotoNearest;
      end;
end;
```

This code starts by prompting the user for the Company to find. If the user closes the InputQuery dialog by clicking the **OK** button then two with statements provide the name of the form and the name of the TTable to use for the search. Without these statements any reference to a property or method of the CustTbl TTable component would have to include both the form's name and the TTable's name. For example, the statement

```
IndexName := 'ByCompany';
```

would have to be written:

```
CustForm.CustTbl.IndexName := 'ByCompany';
```

As you can see, using with saves a lot of typing. You can only search the current index so the first step in performing the search is to switch to the ByCompany index by setting CustTbl's IndexName property to ByCompany.

The next step is the call to the SetKey method. In order to search an index you have to put the value or values you want to find into a special record buffer. Calling SetKey creates the record buffer and makes it the current buffer. Once you call SetKey and reference to CustTbl's fields will refer to the values in this search buffer. The statement

```
FieldByName('Company').AsString := companyToFind;
```

assigns the company name to find to the Company field in the search buffer. If you were searching on a multi-field composite index you could assign a value to any of the first *n* fields in the index.

Finally, the call to GotoNearest searches for a matching record. There are actually two methods you can use to perform the search. GotoKey performs an exact match search. This search will fail unless Delphi finds a record with the exact value you are searching for. GotoNearest will find a record with a value equal to or greater than the value you are searching for.

T I P

You can cause FindNearest and GotoNearest to position you to the record after the record you are searching for instead of on it by setting the table's KeyExclusive property to True.

There is no need for a Find Next button for the Company search because this procedure leaves ByCompany as the current index. Therefore, all you have to do to see the next record is click the Next button on the Navigator.

Finding Groups of Records With ApplyRange

You can also filter your view of a table using the current index so that only the records you specify will be visible. A good example of doing this is to provide a way to filter the Customer records by letters of the alphabet. That is, let the user pick a letter and then display only those customers whose company name starts with that letter.

Notice that this example does not use the SetRange method described in the "Creating a Calculated Field" section earlier in this chapter. SetRange could be used but SetRangeStart, SetRangeEnd, and ApplyRange are used here to introduce them.

A handy tool for letting users select which records they want to see is a TabSet as shown in Figure 17.15.

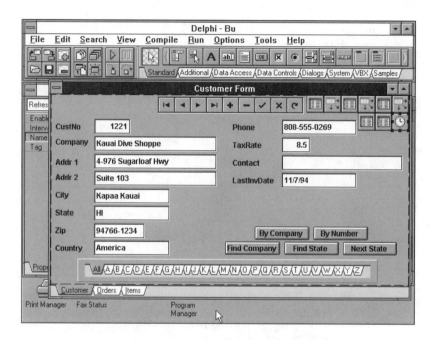

FIGURE 17.15 A TABSET FOR SELECTING RECORDS.

The raised TabSet was created by first placing a Panel component on the form then placing a TabSet within it. The Panel serves no purpose other than appearance. The TabSet is named CompanyTab and its Tabs property, which is a string list, was set using the Object Inspector to the word All followed by the capital letters of the alphabet. The following code was placed in the TabSet's OnChange event handler to filter the customer records.

```
procedure TCustForm.CompanyTabChange(Sender: TObject; NewTab: Integer;
  var AllowChange: Boolean);
var
  letter:      String[1];
begin
  with CompanyTab do
    if NewTab = 0 then
      {If the first tab was clicked show all
       records in the table.}
      CustTbl.CancelRange
    else
    begin
      with CustTbl do
      begin
        {Disable the data aware controls
         to avoid screen flicker while
         setting the range.}
        DisableControls;
        try
          {Get the letter using the tab index.}
          letter := Tabs[NewTab];
          {Switch to the Company index.}
          IndexName := 'ByCompany';
          {Set the minimum value.}
          SetRangeStart;
          FieldByName('Company').AsString := letter;
          {Set the maximum value.}
          SetRangeEnd;
          FieldByName('Company').AsString :=
            letter + 'zzzzzzzzzzzzzzzzzzzzzzzzzzzz';
          {Apply the range to the table.}
          KeyFieldCount := 1;
          ApplyRange;
        finally
          EnableControls;
        end;
      end;
    end;
end;
```

A String variable, letter, is declared to hold the letter the user selects from the TabSet. The tabs in a TabSet are identified by a zero based property, TabIndex. The code

```
if NewTab = 0 then
{If the first tab was clicked show all
 records in the table.}
CustTbl.CancelRange
```

calls the CustTbl's CancelRange method if the user selects the first tab. This removes any filter set with ApplyRange so that all of the records in the table will be visible.

If the user clicks any tab but the first one the code gets the letter of the tab and applies the filter. The text on tabs is stored in the TabSet's Tabs property as a string list. The statement

```
letter := Tabs[TabIndex];
```

retrieves the text from the currently selected tab and stores it in the variable letter. This captures the letter the user clicked. Next, CustTbl's IndexName property is changed to ByCompany. This makes ByCompany the active index.

The final step is to actually set the range of values to display by calling three more TTable methods, SetRangeStart, SetRangeEnd, and ApplyRange. SetRangeStart and SetRangeEnd work much like the SetKey method described in the last section. When you call SetRangeStart Delphi creates a special record buffer to hold the minimum value(s) for the range. After calling SetRangeStart the table's Fields property and FieldByName function refer to the fields in the minimum value record buffer. So the code

```
SetRangeStart;
FieldByName('Company').AsString := letter;
```

sets the minimum value in the Company field to the letter the user selected with the TabSet and

```
SetRangeEnd;
FieldByName('Company').AsString :=
  letter + 'zzzzzzzzzzzzzzzzzzzzzzzzzzzzz';
```

sets the maximum value for the Company field. SetRangeEnd, like SetRangeStart, opens a new record buffer to hold the maximum value(s) for the fields you are filtering on. In this case the maximum value is the letter the user chose plus 29 lower case z's since this is the greatest value that can be present in the 30 character Company field. Next, the table's KeyFieldCount property is set to one to indicate the number of fields in the index that you are using for the range. Finally, calling the table's ApplyRange method imposes the filter on your view of the table. If you did not create the project described in this chapter, run CUSTORD.DPR on your code disk and try the tabs to see how it works.

Notice that the code that sets the range first calls DisableControls to disconnect all data display controls from the TTable. This prevents screen updates until the new range has been set and avoids the annoying screen flicker that can occur if the screen is repainted several times in rapid succession to show each change that occurs as the range is set and calculated fields are updated.

Once a range has been applied you can use EditRangeStart and EditRangeEnd in place of SetRangeStart and SetRangeEnd to modify the range parameters. When you call SetRangeStart or SetRangeEnd the criteria buffer is cleared of all values. When you call EditRangeStart or EditRangeEnd the current values are not cleared.

Refreshing Data

One problem you need to consider in a multiuser database application is that a user may not be looking at accurate data because someone else has changed it. You can update the data for any table at any time by calling TTable's Refresh method.

How you decide to handle the possibility of data changing depends on your particular application. In many database applications the volume of data is large in relation to the number of updates being processed at any one time and, therefore, the chance that another user will change the record you are editing is very slight. On the other hand, if your application is displaying data that is being updated rapidly, for example by a real time data feed from laboratory information or a securities trading service, it may be critical that the data be refreshed every few seconds.

Another consideration in formulating your refresh strategy is how fast your network is and how heavy the traffic load on the network is. The only way to update the data on users' screens is to reread the data from the server. If you have a heavily loaded network or many workstations active at the same time all calling Refresh frequently, you can generate a lot of network traffic and hurt performance.

You have a lot of control over how often data is refreshed. The least demanding strategy from your perspective as a developer is to let the user handle it. The DBNavigator component has a refresh button. If users are concerned that data they are viewing may be out of date they can click the **Refresh** button at any time.

At the other extreme you can force a refresh to occur at regular intervals by using a TTimer component. To see this technique in action proceed as follows.

1. Add a Timer component to the form. The Timer component is on the System page of the Component Palette.

2. Use the Object Inspector to set the Timer's Enabled property to False and its Interval property to 5000. The Interval property determines how often the timer generates an OnTimer event if its Enabled property is True.

3. Add Two buttons to the form. Name them RefreshOnBtn and RefreshOffBtn. Make their captions Refresh On and Refresh Off.

4. Drag the bottom of the Window frame down about 3/8" and add a Panel component from the Standard page of the palette. You will use the Panel as a status bar to display messages.

5. Set the Panel's properties as follows:

Align	= alTop
Alignment	= taLeftJustify
BevelInner	= bvLowered
BevelOuter	= bvRaised
Caption	= blank
Name	= MsgPanel

6. Drag the bottom of the form's frame up to the bottom of the Panel. The form should now look like Figure 17.16.

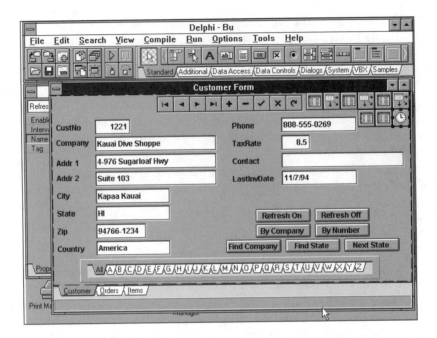

FIGURE 17.16 THE CUSTOMER FOR WITH A TIMER AND PANEL ADDED.

The Timer only has one event, OnTimer. When the Timer's Enabled property is True it generates an OnTimer event every Interval in milliseconds. In this case since the Interval property is set to 5,000 an Ontimer event occurs ever five seconds. Add the following code to the OnTimer event handler.

```
procedure TCustForm.RefreshTimerTimer(Sender: TObject);
begin
  {Display a message on the panel to let the
   user know that the data is being refreshed.}
  MsgPanel.Caption := 'Refreshing...';
  MsgPanel.Update;
  {Refresh the data for all tables in case
   another user has made changes.}
  CustTbl.Refresh;
  OrdersTbl.Refresh;
  ItemsTbl.Refresh;
  {Clear the message on the panel.}
  MsgPanel.Caption := '';
end;
```

This code begins by displaying the message "Refreshing..." in the Panel at the bottom of the screen. It is a good idea to let users know when a refresh takes place because the system will stop responding to user actions while the refresh takes place. For tables on your local hard disk the refresh will be very fast. For server tables there may be a brief delay depending on the speed of your network and the speed of the server. It is also important to let users know a refresh is occurring because the data they are viewing may suddenly change.

WARNING

There is one danger to this approach. Calling Refresh posts any new or changed records. One way to avoid this problem if you call Refresh using a Timer is to check that the table's DataSource component is in the browse state. For example:

```
if CustSrc.State = dsBrowse then CustTbl.Refresh;
```

This ensures that you will not call Refresh while the user is editing or inserting a record.

T I P

If you also want to provide an audible alert use the statement MessageBeep(0);. MessageBeep is described in detail in the Windows API help file.

Displaying the message requires the following two lines of code.

```
MsgPanel.Caption := 'Refreshing...';
MsgPanel.Update;
```

The first line changes the Panel's Caption property. The second line calls the Panel's Update method which which tells Windows to process any pending screen updates. If you do not call Update you will never see the message because Windows does not waste time updating the screen if there is other code waiting to execute.

T I P

You can force any control that is visible when your form runs to update its appearance immediately by calling its Update method.

The next three statements simply call the Refresh method of each TTable component in the form. Finally

```
MsgPanel.Caption := '';
```

clears the Refreshing message from the Panel. Notice that you do not need to call the Panel's Update method here because this is the end of the code so Windows will redraw the screen since it has nothing else to do.

The Refresh On button's OnClick event handler contains a single line of code.

```
RefreshTimer.Enabled := True;
```

This sets the Timer's Enabled property to True. Add the same line to the Refresh off button but set the Enabled property to False. Now you can run the form, click the Refresh On button, and listen to the speaker beep every five seconds as Refresh is called for all of the tables. In a real application you might want to have an INI file that contains the refresh interval and provides the user with a way to change the interval. You could also store the timer interval in an application control table in your database. Run your code or the CUSTORD.DPR project on your code disk, press the Refresh On button, and watch the panel. After five seconds you will see the Refreshing... message flash briefly in the panel.

While using a Timer in this way ensures that all of the tables are refreshed periodically it may not be necessary to keep all of the tables refreshed all of the time. If you are only worried about refreshing the table the user is looking at, another approach would be to add code to the OnClick handler of the TabSet that moves you between Notebook pages. This code could refresh the table on each page when you move to that page.

Saving Data on Close

What happens when a user inserts a new record in a table or changes an existing record and closes the form without explicitly posting the record? Delphi treats these actions as incomplete transactions and rolls them back on a server, or does not post them if you are working with local tables.

If you want your program to automatically save new or changed records when you close the form you need to add some code to the TTable or TQuery's BeforeClose event handler. The following code is from the CustTbl's BeforeClose handler in the CUSTORD.DPR project.

```
procedure TCustForm.CustTblBeforeClose(DataSet: TDataset);
begin
  with CustTbl do
    if State in dsEditModes then
```

```
    Post;
end;
```

This code checks the State property of the TTable or TQuery to determine if it is in the dsEditModes set. If the dataset is in one of these modes then Post is called to save any pending changes before the form closes.

Initializing Fields

In many applications you need to assign an initial default value to one or more fields in each new record. Delphi provides a particularly elegant way to do this using the OnNewRecord event of TTable. Suppose that whenever you add a new record to the Customer table you want to default the State to Hawaii, the TaxRate to 8.5%, and the Country to America. Just add the following code to CustTbl's OnNewRecord event handler.

```
procedure TCustForm.CustTblNewRecord(DataSet: TDataset);
begin
  CustTblState.Value := 'HI';
  CustTblTaxRate.Value := 8.5;
  CustTblCountry.Value := 'America';
end;
```

You could could put the same code in the AfterInsert event handler but you probably do not want to. The reason is that any field assignments you make in the OnNewRecord handler do not cause the field to be flagged as modified. That means that if you insert a new record, then move to another record without changing the value in a field, the record will not be posted.

Printing Your Form

The TForm object has a Print method that lets you print a form as it appears on the screen. You can easily add this capability to the CustOrd form by adding a button to each page of the notebook. Name the button on the Customer page PrintCustBtn and add the following line of code to the Button's OnClick event handler.

```
procedure TCustForm.PrintCustBtnClick(Sender: TObject);
begin
  CustForm.Print;
end;
```

This will print the form to the current printer. You can add print buttons to the Orders and Items pages and set their OnClick handlers to use the handler for the PrintCustBtn.

Using Other Data-Related Events

Data related events are the events that belong to TTable, TQuery, TDataSource, and TField objects. TQuery events are covered in chapter 19. You have used many data related events already in this chapter. This section will focus on the events that have not been used so far and that you may find useful.

TField

TField includes two events you will find useful. The first is OnValidate and the second is OnChange. TField generates both an OnValidate and an OnChange event anytime the user changes the value in the field, and the new value is written to the table's record buffer. This happens when the user does any of the following. These events will also occur if your code performs any of these actions.

1. The user moves to another field after entering a new value.
2. The user moves to another record after entering a new value.
3. The user posts the record by clicking the Post button on the Navigator for the table.

OnValidate occurs before the value is written to the record buffer and is the ideal place to handle custom data validation. If the value the user entered is not valid just call the Abort runtime library procedure to prevent the user from posting the record or leaving the field. For example, you could create an OnValidate event handler for the CustTblState field and add the following code.

```
if CustTblState.Value = 'XX' then
  Abort;
```

Remember, however, that it is better to handle data validation on the server to ensure that the data is validated whether it is changed by your program or by some other means. If you are working with local Paradox tables you may be able to validate values with the validity check features, particularly lookup tables. If you use dBase tables you will have to do all data validation in code.

The OnChange event occurs after the data has been validated and written to the record buffer. This is the place to put code that must execute when the field's value has been successfully changed. One example would be code that makes an entry in another table when the value of this field changes.

TTable

Although this section focuses mainly on events two properties of TTable should be mentioned since they have not been used in any example so far. They are TableName and ReadOnly.

TableName is useful because it lets you change the table whose data your form displays on-the-fly. Suppose you have a form that lets users view current sales data. However, you also have separate tables that contain historical sales data for prior years. Using the GetTableNames method you could display a list of the historical tables, let the user pick one and then switch to that table. Note, however, that you cannot change the TableName property while the TTable is active. To change the TableName a TTable in an open form do the following.

```
with CustTbl do
begin
  DisableControls;
  try
    Active := False;
    TableName := 'oldcust.db';
    Active := True;
  finally
    EnableControls;
  end;
end;
```

ReadOnly is another property that can only be changed when the TTable is not active. The following code will make the Customer table ReadOnly.

```
with CustTbl do
begin
  DisableControls;
  try
    Active := False;
    ReadOnly := True;
    Active := True;
  finally
    EnableControls;
  end;
end;
```

You can use it to prevent unauthorized users from changing data as part of a security system in your program if you are working with local tables, or with server tables where you only need to restrict access for this user at certain times. If you can, it is safer to use the security features built into your database server to control access to data. Doing so protects the data no matter what program is used to access it.

Even if you are working with local Paradox tables you should use their master and auxiliary password system, if possible, to control data access. While the security system for Paradox tables is not as flexible as most database servers it does offer the advantage of protecting the data no matter how many users attempt to get to it. DBase tables have no built-in security. If you must use local dBase tables you will have to code the security into your program.

 If you change TableName or ReadOnly in a client/server program remember to use a Database component in your form to hold the server connection open when you close the table by setting its Active property to False.

T I P

TTable has a rich set of events of which you can take advantage. They are as follows:

- AfterCancel
- AfterClose
- AfterDelete
- AfterEdit
- AfterInsert
- AfterOpen
- AfterPost
- BeforeCancel
- BeforeClose
- BeforeDelete
- BeforeEdit
- BeforeInsert
- BeforeOpen
- BeforePost
- OnCalcFields
- OnNewRecord

Of these events the most useful are OnCalcFields, BeforePost, and AfterInsert. You have already seen examples of using OnCalcFields in the Creating Calculated Fields section earlier in this chapter.

BeforePost

BeforePost is a good place to compute the value of any fields that are calculated from other fields instead of being entered by the user. One example might be a computed primary key that is derived from data in other fields.

BeforePost is also an ideal place to validate the values in fields before the record is actually posted to the table. If you find invalid values you can display a message to warn the user and prevent the record from posting. For example, you can add a test to the Customer table that requires that if the State is two characters in length the Country must be America. Just add the following code to the CustTbl component's BeforePost event handler.

```
procedure TCustForm.CustTblBeforePost(DataSet: TDataset);
var
  State:      String;
begin
  State := CustTbl.FieldByName('State').AsString;
  if (Length(State) = 2) and
     (CustTbl.FieldByName('Country').AsString <>
     'America') then
  begin
    MessageDlg('Country must be America for this State.',
             mtError, [mbOk], 0);
    Abort;
  end;
end;
```

This code displays a dialog box with an error message and then prevents the record from being posted by calling the runtime library Abort procedure. If you add this code and run the program from inside Delphi and cause this error to occur you will first see the MessageDlg dialog box displayed by this code. However, when you click the **OK** button to close it the dialog shown in Figure 17.17 will appear. This dialog will not appear if you run your program from Program Manager outside of the Delphi IDE.

The reason this dialog appears is that Abort generates something called a silent exception. An exception is a runtime error. A silent exception is an error that does not display the error dialog in Figure 17.17. However, the error dialog is shown when you run the program in the IDE because you are running under the interactive debugger and the debugger stops your program anytime an exception occurs, and indicates the line of code responsible. To continue running the program just click the **OK** button to close the dialog, and press **F9** to tell the debugger to continue running.

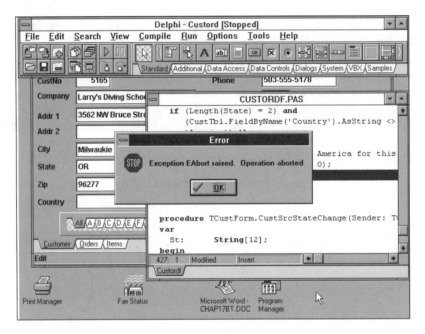

FIGURE 17.17 THE EABORT EXCEPTION DIALOG.

AfterInsert

AfterInsert is very handy for initializing fields in a new record. Suppose that users of your application only enter new customer records from one state. You could provide a menu choice that would allow each user to select the state they want to work with and from then on automatically insert the state code into each new Customer record. The following code in the Customer table's AfterInsert event handler initializes the State field in each new record to HI for Hawaii.

```
procedure TCustForm.CustTblAfterInsert(DataSet: TDataset);
begin
  CustTblState.Value := 'HI';
end;
```

Initializing the value of a field does not prevent users from changing the value if they wish. All a user has to do to override the value you supplied in your AfterInsert handler is move to the field and type a new value. If you do not want users to change the value you supply set the DBEdit's ReadOnly property to True. This lets you change the value of the field in code but prevents users from making changes interactively.

TDataSet

TDataSet only has three events:

- OnDataChange
- OnStateChange
- OnUpdateData

OnDataChange occurs whenever you move to a new record. Therefore, you will get an OnDataChange event when the user moves to the next or prior record, inserts a new record or deletes the current record.

NOTE

Because OnDataChange is a TDataSource event it will not occur if you set the TDataSource's Enabled property to False and move through the table by calling the associated TTables methods.

OnStateChange occurs whenever the the state of the dataset that the TDataSource is connected to changes. A dataset, such as a TTable, can be in any one of the following states:

- dsBrowse
- dsCalcFields
- dsEdit
- dsInactive
- dsInsert
- dsSetKey

The following code in the CustSrc TDataSource's OnStateChange event handler will display the current state of the CustTbl component on the status line.

```
procedure TCustForm.CustSrcStateChange(Sender: TObject);
var
  St:        String[12];
begin
  with CustTbl do
  begin
    case State of
```

```
        dsBrowse:     St := 'Browse';
        dsCalcFields: St := 'Calc Fields';
        dsEdit:       St := 'Edit';
        dsInactive:   St := 'Inactive';
        dsInsert:     St := 'Insert';
        dsSetKey:     St := 'SetKey';
      end;
    end;
    MsgPanel.Caption := St;
    MsgPanel.Update;
end;
```

TDataSource's OnUpdateData event is essentially the same as TTable's BeforePost event. OnUpdateData occurs whenever TTable's Post method is called but before the data is actually posted to the table.

Use TDataSource's OnUpdateData event instead of TTable's BeforePost event if you want to be able to set the DataDource's Enabled property to False, and update the table with code without triggering the event.

T I P

Summary

This chapter has explored how to connect Delphi components to a table in a database so that users can manipulate the data and so that you can access data directly from your code. You have also seen how to use the events that are part of each component to control what users can and cannot do, and to add features by adding code to event handlers.

CHAPTER 18

Understanding SQL

SQL stands for Structured Query Language. The most common pronunciation is "Es que El". Regardless of how you refer to it, SQL is a very powerful data definition query language and manipulation sub-language which you can use to view or modify your data.

SQL can be used to perform the following actions:

- View data based on selection criteria.
- Perform joins on related tables.
- Update, Insert, or Delete data.
- Many other data related activities.

Time and experimentation are necessary to become truly proficient in the use and knowledge of the full capabilities of the SQL engine that is incorporated into the Delphi programming environment and receive its true value as a development tool.

Several other features of SQL give good reason to learn and work with this powerful query language.

- Delphi and most servers can readily process SQL.
- SQL is used by many other database tools other than Delphi. The knowledge gained in working with SQL in Delphi can be transferred to other development environments.
- SQL can be used to request a server to perform actions not normally available through Delphi.

All of the examples in this chapter will be referencing local tables. Therefore, the following SQL examples are considered local SQL. The difference between SQL types will be discussed later in this chapter.

TQuery Component and the SQL Property

All of the techniques demonstrated in this chapter are on the accompanying code disk. The project name is SQLDEMO.DPR and the form (shown in Figure 18.1) is called SQL Demo.

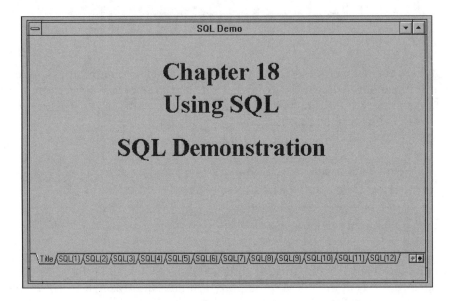

FIGURE 18.1 TAB 'TITLE': THE SQL DEMO FORM.

In order to create SQL statements, you need to use the TQuery object and its SQL property. The SQL property is a member of the TStrings class. This means the property can hold a list of strings which together compromise the SQL command to be performed on a particular data table.

The steps to prepare a simple example of the TQuery object and its SQL property are as follows:

- Place a TQuery, TDataSource, and a DBGrid object on a form. Delphi will name them Query1, Datasource1, and DBGrid1, respectively.
- Using the Object Inspector, set the Database name of the TQuery object to an Alias pointing to DBDEMes included with Delphi, the DataSet property of the DataSource to the name of the TQuery object, and the DataSource property of the DBGrid object to the name of the DataSource object.

- Set the SQL property of the TQuery object to the following: Select * from "Customers.db".
- The last steps are to set the Active property of the TQuery object and the DataSource to True.

When this is complete, the DBGrid object will give a view of the resulting data selected by your SQL statement. Now you can run the form and scroll through the DBGrid object to see the entire data set shown in Figure 18.2.

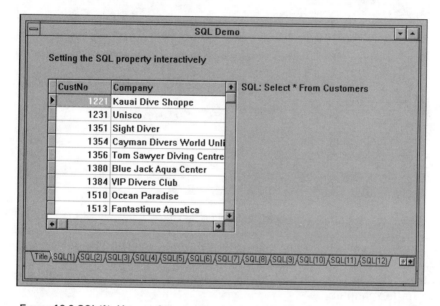

FIGURE 18.2 SQL(1): VIEW OF CUSTOMER DATA THROUGH TQUERY OBJECT SET INTERACTIVELY.

In most applications, you will not want to see all fields of the table you are viewing. In order to limit the fields that are displayed in the DBGrid perform the following steps:

- Select the TQuery object, **Query1**, in design mode.
- Click the right mouse button and select **Fields editor**, or double-click on it.
- Click the **Add** button and select the desired fields from the Available fields list.
- Click the **OK** button to confirm your selection.

Your table view will now display the field selected in the Fields editor, shown in Figure 18.3.

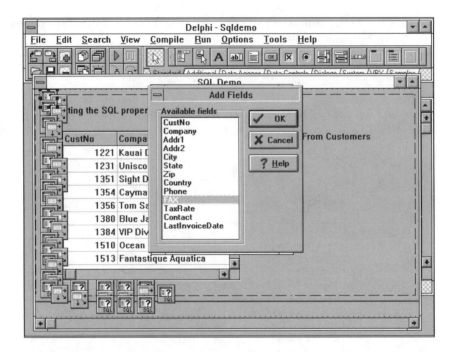

FIGURE 18.3 THE FIELDS EDITOR.

Of course, if you do not ever need to see fields returned by the SQL statement, you can explicitly state which fields ought to be returned. This can
improve the performance of your queries dramatically. This is discussed
later in this chapter.

Data Manipulation Language (DML)

The Data Manipulation Language of Delphi's SQL engine is used to insert,
delete, and change data stored either in local tables or remotely on a server.

Delphi's SQL engine allows the DML items listed in Table 18.1.

TABLE 18.1 VALID SQL DML KEYWORDS

SQL Statements:	SELECT, UPDATE, INSERT, DELETE.
SQL Aggregates:	SUM, AVG, MIN, MAX, COUNT.
SQL Clauses:	FROM, WHERE, ORDER BY, GROUP BY, HAVING.
SQL Operators:	+, -, *, /, =, <, <=, >, >=, <>, IS NULL, AND, OR, NOT, | | (String concatenation).

449

Select and Other SQL Statements

The most commonly used SQL statement is the Select statement. The Select statement tells the SQL engine which field(s) to extract from the table or tables in the current query. While a simple select statement such as

```
Select * from Customer
```

is nice, it is not nearly as powerful as a select statement which has additional selection criteria, aggregate functions, and operators. We will review each of these as well.

The TQuery object and the SQL property do not need to be set interactively. They both work the same when set and operated through code. Most of the examples throughout the rest of this chapter will focus on managing the TQuery object through code.

The next example will refer to Tab SQL(2) on the SQL Demo form (included in the accompanying code disk). In order to set and open a TQuery object during program execution, we have added the following code to the Run button (see Listing 18.1).

LISTING 18.1 SETTING THE SQL PROPERTY THROUGH CODE

```
Query2.Close;
Query2.SQL.Clear;
Query2.SQL.Add('Select * "From Orders.db"');
Query2.Open;
```

Since this is the first example of setting the SQL property through code, this next section will go through Listing 18.1 one line at a time.

Line 1 closes the TQuery object. Delphi will not let you set the SQL property with the TQuery object open. Line 2 clears the SQL property in order to remove any previous value. Line 3 sets the SQL property for our current query and Line 4 opens and runs the query in order to select our order information.

When the demo form is run, and the Run button on tab SQL(2) is clicked, the code will set the SQL property, open the TQuery object and then the corresponding DBGrid object will display all order information.

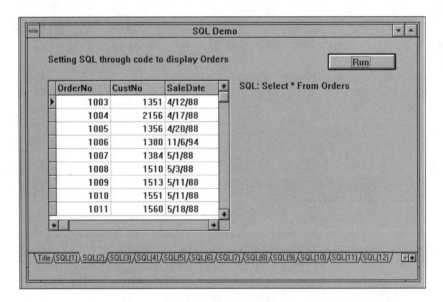

FIGURE 18.4 SQL(2): DISPLAY OF ORDERS DATA.

Special Operators

The list of valid SQL operators listed above (Table 18.1) can be used to restrict the order information that is displayed in our DBGrid. For example, if you are interested only in orders for Customer number 1351, you can change the code on the Run button to return records that belong to Customer number 1351. This example uses tab SQL(3). The Run button code is shown in Listing 18.2. (See Figure 18.5.)

LISTING 18.2 DISPLAYING ORDERS FOR CUSTOMER # 1351

```
Query3.Close;
Query3.SQL.Clear;
Query3.SQL.Add('Select * From Orders Where CustNo = 1351');
Query3.Open;
```

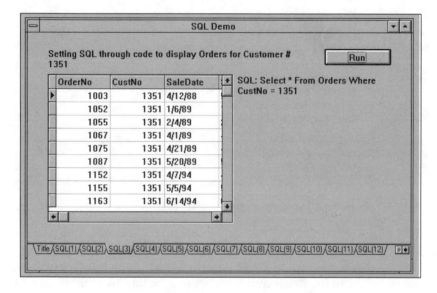

FIGURE 18.5 SQL(3): ORDERS FOR CUSTOMER NUMBER 1351.

Often you will want to see an Order that exceeds a particular total amount. The Run button on Tab SQL(4) sets the SQL property to select those orders whose items total more than $50,000 (see Listing 18.3 and Figure 18.6).

LISTING 18.3 DISPLAYING ORDERS WITH ITEMS TOTALING MORE THAN $50,000

```
Query4.Close;
Query4.SQL.Clear;
Query4.SQL.Add('Select OrderNo, ItemsTotal From Orders Where ItemsTotal >
50000');
Query4.Open;
```

You will notice a slight variation on the Select statement in Listing 18.3. The fields listed after the Select statement tell the SQL compiler to select only the two fields OrderNo and ItemsTotal. This gives the same result as selecting the field list interactively as demonstrated earlier in this chapter.

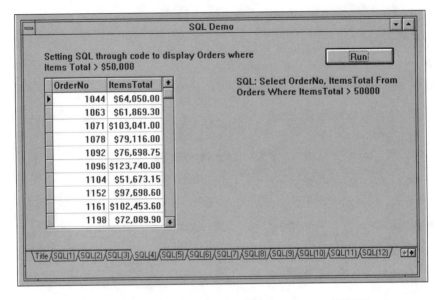

FIGURE 18.6 SQL(4): ORDERS WITH TOTALS GREATER THAN $50,000.

An important feature of SQL is the ability to combine several restrictions at the same time on the data selected through the use of keywords like AND and OR. Tab SQL(5) shows us how to select records which have a total greater than $50,000 or belong to Customer number 1351 (see Listing 18.4 and Figure 18.7).

LISTING 18.4 DISPLAYING ORDERS WITH TOTALING > $50,000 OR CUSTOMER NUMBER = 1351

```
Query5.Close;
Query5.SQL.Clear;
Query5.SQL.Add('Select CustNo,OrderNo, ItemsTotal From Orders Where
ItemsTotal > 50000 OR
      CustNo = 1351');
Query5.Open;
```

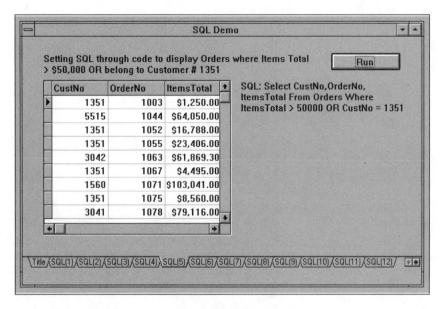

FIGURE 18.7 SQL(5): ORDERS WITH TOTALS GREATER THAN $50,000 OR BELONGING TO CUSTOMER NUMBER 1351.

Aggregators

Aggregate functions are used to summarize data for reporting and analysis purposes. As listed previously, we will be working with the following aggregate functions : COUNT,SUM, MIN, MAX, and AVG.

COUNT

The example on Tab SQL(6) will use the Count function to calculate the number of orders per customer. As usual, the Run button will fill the associated DBGrid (see Listing 18.5 and Figure 18.8).

LISTING 18.5 DISPLAYING THE TOTAL NUMBER OF ORDERS

```
Query6.Close;
Query6.SQL.Clear;
Query6.SQL.Add('Select Custno,COUNT(OrderNo) as TotalOrders From Orders
Group By Custno');
Query6.Open;
```

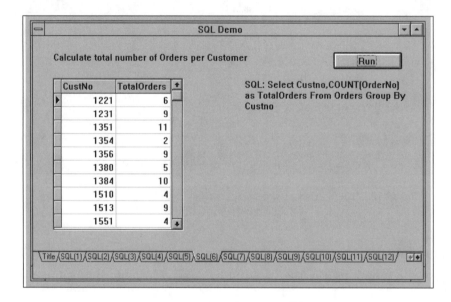

FIGURE 18.8 SQL(6): CALCULATING THE NUMBER OF ORDERS PER CUSTOMER.

An analysis of the previous SQL statement finds two additions to previous examples. First, the COUNT(OrderNo) creates a calculated field in the query result that will calculate the number of orders per customer. Secondly, the Group By Custno clause tells the SQL compiler to group the results by the customer number.

Whenever an aggregate function is used in a select statement, at least one non-aggregate field included in the query result must also be included in the Group By clause.

WARNING

SUM

Most companies that have an order-entry system would want to know at one time or another the total dollar amount of current orders. Tab SQL(7) will use the SUM function to calculate the total value of all orders per customer (see Listing 18.6 and Figure 18.9).

LISTING **18.6** DISPLAYING THE TOTAL DOLLAR AMOUNT OF ORDERS

```
Query7.Close;
Query7.SQL.Clear;
Query7.SQL.Add('Select Custno,SUM(ItemsTotal) as TotalOrderValue From
Orders Group By Custno');
Query7.Open;
```

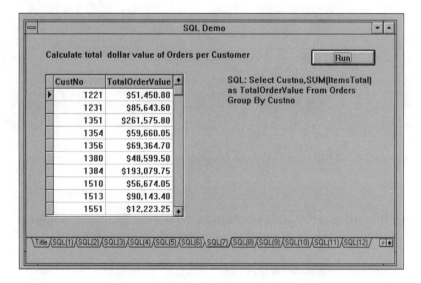

FIGURE **18.9** SQL(7): CALCULATING THE TOTAL ORDERS VALUE FOR ALL CUSTOMERS.

AVG

In order to analyze the order amount of the average order, you will use the AVG function to calculate the average of the ItemsTotal field for all current orders. Tab SQL(8) will use the AVG function to determine the total of the ItemsTotal field of the orders currently in the Orders table (see Listing 18.7 and Figure 8.10).

LISTING **18.7** DISPLAYING THE AVERAGE DOLLAR AMOUNT OF ORDERS

```
Query8.Close;
Query8.SQL.Clear;
Query8.SQL.Add('Select AVG(ItemsTotal) as AverageOrderValue From Orders');
Query8.Open;
```

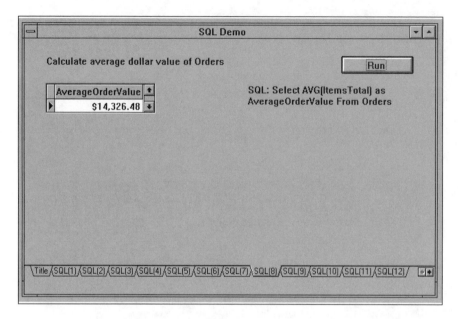

FIGURE 18.10 SQL(8): CALCULATING THE AVERAGE DOLLAR AMOUNT OF ALL ORDERS.

MIN

Tab SQL(9) will use the MIN function to determine the dollar amount of the smallest order currently in the Orders table (see Listing 18.8).

LISTING 18.8 DISPLAYING THE MINIMUM DOLLAR AMOUNT OF ORDERS

```
Query9.Close;
Query9.SQL.Clear;
Query9.SQL.Add('Select MIN(ItemsTotal) as AverageOrderValue From
Orders');
Query9.Open;
```

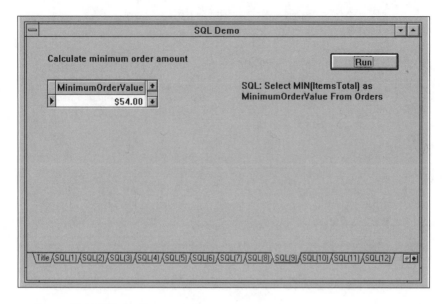

FIGURE 18.11 SQL(9): DETERMINING THE ORDER WITH THE SMALLEST DOLLAR AMOUNT.

MAX

As a parallel to the MIN function and finding the order with the least value, we can also use the MAX function to find the order with the largest total. Tab SQL(10) will use the MAX function to determine the dollar amount of the largest order currently in the Orders table (see Listing 18.9 and Figure 8.12).

LISTING 18.9 DISPLAYING THE LARGEST DOLLAR AMOUNT OF ORDERS

```
Query10.Close;
Query10.SQL.Clear;
Query10.SQL.Add('Select MAX(ItemsTotal) as MaxOrderValue From Orders');
Query10.Open;
```

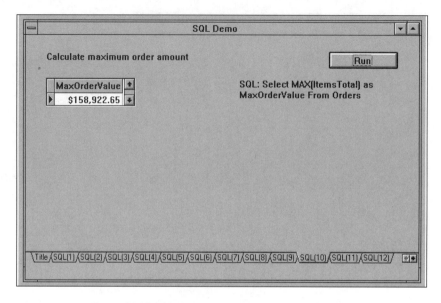

FIGURE 18.12 SQL(10): CALCULATING THE LARGEST ORDER.

Multi-Table Joins

Multi-table joins are used to display data from two or more tables instead of a single table. The requirement for a multi-table join is that all tables involved in the join must have a field with which you can set a logical link to one or more of the other tables involved in the join.

The examples up until this point have focused on single table queries along with aggregate functions and operators. When developing a Delphi application, you will run into instances where you will want to display data from several tables in one query.

For example, it would probably make life easier for the user of your application if he or she could see the name of the company instead of just the customer number, since few users will remember any individual customer's number. Names on the other hand are much easier to recall.

Tab SQL(11) will perform a join between the customer table and the Orders table in order to display customer information along with the customer's associated Order information (see Listing 18.10 and Figure 18.13).

LISTING 18.10 DISPLAYING DATA FROM BOTH THE CUSTOMER TABLE AND THE ORDERS TABLE

```
Query11.Close;
Query11.SQL.Clear;
Query11.SQL.Add('Select C.Company, O.OrderNo From Customer C, Orders O
Where O.CustNo =       C.CustNo Order By C.Company');
Query11.Open;
```

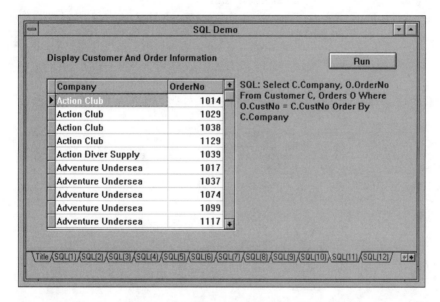

FIGURE 18.13 SQL(11): DISPLAYING DATA FROM BOTH THE CUSTOMER AND ORDER TABLES THROUGH A MULTI-TABLE JOIN.

This code listing merits a moment of discussion due to three new factors in our SQL statement.

First, you will notice the item 'C' in the From clause after the Customer table. This is called a table alias. A table alias is nothing more than a shorthand way of referring to a table in an SQL statement. Since 'C' is defined as an alias to the Customer table, you can refer to fields in the Select clause in the form AliasName.FieldName:

```
Select C.Company
```

Secondly, you will notice a change to the Where clause. The item <u>O.CustNo = C.CustNo</u> is our link between the Customer and the Orders tables. Each order record will display a Company name based on the Customer number in the Orders table.

Finally, the code listing includes an ORDER BY clause. The ORDER By clause is used for sorting the resulting data. The records will be sorted by the Company field in the Customers table.

Even though this gives you much greater ability to display data to your end-user, a two table join may not always be enough. In this vein, Tab SQL(12) will display how easy it is to join yet another table into our previous SQL statement Listing 18.11 provides an example. Figure 18.14 shows the results.

LISTING 18.11 DISPLAYING DATA FROM THE CUSTOMER, ORDERS, AND ITEM TABLES

```
Query12.Close;
Query12.SQL.Clear;
Query12.SQL.Add('Select C.Company, O.OrderNo, I.Description');
Query12.SQL.Add('From Customer C, Orders O, Items I');
Query12.SQL.Add('Where O.CustNo = C.CustNo AND O.OrderNo = I.OrderNo
Order By C.Company');
Query12.Open;
```

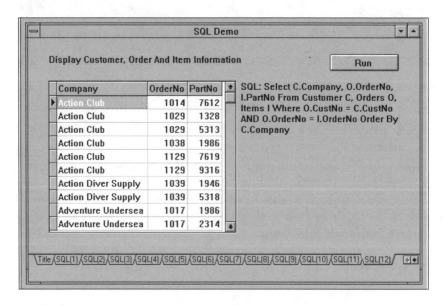

FIGURE 18.14 SQL(12): DISPLAY DATA FROM A THREE-TABLE JOIN.

Self Joins

The BDE, as does standard SQL, allows you to join a table to itself. If you were looking over your vendor information and wanted to find all vendors that operate in the same state as vendor number 3511, Scuba Professionals, you could use Listing 18.12 from Tab SQL(13), which shows a self join. Figure 18.15 shows the results.

Listing 18.12 Self Joins

```
Query13.Close;
Query13.SQL.Clear;
Query13.SQL.Add('Select D1.VendorName, D1.VendorNo, D1.State');
Query13.SQL.Add('From Vendors D, Vendors D1');
Query13.SQL.Add('Where (D.VendorNo = 3511) And (D.State = D1.State)');
Query13.SQL.Add('Order By D1.VendorNo');
Query13.Open;
```

Listing 18.12 tells the SQL compiler to determine the operating state of vendor number 3511. The SQL compiler then uses this state as a link to another copy of the Vendor table to find all vendors in that state.

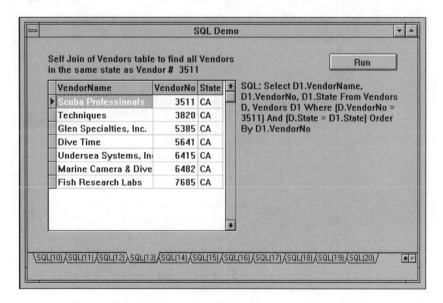

Figure 18.15 SQL(13): Finding all vendors in the same state as vendor number 3511.

Subqueries

Subqueries, or 'Nested Queries', are not allowed in the BDE on local Paradox tables. For this example we will use local Interbase tables. The Databasename property for the TQuery object Query14 is set to IBLOCAL to reference the local Interbase tables included with Delphi. Listing 18.13 contains the code to perform our subquery and Figure 18.16 shows the results.

LISTING 18.13 SUBQUERY STATEMENTS ARE NOT CURRENTLY SUPPORTED BY THE DELPHI SQL COMPILER

```
Query14.Close;
Query14.SQL.Clear;
Query14.SQL.Add('Select * From Customer Where Country in');
Query14.SQL.Add(' (Select Country From Customer Where Customer =
"Signature Design") ');
Query14.Open;
```

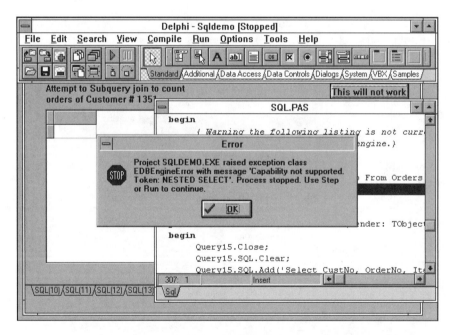

FIGURE 18.16 SQL(14): USING A SUBQUERY TO FIND ALL CUSTOMERS IN THE SAME COUNTRY AS SIGNATURE DESIGN.

Any and All

Any

The ANY keyword is not directly supported by Delphi, but a comparable SQL substitution will do the trick. By using the keyword 'IN', you can restrict your query result based on a selection of values in a particular list. If you frequently looked at the order information for a particular set of customers, then Listing 18.14 will help. Also, see tab SQL(15) and Figure 18.17.

LISTING 18.14 USING THE IN KEYWORD TO SEE ORDER INFORMATION FOR A SELECT LIST OF
          CUSTOMERS

```
Query15.Close;
Query15.SQL.Clear;
Query15.SQL.Add('Select CustNo, OrderNo, ItemsTotal From Orders Where
      Custno IN (1221, 1231, 1351, 1354)');
Query15.Open;
```

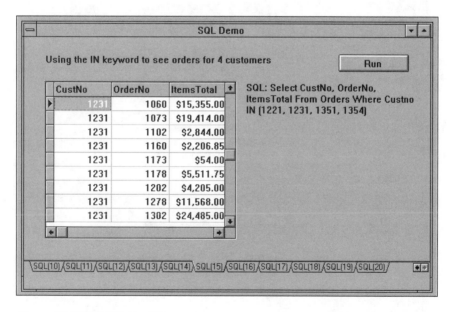

FIGURE 18.17 SQL(15): THE IN KEYWORD USES A CUSTOMER LIST TO FIND ORDER INFORMATION.

All

The All keyword is also not directly supported. With a bit of creative coding you can still obtain the same effect. What if you wanted to see all order information for all customers except those in a given list? Listing 18.15 shows you a way and Figure 18.18 shows the results.

LISTING 18.15 USING THE NOT IN KEYWORD TO SEE ORDER INFORMATION ALL
                CUSTOMERS BUT 4

```
Query16.Close;
Query16.SQL.Clear;
Query16.SQL.Add('Select CustNo, OrderNo, ItemsTotal From Orders');
Query16.SQL.Add('Where Custno NOT IN (1221, 1231, 1351, 1354) Order By
CustNo');
Query16.Open;
```

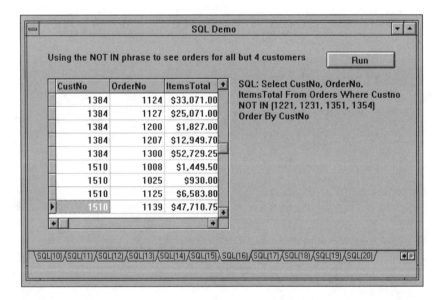

FIGURE 18.18 SQL(16): THE NOT IN PHRASE FINDS ORDER INFORMATION FOR SELECT CUSTOMERS.

Update

Delphi supports the standard Update statement. No extensions have been added to Update statement in Delphi's SQL engine.

The Update feature allows you to modify data by updating or changing the value in a particular field using the Where clause to find the set of records you want to modify.

If a data entry error resulted in customer number 1231 having a variety of SHIPVia values instead of the correct value of UPS, a query using the SQL statement UPDATE can remedy the situation (see Listing 18.16 and Figure 18.19).

LISTING 18.16 UPDATE THE SHIPVIA FIELD FOR CUSTOMER # 1231

```
Query17.Close;
Query17.SQL.Clear;
Query17.SQL.Add('Update Orders SET ShipVIA = "UPS" Where CustNo = 1231');
Query17.ExecSQL;
Query17b.refresh;
```

The line Query17b.refresh refreshes the source for the DBGrid on tab SQL(17) so you can see the effects of the UPDATE query immediately.

Another difference in this query is the use of the ExecSQL method. The ExecSQL method is used to execute a query with an SQL source that does not return a set of records. Use this with the INSERT, DELETE, and UPDATE statements.

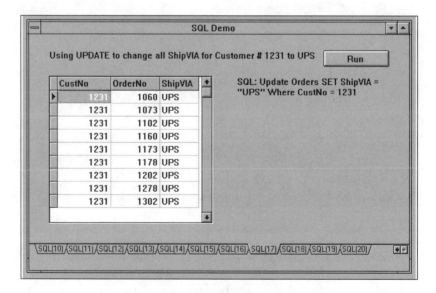

FIGURE 18.19 SQL(17): THE UPDATE STATEMENT LETS YOU DO DATA UPDATES.

465

Insert

Delphi's SQL compiler supports the INSERT statement. The INSERT statement gives you the ability to insert records into a table through the execution of an SQL statement. You can easily add a new vendor while running an application (see Listing 18.17 and Figure 18.20).

LISTING 18.17 INSERT A NEW VENDOR WITH THE INSERT STATEMENT

```
Query18.Close;
Query18.SQL.Clear;
Query18.SQL.Add('INSERT into Vendors (VendorNo,VendorName) Values
(1,"JunkName")');
Query18.ExecSQL;
Query18b.refresh;
Query19b.refresh; (refresh needed to update listing on following page)
```

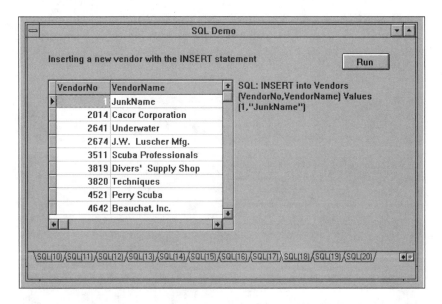

FIGURE 18.20 SQL(18): INSERT NEW RECORDS INTO A TABLE WITH THE INSERT STATEMENT.

The INSERT statement includes, immediately after the name of the destination table, a comma separated list of the fields you wish to fill in for the current insertion. Following the field list comes the Values clause which tells the SQL compiler what values to insert into each field in the field list.

Delete

In conjunction with the INSERT statement, the Delphi SQL compiler allows the deletion of records through the execution of an SQL statement. Execution of Listing 18.18 will remove the record for vendor number 1 that was inserted in the last example. Figure 18.21 shows the results.

LISTING 18.18 DELETE VENDOR # 1

```
Query19.Close;
Query19.SQL.Clear;
Query19.SQL.Add('DELETE From Vendors Where VendorNo = 1');
Query19.ExecSQL;
Query19b.refresh;
Query18b.refresh; (needed to refresh previous page)
```

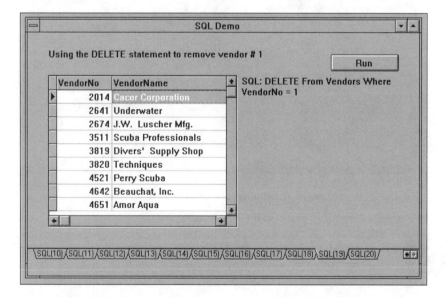

FIGURE 18.21 SQL(19): DELETE UNWANTED RECORDS BY INCLUDING THE DELETE STATEMENT.

Data Definition Language

The Data Definition Language in Delphi's SQL compiler gives you the following abilities:

- Create tables
- Alter tables
- Drop tables
- Create indexes
- Drop indexes

Tab SQL(20) has a Run button for each of the five DDL operations supported by the Borland Database Engine. See Figure 18.22.

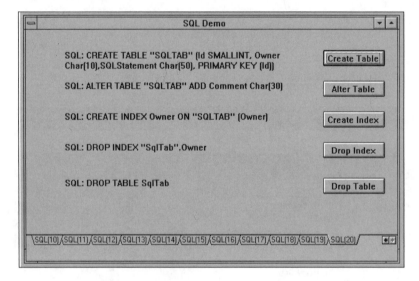

FIGURE 18.22 SQL(20): EXECUTION OF DDL ACTIONS.

The following Data Definition Language examples are meant to be executed in the sequence of the buttons on tab SQL(20) from top to bottom. For example, you should not attempt to create a secondary index unless the table has been created.

WARNING

Creating Tables

The ability to create a table while an application is running is a very useful utility. Delphi's SQL engine makes it a very simple matter to create a new table (see Listing 18.19).

LISTING 18.19 CREATING THE **SQLTAB** TABLE

```
Query20.Close;
Query20.SQL.Clear;
Query20.SQL.Add('CREATE TABLE ''SQLTAB'' (Id SMALLINT,');
Query20.SQL.Add('Owner Char(10),SQLStatement Char(50), PRIMARY KEY
(Id))');
Query20.ExecSQL;
```

The Create statement includes the name of the table to create and a list of fields to be included in the new table along with the type and size of each field. If a table extension is not explicitly included in the table name, the current version of Delphi will create a Paradox table.

Altering Tables

Under certain conditions it might be desirable to restructure a table while an application is running in order to add or remove a field from that table. The Alter Table button adds the field Comment to the SQLTab table (see Listing 18.20).

LISTING 18.20 ALTERING THE **SQLTAB** TABLE TO ADD THE **COMMENT** FIELD

```
Query20.Close;
Query20.SQL.Clear;
Query20.SQL.Add('ALTER TABLE ''SQLTAB'' ADD Comment Char(30)');
Query20.ExecSQL;
```

Create Indexes

Delphi's SQL Engine also lets you create secondary indexes on your tables. Secondary indexes are not in the scope of this chapter. You can refer to Delphi's on-line help on indexes. Listing 18.21 shows you how to add a secondary index to the SQLTab table.

LISTING 18.21 ADDING A SECONDARY INDEX TO THE **SQLTAB** TABLE

```
Query20.Close;
Query20.SQL.Clear;
Query20.SQL.Add('CREATE INDEX Owner ON ''SQLTAB'' (Owner)');
Query20.ExecSQL;
```

Dropping Indexes

Delphi also gives you the ability to drop or delete indexes. Listing 18.22 shows you how.

LISTING 18.22 DELETING A TABLE INDEX

```
Query20.Close;
Query20.SQL.Clear;
Query20.SQL.Add('DROP INDEX ''SqlTab''.Owner');
Query20.ExecSQL;
```

Dropping Tables

The last DDL option supported is the dropping or deletion of tables. This operation will remove or delete the table from your database (see Listing 18.23).

LISTING 18.23 DROPPING A TABLE

```
Query20.Close;
Query20.SQL.Clear;
Query20.SQL.Add('DROP TABLE SqlTab');
Query20.ExecSQL;
```

Local SQL

Local or "client-based" SQL is a subset of the ANSI-standard SQL 92. SQL modifications have been made to the Borland Database Engine SQL to work with Paradox and dBase tables. Due to the fact that Delphi's SQL is a subset of standard SQL, there are certain limitations to its capabilities.

TIP

Many of the limitations of working of local tables are removed if you use the Borland Database Engine to set the SQLPASSTHRU MODE. This feature allows you to specify that SQL statements be passed straight through and processed by your server. The limitations of the SQL statements will be determined by your server and not Delphi's SQL compiler.

Syntax Differences

The SQL syntax used in Delphi is compatible with the ANSI standard of SQL, but of course it has a Borland flavor. Use the on-line help for sample

SQL statements. Other references of standard SQL will also be very useful, but examples of standard SQL may need to be modified to work in Delphi.

If you pass the SQL directly through to your server, you should refer to a SQL reference manual for your particular server when formatting your SQL requests.

Limitations

The following list gives a few of the limitations to the current version of the SQL engine:

- Nested queries
- Using aggregate calculations as a selection criteria
- Multi-join update queries
- Multi-join delete queries

Summary

The SQL compiler is a very powerful database tool and as mentioned earlier will take a little time to get comfortable with and use to its full potential.

The sample program included used a separate TQuery object for each page of the notebook. This is not always necessary in your applications, particularly when performing the DDL functions. It is much easier to use a single TQuery object for all of your table and index creating and dropping.

Most of the differences between Delphi's SQL and the ANSI standard can be worked around either through creative programming or using the SQL processor on your server. Hopefully, as Delphi matures, it will grow closer and closer to the ANSI standard.

CHAPTER 19

Delphi Query Component

The Delphi TQuery component is the other descendant of TDataSet. Since it has the same ancestor as TTable it shares many of the same properties and methods. However, a Query component has one significant difference. The data that a TQuery displays is determined by a SQL statement. This means that you have all the power and flexibility offered by your server's SQL dialect available to control which rows and columns are accessible.

This chapter will explore using Query components to display a subset of data, join tables, link cursors, provide live updatable views, create tables, and more.

Connecting TQuery Components

Using Query components is very similar to using Table components. Figure 19.1 shows the form from the CUSTQ.DPR project. The form contains a Query, a DataSource, a DBNavigator, and a DBGrid. Connect the components as follows:

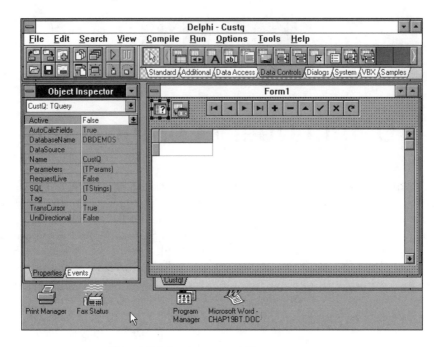

FIGURE 19.1 A FORM USING A TQUERY COMPONENT.

1. Set the Query's DatabaseName to DBDEMOS and its name to CustQ.
2. Set the DataSource's DataSet to CustQ and its name to CustSrc.
3. · Set the DBGrid's DataSource to CustSrc.
4. Set the DBNavigator's DataSource to CustSrc.

Now return to the Query component, select its SQL property, and click the button to display the String List Editor. Now enter the following SQL statement:

```
select * from "customer.db"
```

as shown in Figure 19.2, and click **OK**.

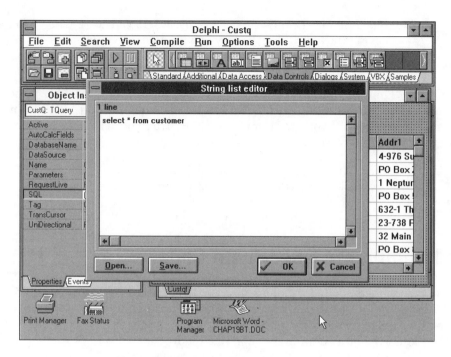

FIGURE 19.2 SETTING A TQUERY'S SQL PROPERTY.

Now set the Query's Active property to True and you will see the data from the query in the DBGrid. Run the form and move around. You will see that everything works just as it did with a Table component but the data is being supplied by the query. However, you cannot edit the result set returned by a query. There is one exception and that is if you request a live query. Live queries are discussed in the "Using Live Queries" section later in this chapter.

If you look at the properties and events for a TQuery component you will see that they are almost identical to the properties and events of a TTable. This means that you can do virtually anything with a TQuery that you can do with a TTable.

The examples in this chapter use local SQL and work with Paradox tables. Since SQL dialects vary slightly from server to server the SQL statements may be different on your server.

N O T E

TQuery's Unidirectional property can have a substantial impact on performance if you are working with a server that does not support bidirectional scrollable cursors. If you set Unidirectional to True you will only be able to move forward in the query result set.

The Unidirectional property has no effect on performance with local tables because local tables are row oriented and provide bidirectional cursors.

N O T E

Changing the Query with Code

You can change the query statement at any time using code. To see this add a Button and an Edit control to the form. These components are on the Standard page of the palette. Set the Edit component's Name property to StateEdit. The form should now look like Figure 19.3.

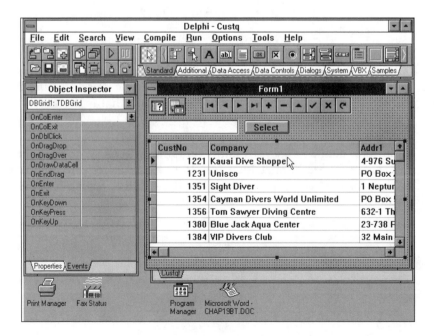

FIGURE 19.3 CHANGING A QUERY AT RUNTIME.

Name the Edit control StateEdit and set the button's Caption to Select. Now add the following code to the button's OnClick event handler:

```
procedure TForm1.Button1Click(Sender: TObject);
begin
  {Disconnect the TQuery from its DataSources so the
   screen will not update while changing the query.}
  try
    CustQ.DisableControls;
    {Close the query by setting its Active
     property to False.}
    CustQ.Active := False;
    {Empty the string list that contains the SQL
     query by calling its Clear method.}
    CustQ.SQL.Clear;
    {Add a new query to the SQL property's string
     list.}
    if StateEdit.Text = '' then
      CustQ.SQL.Add('select * from customer')
    else
      CustQ.SQL.Add('select * from customer where State = "'
        + StateEdit.Text + '"');
    {Open the query by making it active again.}
    CustQ.Active := True;
  finally
    {Reconnect the TQuery to its DataSources so the
     new answer set will be displayed.}
    CustQ.EnableControls;
  end;
end;
```

The purpose of this code is to let you type a State into the Edit control, click the button, and provide a list of customers that live in the state you entered.

You cannot change the Query's SQL property while the Query is active. However, setting the query's Active property to False has an annoying side effect. When Active is set to False the screen will repaint showing the DBGrid blank. When Active is set to True again the screen will repaint a second time with the DBGrid showing the new answer set. This rapid repainting of the screen is very annoying to most users. To prevent this the code starts by calling the query's DisableControls method.

Calling DisableControls has the same effect for a TQuery that it does for a TTable. It disconnects the TQuery from all DataSource components and freezes the data displayed by any data display components. This lets you change the SQL property without any annoying screen flicker. As with a TTable, the code following the DisableControls call is enclosed in a try/finally block to ensure that the EnableControls call executes even if a runtime error occurs.

The next line of code sets the Active property to False. The string list that holds the SQL statement works exactly like all of the other string lists you have encountered in this book. Before you add the new statement you need to empty the SQL property's string list by calling its Clear method.

The value you enter in an Edit component is contained in its Text property. The if statement in this code examines the value of the Text property and adds one of two SQL statements to the Query component. If the Edit control is blank

```
select * from customer
```

is used to display all rows and columns in the customer table. If the Edit component contains a value then

```
select * from customer
  where State = "??"
```

is used with the ?? replaced by the value in the Edit component. The SQL statement is added to the Query component's SQL property by calling its Add method. In the call to Add that adds the query for a particular state

```
CustQ.SQL.Add('select * from customer where State = "'
      + StateEdit.Text + '"');
```

note that the value from StateEdit is enclosed in double quotation marks. For example, if you enter **HI** in the Edit control and click the **Select** button, the value added to the Query's SQL property is:

```
select * from customer where state = "HI"
```

In this example the entire SQL statement appears on one line, however, this need not be the case. In fact, for a complex query it may be easier and clearer to spread the query across multiple lines. To enter the SQL statement as

```
select * from customer
  where State = "HI"
```

change the code as follows:

```
  if StateEdit.Text = '' then
    CustQ.SQL.Add('select * from customer')
  else
  begin
    CustQ.SQL.Add('select * from customer');
    CustQ.SQL.Add('  where State = "' + StateEdit.Text + '"');
  end;
```

Since the number of lines that a string list can hold is limited only by available memory there is no practical limit to the size or complexity of the SQL statement you can use. Finally, EnableControls is called to reconnect the DataSource to the Query and display the new answer set in the DBGrid.

There is one other thing that you may want to change in this code. Both the TTable and TQuery objects have an Open and a Close method. Many programmers find it more intuitive to write

```
CustQ.Close;
```

than to write

```
CustQ.Active := False;
```

Calling the Close method sets the Active property to False. Calling the Open method sets the Active property to True. You may have heard that it is more efficient to set the Active property directly than to call a method that sets it. While this is technically true, Object Pascal is so fast that the difference in time is a fraction of a millisecond and is of no consequence. Use whichever method is most intuitive to you.

Using the Format Function

The preceding example showed that SQL statements are just strings and you can manipulate them like any other string. In the statement

```
CustQ.SQL.Add('select * from customer where State = "'
    + StateEdit.Text + '"');
```

variable information was included in the SQL statement by concatenation with the literal text to form the complete SQL query.

Another convenient way to insert variable information into any location within a string is to use the runtime library format function. Format lets you include placeholders, or replaceable parameters, in a string and substitute variable information for each of the placeholders. In the string

```
'The number %d Windows development tool is %s.'
```

the %d and %s are placeholders for a number and a string, respectively. The following code from the FORMAT.DRP project on your code disk shows how format works.

```
procedure TForm1.Button1Click(Sender: TObject);
var
  a:        Word;
  b,c:      String;
begin
  a := 1;
  b := 'Delphi';
  c := format('The number %d Windows development tool is %s.', [a, b]);
  MessageDlg(c, mtInformation, [mbOK], 0);
end;
```

This code assigns the value 1 to the variable a and the string 'Delphi' to the varible b. When format is called in the statement

```
c := format('The number %d Windows development tool is %s.', [a, b]);
```

it replaces the placeholders with the variables in the argument array, [a,b], and returns the resultant string. The resultant string is <u>The number 1 Windows development tool is Delphi</u>. Format matches the placeholders with the members of the array by position. The first placeholder is replaced by the first member of the array, and so on.

Now that you see how format works you can see that you can use it to put variable information into any location in a SQL query statement. Using the format function you can rewrite the preceding example as follows. This project is FORMATQ.DPR on your code disk.

```
procedure TForm1.Button1Click(Sender: TObject);
begin
  {Disconnect the Query from all DataSources so the
   screen will not repaint while changing the query.}
  CustQ.DisableControls;
  try
    {Close the query.}
    CustQ.Close;
    {Empty the string list that contains the SQL
     query by calling its Clear method.}
    CustQ.SQL.Clear;
    {Add a new query to the SQL property's string
     list.}
    if StateEdit.Text = '' then
      CustQ.SQL.Add('select * from customer')
    else
      CustQ.SQL.Add(format('select * from customer where State = "%s"',
        [StateEdit.Text]));
    {Open the query.}
    CustQ.Open;
```

```
finally
  {Reconnect the Query to the DataSource so the new
   set of records will be visible.}
  CustQ.EnableControls;
  end;
end;
```

Here the state to be found is substituted into the query statement by the call to format in the Add method call shown below.

```
CustQ.SQL.Add(format('select * from customer where State = "%s"',
  [StateEdit.Text]));
```

This can be an easier way to build a query statement than concatenating strings if there are several variables involved or if some of the variables are numeric.

Assigning Values Directly to the SQL Property

Another very easy way to vary information in a query is to take advantage of the free form formatting of SQL. You can spread a SQL statement across as many lines as you like. Therefore, at design time you can set the TQuery's SQL property as shown in Figure 19.4.

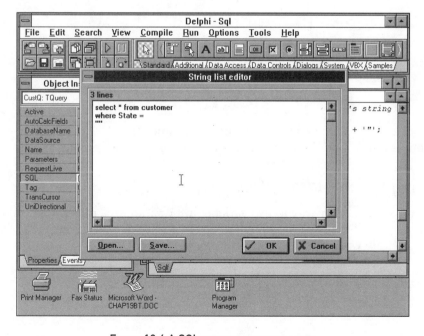

FIGURE 19.4 A SQL QUERY ON MULTIPLE LINES.

Remember that in a string list you can access any line by using its index number. By putting the state to select on a line by itself you can change the value as shown in the following code from SQL.DPR on your code disk.

```
procedure TForm1.Button1Click(Sender: TObject);
begin
  CustQ.DisableControls;
  try
    {Close the query.}
    CustQ.Close;
    {Add a new query to the SQL property's string
     list.}
    CustQ.SQL[2] := '"' + StateEdit.Text + '"';
    {Open the query.}
    CustQ.Open;
  finally
    CustQ.EnableControls;
  end;
end;
```

In this example the first two lines of the query remain the same. Only the state to be selected, which appears on the third line, is changed by the statement:

```
CustQ.SQL[2] := '"' + StateEdit.Text + '"';
```

Remember that the index of a string list is zero based. The first string in the list is 0, the second 1, and so on.

NOTE

If you can structure your query so that the values that need to be changed at runtime are on lines by themselves this is a very easy technique to use.

Using Parameters in Queries

There is yet another way to use variable information in a query. It is called a parameterized query. A parameterized version of the query from the preceding example would look like this:

```
select * from customer
  where State = :StateName
```

In this SQL statement :StateName is a parameter and you can supply its value either at design time or at runtime be setting the TQuery component's Parameters property. To see this in action look at the PARAM.DPR project on your code disk. Figure 19.5 shows the SQL property in the String List Editor set to the SQL statement above.

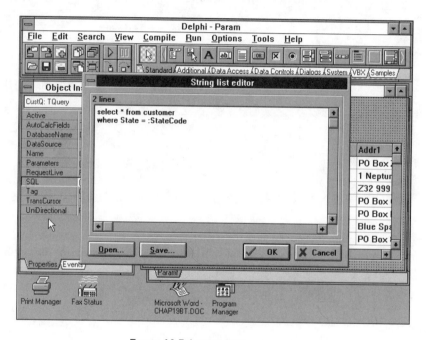

FIGURE 19.5 A PARAMETERIZED QUERY.

The next step in using a parameterized query is to assign initial values to the parameters using the TQuery's Params property. Select the Params property and click its button to display the Define Parameters dialog shown in Figure 19.6. The dialog will contain a list of all of the parameters in the SQL property. You can select each in turn to see their type and value. If you want the parameter to have a null value leave the value field blank and check the Null Value checkbox as shown in Figure 19.6.

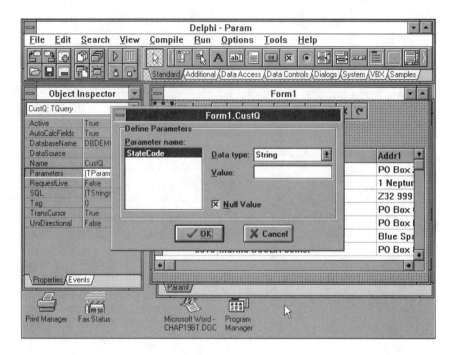

FIGURE 19.6 THE DEFINE PARAMETERS DIALOG BOX.

Finally, change the code in the Select buttons OnClick event handler as shown below.

```
procedure TForm1.Button1Click(Sender: TObject);
begin
  with CustQ do
  begin
    DisableControls;
    try
      {Close the query.}
      CustQ.Close;
      {Set the value of the parameter.}
      Prepare;
      Params[0].AsString := StateEdit.Text;
      {Open the query.}
      CustQ.Open;
    finally
      EnableControls;
    end;
```

```
  end;
end;
```

This code demonstrates the four steps necessary to change the value of parameters in a query.

1. Close the query by calling its Close method or setting its active property to False.

2. Call the TQuery's Prepare method. This causes the Query to parse the SQL statement and identify the parameters.

3. Assign the value for each parameter. The Params property is actually a string list that contains each parameter value as a separate string. The values are related to the parameters in the SQL statement by position only. The first string in Params is assigned to the first parameter in the SQL statement, and so on. In the code above you can see that the syntax for assigning a value to a Query's Params property is identical to that use to assigning a value to a Table's Fields property.

4. Call the Query's open procedure. When you call Open the Query object passes the parameters to the server and runs the query.

While you can change any part of a SQL statement by string manipulation or changing strings in the SQL property this may not be true with parameters. Parameter substitution actually takes place on the server and many servers only allow parameters in the where or insert clauses of a SQL statement.

NOTE

If you are working with local tables instead of a database server these restrictions do not apply. Local SQL lets you use parameters anywhere in your SQL statement.

Reading a Query from a File

TQuery type components offer yet another way to vary the query at runtime. SQL statements can be stored in text files and read into the Query's SQL property when you want to change the query. The FILE.DPR project on your code disk demonstrates this technique. FILE.DPR is very similar to the CUSTQ.DPR project discussed earlier in this chapter. The form is shown in Figure 19.7.

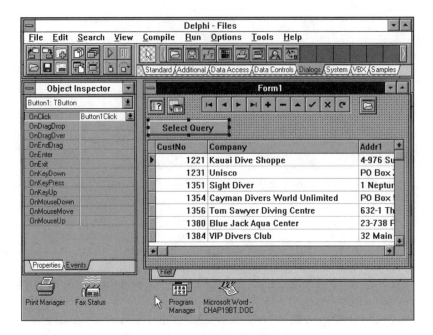

FIGURE 19.7 THE FILE.DPR PROJECT FORM.

This form contains a Query component, a DataSource component, a DBNavigator, and a Button labeled Select Query. The Query component's DatabaseName property is set to DBDEMOS and its SQL property is set to:

```
select * from customer
```

The DataSource's DataSet is set to CustQ, the name of the Query component. In the upper-right corner this form also contains an OpenDialog component from the Dialogs page of the Component Palette. The OpenDialog displays a standard Windows Open File dialog when you call its Execute method. The OpenDialog has the following property settings:

DefaultExtension	= SQL
Filter	= SQL Files	*.sql
Name	= SelectQuery
Title	= Select a Query

The directory on your code disk for this chapter contains three text files that each contain a different SQL statement. The file ALL.SQL contains:

```
select * from customer
```

The file HI.SQL contains:

```
select * from customer where State = "HI"
```

The file FL.SQL contains:

```
select * from customer where State = "FL"
```

The Button contains the following code:

```
procedure TForm1.Button1Click(Sender: TObject);
begin
  {If the user picks a file from the open
  dialog.}
  if SelectQuery.Execute then
    with CustQ do
    begin
      DisableControls;
      try
        {Close the query.}
        Close;
        {Load a new SQL statement from the
         user selected file.}
        SQL.LoadFromFile(SelectQuery.FileName);
        {Open the query.}
        Open;
      finally
        EnableControls;
      end;
    end;
end;
```

This code begins by calling the OpenDialog's Execute method. This displays the dialog and lets you select a file. The Execute method returns True if you select a file and press **OK** and False otherwise. If you do select a file then the Query is closed and the SQL property's LoadFromFile method is called with the file name you selected in the OpenDialog as its parameter. This loads the contents of the file into the Query object's SQL property. Finally, the Query is opened again and the resultant set of the new query appears in the DBGrid.

If you look at TQuery in the on-line help you will not find a LoadFromFile method listed. Load from file is not a method of the TQuery component but of its SQL property, which is a String List.

String Lists also have a SaveToFile method. You could use this by allowing users to enter their own SQL statements into a Memo component, copying the SQL statement from the memo to the Query's SQL property and reopening the query. You could also give users the option to save this new query to a file so they could use it again later without having to enter it again.

Linking Cursors with SQL

One of the really neat things you can do with parameterized queries is to link cursors. In Chapter 17 you saw one way to link cursors using TTable components and indices. Here is how to do it with SQL. This is the LINK.DPR project on your code disk. To create this project yourself follow these steps.

1. Create a new project.
2. Place a TabbedNotebook component from the Additional page of the palette on the form. The TabbedNotebook should have its Align property set to alClient by default so that it will expand to fill the form.
3. Set the notebook's Name property to CustBook.
4. Select the notebook's Pages property and click the button to open the String List Editor. Enter three pages as shown in Figure 19.8. Name the pages **&Customer**, **&Orders**, and **&Items**.

5. Place three Query components and three DataSource Components on the form. Name the first Query **CustQ**, set its DatabaseName to DBDEMOS, and set its SQL property to:

```
select * from customer
```

Then set the Query's Active property to True.

6. Name the first DataSource **CustSrc** and set its DataSet property to CustQ.

7. Place a DBGrid and a DBNavigator on the Customer page of the notebook and set their DataSource Properties to CustSrc. Your form should now look like Figure 19.9.

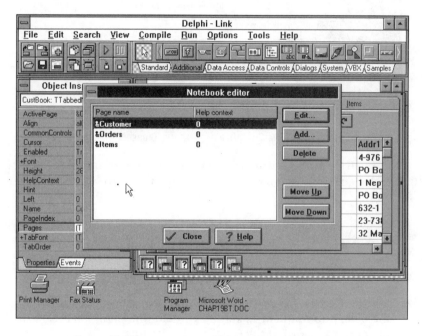

FIGURE 19.8 THE TABS FOR THE TABBEDNOTEBOOK COMPONENT.

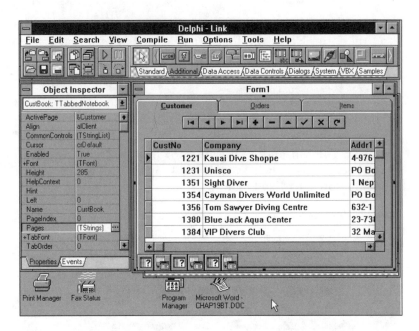

FIGURE 19.9 THE CUSTOMER PAGE OF THE TABBEDNOTEBOOK.

Next you need to perform the same steps for the Orders table. Select the TabbedNotebook and set its ActivePage property to &Orders. Then do the following:

1. Select the second TQuery, set its Name to **OrdersQ**, its DatabaseName to DBDEMOS, and its SQL property to:

```
select * from orders where CustNo = :CustNo
```

2. Set the OrdersQ Query's DataSource property to **CustSrc**. This tells the Query component to get the value of the parameter :CustNo from the current record of the CustSrc DataSource.

3. Set OrderQ's Active property to True.

4. Name the second DataSource **OrdersSrc** and set its DataSet property to OrdersQ.

5. Add two DBNavigators and a DBGrid and set the DataSource property of one navigator and one grid to OrdersSrc. Remove all of the buttons except the movement buttons from the second navigator and set its DataSource to CustSrc. The Orders page should now look like Figure 19.10.

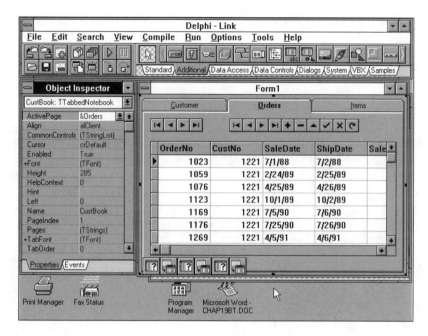

FIGURE 19.10 THE ORDERS PAGE OF THE TABBEDNOTEBOOK.

If you run the program you will see that the orders DBGrid displays the order records for the current customer only. This happens because you used a parameterized query

```
select * from orders
  where CustNo = :CustNo
```

and told the query component to get the value of the parameter :CustNo from the CustSrc DataSource, instead of from its own Params property by setting the OrdersQ Query's DataSource property to CustSrc.

When you use a parameterized query with a DataSource the name of the parameter in the SQL statement must be identical to the name of a column in the DataSource.

N O T E

You can link the Items table to the Orders table in a similar fashion. Connect the third Query on the form to Items, set its SQL property to

```
select * from Items
  where OrderNo = :OrderNo
```

and set its DataSource property to OrdersSrc. Connect the third DataSource to the Items Query. Finally, add two DBNavigators and a DBGrid to the Items page of the notebook and connect them. The Items page should look like Figure 19.11.

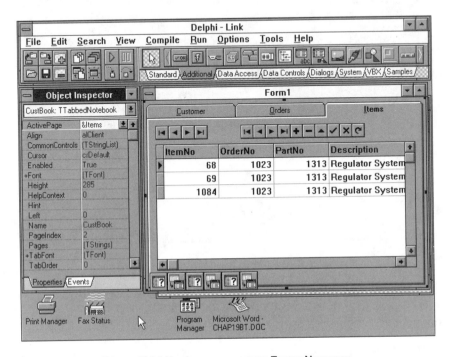

FIGURE 19.11 THE ITEMS PAGE OF THE TABBEDNOTEBOOK.

Although this example linked three TQuerys together you can use any combination of TTable and TQuery components when you build a form that uses linked cursors. The TLINK.DPR project on your code disk is identical to LINK.DPR but it uses a TTable for the Customer table and TQuerys for the Orders and Items.

Using Live Queries

So far, the query examples have produced static answer sets. You cannot edit them. However, TQuery components can return live datasets under certain conditions. The LIVE.DPR project on your code disk is identical to LINK.DPR except that the RequestLive property of all three Query components has been set to True. When you run this program and change the values you are changing the data in the underlying table just as if you were working with TTable components.

TQuery components also have a read only Boolean property called CanModify. You can check the value of CanModify to determine if the query answer set is live or not.

For local tables you must meet all of the following conditions to get a live resultant set:

1. The query must return values from a single table.
2. The table must not use aggregates such as Sum.
3. The query must not include calculations.
4. The query cannot have an Order By clause.
5. The query cannot include the Distinct keyword.
6. The Where clause must contain only comparisons between column values and constants using Like and the relational operators.

Server tables will return a live result set if the following conditions are met:

1. The query returns values from a single table.
2. The query does not include the Distinct keyword.
3. The query does not include aggregates such as Sum.
4. The table has a unique index if it resides on a Sybase server.

T I P

Live queries on local tables never use indices for selecting rows, therefore, a live query may be slow if you are selecting a small percentage of the rows in a large table.

You can determine if a query did in fact return a live resultant set by testing the Query objects CanModify property. If it is true, the resultant set is live and you can edit the data.

Creating Joins

Since you can set a Query's SQL property to any valid SQL statement, creating a join is no different than any of the other examples in this chapter. JOIN.DPR on your code disk provides an example. The form is shown in Figure 19.12.

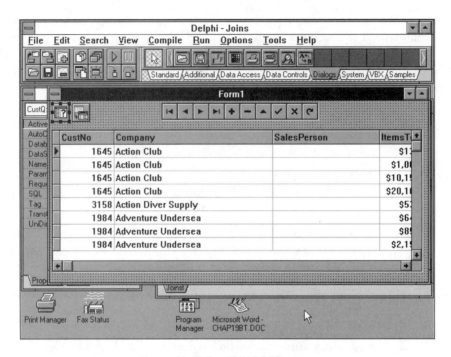

FIGURE 19.12 THE **JOINS.DPR** FORM.

This form contains a Query, a DataSource, a DBNavigator, and a DBGrid connected as in previous examples. What is different here is the Query's SQL property. It contains:

```
select C.CustNo, C.Company,  O.OrderNo, O.ItemsTotal
  from customer C, orders O
  where C.CustNo = O.CustNo
  order by C.Company
```

This query creates a join between the Customer and Orders tables and projects four columns, CustNo and Company from Customer and OrderNo and

ItemsTotal from Orders. The answer set is sorted by Company. Run the program and you will see the result in the DBGrid as shown in Figure 19.13.

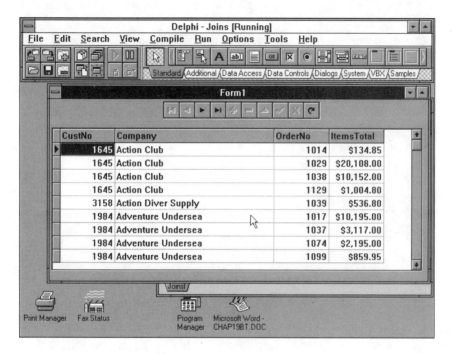

FIGURE 19.13 THE JOINS.DPR PROJECT RUNNING.

Using Data Definition Language

You can use a TQuery object to create and delete tables using the appropriate SQL statements for your server. DDL.DPR is a project that deletes then recreates the TEST.DB table on your code disk. Figure 19.14 shows the form for this project.

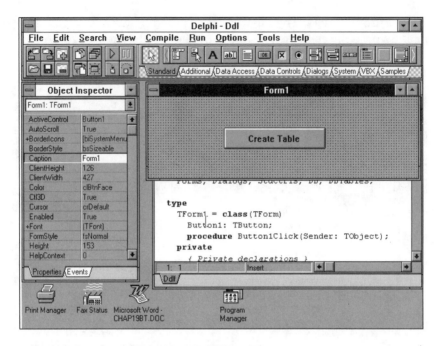

FIGURE 19.14 THE DDL PROJECT'S FORM.

The first thing you will notice about this form is that the only thing on it is a Button. There is no Query component. In this program you will create the Query object in your code, use it, and destroy it. Here is the code from the Button's OnClick event handler.

```
procedure TForm1.Button1Click(Sender: TObject);
var
  TestQ:     TQuery;
begin
  TestQ := TQuery.Create(Form1);
  with TestQ do
  begin
    {Set the DatabaseName.}
    DatabaseName := 'c:\ap\delphi\19c';
    {Empty the SQL property string list.}
    SQL.Clear;
    {Add the SQL statement to delete the table.}
    SQL.Add('drop table "test.db"');
    {Execute the SQL statement to delete the
     table.}
    ExecSQL;
```

```
  {Clear the SQL string list and load the
   create table statement.}
  SQL.Clear;
  SQL.LoadFromFile('create.ddl');
  {Create the table test.db.}
  ExecSQL;
  TestQ.Free;
  end;
end;
```

The procedure begins by declaring a variable, TestQ, of type TQuery. The first statement in the procedure calls TQuery's constructor, Create, to create the instance named TestQ. In the statement

```
TestQ := TQuery.Create(Form1);
```

the Create method takes one parameter, the name of the component that owns this instance of TQuery. Since all components on a form are owned by the form, the form's name is passed as the parameter.

The next step is to set up the SQL statement that will delete the existing table. This is done by the following statements, which assign a value to TestQ's DatabaseName property, clear the SQL property's string list and add the SQL statement to delete the table.

```
  {Set the DatabaseName.}
  DatabaseName := 'c:\ap\delphi\19c';
  {Empty the SQL property string list.}
  SQL.Clear;
  {Add the SQL statement to delete the table.}
  SQL.Add('drop table "test.db"');
```

Remember that each of these statements would have to be prefixed with TestQ. if they were not inside the with statement. Once the SQL statement

```
drop table "test.db"
```

has been assigned to TestQ's SQL property you can run the query but not by calling its open method as you have in all of the preceding examples. The reason is that the Open method expects the query to return a cursor to the resultatn set generated by the SQL statement. However, in this case, there is no resultant set so you will get a runtime error, an exception, if you use the Open method to run the query.

To solve this problem TQuery has a second method, ExecSQL, that will run the query and does not expect a cursor to be returned. This is the method used in the code above. You should always use ExecSQL with SQL statements that do not generate a result set. Examples include DDL statements, insert statements, and delete statements.

NOTE Local SQL requires that table names which contain a period, such as TEST.DB, be enclosed in quotation marks.

The next step is to create the new table using the SQL statement

```
create table "test.db"
  (Name char(30),
   Address char(30),
   City char(20),
   State char(2),
   Zip char(10))
```

which is in the file CREATE.DDL on your code disk. The following code

```
{Clear the SQL string list and load the
 create table statement.}
SQL.Clear;
SQL.LoadFromFile('create.ddl');
{Create the table test.db.}
ExecSQL;
```

clears the SQL string list, reads the create table statement from its file on disk into the SQL string list and executes it by calling ExecSQL. The last statement

```
TestQ.Free;
```

calls TestQ's destructor method, Free, to destroy the TQuery object by performing any necessary operations and releasing its memory. Remember, when you create an object in your code you are responsible for destroying it so that any resources it was using will be available for reuse.

TIP When you need to use a component briefly, create and destroy it in your code, instead of placing it on the form at design time. This way, it will not exist and consume memory all the time the form is open.

Building Queries If You do Not Know SQL

Delphi includes a Visual Query Builder that helps you build a valid SQL statement without knowing the correct syntax. To access the Visual Query Builder select a TQuery component in a form, right-click and select **Query Builder**.

While the Visual Query Builder may be helpful when you are learning SQL or if you are having trouble getting a particular query right you will find it a lot slower than just typing your SQL statement directly into the SQL String List Editor or into your code. If you are going to do a lot of development in Delphi, learn SQL. It will save you a lot of time in the long run.

For more information on the Visual Query Builder, consult the Delphi manuals. The Visual Query Builder also has extensive on-line help that you can access when you are using it.

Summary

Delphi's TQuery component provides a very flexible way to access a subset of your data. You can change the query dynamically at runtime, link TQueries and TTables in any combination to show-one-to-many and one-to-one relationships and even get live editable views of subsets of your data. TQueries combined with SQL's data definition language also lets you create and drop tables and indexes within your application.

CHAPTER 20

Error Handling

Handling errors that occur while your programming is running is something you have to worry about no matter what language or environment you develop in and Delphi is no exception. Delphi handles errors through an object called an Exception. When an error occurs at runtime Delphi raises (creates) an exception and, if your code does not handle the exception, an OnException event.

In this chapter you will learn about handling exceptions, ensuring that cleanup code always executes, and creating your own exceptions.

Handling Resource Allocations and Cleanup

One type of problem that you can handle very easily in Delphi is cleanup code. By cleanup code I mean code that must execute to restore the system to a safe stable state even if a runtime error occurs. One example of this is disabling all of the data aware controls so you can open and close the Table or Query, or so you can change the active index for a Table without annoying screen flicker.

To handle cleanup chores Delphi provides the try/finally construct. The easiest way to understand it is to look at the example in CLEAN.DPR on your code disk. Figure 20.1 shows the form from this project.

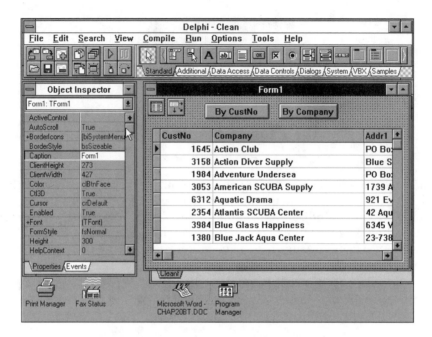

FIGURE 20.1 A FORM THAT CHANGES THE ACTIVE INDEX.

This form contains a Table, DataSource and DBGrid connected as described in Chapter 17. The Table component is connected to the Customer table in the DBDEMOS database. It also contains two buttons that let you change the active index from the primary index, CustNo, to the secondary index ByCompany. One way to make the change to the ByCompany index is with the following code. This code is from the OnClick handler for Button2, the Button with the caption By Company, in the NOCLN.DPR project.

```
procedure TForm1.Button2Click(Sender: TObject);
begin
  with Table1 do
  begin
    DisableControls;
    IndexName := 'x';
    EnableControls;
  end;
end;
```

The problem with this code is that if the statement that changes the IndexName property fails because the index does not exist, an exception will automatically be generated, and execution of the procedure will termi-nate. That means that the EnableControls call will not execute. The result is that you will be in the form and the DBGrid will no longer be connected to the Table. Try it. Run the NOCLN.EXE program, click the By Company but-ton, and then try to move around in the grid. This is not a condition you want to leave a user in.

Delphi's solution to this problem is very elegant in that it gives you a way to guarantee that your cleanup code will execute in spite of any run-time errors that occur. Here is the By Company Button's OnClick handler code from CLEAN.DPR.

```
procedure TForm1.Button2Click(Sender: TObject);
begin
  with Table1 do
  begin
    DisableControls;
    try
      IndexName := 'ByCompany';
    finally
      EnableControls;
    end;
  end;
end;
```

Here the code after the DisableControls method call is enclosed in a try/finally block. If an exception occurs in any of the code between try and finally, the code in the finally block will execute. This means that even if the change to the IndexName property fails the EnableControls call will exe-cute. You can see this by changing the index name to X and running this code. After you click the By Company button and clear the error dialog you will still be able to move around in the grid.

Another case where it is critical that code execute is when your code allocates resources and you must ensure that they are released. Resources that you must recover if an error occurs include:

- Memory
- Files
- Windows resources

In an object-oriented environment there is no better example than creating an instance of an object in your code. Figure 20.2 shows the form from ALLOC.DPR on your code disk.

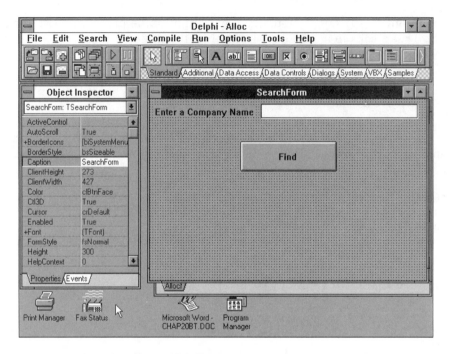

FIGURE 20.2 DYNAMIC OBJECT CREATION.

This form lets you enter a Company name then searches the customer table and reports whether a match was found or not. Here is the code from the Find buttons OnClick handler.

```
procedure TSearchForm.FindBtnClick(Sender: TObject);
var
  CustTbl:    TTable;
begin
  {Create a TTable object.}
  CustTbl := TTable.Create(SearchForm);
  {Make sure the TTable's destructor gets called no
   no matter what happens in the following code.}
  try
    with CustTbl do
    begin
      {Assign the DatabaseName and TableName.}
      DatabaseName := 'DBDEMOS';
```

```
      TableName := 'customer.db';
      {Open the table.}
      Open;
      {Search for the requested name.}
      while (EOF = False) and
            (ToFind.Text <> FieldByName('Company').AsString) do
        Next;
      {Display a message.}
      if ToFind.Text = FieldByName('Company').AsString then
        MessageDlg('Found', mtInformation, [mbOK], 0)
      else
        MessageDlg('Not Found', mtInformation, [mbOK], 0);
    end;
  finally
    {Call the TTable's destructor to fee its memory.}
    CustTbl.Free;
  end;
end;
```

This code declares a variable named CustTbl of type TTable that is used to search the customer table. However, first, this instance of the TTable type must be created by calling its constructor method which is named Create. The important issue here is that any time you create a new instance of an object by calling its constructor you are allocating memory. You are responsible for deallocating that memory by calling the object's destructor method. If you do not the memory will not be available until you restart Windows.

To ensure that CustTbl's Free method is called all of the code in this procedure following the call to TTable's Create method is enclosed in a try/finally block. The call to the destructor, Free, follows the finally keyword so that it will execute even if an exception is raised by any of the code between try and finally.

You can nest try-finally blocks to any depth.

T I P

An example of protecting both file and memory resources is contained in the following code from the FASTE.DPR project. Figure 20.3 shows the form for this project. This is identical to the FAST.DPR project described in chapter 11 with the addition of error-handling code.

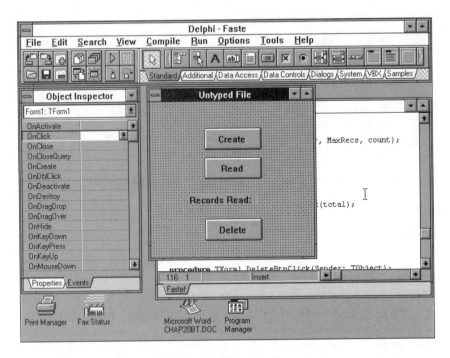

FIGURE 20.3 THE FASTE PROJECT'S MAIN FORM.

The following code is from the Create button's OnClick event handler.

```
procedure TForm1.CreateBtnClick(Sender: TObject);
const
  MaxRecs = 100;
var
  buff:        array[1..MaxRecs] of TAddress;
  addrFile:    File;
  i, count:    Word;
begin
  AssignFile(addrFile, 'addr.dat');
  Rewrite(addrFile, SizeOf(TAddress));
  try
    {Put 100 records into the buffer.}
    for i := 1 to MaxRecs do
      with buff[i] do
      begin
        PasToArray('John Doe', name);
        PasToArray('123 East Main Street', addr);
        PasToArray('New York', city);
        PasToArray('NY', state);
```

```
      PasToArray('55555-5555', zip);
    end;
    {Write 100 buffers (10,000 records.}
    for i := 1 to 100 do
      BlockWrite(addrFile, buff, MaxRecs, count);
  finally
    System.Close(addrFile);
  end;
end;
```

This procedure opens a new file by calling the Rewrite runtime library procedure. Once the file has been opened the code makes sure that it is closed by enclosing the subsequent statements in a try/finally block. If an error occurs the call to System.Close(addrFile) in the finally block will be made.

The following code is from the Read button's OnClick event handler. This procedure has two resource allocations that must be protected and uses nested try finally blocks.

```
procedure TForm1.ReadBtnClick(Sender: TObject);
const
  MaxRecs = 500;
type
  Tbuff =        array[1..MaxRecs] of TAddress;
var
  buff:          ^Tbuff;
  addrFile:      File;
  total,
  count:         Word;
begin
  New(buff);
  try
    AssignFile(addrFile, 'addr.dat');
    Reset(addrFile, SizeOf(TAddress));
    try
      {Read the file MaxRecs records at a time.}
      total := 0;
      repeat
        count := 0;
        BlockRead(addrFile, buff^, MaxRecs, count);
        total := total + count;
      until count = 0;
    finally
      System.Close(addrFile);
    end;
    ReadCount.Caption := IntToStr(total);
  finally
```

```
    Dispose(buff);
  end;
end;
```

508

The first resource that is allocated is memory when New is called in the statement

```
New(buff);
```

to allocate the buffer array that the records will be read into. The try keyword after this statement begins a block that ends with the call to Dispose(buff) after the finally keyword.

Within this outer try/finally block the call to Reset in the statement

```
Reset(addrFile, SizeOf(TAddress));
```

opens a file. The try keyword following this statement begins a try/finally block that protects the file resource by ensuring that

```
System.Close(addrFile);
```

is called in the finally section. If a runtime error occurs in this code neither global heap memory nor file handles will be lost.

Trapping Runtime Library Exceptions

Calling runtime library procedures and functions can generate exceptions. Runtime library exceptions fall into one of the following categories.

- Conversion
- Floating point math
- Hardware
- Heap (memory allocation)
- Input/Output
- Integer math
- Typecast

Before delving into the details of runtime library exception handling, look at the INTERR.DPR project on your code disk to get an overview of the process. Figure 20.4 shows the form for INTERR.DPR.

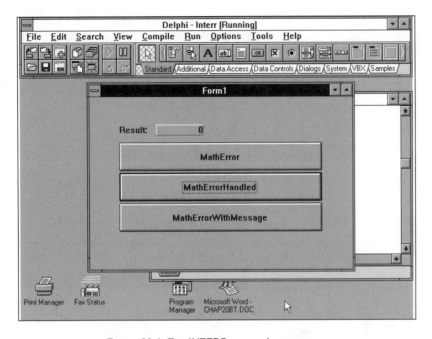

FIGURE 20.4 THE INTERR PROJECT'S MAIN FORM.

This form contains five controls, a Label, a Panel, and three Buttons. The following code is from the MathError Button's OnClick event handler.

```
procedure TForm1.MathErrorClick(Sender: TObject);
var
  i,j,k,l,m:        Integer;
begin
  i := 23;
  j := 0;
  l := 2;
  m := 4;
  {Make a calculation.}
  k := i div j * (l div m);
  {Display the result.}
  Result.Caption := IntToStr(k);
end;
```

This code declares five integer variables and assigns values to all of them except k. When the expression

```
k := i div j * (l div m);
```

510

is evaluated a runtime library exception is raised because the value of j is zero, and division by zero is not allowed. In this case Delphi's default exception handler will handle the error by displaying an error message in a dialog box and ending execution of this procedure.

The following code is from the MathErrorHandled button's OnClick handler.

```
procedure TForm1.MathErrorClick(Sender: TObject);
var
  i,j,k,l,m:          Integer;
begin
  i := 23;
  j := 0;
  l := 2;
  m := 4;
  try
    k := i div j * (l div m);
  except
    on EIntError do k := 0;
  end;
  {Display the result.}
  Result.Caption := IntToStr(k);
end;
```

This code will not display the normal error dialog that appears when an exception is raised and your code does not handle it, because the calculation is enclosed in a try/except block. The except code sets the result to zero and that is the end of the exception.

Notice how much easier this is than handling the possibility of division being zero without try/except. To detect the possibility of either j or m being zero would require the following.

```
if (j = 0) or (m = 0) then
  k := 0
else
  k := i div j * (l div m);
```

If the computation were more complex, testing for all possible integer math errors would require a lot of code.

N O T E When you run a program in the IDE, the program is being run under the control of the Interactive Debugger. You will always see the debugger's exception dialog whether your code handles the exception or not. To see what the user will see run the program from Program Manager.

When an exception is raised in a try/except block Delphi looks to see if the exception is listed in the except section. If it is then that the code for that exception is executed. In this example if any integer math exception occurs, the value of k is set to zero.

Understanding the Runtime Library Exception Hierarchy

Before continuing you need to understand how the seven classes of run-time library exceptions are organized. Three of the categories, integer math exceptions, floating point math exceptions, and hardware exceptions have a hierarchy.

EIntError is a generic integer math exception. You can test for it or for the specific integer math errors shown in Table 20.1.

Table 20.1 Integer Math Exceptions

Exception	Description
EDivByZero	An attempt to divide by zero.
ERangeError	The number or expression result is beyond the range of the integer type.
EIntOverflow	A mathematical operation caused an integer overflow.

For floating point math operations the generic exception is EMathError. The individual floating point errors are listed in table 20.2.

TABLE 20.2 FLOATING POINT MATH EXCEPTIONS

Exception	Description
EInvalidOp	The processor encountered an invalid instruction. This usually means the processor is trying to execute data due to a pointer error.
EZeroDivide	Attempt to divide by zero.
EOverflow	A floating point operation overflowed.
EUnderflow	A floating point operation underflowed.

The generic hardware exception is EProcessorException and its specific descendants are listed in Table 20.3.

TABLE 20.3 HARDWARE EXCEPTIONS

Exception	Description
EFault	The base exception object for all faults.
EGPFault	General protection fault. The most common cause of GP faults is an uninitialized pointer.
EStackFault	Illegal access to the stack segment.
EPageFault	The Windows memory manager could not access the swap file.
EInvalidOpCode	The processor encountered an undefined instruction. This is usually caused by trying to execute data.
EBreakpoint	The program generated a breakpoint interrupt.
ESingleStep	The program generated a single step interrupt.

With the exception of EGPFault you should never encounter or need to worry about any of the hardware exceptions. They will only occur if a serious hardware or operating system failure has occurred, or if you are running under a debugger.

The remaining four categories of exception do not have a generic exception. You must test for each specific exception that you want to handle. For input/output errors there is a single exception, EInOutError, which contains a field named ErrorCode, that contains the operating system error code for the error that occurred.

There is a single typecast exception, EInvalidCast, that occurs anytime you attempt a typecast using the as operator and the typecast fails.

All conversion exceptions raise the EConvertError exception. For example, if you call StrToInt and the string cannot be converted, EConvertError will be raised.

There are two heap exceptions that can occur when you try to use dynamic memory. They are listed in Table 20.4.

TABLE 20.4 HEAP EXCEPTIONS

Exception	Description
EOutOfMemory	An attempt to allocate memory on the heap failed.
EInvalidPointer	An attempt was made to dispose of a pointer that points to an address outside of the heap.

Handling Multiple Exceptions

The third button on the INTERR.DPR form, MathErrorWithMessage, shows how to handle multiple exceptions in a single try/except block. The following code is from the Button's OnClick handler.

```
procedure TForm1.MathErrorWithMessageClick(Sender: TObject);
var
  i,j,k,l,m:         Integer;
begin
  i := 23;
  j := 0;
  l := 2;
  m := 4;
  try
    k := i div j * (l div m);
  except
    on EDivByZero do
    begin
      k := 0;
      MessageDlg('Divide by zero error',
              mtError, [mbOK], 0);
    end;
    on EIntError do
    begin
      k := 0;
      MessageDlg('Integer math error.',
              mtError, [mbOK], 0);
    end;
  end;
  {Display the result.}
  Result.Caption := IntToStr(k);
end;
```

Examine the except clause and you will note that it contains checks for two different exceptions, EDivByZero, and EIntError. In this case a specific message is displayed for EDivByZero and another message for all other integer math exceptions.

NOTE The order of the tests in this code is critical. If you test for EIntError first you will never see the EDivByZero message because EIntError includes all integer math exceptions including EDivByZero.

This construct lets you handle as many exceptions as you wish in a single try/except block.

Understanding Exception Scope

You must understand the scope of exceptions to determine where you need try/except blocks in your application, and what will happen if you do not handle an exception. Consider the following procedures.

```
procedure procB;
var
  i:    Integer;
begin
  i := 2 div 0;
end;

procedure procA;
begin
  try
    procB;
  except
    on EIntError do
      MessageDlg('Integer math error.', mtError, [mbOK], 0);
  end;
end;
```

When procA calls procB, an integer math exception will be raised by the attempt to divide by zero. When an exception is not handled in the block where it occurs, execution in the block that caused the exception ends and control returns to the block that called it. In this case, when the divide by zero exception occurs in procB, control returns to procA and execution resumes with the exception still raised. Therefore, the code in the except clause in procA will execute.

In other words exceptions travel out through each nested try/except block, and moving back up the procedure and function calling chain until they are handled by one of your try/except blocks, or until they reach Delphi's default exception handler.

You can provide a default exception handling mechanism, however, doing so is dangerous. In the following code notice that an else clause appears in the except block.

```
procedure procA;
begin
  try
```

```
    procB;
  except
    on EIntError do
      MessageDlg('Integer math error.', mtError, [mbOK], 0);
    else
      MessageDlg('Some other exception occurred.', mtError, [mbOK], 0);
  end;
end;
```

The else clause will handle all exceptions other than the integer math exceptions handled by the on EIntError do. Since you may not know how to handle every type of exception safely, you almost certainly do not want to write a try/except with an else clause.

Raising Exceptions Again

When you handle an exception with a try/except block the exception ends there because Delphi destroys the exception object. You can raise the exception again with the keyword raise. This code

```
procedure procA;
begin
  try
    procB;
  except
    on EIntError do
      MessageDlg('Integer math error.', mtError, [mbOK], 0);
    else
    begin
      MessageDlg('Some other exception occurred.', mtError, [mbOK], 0);
      raise;
    end;
  end;
end;
```

has an else clause that displays a message for all exceptions except integer math exceptions, however, after the message dialog has been displayed, the call to raise reraises the exception so that it will be handled again farther up the calling chain.

The ability to reraise an exception lets you easily write nested try/except blocks without having to duplicate code. You can provide specific handling in the inner block, then reraise the exception to let the more generic code in the outer try/except block execute. Take a look at the following code from NEST.DPR on your code disk. The main form is shown in Figure 20.5 and the code is from the Button's OnClick event.

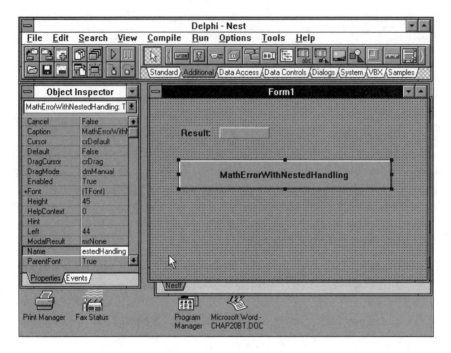

FIGURE 20.5 THE NEST PROJECT'S MAIN FORM.

```
procedure TForm1.MathErrorWithNestedHandlingClick(Sender: TObject);
var
  i,j,k,l,m:          Integer;
begin
  i := 23;
  j := 0;
  l := 2;
  m := 4;
  try
    try
      k := i + j;
    except
      on EIntError do
      begin
        k := 23;
        raise;
```

```
      end;
    end;
    try
      k := k + i div j * (1 div m);
    except
      on EIntError do
      begin
        k := 0;
        raise
      end;
    end;
  except
    on EDivByZero do
      MessageDlg('Divide by zero error',
                 mtError, [mbOK], 0);
    on EIntError do
      MessageDlg('Integer math error.',
                 mtError, [mbOK], 0);
  end;
  {Display the result.}
  Result.Caption := IntToStr(k);
end;
```

This code involves a two step calculation. The value assigned to the variable k must be 23, if an error occurs in the first step of the computation and zero of an error occurs in the second step. Therefore, each of the computation statements is enclosed in its own try/except block that sets k to the proper value, if an error occurs and reraises the exception.

The outer try/except block handles displaying the correct message so that the message display code does not have to be duplicated in the try/except for each step in the calculation.

Using the Exception Object

One of the most useful features of the exception mechanism in Delphi concerns the fact that you can access the Message field in the Exception object using a special form of the on..do syntax in try/except. The project IOERR.DPR on your code disk demonstrates this. Figure 20.6 shows the form for IOERR.DPR. It consists of two buttons, both of which contain code that tries to open a nonexistent file.

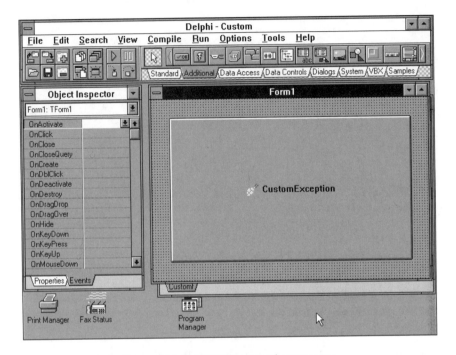

FIGURE 20.6 THE **IOERR** PROJECT'S MAIN FORM.

The following code is from the I/O Error Button's OnClick event handler.

```
procedure TForm1.IOErrorBtnClick(Sender: TObject);
var
  TestFile:      TextFile;
begin
  AssignFile(TestFile, 'foo.txt');
  try
    Reset(TestFile);
  except
    on Ex: EInOutError do
    begin
      MessageBeep(0);
      MessageDlg(Ex.Message + '  Code: ' +
                 IntToStr(Ex.ErrorCode), mtError,
                 [mbOK], 0);
    end;
  end;
end;
```

This code tries to open the file FOO.TXT, which does not exist. In the except block the statement

```
on Ex: EInOutError do
```

performs two functions. First, it traps the EInOutError exception. Second, it initializes the variable Ex to give you access to the Exception object. The type of the variable Ex is the type of the Exception object that you are are trapping, in this case, EInOutError.

In the MessageDlg call Ex.Message inserts the message text so that the standard message text for this error is displayed in the custom dialog box. This field is available for all exceptions. In addition, Ex.ErrorCode is used to add the operating system error code to the message. ErrorCode is available in EInOutError exceptions only. If that was all you could do with the message text it would not be very useful. However, you can change the text of the message and reraise the exception. Look at the following code from the CustomMessage button.

```
procedure TForm1.CustomMessageBtnClick(Sender: TObject);
var
  TestFile:      TextFile;
begin
  AssignFile(TestFile, 'foo.txt');
  try
    Reset(TestFile);
  except
   on Ex: EInOutError do
   begin
     Ex.Message := 'The file FOO.TXT could not be found';
     raise;
   end;
  end;
end;
```

In this case the code changes the text of the Message property and reraises the exception. This means that the standard exception dialog will appear, but with a more descriptive customized message. This allows you to take full advantage of the default exception handling in Delphi, and still easily provide customized error messages that will be more helpful to your users, and yourself.

There is one final piece of information that you can use when working with an exception. When an exception is raised the variable ErrorAddr in the System unit is set to the address in your code where the error occurred. You can display this information to the user just as the default exception handler does.

Using Silent Exceptions

As you have seen, the default exception handling mechanism in Delphi displays a dialog box that contains an error message. However, there is another class of exception, EAbort, that does not display any error dialog. This is called a silent exception and is so useful that a special procedure, Abort, is provided so that you can easily raise a silent exception in your code.

The most common use for Abort in database applications is to block an event, as in the following code from the CUSTORD.DPR project in Chapter 17. This code is from the Customer table's BeforePost event handler.

```
procedure TCustForm.CustTblBeforePost(DataSet: TDataset);
var
  State:      String;
begin
  State := CustTbl.FieldByName('State').AsString;
  if (Length(State) = 2) and
     (CustTbl.FieldByName('Country').AsString <>
     'America') then
  begin
    MessageDlg('Country must be America for this State.',
               mtError, [mbOk], 0);
    Abort;
  end;
end;
```

In this case the code ensures that if the State field value is two characters long and the Country field does not contain "America," the record cannot be posted. The call to the Abort runtime library procedure prevents the record from being posted by raising a silent exception.

Creating Your Own Exceptions

You can create your own exception objects and raise them to handle error conditions. The following code from the CUSTOM.DPR project shows how. Figure 20.7 shows the main form.

```
implementation

{$R *.DFM}

type
```

```
ETestError = class(Exception);

procedure TForm1.CustomExceptionClick(Sender: TObject);
begin
  try
    raise ETestError.Create('This is a custom exception');
  except
    on ETestError do
      MessageDlg('A custom exception occurred at '
                 + IntToHex(Seg(ErrorAddr),4) + ':'
                 + IntToHex(Ofs(ErrorAddr),4),
                 mtError, [mbOK], 0);
  end;
end;
```

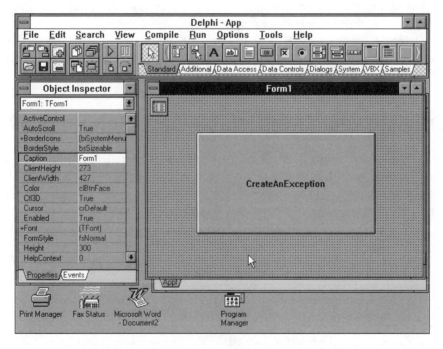

FIGURE 20.7 THE CUSTOM PROJECT'S MAIN FORM.

Exceptions are objects and you can raise any object as an exception, however, there is no reason to do so. Delphi's exception handling mechanism will only handle exception objects that are decendants of Exception, so you should derive your exceptions from the Exception base class.

The code above derives a new exception, ETestError from the Exception class in the type declaration at the beginning of the implementation section of the unit.

N O T E   Your custom exception type declaration must be global to the unit.

To raise your custom exception use the raise command to raise the exception, and call its constructor as in the statement:

```
raise ETestError.Create('This is a custom exception');
```

Raising the exception causes the try/except to handle the exception, and display the custom error dialog. Note the use of the ErrorAddr variable to display the address where the exception was raised.

Delphi's components handle errors with their own custom exceptions, and you can trap and handle those exceptions just as you can trap and handle runtime library exceptions.

Creating Your Own Default Exception Handler

So far this discussion of error handling has been limited to handling errors where they occur in your code. If an error occurs that you do not explicitly trap for in your code, it gets handled by the default exception handler. So what is the default exception handler? It is a method of the Application object.

The top of the hierarchy in a Delphi application is the application object, an object whose type is TApplication, and whose name is always Application. If you look at the project file for a Delphi application you will find the following two lines in the begin/end block.

```
Application.CreateForm(TForm1, Form1);
Application.Run;
```

Delphi starts your application by calling the application object's CreateForm method to create the main form and the application's Run method to start the application. For more information about the TApplication object, see TApplication in the Delphi on-line help.

Another TApplication method is HandleExecption. This is the default exception handler for an application. TApplication also generates an OnException event whenever an exception occurs that your code does not handle. If you write an event handler for the OnException event then your event handler will be used in place of the default handler.

Creating an event handler for one of the Application object's events is a bit more difficult than creating other event handlers. This is because Application does not appear in the Object Inspector. To create an event handler for an Application event you must perform the following three steps.

1. Write the procedure to handle the event.
2. Add the event handler as a method to the type declaration for the main form.
3. Assign the name of the event handler to the event in the main form's OnCreate event handler.

The easiest way to understand this process is to look at an example. The project is APP.DPR on your code disk. The only trick to writing the event handler is knowing the parameters. For OnException the event handler declaration is:

```
procedure TForm1.AppOnException(Sender: TObject; E: Exception);
```

The OnException handler takes two parameters. The first is the object that called it. The second is the Exception object that contains the error message for the exception.

The second step is to add the handler, named AppOnException in this example, to the main form's type declaration. In APP.DPR the main form's type declaration is as follows.

```
type
  TForm1 = class(TForm)
    Table1: TTable;
    CreateAnException: TButton;
    procedure AppOnException(Sender: TObject; E: Exception);
    procedure CreateAnExceptionClick(Sender: TObject);
    procedure FormCreate(Sender: TObject);
  private
    { Private declarations }
  public
    { Public declarations }
  end;
```

Notice that AppOnException has been added to the form's list of methods.

The third step is to assign the name of the exception handler to the OnException event in the form's OnCreate handler. Select the form and double-click the OnCreate event in the Object Inspector. Then add the following code.

```
procedure TForm1.FormCreate(Sender: TObject);
begin
  {Assign the custom OnException handler.}
  Application.OnException := AppOnException;
end;
```

This tells the Application object to call AppOnException whenever an unhandled exception occurs. Figure 20.7 shows the main form for APP.DPR. The form contains a TTable object with its DatabaseName property set to DBDEMOS. It also contains a Button with the following code in its OnClick handler.

```
procedure TForm1.CreateAnExceptionClick(Sender: TObject);
begin
  Table1.TableName := 'foo.db';
  Table1.Open;
end;
```

This code causes an exception by trying to open a table that does not exist. The exception handler itself, AppOnException, contains the following code.

```
procedure TForm1.AppOnException(Sender: TObject; E: Exception);
var
  Addr:          String[9];
  ErrorLog:      System.Text;
begin
  AssignFile(ErrorLog, 'errorlog.txt');
  {Open the file for appending. If it does not exist
   then create it.}
  try
    System.Append(ErrorLog);
  except
    on EInOutError do
      Rewrite(ErrorLog);
  end;
  {Write the date, time, user name, error message
   and address to the error log file.}
  Addr := IntToHex(Seg(ErrorAddr),4) + ':' +
          IntToHex(Ofs(ErrorAddr),4);
  Writeln(ErrorLog, format('%s [%s] %s %s',
    [DateTimeToStr(Now), GetNetUserName, E.Message,
      Addr]));
  {Close the error log file.}
  System.Close(ErrorLog);
  {Display the error message dialog.}
```

```
MessageDlg(E.Message + '. Occurred at: ' +
           Addr, mtError, [mbOK], 0);
end;
```

This exception handler displays the error message in a dialog box and also
writes an entry to an error log text file. The log file entry includes the date,
time, user's network login name, the error message and the address at which
the exception occurred. The first task that this code performs is to open the
error log file.

```
AssignFile(ErrorLog, 'errorlog.txt');
{Open the file for appending. If it does not exist
 then create it.}
try
  System.Append(ErrorLog);
except
  on EInOutError do
    Rewrite(ErrorLog);
end;
```

This code tries to open the file for appending. If the file does not exist, the
call to Append raises an EInOutError exception which is handled in the
except block by calling Rewrite to create, and then open the file.

The next code

```
Addr := IntToHex(Seg(ErrorAddr),4) + ':' +
        IntToHex(Ofs(ErrorAddr),4);
```

converts the ErrorAddr pointer to a hex string by extracting and converting
first the Segment, then the Offset. The next step is to write the date, time,
user name, error message, and address to the file and close the file.

```
Writeln(ErrorLog, format('%s [%s] %s %s',
  [DateTimeToStr(Now), GetNetUserName, E.Message,
   Addr]));
{Close the error log file.}
System.Close(ErrorLog);
```

GetNetUserName is a customer procedure that gets the user's network login
name by making a direct call to a Borland Database Engine function. This is
explained in detail in Chapter 22. The final step in this OnException handler is to display the dialog with the error message to the user.

You could also log exceptions to a table in your database as an alternative to using a text file.

Summary

This chapter has explored Delphi's exception mechanism for handling run-time errors. As you have seen exceptions provide a flexible way to implement error handling in your Delphi programs. You can handle exceptions yourself, let Delphi handle them, take some custom action and then reraise the exception to let the default exception handler process it, or just change the text of the message to add information.

CHAPTER 21

Building a Simple Database Application

It is surprisingly easy to build a simple database application in Delphi. In this chapter, you will apply your new knowledge of Delphi's language and components into a real, working application.

The sample application is a project tracking system you can use to record your progress on any programming project. It includes tables and forms for managing clients, projects, tasks within projects, and recording daily activities on those tasks. The application uses Paradox tables, a simple security system, and a sample help file.

Read and compile the code in this sample application as you have in the previous chapters: by copying all the files to a single directory on your hard disk. This example is also used in chapter 32 on packaging Delphi applications. You can run the chapter 32 install program to install a compiled, working version of the application.

System Analysis and Design

While this is not a system analysis and design text, it will be helpful to briefly review the steps you need to take to build a database application. The example application is simple enough that formal analysis and design are probably not necessary. A rather informal specification of system tasks and data design is used. In a large, real world application, a significant portion of the time spent on a project will be in the analysis and design phase. You would be likely to use a formal analysis and design methodology.

Define System Functions

The most obvious requirement in analysis is to determine exactly what the system is supposed to do. An overall system goal statement is useful:

'The project tracking system will manage data on clients, programming projects, and billable time spent on projects. It will permit us to monitor performance against estimates, alert us to problem tasks, and provide historical data for future estimates.'

This statement lets you know that the system function is primarily data collection and reporting. Other systems may have farther reaching goal statements. For example, a mission critical order entry system would be focused on quick response to customer requests, accurate checking of current inventory, etc. in addition to the data collection and reporting functions.

Once you have the basic goals in mind, you can determine the specific tasks the users will perform with the system. To create an accurate list, you must be sure to consult with everyone involved in the system, from the manager(s) who commissioned the system, to the people who will actually use it.

In the example, the major system tasks are:

- Enter, edit and view client data
- Enter, edit and view project data
- Enter, edit and view task data for each project
- Enter, edit and view task activities
- Print various reports, listing all the above data
- Manage system data (users, lookup tables, configuration data)

With this list of tasks, you can begin designing the data structures of the application.

Define Data Requirements

It is critical to design data structures for an application which properly represent the business needs of the users, allow good performance in data entry, searches, and reporting, make efficient use of computer resources, and are flexible enough to allow for future expansion. The data types required may include text files, binary files, relational tables, Pascal records (or structures in C), objects and their hierarchy (in an object oriented system), etc.

You should also specify the access methods used to get at the system data. The interface could be the simple Delphi LoadFromFile and SaveToFile methods on a memo field, a complex object oriented class interface, or a commercial database engine.

Since this book focuses on database applications, the example application uses relational tables to store its data. The Borland Database Engine (BDE) is an easy way to incorporate tables in a Delphi application, combining a flexible data structure with a powerful interface.

You must determine what tables are required, which tables need primary keys and/or indexes, where foreign keys will be used, where lookup tables will be helpful to the users, and which fields require referential integrity. See chapter 2 for information on designing and normalizing relational data tables, and chapter 26 for information on referential integrity.

The example uses several data, lookup, and system tables. Each table corresponds roughly to one of the system tasks listed above.

- The client table contains the name, address, etc. for each client. It is keyed with a sequential integer, which is used as a foreign key in the projects table. The state field is a foreign key from the states lookup table.

- The project table contains the name, description, status, etc. for each project. It is keyed with a sequential integer, which is used as a foreign key in the task table. The client field is a foreign key from the clients table. The status field is a foreign key from the project status lookup table.

- The task table contains the name, description, status, etc. for each task within a project. It has a composite key consisting of the project ID (a foreign key from the project table) and a sequential integer. The composite key is used as a foreign key in the task table. The status field is a foreign key from the task status lookup table.

- The activity table contains the amount of time spent, description, etc. for a day's activity on a task. It has a composite key consisting of the project ID and task ID (a composite foreign key from the task table), and the date the activity took place. The user name field is a foreign key from the user table.

- The user table contains the login name and password for each authorized user of the system. The key is the user's login name. This is used as a foreign key in the activity table.

- There are four lookup tables used in the system: project status codes, task status codes, task type codes, and state abbreviations. Each of these is keyed by the code or abbreviation represented, and each is used as a foreign key in one of the data tables.

- The system configuration table contains data on user preferences and installation specific settings.

For brevity, detailed descriptions of each table field and its validity constraints have been omitted. These are very important to describe in detail for a real world project. For example, user names are restricted to upper case characters, and client phone numbers must follow the standard '###-####' pattern.

Define Security Requirements

Every application has different security requirements. A simple task database like the example probably doesn't need any security measures at all. A payroll system generally needs very tight security. Chapter 25 gives a thorough discussion on security measures for local and remote databases.

For the example application, two types of security are used. All the data tables are encrypted, and can be accessed only with the proper password. In addition, each user has a personal password which must be entered when logging into the system. This is usually enough protection for all but the most sensitive data.

Selecting the Table Type

After reviewing the data requirements above, Paradox tables were chosen for the example application. There are several reasons for this decision:

- Primary keys are required on all the data tables
- Password security is required on all the data tables
- Field validity checking is supported at the table level
- Referential integrity is supported at the table level
- Paradox tables are available through Delphi (and the BDE) without any add-ins or site licensing fees

A number of other options were available. For example, dBase tables are also readily available through the BDE, but they do not support primary keys or password security. Some valuable features of dBase tables (descending indexes, un-deleting records, compatibility with existing dBase installations) were not important to this application.

Another option was to use a SQL database such as Interbase or Oracle. These support all the necessary data features (and more), but require additional software and site licensing. For a simple task database, the extra expense is unnecessary. See Part 4 for detailed information on the capabilities of SQL databases.

Design System Interface

Before you get down to coding the application, put some serious thought into the user interface. The interface between the user and the program is critical to the success of the program. If the user can't find a task, or can't figure out how to perform a task, the program is a failure.

In a Windows environment, the logical place to start an interface design is the application menu. In many cases, most of the menu items will come directly from the system task list. The task list should be merged into the standard Windows menu format (File, Edit, Window, Help) to provide a familiar starting point for the user.

As easy as Delphi makes it to build a form and start playing with the design, it is still a good idea to do your initial form designs on paper. It is psychologically easier to throw out a piece of paper with a bad design than it is to delete a form with a bad design. Get some sketches down and discuss them with your users before you start building real forms.

Keep in mind that system design is a dynamic process. Your first design won't be your best. New ideas will be popping up throughout the build process.

Design System Structure

A simple application like the example keeps all its files in the same directory. The whole application is a single Delphi project. Each form has its own unit. No external interfaces are required, and no external modules are used (except the BDE). A more complex application will require that you put some thought into the physical layout of the files and code. While a full discussion of application design is beyond the scope of this book, here are several points you should consider:

- While each form generally has its own unit file, you may wish to create additional units not associated with forms which contain objects, methods, and data shared by the entire application.

- Separate portions of the application which are likely to change in the future as much as possible from the more stable areas. For example, if you expect that you may someday convert the application to use a SQL database, isolate the data access routines in a separate unit. You can then make changes in one place without disturbing the rest of the application.

- Keep interfaces to external applications or DLL's (communications servers, graphics engines, etc.) in separate units. When new versions of the external modules are incorporated, the changes to the system are localized.

- Keep prewritten custom routines, or routines which may be used by other applications in the future in separate units. For example, if you have designed a series of special date manipulation functions which could be used by many applications, keep them in a separate unit to make them more portable.

- Applications with multiple executable files (.EXE and .DLL files) will need to be divided into multiple projects. Keep future projects in mind as you separate application functions into .DLL projects.

Building the Application

You've got a solid data design and plans for a nice user interface. Now it's time to start building the system. For all but the simplest programs, an incremental approach works well.

Using a Project Template

Object oriented design and programming stresses re-use of previously designed objects. With Delphi project templates, you can re-use an entire project! Most every database application needs a main form, a menu, a TDatabase component, lookup tables, a configuration table (or .INI file) with access methods, a print setup dialog box, etc. By building a template project containing forms and code to handle all these common needs, you will be able to deliver the first prototype system to your client in no time at all.

The sample application was built from a project template containing all these basic functions (the original template is on the sample disk in a sub directory under the chapter 21 example files directory). Most of the forms and components can be re-used with very few changes. For example, to re-use the lookup editing form, you only have to fill in the 'LOOKUP.DB' table with the names of the application's lookup tables. The user table and form may require a few different fields in a more sophisticated application, but the basic function is built in and ready to go.

The main form contains a number of re-usable objects. You can easily customize the main menu by adding application specific items to the prewritten menu and menu handling code. Code to call the lookup, user, and configuration editing forms is built in. Accessing a help system requires only that you add the name of the proper help file, and set the help context property of any component requiring context sensitive help.

Even though tables are not Delphi objects, you can include them in a project template. Simply copy the tables into the template sub-directory (usually under Delphi\Gallery). When Delphi creates a new project based on the template, all the files in the template directory are copied to the new project, whether or not they are Delphi files.

533

Incremental Development

Using incremental development, you will deliver several versions of the application to the users, each more complete than the last. Feedback from the users at each stage of the build process can help find problems early, when they are relatively easy and inexpensive to fix. If you wait until an application is complete before delivering it, you may find that fundamental design errors were made that require a major system rewrite to fix.

For the first version, build the system shell (the main form and its menu) and some of the data tables. Using a project template as discussed above will save a lot of time in this first step. Create prototypes of the most important forms and attach them to the menu. This first version should contain minimal code. The idea is to let the users get a feel for the overall system design, the menu, and the user interface for the major tasks. They don't have to be able to get any real work done with it.

Deliver this skeleton application to your users for review. Watch them as they use the menu and navigate through the data tables on the forms. Get as much feedback from the users as possible to help you make the interface and the data meet their business needs. Incorporate the users ideas and complaints into subsequent versions.

Each time you complete a major system module or task, deliver a new version to the users and get more feedback. Before you know it, you deliver the final version, and your users are thrilled.

Building the Tables

Since the example uses Paradox tables, the tables were built using the Database Desktop (DBD) supplied with Delphi. The DDB is sort of a mini-Paradox which you can use to create Paradox or dBase tables, enter sample data, run queries, and check the results of your program's database activities (see the appendix for more information on using the DBD).

Populate your tables with representative sample data. This data should mimic the real data to be used by the application as closely as possible. Be sure to include invalid data, and data to test boundary conditions in your application. Don't forget to remove the sample data before shipping the application!

Designing Forms

Designing database application forms is really no different that designing any Delphi form. Particular attention should be paid to the positions of the data controls and the tab order. If, for example, the users will be entering data from a printed, fill-in-the-blanks form, the data entry forms should mimic the printed form as much as possible. It is generally good practice to put the most often used fields near the top of the form (and the beginning of the tab order), and the less used fields below.

This is where delivering prototype systems really pays off. It gives the users the opportunity to help you design the best possible forms for their needs.

Programming

Programming should be the last task to start in the build process. The first version of the system should have very little code: the menu response code to open the forms, pre-existing project template code (if any), and maybe a couple of 'Close' buttons. Be sure that your users are satisfied with the system prototypes before you start any heavy duty coding.

Testing

Another benefit of incremental development is that the users are testing the application for you in real world situations. This does not relieve you of the responsibility for thorough testing, however. On all but the smallest applications, both informal and formal testing is required.

You should be performing informal testing of the system as you go along. For example, suppose you have just completed a function which inserts a new record into a table, and fills in some default values. Test your new function by running the system, inserting the record, and using the Database Desktop to look at the table and verify the new record. Informally verify each new system function before delivering it for formal testing.

Formal testing should be done on a copy of the system installed on another PC, in an environment which mimics, as much as possible, the end user's PC environment. Have someone who is not intimately familiar with the system do the testing. Because of your deep knowledge of the program, it is too easy for you to use it in the 'proper' manner, and not give the system the stress test it needs.

The Sample Application Code

You have seen most of the code in the sample application in previous chapters. A few new items are demonstrated in the following pages.

Checking Passwords

A prospective user must present a valid user name and password combination to be allowed to use the system. In order to do this before the main form is displayed on the screen, you must modify the code in the project (.DPR) file. The entire project file is shown in Listing 21.1.

WARNING

Modifying the project file can be hazardous to your sanity! The Delphi documentation advises against it, and with good reason. Delphi's automatic code maintenance can, and probably will, interfere with your own code in the .DPR file. Proceed with caution.

LISTING 21.1. THE PROJECT FILE - PROJTRAK.DPR

```
program Projtrak;

uses
  Forms,
  Controls,
  Wintypes,
  Clproj in 'CLPROJ.PAS' {ClientProjectForm},
  Main in 'MAIN.PAS' {MainForm},
  About in 'ABOUT.PAS' {AboutBox},
  Pass in 'PASS.PAS' {PasswordDlg},
  User in 'USER.PAS' {UserForm},
  Lookup in 'LOOKUP.PAS' {LookupForm},
  Project in 'PROJECT.PAS' {ProjectForm},
  Client in 'CLIENT.PAS' {ClientForm},
  Task in 'TASK.PAS' {TaskForm},

  { these two units added manually for AllowAccess function }
  SysUtils,
  DB;

{$R *.RES}
```

```
const
   AppPassword = 'Delphi';

{ get password and verify }
function AllowAccess: Boolean;
begin
   { start with false default result -
     change to true if good password entered }
   Result := False;

   { add password to session to permit access to tables }
   Session.AddPassword(AppPassword);

   try
      { activate the user table }
      MainForm.UserTable.Open;

      { create the password form }
      PasswordDlg := TPasswordDlg.Create(Application);

      { keep asking for password until good one is entered
        or user presses cancel button }
      repeat
        if PasswordDlg.ShowModal = mrOK then
           begin
           { locate user name in user table }
           if
MainForm.UserTable.FindKey([UpperCase(PasswordDlg.UserNameEdit.Text)])
then
                 { user name found -
                   if password matches, result is true and loop is done -
                   other wise, display message and display form again }
                 if MainForm.UserTable.FieldByName('Password').AsString
= PasswordDlg.PasswordEdit.Text then
                       Result := True
                 else
                       { password does not match - display message and dis-
play form again }
                       Application.MessageBox('Invalid password - Please
try again', 'Error', MB_ICONSTOP)
              else
                    { user name found - display message and display form again
}
              Application.MessageBox('Invalid user name - Please try
again', 'Error', MB_ICONSTOP);
              end
           else
```

```
            { user pressed cancel button - break out of loop - result
remains false }
            begin
            Application.MessageBox('Application Canceled', 'Cancel',
MB_OK);
            break;
            end;
        until Result = True;
    finally
        { free form memory - de-activate user table }
        PasswordDlg.Free;
        MainForm.UserTable.Close;

        { remove password if access to system denied }
        if Result = False then
            Session.RemovePassword(AppPassword);
    end;
end;

{ original .DPR code starts here }
begin
    Application.Title := 'Project Tracking System';

    { main form is auto create - only one in this app }
    Application.CreateForm(TMainForm, MainForm);
    if AllowAccess then
        Application.Run;

end.
```

The sample project uses a table of user names and passwords to verify a prospective user's access rights. Since all the tables in this application are encrypted, the AllowAccess method must present the table password ('Delphi') before it can access the user table to verify your user password entry. To present a password, the code uses the global variable Session, which is created by automatically by Delphi. It provides control over all database access by the application. In this example, the AddPassword method is used to gain access to the encrypted tables. See chapter 25 for more information on application security and passwords.

The user table on the main form is opened, and the password entry form is created. Code in the OnCreate event handler in the password form fills in the user name field by getting the network login name, if any, from the BDE (this code is not shown here; see chapter 22 for a discussion of direct calls to the BDE).

The password entry form is displayed inside a Repeat loop. Enter or correct your user name, if necessary, and enter your password (on your first login to the example, use 'test' as both user name and password). The code tries to locate the user name (converted to upper case) in the user table. If it is found, the password entered is compared to the password in the user table. If they match, the application is run. If the password does not match, or the user name could not be found in the user table, an error message is shown, and the password entry form is displayed again.

The program exits the loop only after you enter a valid user name and password combination, or press the Cancel button on the password form. If you have canceled, the table password is removed from the session. In this application, this is an unnecessary precaution, since the database engine session will be closed when the application closes. In an application where different table passwords can be presented and removed during a user's session, this is an important technique.

Note that the main form must be created before the AllowAccess method is executed. The code uses the user table and database components on the main form, which must be created before they can be used. The call to CreateForm creates the main form, but does not display it. It is displayed only if Application.Run is called.

Use a table password which is different from any of the user passwords. None of the users need to know the actual password to the tables to access the system. This prevents any unauthorized person from accessing the data tables through the DBD, Paradox, or some other application.

Sharing Tables Among Forms

It is sometimes useful to share database objects across multiple forms. All of the tables in the application share a single Database component on the main form. when the main form is created, the database component's DatabaseName property is set (using a technique covered in the outline example in chapter 15). Since the application does not use BDE aliases to locate the tables, it was considerably easier and more efficient to centralize table access in a single location, rather than have to figure out the proper directory on each form.

Several table components on the main form are used by other forms. The AllowAccess method in the project file uses the user table and data source components on the main form. These components are also used by the user table editing form. It is likely that future modifications to the system would also require access to the user table from other forms. With the user table components on the main form, future enhancements will be able to access the user table more easily.

The configuration table component is kept on the main form since it is likely to be used in a number of places. The data source component, however, is placed on the configuration editing form. This was done as a matter of convenience to the programmer. Since a configuration table may have many fields, it is easier to set all the controls' DataSource properties in the Object Inspector at design time, rather than in code at run time.

Another good use for shared tables is synchronizing two forms at run time. If you have two forms which must display the same record from the same table at all times, the shared table component synchronizes the forms without writing any code.

This method can also be used to centralize all table access in a single unit as an aid to future database changes, such as moving to a SQL database from Paradox. In fact, it is not even necessary to use a form for this purpose. A unit with TTables, etc. created in code works just as well, though it's not quite as convenient to program.

Configuration Data

Most applications need some central system configuration data. This may be as simple as a version number and a date, or it may include user preference settings, environment information, etc. In Windows applications, these data are commonly stored in .INI files. Since this is a database programming book, the configuration data for the sample application are stored in a Paradox table.

There is a configuration TTable component and several access methods on the main form. One of the access methods, and an example of its use is shown in Listing 21.2.

LISTING 21.2. ACCESSING CONFIGURATION TABLE DATA

```
{ get a boolean value from the config table }
function TMainForm.GetConfigBoolean(FieldName: String): Boolean;
begin
    Result := ConfigTable.FieldByName(FieldName).AsBoolean;
end;

{ method on project editing form - called when form is opened }
procedure TProjectForm.SetProject(ProjectID: Integer);
begin

    { code to setup project form }
```

```
    .
    .
    .
    { run the queries to get the hours, if the auto queries flag is set -
these queries
        take some time to run, so we don't unless the user has specified it
    }
    if MainForm.GetConfigBoolean('AutoQueries') then
        GetHours;
end;
```

There are methods on the main form to access boolean, string, number, and date values from the configuration table. As shown above, you can use these methods to retrieve configuration data without having to know how the data is stored. If you decide to store the configuration data in an .INI file, or with some other method, you won't have to change the units which call the access methods, just the internals of the access methods themselves.

The basic configuration table is included in the project template. Just add any new fields required for your application to the table (and the configuration editing form). You may need to add some additional access methods if the basic ones used here aren't enough.

Changing Tables at Run-time

There are several lookup tables used in the system. Once these tables are populated, they will be edited infrequently. Spending time to create a polished data entry form for each table would be wasteful. Instead, the example application uses a single form to edit all these tables.

A table containing a list of the system lookup tables is displayed as the form opens. Select a lookup table to edit by pressing the Edit button, or by double-clicking on the desired table name. The selected table is displayed in the grid. The grid and field sizes change to suit the new table. When you are finished editing the lookup table, press the Save button to return to the lookup table list. The code in Listing 21.3 shows how this is done.

LISTING 21.3. LOOKUP TABLE EDITING

```
{ EditButton OnClick event handler }
procedure TLookupForm.EditButtonClick(Sender: TObject);
begin
    SelectTable;
end;
```

```
{ select a lookup table to edit, or return to lookup table list -
  called by EditButton and grid double click }
procedure TLookupForm.SelectTable;
var
    NewTableName: String;

begin
    with LookupTable do
        begin
            { get the name of the selected table when viewing lookup list -
              if editing a lookup table, this value will not be used }
            NewTableName := Fields[0].AsString;

            { de-activate the table so we can change its table }
            Close;

            { if viewing the lookup list, change to the selected table }
            if TableName = LookupTableName then
                begin
                { set the table name, the button caption, and allow editing }
                TableName := NewTableName;
                EditButton.Caption := '&Save';
                LookupDBGrid.ReadOnly := False;
                LookupForm.Caption := 'Editing ' + NewTableName;
                end
            else    { must be editing a lookup table }
                begin
                { set the table name, the button caption, and disallow editing }
                TableName := LookupTableName;
                EditButton.Caption := '&Edit';
                LookupDBGrid.ReadOnly := True;
                LookupForm.Caption := 'Lookup Tables';
                end;

            { re-activate table }
            Open;
        end;
end;
```

Changing the table displayed on a form is quite simple. Just close the current table, change the TableName property, and re-open it. The code in Listing 21.3 also changes the edit button label to 'Save' when editing a lookup table. The form caption is changed to let the user know which lookup table is displayed. Note that when the lookup table list (from the

LOOKUP.DB table) is displayed, the grid is set to read only so that users cannot change the list of available lookup tables.

Accessing Help Systems

Delphi makes it easy for you to connect context sensitive help to your applications. The example uses a very simple (and not very helpful!) help file as a demonstration. To enable context sensitive help, you need to do three things:

- Create a Windows help file with integer context ID's mapped to each topic you need to access directly from the application.
- Set the applications HelpFile property to the name of the help file (in code, or through the project options dialog box in the IDE).
- Set the HelpContext property of each form and/or component which requires context sensitive help.

With these items in place, pressing F1 in any form or component with a HelpContext property assigned will display the matching help topic. No code is necessary.

Help can also be accessed from the menu. Listing 21.4 shows how the help system is called.

LISTING 21.4. HELP SYSTEM ACCESS

```
{ display help contents from menu choice }
procedure TMainForm.Contents2Click(Sender: TObject);
begin
    Application.HelpCommand(HELP_CONTENTS, 0);
end;

{ display help search from menu choice }
procedure TMainForm.SearchforHelpOn2Click(Sender: TObject);
begin
    Application.HelpCommand(HELP_PARTIALKEY, 0);
end;

{ show the help-on-help contents page }
procedure TMainForm.HowtoUseHelp2Click(Sender: TObject);
var
    OrigHelpFile: string;
begin
    { save the current help file, and set the app help file
      to winhelp - call it, then restore the orig help file setting }
```

```
    OrigHelpFile := Application.HelpFile;
    Application.HelpFile := 'winhelp.hlp';
    Application.HelpCommand(HELP_CONTENTS, 0);
    Application.HelpFile := OrigHelpFile;
end;

{ main form's OnClose event handler -
  close the help system when the app closes }
procedure TMainForm.FormClose(Sender: TObject; var Action: TCloseAction);
begin
    Application.HelpCommand(HELP_QUIT, 0);
end;
```

The HelpCommand method is a wrapper around the Windows API help functions. The first of the menu handlers in Listing 21.4 displays the contents page of the application help file. Call the HelpCommand method with the Windows help command HELP_CONTENTS as the first parameter, and the current help file's contents page will be displayed (the second parameter is ignored, in this case).

The help search dialog box can be displayed by using the HELP_PARTIALKEY command with a second parameter of 0 (zero) This command can also be used to initialize the search dialog box to a partial search string by passing a pointer to a string as the second parameter. A specific topic can be displayed by using the HELP_CONTEXT command, and passing the context ID as the second parameter (not shown in example).

The Windows help-on-help file is called WINHELP.HLP. It is generally found in the Windows directory. The third example in Listing 21.4 changes the application HelpFile to point to WINHELP.HLP and displays its contents page. The original application HelpFile name is then restored.

Finally, a well mannered Windows program should, as it closes, close its help file. The main form's OnClose event handler shown above calls HelpCommand with the HELP_QUIT command.

MDI Applications

The example is implemented as a multiple document interface (MDI) application. This means that the user can have multiple forms open at once, all contained within the main form. There are four types of forms commonly used in an MDI application:

- The main form is the form which contains all the other forms, and displays the application menu.

- Child (multiple instance or document) forms are generally data entry and viewing forms. Multiple copies (or instances) of each form can be open at one time, each viewing a different document or record.
- Single instance forms are a special case of the child forms described above. These are forms which you wish to restrict to single instance at a time.
- Modal dialog boxes are forms which must be dealt with and closed before the user can do anything else. Access to other forms and to the menu are denied while a modal dialog box is displayed. Non-modal dialog boxes are used in special cases where a form needs to stay on top at all times, but the user must be allowed to access another form at the same time. An example is the Windows common search dialog used in many applications.

There can be only one main form in an MDI application, and it must be designated as the main form in your Delphi project. There will generally be a window management menu on the main form's menu bar (usually &Window). This should contain selections to arrange icons, and cascade, tile, and close all open child windows. Set the WindowMenu property of the main form to the window menu object to add a list of all open child windows to the window menu. The code in Listing 21.5 shows how the forms are opened, closed, and tiled.

LISTING 21.5. MDI WINDOW MANAGEMENT

```
{ from clproj.pas -
  create and show a new instance of the client editing form -
  pass the selected client key value }
procedure TClientProjectForm.ClientButtonClick(Sender: TObject);
begin
    ClientForm := TClientForm.Create(Application);
    ClientForm.SetClient(MainForm.ClientTable.Fields[0].AsInteger);
    ClientForm.Show;
end;

{ create and show the lookup form - it will free itself }
procedure TMainForm.LookupTables1Click(Sender: TObject);
begin
    { if the form has not yet been displayed (nil) or
      it has no handle (has been created and freed), then create it -
      otherwise, form is open, just show it }
    if (LookupForm = nil) or (not LookupForm.HandleAllocated) then
      LookupForm := TLookupForm.Create(Application);
```

```
{ bring the lookup form to the top - if it is new, this will show it -
  if it is minimized or overlapped, this will bring it to the front }
LookupForm.BringToFront;
end;
```

```
{ tile the child windows }
procedure TMainForm.Tile1Click(Sender: TObject);
begin
  Tile;
end;

{ close all open child forms }
procedure TMainForm.CloseAll1Click(Sender: TObject);
var
  I: Integer;
begin
  { loop through all open child forms }
  for I := 0 to MDIChildCount-1 do
    MDIChildren[I].Close;
end;
```

The first code block in Listing 21.5 shows how an instance of a multiple instance child form is displayed. The code is called from the Client button on the client/project form. A new copy of the client editing form is created and shown, without regard to the number of copies already created. The SetClient method on the client editing form ensures that the selected client is displayed when the form is shown (this code is not listed here). It also changes the caption of the form to shown the client name so that it can be easily found on the window menu, or among a group of minimized form icons.

Since there is no provision for single-instance forms in the MDI application model, you must handle them in code. The second code block shows how a single instance form is created and managed. If the form is not currently open, it should be created and shown. If it is currently open, it should be brought to the from of all other forms.

The code uses two tests on the form variable to see if it is pointing to an open form. First, if the form variable is equal to nil, then the form has never been created. Second, if the form does not have a window handle (the HandleAllocated property is False), then it may have been created, but has since been destroyed. If the form variable fails both of these tests, then the form must be open. The BringToFront method displays the form.

The standard window menu commands Tile, Cascade, and Arrange Icons are easy to implement. The third code block above show how the Tilemethod is called as an example. Simple methods are provided which you can call from the application's main form.

The standard Close All window menu item is not provided for you. Fortunately, it's not too difficult to implement. The MDI farme form has an MDIChildren property, which is an array of type TForm, including all open child forms, and an MDIChildCount property which is the number of child forms currently open. The array indexes range from 0 (zero) to 'MDIChildCount - 1'. By merely iterating the array, you can close each form in turn.

Reporting

A single ReportSmith report is included with the sample application to demonstrate how easy it is to add sophisticated reports to a Delphi database application. Since ReportSmith was used to create this report, all you need to do is drop a TReport component on a form, set the report name and directory properties, and call its Run method, as shown in Listing 21.6. Of course, your users must have ReportSmith or the ReportSmith run time module installed at their workstations. For more information, see chapter 23 on ReportSmith, and chapter 32 on packaging the application.

LISTING 21.6. RUNNING A REPORT

```
{ run project list report }
procedure TMainForm.ProjectList1Click(Sender: TObject);
begin
    { set the path to the report }
    ProjectListReport.ReportDir := DatabasePath;

    { run report - will fail if ReportSmith not installed }
    try
        ProjectListReport.Run;
    except
        Application.MessageBox('Error running report', 'Error', MB_OK);
    end;
end;
```

Summary

Delphi provides a powerful set of tools for building database applications. Delphi's encapsulation of the Borland Database Engine permits you to include relational data tables and SQL queries in your applications with very little code. Delphi's encapsulation of the complexities of the Windows API make it easy for you to build MDI applications, attach a help system, and do other tasks which are quite difficult (or at least tedious) in traditional Windows programming. By using a project template, you can start with a complete working mini-application, and customize it to meet your client's needs.

CHAPTER 22

Direct Calls to the Borland Database Engine

Most of the important functionality provided by the Borland Database Engine (BDE) is encapsulated in various Delphi components. However, if you have worked with other BDE based products, such as Paradox for Windows, you will find some functions that you are accustomed to missing. These include:

- Filters
- QBE queries
- Semaphore locks
- Getting the user's network username
- Getting the sequence number of the current record in a Paradox table

Implementing Filters and QBE queries is beyond the scope of this book. If you need these features the best way to get them is by purchasing InfoPower from Woll2Woll Software. InfoPower includes table and query components implement Filters and QBE very elegantly.

The last three items in this list are easy to implement, useful and provide good examples of the basics of calling BDE functions from your Delphi programs. They will be described in detail in this chapter.

Getting Access to the BDE

The BDE ships with every copy of Delphi. In addition to the BDE that is installed as part of Delphi you also get the BDE redistribution diskette which you can distribute with your applications so users can install the BDE on their systems.

The BDE consists of a series of DLL's and Delphi includes a complete set of interface units to all of the functions in the BDE. What you do not get with Delphi is the BDE manuals. If you plan to work directly with the BDE you will probably want to order the manuals from Borland.

Delphi's interface to the BDE is implemented as a set of units. In order to call BDE functions from your Delphi programs you must include the following units in the Uses clause of each unit in your program that makes BDE function calls.

```
DbiProcs
DbiErrs
DbiTypes
```

Once you have these units in your uses clause you can call any BDE function. However, you must be very careful calling BDE functions directly for tables that Delphi is using. Delphi maintains a lot of critical information about the state of the tables it is accessing. If you bypass Delphi and call the BDE directly you may have problems when Delphi tries to access the tables. The calls presented in this chapter do not cause conflicts with Delphi.

Getting the Network User Name

DbiGetNetUserName is the BDE function that returns the current users network login name. Figure 22.1 shows the main form for USERNAME.DPR which demonstrates how to use this function.

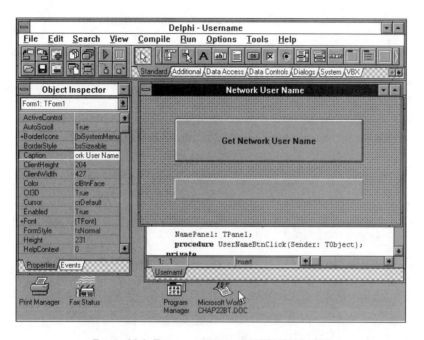

FIGURE 22.1 THE MAIN FOR FORM USERNAME.DPR

The following code is from the Get Network User Name button's OnClick event handler.

```
procedure TForm1.UserNameBtnClick(Sender: TObject);
var
  UserName:    array[0..63] of Char;
begin
  {Get and display the network user name.}
  if DbiGetNetUserName(UserName) <> DBIERR_NONE then
    NamePanel.Caption := 'No Name'
  else
    NamePanel.Caption := UserName;
end;
```

DbiGetNetUserName takes one parameter, the variable to receive the network user name. Any string parameter used by a BDE function must be a null terminated string, not a Pascal string. In this case a character array is used to receive the user name.

Like all BDE functions DbiGetNetUsername returns an error code that you can use to determine if the function succeeded or not. If the returned value is equal to DBIERR_NONE then the call was succesful. If not, then there was an error.

In this case the only thing that can cause an error is if no network username is returned. In this case a null string is returned and DbiGetNetUserName returns DBIERR_INVALIDHNDL. The sample form includes a Panel component and the code above displays the username in the Panel, UserNamePnl, if one is returned. Otherwise the message "No Name" is displayed in the Panel. Figure 22.2 show the program running with a network username displayed.

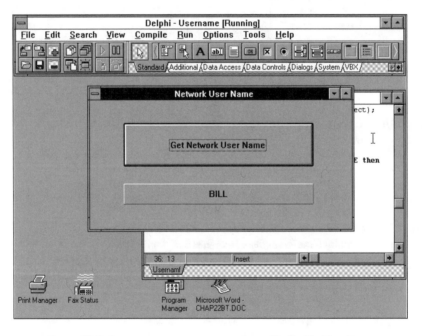

FIGURE 22.2 A NETWORK USERNAME RETURNED BY DBIGETNETUSERNAME

Locking Tables

The TTable component includes two methods, LockTable and UnlockTable, that were added at the last minute to let you place table level locks. These methods are intended primarily for use with Paradox and dBase tables and are not described in any of the Delphi manuals or the on-line help. For information about these methods see the MANUALS.TXT file in your Delphi directory.

These methods and the Exclusive property of TTable let you place Exclusive, Read or Write locks on an open table. However, you cannot place an exclusive lock on a table that does not exist. There are two reasons that you may want to place an exclusive lock on a table that does not exist.

The first is to reserve the table name. If you place an exclusive lock on a table that does not exist then no other user can create a table with that name. Only you will be able to create the table. This is not a common requirement but the capability exists if you ever do need it.

The second, and mose useful, reason to lock a non-existent table is as a semaphore. The best way to explain a semaphore lock is with an example. Suppose you have a multiuser application. Every night the mainframe operations department downloads a file that someone must import into your database. Any user on your network can run the import routine but you certainly do not want two users to try to do it at the same time. The easy way to ensure that two users cannot run the import process at the same time is to place a semaphore lock on a non-existent table. If you get the lock it is safe to proceed with the import. If a second user tries to run the import process they will not be able to lock the non-existent table and your code can prevent the import from executing.

Placing and Clearing Persistent Exclusive Table Locks

The PERSIST.DPR project demonstrates placing and clearing locks on a non-existent table. Figure 22.3 shows the main form which contains a TDatabase component, two buttons and a memo. The memo component is not used in the code. It just displays instructions.

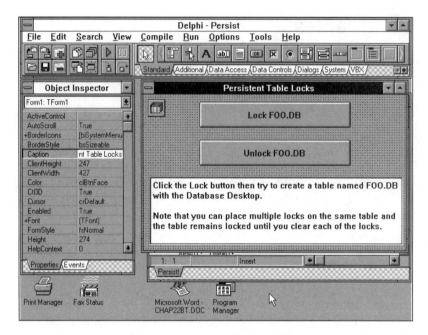

FIGURE 22.3 THE PERSIST.DPR FORM

The TDatabase component is named DemoDb and its Alias and DatabaseName properties are both set to DBDEMOS, the alias of the directory where the locks on the non-existent table will be placed. This must be an alias that points to a directory on your network, not to a database on a database server. Set the DemoDb component's Connected property to True. Setting Connected to True causes the BDE to establish a connection to the database as soon as the form is opened. Establishing the connection gets a handle to the database which is stored in the Database component's Handle property.

As described earlier in this chapter you must include the three BDE units in your program. Figure 22.4 shows the Uses clause in the interface section of the unit for the main form. Note that DbiProcs, DbiErrs and DbiTypes have been added.

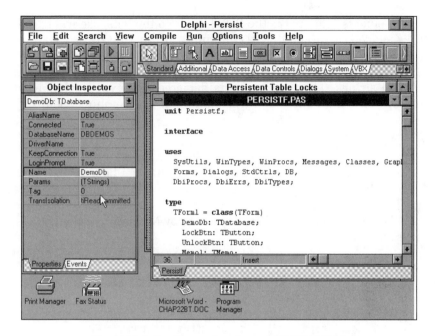

FIGURE 22.4 THE USES DECLARATION IN **PERSISTF.PAS**

The following code is from the OnClick event handler of the Lock FOO.DB button.

```
procedure TForm1.LockBtnClick(Sender: TObject);
begin
  {Place a persistent exclusive lock on the non-
   existent table FOO.DB}
  if DbiAcqPersistTableLock(DemoDb.Handle, TblName, '')
    <> DBIERR_NONE then
    ShowMessage('Lock Failed');
end;
```

This code calls the BDE function DbiAcqPersistTableLock to place an exclusive lock on the non-existent table FOO.DB. DbiAcqPersistTableLock takes three arguements. The first is the BDE handle to the database where the lock is to be placed. This handle is contained in the Handle property of the DemoDb database component. The second parameter is the table name. Once again, strings passed to BDE functions must be null terminated strings, not Pascal strings. The table name is declared as a typed constant at the beginning of the implementationn section of the unit as shown below.

```
const
   TblName: array[0..15] of Char = 'foo.db'#0;
```

The third parameter is the table driver type. This can be a null string since BDE knows to use the Paradox driver from the .DB extension on the table name. This code checks the value returned by DbiAcqPersistTableLock to see if it is DBERR_NONE and if it is not ShowMessage is called to display an error message.

The following code is from the Unlock FOO.DB button's OnClick handler and shows how to remove the lock.

```
procedure TForm1.UnlockBtnClick(Sender: TObject);
begin
   {Release a persistent exclusive lock from the non-
    existent table FOO.DB}
   if DbiRelPersistTableLock(DemoDb.Handle, TblName, '')
     <> DBIERR_NONE then
     ShowMessage('Unlock Failed');
end;
```

To see how this works run PERSIST.DPR and click the Lock FOO.DB button. Next, start the Database Desktop, change your working directory to the DBDEMOS alias and try to create a table named FOO.DB. You will get an error message stating that the table is locked.

One of the interesting things about locks is that you can place more than one of the same kind of lock on the same table. If you do, make sure you clear all of your locks when you are done. You can see this by clicking the Lock FOO.DB button three times. Now start clicking the Unlock FOO.DB button. Notice that you do not get an error message until the fourth click.

Getting the Record Number

If you are a Paradox user you will discover that there is no way in Delphi to get the current record's sequence number when you are working with a Paradox table. You can get the number of records in a table from the TTable

RecordCount property but there is no property that gives the sequence number of the current record. This feature was probably omitted since Delphi was designed primarily as a client/server development tool and the concept of a record number does not exist on database servers.

If you work with Paradox tables and need the record number of the current record you can get it easily with a BDE call. Figure 22.5 shows the main form for RECNO.DPR. This form shows the sample Customer table that ships with Delphi in a grid and displays the current record number in a panel at the bottom of the form.

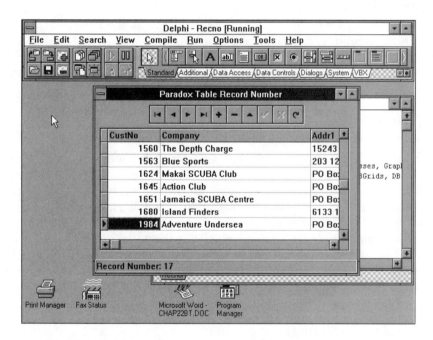

FIGURE 22.5 THE RECNO.DPR MAIN FORM SHOWNING THE CURRENT RECORD NUMBER

This form contains a TTable and a TDataSource connected in the usual way. The following code is from the TDataSource component's OnDataChange event handler.

```
procedure TForm1.CustSrcDataChange(Sender: TObject; Field: TField);
var
  RecNo:     LongInt;
begin
  {Make sure the BDE cursor points to the same record
   that is current in the TTable.}
  CustTbl.UpdateCursorPos;
```

```
{Get the current record's sequence number.}
DbiGetSeqNo(CustTbl.Handle, RecNo);
{Display the record number in the panel.}
  Panel1.Caption := 'Record Number: ' + IntToStr(RecNo);
end;
```

This code calls DbiGetSeqNo to get the sequence number of the current record. Note, however, that before calling DbiGetSeqNo the code calls the TTable method UpdateCursorPos. This method updates the position of the BDE cursor for this table to make sure that it is on the same record that is current in the TTable.

DbiGetSeqNo takes two parameters. The first is the handle property of the TTable component. The second is a LongInt variable that will be set to the sequence number of the current record. The last line in the method displays the record number in the Panel component at the bottom of the form.

Summary

This chapter has shown how to use persistent table locks on tables that do not exist by making direct calls to the BDE. It has also presented examples of getting the users network username and the record number of the current record in a Paradox table. The basic structure of BDE function calls has also been introduced. However, remember that calling other BDE functions directly to manipulate tables that Delphi has open may produce undesirable results since Delphi will not be aware of the change you have made. Study the VCL source code and the BDE manual carefully to be sure you understand the effects of any calls you make.

CHAPTER 23

Overview of ReportSmith

Nearly every application you develop will include reports to present information. No matter how one tries to work toward a paperless office, there will always be a need for hard copy at some point.

The Delphi programming environment includes Borland's ReportSmith report development tool. Just as Delphi gives you a visual programming environment to develop custom applications, so does ReportSmith give you a powerful visual reporting tool, which you can use along with database tables or SQL statements as data sources to create ReportSmith reports.

Top ReportSmith Features

ReportSmith has many tools to make use of when developing reports for a database. Also, the ReportSmith environment is very intuitive, making for quick and easy report creation.

The following list will explain a few of ReportSmiths most important features:

- View data from one or more tables at once.
- View actual data without running a report and see format changes instantly.
- Sort data by any field in your selection.
- Insert group, page and report headers, and footers.
- Use OLE objects for a more visual interpretation of data.
- Create ReportSmith macros to perform many different tasks, such as loading reports or creating derived fields.
- Use one of the four standard ReportSmith report types with style variations of each report type predefined by ReportSmith.
- Access data from a large variety of data sources.

As you can see, ReportSmith gives you a way to perform all of the necessary tasks to create top-quality comprehensive reports.

This chapter assumes you have installed ReportSmith as part of your Delphi installation. If you have not already done this, please do so before proceeding with this chapter.

Design Tools

ReportSmith includes an entire host of development tools to help you develop the ideal report for your particular database situation. This includes connections to your various datasources, assorted dialog boxes to enter your reports criteria, and tools to modify the visual appearance of your finished report.

Connections

Connections are used to define a data source for a ReportSmith report. A connection attaches ReportSmith to a server or gives ReportSmith the directory path of the local tables you intend to use as your report source. Each connection tells ReportSmith the connection type (Paradox, Access, and so on), the name of your connection, and other information such as User id and password when accessing data stored on a server.

ReportSmith can access the following list of sources:

- Access
- Btrieve
- DB2
- dBase
- Excel
- FoxPro
- INGRES
- Informix
- InterBase
- ORACLE
- Paradox
- Raima
- AS/400
- SQL Server

- SQLBase
- Sybase
- Teradata
- Text Files
- Unify
- Watcom SQL

Since a connection reference will be needed to create reports later in this chapter, the next task is to create the DBDEMOS connection.

If you have not already started ReportSmith, please do so now by double-clicking the **ReportSmith** icon in your Delphi Windows group.

Perform the following steps in order to create a ReportSmith connection to the local tables included with Delphi:

1. From the main menu, select the menu option **File|Connections**. (See Figure 23.1.)

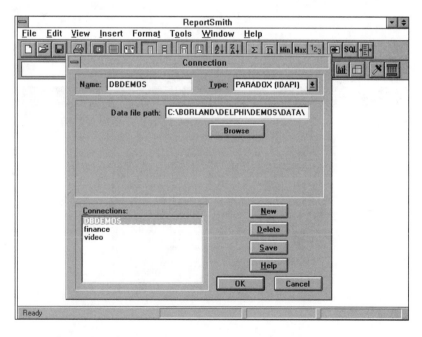

FIGURE 23.1 CREATE A CONNECTION TO REFERENCE TABLES IN A REPORT.

2. Assign DBDEMOS as the name for your connection.

3. Select **Paradox (IDAPI)** as the connection type, since we will be accessing the Paradox tables included with Delphi.

4. Click the **Browse** button and select the path of the Delphi demo data ables. If you did a standard install, these tables will be in **C:\Delphi\Demos\Data**.

5. Click the **Save** button and then the **OK** button to save and complete the connection. This connection information will be stored for future sessions of ReportSmith.

Report Types

Four different report types are packaged with ReportSmit (see Figure 23.2). They are as follows:

- Columnar report
- Crosstab report
- Form report
- Label report

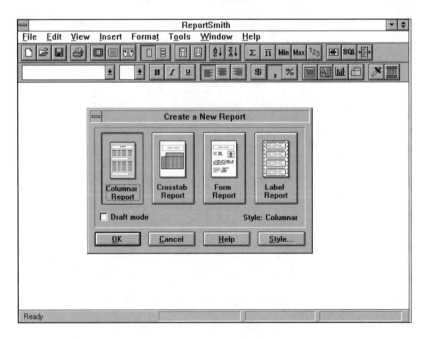

FIGURE 23.2 REPORT TYPE SELECTION.

A Columnar report will display a series of columns on your report representing the various fields you have selected from your report tables.

A Crosstab report will display your data in a spreadsheet-type fashion. This is very useful for analysis reports.

A Form report gives you the ability to place your fields in a noncolumnar fashion. You can place them on your report in the same way you would on a data-entry form.

A Label report displays your data in a label format. This is ideal for creating mailing labels.

If one of these report types is not quite suited for your reporting needs, you can select from several different styles of each report type in order to remedy this situation.

Report Query Dialog Boxes

ReportSmith uses a series of Report Query dialog box pages to allow you to enter your report specifications before your report is actually created on the workspace.

You can use one or more of the seven Report Query dialog boxes to enter information specific to your report.

These are the seven Report Query dialog boxes:

- Tables
- Selections
- Sorting
- Derived fields
- Report variables
- Database grouping
- SQL

Tables

You can use the Tables page of the Report Query dialog box to perform the following tasks:

- Add, replace, or remove tables from your report design.
- Select which fields or columns should be displayed from each table.
- Add, edit, or remove links between tables included in your report.
- Assign an alias to each table in your report. (See Figure 23.3.)

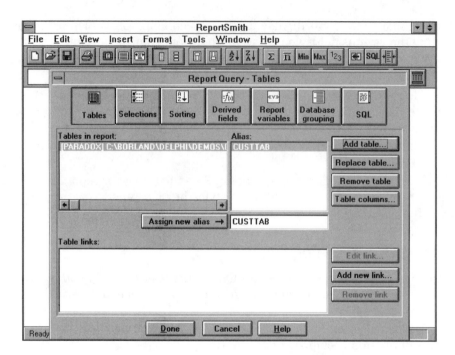

FIGURE 23.3 THE REPORT QUERY—TABLES DIALOG BOX.

Selections

The Selections dialog box is used to create, modify, or delete selection criteria on the data included in your report. You can add a single criterion or an entire list of criteria to select the appropriate records for your report. Each criterion is very sentence-like in structure, allowing for easy readability and understanding. (See Figure 23.4.)

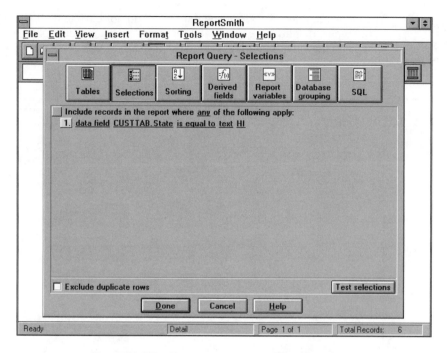

FIGURE 23.4 THE REPORT QUERY—SELECTIONS DIALOG BOX.

Sorting

Use the Sorting dialog box to add, remove, or modify a list of fields to be used for sorting and subsorting data included in the report. The fields selection for sorting consists of all fields selected in the Tables dialog box. (See Figure 23.5.)

The fields included in the Sorting dialog box do not have to be included in the report display. The column(s) representing the sorting field(s) can be deleted once the report is created and placed on the workspace.

T I P

564

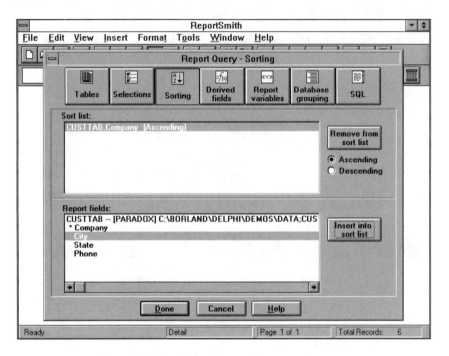

FIGURE 23.5 THE REPORT QUERY—SORTING DIALOG BOX.

Derived Fields

Derived fields are calculated fields that can be placed on your report. These fields can be created either through the use of ReportSmith's macro language or through an SQL statement. Derived fields are very useful for displaying data that is not stored in tables but is required for reporting purposes. (See Figure 23.6.)

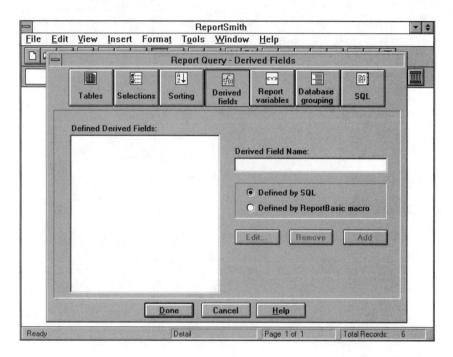

FIGURE 23.6 THE REPORT QUERY—DERIVED FIELDS DIALOG BOX.

Report Variables

With the Report Variables dialog box you can create, modify, or delete report variables. Report variables can be used to insert values at any place in the report. This is useful for displaying the date range for a given report in the report header or other information that is not included in your report data source(s). (See Figure 23.7.)

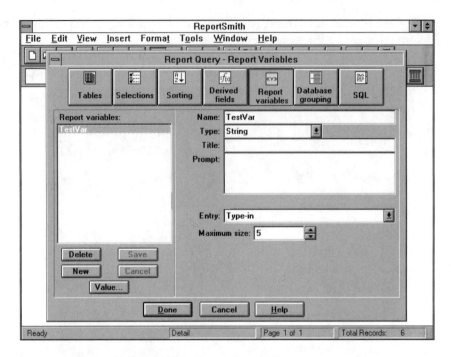

FIGURE 23.7 THE REPORT QUERY—REPORT VARIABLES DIALOG BOX.

Database Grouping

The Database Grouping dialog box gives you the option of grouping data before it is loaded into your report. You can also create selection criteria to be applied to your data groupings. (See Figure 23.8.)

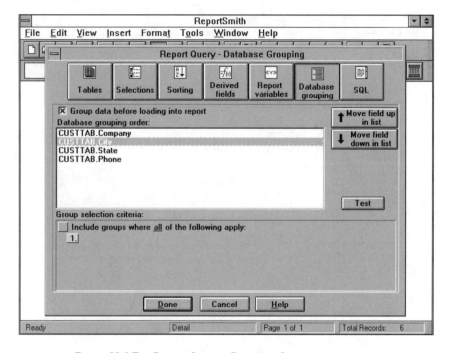

FIGURE 23.8 THE REPORT QUERY—DATABASE GROUPING DIALOG BOX.

SQL

With the SQL dialog box you can enter valid SQL statements and select which fields from your report tables to include in the report. You may also include sorting and grouping criteria in the SQL dialog box. In addition, as mentioned earlier, you can create calculated fields as part of your report data. (See Figure 23.9.)

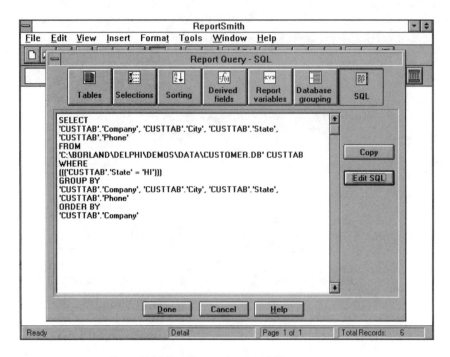

FIGURE 23.9 THE REPORT QUERY—SQL DIALOG BOX.

Data Access and Formatting

ReportSmith, like Delphi, gives you access to your report data without even running the report. Once you've entered your specific report information, you receive a snapshot view of the first page of your report.

Format Quick Menu

Once your report is created, you can use the format options to fine-tune the visual appearance of your report before incorporating it into your application.

In order to create the report samples in this chapter, we will access the format options through the Format Quick menu. This menu can be accessed by clicking the right mouse button after you have selected a column of data or any other item on the report. The quick menu includes the following options:

- Character
- Border

- Field formats
- Text alignment
- Display as picture
- Column width
- Field height
- Selection criteria
- Deselect

Character

The Character formatting option displays the Font dialog box from which you can perform the following font modifications:

- Select font type, style, and size
- Apply effects such as underline and strikeout
- Change the color of the current font

Figure 23.10 shows the Font dialog box.

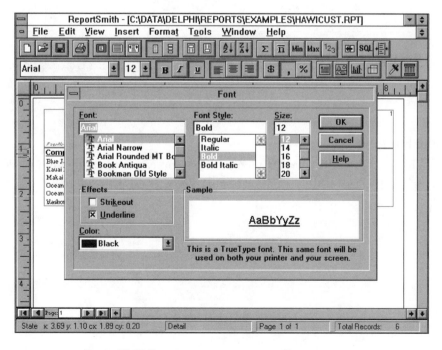

FIGURE 23.10 FORMATTING FONTS USING THE FONT DIALOG BOX.

Border

Using the **Border** choice from the Format Quick menu, you can create a border around field columns, column headers, or any other report object. (See Figure 23.11.)

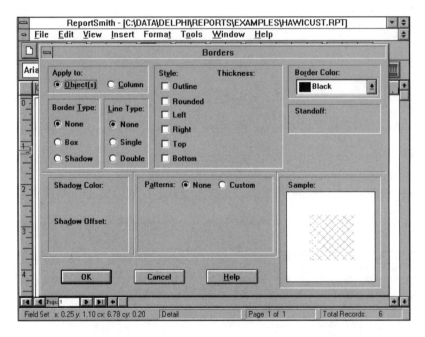

FIGURE 23.11 CREATE BORDERS USING THE BORDERS DIALOG BOX.

Field Formats

By selecting the **Field Formats** menu option you can format any field placed on the report. Number fields are generally ideal candidates for formatting on reports using one of the four ReportSmith formatting categories: Number, Currency, Percentage, or Scientific. (See Figure 23.12.)

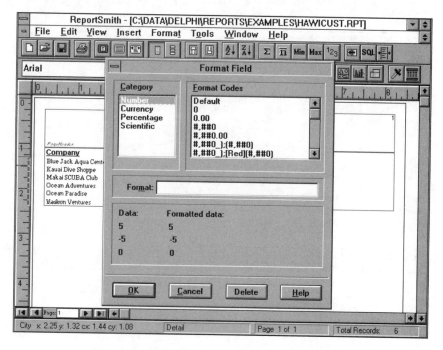

FIGURE 23.12 FORMAT FIELDS USING THE FORMAT FIELD DIALOG BOX.

Text Alignment

You can use the **Text Alignment** menu option on the Format Quick menu to format the alignment of the currently selected column or object to left, center, or right. (See Figure 12.13.)

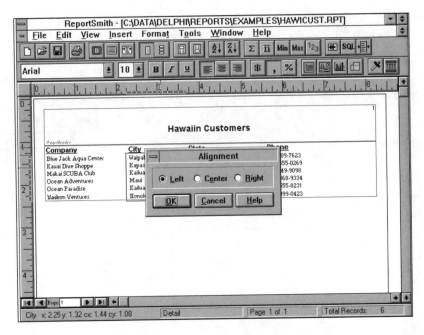

FIGURE 23.13 FORMAT FIELDS USING THE ALIGNMENT DIALOG BOX.

Column Width

Formatting of a columns width can also be done from the Quick Format menu. Simply select the **Column Width** menu option, set the desired column width, check the **Use Default Width** checkbox, or click the **Best Fit** button. (See Figure 12.14.)

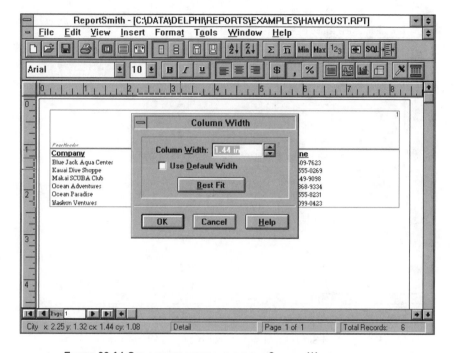

FIGURE 23.14 SET COLUMN WIDTHS USING THE COLUMN WIDTH DIALOG BOX.

Field Height

The height of a specific field can be set by using the **Field Height** option on the Format Quick menu. (See Figure 12.15.)

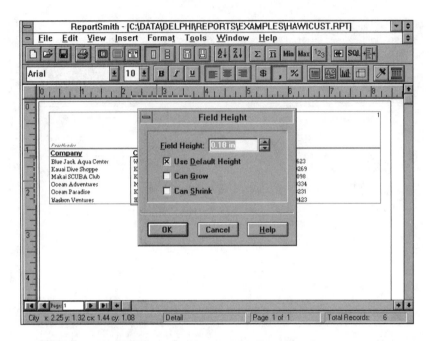

FIGURE 23.15 SET FIELD HEIGHTS USING THE FIELD HEIGHT DIALOG BOX.

Selection Criteria

Using the **Selection Criteria** option gives you the ability to add additional selection criteria to those created in the Report Query. This gives even greater capabilities in report development. You can actually change the data you view while you're viewing it. (See Figure 23.16.)

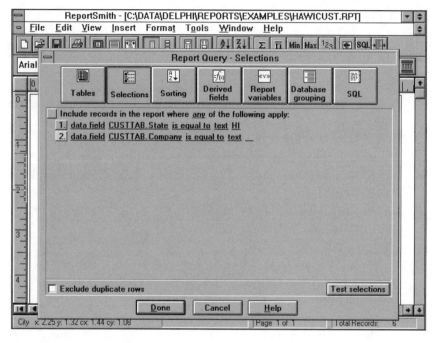

FIGURE 23.16 SET ADDITIONAL SELECTION CRITERIA USING THE SELECTION CRITERIA DIALOG BOX.

Deselect

You can deselect selected objects or columns by bringing up the Format Quick menu and choosing **Deselect**.

Building a Customer Report

Now that we have reviewed the basic parts of the ReportSmith work area, you can use the tools documented above to create a simple customer report using ReportSmith. The steps are as follows:

1. Start the ReportSmith program by double-clicking the **ReportSmith** icon.
2. Select **File|New** from the main menu.
3. Select **Columnar Report** from the Create a New Report dialog box.
4. From the Tables page of the Report Query dialog box, click the **Add Table** button.
5. Select **DBDEMOS** as your connection.
6. Select **Customer.db** as your table.
7. Click the **OK** button.
8. Click the **Assign New Alias** button and type in **CUSTTAB** as the alias name for the Customer table. After typing in the table alias, press the **Enter** key to confirm your entry.
9. Click the **Table Columns** button.
10. Double-click all fields except Company, City, State, and Phone in order to exclude them from the report.
11. Click the **OK** button to return to the Tables page of the Report Query dialog box.
12. Click the **Sorting** button to move to the Sorting page.
13. From the Report Fields section, double-click the **Company** field. This will sort the records by company name.
14. Click the **Selections** button to go to the Selections page.
15. Click the yellow square on the upper-left corner of the Selections page and select **Add New Selection Criteria to this List**.
16. In the first column of the criteria statement, select a data field in order to put a selection criteria on a report field. You also have the option of using a formula for selection criteria.
17. In the second column of the criteria statement, select **State** as your criteria field.
18. In the third column, select the verb **Is Equal to** for an exact match in your criteria.
19. In the fourth column, select **Text** as the object of the verb.
20. In the fifth column of the criteria statement, type in **HI** in order to restrict the records selected to those customers in Hawaii.

Figure 23.17 shows the selection criteria for Hawaiian Customer Report.

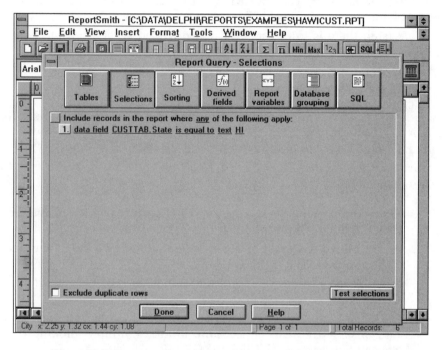

FIGURE 23.17 THE SELECTION CRITERIA FOR THE HAWAIIAN CUSTOMER REPORT.

21. Click the **Done** button to create your Hawaiian customer report.

22. Select the **Column Header** and **Data Column** for the State field and press the **Delete** key. To select multiple items, hold down the shift key as you click the items. There is no point in displaying the state field for a report that is only looking at Hawaiian customers.

You have now created a ReportSmith report. Now you can add a few finishing touches in order to complete the Hawaiian customer report.

Hold down the **Shift** key and click each of the column headers. After selecting all column headers, release the Shift key, click the right mouse button on the highlighted region and select **Character** from the menu. This will display the Font dialog box.

Select **Bold** as your font style and **12** as your font size. Click the **OK** button to confirm your selections.

The last step is to double-click the default title and replace the text with **Hawaiian Customers**.

Save the report by selecting **File|Save** from the menu and giving the report file the name **HAWICUST.RPT**. An example of this report is on the code disk included with this book.

That is all there is to it. As you can see with this report example, with just a little bit of learning, ReportSmith is very easy to use.

Multi-Table Reports

Not all reports are a simple one-table report. Many reports need data from two or more tables joined together; the next report example illustrates this point by including order information for the Hawaiian customers.

Perform the following steps in order to create an order report for the Hawaiian customers:

1. Open the previously created report **HAWICUST.RPT** on the code disk included with this book.

2. Select **File|Save As** from the main menu and give the new report a file name of **HAWIORDS.RPT**.

3. Select **Tools|Tables** to access the Tables page of the Report Query dialog box.

4. With the Customer table selected, click the **Table Columns** button and deselect the **City** and **Phone** fields by double-clicking them. Select the **Custno** field. Click the **OK** button.

5. Click the **Add Table** button and select the **Orders Table** and click the **OK** button. If the connection for the Orders table is not **DBDEMOS**, then select this as your connection before clicking **OK**.

6. Click the **Table Columns** button and select only the following fields from the Orders table: **OrderNo**, **CustNo**, and **ItemsTotal**, deselect all others. Click the **OK** button.

7. Assign a table alias of **ORDERTAB** to the Orders table.

8. Click the **Add New Link** button on the Tables page.

Figure 23.18 shows how to edit a table link.

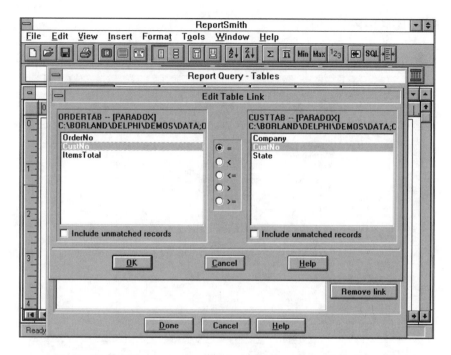

FIGURE 23.18 CREATING A LINK BETWEEN THE CUSTOMER AND ORDER TABLES.

9. Select the **Custno** field for both the Customer table and the Order table. Click the **OK** button to confirm your table link. You have now joined the Customer and Order tables.

10. Click the **Done** button to create your Order report.

11. Select **Insert I Headers/Footers** from the main menu.

12. Choose **Entire Report Group**, check **Footer**, and click the **OK** button.

13. Once the report footer has been inserted at the bottom of your report, select the **ItemsTotal Data Column**, click the right mouse button, and select **Field Formats**. This will display the Format Field dialog box. Select the **Currency** category and select **$#,##0.00** as your format code. Click the **OK** button to confirm your format

See Figure 23.19.

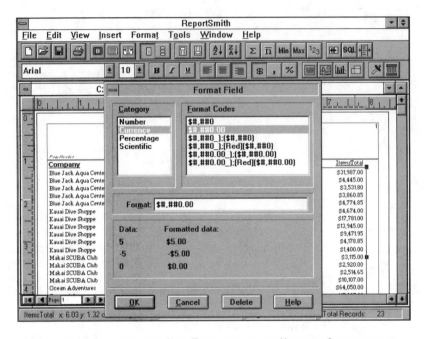

FIGURE 23.19 FORMATTING THE ITEMSTOTAL FIELD IN THE HAWAIIAN ORDERS REPORT.

To add more useful information, click all five of the aggregate function tool bar buttons—**Sum**, **Average**, **Min**, **Max**, and **Count**. Your report now includes totals in your report footer that can be used for customer studies.

You will notice that you have two columns that include the Customer number field. Select one of the **Custno** column headers and its column of data and press the **Delete** key to remove them from your report.

WARNING

You must include the linking Custno field in both the Customer table and the Order table in order to perform a link between the two tables. Once the report is created, you can readily delete one of them, but if you do not include the field from both tables in your Table column selections, you will not be able to make a logical join between the two tables. Also, any fields involved in a criteria statement must be included from its respective tables. These may also be deleted from the report display once the report has been created.

The last step in our order report is to double-click the report title and change it to **Hawaiian Orders**. Select **File | Save** to save the changes you have made to the Order report.

The Hawaiian Orders report is included on the accompanying code disk.

Running Reports in Your Application

Once reports have been designed and created, they can be incorporated into your database applications and included with your delivered application. There are several ways to access ReportSmith or ReportSmith reports from a Windows application:

- DDE—Dynamic Data Exchange calls
- OLE—Object linking and embedding
- ReportSmith Runtime
- Using the Delphi TReport component

Printing a Report with ReportSmith Runtime

In order to set up your Hawaiian customer report for anyone with ReportSmith Runtime installed to access through Windows, you can follow these steps:

1. Select **File | New** from your Windows menu and choose **Create a New Program Item.**
2. Set the description of the program item to **Hawaiian Customer Report**.
3. Set the command line to the full path and .exe name of the file **RS_RUN.exe**, which will be found in your ReportSmith Runtime directory. Also on the command line, after the .exe file name, insert a space and then give the full path and file name for your **hawicust.rpt** file. A sample command line would look as follows:

```
C:\RS_RUN\RS_RUN.EXE C:\REPORTS\HAWICUST.RPT
```

4. Click the **OK** button.

Now, when anyone executes your program item in Windows, they will have access to your Customer report.

Printing a Report from a Delphi Application

In order to access reports through a Delphi application, you need to place a TReport component on our report form and give it the name **RptObject**. All of the following code is included on the code disk. With the TReport object on a form, and with a few simple lines of code attached to a form button, you can display the Customer report you developed earlier in the chapter (see Listing 23.1).

LISTING 23.1 DISPLAYING THE HAWAIIAN CUSTOMERS REPORT

```
RptObject.Preview := True;
RptObject.ReportName := 'hawicust.rpt';
RptObject.Run;
```

The first line of Listing 23.1 sets the report object's preview property to True, which tells the object to send the report to the screen when the report is run. Line 2 tells the report object the name of the report file to display when the report is run. Line 3 runs the report object. This will start ReportSmith Runtime and will open the report file **HAWICUST.RPT**.

Listing 23.2 displays the modifications to Listing 23.1 that are necessary to send the report directly to the printer.

LISTING 23.2 PRINTING THE HAWAIIAN CUSTOMERS REPORT

```
RptObject.Preview := False;
RptObject.ReportName := 'hawicust.rpt';
RptObject.Run;
```

Simply by setting the preview property to False, the report will be sent directly to the printer instead of being displayed on the screen.

In order to display or print the Order report you created earlier in this chapter, you simply need to change line 2 of the previous listing to

```
RptObject.ReportName := 'hawiords.rpt';
```

To allow users of your application direct access through the application to their Windows printer setup is a very easy operation.

Add a PrinterSetupDialog component to the Reports form and give it the name **PrinterSetupDialog**. The following line shows the single line of code needed to operate this component:

```
PrinterSetupDialog.execute;
```

That's all there is to it. You have now allowed your users complete control over redirecting their print job to a different printer.

Summary

This chapter has given you an overview of the ReportSmith report development environment and its capabilities. To become truly proficient in the development of ReportSmith reports, experimentation and a bit of experience are required, but since ReportSmith is very intuitive, it is easy to create complex reports with a minimal amount of work.

Those who need even more from their reporting tool should look into the ReportSmith macro language to give reports even more complex features.

CHAPTER 24

Managing Transactions

Perhaps the most significant difference between client-server applications and file-server applications is transactions. Two of the Borland database formats that Delphi supports, Paradox tables and Interbase databases, are quite different when it comes to transactions and concurrent access.

Local file formats usually do not support transactions, SQL-database servers do. Local file formats usually assume record-at-a-time, pessimistic locking mechanisms, SQL database servers usually implement optimistic and often page-locking mechanisms. Local file formats are optimized for updating individual records in small to medium-sized tables. SQL database servers are optimized for accessing tables with a large number of records.

Those familiar with SQL database servers will find most of this chapter quite familiar. Those developers new to client-server application development will find this chapter illuminating, since the Borland Database Engine does not support any form of transaction management for both Paradox and dBase file formats.

Definition of a Transaction

A *transaction* is an atomic unit of work. Suppose a transaction contains steps to write data to seven different tables. Assume these seven steps, which represent a routine financial transaction, such as a customer paying a portion of a bill, might include writing data to a customer master table, a customer orders table, a customer payments table, a general ledger table, and other tables. Now suppose one of the tables in Step 3 of the transaction is damaged and can not be updated. With transaction management, when this occurs, the entire transaction is *rolled-back* so that it is as if it never took place. If three of the seven tables have been updated as part of the transaction, the changes to those three tables are undone. The database maintains its consistency.

Transaction management improves data integrity dramatically. It also removes from the database programmer the arduous task of hand-coding a transaction management system. Perhaps the most important reason for client-server database development is to ensure transaction integrity.

Transactions have other properties besides atomicity. Transactions must exhibit consistency in which the programmer can set consistency checkpoints and verify transaction integrity. Transactions must exhibit durability. Once the database system commits a transaction, it must persist even in the event of power, hardware, or software. The database system must be able to correctly handle multiple simultaneous transactions initiated by multiple users. In multi-user environments, data can be temporarily inconsistent during a transaction (discussed in the next section). The database system must give the developer tools to determine what level of inconsistency is tolerable. This attribute is called *isolation* and is the most important aspect of managing transactions in Delphi.

SQL-92 Isolation Levels

Isolation levels arose because database programmers need to handle concurrent access, chiefly writing access, to tables in different ways. For example, if one user is querying a large number of records, should the database system let another user make changes to the records being queried? If it does, what does this mean for the user running a query? Do they get to see the changes? Does the query abort because records have changed? This is just one problem with multi-user access to data.

The SQL-92 standard identifies several isolation levels for transactions. These are:

- Read uncommitted
- Read committed
- Repeatable read
- Serializable

In order to understand these isolation levels, it is important for you to understand the consistency anomalies that these levels address. These anomalies are:

- Dirty read
- Nonrepeatable read
- Phantom

Dirty reads refer to transactions (or read accesses to data) which run with no regard for other transactions. Consider the following example:

1. One user starts a transaction T1 on the Customer table which changes the credit limit for four customers in Arizona.

2. During this transaction, another user starts a transaction T2 on the Customer table which queries the credit limit for all customers in Arizona.

3. Transactions T1 fails and rolls back the changes to the credit limits for the four customers.

When step 3 occurs, then transaction T2 has read changes that were never committed. These changes did not really exist and should not have been read by transaction T1.

Nonrepeatable reads are reads that handle transaction roll back properly but do not read the exact same data twice. Given the example described above for dirty reads, assume the following sequence of actions:

1. User A starts transaction T1 which, as a first of a two-step transaction, queries for customers in Arizona, returning credit limits.

2. User B starts and completes transaction T2 which changes the credit limit for four customers in Arizona.

3. User A completes transaction T1 which, as the final step, queries customers in Arizona, returning outstanding balances. After all, User A wants to compare the account balances with the total credit limits.

Without the proper isolation level set, User A will have read the same customer records twice, but with different information. Hence, the read for data was non-repeatable.

The phantom anomaly is just a variation on the repeatable read problem. It goes like this:

1. User A starts transaction T1, which first queries for customers in Arizona, returning credit limits.

2. User B starts and completes transaction T2, which adds a new customer account in Arizona.

3. User A completes transaction T1 which, as the final step, queries customers in Arizona, returning outstanding balances. After all, User A wants to compare the account balances with the total credit limits.

User A will see in the final step of transaction T1 a new record (a phantom) which did not exist in the prior read. This can occur if User B adds a new record, or if User B changes other customer records, which now causes them to land in the set of customer records in Arizona. The second part of transaction T1 returns a different set of records, not the same set with different data.

This sets up the following matrix of isolation levels and consistency anomalies in Table 24.1.

TABLE 24.1 ISOLATION LEVEL AND CONSISTENCY

Isolation Level	Dirty Read	Non-repeatable Read	Phantom
Read uncommitted	Y	Y	Y
Read committed	N	Y	Y
Repeatable read	N	N	Y
Serializable	N	N	N

This table shows that if you choose an isolation level of read uncommitted, then you will not be able to stop any of the consistency anomalies. If you choose read committed, then your transaction will only read committed records, but will not stop the non-repeatable read or phantom problem. If you choose the repeatable real isolation level, then you solve the first two consistency anomalies but fail to stop phantoms. The highest level of isolation is serializable. This stops all three consistency anomalies.

Delphi Isolation Levels

Delphi supports the first three of the SQL-92 isolation levels: read uncommitted (Delphi calls it dirty read), read committed, and repeatable read. However, your back end server may not implement these three levels, or may implement them differently. For example, an Oracle server only supports a read committed and a repeatable read isolation level. If you set the isolation level to dirty read on an Oracle database, Delphi will use the next highest isolation level since Oracle does not support dirty reads.

For Sybase and Microsoft SQL servers, Delphi will use the read committed isolation level, since that is the only isolation level supported by the back end. Interbase uses two isolation levels: read committed and repeatable read. If you set the isolation level to dirty read on an Interbase database, Interbase will treat it as a read committed.

To confuse matters more, each server may implement an isolation level differently. One server uses a repeatable read isolation level by actually implementing it as a serializable transaction. You will need to read your server software manuals to learn exactly how it implements each isolation level.

To set the isolation level in a Delphi application, you will need to use a TDatabase component and modify its TransIsolation property (see Figure 24.1).

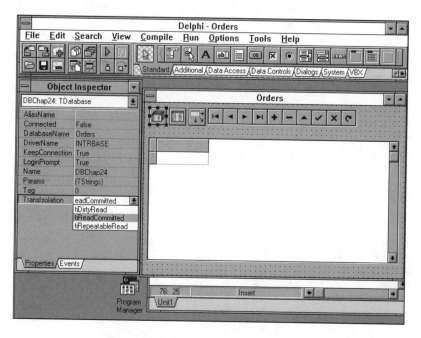

FIGURE 24.1 THE TRANSISOLATION PROPERTY.

The example in figure 24.1 is included on your code disk. The example includes an Interbase database with customer and orders tables. These tables were created from the same tables in the Delphi DBDEMOS directory included in your Delphi installation.

Using Transactions: Implicit Versus Explicit

Whenever your application adds, deletes, or changes records without any programmatic transaction control, Delphi places these changes in an implicit transaction. However, for batch updates to data, especially where you are updating several rows in several tables, you can not rely on Delphi's implicit transaction management.

Delphi places each record update in a transaction. Sometimes you might want to place many changes to several rows or several tables in one transaction. If any update fails, they all fail. To do this, you will need to use the TDatabase components StartTransaction and Commit methods. The following code, which is included in the example for this chapter on the code disk, shows how to do this.

```
procedure TForm1.IncreaseButtonClick(Sender: TObject);
begin
    ChangeAmount(2.0)
end;

procedure TForm1.DecreaseButtonClick(Sender: TObject);
begin
    ChangeAmount(0.5)
end;

procedure TForm1.ChangeAmount(amt: real);
begin

    {Start a transaction and disable
    to prevent screen flicker}
    DBChap24.StartTransaction;
    TBOrders.DisableControls;
    TBOrders.First;

    {iterate through all records}
    While not TBOrders.EOF do
    begin
        {update the status line}
        StatusPanel.Caption := 'Updating order ' +
            TBOrdersORDERNO.AsString;
        StatusPanel.Repaint;
        {edit the current record, increase
        the amount, move to next record}
        TBOrders.Edit;
        TBOrdersAmountPaid.value :=
                TBOrdersAmountPaid.value * amt;
        TBOrders.Next;
    end;

    {ask user to save changes}
```

```
if messageDlg('Commit these changes?',
   mtConfirmation,[mbYes,mbNo],0)=mrYes then
   begin
      DbChap24.Commit;
      StatusPanel.Caption := 'Changes committed.';
   end
else
   begin
      DbChap24.Rollback;
      StatusPanel.Caption := 'Changes rolled back.';
   end;

{enable the grid}
TBOrders.EnableControls;

end;
```

The Orders form (Figure 24.2) has two buttons: one to increase each order's Amount paid field by 100%, the other to decrease that field by 50%.

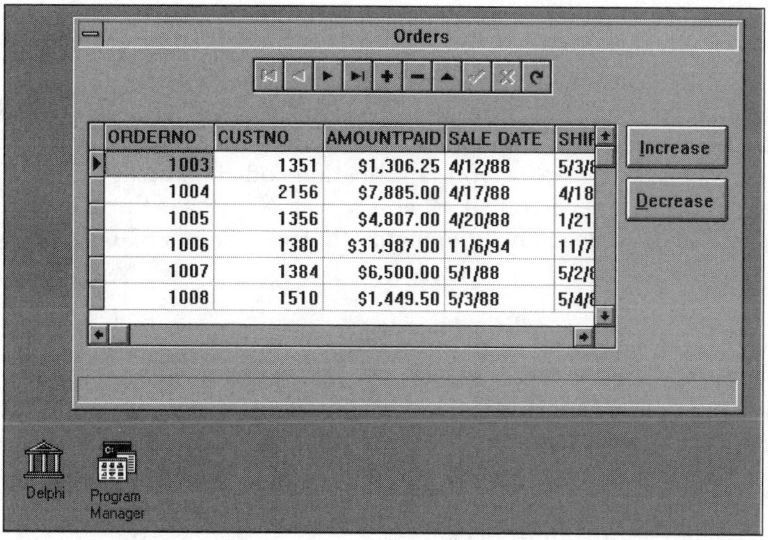

FIGURE 24.2 ORDERS FORM WITH INCREASE/DECREASE BUTTONS.

The code starts a transaction and then asks the user if they want to commit the transaction. If they do, then all changes are written out. If not, then all the changes are rolled back.

Keep in mind, that in real-world applications, you would not ask the user to save changes after they have been made. First, it is wise to ask the user before running the transaction, rather than after. Second, it is unwise to keep a transaction pending because you are waiting for user input. What if the user leaves for lunch, or worse yet, for vacation, while the dialog box asking for permission to commit the changes is up? The database server places locks on the tables and records in order to handle the transactions. Until the transactions are committed or rolled back, these locks remain in place, and other transactions might be blocked from accessing the data. This example simply illustrates transaction management so you can see how it works.

Knowing when and where you use explicit or implicit transaction management is crucial to building a good client server application. First, you need to understand the transaction management capabilities of your back-end server. Second, you need to understand how Delphi maps its isolation levels to your servers isolation levels. Third, you need to understand the performance characteristics of your application.

For example, Delphi's implicit transaction management can cause undue network traffic, especially if you can update many rows in an explicit transaction. Batch update processes and reporting processes will undoubtedly require explicit transaction control. When in doubt, it is probably best to control the transactions yourself.

Delphi offers you a third alternative. You can use pass-through SQL to send transaction control commands directly to the back-end server. Keep in mind that when you do this, your application code is now dependent on the back end. If you change your back-end server, your pass-through SQL commands will need to be changed to match the new servers SQL syntax.

Other Concurrency Issues

Establishing transaction isolation levels is just one aspect of controlling concurrency. Database servers also have a default locking mechanism which you need to understand. Each server uses its locking mechanisms to implement transaction isolation and the implementation can have profound effects on your applications design.

For example, when you update a record in a Microsoft SQL Server environment, SQL Server does not lock the row or rows in question. Instead, it locks the page in which the row is situated. This means that if the database page contains ten rows, then all ten rows are locked as well. Oracle servers, on the other hand, implement row-level locking. In this scheme, just the row updated is locked, not the entire database page.

In addition, you need to understand exactly when a record or page gets locked during a data entry session. Delphi uses an optimistic locking scheme where a record is locked at the moment the changes are posted to the database, not when the user begins editing data. On local Paradox tables, just the opposite is true. Paradox tables use a pessimistic locking scheme in which the record being changed is locked the moment a user starts typing in a change.

To give us some control over the optimistic updating scheme on client-server data, Delphi gives us the UpdateMode property on the TTable and TQuery objects. This property has the following values:

Constant	Meaning
upWhereAll	Delphi performs the update by using every column to find the record to update. If another user changed any field in the record, the update will fail because it will not find the record.
upWhereChanged	Delphi performs the update by using only changed columns to find the record to update. If another user (user B) changed any field that user A changed, then user As attempt to post will fail because Delphi will not find the record. This lets users change different fields in the same record.
upWhereKeyOnly	Delphi performs the update by using only the key fields to find the record to update. As long as other users do not change the key fields, then each user will overwrite changes to the other. In effect, this is a last one wins strategy.

Developers familiar with local database development tactics that include pessimistic record locking will be disappointed, at first, by the lack of control over when records get locked. In addition, some database drivers, such as the Microsoft ODBC drivers for Access get confused by the upWhereAll update mode. This update mode constructs a potentially complex and long SQL statement. You might encounter a **SQL is too complex** error (Figure 24.3) when you attempt to post records in this mode. If this happens, you will need to use the upWhereChanged or upWhereKeyOnly modes.

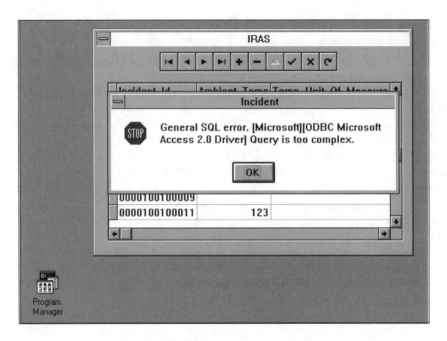

FIGURE 24.3 SQL IS TOO COMPLEX AN ERROR

If not having a pessimistic record locking scheme worries you, consider this. In client-server databases with large tables and many concurrent users, the performance overhead of a pessimistic locking scheme must be weighed against the chance of two users editing the same records at the same time. Through transaction isolation levels and the UpdateMode property, Delphi gives the user flexibility. You could keep a repeatable read transaction open which contains three steps: a query to read the data, a data entry session to let the user change the record, and a query to update the record. This will ensure that no other user can change the record.

In addition, you can always use SQL pass-through to send back-end specific SQL commands to the server to control concurrency. Some database servers let you implement a hold lock which keeps a record or page locked even though you are not posting a change. The problem with a hold lock, is that since it keeps the page or record locked for potentially long periods of time, it can block other users or processes from accessing the page or record, reducing concurrency and increasing locking activity.

Summary

Delphi provides three main mechanisms for transactions: implicit transactions, explicit transactions, and SQL pass-through. Unless you explicitly create transactions, Delphi automatically wraps record posts and updates in a transaction. However, if you want to improve database performance or you need to control updates to multiple rows or multiple tables, explicit transaction control is preferred. If neither explicit nor implicit transaction control is suitable, then you can use SQL pass-through to take advantage of specific back-end transaction features not supported in the Delphi TDatabase, TTable, or TQuery components. Finally, the TTable component has an UpdateMode property which lets you implement three levels of optimistic updates: WhereAll, WhereChanged, and WhereKeyOnly.

595

CHAPTER 25

Data Security Overview

Heavy-duty applications require tight security. *Data security* is different from *data integrity*. The latter refers to the data validity and correctness. The former refers to data visibility and the scope of changes. If your application maintains data integrity properly, those who use the data will rest at night knowing that referential integrity constraints are not being violated or that domain constraints are not being subverted. If your application is properly secured, then those who are not supposed to use the data will not be able to get at it. And if your application is elegantly secured, then the security systems will not interfere with those who must access the data. Data integrity and data security often go hand-in-hand, yet the features which manage them are quite distinct.

When it comes to data security, with Delphi you have options. For local or file-server applications, you can use the security features in the Paradox file format (the DB format). Or, if no security is required, you can use the DBase file format (the DBF format). For client-server applications, you can use the security facilities the server provides. This chapter will review security features and security design options for both local and client-server applications.

Local Data

When it comes to security, the best choice for a local data is the Paradox file format. With the Paradox file format, you can encrypt the table, set table-level rights, and field-level rights. The DBase file format has no security provisions built-in. You can not encrypt a DBase file nor can you assign table-level or field-level rights.

Encrypting a Paradox Table

You can use the Database Desktop to create and maintain Paradox and DBase local tables. The Database Desktop is discussed more fully in Chapter 33. This chapter assumes you have some familiarity with the Database Desktop or that you have read the chapter on the Database Desktop at the end of the book to learn more.

You can encrypt a Paradox table when you create it or, if it is already created, you can use the **Tools I Utilities I Restructure** menu commands. Once you are in the restructure dialog box (Figure 25.1), you can select **Password Security** from the table properties drop-down list in the upper-right corner.

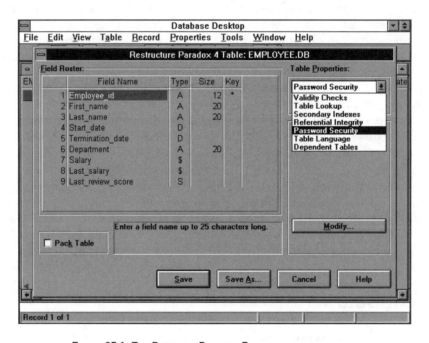

FIGURE 25.1 THE DATABASE DESKTOP RESTRUCTURE DIALOG BOX.

Once you choose **Password Security**, a **Define** button appears in the Restructure dialog box. Press this button to define a master password (Figure 25.2).

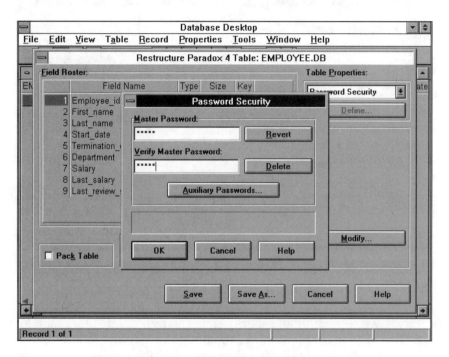

FIGURE 25.2 DEFINING A MASTER PASSWORD DIALOG BOX.

With Paradox tables, the Master Password gives you all rights to the table, including the right to change or remove the master password. If you forget your password, you will not be able to access the table. Once you have entered a master password, you can press the **Auxiliary Passwords** button in the Password Security dialog box. The Database Desktop brings up Auxiliary Passwords dialog box (Figure 25.3)

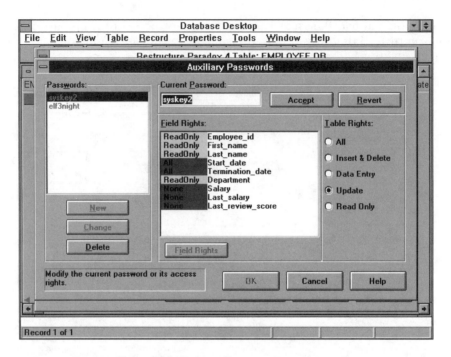

FIGURE 25.3 AUXILIARY PASSWORDS DIALOG BOX.

Master passwords control all security rights as well as any other table properties. Obviously master passwords should not be passed around for general use. Usually only the application developer and the person responsible for the data security know the master password. Auxiliary passwords let you give users partial access to the table. Auxiliary passwords are frequently passed around.

Assigning Table-Level and Field-Level Rights

You assign table-level and field-level rights with the Auxiliary Passwords dialog box. The table-level rights include:

All	User can add, edit, and delete records, restructure the table, change all table properties except the master password.
Insert and delete	User can add, edit, and delete records, but cannot delete the table.
Data entry	User can add and edit records, but cannot delete records, empty the table, or restructure the table.
Update	User can only edit nonkey fields.
Read-only	User cannot edit or add records.

The field level rights include:

All	User can view and edit the field.
Read only	User cannot edit the field.
None	User cannot view or edit the field.

Some of the field-level and table-level rights are mutually exclusive. For example, if you assign an auxiliary password All or Insert & Delete table rights, then you cannot assign field-level rights of Read Only or None.

Entering and Clearing Passwords

With the Database Desktop, the first time you access an encrypted table, it asks for a password. Your rights to the table depend on the password you enter. The next time you access the table, the Database Desktop does not ask for a password. This eliminates pesky password dialog boxes that would otherwise appear every time you access a table. This can be annoying at times.

The code disk for this book contains an encrypted table (used in this chapter) as an example. The table, **EMPLOYEE.DB**, has the master password **charm** and two auxiliary passwords, **elf3night** and **syskey2**.

The Database Desktop lets you enter a password before you access a table. Use the menu command **Tools | Utilities | Passwords** to add a password to the current Database Desktop session (see Figure 25.4).

This dialog box also lets you remove any password(s) you have entered in the current Database Desktop session. You remove passwords if you want to open a table and have the Database Desktop prompt you for a password.

FIGURE 25.4 ENTER PASSWORD(S) DIALOG BOX.

Just like the Database Desktop, Delphi lets you control passwords to local Paradox tables. The TSession object is useful here. Although Delphi automatically creates and manages the TSession object (there is one for each application) for you, you can use the following methods to control adding and removing passwords:

```
AddPassword(const Password: String)
GetPassword: Boolean
RemovePassword(const Password: String)
RemoveAllPasswords
```

Just like the Enter Password(s) dialog box in Figure 25.5, the AddPassword() method adds a password to the current session (the TSession object).

Controlling Passwords in Code

If you need to add passwords to access tables in code, you need to use the Session object, which Delphi automatically creates and manages for you. The TSession object is not a visual component that is accessible from the Component palette. The code in Figure 25.5 is associated with TBEmployee table object's BeforeOpen event. This code adds a password to the current session, eliminating the need for the password dialog box that normally appears the first time the user (or programmer) accesses an encrypted table.

603

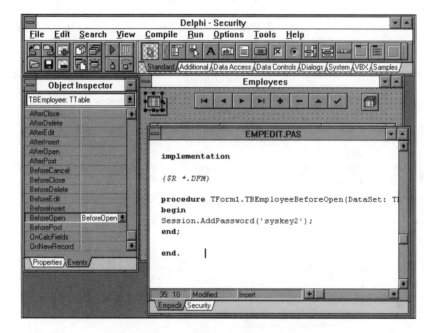

FIGURE 25.5 ADDING PASSWORD UNDER CODE CONTROL.

You will not be able to use the TDatabase objects OnLogin event on Paradox tables. This event is only activated for client-server tables. Instead, you will have to add the password to the TSession object when Delphi creates the form or the TTable object.

Using Microsoft Access tables

Your Delphi application can use Microsoft Access tables. Like Paradox tables, you can secure and encrypt Microsoft Access databases. To read and write Access databases you will need at least version 2 of the Microsoft ODBC drivers. Delphi and the Database Desktop work with ODBC drivers quite easily.

Setting Up ODBC Drivers

If you do not have the Microsoft ODBC drivers (at least version 2), you can call Microsoft and purchase these drivers; they are very inexpensive. The Microsoft ODBC disks contain installation software that installs the drivers onto your PC. Once you have installed the drivers, perform the following steps to let Delphi read and write Access databases:

1. Open up the Control Panel icon in the Main program group and click the **ODBC** icon (Figure 25.6).

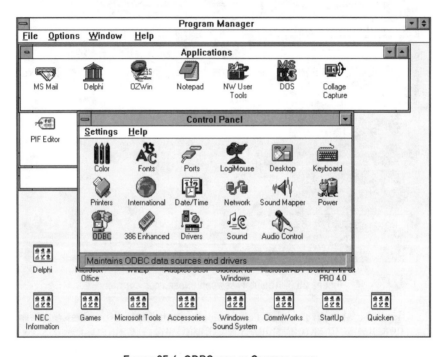

FIGURE 25.6 ODBC ICON IN CONTROL PANEL.

2. From the ODBC Data Sources dialog box, press the **Add** button to bring up the dialog box, Add **Data Source**, shown in Figure 25.7.

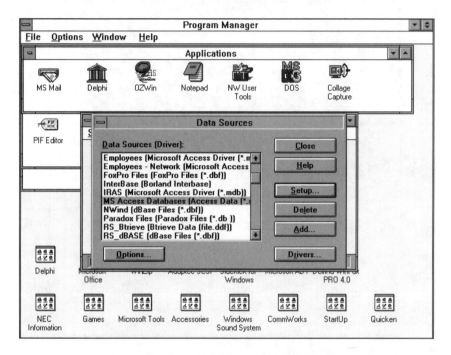

FIGURE 25.7 ADD **ODBC** DATA SOURCE DIALOG BOX.

3. Select **Microsoft Access driver**, and press **OK**. This brings up the ODBC Setup dialog box (Figure 25.8). Give the ODBC driver a descriptive name, such as **Employees**. Select the **Access** database and the system database (**SYSTEM.MDA**) from this dialog box using the select button. When you are done, press **OK** and close the Data Sources dialog box. This saves the ODBC driver name as part of the ODBC settings.

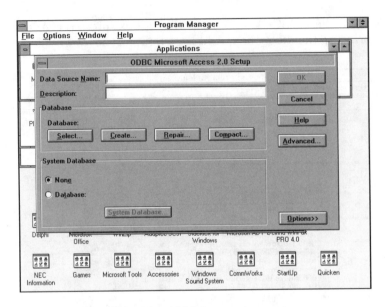

FIGURE 25.8 ODBC SETUP DIALOG BOX.

4. Open up the BDE Configuration Utility in the Delphi program group (Figure 25.9).

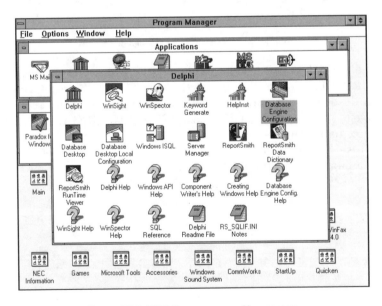

FIGURE 25.9 BDE CONFIGURATION UTILITY ICON.

5. From the BDE Configuration Utility Drivers page, click on the **New ODBC Driver** button. This brings up the Add ODBC Driver dialog box (Figure 25.10). Type in a descriptive name (such as **Employee**) for the SQL-Link driver. This name is used to refer to the actual ODBC data source. The name you type in does not have any special meaning to the ODBC setup or the BDE Configuration Utility. Select the **Microsoft Access driver** as the Default ODBC driver. Once you select **Microsoft Access driver**, the Default Data Source Name drop-down list will contain the ODBC data source you set up in step 3. Select that data source and press **OK** to save the new ODBC driver.

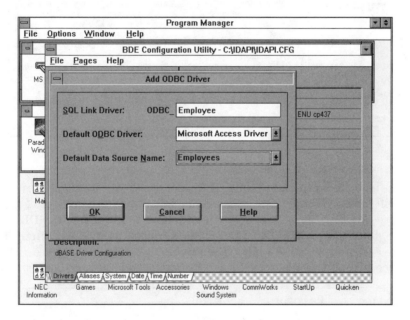

FIGURE 25.10 ADD ODBC DRIVER DIALOG BOX IN BDE CONFIG UTILITY.

6. Select the **Aliases** page in the BDE Configuration utility and press the **New Alias** button to create a new alias for the ODBC data source. This brings up the Add New Alias Name dialog box (Figure 25.11). Enter the alias name and choose the **ODBC_Employee** alias type created in step 5. Press **OK** to accept the new alias.

7. Choose **File | Save** to save the new alias information as part of the BDE configuration. The next time you start Delphi, this alias will be available as a database name, just like other aliases you might have created.

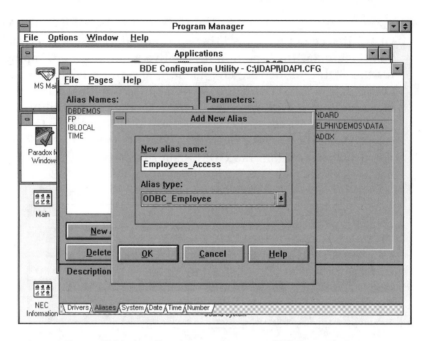

FIGURE 25.11 ADD NEW ALIAS DIALOG BOX IN BDE CONFIG UTILITY.

Despite the number of steps required to connect to Access databases via the Microsoft ODBC data drivers, it can be done. In fact, the code disk for this chapter contains a Microsoft Access 2.0 database (**EMPLOYEE.MDB**) and a System database (**SYSTEM.MDA**). The database contains a single table (**Employees**) and a single query, **EmployeeView**. The database does have security assigned with the following user names and passwords:

User Name	Password	Rights
Admin	admin	All
Vince	vince	Read-only
Brad	brad	Add, edit, delete records

SYSTEM.MDA

Each copy of Access (or Access Runtime) has a SYSTEM.MDA file that contains three built-in groups and two built-in user accounts. The three groups are Admin, Users, and Guests. The two user accounts are Admin and Guest. The password for the Admin and User accounts are initially null (blank).

You can use the ODBC maintenance facility in the Control Panel or Access to create a SYSTEM.MDA (you do not have to call it SYSTEM.MDA), and you can configure the Windows ODBC Access drivers to use any system database, no matter what it is called (step 3 above). The purpose of the system database is to control access to tables and other objects in the Access database.

Users and Groups

Using Access, you can create additional users and groups for an Access database. Each user and/or group can have the following rights to tables and other objects in an Access database:

- Read design
- Modify design
- Administer
- Read data
- Update data
- Insert data
- Delete data

The last four rights—read, update, insert, and delete data—are significant for Delphi applications that need to read and write Access data, because your application will only be allowed those operations if it logs in with a proper user id and password. If the Access database does not have any security restrictions assigned, then you probably will not need to worry about security. If the Access database does, you will need to present the proper name and password before you can access any data in the database.

In Access security, users belong to groups. Since both users and groups have rights, you can have conflicts between the two. Access resolves this in a rather simple manner. If a user belongs to a group with less restrictive rights, then the group rights prevail. If the user belongs to two groups, one with less restrictive rights, then the less restrictive group rights prevail. To assign rights to users and groups in an Access database, you will need a copy of Microsoft Access. Be careful when assigning rights to a user in Access. If the group a user belongs to has more rights to tables than what you have given the user, the less restrictive rights prevail.

To display and edit data in an Access table, you can connect a TTable component to the Access alias (created in step 6 above) via the DatabaseName property. Alternatively, you can use a TDatabase component to connect to the Access alias via the DatabaseName property, or you can connect directly to the ODBC driver (created in step 3 above) via the DriverName property. The TDatabase, DatabaseName, and DriverName properties are mutually exclusive. You can only specify one or the other, not both.

The example project for this chapter (**ACCESS.DPR**) on the included code disk uses a TDatabase component that needs an Employees_Access alias defined for the Access database and **SYSTEM.MDA** file on disk. Unlike the example shown in Figure 25.5, this example uses code on the TDatabase OnLogin event to set the user name and password so the application does not display the password dialog box at startup. Figure 25.12 shows the form, in design mode. The following code is in the TDatabase objects OnLogin event handler:

```
procedure TForm1.DBEmployeesLogin(Database: TDatabase;
  LoginParams: TStrings);
begin
LoginParams.Values['USER NAME'] := 'Vince';
LoginParams.Values['PASSWORD'] := 'vince';
end;
```

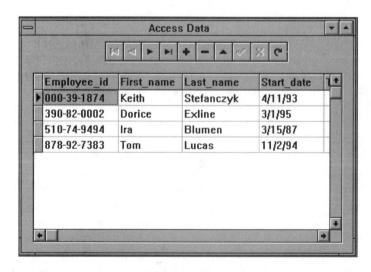

FIGURE 25.12 ACCESS.DPR FORM WITH A SECURED ACCESS TABLE.

As you might have noticed, Microsoft Access does not have built-in field-level security, unlike Paradox tables. You will have to provide any field-level security via ObjectPascal code.

Microsoft Access has more in it concerning security. This chapter provides the basics of accessing Microsoft Access databases and handling security. For further information, check the Microsoft Access manuals.

611

Client-Server Security

Handling security in a client-server environment is very similar to handling security in Access tables. In fact, from the Delphi programmer's perspective, there is very little difference between the two. All you have to do is connect the TTable object to the proper alias or a TDatabase object, present the correct user name and password, and you gain access to tables.

However, different database packages and servers have different dialects of SQL and hence, different security implementations. Subsequently, some large differences in implementation remain. While this does not always affect ObjectPascal code in your applications, it does affect your application design. You will have to make sure that you can in fact implement, in a cost-effective way, the security that your users are expecting or requesting.

Fortunately, database software manufacturers are working toward an industry SQL standard. This section of the chapter discusses the SQL-92 security standards. The goal is to give some background on typical client-server security issues and shed some insight on the actual SQL commands to implement server security. We also suggest that you take a look at the SQL-92 standard (and any SQL standards later than SQL-92) and learn as much as you can about SQL syntax. This will help you build front-end Delphi applications that require fewer changes when moving the data to a different back-end database server.

Privileges, Users, and Security

The SQL-92 standard lets you assign security for several objects including:

- Tables
- Columns in tables
- Views (Query-based tables)
- Domains

The security rights include the following:

Rights	SQL feature
Seeing	SELECT
Adding	INSERT
Modifying	UPDATE
Deleting	DELETE
Referencing	Referential integrity
Using	Domains

Each database server lets you create new user accounts. When setting up a database server, this is one of the first tasks database administrators or developers complete. Without an accurate list of user names, database security cannot be implemented.

Once the administrator establishes the user accounts, each account can be given specific rights to the tables, fields, views, and other objects. Chapter 26, "Data Integrity Overview," discusses some of the basic operations on assigning security. This chapter discusses additional security issues.

Granting Privileges

As shown in Chapter 26, the GRANT SQL keyword lets you link privileges between users and objects in the server database. When establishing privileges on an object, you need to understand that in SQL the person who creates an object is considered the owner of the object; and the owner of an object has all privileges to that object, including the ability to pass some or all of those privileges on to other users.

As an example, consider an Employees table that contains sensitive information and a user, called Brad. To let Brad query the Employees table, you would use the following SQL-92 syntax:

```
GRANT SELECT ON Employees TO BRAD;
```

Likewise, the syntax to let Brad add records to the Employees table is similar:

```
GRANT INSERT ON Employees TO BRAD;
```

If you want Brad to be able to pass on his new rights to other users, you would use the WITH GRANT OPTION phrase:

```
GRANT SELECT ON Employees TO BRAD WITH GRANT OPTION;
```

If you want Brad to be able to update only the First_name and Last_name columns in the Employees table, then you will need to issue the following SQL command:

```
GRANT UPDATE (First_name, Last_name) ON Employees TO BRAD;
```

Likewise, if you wanted to restrict what columns Brad can update in the Employees table, you can use the following syntax:

```
GRANT UPDATE (Employee_id, First_name, Last_name) ON Employees TO BRAD;
```

This command lets Brad enter only the employee id and name. All other columns in the Employees table will be blank or assigned default values, if any default values have been established as part of the table definition.

If you wanted to give Brad all privileges to the Employees table, you can use the following command:

```
GRANT ALL PRIVILEGES ON Employees TO BRAD;
```

When you assign table privileges, the SQL-92 standard assumes that if columns are added to the table in the future, then the rights are granted to these new fields automatically. Unless you want to restrict access to new columns, you do not need to assign new privileges simply because you have added columns to a table.

Since you can let users pass on table privileges to other users, you must be aware that the SQL-92 standard will prevent someone from passing on privileges that they have not been granted. For example, if Brad has been given the SELECT privilege on the Employees table with the grant option and he has been given the UPDATE privilege without the grant option, then he will be unable to pass UPDATE privilege to other users. He will not be able to issue the following command to pass on the UPDATE privilege to others:

```
GRANT ALL PRIVILEGES ON Employees TO MyGoodFriendAl;
```

SQL-92 lets you control who can establish a referential integrity relationship. For example, suppose the Employees database contained a table called Disciplined_Employees, which contained a list of employees who have received written disciplinary notices. Another user could establish a referential integrity relationship (via the REFERENCES keyword in the CREATE TABLE command) to a new table. This user could then attempt to add records to this new table, and depending on whether or not the records were successfully added to the table, determine who has been disciplined. By default, users would not be able to establish a referential integrity link, effectively preventing this subtle security hole. But if a user (Brad) needed to establish one, you could issue the following command:

```
GRANT REFERENCES (Employee_id) ON DISCIPLINED_EMPLOYEES TO Brad;
```

Revoking Privileges

Obviously if you have granted privileges, you want to be able to remove them as well. The REVOKE statement handles this.

If you wanted to remove Brad's INSERT privileges on the Employees table, the following command will do:

```
REVOKE INSERT PRIVILEGES ON Employees FROM Brad;
```

If you had given Brad the GRANT OPTION for the DELETE privilege on the Employees table and you wanted to revoke only his ability to pass the DELETE privilege on to others, the following command works:

```
REVOKE GRANT OPTION FOR DELETE ON Employees FROM Brad;
```

If you wanted to revoke Brad's DELETE privileges on the Employee table and any DELETE privileges Brad passed on to others, you will need to use the CASCADE keyword:

```
REVOKE DELETE ON Employees FROM Brad CASCADE;
```

If you use the RESTRICT keyword, then the privilege will only be revoked if Brad had not passed on the DELETE privilege to other users.

Using Views

Many client-server developers use views to implement additional security. Views are actually SQL SELECT statements that act just like a table. In fact, to the user, they are indistinguishable from a table. When setting up client-server system security, consider using views to prevent the user from seeing all the records in a table. Then grant users the rights they need for the view, not the table.

Views provide an additional layer of security. The SQL-92 standard commands GRANT and REVOKE do not control access to a region of rows within a table, just the columns. Views, on the other hand, let you carve up your data tables into smaller pieces so that users can only see the portion of data they need to see.

An Application Security Framework

The biggest problem with security in client-server systems is that you often need to build a layer that stands between the database server security mechanism and the application itself. The reason: to manage application security complexity.

Since the SQL-92 standard does not have a notion of groups, nor can it always have knowledge of the major groupings of related tables in your application, developers frequently build additional tables that map user accounts to areas of the application's functionality. Sometimes it is much easier to do this than to manage 200 user accounts with privileges explicitly stated for each user.

And when it comes to local Paradox tables, it is not always feasible or practical to give the user even the auxiliary passwords to all the tables in the application. Rather, you might consider giving all tables in your application a carefully controlled set of master and auxiliary passwords and manage user accounts through tables and codes yourself.

Users and Groups

The biggest problem with managing security in large applications with a large user base is managing the number of privileges for each user. Many application developers use the concept of a group to reduce this maintenance overhead. Users belong to groups (as in the Access security scheme) and groups can be assigned privileges. So instead of entering privileges for hundreds of users, the security administrator enters privileges for perhaps a dozen or so groups and assigns users to groups, thereby reducing security overhead by a factor of 10.

The problem with this scheme is that you must design a few tables to hold the list of valid groups, the list of valid users, and the list of users in each group. In addition, you need to maintain a set of privileges on the back-end server that maps to your application-layer groups. Your application will maintain the back-end privileges for the application user while maintaining the list of users and groups in the front-end application.

Creating an application-layer of security is desirable if the following conditions are true:

- Security administration for the data tables can be moved from exclusively on the back-end to partly on the front-end application and partly on the back-end server. In some organizations and environments, this arrangement might not be possible due to past policy, procedures, or the design of existing tables.
- The number of users is high enough to warrant the front-end work. If not adding an application layer of security costs more than simply using the back-end server security, then why bother with the front-end work?
- Users can be grouped into a manageable number of groups, and privileges can be assigned to the groups rather than to the users. If the user community does not fall neatly into a small number of groups and requires special security considerations, then the cost of creating an application layer of security while managing a high number of security exceptions might be too great.

There are other approaches to application-level security. The schemes used in SQL-92 and in the user/group scheme discussed above, are static. Privileges, while they can be changed, are etched in stone while the application runs.

Quite frequently, developers are called on to write *dynamic security* requirements: security that changes depending on the content of the data. The security rules might change as the user scrolls from record to record in a table.

Usually this involves writing either stored procedures on the back end (usually in response to triggers) or by writing ObjectPascal code in the front-end application. Additionally, one could construct a table-based, rule-based system that lets users change the security business rules without additional programming. However, that leaves you the task of writing a component or components that algorithmically handle dynamic security requirements.

Security, like virtue, often remains local. What one organization considers secure another considers too open. One organization will think the SQL-92 GRANT and REVOKE mechanisms are too limiting, another will think that these commands are sufficient. Your job is to understand the back-end and front-end options and to design a security mechanism that meets your customer's requirements.

Limits to Database Security

Devising database protection schemes is important, but there is much more to securing data. Just because your data is encrypted or tucked away in a database server with security assigned does not mean it is secure.

Password-protected Paradox tables are encrypted, preventing users from using a text editor or some other utility to see the data in the files that comprise the table. While this makes Paradox tables more secure than they would otherwise be, it does not mean that they are impenetrable. You can purchase utilities that decrypt Paradox tables, which means that a determined hacker can, too.

The encryption algorithm that Borland uses in Paradox tables is not considered highly secure. It is not in the same league as a DES-compliant or public-key encryption algorithm. While Paradox encryption is good enough for nearly all business data, you should be wary of using it for data that requires extremely high security.

In addition, just because your data resides in a database server such as Interbase or SQL Server does not make it secure. Data encryption and password protection are just two pieces in the security puzzle. Customers that require data security that cannot be busted will also need several other important security measures.

The following areas are security weak spots:

- Local area network wires. A determined person can easily tap into the wires that connect computers together. Once attached, a data thief can view all the packets transmitted between computers, gathering important sensitive data. To be totally secure, data should be encrypted before it is transmitted down the network wire. Some network operating systems let you encrypt or secure network packets to prevent unauthorized access.

- Server passwords. If written down, users must store all their passwords in secured locations. In addition, a thief must not be able to easily guess the users' passwords. Passwords based on family member names, pets, or other easy words must be forbidden. Passwords that are too short can be busted with brute force. Passwords that do not change frequently enough are more apt to be shared.

- Server machines. File and database server machines must be placed in secured areas so that a thief cannot access them. If a server lets you control it remotely, that remote access software must be carefully secured.

- Temporary files on workstations. If the application creates temporary files on the workstation's local hard drive and these temporary files contain data that needs to be secured, these temporary files need to be deleted and the blocks on the hard disk the files occupied must be wiped. Otherwise, a thief can use disk utilities (included in Windows and DOS) to recover these deleted temporary files.

- Source code or table-driven passwords. If the application stores passwords in source code or application tables, then these passwords must also be protected. Source code should not remain accessible, and tables that hold passwords need to be protected.

- Data backups. Data backup on tape is a potential security risk, especially if any sensitive data backed up is not encrypted. Backup tapes must be placed in a secure environment.

These areas of weakness just scratch the surface. If your customers require stringent security measures, either get in touch with a security expert or become one yourself. For local data, using encrypted Paradox tables will deter casual data thieves, disgruntled employees, and others. It will not stop the very knowledgeable professional data thief. If your customers want to stop the security pro, then the cost of security goes up significantly.

Summary

Managing security in database applications can be a difficult task, depending on the user's requirements. Between the variety of back ends that Delphi supports and the front-end programming tools, you have everything you need to handle just about any security requirement.

CHAPTER 26

Data Integrity Overview

Whether you are developing a client/server application or a file server application that uses local tables, perhaps the single most important aspect of your design is ensuring data integrity. It makes no difference how user friendly your interface is or how fast your program is if the data in the database is not accurate and accessible.

Up to this point, this book has used local tables for most of the examples and has emphasized, correctly, that with Delphi there is virtually no difference between working with local tables and working with server tables. That is one of Delphi's strengths. However, this database-independence does not apply to data integrity. The techniques you use to ensure the validity and consistency of your data are very different for client/server applications and for local table applications. This chapter will present a general overview of client/server data-integrity techniques and then local table techniques. Specific examples for Interbase and Microsoft SQL are presented in Chapters 27 and 28, respectively.

Controlling Data Integrity

The most critical part of any database application is to ensure that all of the data in the database is valid all the time. How you do this is very dependent on your environment.

To be sure that the data in your database is valid, you need to enforce two types of constraints. The first is domain integrity constraints. *Domain integrity constraints* ensure that all of the values in a column in a table are valid. Examples of domain integrity constraints include:

- The value must be greater than or equal to a minimum value.
- The value must be less than or equal to a maximum value.
- If no value is entered a default value must be assigned.
- The data must be of a particular type, such as alphanumeric, numeric. or date.
- A value is required; the field cannot be left blank.
- The value must exist in another table. For example, the State field can only contain values from a valid list of two-character state codes in a validation table.
- The value must match a pattern. For example, a zip code must consist of either five digits or five digits, a hyphen, and four more digits.
- Duplicate values are not allowed. That is, no two rows in a table can have the same value in one or more columns.

The second type of constraint that ensures valid data is a referential integrity constraint. *Referential integrity* requires that the values in a column in one table exist in a column in another table. The most common example of referential integrity is a foreign key in one table referring to the primary key in another table. For example, using the sample Customer and Order tables, you would not want a user to be able to enter an order record that contains a Customer Number that does not exist in the Customer table.

Referential integrity also requires that users not be allowed to orphan detail records by deleting the parent or changing the parent's key. Consider the Customer and Order table again; if users could delete a Customer record that had dependent Order records in the Order table the Order records would be *orphaned*. The same thing would happen if users could change the primary key, CustomerNo, of a Customer record without changing the CustomerNo foreign key in all of the related Order records. To ensure referential integrity, the database must either cascade primary key changes to dependent detail records or prohibit changes in the key of the parent record.

Most databases, particularly in larger organizations, are accessed by more than one application. If each application enforces its own rules, it is very difficult to ensure that each enforces exactly the same rules. It is also difficult to ensure that all of the rules are enforced in every part of your application that accesses the database. The way to avoid that problem is to let the database management software—not your application—enforce the rules. The problem with letting the database manager enforce the rules is that every database management package does it differently.

If you are working with local dBase tables, you have to provide all data-integrity constraints in your application. Local Paradox tables, on the other hand, provide the following data-integrity features that are enforced automatically by the Borland Database Engine (BDE) regardless of what application is accessing the tables.

- Minimum value
- Maximum value
- Default value
- Table lookup validation
- Referential integrity
- Pictures (pattern masks)

Database servers provide even more powerful capabilities through triggers. *Triggers* are programs you write that are part of the database and that you can use to enforce data-integrity constraints. Because triggers are programs you write, you can use them to enforce virtually any data-integrity constraint you can conceive.

Always enforce data integrity at the database level, not in your application. This eliminates redundant code across applications and ensures that the data is valid no matter what application is used to access the database.

There may be cases where you need to enforce a constraint in your application that only applies when that particular application is used to access the data, but this is not likely.

Preventing Duplicate Values

In a relational database each table must have a primary key. The primary key is a column whose value, or a combination of columns whose values taken together, uniquely identifies one row. Put another way, duplicate primary key values are not allowed in a table. In addition, you may want to enforce uniqueness on one or a combination of fields other than the primary key.

To enforce uniqueness, you must define an index on the field or fields involved and declare the index to be unique. Using Interbase you can create an index in one of the following ways:

- Using a Create Table statement.
- Using a Create Index statement.
- Specifying a primary key, foreign key, or unique constraint when you define a column. When you specify one of these constraints Interbase automatically creates an index on the column.

The syntax for Create Index is:

```
CREATE [unique] [ascending] [descending]
       INDEX IndexName ON TableName (col1[, col2,...])
```

If you have an Employee table whose primary key is EmployeeNumber, then you might want to create the following index:

```
CREATE UNIQUE INDEX SSNX ON EMPLOYEE (SOCIAL_SECURITY)
```

This statement will create a unique ascending index on the Social Security Number column in the Employee table. Any column in any table where uniqueness is a natural property of the data is a candidate for a unique index. In addition to Social Security Number and employee number, other values that may be naturally unique are part numbers, purchase order numbers, check numbers, and vendor numbers.

There is another advantage to creating a unique index on a column or group of columns. Values that are unique are likely to be used as search criteria to find specific rows in a table, and the presence of an index will dramatically improve search performance.

There is only one disadvantage to creating an index to enforce uniqueness. Each index imposes overhead when adding or changing records because the index must be updated each time a record is added or a value in the indexed field is changed.

Creating Domains and Check Constraints

Domains are a feature of Interbase that makes enforcing data integrity easier. A *domain* is simply a user-defined column type. Typically, you will define domains before you create the tables in your database and then use the domains to define the columns in your tables. Domains offer no benefit unless you will be creating two or more columns in the same or different tables that will have the same characteristics. Anything you can include in a domain definition you can also include in a column's definition in a Create Table statement. A domain definition can include any of the following:

- A data type. The data type is required.
- A default value.
- Not null. If not null is included, users must enter a value in any column based on this domain.

- A check condition. Check conditions allow you to define conditions that values in this column must satisfy. Check conditions are described in more detail later in this section.
- Collation order for the column.

Selecting a data type is usually the first step in enforcing data integrity. By selecting a **Numeric** data type you ensure that the column will not contain alpha characters. By selecting an **Integer** type you restrict the column's contents to whole numbers. Selecting **Date** instead of Char as the type for a field that will hold dates guarantees that only valid dates will be allowed.

Selecting a default value for a column not only helps ensure data integrity but can also speed data entry. The default value is automatically entered into the field in a new record if the user does not enter a value. The default value can be null, any literal constant, or, in the case of Interbase, the user's username.

Specifying Not Null for a column forces the user to enter a value. This ensures that the field is not left blank in either a new or an existing record.

Be careful not to create an impossible condition by specifying Null as the default value and also specifying Not Null.

T I P

For example, the following statement creates a domain for the City portion of an address:

```
CREATE DOMAIN CITYD AS VARCHAR(20) NOT NULL
```

This domain can be used to define any city name column in any table and to ensure that all columns that contain city names will have a data type of **VARCHAR(20)** and that a value must be entered. Domains are particularly useful for the components of addresses, which can appear in many tables. For example, in one database you might have addresses for employees, customers, and vendors. By basing all addresses on the same domains, you ensure that they will have the same properties.

Check constraints allow you to construct custom data-validation rules. Check constraints are not as powerful as triggers, but they are much easier to define. Interbase check constraints let you validate the value entered in a field against one or more literal values. The best way to get a feeling for check constraints is to look at some examples. This section is not an exhaustive treatment of the syntax of check constraints. For that, see your Interbase manuals.

```
CREATE DOMAINT PROJSTATUS
        AS VARCHAR(16)
        CHECK (VALUE IN ("Active", "Wait Client", "Proposal", "Done"))
```

This statement creates a domain named **PROJSTATUS** whose value must be in the set of four values in the check constraint. If you want the user to be able to leave the field blank you must include Null in the check constraint, as shown here:

```
CREATE DOMAIN PROJSTATUSD
        AS VARCHAR(16)
        CHECK ((VALUE IN ("Active", "Wait Client", "Proposal", "Done"))
OR
            (VALUE IS NULL))
```

You can also specify ranges of values, as in the following example:

```
CREATE DOMAIN SEQUENCED
        AS INTEGER
        CHECK (VALUE NOT BETWEEN 1 AND 1000)
```

You can also use the LIKE, CONTAINING, and STARTING WITH keywords, as shown in the following examples:

```
CREATE DOMAIN PARTNOD
        AS VARCHAR(20)
        CHECK (VALUE STARTING WITH "PXD")
CREATE DOMAIN PARTNOD
        AS VARCHAR(20)
        CHECK (VALUE CONTAINING "PXD")
```

You can create very complex check constraints by using the NOT, AND, and OR operators in combination with parentheses for grouping.

Check constraints provide a fast and easy way to specify many domain-integrity constraints. You can include a check constraint as part of a domain definition, as shown in the preceding examples. You can also include check constraints in a CREATE TABLE statement to apply checks to one or more columns.

If your server supports domains and check constraints, use them to prevent redundant definitions of domain-integrity constraints and to centralize your data validation on the server. This is just one more example of the need to know all the features of the database server you are using before you begin designing and implementing your application. Most servers have server-specific features that will aid in implementing data integrity.

Using Referential Integrity

Referential integrity is probably the most critical integrity constraint in a relational database. Referential integrity ensures that there are no orphaned records in related tables. Consider a Customer table and an Order table. Customer_Number is the primary key of the Customer table and is a foreign key in the Order table. Given these tables, you do not want users to be able to do any of the following:

625

- Insert a new Order row that contains a Customer_Number that does not exist in the Customer table.
- Change the Customer_Number of a record in the Customer table without changing the Customer_Number in each Order record for that customer.
- Delete a row from the Customer table without first deleting all of the Order rows for that Customer.

Once again, how referential integrity is implemented varies from server to server. With Interbase, defining a referential integrity constraint between the Customer and Order tables will prevent all of these actions. For example, the following clause in the CREATE TABLE statement for the Order table will define referential integrity between Customer and Order.

```
FOREIGN KEY (CUSTOMER_NUMBER) REFERENCES CUSTOMER (CUSTOMER_NO)
```

This clause not only defines referential integrity between the tables but also creates an index on the Customer_Number foreign key field in the Order table. If your server does not support a similar direct method of defining referential integrity you will have to implement referential integrity yourself using triggers.

While this example shows the most common implementation of referential integrity, a foreign key in the child table linked to the primary key in the parent table, Interbase also lets you define referential integrity between a foreign key in the child table and a unique key that is not the primary key in the parent table. For example, suppose you have an Employee table whose primary key is EmployeeNumber and that also contains a SocialSecurityNumber column. You can create a unique index on SocialSecurityNumber and then define referential integrity between the SocialSecurityNumber column of a Payroll table and the SocialSecurityNumber Column of the Employee table.

Using Triggers

Triggers are programs that are part of the database. You write these programs in the trigger language provided by your database server. The trigger language is typically SQL with extensions. Triggers are unique in that they are executed automatically whenever any application makes a change to the table to which the trigger is attached.

Typically, you can attach a trigger to one of the following events:

- Insert
- Update
- Delete

You can also specify whether the trigger executes before or after the event. Triggers can be used for a variety of tasks. Obviously, you can use them for complex data validation. For example, you could write a trigger that would only allow a value in one field if a value had already been entered in another field. Because triggers are implemented with a full featured programming language that includes SQL data manipulation, what a trigger can do is limited only by your imagination.

Another use for triggers is logging changes. For example, you could write a trigger that would automatically create a log record in a table any time a user made a change to the salary field in an Employee table. The log table could contain the original value of the salary field, the date and time of the change, and the name of the user who made the change.

Triggers can also be used to extend the functionality of the server's referential integrity support. For example, suppose you had an Employee table and an Assignment table that shows which projects employees are assigned to. Naturally, you would define referential integrity between the parent Employee table and the Assignment table to ensure that someone could not assign a nonexistent employee to a project. Using Interbase referential integrity prevents any user from deleting an employee who is assigned to any projects. However, you could make it possible for a user to delete an employee by attaching a trigger to the before delete event of the Employee table. The trigger would delete all the records in the Assignment table for the employee so that the employee record would be deleted.

Triggers allow you to customize the data integrity rules for a table in any way that meets your needs. As with all of the other server-based data integrity features described in this chapter, triggers offer the advantage of centralizing code on the server so that the rules you program in triggers will be enforced no matter what application accesses the data. Triggers also allow you to change the rules for all applications by making a single change in one place.

Most servers also support stored procedures. A *stored procedure* is essentially the same as a trigger in that it is an object in the database that contains code written by you. The difference is that stored procedures, unlike triggers, are never called automatically by the database server in response to an event. Instead, stored procedures only execute when they are explicitly called from your application.

Chapter 27 shows examples of writing triggers and stored procedures using Interbase.

Using Views

Views can help you control data integrity by limiting a user's access to certain rows and/or columns in a table. Users cannot corrupt data they cannot access. By providing access to data through an updatable view, you can control what data a user or group of users can change.

For example, consider an Employee table that contains salary information. By defining a view that excludes the salary columns and granting certain users access to the view but not to the table, you can ensure that they do not make changes to the salary information.

Another example might be a Customer table that contains information about all customers. Assume that you have the country divided into four regions and you have a separate sales administration team for each region. You could define four views, one for each region; each would display only the records for customers in a single region. By granting users access to the appropriate view and not to the table, you ensure that the members of each sales administration team can only change records for the customers in their region.

It may seem that using views to control access to rows and columns in a table is a security issue. However, security is really just one aspect of data integrity. To ensure that data is valid, you must guarantee that:

- Invalid values are not entered into the database.
- Unauthorized users do not make changes to the database.

The next section explores using your server's security features to protect your data.

Both creating a view on the server and using a Tquery object in Delphi provide a way to use SQL statements to access a subset of the rows and/or columns in a table. If you need to dynamically change the SQL select conditions as your application runs, then a Tquery is the right tool.

627

However, in most other cases creating a view on the server is a better solution. First, creating a view on the server makes the view available to every application that uses the database. Second, you can change the selection criteria in the view without having to recompile any of your applications. Third, your server may let you create an updatable view under conditions where a Tquery will not be updatable. Keep these advantages in mind when you decide whether to use a Tquery or a Ttable and a view.

Security to Enforce Data Integrity

Database servers have powerful and flexible security systems that let you protect your data by controlling access to it. You can grant a user any of the following privileges in any combination:

- Select
- Delete
- Insert
- Update
- All of the above

In addition, you can grant a user Execute access to a stored procedure. *Execute access* grants the user the right to call the stored procedure.

You can also grant any of these rights to a stored procedure or trigger instead of to a user. This lets you write stored procedures and triggers that can perform operations that the user cannot. This is a very powerful feature, because it lets you grant users very limited access to data through a stored procedure. The only privilege the user needs is Execute for the stored procedure, and the only thing the user can do is call the stored procedure.

The privileges that a stored procedure or trigger has is the combination of the privileges that have been granted to the stored procedure or trigger and the privileges that have been granted to the user.

You give privileges to users, stored procedures, and triggers with the SQL **GRANT** command:

```
GRANT ALL ON CUSTOMER TO FRED
```

This grants all rights on the Customer table to user Fred. You can also grant multiple privileges to multiple users in a single command, as shown in the following statement:

```
GRANT INSERT, UPDATE ON CUSTOMER TO FRED, JANE, AL, SARAH, PROCEDURE
DELETE_JOB
```

This statement grants insert and update privileges to four users and one
stored procedure.

You can also grant one or more privileges to users and grant the user the
right to grant these privileges to other users with the following syntax:

```
GRANT UPDATE ON CUSTOMER TO FRED WITH GRANT OPTION
```

This not only grants Fred the ability to make changes to the Customer table,
but it also allows Fred to grant update to any other user. This is very dangerous because privileges granted by different users are cumulative.
Consider the following situation. You grant update rights to Fred and Jane
with the grant option. Fred now grants update rights to Jane and Jane grants
update rights to Fred.

Now suppose you want to revoke Fred's and Jane's update privileges.
You issue the following SQL command:

```
REVOKE UPDATE ON CUSTOMER FROM FRED, JANE
```

Can Fred and Jane still update the Customer table? Yes, because they still
have the update privileges they granted each other. You can see the night-
mare that this can lead to. Soon you will have no idea how many times a
user has been granted rights by others. When this happens, the only way to
truly revoke someone's rights to a table is to have the table's owner revoke
all rights for all users and then grant rights again for those users that are
supposed to have them.

If you are serious about security, you should have have one and only one
user grant rights. Even if you need to have more than one person grant
rights, have them do so using the same user name. That way, you will
know that you can easily and reliably revoke a user's rights if necessary.

Enforcing Data Integrity on Local Tables

Enforcing data integrity on local tables is much more difficult than on database server tables. As you have seen in the previous sections, servers provide powerful flexible tools that let you enforce any rules you can conceive
at the server so that they cannot be bypassed by any application.

This is not the case with local dBase and Paradox tables. Dbase tables have no data-integrity features of any kind. All data integrity must be enforced by code in each application that accesses the tables.

The situation is much better with Paradox tables. Paradox tables let you define the following data-integrity constraints. Once defined, these constraints are enforced by the Borland Database Engine for all applications that access the table. The Paradox constraints are:

- Minimum value for a column
- Maximum value for a column
- Default value for a column
- Lookup table (value in a column must exist in another table)
- Picture marks
- Referential integrity

While these constraints will meet many of your needs, you will probably find that most applications contain some constraints that you will have to code into the application.

Summary

A database is worthless unless the data is valid. The most important part of designing any database is careful consideration of how you will ensure data integrity. Database servers offer a wide variety of tools including triggers and constraints to help protect your data. Local table applications are more challenging because they do not support the variety of integrity features found on servers.

When considering how to enforce data integrity in your application remember that the cardinal rule is to enforce data integrity on the server whenever possible. Placing data integrity enforcement on the server ensures that the data is protected no matter how it is accessed.

Using Interbase

This chapter will introduce you to Borland's Interbase database server. If you do not have the client/server version of Delphi, you may want to skip this chapter and the next, which covers Microsoft SQL Server.

Interbase is a server worth learning about for several reasons. Perhaps the most important is that Delphi includes the local Interbase server. The *local Interbase server* is a single-user 16-bit version of Interbase that runs under Windows. Using the local Interbase server, you can develop and test complete client/server applications on a single machine before moving them to the production server.

This chapter will explore Interbase's features through the local Interbase server by creating a small database. After creating the database, you will get to use it in a Delphi program.

Understanding Interbase

Interbase is a unique database server due to its multi-versioning architecture. When multiple users are both reading and writing an Interbase database, readers are not prevented from reading while update transactions are committed, to ensure that they get a consistent view of the data. Instead, Interbase maintains multiple versions of records as necessary to guarantee that database readers always see a consistent view of the data. This approach lets both readers and writers access the data simultaneously with the best possible performance.

Interbase is highly scalable. It runs as a NetWare NLM, under Windows NT, and under many flavors of UNIX. In addition, Delphi includes a single-user 16-bit version of Interbase that you can use to develop and test a client-server application on a single PC. Once your application is ready, you simply backup the database and restore it to the production server and you are ready to go. If the number of users grows over time and you need more power on the server than a PC can deliver, you can easily scale up to a UNIX workstation as your server. The local Interbase server is also valuable because you can develop and test changes to a production application without having to have a test server or a test database on your production server.

Interbase also supports multifile databases. Using a multifile database that spans multiple disk drives can improve performance and allow you to create a database that is larger than any single drive.

One of the most impressive characteristics of Interbase is its small size. It ships on just two diskettes and requires much less disk space and memory than other servers. Using Interbase under Windows NT, NetWare, and, in the near future, Windows 95, you will be able to develop client-server systems for small and medium-size clients at a cost not much greater than the cost of using local Paradox or dBase tables.

Using ISQL

Windows ISQL is the Interbase interactive SQL tool that runs under Windows and lets you interact with a local, or remote, Interbase server through SQL statements. Using SQL you can create databases, tables, views, indexes, domains, and other Interbase objects; view the structure of database objects; and query and manipulate data in your database. You start **ISQL** by double-clicking its icon in the Delphi program group to display the screen shown in Figure 27.1.

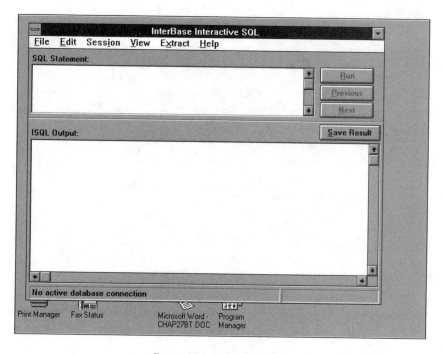

FIGURE 27.1 WINDOWS ISQL.

The ISQL screen consists of a menu, two windows, and four buttons. To use ISQL you type SQL statements in the top window and see the result in the bottom window. However, before you can do anything in ISQL except create a database you must connect to a database. To do so select **Connect To Database** from the File menu to display the Database Connect dialog box shown in Figure 27.2.

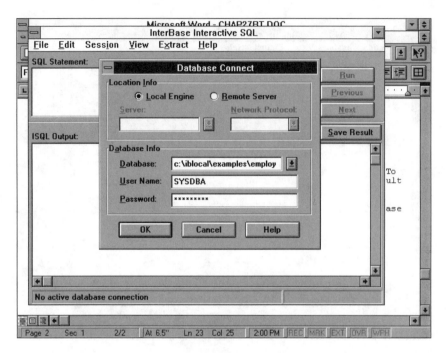

FIGURE 27.2 CONNECTING TO A DATABASE.

Enter the full path to the database, in this case C:\IBLOCAL
\EXAMPLES\EMPLOYEE.GDB, the username, and the password. When
Interbase is installed there is one valid user name, **SYSDBA**, and the
password is **masterkey**. Click **OK**, and you should see a message on the
status bar at the bottom of the window showing the database you are
connected to.

Now that you are connected, you can type a SQL statement in the SQL
Statement window, click **Run**, and see the result in the ISQL Output window, as shown in Figure 27.3.

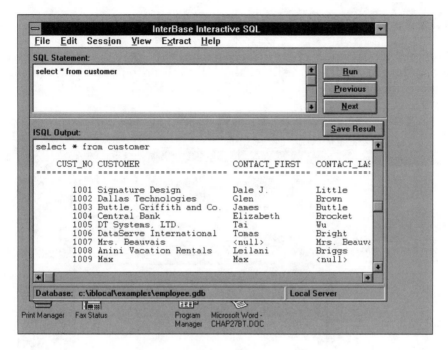

FIGURE 27.3 A SQL STATEMENT AND ITS OUTPUT.

The **Previous** and **Next** buttons below the **Run** button let you scroll through the SQL commands you have entered during this session and re-execute them at will. The **Save Result** button at the top of the ISQL Output window lets you save the contents of the output file to a text file.

You can disconnect from the current database or exit ISQL by selecting the appropriate choice from the File menu. If you have made changes to the database and the changes have not been committed, ISQL will ask if you want to commit them. You can commit or roll back transactions at any time during an ISQL session by selecting **Commit Work** or **Rollback Work** from the File menu.

Creating and Dropping a Database

From the File menu, choose **Create Database** to display the Create Database dialog box in Figure 27.4. Enter the full path to the database, your user name, and your password.

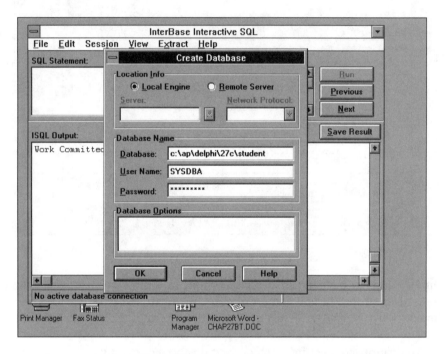

FIGURE 27.4 CREATING A DATABASE.

You can enter any of the options for the CREATE DATABASE statement in the Options area. Table 27.1 provides a brief description of the options.

TABLE 27.1 Create Database Options

Option	Description
Page =	The default page size is 1024. Options are 2048, 4096, and 8192.
Default Character Set	Lets you pick an international character set for the database.
File	Lets you define one or more secondary files so that large databases can be placed on multiple disk drives.
Starting	Sets the starting page for a secondary file.
Length =	Sets the length in pages of a secondary file. You do not need to specify a length for single-file databases, because Interbase databases will grow automatically as you add rows.

The option that needs some explanation is page size. To decide if you need to change the page size, consider the following:

- Performance is generally better if one record fits on one page. If a record spans two pages, two disk reads will be required to retrieve it.
- If the index depth exceeds four levels, increasing the page size will decrease the depth of the index and help performance.
- BLOBs are handled more efficiently if they fit on a single page. If most rows have BLOB data, consider the BLOB size in determining the page size.
- Large page sizes require more data to be transferred across the network for each read and consume more space in the disk cache.

Once you have entered any options for the database, click **OK** and Interbase will create the database and connect you to it.

If a database grows to the point that it will exceed the capacity of the drive that it is on, you can use the **ALTER DATABASE** command to add one or more secondary files to an existing database. You can also drop (delete) an existing database with the **DROP DATABASE** command or by selecting **Drop Database** from the File menu in ISQL.

Dropping a database deletes the database, all of its data, and all information about its structure.

WARNING

Shadowing a Database

Interbase lets you create a shadow copy of your database with the **CREATE SHADOW** command. By creating a shadow of your database on a different disk drive, you can continue to operate using the shadow if the drive that contains the database fails.

Shadowing does for your database what using a redundant drive array does for all your files; it protects you from a hard disk failure. Using shadowing requires twice the disk space because it stores a complete copy of your database. If you are already using a redundant drive array to store your database, the additional cost may not be worth it.

Remember that shadowing is worthless unless the shadow is not on the same drive as the database.

WARNING

Creating Tables

As with all other servers, you create Interbase tables with the SQL **CREATE TABLE** statement. You can type CREATE TABLE statements in the SQL Statement window of ISQL, but you probably will not want to. CREATE TABLE statements are frequently long and complex, and you may want to save and modify them during development. To meet this need, ISQL lets you create and run ISQL scripts.

ISQL Scripts

An ISQL *script* is a text file that contains a series of SQL statements. By default, ISQL expects a file extension of .SQL. The following code is a simple ISQL script to create the Student, Course, and Registration tables. This script is **CRETBL.SQL** on the included program disk. The following sections will examine this script in detail and describe all of the features and options it uses.

```
CONNECT "c:\ap\delphi\27c\student.gdb"
  USER "SYSDBA" PASSWORD "masterkey";

CREATE DOMAIN DSTUDENT_ID INTEGER NOT NULL;
CREATE DOMAIN DCOURSE_ID CHAR(4) NOT NULL;

CREATE TABLE STUDENT
  (STUDENT_ID DSTUDENT_ID,
   LAST_NAME VARCHAR(24) NOT NULL,
   FIRST_NAME VARCHAR(20) NOT NULL,
   SSN CHAR(9) NOT NULL,
   CLASS_YEAR SMALLINT NOT NULL,
   STUDENT_NAME COMPUTED BY (FIRST_NAME || " " || LAST_NAME),
   CONSTRAINT STUDENT_PRIMARY_KEY PRIMARY KEY (STUDENT_ID),
   CONSTRAINT SSN_UNIQUE UNIQUE (SSN),
   CONSTRAINT CLASS_YEAR_RANGE CHECK (CLASS_YEAR >= 1 AND CLASS_YEAR <=
4));

CREATE TABLE COURSE
  (COURSE_ID DCOURSE_ID,
   COURSE_DESC VARCHAR(40) NOT NULL,
   COURSE_DEPARTMENT CHAR(12) NOT NULL,
   CONSTRAINT COURSE_PRIMARY_KEY PRIMARY KEY (COURSE_ID));

CREATE TABLE REGISTRATION
  (STUDENT_ID DSTUDENT_ID,
   COURSE_ID DCOURSE_ID,
   CONSTRAINT REG_PRIMARY_KEY PRIMARY KEY (STUDENT_ID, COURSE_ID),
   CONSTRAINT REG_FOREIGN_KEY_STUDENT_ID
     FOREIGN KEY (STUDENT_ID) REFERENCES STUDENT,
   CONSTRAINT REG_FOREIGN_KEY_COURSE_ID
     FOREIGN KEY (COURSE_ID) REFERENCES COURSE);

EXIT;
```

When you write an ISQL script, remember that:

- The script must begin by either creating or connecting to a database.
- Each SQL statement in the script file must end with a semicolon.

- The script should end with **Exit** to commit the changes made by the script or **Quit** to rollback the changes. If you do not include either, ISQL commits your changes by default.

To run the script select **File | Run an ISQL script...** from the ISQL menu. After selecting the script file to run, you will be asked if you want to save the output to a file as shown in Figure 27.5. Always click **Yes**.

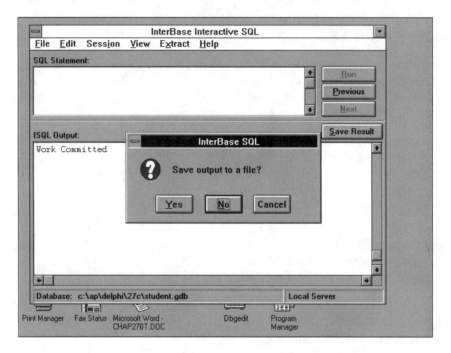

FIGURE 27.5 SAVE SCRIPT OUTPUT TO A FILE.

If errors occur when your script runs, you will have no way to find out what they were if you do not save the output to a file. If you choose **Yes**, then the SQL statements from your script file will be written to the output file, interspersed with any error messages generated by Interbase. ISQL processes your script and displays a dialog box telling you that your script completed and whether errors occurred. If there are errors you can review the output file, edit your script file to correct them, and try again.

The Sample Tables

The script in the preceding section creates three tables: Student, Course, and Registration. These tables comprise the classic solution to a many-to-many relationship in a relational database. In this case, one student can take many courses and one course can be taken by many students. The Registration table provides the link between them by showing which students are registered for which courses. The relationships are shown in Figure 27.6.

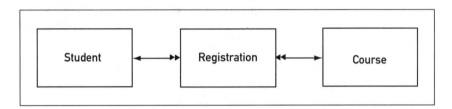

FIGURE 27.6 STUDENT, COURSE, AND REGISTRATION RELATIONSHIPS.

Understanding the CRETBL.SQL Script

This section will examine the ISQL script that creates the Student, Course, and Registration tables in order from top to bottom starting with the following CONNECT statement:

```
CONNECT "c:\ap\delphi\27c\student.gdb"
  USER "SYSDBA" PASSWORD "masterkey";
```

Before your script can do anything with the objects in a database it must connect to the database. You can either connect to an existing database, as shown above, or create a new one with CREATE DATABASE. The remaining statements in the script create objects in the database. However, before creating any tables you need to be familiar with the Interbase data types.

Data Types

Interbase provides a rich set of data types that allow you to store virtually anything in your database.

BLOB	The BLOB, for Binary Large Object, type is designed to store unlimited amounts of any type of data. Interbase neither knows nor cares what the data represents. You can store graphical images or drawings, sound files, full-motion video, satellite telemetry data, text, or anything else you can convert to digital form.
CHAR	The char data type stores a fixed amount of text, from 1 to 32,767 bytes. This is a good choice for alphanumeric information where the amount of text in each row is identical, or nearly so. Part numbers or social security numbers are examples. If the value is less than the column size, Interbase pads the value with trailing blanks.
DATE	The date type stores date and time information. Dates can range from January 1, 100 to December 11, 5941.
Decimal	Decimal is a SQL data type that stores a number with a fixed number of digits to the right of the decimal point. When you define a Decimal column, you can specify the precision of the value, that is, the total number of digits to be stored. Optionally, you can also specify a scale that is the number of fractional digits. For example, Decimal(10,2) specifies a ten-digit number with two digits to the right of the decimal and eight to the left. With the Decimal type the number of digits stored is at least the precision you specified.
Double Precision	Doubles store floating-point numbers to 15 digits of precision in 64 bits on most platforms.
Float	The Float type is a single-precision 32-bit floating-point number that stores values to seven digits of precision.
Integer	The Integer type is a 32-bit signed binary integer with a range from −2,147,483,648 to 2,147,483,648.
Numeric	Like Decimal, Numeric is a SQL data type. The only difference between Decimal and Numeric is that Numeric stores exactly the number of digits specified by its precision, while a Decimal stores at least the number of digits specified by its precision.
SmallInt	SmallInt is a 16-bit binary integer with a range from −32,768 to 32,767.
Varchar	Use the Varchar type to store strings of text whose length varies from row to row. Interbase stores only the characters you enter, so short values consume less disk space than long ones. The maximum size for Varchar is 32,765 characters.

Domains

Domains are templates for columns in tables. In most databases there are columns that appear in one table as the primary key and in one or more others as foreign keys. To ensure that these columns are declared consistently wherever they appear, define a domain and use the domain to define the column. The **CRETBL.SQL** script defines two domains with the following CREATE DOMAIN statements:

```
CREATE DOMAIN DSTUDENT_ID INTEGER NOT NULL;
CREATE DOMAIN DCOURSE_ID CHAR(4) NOT NULL;
```

The first statement defines the DSTUDENT_ID domain with a data type of Integer and the Not Null constraint. Not Null ensures that the column cannot be left blank. This domain is used later in the script to define the primary key of the Student table and a foreign key in Registration.

The second domain is DCOURSE_ID, which is a four-character field that has the Not Null constraint. This domain is used to define the primary key of the Course table and a foreign key in Registration.

While ensuring consistency between primary and foreign key declarations is important, domains can play a much more important role in your database strategy. You can also define domains for types of columns, even though they will not necessarily hold the same data. For example, you could define domains for all of the following:

```
Last_Name
First_Name
Middle_Initial
Salutation
Title
Social_Security_Number
Company_Name
Address_Line
City
State
Zip_Code
Country
```

Defining a robust set of domains will ensure that similar data is stored the same way in all of your tables across all of your databases. This will make the data easier to relate and use.

Tables, Indexes, Computed Columns, and Constraints

The next three statements in the **CRETBL.SQL** script create the three tables. The following statement creates the Student table:

```
CREATE TABLE STUDENT
  (STUDENT_ID DSTUDENT_ID,
   LAST_NAME VARCHAR(24) NOT NULL,
   FIRST_NAME VARCHAR(20) NOT NULL,
   SSN CHAR(9) NOT NULL,
   CLASS_YEAR SMALLINT NOT NULL,
   STUDENT_NAME COMPUTED BY (FIRST_NAME || " " || LAST_NAME),
   CONSTRAINT STUDENT_PRIMARY_KEY PRIMARY KEY (STUDENT_ID),
   CONSTRAINT SSN_UNIQUE UNIQUE (SSN),
   CONSTRAINT CLASS_YEAR_RANGE CHECK (CLASS_YEAR >= 1 AND CLASS_YEAR <= 4));
```

The table consists of six columns, STUDENT_ID, LAST_NAME, FIRST_NAME, SSN, CLASS_YEAR, and STUDENT_NAME. Note that no data type is given for STUDENT_ID. The domain name DSTUDENT_ID is used instead to specify both the type and the Not Null constraint. You can add constraints to or override the domain definition in the CREATE TABLE statement. The SSN and CLASS_YEAR columns also include the NOT NULL constraint.

STUDENT_NAME is a computed field. It is not actually stored in the table. Instead it is computed from other fields in the table and from literals. In this case, STUDENT_NAME is computed as FIRST_NAME plus a space plus LAST_NAME.

Never store a value in a table that can be computed from other values. It wastes disk space and requires you to write code to update the column whenever one of the values it is derived from changes.

T I P

Following the column definitions are a series of constraint clauses. Many of the constraints could also have been defined as part of the column definition. For example, to make STUDENT_ID the primary key, the column definition could have been changed to:

```
(STUDENT_ID DSTUDENT_ID PRIMARY KEY,
```

However, in Interbase you should not do it this way, even though it involves less typing. Constraints are identified by name, and you cannot assign a name when you include a constraint as part of the column definition. If you do not or cannot provide a name for a constraint, Interbase creates one for you. Unfortunately,, the names that Interbase creates make no sense in terms of what the constraint is. Therefore, when a user violates the constraint, he or she will get an error message something like **Key violation $RDB_INTEG0043**, which is not a big help. It is much better to define your constraints in a CONSTRAINT clause, where you can assign a meaningful name. By declaring the primary key for the Student table with the line

```
CONSTRAINT STUDENT_PRIMARY_KEY PRIMARY KEY (STUDENT_ID),
```

the message will become something like **Key violation STUDENT_PRI-MARY_KEY**, which is much more helpful.

Defining STUDENT_ID as the primary key tells Interbase to create a unique index on this field. In addition, the primary key can never be null so you cannot use the Primary Key constraint on a column in Interbase unless that column also has the Not Null constraint.

The SSN (social security number) column is defined as nine characters with both the Not Null and Unique constraints. The Unique constraint is defined in the second CONSTRAINT clause and makes Interbase create a unique index on this column. Interbase will use the index to ensure uniqueness when rows are added or changed.

This table also includes a Check constraint on CLASS_YEAR. This constraint prevents any value from being entered in the CLASS_YEAR field except 1, 2, 3, or 4. You can also use Check constraints to validate data between fields. For example, you could use a Check constraint to make sure that the ship date is greater than the order date.

The CREATE TABLE statement for the Course table is shown below and does not use any new features.

```
CREATE TABLE COURSE
  (COURSE_ID DCOURSE_ID,
   COURSE_DESC VARCHAR(40) NOT NULL,
   COURSE_DEPARTMENT CHAR(12) NOT NULL,
   CONSTRAINT COURSE_PRIMARY_KEY PRIMARY KEY (COURSE_ID));
```

The table consists of three columns with COURSE_ID as the primary key. The final CREATE TABLE statement creates the Registration table as follows:

```
CREATE TABLE REGISTRATION
  (STUDENT_ID DSTUDENT_ID,
   COURSE_ID DCOURSE_ID,
   CONSTRAINT REG_PRIMARY_KEY PRIMARY KEY (STUDENT_ID, COURSE_ID),
   CONSTRAINT REG_FOREIGN_KEY_STUDENT_ID
     FOREIGN KEY (STUDENT_ID) REFERENCES STUDENT,
```

```
CONSTRAINT REG_FOREIGN_KEY_COURSE_ID
   FOREIGN KEY (COURSE_ID) REFERENCES COURSE);
```

The Registration table also contains the STUDENT_ID and COURSE_ID columns, which are defined by their respective domains. Here, the table's primary key must be defined in the PRIMARY KEY clause at the end of the column definitions because the primary key consists of both the STUDENT_ID and COURSE_ID columns.

In addition, two CONSTRAINT clauses define the STUDENT_ID and COURSE_ID as foreign keys of Student and Course, respectively. Foreign keys are used by Interbase to implement referential integrity.

Foreign Keys and Referential Integrity

Interbase lets you define foreign keys to implement referential integrity as part of the CREATE TABLE syntax. The concept of foreign keys and referential integrity was discussed in Chapter 26 and is not repeated here.

When you define a foreign key for a table, Interbase automatically creates an index for the foreign key field or fields. The index allows Interbase to quickly find the rows that contain a particular foreign key value.

One problem with foreign keys is a circular reference. To enforce referential integrity, Interbase will not allow you to use a foreign key value that does not yet exist in the parent table. The problem occurs when you have two tables, both of which contain each other's primary keys as foreign keys. If you need to add a new record to both tables and the two new records reference each other, you are stuck.

The Employee database that ships with Interbase contains an example using the Employee and Department tables. The primary keys are Emp_No and Dept_No, respectively. The Employee table contains Dept_No as a foreign key to identify the department the employee is assigned to. The Department table contains Emp_No as a foreign key to identify the person who is the head of the department. When you hire a new person to head a new department you have a problem. You cannot add the Department row first because the Employee row does not exist and you cannot add the Employee row first because the Department row does not exist.

Interbase solves this problem by letting you insert a new row with a blank foreign key value. In this example, you could insert a new row in the Department table and leave the Emp_No field blank. Then insert the new row in the Employee table including the new Dept_No. Finally you can update the Department entry to add the new Emp_No.

Indexes

Index design is one of the most important aspects of database design because it has a powerful impact on performance. However, Interbase also uses indexes to:

- Provide links between tables.
- Control the order in which data is viewed.
- Enforce uniqueness on the values in one or more columns.

When processing SQL select statements, the Interbase query optimizer always determines which indexes are available. That can be used to speed selection of the records you requested. Indexes can be built on either single or multiple columns.

Multicolumn indexes are also used to select records based on the value of a single column if the single column is the first column of the index. For example, given a composite index on the City and State columns, the index will be used to select records by either City alone or by the combination of City and State. The index cannot be used to select records by State alone because it is not in order by State.

Indexes are a two-edged sword. When you add an index to a table, you increase the time it takes to add and delete rows and to change rows, if one or more of the fields in the index is modified. Indexes also consume disk space. However, the increase in time to add, delete, or update a row is only a fraction of a second per index; the savings in retrieval time can be very large on large tables. Therefore, if an index will improve row-selection speed, you should create it. Interbase uses indexes to improve performance in the following situations:

- The column is used to join this table with others.
- The column is used to select rows.
- The column is used in the ORDER BY clause of a SQL statement.

There is one case where you may need to do some testing to determine whether an index will improve performance. When a column contains a small number of unique values, then a large percentage of the rows will be selected for any value. In this case, it may be faster to omit the index and let Interbase scan the table sequentially. One example is a column that contains only Yes or No. When working with a small number of unique values, the only way to find out whether an index improves speed is to test with and without the index.

If the number of unique values in an indexed column changes greatly, you should recompute the index selectivity using the **SET STATISTICS** command.

TIP

For example, SET STATISTICS INDEX NAMEX recomputes the selectivity of the NAMEX index. Selectivity is a value that the query optimizer uses to decide whether to use an index for a particular query. If the number of unique values in an index changes substantially and you do not recompute selectivity, the optimizer may not use the index when it should.

Enforcing Uniqueness

One reason to create an index, even if you will never use it to select or order records, is to enforce uniqueness on a column or a combination of columns. By default, Interbase indexes are not unique; however, you can specify uniqueness as a property of the index when you create it. For example, if you have an Employee table that is keyed by EmployeeNumber and the table also contains the employee's social security number, you may want to create a unique index on the SSN field to ensure that duplicate social security numbers cannot be entered. The statement

```
CREATE UNIQUE INDEX SSNX ON EMPLOYEE (SSN)
```

will create a unique index on the SSN column because it contains the UNIQUE keyword. If you define a column as unique in a CREATE TABLE statement, Interbase will create a unique index on that column automatically. Interbase will also automatically create a unique index on the column or columns that you define as the primary key in your CREATE TABLE statement.

You cannot create a unique index on a column or group of columns that already contain duplicate values.

NOTE

Specifying Index Sort Order

You can also specify the sort order of an index when you create it. By default, the index will be in ascending order. Although you can include the ASCENDING keyword in a CREATE INDEX statement, it is not necessary. To make the index descending, use the DESCENDING keyword, as in the following example:

```
CREATE DESCENDING INDEX SHIPX ON ORDERS (SHIP_DATE)
```

This statement creates a descending index on the Ship_Date column of the Orders table. Descending indexes are particularly useful on dates, where users frequently want to see the most recent information first.

649

Using Multicolumn Versus Single-Column Indexes

There are two reasons to use composite (multicolumn) indexes. The first is to enforce uniqueness on a combination of columns. In a table that records which students are taking which courses, both the Student_ID and the Course_Id can occur many times; however, the combination of Student_ID and Course_Id should be unique. You would not want the same student registered for the same course multiple times.

The second use for composite indexes is to speed searches on more than one column. Using a table that records the inventory of cars at several showrooms, you might want to run queries similar to the following:

```
SELECT * FROM INVENTORY
  WHERE MODEL = 'Mustang' AND COLOR = 'Blue'
```

This query will run faster with a single composite index on both the Model and Color columns than with a single field index on each column. That is not true, however, of the following query:

```
SELECT * FROM INVENTORY
  WHERE MODEL = 'Mustang' OR COLOR = 'Blue'
```

TIP

If a query includes a logical OR condition between two columns, Interbase will perform faster if each column has its own index.

Remember also that a query does not have to select rows based on all of the columns of a composite index in order to use the index effectively. The index will help as long as the query uses the first N columns of the index, where N is any number from one through the number of columns in the index. So, if an index includes the Student_ID, Course_ID, and Campus fields, a query that selects records on the Student_ID field will use the index and so will a query that selects records using Student_ID and Course_ID. However, a query that selects on Course_ID alone will derive no benefit from the index.

NOTE

An index will speed up a query if the indexed fields are only referenced in the ORDER BY clause and are not used in the WHERE clause, because Interbase will not have to sort the result set.

Inactivating and Activating Indexes for Performance

You can inactivate and activate an index at any time using the **ALTER INDEX** command as follows:

```
ALTER INDEX NAMEX INACTIVE
ALTER INDEX NAMEX ACTIVE
```

There are two reasons to do this. The first is to balance the index. Over time, as many records are added to and deleted from a table, the organization of the index can become less efficient. When you inactivate an index and then activate it again, Interbase rebuilds it in the most efficient way for the records that exist in the table at that time. Tables that undergo many of changes should have their indexes rebuilt periodically to provide the best possible performance. If a table is fairly static, rebuilding the indexes is not necessary.

The second reason to inactivate an index is to improve performance when you make many changes at one time. For example, suppose you are going to add a large number of records to a table in a single insert operation or change an indexed column in a very large number of rows with a single update. Interbase will update the index each time a row is inserted or changed. When you make bulk changes that will affect many rows, it will be faster to inactivate the affected indexes, make the changes, and activate the indexes again.

Remember that views are based on SELECT statements, and their performance will improve if you create the appropriate indexes.

T I P

Using Views

Like most servers, Interbase lets you create views that consist of selected rows and columns from one or more existing tables or from other views. A view may be either read only or updatable. To be updatable, an Interbase view must meet all of the following conditions:

- The view must be derived from a single table or from another updatable view.
- Any columns that are not included in the view must allow null values.
- The view's select statement cannot include subqueries, DISTINCT, HAVING, aggregate functions, joined tables, user-defined functions, or stored procedures.

The Student database includes a single view that shows the courses for the Math department. The view is created using the **CREATE VIEW** command in the ISQL script **CREVIEW.SQL** shown in Figure 27.7.

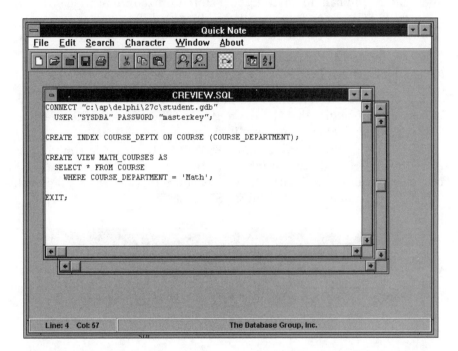

FIGURE 27.7 ISQL SCRIPT TO CREATE THE **MATH_COURSES** VIEW.

Note that the script not only creates the view but also creates an index on the COURSE_DEPARTMENT column of the Course table. The index improves the performance of the select for the view dramatically if the table is large and there are many unique values in the column.

Using Stored Procedures, Triggers, and Generators

Interbase supports both stored procedures and triggers. Both are code modules that you write in the Interbase Procedure and Trigger Language and that become part of the metadata of your database. The difference between a stored procedure and a trigger is how and when they are called.

Stored procedures are explicitly called by your code. Triggers are called automatically when some event occurs in the database. For example, you could create a trigger that is called every time a new row is inserted into the Student table. You can do anything in a stored procedure or trigger that you can do with SQL since Interbase Procedure and Trigger Language is an extended version of SQL with flow control statements added.

Stored Procedures

Stored procedures can return one or more values or they can return no values. A stored procedure that returns multiple values behaves like a table in that you can view its data and query it to get a subset of its data.

The ISQL script in Figure 27.8, **CRESTOR.SQL**, creates a simple stored procedure that returns the number of students that have registered for classes. This is an example of a stored procedure that returns a single value via the return parameter REGISTERED_STUDENTS.

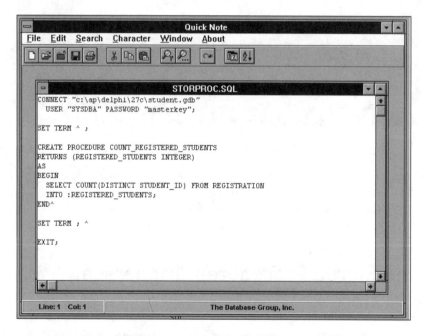

FIGURE 27.8 ISQL SCRIPT TO CREATE A STORED PROCEDURE.

This script is different from the others in this chapter because it uses the command

```
SET TERM ^ ;
```

to overcome a problem that occurs when you define stored procedures and triggers. The problem occurs because in an ISQL script a semicolon terminates a SQL statement. The problem is that the CREATE PROCEDURE and CREATE TRIGGER statements contain other statements that end with a semicolon. ISQL will assume that the first semicolon it encounters is the end of the CREATE statement, and that is not true.

The solution is to use SET TERM to change the termination character to something other than a semicolon, in this case a caret. After all of the CREATE statements, SET TERM is used again to set the terminator back to a semicolon.

Generators

A generator is an object you define to generate unique numbers in an Interbase database. Once you create a generator, it becomes part of the database's metadata and cannot be removed. The Student database uses a generator named STUDENT_ID_GEN to generate a unique new id number for each new row in the Student table. The following code is the complete listing of CRESTOR.SQL.

```
CONNECT "c:\ap\delphi\27c\student.gdb"
  USER "SYSDBA" PASSWORD "masterkey";

SET TERM ^ ;

CREATE PROCEDURE COUNT_REGISTERED_STUDENTS
RETURNS (REGISTERED_STUDENTS INTEGER)
AS
BEGIN
  SELECT COUNT(DISTINCT STUDENT_ID) FROM REGISTRATION
  INTO :REGISTERED_STUDENTS;
END^

CREATE GENERATOR STUDENT_ID_GEN^
SET GENERATOR STUDENT_ID_GEN TO 200^

CREATE PROCEDURE GET_NEW_STUDENT_ID
RETURNS (NEW_STUDENT_ID INTEGER)
AS
BEGIN
  NEW_STUDENT_ID = GEN_ID (STUDENT_ID_GEN, 1);
END^

SET TERM ; ^

EXIT;
```

The first CREATE PROCEDURE statement counts the number of registered students and was described briefly in the preceding section. The next statement creates a generator named STUDENT_ID_GEN, and the following statement sets its initial value to 200.

The last CREATE PROCEDURE statement defines the GET_NEW_STUDENT_ID stored procedure. When you call this stored procedure, it calls the Interbase GEN_ID() function to get the next unique value from the STUDENT_ID_GEN generator and returns that value via the NEW_STUDENT_ID return parameter.

Triggers

Triggers are also written in the Interbase Procedure and Trigger Language. However, triggers are executed automatically when data is changed. A trigger can be defined to execute either before or after an insert, delete, or update operation on a table.

Figure 27.9 shows the script that creates the STUDENT_DELETE trigger for the Student database. This trigger performs a cascaded delete on the Student table.

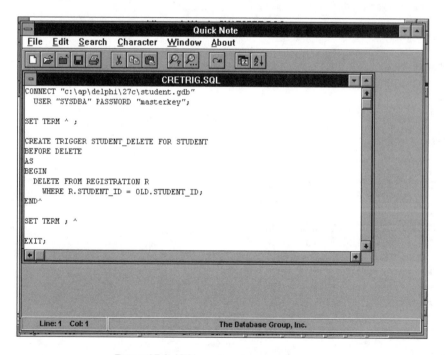

FIGURE 27.9 ISQL SCRIPT TO CREATE A TRIGGER.

Since referential integrity is defined by the foreign key declaration on STU-DENT_ID in the Registration table you cannot delete a row from the Student table if that student has records in the Registration table. This trigger solves that problem by cascading the delete of a Student record to the Registration table.

The STUDENT_DELETE trigger occurs before a delete in the Student table. The trigger deletes all records from the Registration table that have the same STUDENT_ID as the record in the Student table that is about to be deleted. The OLD context variable lets you refer to the values in the columns of a record that is being deleted or updated, so in this trigger OLD.STUDENT_ID refers to the value of STUDENT_ID in the Student table. Interbase also provides a NEW context variable that lets you refer to the new values during an insert or update operation.

Using the Student Database in Delphi

This section describes the steps to build a complete client/server application that uses the student database. Start by selecting **File** I **A_lias** from the Database Desktop menu to create an alias named **Student** that points to the **STUDENT.GDB** database. Figure 27.10 shows the alias definition.

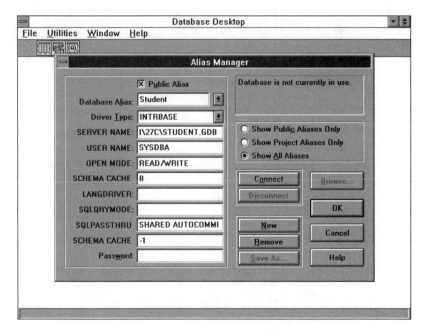

FIGURE 27.10 STUDENT ALIAS DEFINITION

Figure 27.11 shows the form for the **STUDENT.DPR** project on the included code disk.

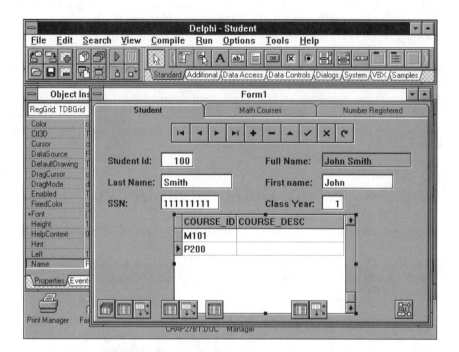

FIGURE 27.11 STUDENT PAGE OF THE **STUDENT.DPR** FORM

To create this form, follow these steps:

1. Start by placing a TabbedNotebook from the Additional page of the Component palette on the form. Set its Align property to **alClient** so it fills the form. Create three tabs—**Student**, **Math Courses**, and **Number Registered**—by setting the notebook's Pages property.

2. Add a Database component from the Data Access page of the form. Set the AliasName property to **Student** and the DatabaseName property to **Student.gdb**. Finally, set the Connected property to **True** and name the component **StudentDb**.

3. Add two Table components and two DataSource components from the Data Controls page to the form.

4. Name the first Table **StudentTbl**. Set its DatabaseName to **Student.gdb** and its TableName to **Student**. Last, set its Active property to **True**.

5. Name the first DataSource **StudentSrc** and set its DataSet property to **StudentTbl**.

6. Name the second Table **RegistrationTbl**. Set its DatabaseName to **Student.gdb** and its TableName to **Registration**. Next, link it to StudentTbl by setting its MasterSource property to **StudentSrc** and its MasterFields property to **STUDENT_ID**. Finally, set the Active property to **True**.

7. Select the **RegistrationTbl** object, right-click, and open the **Fields Editor**. Click the **Add** button, then click **OK** to create a TField object for each column in the table. Select the **STUDENT_ID** field, then set its Visible property to **False** in the Object Inspector. This will prevent this field from being displayed in a DBGrid. Since it will be the same as the STUDENT_ID shown for the Student table, there is no need to display it again for every record in the Registration table grid.

8. Click the **Define** button in the Fields Editor and define a calculated field named **COURSE_DESC**. Since it is not very meaningful to show only the course number, this will add a field you can use to get the description from the Course table.

9. Name the second DataSource **RegistrationSrc** and set its DataSet to **RegistrationTbl**.

10. Add six Labels and six DBEdits as arranged as shown in Figure 27.11. Set the DataSource property for all six DBEdits to **StudentSrc** and set the FieldName for each DBEdit to the appropriate field. Set the ReadOnly property for the Full Name edit control to **True**. Since the FULL_NAME column is a computed column. you cannot edit it.

11. Add a DBNavigator and set its DataSource to **StudentSrc**. Also set its ShowHints property to **True** to enable fly-by help for the navigator buttons.

12. Add a DBGrid to the bottom of the form as shown in Figure 27.11 and set its DataSource property to **RegistrationSrc**. Name the grid **RegGrid**.

At this point you should be able to compile and run your program. When you run, it you will be prompted for a user name and password to login to the server. If you do not want to be bothered with the login prompt while you are testing you can add your user name and password to the Database component's Params property, as shown in Figure 27.12. Just click the **Params** property, then click the ellipsis button to open the String List Editor. After you have entered your user name and password, set the LoginPrompt property to **False**. While this is handy during development, be sure to remove these parameters and turn the login prompt back on before giving the program to users so that server security is not compromised.

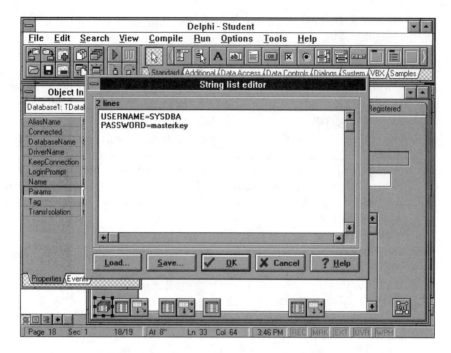

FIGURE 27.12 SETTING THE DATABASE COMPONENTS PARAMS PROPERTY.

The next step is to add another Table component to the form as follows:

1. Add a Table component to the form.
2. Set its DataBase property to **Student.gdb** and its TableName to **COURSE**.
3. Name the Table component **CourseTbl**.

Now add the following code to the OnCalcFields event handler for RegistrationTbl:

```
procedure TForm1.RegistrationTblCalcFields(DataSet: TDataset);
begin
  {Find the record for this course in the Course
   table.}
  if CourseTbl.FindKey([RegistrationTblCOURSE_ID]) then
```

```
begin
  RegistrationTblCOURSE_DESC.Value :=
    CourseTblCOURSE_DESC.Value;
  end;
end;
```

This code uses the FindKey method to locate the record in the Course table with the same COURSE_ID as the current record in the grid and then assigns the value of the COURSE_DESC field in Course to the calculated COURSE_DESC field in the grid.

Since the COURSE_DESC field in the grid is calculated and cannot be edited, you may want to display it in a different color. To do so, add the following code to the DBGrid's OnDrawDataCell event handler:

```
procedure TForm1.RegGridDrawDataCell(Sender: TObject; const Rect: TRect;
  Field: TField; State: TGridDrawState);
begin
  with RegGrid do
    if Field = RegistrationTblCourse_Desc then
    begin
      Canvas.Brush.Color := clGray;
      Canvas.Font.Color := clWhite;
      DefaultDrawDataCell(Rect,Field,State);
    end;
end;
```

This code checks to see if the grid cell being drawn is RegistrationTblCourse_Desc. If it is, the code changes the canvas brush color to gray. The brush color is the background color for the cell. Next, the code changes the font color to white, and finally it calls the DefaultDrawDataCell method to draw the cell with these colors.

Using Views

You will use the second page of the notebook to display the MATH_COURSES view. Recall that this is an editable view of the Courses table that shows only the courses offered by the Math department. Create the second page as follows (Figure 27.13 shows the finished Math Courses page):

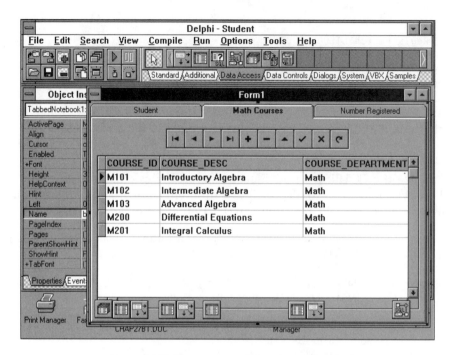

FIGURE 27.13 THE COMPLETED MATH COURSES PAGE.

1. Select the notebook, right-click, and select **Next Page**.
2. Add a Table component and a DataSource component to the form.
3. Set the Table component's name to **MathCoursesTbl**, its DatabaseName to **Student.gdb**, and its TableName to **MATH_COURSES**. Notice that although MATH_COURSES is a view, it appears in the TableName drop-down list with the rest of the tables. A view is indistinguishable from a table to Delphi.
4. Set the DataSource's name to **MathCoursesSrc** and its DataSet to **MathCoursesTbl**.
5. Add a DBGrid to the form and set its DataSource property to **MathCoursesSrc**.
6. Add a DBNavigator to the form and set its DataSource property to **MathCoursesSrc**.

Run the program and you should be able to select the **Math Courses** tab and scroll through the view. Working with an Interbase view is no different than working with a table in your Delphi applications. Views let you control access for increased security and better performance.

Using Stored Procedures

The third page of the form, Number Registered, shows how to use a stored procedure in your form. The following steps will complete the Number Registered page, as shown in Figure 27.14:

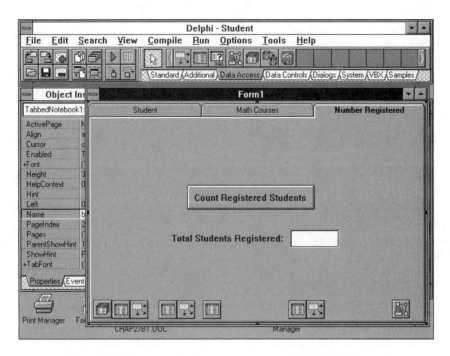

FIGURE 27.14 NUMBER REGISTERED PAGE OF THE STUDENT.DPR FORM.

1. Select the **TabbedNotbook**, right-click, and select **Next Page** until you reach the Number Registered page.

2. Add a StoredProc component from the Data Access page of the palette to the form. Set the DatabaseName to **Student.gdb** and select the **COUNT_REGISTERED_STUDENTS** stored procedure from the StoredProcName drop-down list. Last, set the StoredProc's Name to **RegCountProc**.

3. Add a Label and an Edit component as shown in Figure 27.14. Name the Edit component **RegCountEdit**.

4. Add a button, name it **RegCountBtn**, and set its caption to **Count Registered Students**.

Now that all of the components are in position, add the following code to the OnClick handler for RegCountBtn:

```
procedure TForm1.RegCountBtnClick(Sender: TObject);
begin
  with RegCountProc do
  begin
    Prepare;
    ExecProc;
    RegCountEdit.Text := Params[0].AsString;
  end;
end;
```

This code prepares and executes the stored procedure and then retrieves the count of registered students from its single parameter.

Generating a Unique ID

When a new Student record is inserted, the system must generate a unique new value for the STUDENT_ID field. The following code from the StudentTbl Table's OnNewRecord event handle does the job:

```
procedure TForm1.StudentTblNewRecord(DataSet: TDataset);
begin
  {When a new record is inserted call the
   NewStudentIdProc stored procedure which uses a
   generator in the database to get a unique
   Studetn_Id.}
  with NewStudentIdProc do
  begin
    Prepare;
    ExecProc;
    StudentTblSTUDENT_ID.Value := Params[0].AsInteger;
  end;
end;
```

This code calls a second StoredProc component that you must add to the form. This StoredProc, named NewStudentIdProc, calls the GET_NEW_STUDENT_ID stored procedure, which returns the next value from the STUDENT_ID_GEN generator. The returned value is assigned to the STUDENT_ID field of the new record.

You may be wondering why we do not use a trigger to insert the new value into the STUDENT_ID field automatically on the server. This will not work in Delphi if you have added the STUDENT_ID field to the list of fields in the fields editor. To understand why, you need to follow the steps that the BDE performs when you insert a new row:

1. You insert a new row.
2. BDE posts the row with a blank key.
3. Unbeknown to BDE, Interbase changes the primary key from blank to a new unique number.
4. BDE tries to reread the record to maintain position on the new record after it has been posted. When it tries to read the record using the value blank for the key, it cannot find it and generates an error.

To avoid this problem, use the technique described earlier or do not add the key field in the fields editor.

Using Transactions

Delphi will implicitly start a transaction whenever you change a row in a table on a database server and will automatically commit the transaction when you post the changed row. However, this is not the best way to handle transaction processing if transactions involve multiple changes. If a transaction includes many changes to a single table or changes to multiple tables, all the changes should be part of a single transaction.

Delphi's Database component provides three methods that let you explicitly control transactions with any database server. The three methods are StartTransaction, Commit, and Rollback. The Student application uses explicit transaction control by ensuring that there is always an active transaction. It begins by starting a transaction when the form opens using the following code on the form's OnShow event handler:

```
procedure TForm1.FormShow(Sender: TObject);
begin
  {Start a transaction immediately when the form
   is opened.}
  StudentDb.StartTransaction;
end;
```

To manage the transaction as users make changes to the tables, the following code is added to the AfterEdit and AfterCanel event handlers for each of the tables displayed on the form. The following code is from the StudentTbl component:

```
procedure TForm1.StudentTblAfterEdit(DataSet: TDataset);
begin
  StudentDb.Commit;
  StudentDb.StartTransaction;
end;

procedure TForm1.StudentTblAfterCancel(DataSet: TDataset);
begin
  RollbackAndRefresh;
end;
```

The AfterEdit code commits the changes the user has made and starts a new transaction. The code in the AfterCancel procedure calls a custom method, RollbackAndRefresh, which rolls back the current transactions and refreshes all of the TTable components so that they reflect the current state of the database. This method also starts a new transaction. Here is the code for RollbackAndRefresh:

```
procedure TForm1.RollbackAndRefresh;
begin
  {Rollback the current transaction, start a new
   transaction and refresh all tables.}
  StudentDb.Rollback;
  StudentDb.StartTransaction;
  StudentTbl.Refresh;
  RegistrationTbl.Refresh;
  MathCoursesTbl.Refresh;
end;
```

That leaves only one problem. What happens if something unexpected happens that causes an exception during a transaction? For example, suppose a user tries to delete a student's record. This will fire the STUDENT_DELETE trigger, which will delete the Registration records for the student. Suppose an error occurs and the Registration records are deleted but the Student record is not. You need to detect the exception and rollback the transaction. To handle this, the Student program uses a custom exception handler, as described in Chapter 20. The following method is the customer exception handler:

```
procedure TForm1.AppOnException(Sender: TObject; E: Exception);
begin
  {Display the error message.}
  MessageDlg(E.Message, mtError, [mbOK], 0);
  {If this is a database exception rollback the
   current transaction and refresh the tables.}
  if E is EDatabaseError then
    try
      RollbackAndRefresh;
    except
      on EDatabaseError do
    end;
end;
```

Whenever an exception occurs that is not handled by a try/except block, this default exception handler is called. It begins by displaying the error message in a dialog box. It then checks to see if this exception is of the EDatabaseError class, and if it is, the code calls RollbackAndRefresh to roll-back the current transactions.

Notice that the call to RollbackAndRefresh is enclosed in a try/except block. This is done in case there is no active transaction and the call to Rollback generates an exception. By using the try/except block, you force any exception that occurs during the rollback attempt to be ignored.

If your code makes changes to multiple rows or multiple tables you can easily control the transaction using a try/except block as in the following code. This code assumes that there is already an active transaction:

```
try
   ...make some changes here...
  Database1.Commit;
  Database1.StartTransaction;
except
  Database1.Rollback;
  Database1.StartTransaction
end;
```

If the changes are successful they are committed and a new transaction is started. If an exception is raised, the transaction is rolled back and a new transaction is started.

WARNING

Do not use this technique of holding a transaction open for a long period of time if your server holds locks on pages or records during the time a transaction is open. If the server locks pages or records while a transaction is open, transactions must be very short or you will interfere with other users' access to the data.

The transaction-handling approach described in this section for the Student application works fine with Interbase because of its multigenerational architecture. Interbase can provide repeatable reads during a transaction without locks. That is not true of all servers. If your server maintains locks during the time a transaction is open then you will need to design your transaction handling to minimize the duration of the transaction.

Maintaining an Interbase Database

Interbase, unlike many other servers, requires very little configuration and maintenance. The main things you will need to do to maintain your database are:

- Add users to the database.
- Periodically back up and restore the database.
- Verify the integrity of the database and repair it if necessary.
- Seep the database to remove out-of-date records.

Using Server Manager

Server Manager is a Windows utility that allows you to manage all of your Interbase databases on multiple servers. Figure 27.15 shows the Server Manager main window with the File menu displayed.

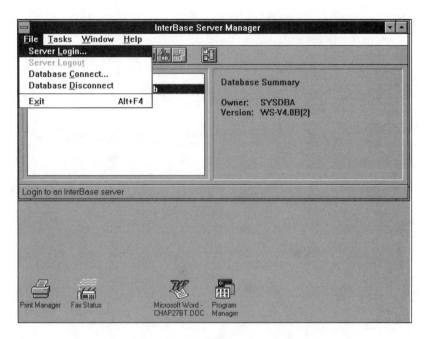

FIGURE 27.15 SERVER MANAGER.

The File menu provides choices to login and logout of various servers and to connect to and disconnect from databases. Server Manager lets you login to multiple servers and connect to multiple databases simultaneously. You can move freely from server to server and database to database. The servers and databases you are connected to are shown in outline format in the left pane of the Server Manager window. Just click the database you want to work with. You can expand and contract this tree by double-clicking in the same way that you manipulate the directory tree in Windows File Manager.

Figure 27.16 shows the <u>T</u>asks menu. It lets you maintain security by adding and removing users for a database, back up and restore the database, open the database maintenance dialog box, verify the database, or start the Windows ISQL utility. In addition, there are three options that are not available for the local Interbase server. The first allows you to enable or disable the write ahead log. The other two allow you to view database and lock manager statistics.

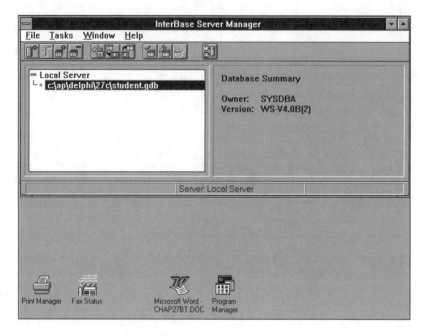

FIGURE 27.16 SERVER MANAGER TASKS MENU.

Maintaining Security

Server Manager allows you to add users to and remove users from a database. Once a user has been added to the database, you can use the SQL **GRANT** and **REVOKE** commands to grant a user any of the following privileges in any combination:

- Select
- Delete
- Insert
- Update
- All of the above

In addition, you can grant a user Execute access to a stored procedure. *Execute access* grants the user the right to call the stored procedure.

Sweeping the Database

Interbase's unique multigenerational architecture allows it to provide consistent concurrent reading and writing by creating multiple versions of a database record on a page. This can cause the database to grow.

To control growth, Interbase performs automatic garbage collection. Each time a record is accessed, Interbase checks for obsolete versions of that record. If any are found, they are deleted, freeing their space for reuse. However, old versions of records that are infrequently accessed can accumulate. In addition, records left from transactions that are rolled back will not be released by the garbage collection process.

There are two ways to release all of the out-of-date records in a database. The first is to perform a sweep. To *sweep* a database select **Database Maintenance** from the <u>T</u>asks menu in Server Manager. Doing so will open the Database Maintenance window shown in Figure 27.17.

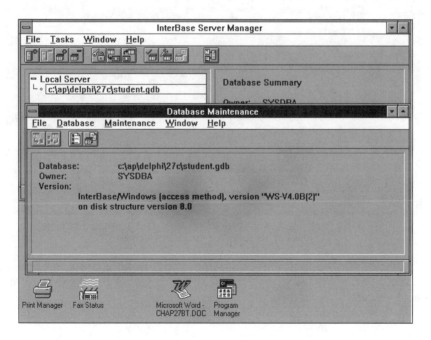

FIGURE 27.17 DATABASE MAINTENANCE WINDOW.

Select **Database Sweep** to sweep the database. You do not have to restrict users in any way during a sweep operation. They can continue working normally in the database. However, performance may suffer during a sweep, so it is best to sweep the database during periods of low activity.

To ensure that the database gets swept periodically, Interbase maintains a sweep interval for each database. By default, the interval is set to 20,000 transactions. When the database reaches its sweep interval you will see a message asking if you want to sweep the database. You can change the sweep interval by selecting **Database\|Properties** from the Server Manager menu. The Database Properties dialog box shown in Figure 27.18 shows the current sweep interval and lets you change it.

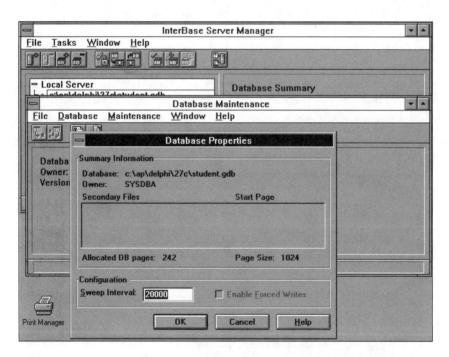

FIGURE 27.18 CHANGING THE SWEEP INTERVAL.

You can also effectively sweep the database by backing it up and restoring it. Since a backup reads every record, it forces garbage collection to occur for every record.

Backing Up

You can back up and restore a database from the Server Manager Tasks menu. A backup can be directed to a disk file or any other valid device. Remember that a backup has little value if it is on the same disk drive as the database itself, since a disk failure could destroy both.

671

Backing up also has other uses. First, the backup will always be smaller than the database itself because the backup includes only the current version of each record and does not include any unused space. Second, Interbase backups are portable from one platform to another. That means you can back up a database from an NT server and restore it on a UNIX server. Third, you can perform a metadata-only backup to save the database structure without the data. This is an easy way to create a new empty database on another server.

Summary

Interbase is an important database to be familiar with for two reasons. First, the Interbase Local Server makes it possible to develop and test client-server applications on a local machine.

Second, Interbase has very low resource requirements and is very easy to install, use, and maintain. Using Interbase you can economically build client/server applications for smaller workgroups than has been possible in the past. In addition, Interbase is the only server with multigenerational architecture, so it provides the best performance in mixed read/write environments.

CHAPTER 28

Using Microsoft SQL-Server

Database servers are improving rapidly as of late. As of this writing in 1995, Microsoft is about to release Microsoft SQL-Server 6.0. Borland has released versions of Interbase that run on Windows NT server and Novell server platforms. Oracle is readying newer versions of its product. Things are getting interesting.

This chapter will familiarize you with version 4.2X of Microsoft SQL-Server. In 1992, Microsoft released version 4.2 of the server, and it has provided minor revisions since then. You can see why version 6.0 has been eagerly awaited. Microsoft SQL-Server 4.2X is one of the supported servers for Borland SQL links, which Delphi can access. In addition, Microsoft makes ODBC drivers for SQL-Server, which you use as well.

SQL-Server is gaining popularity. Since Delphi can connect to a variety of back ends and since SQL-Server has found its way onto many PC server platforms in Windows NT and OS/2, it makes sense to show how Delphi can work with SQL-Server. This chapter will review the basic features and conclude with a quick look at some of the enhancements coming in the new version.

Installing and Configuring SQL-Server

Developing client/server applications requires spending long hours getting familiar with your database server installation and configuration. Perhaps the trickiest part of installing and configuring a database server is making sure you have all the network software (*the middleware*) installed properly. For example, the environment development for this book included SQL-Server 4.2 for OS/2 on a Novell 3.12 network, Novell's ODI drivers, and the Novell named pipes software, Borland's SQL Links (for Sybase), Microsoft SQL-Server client named pipes drivers for Windows, and Microsoft ODBC 2.0 drivers for SQL-Server. Needless to say, this configuration requires about eight pieces of middleware that all need to be installed and configured properly. In addition, three vendors are involved: Borland, Microsoft, and Novell with different versions of each of the middleware drivers.

If you are new to client/server development, prepare to spend several days getting familiar with all the pieces of software required to communicate to SQL-Server. Although it is relatively easy to install each of these drivers, trying to find out why the drivers on one PC cannot talk to the SQL-Server can be a hair-raising experience. It will make creating the application interface with Delphi seem terribly easy. In fact, client/server development is often one part real application development and five parts of middleware configuration and troubleshooting.

Determining Hardware Requirements for SQL-Server

Perhaps the most important performance issue with database servers—and SQL-Server is no exception—is making sure your hardware is chosen properly. While deciding on the proper hardware is a detailed science that would require more space than is warranted here, we offer the following tips:

- Try to purchase the fastest CPU you can for the server. The recommended minimum is a 486/50 processor. SQL-Server is CPU-bound, with large amounts of memory and cache used properly, or with small amounts of memory and lots of disk I/O. Look for a fast single CPU before exploring multiprocessor solutions (for operating systems such as NT that support them).
- Make sure you have sufficient memory for SQL-Server. Make sure you know the memory footprint for your operating system and that you have physical memory to accommodate both SQL-Server and the operating system. This will prevent the operating system from swapping either itself or SQL-Server out of memory. A minimum recommended memory configuration is 32 megabytes of RAM. How much memory you actually need depends on the volume of data and the number of users accessing SQL-Server.
- Get a fast disk subsystem. Look for Fast SCSI-2 32-bit disk controllers and Fast SCSI-2 hard drives. Hardware-level RAID with data striping and intelligent disk controller duplexing can improve performance significantly, often by a factor of two.
- Get a handle on how big your database is and how fast it will grow to make sure you have sufficient hard disk space.
- Place the SQL-Server transaction logs (which are temporary tables used to maintain database integrity during database updates) and the

application databases on separate physical devices. This will improve transaction performance for databases with read and write access.

- Make sure your network cabling and routing systems are fast enough and configured properly. Defective or damaged routers, hubs, or network interface cards can slow down a network significantly, giving the appearance that SQL-Server is performing poorly.

From these notes, you can see that size of the data and the transaction rate usually drive an application to a client/server solution. If your database is in the tens of megabytes in size, perhaps it is most appropriately handled with local tables. When your database is hundreds of megabytes or gigabytes in size, you most certainly should be looking at client/server solutions.

These hardware configuration issues are just an overview of typical hardware issues. They are guidelines, not absolutes. Serious database applications will require serious resource planning. For example, you can determine transaction rates for your application to determine how fast the disk subsystem and network architecture should be. You can do detailed application database size estimates on every application table to determine how much hard disk space you will need. For large databases in a Microsoft SQL-Server environment, it is important to plan ahead and make sure you have the proper hardware in place before you begin deploying serious applications.

Installing SQL-Server Software and Drivers

Installing Microsoft SQL-Server and the drivers required to access it requires, at the least, the following steps:

1. Install the SQL-Server software on an OS/2 or Windows NT server (depending on the version of SQL-Server).
2. Install the network operating system drivers on the server. For Novell networks and the OS/2 server version, you will need the NetWare Requester for OS/2 and named pipes driver for OS/2 from Novell.
3. Install the necessary drivers on the client PC. For Novell networks accessing SQL-Server for OS/2, you will need the DOSNP.EXE driver from Novell and the DBNMPIPE.EXE driver (so you can access SQL-Server from DOS using Microsoft DOS client software) or the DBNMP3.DLL (so you can access SQL-Server from Windows) from Microsoft. You do not need DBNMPIPE.EXE if you are only going to use Windows to access SQL-Server. These drivers come with the client software tools shipped with SQL-Server. For SQL-Server for NT and other networks, you will need to consult the SQL-Server installation guide.

4. Install Borland SQL Link for Sybase (or the Microsoft ODBC 2.0 drivers for SQL-Server) on the client PC.

5. Review the Sybase driver configuration on the drivers page of the Borland Database Engine configuration utility that comes with Delphi.

6. If you are using ODBC to access SQL-Server, install the Microsoft ODBC drivers and set up a data source for the SQL-Server using the ODBC setup utility in the Control Panel.

In order to execute these steps, you will need to consult the appropriate installation guide with each vendor's software. This listing here is to give you an overview of what is involved in installing SQL-Server.

Creating Disk Devices and Databases

SQL-Server ships with a Windows utility that lets you administer the various server resources. This tool is called *Microsoft SQL Administrator.*

In order to create an application database, you need to create what SQL-Server calls a database device. *Database devices* are physical files that hold databases. Databases, in turn, hold tables. When SQL-Server is installed, it automatically creates a database device called MASTER. This device holds the Master database, the tempdb database, and the model database.

Each database device consumes operating system resources, so when you create database devices, make sure you consult the SQL System Administrator guidelines to determine how many physical devices you can create. For example, the OS/2 version of SQL-Server is limited to about 40 to 45 devices. For most installations, this should be more than enough.

Creating Disk Devices

Creating a database device is easy. SQL-Server has a SQL command, **DISK INIT**, for this task. To create a device called *customer* that is 100 MB in size, you can type the following in the query window in SQL Administrator Tools:

```
DISK INIT
NAME = 'customer',
PHYSNAME = 'c:\sql\data\cust.dat',
VDEVNO = 5,
SIZE = 51200
```

NAME is the logical device name. This can be a longer more descriptive name than PHYSNAME, which refers to the actual file on disk. VDEVNO refers to the virtual device number for the device. Each device must have its own unique VDEVNO. You can use SQL Administrator Tools **Manage | Devices** menu option to display all the devices and their VDEVNO to determine the next available device number (see Figure 28.1).

677

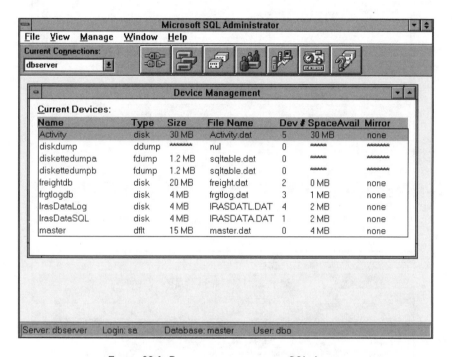

FIGURE 28.1 DISPLAYING DEVICES USING SQL ADMIN.

The SIZE argument is the number of 2K blocks SQL-Server will initialize in the device. In this example, 51200 * 2K = 100MB. There are 512 2K blocks in a megabyte.

However, the SQL Administrator Tools includes an option to let you create a device via a dialog box (Figure 28.2). In most administrative tasks in SQL-Server, you can either use the SQL-Server Transact-SQL commands in the query window (Figure 28.2), or you can use a dialog box in the SQL Administrator Tool to perform the task (Figure 28.3).

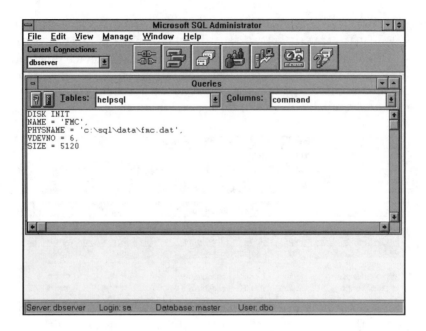

FIGURE 28.2 CREATING A DISK DEVICE VIA SQL ADMINISTRATOR QUERY WINDOW.

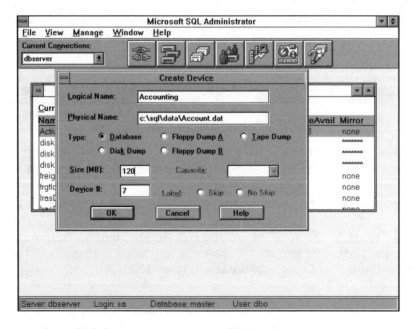

FIGURE 28.3 CREATING A DISK DEVICE VIA SQL ADMINISTRATOR DIALOG BOX.

Creating, Altering and Dropping Databases

After you have created your database device, you can create a database on the device. A database can contain tables, views, stored procedures, and other objects. Transact-SQL has commands for creating, altering, and deleting a database.

679

Creating a database is easy. In the SQL Administrator query window, you can type the following:

```
create database 'billing'
on customer = 12
log on customerlog = 2
```

This command creates a database called **billing** on the **customer** device with a size of 12 megabytes. Notice that when you create a database in Transact-SQL, you specify the size in megabytes, not in 2K pages. This billing database will allocate 2MB and store its transaction logs on the **customerlog** device (transaction logs are discussed in the next paragraph). You can also use the Database window to create a database by selecting **Database | Window** from the menu in SQL Administrator. This brings up a dialog box that asks for the information and creates the database for you (Figure 28.4).

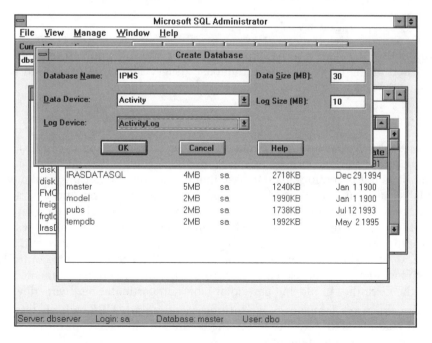

FIGURE 28.4 CREATING A DISK DEVICE VIA SQL ADMINISTRATOR DIALOG.

Whenever you create a database, you should assign the transaction log for that database to another device. SQL-Server maintains all changes to a database in a transaction log. This log is used to restore the database to a consistent state during automatic recovery. As users update data, these transaction logs can fill up. Transaction logs are backed up frequently, usually once a day, and the backed-up portion of the log is reclaimed for use by new transaction entries. Since a lot of activity goes on in a transaction log, for performance reasons, it is a good idea to put it on separate devices.

Databases can span multiple disk devices. If a database grows beyond a single physical disk, this scheme lets you allocate space for a database on an additional disk device. The Transact-SQL code for this is listed below:

```
create database inventory on device1 = 25, device2 = 30.
```

Expanding or dropping a database is also easy. The Transact SQL for allocating an additional 10 MB for the inventory database is:

```
alter database inventory on device1 = 10.
```

The code to drop the inventory and customer databases is:

```
drop database inventory, customer.
```

Transaction logs can also be expanded. You may find yourself expanding a transaction log as you observe database usage. The code to add an additional 10 MB for the billing database's transaction log is:

```
alter database billing on tranlog = 10.
```

If a database spans multiple database devices, you can control what objects get placed on each device by using segments. *Segments* let you create a label that refers to the section of a database that resides on another physical device. This is handy if you want to place some database tables on one device and another set of tables on another device. For example, one database might have tables that hold text and other tables that hold images. You might want to place the image data on a different high-speed large capacity device and leave the text on a different device. Having multiple disks and multiple controllers servicing a single database can improve performance. Having segments gives you the flexibility in placing particular tables on particular hardware devices.

By the way, Transact-SQL defines a command, **USE**, which lets you select a database to use. The following command changes your current database to the customer database:

```
use customer
```

This is similar to changing current directories in DOS with the **CD** command.

User Accounts and Groups

SQL-Server lets you establish user accounts and assign users to groups. Again, like just about all administrative tasks in SQL-Server, you can use either the interactive tools in SQL Administrator or the appropriate Transact-SQL command or stored procedure. A *stored procedure* is nothing more than a series of Transact-SQL commands placed in one file and executed as a single program. In fact, many parts of the interactive interface of SQL Administrator simply calls stored procedures.

To create a login id, you use the stored procedure sp_addlogin. This procedure takes up to four arguments:

- user id (it must be unique)
- user's password
- the name of the default database the user will be automatically connected to when he or she logs in. If no default is given, master is assumed.
- the user's default language. If none is given, SQL-Server's default language is used.

To create a login id for sharonl with a password of *spin* with a database default of *customer*, type the following:

```
sp_addlogin sharonl, spin, customer
```

Users, by default, always belong to the group **public**. You can assign users to one other group. Groups make it easy to grant or revoke permissions for several user ids at a time. To add a group to the database, use the sp_addgroup stored procedure:

```
sp_addgroup marketing
```

Whenever you add a group in SQL-Server, you are adding a group to the current database. This means that each database can have its own groups of users. Creating a login id only ensures the user can log into SQL-Server, not that he or she can access any databases or objects in a database. In order to let a user access a database, you must do the following:

1. Create the login id with sp_addlogin.
2. Create any groups for the databases in the server with sp_addgroup.
3. Add users to databases and optionally a group in a database with sp_adduser.
4. Grant permissions on specific objects for a user or a group the user belongs to with GRANT.

The sp_adduser stored procedure can take up to three arguments (the last two arguments are optional). The following command adds a user id, sharonl, to a group called **marketing** in the current database:

```
sp_adduser sharonl, sharonlu, marketing
```

The second argument to this stored procedure is a nickname for the user id. Very often, users may want to use a more descriptive name inside a database. After all, you might have defined hundreds of login ids for a server installation but only a few users in the marketing database.

Behind the scenes, these stored procedures add records to system tables. SQL-Server stored nearly every configuration item such as login ids, database names, device names, groups, user names, and so on, in these system tables. These system tables are just like data tables. You can query them, but certainly not update all of them without calling the appropriate stored procedure.

Creating Tables

Like Interbase, SQL-Server lets you create tables with a **CREATE TABLE** command. To create an employee table with three fields—employee_id, first_name, and last_name—you would enter the following:

```
create table employee
(employee_id char(4),
first_name varchar(40),
last_name varchar(40))
```

SQL-Server Data Types

In the prior example, all three fields in the employee table are alphanumeric. The first and last name fields are of type varchar, whereas the id field is of type char. SQL-Server supports seven basic data types that have a total of 17 different implementations. Table 28.1 lists the various data types, and Table 28.2 lists the size of each data type implementation.

TABLE 28.1 SQL-SERVER DATATYPES

Types	Implementations
Integer	int, smallint, tinyint
Floating-point	float, real
Money	money, smallmoney
Character	char(n), varchar(n), text
Binary	binary(n), varbinary(n), image
Date and time	datetime, smalldatetime
Other	bit, timestamp, sysname

683

TABLE 28.2 SQL-SERVER DATATYPE SIZES

int	−2,147,483,648 to +2,147,483,647	4 bytes
smallint	−32,768 to +32,767	2 bytes
tinyint	0 to 255	1 byte
float	1.7E-308 to 1.7E+308, 15 digits of precision	8 bytes
real	3.4E-38 to 2.4E+38, 7 digits of precision	4 bytes
money	±922,337,203,658,477.5807, accurate to 1/10,000 of a monetary unit, stored as double precision integers	8 bytes
smallmoney	±214,748.3647, accurate to 1/10,000 of a monetary unit	4 bytes
char	up to 255 characters	size specified
varchar	up to 255 characters. This type is for character fields in which actual lengths vary greatly	depends on actual size of data
text	up to 2,147,483,647 characters	varying
binary	up to 255 bytes of binary data	size specified
varbinary	up to 255 bytes of binary data	varying
image	up to 2,147,483,647 bytes of binary data	varying
datetime	1/1/1753 to 12/31/1999, accurate to 3.33 milliseconds	8 bytes
smalldatetime	1/1/1900 to 6/6/2079, accurate to 1 minute	4 bytes
bit	0 or 1	1 bit
timestamp	this is not a datetime data type, but rather a varbinary(8); a column of this type is automatically updated every time a row is inserted or updated	8 bytes
sysname	A user-defined data type: varchar(30)	varying

Null Values

When you create a table, you can tell SQL-Server whether or not null values are allowed in a column:

```
create table employee
(employee_id char(4)not null,
first_name varchar(40),
last_name varchar(40),
division char(20),
age tinyint)
```

In this example, the **not null** clause indicates the employee_id field must contain a value. If the user attempts to create a record without supplying a value or attempts to change a field value to null, SQL-Server will generate an error and prevent the action. If you do not specify null and if the user does not make an entry into the column when a record is inserted, SQL-Server assigns the field a value of null. If you don't specify null or not null when you create a table, not null is assumed.

This explanation of nulls in column definitions fails to describe the complexities in dealing with null values. A null value represents the absence of information, which has varying implications depending on the data type. For example, when adding three numbers and a null value, what should the system do? Throw out the entire calculation or disregard the null value? It depends on whether the null value is required for the formula to be considered reasonable. However, you can also come up with multiple reasons or categories of null values. Does your application need to consider why the values are null? The treatment of nulls has been discussed at great length in many books and articles on relational theory.

You can easily remove tables from SQL-Server with the **DROP** command and you can add columns to an existing table with the **ALTER TABLE** command.

Temporary Tables

You can create temporary tables in SQL-Server. Temporary tables are removed at the end of the current session, unless you drop them explicitly. Temporary tables are always stored in the tempdb database, not the current database. SQL-Server gives temporary tables a name consisting of the name you supply, plus a system-supplied numeric suffix.

You can create a temporary table by preceding the table name with a **#** sign. The name you supply can be no more than 13 characters in length. The following code creates a temporary employee table:

```
create table #employee
(employee_id char(4)not null,
first_name varchar(40),
last_name varchar(40))
```

Creating Indexes

Without indexes, access to large tables would be very slow. Just as trying to find a book in a library without a card catalog is arduous, so is finding a record in a table without an index. In both cases, a sequential scan is required. When creating client/server applications, developing appropriate indexes can make big performance differences.

The following code creates an index, called employee_id_ind, on the employee name field:

```
create index employee_id_ind
on employee( employee_id )
```

A composite index is simply an index based on more than one field. The following example creates an index on the last name and first name fields:

```
create index last_first_ind
on employee( last_name, first_name )
```

Unique Indexes

You can mark an index as unique, which means that SQL-Server will prevent two records from having the same index entry. For example, if the last_first_ind index created above were a unique index, then you would not be able to enter two employees with the name **Henry Higgins**. To create a unique index, simply use the keyword INDEX:

```
create unique index employee_id_ind
on employee( employee_id )
```

SQL-Server will prevent you from creating an index on an existing table with duplicate index entries.

Clustered and Nonclustered Indexes

When you enter a library, the book shelves are not always arranged in sequential order. Sometimes libraries use whatever available space is necessary to house some books. However, some libraries physically order their bookcases in the same order as the card catalog.

SQL-Server lets you do the same. If you declare an index as clustered, the data in the table is stored in the same order as the index. If you specify an index as nonclustered, the order of the rows does not matter.

Clustered indexes speed up sequential access significantly. When you need to collect all books in the range of 300 to 500, you can simply go to the bookcase that starts at 300 and visit all the other bookcases that are arranged in order without ever going back to the card catalog. If an index is clustered, SQL-Server can dispense with looking though the index when a query is sequentially accessing data. Of course, only one index can be clustered. After all, you cannot expect a library to have all books sorted on the bookcases by number and by author simultaneously.

To create a clustered index, simply use the keyword CLUSTERED:

```
create unique clustered index employee_id_ind
on employee( employee_id )
```

Maintaining Database Integrity: Defaults and Rules

SQL-Server provides two tools for helping you maintain database integrity: defaults and rules. A *default* is simply a value that you want inserted into a column if no value is supplied. A *rule* specifies validation criteria for a specific column.

Creating a default is easy. The following code establishes a default called division_dflt, which returns **Marketing**.

```
create default division_dflt as 'Marketing'
```

You can then bind this default to a single column in a single table or as many columns in as many tables as you wish. You need to use the sp_bindefault stored procedure for this. The following code binds the division_dflt default to the division field in the employee table:

```
sp_bindefault division_dflt, 'employee.division'
```

You can disassociate a default from a column in a table with the sp_unbindefault store procedure. You can delete a default by using the **DROP DEFAULT** command.

Rules are a bit more involved. They let you specify simple or elaborate validation criteria that can be applied to columns. You create rules just like you create defaults. The following rule establishes a range of valid employee ages:

```
create rule employee_age_rule as @age between 1 and 150
```

In this rule, age is the rule's parameter. This parameter will be bound to a column in a table with the sp_bindrule stored procedure. The following code binds this rule to the age field in the employee table:

```
sp_bindrule employee_age_rule, 'employee.age'
```

Rules can get elaborate. You can use any Transact-SQL expression that is valid in a where clause, which includes arithmetic and relational operators, built-in functions that do not reference tables or columns, and other operators.

Views: What are They?

Views are queries that look like tables. To define a view, you use the **CREATE VIEW** command. The following view returns only the employee names and ids in the marketing division:

```
create view marketing_employees as
select employee_id, first_name, last_name
from employee
where division = 'Marketing'
```

Views are extremely useful for preventing the user from accessing rows (or columns) in a table and for providing a layer of abstraction between the logical database design and an application. If an application only accesses views (and the application user might not even know he or she is accessing views; after all, they look just like tables), you can rearrange a database's logical design without disrupting the application, provided you can re-create the views to produce the same columns as before.

Views have another important role in terms of Delphi. In Delphi, queries that join tables cannot be live: you cannot update the underlying table in the query. Delphi has this and other restrictions on queries against local tables and Interbase tables. However, SQL-Server does not have the same restrictions.

Most views in SQL-Server are updatable, except for the following restrictions:

- Views with aggregates or row aggregates are not updatable.
- You cannot modify a column in a view that is a computation.
- You cannot delete records in a multitable view.
- You can only update or insert records in a multitable view if the columns inserted or updated are in the same base table.
- You can only insert new records if all not null columns are included in the view.

If you create a multitable query in Delphi, Delphi will not let you update the result set. If you select a view, however, you can update the data.

Stored Procedures

Stored procedures are like DOS batch files. They let you string together several SQL statements, and they provide some basic control-of-flow language constructs. Transact-SQL has the following control-of-flow language constructs:

Construct	Usage
IF..ELSE	provides branching
BEGIN...END	lets you execute a group of statements in a block
WHILE...CONTINUE	looping construct with BREAK to break out of the loop independent of the loop's terminating expression
DECLARE	declare local variable
RETURN	exit from a procedure or query
WAITFOR	execute a block of statements at a particular time

You can use these constructs to create elaborate programs that include queries and many other built-in functions. In order to run a stored procedure, SQL-Server must build two internal data structures:

- a query tree
- an execution plan

When you create a stored procedure, the text of the stored procedure is stored in the syscomments system table, and a normalized form of the query or queries within the stored procedure are stored in the sysproce-dures system table. The first time a stored procedure is executed, the query tree is read from the sysprocedures table into memory. SQL-Server then passes the query tree to the query optimizer, which creates an opti-mal access plan. This access plan remains in memory for all subsequent calls to the stored procedure. This makes subsequent calls to a stored procedure very fast.

In fact, stored procedures are faster than views. Although SQL-Server will cache the query tree for views, it will not cache the access plan for views. However, this is one of the problems with a stored procedure. If the nature of the data changes significantly after the stored procedure's access plan was read into memory, the access plan may no longer be optimal. Fortunately, you can create stored procedures that tell SQL-Server to gener-ate a new access plan upon each execution.

Stored procedures can accept parameters. This lets you pass variable data to the stored procedure, enabling dynamic queries and dynamic con-trol-of-flow. In fact, the Delphi TStoredProc component lets you specify parameters for a stored procedure and the TStoredProc can be used as a data set for a TDataSource component.

The following code is an example of a simple stored procedure that returns all the authors in a given state:

```
create proc authors_in_state @state char(2) as
select * from authors
where state = @state
```

In this stored procedure, @state is an argument of type char(2). This stored procedure can be used in a Delphi application as the data set for a grid in which the user can select a given state (Figure 28.5). The code for the select button is listed below:

```
AuthorsSP.DisableControls;
AuthorsSP.Active:=False;
AuthorsSP.Params.Items[1].AsString := State.Text;
AuthorsSP.Active:=True;
AuthorsSP.EnableControls;
```

The AuthorsSP component is a TStoredProc component. Its StoredProcName property is set to the authors_in_state stored procedure. The Params.Items[1] property refers to the state parameter in the authors_in_name stored procedure. Execution speed of this client/server example is as fast as execution speed of local data.

Triggers

Triggers are stored procedures that fire in response to database operations. These operations are INSERT, DELETE, and UPDATE. Triggers are commonly used to implement referential integrity. Unlike Interbase, which has declarative referential integrity as part of the data definition language, SQL-Server uses triggers. Not only can triggers enforce referential integrity, they can also enforce more complex restrictions than rules can.

The syntax for defining a trigger is more involved than defining a rule or a default. The pubs database that comes with SQL-Server defines the following trigger on the DELETE operation for the titles table:

```
create trigger deltitle
on titles
for delete
as
if (select count(*) from deleted, sales
where sales.title = deleted.title_id) > 0
  begin
  rollback transaction
  print "You can't delete a title with sales"
  end
```

This trigger prevents the user from deleting a title from the titles table if it has any sales records in the sales table. This trigger has four interesting keywords: if, deleted, rollback transaction, and print. The *deleted* keyword refers to a special table, called deleted, which is created whenever records are deleted from a table. In this case, the trigger is firing in the middle of the delete transaction. The *if* keyword checks to see if any records in the deleted table (records from titles) have any corresponding sales records. If so, the transaction is rolled back with the *rollback transaction* keyword and a message is returned with *print*.

Just like stored procedures, triggers can get complex and involved, depending on the application requirements. One of the most important decisions you need to make in client/server development in Delphi is to decide what processing should take place on SQL-Server in the form of triggers, stored procedures, rules, and defaults and what processing should take place in your Delphi code.

The answer to this design problem varies. It depends on your application's performance profile, on the database server data structures, on the cost of implementation in either environment, and on many other factors. Often, critical business rules and core referential integrity processing are delegated to SQL-Server with user-interface or workgroup-specific data manipulation or verification delegated to the Delphi application.

Locking, Transactions, and Concurrency

SQL-Server performs page-level locking, not row-level locking. When accessing local Paradox and dBase tables, the Borland Database Engine in Delphi implements row-level locking. This means that the row being edited is locked, preventing other users from changing that record. In SQL-Server, the database page is locked. A database page can hold many records, depending on the record size. Subsequently, when a record is updated with an UPDATE query, the page containing the record is locked for the duration of the transaction.

Page-level locking often provides better performance than row-level locking since fewer locks are placed. However, if users are continually trying to update (or add) different records on the same page, page-level locking provides less concurrency and performance than row-level locking.

SQL-Server automatically manages locks. Whenever you read data with a SELECT query, SQL-Server places a shared lock on the table and/or database pages. Multiple users can simultaneously place shared locks on the same table or the same database pages. If you try to change data with an UPDATE, INSERT, or DELETE query, SQL-Server will place an exclusive lock on the affected database pages. An exclusive lock prevents any other transaction from placing any other type of lock until the exclusive lock is released at the end of the transaction. (See Chapter 24 for a more detailed discussion on transactions.)

When you write client/server applications, you need to understand what types of locks data operations will be placing on your tables. In addition, you need to understand the consistency problems that can arise in client/server applications.

One such consistency problem is a repeatable read problem. In Delphi, you can set the transaction isolation level on the TDatabase component to address the repeatable read problem. However, Delphi converts the repeatable read isolation level to the highest isolation level supported by SQL-Server: read committed. To get around the repeatable read problem, SQL-Server provides a keyword *HOLDLOCK*, which you can place immediately after the table name in the SELECT statement. Normally, SQL-Server releases all shared locks as soon as it is finished accessing a table, even if the transaction is not complete. The *HOLDLOCK* keyword tells SQL-Server not to release shared locks during the query until the transaction is complete. This ensures that the data you read in the beginning of the transaction will not change if you reread the data at the end of the transaction.

In addition, Delphi provides an UpdateMode property on the TTable and TQuery component, which lets you implement optimistic concurrency control. In *optimistic concurrency control*, you do not try to hold a lock or get an explicit lock in a transaction in order to ensure an update will succeed. Instead, you assume that no other user will change the record and try to find the record by using the upWhereAll setting in the UpdateMode property. With this setting, Delphi will try to find the record based on the original value of all the fields. If it finds it, then no other user has changed the record. If it cannot find it, then someone has changed the record and the update is prohibited.

Accessing SQL Objects with TTable, TQuery, and TStoredProc

With SQL-Server and other database servers, Delphi gives you three components to access data on the server: TTable, TQuery, and TStoredProc. Obviously, there is some overlap among the three.

The TTable component has some advantages. You do not need any SQL commands to access a table. However, you can access only one table. The TQuery component is desirable when you need to join tables together in order to display them. You could use the TQuery component to access a few columns for a single table with potentially very little performance difference compared to the TTable component. On local tables, however, the TTable component is always fastest.

The TStoredProc component is good for high-speed read-only queries that are repeated frequently, such as lookups in which a parameter is passed to the query's WHERE clause. In addition, the TStoredProc is valuable for running a series of queries with other Transact-SQL commands included. You will not be able to update a data set returned with a stored procedure, however. Delphi considers it read only.

You can also use the TQuery.ExecSQL method to send a SQL command directly to the server. This command could create stored procedures or views on the fly. Clearly you have options. No single option will solve all database problems.

Summary

There is much more to SQL-Server than can be effectively discussed here. As of this writing, SQL-Server version 6.0 is waiting in the wings, and it promises more features, such as asynchronous data replication, ANSI-SQL compliance with support for declarative referential integrity, better administration software, better performance on very large databases, easier installation, and more. Clearly, the client/server market is maturing, and the technology is becoming easier to implement. Delphi augments this by providing a great front-end tool with plenty of data-aware controls and database access options.

CHAPTER 29

Improving Performance

One of the unique things about Delphi compared to other database application development tools is that performance is not much of a consideration with respect to Delphi itself. Unlike other products, Delphi does not use an interpreter to process the code you write. Since Delphi is based on an optimizing compiler that produces native-code .EXE files, your Delphi code executes so fast that you do not have to concern yourself with many coding tips and tricks to improve performance.

The performance bottleneck in Delphi database applications is getting data into and out of the database and getting the data across the network from the database server or from the file server to each workstation. This chapter begins with some information on coding techniques but focuses mainly on database access techniques to improve performance.

Minimizing Display Overhead

There is one topic that is more important than data access performance in a Windows database application, and that is updating the screen. Repainting the screen in a graphical environment like Windows is an expensive operation in terms of time.

TIP

When you write code that moves through several records in a table that is being displayed on a form, always call the TTable component's DisableControls method before traversing the table and the EnableControls method when you are done.

Figure 29.1 shows the **ENABLE.DPR** project's main form. The form contains a TTable, a TDataSource, a DBNavigator, and a DBGrid connected to the sample Orders table.

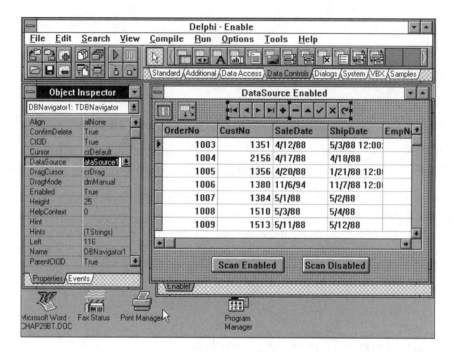

FIGURE 29.1 SCREEN I/O PERFORMANCE DEMONSTRATION.

The following code is from the Scan Enabled button's OnClick event handler. This code moves to the beginning of the table and loops through all of the records in the table:

```
procedure TForm1.ScanBtnClick(Sender: TObject);
begin
  Table1.First;
  while Table1.EOF = False do
    Table1.Next;
end;
```

Run the program, click the button, and you will see the DBGrid update as you move from record to record. Scanning all the records takes several seconds. The following code from the Scan Disabled button is almost identical:

```
procedure TForm1.ScanDisabledBtnClick(Sender: TObject);
begin
  Table1.DisableControls;
  with Table1 do
  begin
    First;
    while EOF = False do
      Next;
  end;
  Table1.EnableControls;
end;
```

The difference is that this code sets the DataSource component's Enabled property to **False** so the grid is not updated as the code moves through the records. Click this button and notice the difference.

Orders is a small table, so the difference between updating the display and not updating the display is only a few seconds; however, the difference is dramatic with larger tables. Using a 78,000-record table, the scan took 40 minutes with the DataSource enabled and 50 seconds with it disabled.

Using Constant Parameters

Whenever possible, use constant parameters in procedures and functions. Constant parameters are particularly more efficient than value parameters for passing structured or string types. For example,

```
procedure MyProc(const MyString: String);
```

is much more efficient than

```
procedure MyProc(MyString: String);
```

Constant parameters generate less code, so procedure and function calls execute faster. If you use value parameters, the compiler must generate code to make a copy of the parameter on the stack so that the actual parameter will not be affected if you change the value of the formal parameter in the procedure or function. Since you are not allowed to change the value of a constant parameter, the compiler does not have to generate the code to make a copy on the stack, which saves both time and memory.

If you need to change the value of the formal parameter in your procedure or function and it is acceptable or necessary to change the value of the actual parameter in the call, use a variable parameter. Variable parameters are still more efficient than value parameters for string and structured types because only a pointer must be passed, not the entire string or structure.

Using Sets

The Delphi compiler generates very efficient code for testing inclusion in sets. You will always get better performance using the in operator to test inclusion in a constant set than using if statements and Boolean logic. For example,

```
if C in ['0'..'9'] then
```

is much more efficient than

```
if (C >= '0') and (C <= '9') then
```

Delphi also generates extremely efficient code for all operations on small sets. A small set is one where the ordinal value of the lower bound is in the range of 0 to 7 and the upper bound is in the range of 0 to 15.

Checking Ranges

Figure 29.2 shows the Compiler page of the Project Options dialog box in Delphi. The first choice in the Runtime Errors group is Range Checking.

It is a good idea to turn this option on during program development. If you do, the compiler generates code to check that all array and string subscipts are within bounds. Without this checking, an errant subscript may cause your program to corrupt memory and produce errors or crashes that are hard to find.

However, once your program has been tested, debugged, and is ready for production, turn this option off and recompile. Range checking generates a significant amount of additional code that increases the size and decreases the speed of your program.

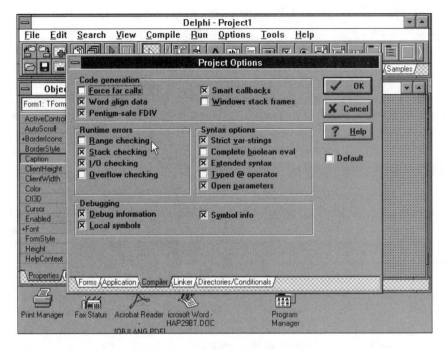

FIGURE 29.2 THE COMPILER PAGE OF THE PROJECT OPTIONS DIALOG BOX.

Using Indexes

Creating indexes is a tradeoff. Creating an index on a field or combination of fields that you use to select records can improve performance dramatically. However, every time you add or delete a record or change the value of any field that is part of an index, the database manager must update all of the affected indexes. Therefore, you want to minimize the number of indexes for the best update performance and create indexes to speed row selection.

When you have to make a choice it is generally better to create the index. Adding an index increases the time required to update a single row by a fraction of a second. Interactive users will never notice the difference; they will only notice the cumulative delay if many indexes must be updated when a row is changed. However, adding an index can reduce the time to find a record in a large table from minutes to a second or less.

The one exception to this advice is when you have code that performs updates to many records at once. In this case, the cumulative time to update an extra index for many records may be significant.

The next question is what indexes and what type of indexes you should create. The answer depends on the database manager you are using and how its query optimizer uses indexes. You have to know your specific server or the BDE well in order to understand how to construct the indexes that will give you the best performance.

Using Indexes with Local Tables

Index usage by the BDE query processor for Paradox tables is a bit complex. The basic rule is that queries will use single-field case-sensitive secondary indexes for searches that do not include wildcards. Queries do not use secondary indexes if the search value includes wildcards, and they never use case-insensitive or composite (multifield) secondary indexes.

Queries will always use the primary index, even if the search value includes trailing wildcards and the index includes more than one field. To get the best performance from queries, select records using the primary index if possible. If you must use, other fields and then pick the field that does not include wildcards in the search value and that offers the most selectivity and then build a single-field case-sensitive index on that field.

The most selective index is the one with the most unique values. Put another way, it is the one that will produce the smallest result set. Consider a query that searches for Chicago in the City field and IL in the state field. Based on the preceding information about how the BDE uses indexes in queries on Paradox tables, what is the fastest way to process this query? The fastest strategy is to have a single- field case-sensitive index on the City field. The BDE can use this index to quickly select all records whose City is Chicago into a temporary table and then sequentially search this much smaller table for the records whose State is IL. If you create an index on the State field instead of the City field, the query will take longer because BDE will first select to a temporary table using the State index. Since there will certainly be more records whose State is IL than whose City is Chicago, the temporary table that must be searched sequentially will be larger and the sequential search will take longer.

The fastest way to find a single record in a Paradox table is with FindKey. FindKey searches the current index for an exact match. You can use FindKey with the primary index or any secondary index regardless of whether or not it is case-sensitive. If the index is case-insensitive, then the search will be case-insensitive. FindKey also allows you to use composite indexes to search for an exact match on more than one field. Using a composite index you can search for an exact match using the first *N* fields of the index.

Another very fast way to find a subset of records in a Paradox table is with SetRange. Like FindKey, SetRange will use both primary and secondary indexes and will use both case-insensitive and composite indexes. SetRange is faster than a query and always gives you an updatable view of the table.

Always use FindKey or SetRange instead of a query to find records in local Paradox tables if you can.

T I P

Do not use live queries on local Paradox tables. Live queries on local tables never use indexes and may, therefore, be slow.

T I P

Using Indexes with Server Tables

To understand how to make the best use of indexes with a database server, read the server's documentation. The types of indexes available vary from server to server, and the way the query optimizer uses indexes also varies from server to server.

For example, with Interbase you should create indexes on columns that are used frequently in the Where or Join clauses of SQL statements or on columns that appear in the Order By clause. Note that for the index to be used in the Order By clause, the first *N* fields of the index must match the fields in the Order By clause. Another thing to watch for with Interbase tables is whether or not the query includes the Or operator. In the query

```
SELECT * FROM Customer
  WHERE City = 'Phoenix' and State = 'AZ'
```

you will get the best performance with a single index that includes the City and State columns. However, if the query is changed to

```
SELECT * FROM Customer
  WHERE City = 'Phoenix' or State = 'AZ'
```

you will get better performance with two single-field indexes, one on the City column and another on the State column.

With servers it makes no difference if you use FindKey, SetRange, or a query. Database servers are designed to process SQL statements fast, so no matter what Delphi method you use to select rows on a server the BDE translates the call to a SQL statement.

Optimizing Performance of Batch Operations

Indexes can hurt performance in batch operations. Consider a large table with an index on the PartNumber field. The company has changed its part numbering scheme, so you have to write a program that will change the format of the part numbers for all 500,000 parts in the PartMaster table.

The problem here is that every time you change the value in the PartNumber column of a row, the PartNumber index must be updated. This operation will be much faster if you drop the PartNumber index, update all of the rows, and then re-create the PartNumber index. The same concept applies to batch operations that add large numbers of rows to a table or delete many rows from a table. It will probably be faster to drop the indexes, perform the update, and then re-create the indexes than to update the indexes for each row as it is processed. The disadvantage of this technique is that you must have exclusive use of the table if you are using local tables.

Using Unidirectional Cursors

One of the properties of the TQuery object is Unidirectional. Most database servers do not support bidirectional scrollable cursors. The reason that you can scroll both forward and backward through a query result set in Delphi is that the BDE caches the records for you. However, if you scroll back too far, BDE must start fetching records again to get the ones it needs to display.

All of this is great because it allows you to have the bidirectional scrolling ability of a desktop database, like Paradox or dBase, with your server. However, there is a price in both time and memory usage to maintain the cache. If you do not need to move backward through the query rows, there is no need to pay the price for this capability.

 If you only need to move forward through a query result, then set the TQuery's Unidirectional property to **True**.

T I P

Minimizing Network Traffic

The slowest thing you do in a database application is move data across the network. To minimize network traffic, do the following.

Always use an index to retrieve rows from a table. Do not do sequential scans or query columns without indexes. This is particularly important with

Paradox or dBase tables on a file server because the entire table will be read across the network to the PC.

When using a query make sure it returns only the rows you need. Never set the SQLQRYMODE option in the BDE Configuration Utility to **Local**. If you do, the BDE will read every record in the table you are querying across the network to the workstation that the query is running on and perform the record selection there.

Knowing Your Server

Perhaps one of the most important aspects of getting the best performance is to know the characteristics of your database server. The characteristics of servers, such as their indexing schemes, locking mechanisms, and query optimizers, can have a powerful impact on performance.

For example, suppose you are working with a server that supports page-level locking and clustered indexes. In your application, many users will be entering new orders, each of which is identified by a unique order number. You create a clustered index on order number and write code to generate the unique order numbers sequentially, as orders are added.

While this sounds all right, the combination of page-level locking, a clustered index, and generating sequential order numbers will produce poor performance; here is why. The clustered index ensures that rows with adjacent order numbers will be placed on the same page. Sequential order numbers ensure that users will be trying to add new records to the same page at the same time. Page-level locking ensures that only one user can add an order to the page at a time. This creates a serious performance bottleneck. One solution would be to generate random order numbers so that many users will not be trying to update the same page at the same time. The point is, if you do not understand how your server works *in detail* you may not be able to spot problems like this at design time.

Summary

The secret to high-performance Delphi database applications is not coding tricks but rather avoiding input and output. Performing operations that require large numbers of screen repaints will be slow in the Windows graphical environment. Even more important, however, is engineering your application carefully to avoid network and disk i/o.

CHAPTER 30

OOP and Delphi

One feature that makes Delphi appealing is that it has a full object-oriented programming (OOP) language, ObjectPascal. ObjectPascal is a very clean and elegant language that in many ways is easier to learn than the C++ language—and it still offers all the important OOP concepts.

While many Delphi developers do not need to learn ObjectPascal's OOP features to produce usable systems, the best developers will take full advantage of OOP. Developers who want to write components need to understand OOP. Developers that want to write large complex applications that need to reuse code effectively also need to understand OOP.

This chapter will review some subtle points not previously discussed concerning how Delphi implements encapsulation, inheritance, polymorphism, and properties. In addition, this chapter reviews some key ObjectPascal classes that you will invariably run into as you work with Delphi.

Encapsulation

As discussed in Chapter 3 on object-oriented programming and Chapter 10 on objects, *encapsulation* means information hiding. Complex applications require some tough decisions about what routines will be considered private or out of view from other programmers (or even yourself). If all code in an application needed to be immediately comprehensible to all programmers, then it would be impossible to construct sophisticated software. By layering into levels of abstraction, programmers can ignore messy details at a low level and concentrate on higher-level problems. Object-oriented programming languages such as ObjectPascal make this abstraction possible through encapsulation.

ObjectPascal lets you control encapsulation in two locations: in the unit itself and in the object. Let us look at the levels of encapsulation Delphi offers in units.

With regard to encapsulation: units have two main sections—an interface section and an implementation section. In Chapter 12 on units, you saw how objects and variables declared in the interface section are visible to all other units. And objects declared in the implementation section are visible only to other functions and procedures in the same unit. In this sense, methods and objects declared in the interface section are public and are available to all other objects and methods in the application. Methods and objects declared in the implementation section are private; these are not to be shared with other parts of the application.

ObjectPascal also lets you control the visibility of properties and methods in objects. The keywords *published*, *public*, *protected*, and *private* determine what other objects can access in the defined object.

The following object declaration (for a new component called TTableAutoKey) has these four sections listed:

```
type
  TTableAutoKey = class(TTable)
  private
    { Private declarations }
  protected
    { Protected declarations }
  public
    { Public declarations }
  published
    { Published declarations }
  end;
```

As discussed in Chapter 10 on objects, you use the private section to declare methods and properties for items that can only be accessed by code in the current unit. The protected section lets objects of TTableAutoKey and its descendants access properties and methods declared here. The public section lets all other objects or code in the application access properties and methods declared here. Finally, the published section is for letting other objects and code access properties and methods declared here during design time. Within each section, you are free to declare variables, methods, procedures, and properties.

WARNING

All code in a unit has free access to all methods or properties declared for an object in that unit. Properties, variables, or methods declared in an object's protected or private section are accessible to all code in the unit. This means that you do not want to place two different objects in the same unit (unless of course, by design, you want them to access each other's private parts). Each object would be able to access the other's private and protected parts, thereby eliminating the desired encapsulation.

Inheritance

Inheritance lets you create objects that inherit properties and methods from a given ancestor. This lets objects pass on their inherited wealth to descendant objects. Delphi lets you create an arbitrarily deep inheritance tree. You simply declare an object based on another object.

For example, the following code fragment (taken from the example above), shows that the TTableAutoKey object is based on the TTable object:

```
type
  TTableAutoKey = class(TTable)
```

Chapter 10, "Objects," goes into a more detailed demonstration of inheritance. This chapter reviews some of the ObjectPascal implementation details.

Multiple Inheritance

ObjectPascal does *not* support multiple inheritance. C++ programmers and programmers familiar with other OOP languages might lament this fact, but there's not much they can do about it. ObjectPascal, even Apple's version of it (the language ObjectPascal was originally designed for Apple computers), has always been this way and most likely always will.

Multiple inheritance lets you declare an object that inherits methods and properties from two or more ancestor classes. Imagine the following fictitious object declaration:

```
type
  TCanvasPicture = class(TCanvas, TPicture)
```

This declaration attempts to create a new object, TCanvasPicture, that inherits properties and methods from TCanvas and TPicture, which are siblings in the inheritance tree. Multiple inheritance, despite its usefulness, has problems. Two classes can have the same method names. How would one call a Print method inherited from TCanvas and TPicture? How would such a Print method work? Should all redundant methods and properties be overridden?

Another problem involves multiple inheritance. Suppose a class, TMyObject, inherits from two other classes, TClassA and TClassG. Suppose TClassG also inherits from TClassA. Should TMyObject access TClassA's methods and properties or TClassG's?

To avoid these complexities, ObjectPascal supports single inheritance only.

Inheriting Visual Components from Form Classes

While you can create objects based on any class, you cannot subclass a TForm object and expect all the visual controls on the ancestor object to automatically appear on the descendant object. For example, many developers would like the ability to create a form class (let's call it TAppForm for the purposes of this discussion) and place, in design mode, several other controls such as buttons, a status line, a graphic object containing a company logo, and other controls that will appear exactly the same in all forms in the application.

When Delphi creates a form during execution, it does not create any of the parent classes' visual objects. However, this is not such a great loss. You can write code for the TAppForm class (or any user-defined class), however, and have the code available to all objects that descend from TAppForm. This code can dynamically create and destroy objects as needed. The following code is from the code disk example for this chapter. This example contains a unit, Appfrm (APPFRMP project), which contains a class, TAppForm, based on the TForm class. Unlike the TForm class, however, this class dynamically creates four objects: OK, Cancel, and Help buttons and a TPanel object that is used as a status line.

```
unit Appfrm;

interface

uses
   SysUtils, WinTypes, WinProcs, Messages, Classes, Graphics, Controls,
   Forms, Dialogs, StdCtrls, ExtCtrls;

type
   TAppForm = class(TForm)
     procedure FormDestroy(Sender: TObject);
     procedure CreateObjects;
     procedure FormCreate(Sender: TObject);
   private
     { Private declarations }
   public
     { Public declarations }
   end;

var
   HelpBtn: TButton;
   OkBtn: TButton;
   CancelBtn: TButton;
   AppForm: TAppForm;
   StatusLine: TPanel;
```

```
implementation

{$R *.DFM}

procedure TAppForm.FormDestroy(Sender: TObject);
begin
OKBtn.Free;
HelpBtn.Free;
CancelBtn.Free;
StatusLine.Free;
end;

procedure TAppForm.FormCreate(Sender: TObject);
begin
CreateObjects;
end;

procedure TAppForm.CreateObjects;
const
   {Set constants for height, etc}
   h = 33;
   t = 10;
   w = 89;
   {offset (hincr) from right edge of form
    and between buttons (vincr)}
   hincr = 17;
   vincr = 5;
begin

{Create OK button using Self as owner}
OkBtn := TButton.Create(Self);
With OKBtn do
begin
   Top := t;
   Width := w;
   Height := h;
   Left := Self.Width - (OkBtn.Width + hincr);
   Caption := '&OK';
   Visible := True;
   Name := 'OKButton';
end;
{make self the parent window}
Self.InsertControl(OkBtn);

{Create Cancel button using Self as owner}
CancelBtn := TButton.Create(Self);
```

```
With CancelBtn do
begin
   Top := vincr + OKBtn.Top+OKBtn.Height;
   Width := w;
   Height := h;
   Left := Self.Width - (CancelBtn.Width + hincr);
   Caption := '&Cancel';
   Visible := True;
   Name := 'CancelButton';
end;
{make self the parent window}
Self.InsertControl(CancelBtn);

{Create Help button using Self as owner}
HelpBtn := TButton.Create(Self);
With HelpBtn do
begin
   Top := vincr + CancelBtn.Top+CancelBtn.Height;
   Width := w;
   Height := h;
   Left := Self.Width - (HelpBtn.Width + hincr);
   Caption := '&Help';
   Visible := True;
   Name := 'HelpButton';
end;
{make self the parent window}
Self.InsertControl(HelpBtn);

{Create StatusLine using Self as owner}
StatusLine := TPanel.Create(Self);
With StatusLine do
begin
    Align := alBottom;
    BevelOuter := bvNone;
    BevelInner := bvLowered;
    Height := 20;
    Caption := 'Status line';
    Alignment := taLeftJustify;
    Name := 'StatusLine';
end;
{make self the parent window}
Self.InsertControl(StatusLine);

end;

end.
```

To create the buttons in the proper relative position, the code simply assigns the Left and Top properties (which dictate the object's position) relative to the right-most window border and the prior button. Figure 30.1 shows a form based on TAppForm. Each control is created using Self as the owner. *Self* is a pointer to the instance of the object through which the method is called. In addition, the code uses Self.InsertControl to associate the new visual component with a parent window.

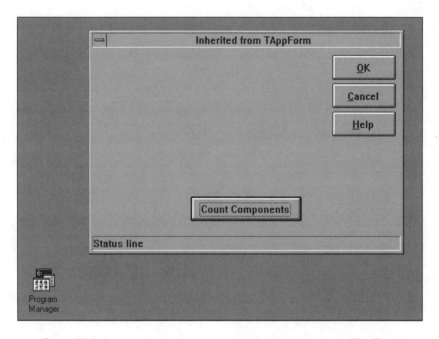

FIGURE 30.1 INHERITING VISUAL COMPONENTS: FORM BASED ON CLASS TAPPFORM

The code for the sample form, shown below, is straightforward:

```
unit Unit1;

interface

uses
  SysUtils, WinTypes, WinProcs, Messages, Classes, Graphics, Controls,
  Forms, Dialogs, AppFrm, StdCtrls;

type
  TTestForm = class(TAppForm)
```

```
    CountBtn: TButton;
    procedure FormCreate(Sender: TObject);
    procedure CountComponents;
    procedure CountBtnClick(Sender: TObject);
  private
    { Private declarations }
  public
    { Public declarations }
  end;

var
  TestForm: TTestForm;

implementation

{$R *.DFM}

procedure TTestForm.FormCreate(Sender: TObject);
begin
Inherited FormCreate(Sender);
end;

procedure TTestForm.CountComponents;
var
  I: Integer;
begin
  for I := 0 to ComponentCount-1 do
  begin
      MessageDlg(Components[I].Name,mtInformation,[mbOk],0);
  end;
end;

procedure TTestForm.CountBtnClick(Sender: TObject);
begin
CountComponents;
end;

end.
```

The key line of code in this example is

```
Inherited FormCreate(Sender);
```

in the TTestForm.FormCreate method. This method invokes the ancestor
class's FormCreate method, which actually creates the three buttons and the

status line. Notice that Unit1 uses the AppFrm unit, which contains the ancestor class declaration and implementation.

Class TTestForm contains some code that enumerates all the components on the form. When you press this button, it displays the name for each component, whether it was inherited or not.

The problem with this technique is that you cannot see the components at design time. However, you can get around this limitation by creating a new TPanel custom control that dynamically creates the objects. Since Delphi lets you see custom controls in design time, this will let you see all the controls with just the added overhead of one panel. This technique is demonstrated in Chapter 31, "Writing Components."

Polymorphism

As discussed in Chapter 10, Delphi supports polymorphism, which lets different objects respond appropriately to methods with the same name. For example, the Create method, which is a method of every object in Delphi, responds appropriately regardless of the object. Without polymorphism, you would need to name each object's Create method differently.

Delphi does not support *parametric polymorphism*, otherwise known as overloading. In C++ you can have the following methods defined for the same object:

```
check.print(1)
check.print(1,"1/1/95")
```

ObjectPascal does not let you create overloaded methods. However, if you look closely at the Create method, you will notice that Delphi does have some overloading as part of the base language. The Create method for the TComponent class always takes one argument, the owner (of TComponent type). However, the Create method for all other objects does not require a parameter. This is because some versions of the Create method (most noticeably the TObject class) are written in assembler language. The bottom line is that if you absolutely need overloading, you can resort to assembler language!

Properties

What makes the Delphi OOP framework nice is that it adds language extensions to read and write object properties. The following code fragment shows an example of the property syntax:

```
property Note: String read GetNote write SetNote;
```

This line of code, which can be placed in an object's published section, establishes a string property, called Note. Two methods, GetNote and SetNote, retrieve and assign a value to the property. With this approach, the two routines, GetNote and SetNote, can be written as follows:

```
function TMyObject.GetNote: String;
begin
    GetNote := FStringNote;
end;
```

In this example, FStringNote is a string variable declared in TMyObject's private section. Alternatively, you could declare the property as follows:

```
property Note: String read FStringNote write FStringNote;
```

This example requires no read or write method. Instead, the FNote variable is accessed directly.

The wonderful thing about properties with methods that set and get values is that the public and published interface to properties can remain constant while the internal representation changes. The read and write methods can convert to the appropriate data type the argument passed in to set the property or returned back as the property. This gives your application a bit more insulation from implementation changes.

Visual Component Library

In order to understand OOP and Delphi, you need to spend time reviewing Delphi's visual component library classes. Since all objects descend from the patriarch TObject, you need to understand how the various subclasses fit together. To help out, open the object browser and collapse all the nodes in the object tree (Figure 30.2).

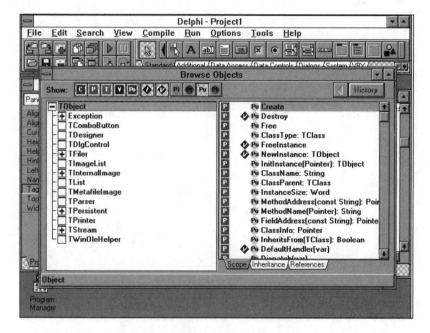

FIGURE 30.2 COLLAPSED OBJECT TREE.

Of direct descendant TObject classes, the important one is TPersistent. It is from this class that all the nonvisual components and the visual controls descend. The direct descendants from the TPersistent class are shown in Figure 30.3.

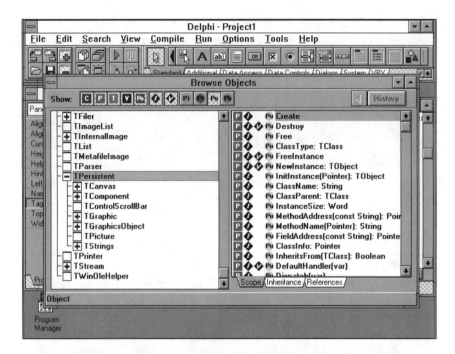

FIGURE 30.3 TPERSISTENT CLASS DESCENDANTS.

From the TPersistent class comes the TComponent class (its direct descendants are shown in Figure 30.4). TControl has two direct descendants: TGraphicControl and TWinControl. A TGraphicControl is a visual object that never receives focus. A TWinControl is a visual object that does receive focus. The direct descendants for TWinControl are shown in Figure 30.5.

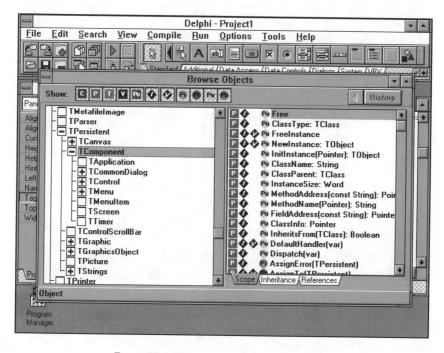

FIGURE 30.4 TCOMPONENT CLASS DESCENDANTS.

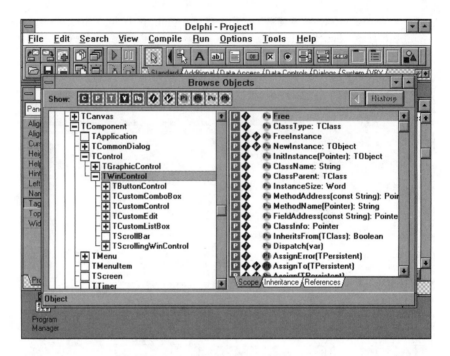

FIGURE 30.5 TWINCONTROL CLASS DESCENDANTS.

The most important family line in Delphi is the TObject-TPersistent-TComponent-TControl line. The reason is simple: perhaps the most important object-oriented work you will do in Delphi is to create new components based on one of the TWinControl classes. Table 30.1 lists the controls that are intermediate classes, which serve as the ancestor classes for the standard Delphi controls, such as TButton.

TABLE 30.1 INTERMEDIATE CLASSES

TButtonControl

TCustomComboBox
TCustomControl
TCustomEdit
TCustomListBox
TScrollingWinControl

When you work with the visual class library, you have to think hard about where your new object fits into the class hierarchy. Keep in mind that all the controls that descend from those in Table 30.1 have almost all the properties and behavior that you would typically need in a new control. Most often, you would create a new control that is a subclass of the standard Delphi control. For example, the TButton class, which descends from TButtonControl, inherits very little from TButtonControl, but offers much to a potential descendant. Most likely, you will base your new object on an existing Delphi standard control, such as TButton.

T I P

When you write object-oriented code in Delphi, it is important to consider on which object to base your new classes. Choose those classes that have the most to offer your new class. In other words, marry a rich family!

The purpose of this discussion of the visual component library is to remind you to use the object browser frequently. The browser clearly details how classes relate to each other and what wealth (properties and methods) passes from generation to generation. At first, you may be overwhelmed by the amount of information the browser conveys. But if you learn how to collapse irrelevant nodes in the browser and filter out unimportant items (such as private properties and methods), you can learn quite a bit about how Delphi implements its object-oriented visual component library.

Summary

Delphi provides direct support for encapsulation, inheritance, and polymorphism. Although it does not support multiple inheritance and parametric polymorphism, it is a complete OOP language.

CHAPTER 31

Writing Components

At first blush, the thought of creating components sounds intimidating. After all, if you create a component, you have to deal with all those messy and complex Windows issues, right?

Wrong. Creating components is very easy. In fact, if you use Delphi for a week without creating a component, you are missing one of the most essential parts of Delphi. It is through the creation of components that you take best advantage of Delphi's OOP capabilities.

Creating Your Own Components: Five Easy Steps

So you want to create your own component? It's easy, and it takes only five easy steps.

1. Choose an existing Delphi component on which to base your new component.
2. Choose **File | New Component** to create a new unit.
3. Modify the component with code.
4. Choose **Options | Install Components** to have Delphi install your component on the Component palette.
5. Place the new component on your form.

The first step is perhaps the most difficult, depending on the component. You have to pick your component wisely. Delphi offers many of components to choose from, and you need to understand the VCL hierarchy in order to pick the best class. In addition, we recommend you use the Object Browser to review the VCL class hierarchy to see what each class contributes.

In this example, we will create a component, TMyLabel, which will be based on the TLabel component. First, make sure that any projects you have opened are closed. To create the component, use the **File | New Component** menu item in step 2. This brings up the Component Expert dialog box (Figure 31.1).

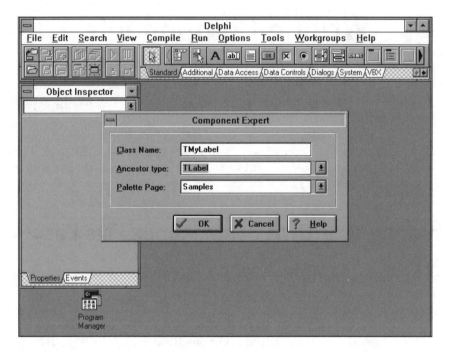

FIGURE 31.1 NEW COMPONENT EXPERT.

This dialog asks for three things:

- The name for the new component class (in this case TMyLabel)
- The name of the parent class (TLabel)
- The Component palette page where Delphi will place the component

After you provide this information and press the **OK** button, Delphi creates a unit with a class declaration for your new component. This unit can be located anywhere: on a network or on your local drive. If you are the sole programmer, you can create a directory in the Delphi directory. If you have several programmers creating custom components, its a good idea to decide on component source-code policies. Most likely, you will maintain a read-only shared central directory of custom component source code, which will then be copied to each developer's Delphi installation. Only developers responsible for the component source code should be allowed to change it.

After Delphi creates the component class template, you are free to add whatever code you want to change the component. In this example, we have added code on the object's constructor, which sets new default values for several properties. The unit source code is listed here:

```
unit Mylabel;

interface

uses
  SysUtils, WinTypes, WinProcs, Messages, Classes, Graphics, Controls,
  Forms, Dialogs, StdCtrls;

type
  TMyLabel = class(TLabel)
  private
    { Private declarations }
  protected
    { Protected declarations }
  public
    { Public declarations }
    constructor Create(AOwner: TComponent); override;
  published
    { Published declarations }
  end;

procedure Register;

implementation

constructor TMyLabel.Create(AOwner: TComponent);
begin
  inherited Create(AOwner);
  Font.Size := 12;
  Font.Color := clBlack;
  Font.Style := [fsBold,fsItalic];
  WordWrap := True;
  Caption := 'MyLabel Caption';
end;


procedure Register;
begin
```

```
    RegisterComponents('Samples', [TMyLabel]);
end;

end.
```

The constructor method declaration

```
constructor Create(AOwner: TComponent); override;
```

matches the constructor for the parent class TLabel. In the constructor, the code calls the create method for the parent class with the following line of code:

```
inherited Create(AOwner);
```

This ensures that the properties and methods for the ancestor classes are properly created before you decide to alter them. If you leave this line of code, your code will fail and report a general protection fault as soon as you place the component on a form because until you call the parent's create method, the object does not fully exist. The object has not allocated memory for its properties and methods. You cannot assign values to properties that do not have memory allocated and valid pointer addresses assigned. In fact, most general protection faults are the result of trying to access memory addresses (properties or methods) that have not been created or properly assigned.

After the parent's create method is invoked, the example replaces several default properties with new values. At the very least, this new component can save you time in resetting label properties each time you add one to a form. In fact, many Delphi developers create custom components to save design time.

When you are finished adding the code for the component, save the source file and then use **Options | Install Components** menu item (step 4) so that Delphi can compile your code and your component to the Component palette.

Choose the **Add** button to select your component source file; this will add the component. Once you select the source file, the path to the source file will automatically be added to the search path. Delphi uses the search path to find all compiled unit files during the component library recompilation and linking. Don't worry about the Installed units and the Component classes list boxes in the Install Components dialog box. These list boxes simply show what units are in the component library (COMPLIB.DCL) and what components are in each unit. (Remember, units can have multiple class declarations, and hence components, in them.)

After you add your source file and press the **OK** button, Delphi will compile your source code and rebuild the **COMPLIB.DCL** file. If any errors are found in your component source file, Delphi will display the error and the source file that contains the error. Delphi will use the DCU file (the compiled unit) when rebuilding the **COMPLIB.DCL**. When you specify a search path for the Install Component dialog box, it only needs to find the new component's DCU file, not the original source file. If a DCU file does not exist, Delphi will compile your source file to make one. If the source file does not exist but the DCU file does, Delphi will use the DCU file to add to the component library.

If the process completes successfully, the component will appear on the palette page you specified in step 3. In fact, if you look at the component declaration template that Delphi creates for you, you will notice the following lines of code:

```
procedure Register;

implementation

procedure Register;
begin
  RegisterComponents('Samples', [TMyLabel]);
end;
```

When you add a component to the component library, Delphi looks for the RegisterComponents procedure. If it does not find one, it reports an error. This procedure places the component on the specified page of the Component palette.

When creating your own components, it is a good idea to make a backup copy of **COMPLIB.DCL**. If the **COMPLIB.DCL** file is damaged, Delphi will not be able to display any components on your Component palette. Since this file holds compiled versions of your components and Delphi writes to it when it installs components, if something should go wrong during the component install, you can quickly restore the prior version.

Once Delphi has installed the component library, you can create a new form and place the component on your form (Figure 31.2). As you can see, the new component appears on the Sample page. When you create components, if you specify a palette page that does not exist (in step 2), Delphi will create a new palette page for you.

As you can see, Delphi automates much of the component registering process. However, Borland could make one improvement to the process, perhaps in a future version of Delphi. The component creation and registering process would be simpler if you could interactively, through the form designer, modify the properties of an existing component first. When you are finished setting the properties, you would then select the **File | New Component** menu item with the component selected, which would create the class declaration template with the constructor code and property assignments already completed.

A More Complex Example

While creating simple components that change default properties is quite simple, creating more sophisticated components requires more work. The next example demonstrates creating two slightly different components based on the TTable class.

This example, which is on the included code disk, demonstrates two components that work together to create an autoincrementing field. Although the Paradox table format has an autoincrementing field type, which increases the counter field by one with each new record, you might consider creating your own autoincrementing field for the following reasons:

- You can increment the field by some other algorithm.
- You want the autoincrement field to be more stable (the Paradox autoincrement field value can get reset during a table repair operation with Paradox for Windows).
- The underlying table format does not support autoincrement fields.
- You want to store the seed for the autoincrementing field in another table for easy access.

This example includes two components: TTableAutoField and TTableAutoSource. The TTableAutoField component is based on the TTable class and adds the following two properties:

AutoKeyField	The name of the field in the TTableAutoField component to write the autoincrement value.
AutoKeyTable	The table object that is connected to the autoincrement seed value.

The TTableAutoSource component is also based on the TTable class and adds a new property, AutoSourceField, which is the name of the field in the autoincrement seed table whose value should be incremented. In addition, this component has a public function that returns the next autoincrement value.

The basic idea is that you place a TTableAutoField object on your form for tables that require an autoincrement field. You then place a TTableAutoSource object on your form and link it to the TTableAutoField object via its AutoKeyTable property. This lets you specify an autoincrement table in another database, either local or remote.

This example demonstrates the following crucial concepts you will need to master in order to create components:

- Creating and registering property editors
- Overriding existing component methods
- Adding new methods
- Overriding existing component events

Figure 31.2 shows the sample form on the included code disk in design mode. The source code for the two components is listed below:

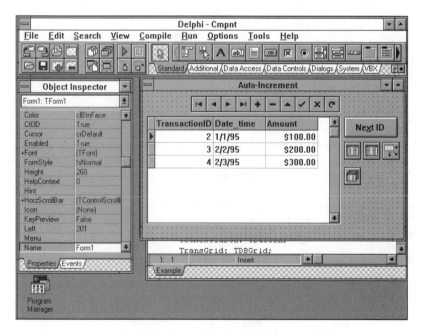

FIGURE 31.2 CHAPTER 31 EXAMPLE FORM.

```
unit Autokey;

interface

uses
  SysUtils, WinTypes, WinProcs, Messages, Classes, Graphics, Controls,
  Forms, Dialogs, DB, DBTables, Dsgnintf;

type

  { TTableAutoField is a TTable object which can be linked
    to a TTableAutoSource object to automatically increment
    a user-defineable counter field }

  TTableAutoField = class(TTable)
  private
    FAutoKeyComponent : TDataSet;
    FAutoKeyField : String;
    FLastKeyRetrieved : Longint;
    { Private declarations }
  protected
    { Protected declarations }
    procedure DoBeforeInsert; override;
    procedure DoAfterInsert; override;
  public
    { Public declarations }
    constructor Create(AOwner: TComponent); override;
    function GetNextKey: Longint;
  published
    { Published declarations }
    property AutoKeyTable: TDataSet
             read FAutoKeyComponent write FAutoKeyComponent;
    property AutoKeyField: String read FAutoKeyField write FAutoKeyField;
  end;

  { TTableAutoSource is a table component which holds
   the incrementing key field }
  TTableAutoSource = class(TTable)
  private
    FAutoSourceField : String;
    { Private declarations }
  protected
    { Protected declarations }
  public
    { Public declarations }
    constructor Create(AOwner: TComponent); override;
```

```
    function GetAutoKey: Longint;
  published
    { Published declarations }
    property AutoSourceField: String read FAutoSourceField write
FAutoSourceField;
  end;

procedure Register;

implementation

type
  EAutoSourceError  = class(EComponentError);

  { TAutoFieldProperty editor }
  TAutoFieldProperty = class(TStringProperty)
  public
    function GetAttributes: TPropertyAttributes; override;
    procedure GetValues(Proc: TGetStrProc); override;
  end;

{ TAutoFieldProperty methods, copied from DBREG.PAS }
function TAutoFieldProperty.GetAttributes: TPropertyAttributes;
begin
  Result := [paValueList, paSortList, paMultiSelect];
end;

procedure TAutoFieldProperty.GetValues(Proc: TGetStrProc);
var
  I: Integer;
  Values: TStringList;
begin
  { create a string list to hold fields }
  Values := TStringList.Create;
  try
    { call the TTable procedure to store fields in a list }
    TTable(GetComponent(0)).GetFieldNames(Values);
    { add the fields to the property drop down list }
    for I := 0 to Values.Count - 1 do Proc(Values[I]);
  finally
    { release the string list }
    Values.Free;
  end;
end;

{ TTableAutoField methods }
```

```
constructor TTableAutoField.Create(AOwner: TComponent);
begin
  inherited Create(AOwner);
end;

function TTableAutoField.GetNextKey: Longint;
begin
   result := TTableAutoSource(FAutoKeyComponent).GetAutoKey;
end;

procedure TTableAutoField.DoBeforeInsert;
begin
   inherited DoBeforeInsert;
   FLastKeyRetrieved := GetNextKey;
end;

procedure TTableAutoField.DoAfterInsert;
begin
   if FAutoKeyField<>'' then
      FieldByName(FAutoKeyField).AsInteger := FLastKeyRetrieved;
   Inherited DoAfterInsert;
end;

{ TTableAutoSource methods}
constructor TTableAutoSource.Create(AOwner: TComponent);
begin
  inherited Create(AOwner);
end;

function TTableAutoSource.GetAutoKey: Longint;
var
   AutoField: TField;
begin
   if FAutoSourceField='' then
      Raise EAutoSourceError.Create('AutoSource field is blank');
   Edit;
   Result := FieldByName(FAutoSourceField).AsInteger+1;
   FieldByName(FAutoSourceField).AsInteger := Result;
   Post;
end;

procedure Register;
begin
  { register the two components }
  RegisterComponents('Data Access', [TTableAutoField,TTableAutoSource]);
  { register the property editors }
```

```
RegisterPropertyEditor(TypeInfo(string), TTableAutoField,
  'AutoKeyField', TAutoFieldProperty);
RegisterPropertyEditor(TypeInfo(string), TTableAutoSource,
  'AutoSourceField', TAutoFieldProperty);
end;
end.
```

Creating and Registering Property Editors

One of the best places to look for good examples of creating components is within the Delphi VCL source code (if you have the client/server edition), since it contains numerous examples of all sorts of components. However, it will take some time for you to understand how the source code files are organized and how the class hierarchies work together.

Perhaps the most important piece is understanding how to add properties to your component with intelligent property editors. A property editor is an object that knows how to assist or validate user input in a component's property. If you want your components to have drop-down lists or dialog boxes that validate property settings, then you will need to know which property/component combinations have property editors already established in Delphi and which property editors you will need to add.

The two components in this example have properties with property editors, both custom and built-in. The TTableAutoField component has two properties of interest:

```
property AutoKeyTable: TDataSet
         read FAutoKeyComponent write FAutoKeyComponent;
property AutoKeyField: String read FAutoKeyField write FAutoKeyField;
```

The AutoKeyTable property is of type TDataSet for one very important reason: *It takes automatic advantage of an existing registered property editor.* When you click on this property's drop-down button, you will see a list of TTable components to choose from. This behavior was created simply by giving the AutoKeyTable property the type TDataSet. Delphi has a property editor for the TDataSet class, which is set to respond to any property of TDataSet type.

The next property, AutoKeyField, also has a property editor associated with it. The AutoKeyField should show a list of field names from the underlying table. However, this property requires a custom property editor. At the end of the code listing above, you will notice the following code:

```
RegisterPropertyEditor(TypeInfo(string), TTableAutoField,
  'AutoKeyField', TAutoFieldProperty);
```

In this example, the RegisterPropertyEditor() procedure instructs Delphi to register in the component library (whenever the menu item **Options** | **Install Components** is chosen) the new property editor class TTableAutoField for the AutoKeyField property of the TAutoFieldProperty class. These are the last three arguments in RegisterPropertyEditor(). The first argument is always a type information pointer to the type of property being registered.

During design time, whenever the user attempts to edit the property, the TTableAutoFieldProperty class will control the setting of the property. The class declaration for this property editor, repeated below, shows the methods needed to construct a property editor that needs to display a list of fields from a table:

```
{ TAutoFieldProperty editor }
  TAutoFieldProperty = class(TStringProperty)
  public
    function GetAttributes: TPropertyAttributes; override;
    procedure GetValues(Proc: TGetStrProc); override;
  end;
```

All property editors descend from TPropertyEditor, which defines the basic events and methods the property editor mechanism will support. The GetAttributes method listed above is initially declared in the class TPropertyEditor. In fact, the TPropertyEditor class is abstract; it simply defines methods that can be overridden by descendant classes.

In this example, the GetAttributes method is called by the property editor mechanism to determine the property's attributes so that it knows how to display and handle the property. The AutoKeyField and AutoSourceField properties have the following properties set: [paValueList, paSortList, paMultiSelect]. This tells the property editor mechanism that the property is chosen from a value list, the list should be sorted, and the property should be available when the user has multiple components selected.

The real work in getting the field list is done in the GetValues method with the following line of code:

```
TTable(GetComponent(0)).GetFieldNames(Values);
```

GetComponent(0) returns a pointer to the current component, which is then cast to a TTable pointer. Once converted to a TTable pointer, the TTable method GetFieldNames() is invoked to fill a string list with the fields from the underlying table. Once the fields are stored in a string list, they can be safely added to the component's drop-down list with the following line of code:

```
for I := 0 to Values.Count - 1 do Proc(Values[I]);
```

Proc() is a method pointer that is supplied by the property editor mechanism. The method Proc() points to a procedure that requires a single argument of type string, which simply adds the string to the property's drop-down list.

From this short example, you can see that if you want to create your own properties that work just like Borland's property editors, you will have to spend time learning advanced ObjectPascal features. All the code you see here is based on techniques derived from Borland's own components. While the amount of code is quite small, learning how the class hierarchies work together is no small task. However, once you learn the details of the VCL class hierarchy, writing sophisticated property editors is much easier. If you are serious about writing many components, it is a good idea to get the VCL source code. In it, you will find many more techniques for handling property editors.

A Property Editor Dialog Box

If you need a more sophisticated property editor than the drop-down list, you can have a dialog box pop up when the user clicks on the button next to the property value. The TPropertyEditor class defines several methods you are free to override for any property. One method, Edit, is called when the user double-clicks the property or clicks on the ... next to the property value.

You can override the Edit method and display your own dialog box to get the user's value. Listed below is the code, taken from the Delphi source code file **DBREG.PAS**, which shows how Delphi brings up a dialog box when you edit the query parameters property for the TQuery component:

```
procedure TQueryParamsProperty.Edit;
var
  List: TParams;
  Query: TQuery;
begin
  Query := GetComponent(0) as TQuery;
  List := TParams.Create;
  try
    List.Assign(Query.Params);
    if EditQueryParams(Query, List) then
    begin
      Query.Params := List;
      if Designer <> nil then Designer.Modified;
    end;
```

```
    finally
      List.Free;
    end;
end;
```

This code example performs a few simple steps:

1. It gets a pointer to the TQuery component (GetComponent(0)).
2. It creates a list of parameters (TParams.Create).
3. It assigns the current vales of the query parameters to List (List.Assign()).
4. It calls EditQueryParams() to display a dialog box to let the user edit the parameters.
5. If the dialog box is accepted, it assigns the new parameters to the Query.Params property (Query.Params := List).

Overriding Methods

You will frequently need to provide custom behavior in your component, as the TTableAutoField component does. It must write a new increment value to each new record. To perform this, the code example overrides two event procedures: DoBeforeInsert and DoAfterInsert. Since a new record does not yet exist after the DoBeforeInsert event, we actually get the new increment value before a record is even inserted. If anything should go wrong, Delphi will raise an exception at this point, before a record is created.

```
procedure TTableAutoField.DoBeforeInsert;
begin
   inherited DoBeforeInsert;
   FLastKeyRetrieved := GetNextKey;
end;

procedure TTableAutoField.DoAfterInsert;
begin
   if FAutoKeyField<>'' then
      FieldByName(FAutoKeyField).AsInteger := FLastKeyRetrieved;
   Inherited DoAfterInsert;
end;
```

Then, in the DoAfterInsert procedure, TTableAutoField places the new increment value into the proper field using the TTable FieldByName method.

Events are Properties

In Delphi, events appear as properties. In fact, events are merely method pointers. For example, the DoBeforeInsert method just discussed has a corresponding property definition for the TDataSet type (an ancestor of the TTable class). The TDataSet object defines the property as

```
property BeforeInsert: TDataSetNotifyEvent read FBeforeInsert write
FBeforeInsert;
```

The FBeforeInsert field is defined as a method pointer:

```
FBeforeInsert: TDataSetNotifyEvent;
```

The Delphi VCL calls our method DoBeforeInsert at the proper time during the insert record sequence. When it does, it calls the TDataSet.DoBeforeInsert procedure:

```
procedure TDataSet.DoBeforeInsert;
begin
  if Assigned(FBeforeInsert) then FBeforeInsert(Self);
end;
```

All this code does is check to make sure the field FBeforeInsert is assigned a pointer before calling that method. To summarize, remember that events are actually properties in which the pointer to the method the user selected for the property is stored in a field. Then, during the event sequence, the Delphi VCL will call a procedure (with the same name as the event, DoBeforeInsert), which in turn calls the method assigned to the property. This scheme lets you override event methods easily.

While it is rare to do so, if you need to create new events for components, Delphi lets you easily tap into the Windows event model. For example, the **CONTROLS.PAS** file in the **SOURCE\VCL** directory (for those who have the source version of Delphi), defines the following private procedure for the class TControl:

```
procedure WMLButtonDblClk(var Message: TWMLButtonDblClk); message
WM_LBUTTONDBLCLK;
```

By virtue of the key word *message*, Delphi will invoke this procedure whenever the Windows message WM_LBUTTONDBLCLK occurs. Windows programmers that are used to dealing with the wParam and lParam message arguments and with the high-order or low-order word in lParam can relax. Delphi has several record structures that place the data in these arguments in appropriately named fields. The Message: TWMLButtonDblClk argument is one example of a predefined message cracker.

Also included in **CONTROL.PAS** is the source code for how TControl responds to the WM_LBUTTONDBLCLK Windows event:

```
procedure TControl.WMLButtonDblClk(var Message: TWMLButtonDblClk);
begin
  SendCancelMode(Self);
  inherited;
  if csCaptureMouse in ControlStyle then MouseCapture := True;
  if csClickEvents in ControlStyle then DblClick;
  DoMouseDown(Message, mbLeft, [ssDouble]);
end;
```

In this procedure, notice the use of the word *inherited*. This calls the message handler inherited from the parent object. If you need to, you can define your own messages outside the range of Windows messages. Delphi ships with a component writer's guide that goes into much more detail about how Windows messages are handled and dispatched. For nearly all components, you won't need this detailed knowledge. But it is important to know that Delphi can easily accommodate even the most arduous Windows programming task.

Other Component Issues

If you want to give your component a different bitmap on the Component palette, make sure you have a Windows resource file with the same name as the unit (but with a DCR extension). Inside the DCR file should be a bitmaps (24 pixels by 24 pixels) for each component registered. The bitmap image name must be the same as the component type. Also, you will need to force Delphi to recompile your component source file. To do this, delete the DCU file or change the date/time stamp on the source code file by making a comment change or some other change. You can also give each component its own help screens. The component writer's guide contains information on how to name your keywords and merge your help file in Delphi.

Summary

By allowing custom components, Delphi offers ultimate flexibility. Developers get to tap into the very same features that Borland programmers used to create all the controls in Delphi. You can create new controls based on existing controls, add new properties, control how those properties should be edited, and rearrange the event model by adding events or over-riding existing events. And since the source code is included in the client/server edition, you can determine exactly how your code can best interact with the existing code.

This chapter just scratches the surface in creating components. No doubt, many developers are busy creating all sorts of custom components. Delphi not only makes it easy to make simple changes to existing components, it has all the tools necessary to make almost any kind of component imaginable.

CHAPTER 32

Packaging your Application

The first impression users will get of your application is through its installation program. The goal of your installation program should be to give users a pleasant "OOBE" (Out-Of-Box Experience). This means that the program should be easily installed by users of any skill level.

This chapter discusses the steps you must take to successfully distribute your Delphi application. The example application from Chapter 21 is used to demonstrate a typical database application installation.

Identify the Required Files

The first step in packaging your application is to determine what files are required for a user to run the program. The following sections describe the different file types you may be using in your application, what they do, and how they are installed.

Executable Files

The obvious requirement for most applications is the main executable, or .EXE file. For small applications, this may be the only file required. It is installed in the application's main directory. Include an icon in the file so that users can easily identify the program in their Windows shell.

More complex applications may require .DLL files. These are usually installed in the main application directory or in the **Windows\System** directory. Unless your application explicitly loads the .DLLs, they should be in a directory where Windows can find them when needed (in the current directory, the Windows or Windows/System directories, or on the DOS or network search path).

T I P

Check the **Optimize for Size and Load Time** option on the linker page in the Project Options dialog box. This will significantly reduce the size of your .EXE or .DLL target file. Also, be sure the **Include TDW Debug Info** option is not checked. Debugging information can more than double the size of your executable file.

If you use VBX controls in your application, you will need to include the .VBX file in the same directory as the .EXE file, in the system path, or in the **Windows\System** directory. The Delphi VBX runtime library (**BIVBX11.DLL**) must be installed into the user's **Windows\System** directory.

Commercial .DLL files can also be used with Delphi applications. These are commonly stored in the application directory or in the **Windows\System** directory. Be certain that you have purchased appropriate distribution licenses before using a commercial .DLL in your application.

For an OLE container application, you must install the Borland OLE support file (**BOLE16D.DLL**) in the **Windows\System** directory. In addition, be sure that the following Microsoft files are present:

OLE2.DLL
OLE2.REG
OLE2CONV.DLL
OLE2DISP.DLL
OLE2NLS.DLL
OLE2PROX.DLL
OLECLI.DLL
OLESVR.DLL
STORAGE.DLL
TYPELIB.DLL
COMPOBJ.DLL

Data Files

Most applications require data files. If your application uses database tables, you will need to include empty tables with their related files in the installation. You may not need to distribute other types of data files. For example, there is no need to distribute empty documents for a word processing program.

Most users find sample files helpful. If it is appropriate to your application, create some sample data files that mimic real-world use of the program as closely as possible.

Auxiliary Files

One of the most important files you will distribute is the **Readme** file, usually called **README.TXT**. This file should contain brief installation instructions (as a supplement to the user manual), information that arrived too late to be included in the manual, troubleshooting tips, technical support procedures, a known bug list, and whatever other information a new user might find useful. It should be available to the user at any time before or after installation.

You may wish to provide a separate file with information specific to the installation procedure. This file is often called **INSTALL.TXT**, and it replaces the installation instruction portion of the **README.TXT** file.

Many Windows programs use initialization files, usually with the extension .INI. These contain startup information and user preference settings for your application. They are normally stored in the main application directory or in the **Windows** directory. The original version of the file distributed with the application should contain reasonable default values. Note that the sample application does not use an .INI file. Instead, a Paradox table is used to store this information.

Windows help files are often part of a complete application. These files have the extension .HLP. They are usually installed in the application's main directory.

Utility Files

Most applications require at least one utility program: the installation program. Other examples of utility programs are a setup utility to allow users to make configuration changes, a utility to repair damaged data files, and an uninstall program.

Delivering Database Applications

Database applications require some or all of the files discussed above. In addition, you will need to provide the database access files. Delphi supports a number of different databases, so you have a number of different installation options.

WARNING

The Delphi standard and client/server editions have very different licensing agreements regarding redistributing database files. Be absolutely certain you have secured the proper licensing for any files you distribute with your Delphi application. The information in this chapter is intended only as a reference to the Borland licensing agreements. Refer to your Delphi documentation (in particular, the Deploy.txt file) for the final word on redistributing Delphi files.

Installing the BDE

All Delphi database applications use the Borland Database Engine (BDE) to access data. The BDE is redistributable without additional licensing fees for use in any Delphi application. The entire BDE must be installed by each user, using the BDE installation program provided with Delphi. You can tell your users to delete any unnecessary BDE files after the installation is complete, but your Delphi licensing agreement requires that the entire BDE be installed first.

The redistributable BDE is on the Delphi CD-ROM in two directories: **\REDIST\BDEINST\DISK1** and **\REDIST\BDEINST\DISK2**. Copy these directories to two floppy disks and instruct your users to run **INSTALL.EXE** on DISK1 (or to run it directly from your installation program).

Use the following table to determine which of the BDE files are required for your application and which can be safely deleted by users.

File Name	Required For
IDAPI01.DLL	All database applications
IDR10009.DLL	All database applications
ILD01.DLL	All database applications
IDAPI.CFG	All database applications
IDQRY01.DLL	SQL queries (with IDPDX01.DLL)
IDBAT01.DLL	SQL queries and batch move operations
IDPDX01.DLL	Paradox tables
IDDBAS01.DLL	dBASE tables
IDASCI01.DLL	ASCII tables
IDODBC01.DLL	ODBC tables
ODBC.NEW	Microsoft ODBC Driver Manager DLL, v2.0
ODBCINST.NEW	Microsoft ODBC Driver Installation DLL, v2.0
BDECFG.EXE	BDE Configuration utility
BDECFG.HLP	BDE Configuration utility help

If your database application requires BDE aliases, be sure to include instructions on how to use the BDE configuration program. It is recommended, however, that you use the technique described in Chapters 15 and 21 to set up database access as the application runs.

Installing SQL Links

If your application uses a SQL database such as Interbase or Oracle, your users must install Borland SQL Link software. This software provides a link between the BDE and the SQL database. Note that your users will also require network communications software, such as TCP/IP, to connect to the database.

The redistributable SQL Link software is on the Delphi CD-ROM in two directories: **\REDIST\SQLINST\DISK1** and **\REDIST\SQLINST\DISK2**. Copy these directories to two floppy disks and instruct your users to run **SETUP.EXE** on DISK1 (or to run it directly from your installation program).

The client/server edition of Delphi includes a redistribution license for these SQL Link files. The files may be used to run applications created in Delphi only. They may not be used to develop or run any other applications. The standard edition of Delphi does not provide the SQL Link files or any licensing. If you are using the standard edition, you will have to license these items separately.

The following tables describe the files required for each supported SQL database.

Interbase	Informix
SQLD_IB.DLL	SQLD_INF.DLL
SQLD_IB.HLP	SQLD_INF.HLP
SQL_IB.CNF	SQL_INF.CNF
CONNECT.EXE	LDLLSQLW.DLL
CONNECT.HLP	ISAM.IEM
GDS.DLL	OS.IEM
REMOTE.DLL	RDS.IEM
INTERBAS.MSG	SECURITY.IEM
IUTLS.DLL	SQL.IEM
DSQL.DLL	ZRDSTERM.IEM
NWIPXSPX.DLL	
NWCALLS.DLL	
NWNETAPI.DLL	

Sybase and Microsoft SQL Server	Oracle
SQLD_SS.DLL	SQLD_ORA.DLL
SQLD_SS.HLP	SQLD_ORA.HLP
SQL_SS.CNF	SQL_ORA.CNF
W3DBLIB.DLL	ORA6WIN.DLL
DBNMP3.DLL	ORA7WIN.DLL
SYDC437.LD	COREWIN.DLL
SYDC850.LD	ORAWE850.LD
NWIPXSPX.DLL	NWIPXSPX.DLL
NWNETAPI.DLL	NWNETAPI.DLL

The Delphi client/server edition also provides a distribution license for the Local Interbase Server (LIBS). The following files are required to use LIBS in your program:

Local Interbase Server

DSQL.DLL
FILEIO.DLL
GDS.DLL
GBAK.DLL
INTL.DLL
IUTLS.DLL
JRD.DLL
REMOTE.DLL
STACK.DLL
INTERBASE.MSG
ISC4.GDB
ISC_LIC.DAT
WISQL.EXE
WISQL.HLP
SQLREF.HLP
IBMGR.EXE
SVRMGR.HLP
COMDIAG.EXE
COMDIAG.INI
COMDIAG.HLP
BLINT04.HLP

Please note that while LIBS is provided with the standard edition of Delphi as a development tool, it does not have a redistribution license. Contact Borland for a local Interbase deployment kit.

Installing ReportSmith RunTime

To use ReportSmith reports in your application, your users will have to have ReportSmith Runtime (or ReportSmith itself) installed on their systems. The redistributable ReportSmith Runtime is on the Delphi CD-ROM in five directories: **\REDIST\RPTINST\DISK1** through **\REDIST\RPTINST \DISK5**. Copy these directories to five floppy disks and instruct your users to run **INSTALL.EXE** on DISK1 (or to run it directly from your installation program).

The following table lists the files required for the ReportSmith Runtime module. The files should be installed to a directory on the user's path so that Delphi can find the runtime module when it is needed.

ReportSmith

RED110.DLL	DRVACCSS.HLP	BTRV110.DLL
DRVBTRV.HLP	RCS0.RST-RCS8.RST	RSCTSFMT.RST
DRVDBASE.HLP	XBS110.DLL	RS_DBLIB.DLL
XLSISAM.DLL	DRVEXCEL.HLP	RVFOX.HLP
RS_GUP.DLL	S_INGR.DLL	4RPT.MAC
DONDFMT.MAC	ATE.MAC	DISABLE.MAC
ENABLE.MAC	GREETING.MAC	ID2NAME.MAC
LOADREP.MAC	OADREPS.MAC	RECNO.MAC
THETIME.MAC	TL3D.DLL	MSJETDSP.DLL
ODBC.DLL	DBCADM.EXE	ODBCINST.DLL
SIMADMIN.DLL	IMBA.DLL	ODBCINST.HLP
COPOBJ.DLL	TDOLE.TLD	DRVTEXT.HLP
RS_ORA6.DLL	S_ORA7.DLL	BIBAS04.DLL
BIFLT04.DLL	IMDS04.DLL	BIUTL04.DL
ODBCCURS.DLL	PXENGCFG.EXE	PXENGWIN.DLL
BIPDX04.DLL	BIPDX04.HLP	QEBI.LIC
README.TXT	BC30RTL.DLL	DATALIB2.DLL
DLOLE2.DLL	IMAGEMAN.DLL	IMGPCX.DIL
IMGTIFF.DIL	RSSQLIF.TXT	RS_FMT.DLL
RS_IDABP.DLL	RS_ODBC.DLL	RS_OGLWL.DLL
RS_OLE2C.DLL	RS_OLE2U.DLL	RS_OWL31.DLL

RS_SIFUT.DLL	RS_SQLIF.DLL	RS_SYS.DLL
RS_SYS.DLL	RS_TBP1.DLL	RS_TBP2.DLL
RS_TCL31.DLL	RS_TKRIB.DLL	RS_DFWEN.DLL
RS_TKSTB.DLL	RS_TKTB.DLL	RS_UTIL.DLL
SSMRTHEAP.DLL	EPVAR.FRM	REPVAR.MAK
RSR_CTAB.DLL	RSR_DBAC.DLL	RSR_DBUI.DLL
RSR_MAIN.DLL	RSR_RPT.DLL	RSR_RUTL.DLL
RSR_XPRT.DLL	RSTEST.FRM	RSTEST.FRM
RS_RUN.EXE	RS_RUN.HLP	RUN_TEST.EXE
RS_SQLIF.INI	CTL3DV2.DLL	TXTISAM.DLL

Creating the Package

Now that you have a list of required files, you need to put together the distribution package. Applications are generally distributed on floppy disks or CD ROM or by downloading from an on-line services such as CompuServe. Depending on the size and complexity of your application, there are several different ways you can set up the distribution package. You will probably want to use file compression to reduce the size of the files you are distributing. Most programs also use an install program to automate the installation process.

File Compression

Windows programs are big—and getting bigger. It is not uncommon for a commercial program to consume 20 MB or more of disk space (a full installation of Delphi is more than 75 MB!). Unless you are distributing on CD-ROM, you will need to minimize the size of the files (and therefore the number of disks) you are distributing. This is particularly important if your customers are going to download your program from an on-line service; it will minimize their connect time charges.

There are a number of file-compression utilities on the market. Perhaps the most commonly used utility is PKZIP, a popular DOS shareware program. There are also several Windows-based compression utilities on the market. Any of these programs will shrink your distribution files to a fraction of their original size (the redistributable BDE and ReportSmith are already compressed). The files can easily be restored by your customers or your installation program.

Earlier in this chapter, we warned you about the licensing of Delphi redistributable files. This warning applies equally to the compression utility you choose. Be certain that you have purchased the appropriate licenses to allow you to distribute files compressed with the selected utility. This includes shareware compression utilities.

 Leave your application's **README.TXT** and/or **INSTALL.TXT** files uncompressed on the installation disk. The users will need to refer to this file before starting the installation program to be sure they have the latest information.

T I P

Documentation

No application is complete without documentation. While most applications still use some paper documentation (such as user manuals), many vendors are moving toward electronic on-line documentation. Be sure to include books, help files, **readme** files, and/or on-line manuals to help customers use your program. Keep in mind that most users still seem to prefer some hard-copy documentation, at least enough to get them started with the program.

Installation Programs

For a simple application, you may be able to distribute a single .EXE file without any other supporting files. For this type of application, an installation program is probably not necessary. For a more complex application, you will need to provide an installation program to help your users get up and running. An installation program should be able to:

- Extract compressed program files.
- Move program files to the selected application directory and the Windows directories. If necessary, the application directory should be created by the installation program.
- Create and/or modify .INI files, and other system control files (such as **AUTOEXEC.BAT**).
- Display the **README.TXT** file.
- Create and/or modify Windows program groups.
- Run other installation programs, such as the BDE or SQL Links.
- Offer the user maximum flexibility in installing and configuring the program (including selecting a directory and creating program groups).

While you can certainly write your own installation program, by far the easiest way to build your installation package is to purchase a commercial installation utility. A good program will automate the entire build process, including selecting the list of files to include in your distribution disks, compressing the files, and creating a setup program for the user.

There are a number of excellent installation program utilities on the market. For the sample program, the Setup Expert from Eschalon Development was used to create the installation program. The Setup Expert guides you through the process of creating the installation disks, prompting you at each step for the necessary information. It is similar in concept to Borland's Experts and Microsoft's Wizards. A demonstration copy is included on the code disk.

Uninstalling

Good Windows manners suggest that your installation program should have an **Uninstall** option, in case the users need to remove the application from their systems. At the very least, provide your users with a complete list of files your application uses, so they can uninstall it themselves, if necessary. This list should include the files in the program's main directory, as well as any files stored in the **Windows** or **Windows\System** directories.

Testing the Installation Program

Even though this is one of the last chapters in the book, the installation program should not be your last task in building your application. As you deliver incremental builds of the application, give your users incremental builds of the installation program to install them. The installation program needs as much testing as any other part of your application. Nothing is more embarrassing than delivering a finely crafted application to your customers, only to have them return it for a refund because they couldn't get the installation program to run.

Sample Program Installation Instructions

The sample application installation files are included on the CD-ROM included with this book in this chapter's directory. There are four files included: **SETUP.EXE**, **SETUP.ARV**, **SETUPMN.ARV**, and **README.TXT**. Take a look at **README.TXT** in case there is any information on the sample program that arrived too late for publication here. Then, run **SETUP.EXE** and enter the application's directory in the dialog box displayed. After the application is installed, the program will ask if you want a Windows Program Manager group created. After creating the group (if requested), the installation is complete. The sample program is started by running **PROJTRAK.EXE**.

Note that the BDE is not a part of the sample program installation. It is assumed that as a reader of this book, you already have Delphi and the BDE installed on your system. If not, install the BDE from the Delphi disk(s) before running the sample program.

Summary

A solid user-friendly installation program will give your users a good first impression of your application. A sloppy installation program will make your users wonder how much attention you paid to the rest of the program. Spend some time to get it right. It will pay off in reduced technical support and increased future business.

CHAPTER 33

Database Desktop Background and Overview

Borland's Delphi includes the Database desktop, which is a development tool that provides the ability to perform the following necessary functions in your database applications:

- Create Paradox, dBase, and local InterBase tables.
- Create other table types, if drivers are available, including ODBC drivers.
- Use table utilities such as Add, Delete, Restructure, and Infostructure to modify, restructure, or analyze a table's structure or data contents.
- Interactively modify the data in your tables.
- Create and execute QBE (Query-By-Example) queries to view or modify data in one or more tables.
- Create and execute SQL (Structured Query Language) statements to perform functions as you would with the QBEs.

With this array of development tools in the Database desktop, you can create and fill the tables needed to create and fully test your Delphi application and test query results before they are included in your application.

The Database desktop also gives you the flexibility of creating just a few tables or queries to start your application and easy addition of other tables and queries as the application matures and grows into the delivered version.

Overview of Database Desktop

Borland's Database desktop has four main menus:

- Files
- Utilities
- Windows
- Help

Figure 33.1 shows the main screen of the Database Desktop.

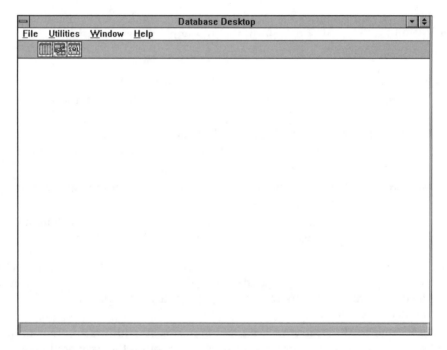

FIGURE 33.1 THE MAIN SCREEN OF THE DATABASE DESKTOP.

Important menu items will be addressed throughout the course of this chapter as you would use them, instead of just walking through the menus and explaining as we go.

Creating Tables

Data for Delphi applications will be stored in database files called *tables*. Each table is made up of columns and rows. Each column represents a data item to be part of each record, or row, stored in your tables.

As previously mentioned, the Database desktop gives you the option of creating Paradox, dBase, and InterBase tables. The following table creations will work with Paradox tables and local InterBase tables.

When creating tables it is important to keep in mind the following guidelines:

- Keep only the information that is absolutely necessary in each table.
- Each field should be unique and not a combination of fields, i.e., keeping a customer's first and last name in the same field makes the data difficult to work with.
- Avoid repeating data in multiple tables.
- Create tables as units that would be referenced in your application. For example in an order-entry system you would keep the customer, order, and order items information separate to prevent data redundancy.
- Choose your table type carefully, as each type has a few characteristics not common to other tables types.

Adding, Editing, and Removing Table Fields

Since we'll now be creating a few Paradox 5.0 tables, a review of the available Paradox data types will help us decide the logical type for each field in our new table. Table 33.1 displays pertinent information for each of the Paradox data types.

TABLE 33.1 REAL TYPES

Type	Symbol	Size Values	Description
Alpha	A	1-255 Required	Comprised of letters, numbers, and special characters
Number	N	None	Numbers in the range of 10^{-307} to 10^{308}

Money	$	None	Same range as Number, but Money fields are formatted to have decimal places and a money symbol
Short	S	None	Whole numbers from -32,767 to 32,768
Long Integer	I	None	Whole Numbers from 2147483647 to -2147483647
BCD	#	0-32	Binary Coded Decimal. (0-32) is the number of digits after the decimal point
Date	D	None	Any date from 1/1/9999 B.C. to 12/31/9999
Time	T	None	Time of day
Timestamp	@	None	Contains date and time values
Memo	M	1-240	Any printable characters. Limited only by disk space. Size value represents number of characters actually stored in table
Formatted Memo	F	1-240	Same as Memo with the addition of ability to save typeface and formatting preferences
Graphic	G	0-240 (Optional)	Contains graphics/pictures
OLE	O	0-240 (Optional)	Contains objects that support Object Linking and Embedding
Logical	L	None	Value representing True/False or Yes/No
Auto-increment	(	None	Long integer value maintained by Paradox. Started at 1 and incremented for each record added
Binary	B	0-240 (Optional)	Paradox can interpret Binary information only through ObjectPal Code
Bytes	Y	1-255	Used to store bar-codes or magnetic strips

As you can see, the Paradox data types cover virtually every conceivable type of data that you will need to store.

Using Table 33.1 as a guideline, you can create your own version of the customer table. This will have the same structure as the customer table in the **\DEMOS\DATA** subdirectory under the directory in which you have installed Delphi, but we will make other modifications. The original customer table can always be used as a reference, but it will have obvious differences.

In order to create a new table, select **File | New | Table** from the main menu. When the Table Type dialog box appears, choose **Paradox 5.0 For Windows**. See Figure 33.2.

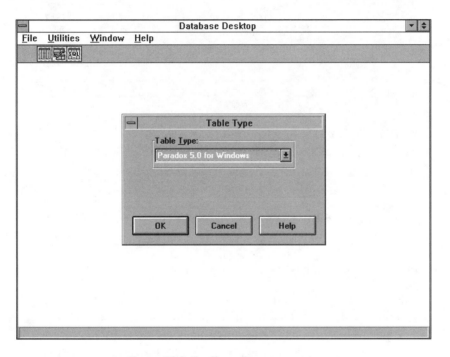

FIGURE 33.2 THE TABLE TYPE DIALOG BOX.

Once you have selected the table type, you will see the Table Structure dialog box. This is where you will define your table's fields and other properties, such as validity checks and secondary indexes. See Figure 33.3.

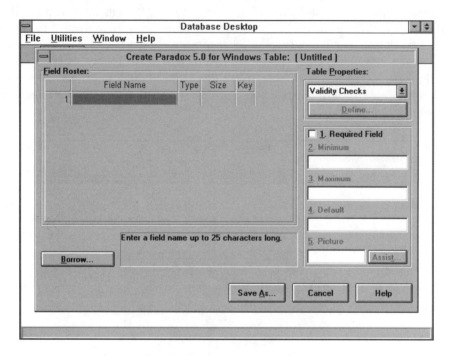

FIGURE 33.3 CREATING A NEW TABLE.

Each field of your table has the following parts:

- Field Name: The name you wish to use to reference that particular field. Field names may not be duplicated in a table.
- Type: The field's data type can be selected from Table 33.1.
- Size: The size of the field (see Table 33.1 for sizes, if required).
- Key: This field is part of the record's key values.

The key you select in the customer table is also known as the *primary key*. A primary key is the field or fields that uniquely identify each record in a table.

To insert the first field in your customer table, enter **CustNo** as the field name and **N** as the type. We want the customer number to be unique for each customer record to prevent multiple customers having the same id number. Double-click the **Key field** of the CustNo field in order to mark that field as our primary key. If you wanted more than the CustNo field to comprise your primary key, you would double-click the **Key field** for each field you want included in your primary key.

WARNING

If you want your primary key to include more than one field, then all fields that will comprise the primary key must be the first group of fields in your table. In other words, if the primary key for your table will be comprised of three fields, then those three fields must be the first three fields of your table.

To add a second field to your table, press the **Down Arrow** key to move to the next row.

To delete a field row from your table, hold down the **Ctrl** key and press the minus key (**-**).

Use the **Delete** or **Backspace** key to modify a field's name.

Table 33.2 shows the fields to enter in order to complete the customer table.

Table 33.2 CUSTOMER TABLE FIELDS

FieldName	Type	Size	Key
CustNo	N		*
Company	A	30	
Addr1	A	30	
Addr2	A	30	
City	A	15	
State	A	20	
Zip	A	10	
Country	A	20	
Phone	A	15	
FAX	A	15	
TaxRate	N		
Contact	A	20	
LastInvoiceDate	@		

You now have all of the fields entered for the customer table. Click the **Save As** button and enter **DELPCUST.DB** as the name for your Paradox table. A copy of the DELPCUST table has been included on the code disk accompanying this book.

Validity Checks

When you design a table, you should give serious thought to validity checks. *Validity checks* verify that the data entered into your tables meets certain restrictions.

If you do not set validity checks when the table is created, you can select **Utilities | Restructure** from the Database desktop main menu and select the table you want to restructure in order to add validity checks. You must select the field you want to add validity checks on before filling in the corresponding validity check field.

Required Field

The **Required Field** checkbox determines whether a field must be filled in before a record is inserted into the table. For example, to make sure that a zip code is entered for each customer record, you can select the **Zip Code field** and then check **Required field**.

Minimum

The **Minimum** checkbox determines what the smallest value for a field can be. This can be used in conjunction with the Maximum validity checkbox to set a range of valid values for a field.

Maximum

The **Maximum** validity checkbox sets the maximum value for a field.

Default

The **Default** validity checkbox contains the value that is entered for a new record if no value is entered by the user. The default value can be changed at any time by the user.

Picture

Picture strings are used to ensure that the data for a particular field is entered according to a specific format.

The following list contains the allowable picture string characters and what they represent:

#	Any digit
?	Any letter (uppercase or lowercase)
&	Any letter (converted to uppercase)
@	Any character
!	Any character (converted to uppercase)
;	Interpret the next character as the literal character it represents, not a picture string character
*	0 or more of the following character
[abc]	Optional character of a, b, or c
{abc}	Optional character of a, b, or c; one must be selected

When creating or restructuring a table, you can select the **Assist** button next to the Picture edit region to get help on creating a picture for the currently selected field. You can create and test your own or use sample pictures included with the Database desktop. See Figure 33.4.

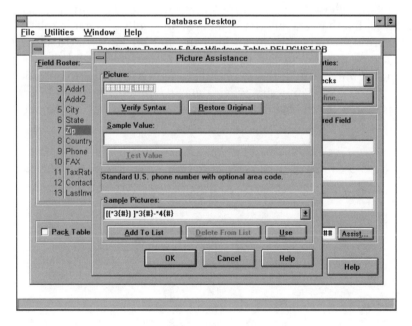

FIGURE 33.4 THE PICTURE ASSISTANCE DIALOG BOX HELPS YOU BUILD AND TEST VALIDATION PICTURE STRINGS.

We can easily add a sample picture clause to our saved DELPCUST table by performing the following steps:

1. Select **Utilities | Restructure** from the main menu and select your **DELPCUST.DB** table as the table to restructure.

2. Use the **Down Arrow** key or the **Scroll bars** to move down to the **Zip** field.

3. Once you're on the **Zip** field, enter the following value into the Picture field in the bottom-right corner of the Restructure dialog box: **#####[-####]**

4. Click the **Save** button to confirm your changes.

Now when data is entered in the zip code field, the data must be either five digits or five digits with a four-digit extension. You can create your own picture clauses for any other field in customer table.

Table Lookups

Table lookups define relationships between tables in your database. This guarantees that the data entered in a particular field exists in a related table. For example, when entering order information you would most likely define a lookup relationship between the Orders table and the Customer table so that only valid customer numbers can be assigned to an order. This helps maintain data integrity when data is entered into the Orders table. You may also want to ensure that the states selected for a customer's record come from a selected list. See Figure 33.5.

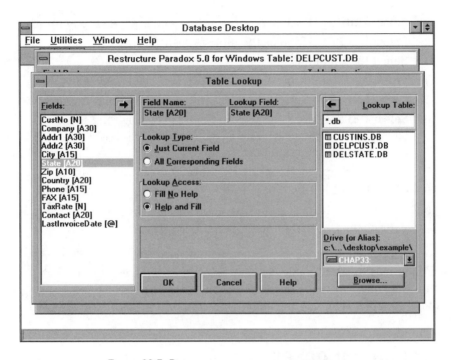

FIGURE 33.5 DEFINING A LOOKUP TABLE RELATIONSHIP.

An additional table named **DELSTATE.DB** is on the included code disk. This table holds the names of a few states and can be defined as a lookup for the DELPCUST table by performing the following steps:

1. Select **Utilities | Restructure** from the Database desktop main menu.
2. Select **DELPCUST.DB** as the table to restructure.
3. Select the **State** field.
4. From the Table Properties drop-down list, select **Table Lookup**.
5. Click the **Define** button to bring up the Table Lookup dialog box.
6. Select **DELSTATE** as the lookup table by highlighting the **DELSTATE** table and double-clicking the selection. The DELSTATE table will be located in the same directory as the DELPCUST table on the code disk.
7. Under Lookup Access, click the **Help and Fill** radio button.
8. Click the **OK** button.
9. Once you're back in the Restructure dialog box, click **Save** to save your changes.

You have now added a lookup relation to your customer table. When you enter data into the DELPCUST table, you can select one of the valid states by moving to the **State** field of the DELPCUST table, pressing **Ctrl-Space** to bring up the lookup table, selecting the state you want, and pressing the **Enter** key.

Secondary Indexes

A secondary index creates another order for viewing or accessing your data. If you often use code at runtime to search through a particular field in a table, it would be to your benefit to create a secondary index on the field or fields you search often. A secondary index will allow for a must faster search.

You can create a secondary index on the State field of our customer table by performing the following steps:

1. Select **Utilities | Restructure** from the Database desktop main menu.
2. Select **DELPCUST.DB** as the table to restructure.
3. Select the **State** field.
4. Select **Secondary Indexes** from the Table Properties drop-down list.
5. Click the **Define** button. See Figure 33.6.

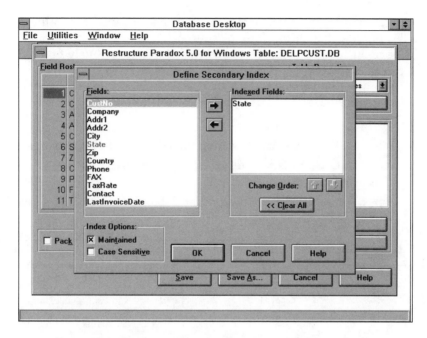

763

FIGURE 33.6 DEFINING A SECONDARY INDEX FOR THE DELPCUST TABLE.

6. Highlight the **State** field in the Fields column.
7. Move the State field over to the Index Fields column by clicking the button with the **Right Arrow (→)**.
8. Click the **OK** button and enter **StateOrder** as the name for your secondary index.
9. Click the **Save** button on the Restructure dialog box to confirm your changes.

Referential Integrity

Referential integrity maintains integrity in your data to make sure the values of a field in one table always have a matching link in a parent table. For example, if you enter a value into the State field of the DELPCUST table for a group of records and then decide you need to change the value in the DELSTATE table that is the lookup source for the DELPCUST table, you would have an invalid value in the State field for previously entered customer records. Referential integrity enables you to have the Database desktop update the State values of the DELPCUST field automatically when the lookup value in the DELSTATE table is changed. To do this, perform the following steps:

1. Select **Utilities | Restructure** from the Database desktop main menu.
2. Select **DELPCUST.DB** as the table to restructure.
3. Select the **State** field.
4. Select **Referential Integrity** from the Table Properties drop-down list. See Figure 33.7.

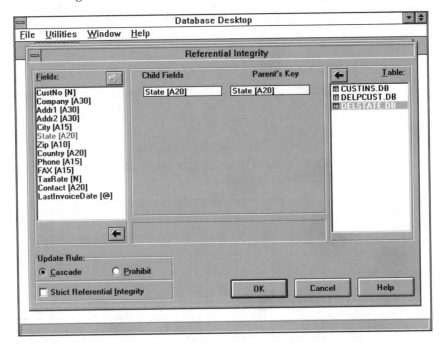

FIGURE 33.7 DEFINING REFERENTIAL INTEGRITY FOR THE DELPCUST TABLE.

5. Select **State** as the Child Field and **DELSTATE** as the Parent's key.
6. Select **Cascade** as the Update Rule.

7. Click the **OK** button and enter **State** as the name for your Referential Integrity.

8. Click the **Save** button on the Restructure dialog box to confirm your table modifications.

Now when the value of the State field in the DELSTATE table is modified, all corresponding state values in your DELPCUST records will also be updated. Also, this will prevent anyone from deleting DELSTATE records if there are customer records assigned to that state.

Password Security

In almost every application that you will develop, security will be a critical issue. Data should not be accessed by just anyone, and while a password form at the start of an application would prevent the casual user from unauthorized access, passwords on the tables themselves present a much more secure environment. Passwords will prevent unauthorized users from trying to access the data tables directly.

Passwords can either be master or auxiliary. While a master password will determine whether or not a user has access to a table, an auxiliary password can be set up to give a user restricted access and rights to a table.

To add a master password to the DELPCUST table, perform the following steps:

1. Select **Utilities | Restructure** from the Database desktop main menu.

2. Select **DELPCUST.DB** as the table to restructure.

3. Select the **State** field.

4. Select **Password Security** from the Table Properties drop-down list.

5. Click the **Define** button. See Figure 33.8.

6. Type the word **customer** into both the Master Password area and the Verify Master Password area. You can use any password you want; just be sure to write it down somewhere safe, or make sure to remember it.

7. Click the **OK** button.

8. Click the **Save** button in the Restructure dialog box to confirm your Password modifications.

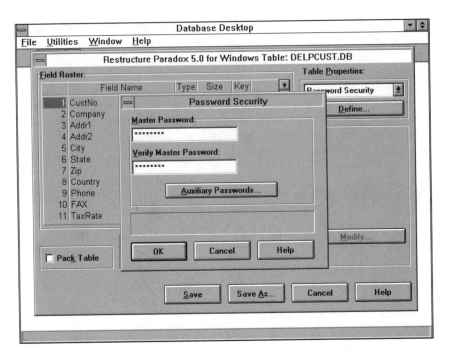

FIGURE 33.8 DEFINING PASSWORD SECURITY FOR THE DELPCUST TABLE.

Now the next time you attempt to access the DELPCUST table, you must enter the password in order to access the customer data. Once a master password is assigned, you can assign auxiliary passwords to have different types of restricted access to your table. For more information on security, see Chapter 25, "Data Security Overview."

Table Language

Selecting the **Table Language** property from the Table Properties in the Restructure dialog box and clicking the **Modify** button allows you to select a different language than that selected in the BDE Configuration utility. See Figure 33.9.

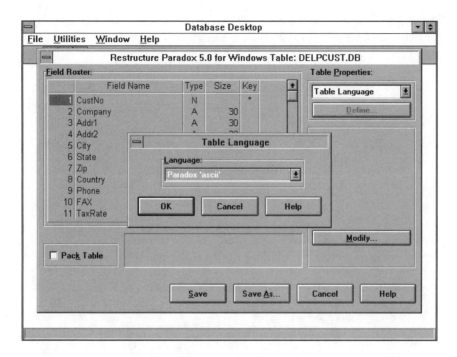

FIGURE 33.9 SELECTING A TABLE LANGUAGE.

Dependent Tables

Selecting the **Dependent Tables** option of the Table Properties drop-down list displays tables related to your current table through referential integrity.

Viewing Table Data

The Database desktop gives you the ability to view data in your tables without working through a Delphi application. Using various keystrokes you can quickly navigate a table, search for a particular record, or just browse.

In order to view a table, select **File | Open | Table** from the main menu. Select the **Customer** table included with the Delphi sample tables. See Figure 33.10.

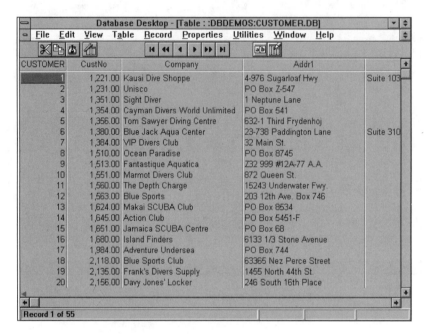

FIGURE 33.10 VIEWING THE CUSTOMER TABLE.

Navigating a Table with Keystrokes

Generally, the quickest way to navigate a table is to use keystrokes or a combination of keystrokes to move through the current table. There are many keystrokes that perform different functions while viewing a table. Table 33.3 lists the most frequently used keystrokes.

TABLE 33.3 COMMON KEYSTROKES FOR TABLE NAVIGATION

Keystroke	Effect
PgUp	Move up one set of records
PgDn	Move down one set of records
Right	Move right one field

Left	Move left one field
Ctrl-PgUp	Move one screen left
Ctrl-PgDn	Move one screen right
Home	Left-most field of current record
End	Right-most field of current record
Ctrl-Home	Left-most field of first record in table
Ctrl-End	Right-most field of last record in table
Up	Move to previous record
Ctrl-R	Rotate columns
Down	Move to next record

With the keystrokes listed in Table 33.3, you can move around the entire Customer table and see each record and each column of each record.

Nonkeystroke Navigation

Even though keystrokes are generally the quickest and easiest way to navigate a table there are several other navigation tools you can use to move through a table.

Scroll Bars

You can use the vertical scroll bar to scroll through the individual records and the horizontal scroll bar to move through the different columns in your table.

Mouse Clicks

As long as part of a column is visible in the table window, you can select that column by clicking it with your mouse. You can also use the mouse to select the row on which you want to focus.

Record Navigation Toolbar

When viewing a table, you will notice a toolbar with six different arrows in the middle. These buttons can be used for table navigation. Their actions are from left to right: First Record, Previous Record Set, Previous Record, Next Record, Next Record Set, and Last Record.

With this array of table navigation tools, moving through a table is a snap.

Editing Table Data

When developing an application and creating tables you will need to create and insert test data in your tables to determine if you have allocated table space for each data item that you will need to store. Creating test data also gives you data with which to test your finished application.

The first step in editing data is to open a table. If you do not have the Customer table, select **File**|**Open**|**Table** from Database desktop main menu and select the **Customer** table from Delphi's sample data tables. Click the **Edit Data** toolbar button, which has the pencil on it.

Table 33.4 shows the typical list of keystrokes that you will use to edit table data.

Table 33.4 COMMON KEYSTROKES FOR TABLE EDITING

Keystroke	Effect
F9	Enter/leave edit mode
Ins	Insert new record
Del	Delete current field value
Ctrl-Del	Delete current record
Ctrl-X	Cut
Ctrl-C	Copy
Ctrl-V	Paste
Alt-BkSp	Undo record edit
Esc	Undo field edit
Tab or Enter	Commit value and move to next field
Shift-Tab	Commit value and move to previous field

In order to enter or leave Field View, to edit the data of the current field without completely replacing it, you can press **F2** or click the **Field View** toolbar button.

Use the **DELPCUST.DB** table created earlier to practice inserting, deleting, and modifying customer data.

Directories

Tables for an application are generally kept in a single directory, unless there are so many that it is easier to keep them in a logically organized group of directories. When you work with tables in the Database desktop, there are two special directories, the working and the private directories.

Working Directory

The easiest way to work with a group of tables in the Database desktop is to set your working directory to that in which the tables reside. Setting your working directory will make your current directory the same as the directory of the files that you wish to reference. Once the working directory is set, you can access your tables without typing in their full paths.

Setting your working directory entails performing the following steps:

1. Select **File | Working Directory** from the main menu. Figure 33.11 shows the Set Working Directory dialog box.

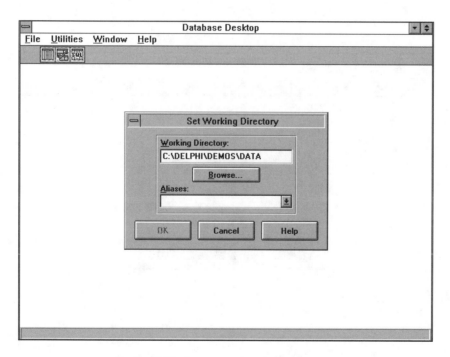

FIGURE 33.11 SETTING YOUR WORKING DIRECTORY.

2. Choose one option. You can either type in the desired path for your working directory, use Browse to select a directory, or use a prede-

fined alias to select your working directory. Aliases will be discussed shortly.

3. Click the **OK** button to confirm your working directory selection.

Private Directory

Your private directory is used to store temporary tables created by the Database desktop that cannot be shared among multiple users. One such table is the Answer table resulting from queries, which will be explained a little later in this chapter. Local drives are generally a good location for defining your private directory.

In order to set your private directory, perform the following steps:

1. Select **File | Private Directory** from the Database desktop main menu. See Figure 33.12.

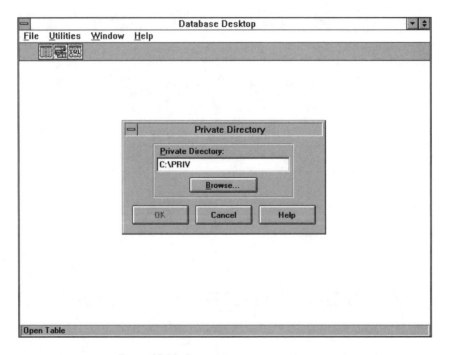

FIGURE 33.12 SETTING YOUR PRIVATE DIRECTORY.

2. Type in the path for your private directory or click the **Browse** button to select a directory path.

3. Click the **OK** button to confirm your Private Directory selection.

Aliases

An *alias* is a shortcut name to a directory that contains your database tables. The two major benefits of using an alias are as follows. First, you do not have to type the full path of a table when you want to reference it, and secondly, when an application is delivered to a client, all you need to do is redefine the aliases to wherever your client is going to store the data. That is all there is to it.

The Database desktop includes a couple of predefined aliases in addition to those that you will define.

:WORK:

All files in your working directory can be referenced by using the working directory alias, **:WORK:**.

:PRIV:

All files in your private directory can be referenced by using the private directory alias, **:PRIV:**.

User-Defined Aliases

As already mentioned, you will want to avoid referencing a table by using the full path and file name for that table. Using your own user-defined aliases will make life much easier in the long run.

For query examples later in this chapter, we will be using the alias DBDEMOS. The DBDEMOS alias will point to the directory containing the sample tables. In this case the directory is **C:\BORLAND\DELPHI\DEMOS\DATA**. When you create your DBDEMOS alias, use the appropriate directory path for your installation of Delphi.

In order to create your DBDEMOS alias, perform the following steps:

1. Select **File | Aliases** from the Database desktop main menu.
2. Click the **New** button.
3. Enter **DBDEMOS** as the Database Alias.
4. Enter the path to your sample tables in the Path field.
5. Click the **SaveAs** button and click **OK** on the Save Configuration dialog box.
6. Click **OK** to confirm the overwriting of your **IDAPI.CFG** file, which h olds alias and other information used by Borland's Database Engine.

Figure 33.13 shows the Alias Manager.

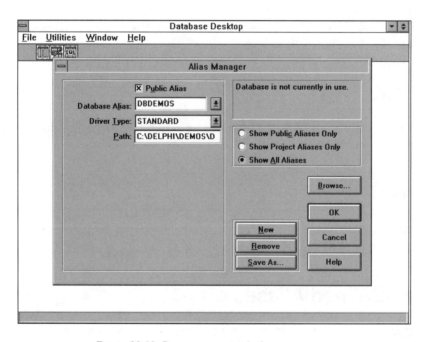

FIGURE 33.13 DATABASE DESKTOP'S ALIAS MANAGER.

Queries

Once data has been entered into your application tables, you can use queries to perform the following actions on your tables:

- Select data from one or more tables.
- Restrict data selected by entering selection criteria.
- Create fields based on calculations of your current field values to give more useful information.
- Insert or delete data from tables.
- Perform calculations based on groups of records.
- Update or change field values.

Selection Queries

When viewing data, it is often preferable to use a restricted view of your data table or tables instead of looking at the entire table. This can be accomplished by looking at selected columns of a table, records based on criteria restrictions, or a combination of both.

When referencing a table in a query, using an alias will make the query portable if you want to use the same query on another system where the tables will not be in the same directory path as they are on your system. Query examples in this section will be using the DBDEMOS alias set up earlier in the chapter. If you have not already created the DBDEMOS alias, refer to the section on aliases earlier in the chapter, before proceeding with the following queries.

To create a new query perform the following steps:

1. Select **File | New | QBE Query** from the main menu.

Figure 33.14 shows the table selection dialog box.

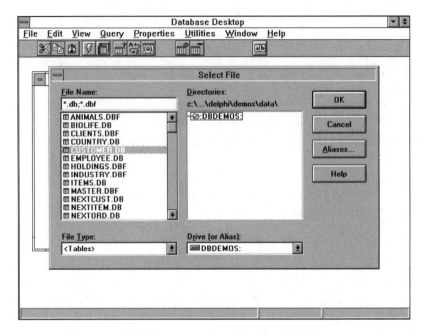

FIGURE 33.14 SELECTING A SOURCE TABLE FOR YOUR QUERY.

2. Select **DBDEMOS** from the Drive (or Alias) drop-down list.
3. Select the table **CUSTOMER.DB** as the source table for the query.
4. Click the **OK** button to confirm your table selection.

You will now have the customer table displayed in the Database desktop's QBE, Query-By-Example, interface.

You will notice that each field of the Customer table is represented in the QBE grid. To select a field to be included as part of the query result, you can check one of the check types next to each field. Table 33.5 gives an explanation of the various check types.

TABLE 33.5 QUERY CHECK TYPES

Checktype	Effect on Query
Check	Includes all unique values for a field, excluding duplicates
Check-Plus	Shows all values for a field, including duplicates
Check-Descending	Shows all unique values for a field in a descending sort order
Check-GroupBy	Specifies a group of records for a Set query
Empty box	To uncheck a field, removing it from the query result

If you want the same check for each field of the query grid, you can select the desired check type in the grid box under the table name in the left-most box of the query grid.

To select a check type for a single field or for the entire table, click the small white square in the lower-left corner of the field's grid box. Hold the mouse button down after clicking the box, and drag the check highlighter down until the desired check type is highlighted. Releasing the mouse button will place the selected check type into the current field's checkbox. Use the horizontal scroll bar to move to any field in the QBE grid.

Selecting Fields: Selection Query Example 1

For the first example, follow the preceding directions to select a check type and place a standard check in the following fields of the Customer.db query grid: **Custno**, **Company**, **City**, and **State**. Your QBE grid should look like Figure 33.15.

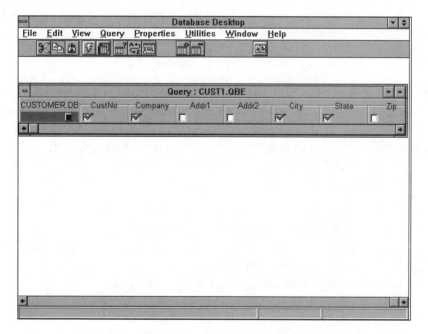

FIGURE 33.15 SELECTION QUERY BASED ON THE CUSTOMER TABLE.

In order to run the query, you can do one of the following actions:

- Select **View | Run Query** from the QBE menu.

- Press the **F8** key.
- Click the **Run** button, the one with the lightening bolt.

After you have run the query, the Database desktop will select those fields from the Customer table that you selected in the QBE grid and create the Answer table.

The *Answer table* is one of the temporary tables that the Database desktop will store in your private directory, which as mentioned earlier can be referenced by the :PRIV: alias. Every time a selection query is run, the Answer table is replaced by a new version of the answer table, which will be based on the query just run.

To close the Answer table, simple double-click the upper-left corner of the window containing the Answer table.

After closing the Answer table, select **File | Save** from the QBE menu. Use **CUST1** as the name for the query. All query examples are included with the code disk.

You can prevent the Answer table being overwritten by renaming the Answer table. This and other Utility menu options will be discussed later in this chapter.

Adding and Joining Tables: Selection Query Example 2

The second selection will show how to join two tables within the same query in order to display order information for the customers in the Customer.db table and how to place selection criteria into your query.

Perform the following steps in order to display order information along with the customer information:

1. Select **File | Open | QBE Query** from the main menu.
2. Select **CUST1.QBE** as the query file to open.
3. Select **File | Save As** from the main menu and enter **CUSTORD.QBE** as the name for your new query.
4. Select **Query | Add Table** from the QBE menu.
5. Select **DBDEMOS** as the alias and select **Order.db** as the table to add to your query.
6. Click the **Join Tables** button from the toolbar.
7. Click once in the **CustNo** field of both tables to place an example element in both fields. This creates a join between the two tables.
8. Check the **OrderNo** field of the Orders table. See Figure 33.16.

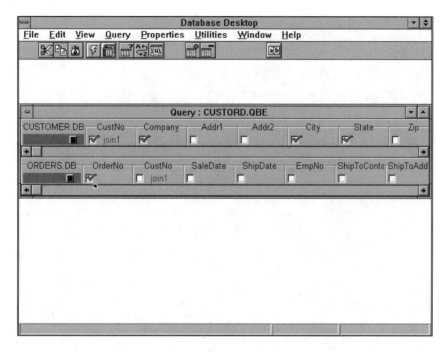

FIGURE 33.16 JOINING THE CUSTOMER AND THE ORDERS TABLES.

9. Select **File | Save** to save the changes to the current query.

10. Run the query.

Data Restrictions

The first two query examples selected all records from their respective tables. This is not always the desired result when you are viewing data. In many instances, you will want to see details for only a selected group of customers or orders.

Exact Matches

In many cases you will want to see the customer and order information for those customers in a particular state. For the next example, open the query **CUSTORD2.QBE**, which is stored on the included disk with all the examples for the current chapter. This is a copy of the CUSTORD query that we will use to restrict the data.

Once the query is open, type **HI** into the state field, and run the query. As you will see, the Answer table will display order numbers and customer

information for all customers in Hawaii. This was an exact match, the value
of the State field had to be exactly HI. See Figure 33.17.

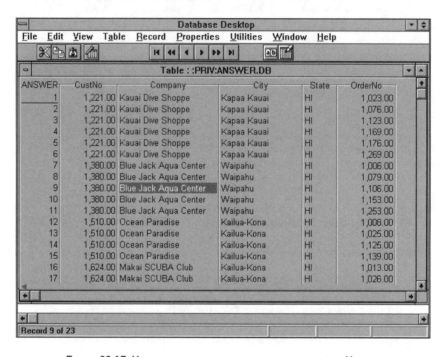

FIGURE 33.17 VIEWING ORDER INFORMATION FOR CUSTOMERS IN HAWAII.

Range Matching

An exact match in a field is not always what you need for a particular
query. For example, if we were querying by SaleDate, we might want
to find all orders after a certain date instead of an exact match for a
particular date.

You can select from the following list of operators to specify a range of
values:

=	Equal
>	Greater than
<	Less than
>=	Greater than or equal to
<=	Less than or equal to

Open the query **CUSTORD2.QBE** and type the following string into the SaleDate field of the Orders table: **> 1/1/94**. Run the query. The resulting Answer table will display orders placed after January 1, 1994. Experiment with the other range operators.

Inexact Matches

Often when creating a query, you will not know the exact value you are querying for. You can use one following operators to resolve your problem:

TODAY	Use today's date
BLANK	No value in field
NOT	Find records without value supplied
LIKE	Find similar but not necessarily an exact match

Open the query **CUSTORD2.QBE** and type the following value into the SaleDate field: **>= TODAY - 180.** Run the query. The Answer table will display information for orders placed within the last 180 days. Figure 33.18 shows the query.

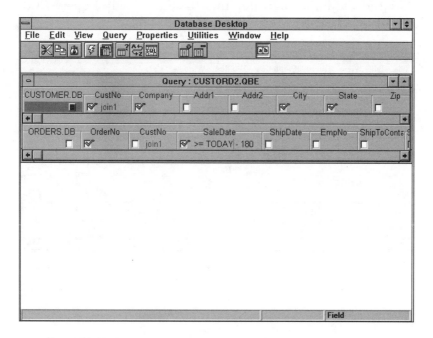

FIGURE 33.18 A SELECT QUERY FOR VIEWING ORDER INFORMATION FOR ORDERS PLACED IN THE LAST 180 DAYS.

Pattern Matching

Another way to query data is to use the Database desktop's pattern operators. They are .., the wildcard operator that matches any string of characters, and the @ wildcard operator that will match a single character.

Open the **CUSTORD2.QBE** query and type the following value in the Company field of the Customer table: **C..**. Run the query. The Answer table will contain information for all customers whose name starts with the letter *C*.

Special Operators

In many cases you will need to join conditions in your queries with the special operators:

,	Use the comma to represent an AND condition
OR	Use OR for OR conditions

For example, if you want to see order information for customers in Hawaii or Florida insert the following value into the State field of query **CUSTORD2.QBE**: **HI OR FL**. Figure 33.19 shows the resulting query.

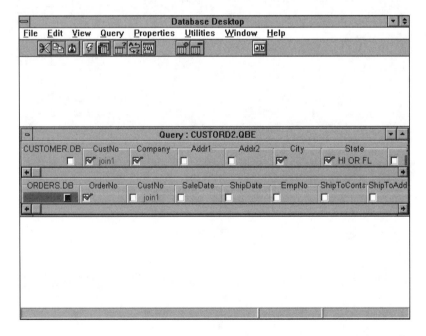

FIGURE 33.19 A SELECT QUERY FOR VIEWING ORDER INFORMATION FOR CUSTOMERS IN HAWAII OR FLORIDA.

Run the query to see the results.

Using CALC with Summary Operators

The Database desktop gives you the ability to calculate fields in the query result. The Summary operators are as follows:

AVERAGE	Find the average value for a field.
COUNT	Count the different values in a field.
MAX	Find the maximum value in a field.
MIN	Find the minimum value in a field.
SUM	Find the sum of values in a field.
ALL	Include all values including duplicates.
UNIQUE	Include only unique values.

A summary operator is the solution if you want to count the number of orders for each customer. To find this data, perform the following steps:

1. Select **File | New | QBE Query** from the main menu.
2. Select **DBDEMOS** as the Alias and select the **Orders** table.
3. Check the **CustNo** field in the query grid.
4. Type **CALC COUNT ALL** into the OrderNo field.
5. Save the query as **TOTORDS.QBE**.
6. Run the query.

The resulting Answer table will contain each customer number and the number of orders for each customer.

Joins

The two main types of join are called *outer* and *inner joins*. The examples so far in this chapter have been based on inner joins, that is, we only saw customers listed who did in fact have orders in the Orders table. If we want to see customer numbers whether or not they currently have an order in the Orders table we need to use the inclusion operator, ! (the exclamation mark), to create an outer join. To see the effects of an outer join perform the following steps:

1. Select **File | New | QBE Query** to create a new query.
2. Select the **Customer** table from the DBDEMOS alias.

3. Hold down the **Ctrl** key and click the **Orders** table.

4. Click the **OK** button to select both tables.

5. Press the **Join Tables** button and place an example element in the CustNo field of both tables.

6. In the CustNo field of the Customer table, type ! directly after the red word join1.

7. Run the query.

8. Save the query as **OUTRJOIN.QBE**. Figure 33.20 shows the query.

The Answer table shows that customer number 3055 does not currently have any orders in the Orders table.

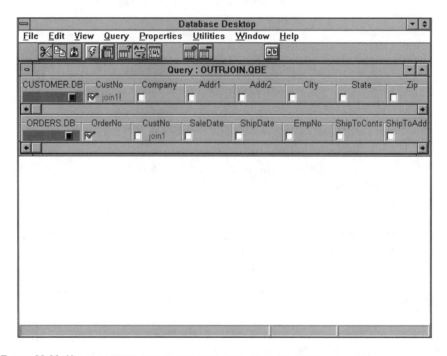

FIGURE 33.20 USING AN OUTER JOIN TO SEE CUSTOMERS AND THEIR ORDER NUMBERS, IF THEY HAVE ANY.

Set Queries

Set queries are used in the event that you want to select a group of records and then ask a further question on those selected records.

To see a set query in action, open the file **SET.QBE**. This query defines a set of customers and calculates the average order for those customers. Therefore, we calculate the value of the average order for a Hawaiian customer.

Action Queries

There is another type of query beyond the selection query, this is the *action query*. Action queries can be used to insert or delete records or to change a field's value.

Insert

Use an *insert query* to insert records into a table. This can include specific values or be based on a selection query. For example, we can insert all customers whose name begins with the letter *C* into our table, DELPCUST.

Perform the following steps in order to select the appropriate records from the Customer table and insert them into our DELPCUST table:

1. Copy the **CUSTINS.DB table** from the code disk to your local hard drive.
2. Create a new query.
3. Select the **DBDEMOS** alias and then select the **Customer** table from that directory.
4. Click the **Add Table** button and add the **CUSTINS.db** table from wherever you copied it to.
5. Use the **Join Tables** button and place an example element in each corresponding field. Be sure to enter the same example element in the same field in each table.
6. In the left-most block of the CUSTINS table, click your mouse in the blank area and drag down the list until the word **Insert** is highlighted. Release your mouse button.

Your query should look similar to Figure 33.21.

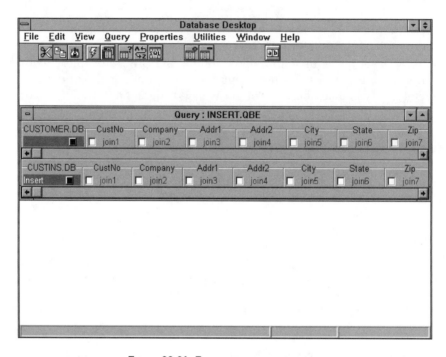

FIGURE 33.21 EXECUTING AN INSERT QUERY.

7. Save the query as **INSERT.QBE**.
8. Run the query.

Notice that we did not get an Answer table, but rather an Inserted.db table. This is another of the Database desktop's temporary tables. You can close it just as you did the Answer table.

Delete

You can also use a query to delete records. For example, if you wanted to delete all of the customers from Hawaii from the **CUSTINS.db** table, you could perform the following steps:

1. Create a new query.
2. Select the **CUSTINS** table as the source table for your query.
3. Type **HI** into the State field.

4. Click your mouse in the area below the table name and drag down the list until you select **Delete**. Release your mouse button.

Your query should look like Figure 33.22.

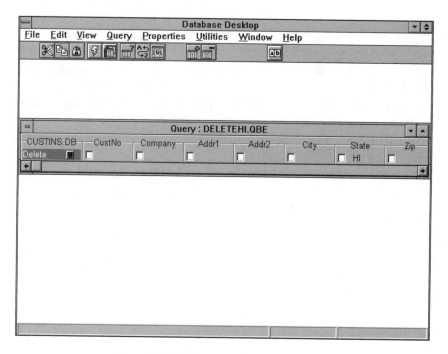

FIGURE 33.22 DELETING HAWAIIAN CUSTOMERS.

5. Save the query as **DELETEHI.QBE**.
6. Run the query.

You will notice the table Deleted.db. This contains all records that were removed from the CUSTINS table.

Changeto Queries

Using the *UPDATE* keyword allows you to change the values in a particular field. For example, if all of your customers decided to move to Illinois you could perform the following steps:

1. Create a new query.
2. Select **CUSTINS.DB** as your source table.

3. Type the following into the State field: **CHANGETO IL.**
4. Save the query as **CHANGEIL.QBE.**
5. Run the query.

SQL

SQL, otherwise known as Structured Query Language, is a language for developing and executing queries. To see the SQL statement for queries you design with the QBE grid, press the **Show SQL** button after you have designed your query.

Choose **File|New** to create a new SQL statement or **File|Open** to view a previously created SQL statement. For a more detailed examination of SQL and its abilities, refer to Chapter 18, "Understanding SQL."

Utilities

The Database desktop includes an array of utilities to work with your data tables. These utilities save time and effort when you are performing essential database tasks.

Add

Select **Add** from the Utilities menu to add the records from a source table into a chosen destination table. The two tables must have the same structure.

In the Add dialog box, select a source table to add records from and a destination table to add them to. See Figure 33.23.

When adding two tables you can select from the following add options:

- Append
- Update
- Append and Update

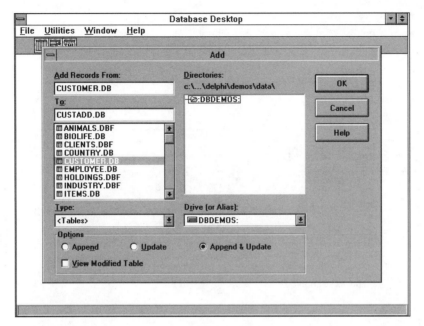

FIGURE 33.23 ADD TABLES.

Using the **Append** option in nonkeyed tables will append the source records after the last record in the destination table, while appending records to a keyed table will only append those records that do not match a key value in the destination table.

Using the **Update** option will update the records that already exist in the destination table.

Using the **Append and Update** option will append those records that do not exist in the destination table and update those that already exist.

Copy

The **Copy** option of the Utilities menu allows you to copy the following items:

- Tables
- Queries
- Text files
- SQL files

See Figure 33.24.

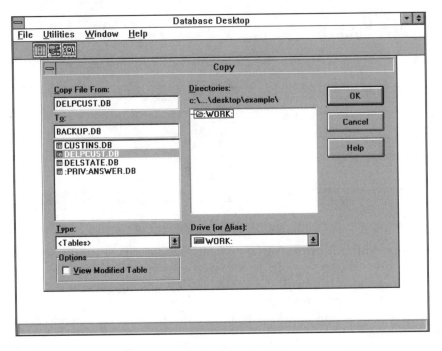

FIGURE 33.24 THE COPY UTILITY.

Select **Utilities | Copy** to access the Copy dialog box.

In the Copy dialog box you must select the type of object you want to copy, the source file to copy from, and the new name to copy the source object to.

Delete

Use the **Delete** menu option to delete one of the following file types:

- Tables
- Queries

- Text files
- SQL files

Simply select the file type and then use the directory list box to select the directory in which the desired file resides. Finally double-click the actual file and click the **OK** button to delete the object.

Empty

Select **Utilities | Empty** in order to empty a table.

Use the directory list box to locate the desired table, select the table to empty, and click the **OK** button to empty the contents of the selected table. See Figure 33.25.

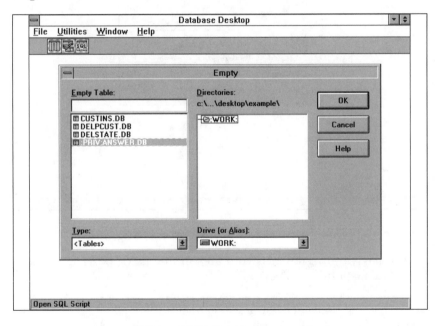

FIGURE 33.25 EMPTYING A TABLE.

Password

Use the **Password** option of the Utilities menu to add or remove passwords from your current session of the Database desktop. See Figure 33.26.

T I P

If you are going to access several tables with different passwords during a session of the Database desktop, you can save time by using the **Password** option to enter all passwords at the beginning of the session. Also, remember that the submission of passwords if valid only for your current session of the Database desktop.

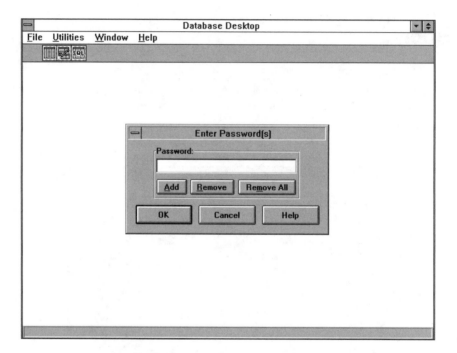

FIGURE 33.26 SUBMITTING PASSWORDS WITH THE PASSWORD DIALOG BOX.

Type your password in the Password area of the dialog box and choose one of the following button choices:

Add	Submit password for current session.
Remove	Remove password from current session.
Remove All	Remove all passwords from current session.

Once a password has been removed from a session, if you try to access a table protected by the removed password, you will need to resubmit the password before obtaining access to the table.

Rename

You can use the **Rename** option to rename the same objects you were able to copy and delete:

- Tables
- Queries
- Text files
- SQL files

Select **Utilities | Rename** from the main menu to bring up the Rename dialog box.

You must select your file type, select a file, and enter a new name for the file. Click the **OK** button to confirm your renaming.

Sort

You can sort tables created with the Database desktop by choosing **Utilities | Sort** from the main menu. After choosing the **Sort** menu option, choose the desired table in the Select File dialog box. See Figure 33.27.

After selecting the table to sort, the Sort Table dialog box will appear.

If the table you want to sort has a primary key, the only option is to sort into a new table. On the other hand, tables without a primary key can be sorted back into themselves.

Double-clicking the field(s) you want to sort by from the Fields list will move the field to your Sort Order list. Use the **Change Order** arrows to arrange the sorting fields in the order that you want your data sorted.

While sorting your data according to your list of sort order fields, the Database desktop will resolve any further ties in succeeding fields unless you check the **Sort Just Selected Fields** checkbox.

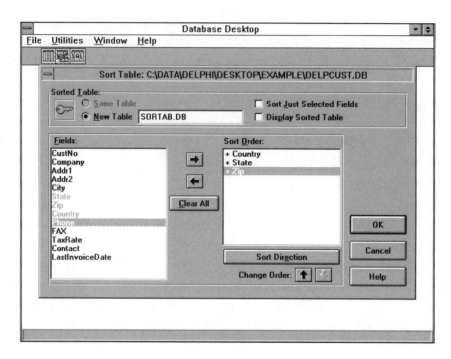

FIGURE 33.27 SORTING A TABLE.

Infostructure

The **Infostructure** menu option allows you to select a table. It will display a Structure Information dialog box. This dialog box is the same one you saw when creating a table. The only difference is that you cannot make any modifications to the table at this point. The **Infostructure** option is for reference only. If you want to add secondary indexes, picture clauses, or any other table properties like those added when the DELPCUST table was created earlier in the chapter, you must restructure the table. See Figure 33.28.

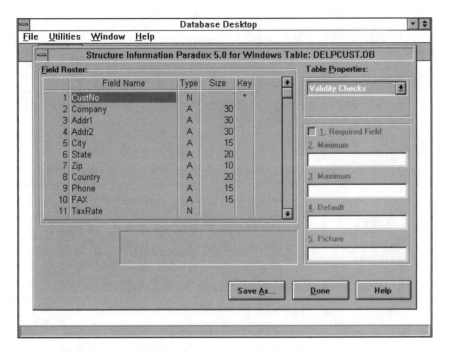

FIGURE 33.28 VIEW A TABLE'S PROPERTY INFORMATION THROUGH INFOSTRUCTURE.

Restructure

Select **Utilities | Restructure** to restructure a table in order to modify its field list or change table properties. When you restructure a table, you will have the same options as when you first created the table.

Subtract

In order to subtract the records from one table to another, choose **Utilities | Subtract** from the main menu. See Figure 33.29.

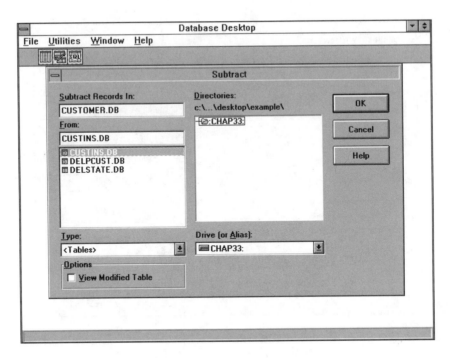

FIGURE 33.29 SUBTRACTING TABLES.

From the Subtract dialog box you must choose one table to subtract and a table to subtract from. The two tables must have the same table structure in order to subtract one from the other.

Creating Local Interbase Tables

Using the Database desktop, you can create a local Interbase table just as easily as you created a Paradox table. Table 33.6 explains the available field types for local Interbase tables.

TABLE 33.6 CUSTOMER TABLE FIELDS

FieldName	Description
SHORT	Integers from −32,768 to 32,767
LONG	Integers from −2,147,483,647 to 2,147,483,647
FLOAT	Floating-point numbers with seven-digit precision

DOUBLE	Floating-point numbers with 15-digit precision
CHAR	Fixed-length Character data up to 32,767 characters
VARCHAR	Variable-length character data up to 32,767 characters
DATE	Date from 1/1/100 to 12/11/5941
BLOB	Binary data
ARRAY	You cannot create the Array field with the Database desktop

In order to create a new Interbase table, select **File | New | Table** from the Database Desktop's main menu, as we did earlier to create our Paradox tables.

As noted in Table 33.6, you cannot create the Array data type with the Database desktop. Also, you can enter data into all of the local Interbase data types except for the BLOB field.

WARNING

Summary

The Database desktop is an excellent supplemental tool to Delphi. Use it to create test tables and aliases with which you can create data to test your application. When the application is delivered, you simply need to redefine the alias' directory path to that in which the users of the application will keep their data.

With all of the tools you have to work with, you can quickly and easily make any necessary modifications to your tables as your application is developed.

The query tools give an easy way to view selected data or make quick data modifications during the development process. This, along with the table tools and other utility options packaged in the Database desktop, gives you all you need to create and populate tables for your Delphi application.

INDEX

S

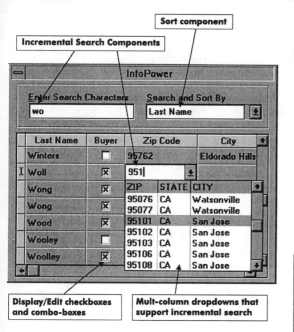

About the CD

The CD-ROM contains all the sample code discussed in the book along with the finished, compiled programs and objects. They have been organized by chapter number in order to be easily located.

Also contained on the CD-ROM are a set of 3rd-party VCLs from Woll2Woll Software. These VCLs are a demo version called Info*Power*. To use them, run the Setup program found in the directory containing the Woll2Woll software. Please follow the licensing rules Woll2Woll gives with the components.